Canada and the Second World War

Geoffrey Hayes, Mike Bechthold, and Matt Symes, Editors

Foreword by John Cleghorn

Canada and the Second World War

Essays in Honour of Terry Copp

Wilfrid Laurier University Press

This book has been published with the help of a grant from the Canadian Federation for the Humanities and Social Sciences, through the Aid to Scholarly Publications Programme, using funds provided by the Social Sciences and Humanities Research Council of Canada. Wilfrid Laurier University Press acknowledges the support of the Canada Council for the Arts for our publishing program. We acknowledge the financial support of the Government of Canada through the Canada Book Fund for our publishing activities.

Library and Archives Canada Cataloguing in Publication

Canada and the Second World War : essays in honour of Terry Copp / Geoffrey Hayes, Mike Bechthold, and Matt Symes, editors.

Includes bibliographical references.
Also issued in electronic format.
ISBN 978-1-55458-629-5

1. World War, 1939–1945—Canada. 2. World War, 1939–1945—Campaigns. 3. Canada—History—1939–1945. I. Copp, Terry, 1938– II. Hayes, Geoffrey, 1961– III. Bechthold, Michael, 1968– IV. Symes, Matt V. Title.

D768.15.C26 2012   940.54'0971   C2012-900658-0

Electronic monograph issued in multiple formats.
Also issued in print format.
ISBN 978-1-55458-645-5 (PDF).—ISBN 978-1-55458-646-2 (EPUB)

1. World War, 1939–1945—Canada. 2. World War, 1939–1945—Campaigns. 3. Canada—History—1939–1945. I. Copp, Terry, 1938– II. Hayes, Geoffrey, 1961– III. Bechthold, Michael, 1968– IV. Symes, Matt V. Title.

D768.15.C26 2012   940.54'0971   C2012-900659-9

Cover design by Blakeley Words+Pictures. Front-cover image: Canadian Forces Joint Imagery Centre ZK-1080-8. Text formatting by Matt Symes. Text design by Catharine Bonas Taylor. Maps by Mike Bechthold. Map on p. 321 adapted from Douglas E. Delaney, *Corps Commanders: Five British and Canadian Generals at War, 1939–1945* (Toronto and Vancouver: University of British Columbia Press, 2011), Map 16.

© 2012 Wilfrid Laurier University Press
Waterloo, Ontario, Canada
www.wlupress.wlu.ca

This book is printed on FSC recycled paper and is certified Ecologo. It is made from 100% post-consumer fibre, processed chlorine free, and manufactured using biogas energy.

Printed in Canada

Every reasonable effort has been made to acquire permission for copyright material used in this text, and to acknowledge all such indebtedness accurately. Any errors and omissions called to the publisher's attention will be corrected in future printings.

No part of this publication may be reproduced, stored in a retrieval system, or transmitted, in any form or by any means, without the prior written consent of the publisher or a licence from the Canadian Copyright Licensing Agency (Access Copyright). For an Access Copyright licence, visit http://www.accesscopyright.ca or call toll free to 1-800-893-5777.

Contents

Foreword ix
John Cleghorn

Acknowledgements xi

1 **Introduction** 1

2 **Terry Copp's Approach to History**
Mark Osborne Humphries 15

The Home Front

3 **"To Hold on High the Torch of Liberty"**
Canadian Youth and the Second World War
Cynthia Comacchio 33

4 **Fighting a White Man's War?**
First Nations Participation in the Canadian War Effort, 1939–1945
Scott Sheffield 67

5 **Harnessing Journalists to the War Machine**
Canada's Domestic Press Censors in the Second World War
Mark Bourrie 93

6 **Dangerous Curves**
Canadian Drivers and Mechanical Transport in Two World Wars
Andrew Iarocci 115

7 **How C.P. Stacey Became the Army's Official Historian**
The Writing of *The Military Problems of Canada*, 1937–1940
Roger Sarty 139

The War of the Scientists

8 **"Strike Hard, Strike Sure"**
Bomber Harris, Precision Bombing, and Decision Making in RAF Bomber Command
Randall Wakelam   159

9 **Leadership and Science at War**
Colonel Omond Solandt and the British Army Operational Research Group, 1943–1945
Jason Ridler   173

10 **Wartime Military Innovation and the Creation of Canada's Defence Research Board**
Andrew Godefroy   199

The Mediterranean Theatre

11 **Overlord's Long Right Flank**
The Battles for Cassino and Anzio, January–June 1944
Lee Windsor   219

12 **A Sharp Tool Blunted**
The First Special Service Force in the Breakout from Anzio
James A. Wood   239

13 **La culture tactique canadienne**
le cas de l'opération Chesterfield, 23 mai 1944
Yves Tremblay   269

14 **Knowing Enough Not to Interfere**
Lieutenant-General Charles Foulkes at the Lamone River, December 1944
Douglas E. Delaney   317

Northwest Europe

15 **No Ambush, No Defeat**
The Advance of the Vanguard of the 9th Canadian Infantry Brigade, 7 June 1944
Marc Milner   335

16 **Defending the Normandy Bridgehead**
The Battles for Putot-en-Bessin, 7–9 June 1944
Mike Bechthold   367

17 **Operation Smash and 4 Canadian Armoured Division's Drive to Trun**
Angelo Caravaggio   391

18 A History of Lieutenant Jones
Geoffrey Hayes   413

The Aftermath

19 A Biography of Major Ronald Edmond Balfour
Michelle Fowler   431

20 The Personality of Memory
The Process of Informal Commemoration in Normandy
Matt Symes   443

21 An Open Door to a Better Future
The Memory of Canada's Second World War
Jonathan F. Vance   461

Contributors   479

Terry Copp: A Select Bibliography   485

Foreword
John Cleghorn

Canada's contribution to the liberation of Europe and the postwar efforts to advance the cause of peace are important parts of the Canadian story. My family and I have a great interest in helping Canadians understand and appreciate the roles played and sacrifices made by the Canadian Forces during some of history's most tragic and troubled times. Terry Copp's excellent series of battlefield guides all start with the same epitaph: "Dedicated to the men and women of the Canadian Forces who fought for the liberation of Europe and the hope of a better world." This sentiment expresses the motivation of a man who has done more than most to educate Canadians about the important role played by Canada's military in the two cataclysmic wars of the twentieth century.

I have known Terry since my days at Laurier when I was Chancellor and sat on the Board of Governors with him. We quickly discovered our shared love for military history and spent hours talking about our mutual interest. Terry's passion is contagious and showed clearly when I sat in on his Second World War course and watched as he captivated a room full of undergraduates. To capture the interest of 200 students during a three-hour night course, and to hold it for an entire term, speaks to Terry's talents as a teacher.

I have had the good fortune to visit Canadian battlefields around the world. Reading about the wars is one thing, but to actually see the ages of the young men on their tombstones is quite another. During our trips following the Maple Leaf Route from Normandy to Germany, Terry's guidebooks have been constant companions for my wife and I and our friends. Terry supplied books and materials so we could follow the routes the Canadians took in Sicily and Italy. On our own we have visited sites in Hong Kong; our inspiration for doing all these visits has been Terry Copp. We have given out countless copies of the Laurier battlefield tour booklets to friends and family and other interested people to help them on their journeys.

The Laurier Centre for Military Strategic and Disarmament Studies was founded by Terry in 1991 and quickly become a centre for excellence in the study of Canadian military history. The publications of the Centre, including *Canadian Military History*, the battlefield guidebooks and a wealth of other books, have made an important contribution to the field. Terry has developed a program of battlefield study tours that take Canadian university students, high school teachers and young military officers to visit the battlefields and study them in a way that is not possible in the classroom. In addition Terry's Centre has provided opportunities to an entire generation of budding military historians who are helping to reenergize the study of Canadian military history. For these reasons my family is proud and honoured to continue my support of the Centre's activities.

This collection of essays is a fitting tribute to a scholar who has made a great contribution to the field of Canadian military history.

Acknowledgements

Many people have contributed to this project. The Laurier Centre for Military Strategic and Disarmament Studies was co-founded in 1991 by Terry Copp and Marc Kilgour. Marc and the Centre's current co-director Alistair Edgar shared their insights and talents with us in support of the project. The Centre's Board of Directors continue to invest countless hours and resources into ensuring its continued operations. Many thanks go to John Cleghorn, Brad Dunkley, Beverly Harris, Peter Kenny, Eric McGeer, Reid Morden, Katherine Sage, Arthur Stephen, Benson Tendler and Shelagh Whitaker.

What inspires Terry most is the energy students bring to the Centre. Two deserve special mention. Geoff Keelan filled his usual role as the last set of eyes to inspect the manuscript before we sent it to the presses. Kellen Kurschinski was involved in every stage of editing and organizing the submissions. A sincere thank you also to Brandey Barton, Elise DeGarie, Kirk Goodlet, Alex Groarke, Ian Haight, Nicholas Lachance, Vanessa McMackin, Caitlin McWilliams, Kathryn Rose, and Jane Whalen. Their enthusiasm was an irreplaceable resource that made a long process more enjoyable.

Many of the authors in this book owe their opportunity to walk the battlefields of Europe to the study tours offered by the Canadian Battlefields Foundation (CBF). A special thanks to past presidents, Charles Belzille, Clive Addy and the Foundation's current president, David Patterson. The staff of the Juno Beach Centre, Courseulles-sur-mer, Calvados, France, especially Natalie Worthington, Rebecca Cline and Marie-Eve Vaillancourt-Deleris, has always offered their full support to the tours and the Centre.

The Centre's close working relationship with WLU Press began with a meeting between Director Brian Henderson and Mark Humphries in 2007.

Since then WLU Press has published and distributed more than 20 of the Centre's titles. This partnership would not be possible without the work of Cheryl Beaupré, Penelope Grows, Clare Hitchens, Cathy Hebbourn, and Leslie Macredie. Ryan Chynces, Acquisitions Editor at WLU Press, was instrumental in patiently guiding us through the ASPP funding and peer-review process. Thanks also to copy editor Matthew Kudelka and to the anonymous readers whose comments strengthened the collection.

John Laband, the current department chair at WLU and Lynne Doyle, warrant special mention. At UW, many thanks go to department chair Gary Bruce, and especially Donna Lang.

Serge Bernier, Paul Dickson, Serge Durflinger, J.L. Granatstein, Chris Madsen, P. Whitney Lackenbauer, Stephen Harris and Michael Neiberg offered sound advice throughout the project.

To our contributors, thank you for your ideas and your patience.

Finally, this collection is dedicated to Terry Copp, teacher, historian, commentator, mentor. Thanks Terry.

1
Introduction

This collection offers new and diverse interpretations of Canada's Second World War experience. It draws from a diverse group of scholars: military, social, and cultural historians, as well as working journalists, graduate students, and serving military officers. Their articles are organized under five headings: The Home Front; The War of the Scientists; The Mediterranean Theatre; Northwest Europe; and the Aftermath. Most address Canadian topics. Some consider the complexity of operations. Others explore new topics, or they introduce readers to people most have never heard of before. Still others are instructive for what they tell us about decision making, leadership, and the construction of memory. Each is exciting for how they question "standard" interpretations through a new reading of the primary documents. The list of the contributors and the breadth of topics speak to the enthusiasm, curiosity, and energy of Professor Terry Copp.

Terry Copp is well-known as a passionate educator and a remarkable scholar. He began his career in 1959 as a lecturer in history at Sir George Williams, now Concordia University in Montreal. After completing his MA at McGill (1962), he embarked upon a career as a teacher, research historian, and writer. As general editor of the Problems in Canadian History series, Copp was responsible for introducing a problem-solving approach to high school history students. In 1974 his book *The Anatomy of Poverty: The Condition of the Working Class in Montreal 1887–1929* launched McClelland and Stewart's Canadian Social History series. After working in the field of labour history, Terry, together with his mentor, the late Professor Robert Vogel of McGill University, embarked on his first foray into military history with the five-volume *Maple Leaf Route* series, published between 1983 and 1988. With Bill McAndrew, Terry wrote *Battle Exhaustion: Soldiers and*

Psychiatrists in the Canadian Army, 1939–1945, in 1990. *The Brigade: The Fifth Canadian Infantry Brigade, 1939–1945* followed in 1992. Both these projects were awarded the C.P. Stacey Prize for the best book in Canadian military history. Never one to shy away from controversy, Terry submitted a brief to the Senate of Canada over the controversial NFB series *The Valour and the Horror* (1992) and later contributed to Richard Nielson's book and film series *No Price Too High: Canadians and the Second World War* (1996), which came out in response. His collaborative works continued with Denis and Shelagh Whitaker in *Victory at Falaise: The Soldiers' Story*, published in 2000. The following year he worked with another veteran, Gordon Brown, to write *Look to Your Front ... Regina Rifles: A Regiment at War, 1944–1945*. Invited to the Joanne Goodman Lecture Series at the University of Western Ontario in 1998, Terry spoke on "*A Citizen Army: The Canadians in Normandy, 1944,*" in which he developed ideas that were published in 2003 as *Fields of Fire: The Canadians in Normandy*. For this work, Terry won a Distinguished Book Award from the Society of Military History in 2004. The companion volume, *Cinderella Army: The Canadians in Northwest Europe, 1944–1945*, came out in 2006. Always curious about the role of operational research, Terry published *Montgomery's Scientists: Operational Research in Northwest Europe: The Work of No. 2 Operational Research Section with 21 Army Group, June 1944 to July 1945* in 2000. Terry published *Guy Simonds and the Art of Command* in 2007. His most recent book, *Combat Stress in the 20th Century: The Commonwealth Perspective* (2010) co-authored with Mark Humphries, revisits his interest in the human cost of war.

It is no exaggeration to say that Professor Copp's passion as a public historian has helped sustain the popularity of military history in Canada. In 1991, Terry and Marc Kilgour started the Laurier Centre for Military Strategic and Disarmament Studies at Wilfrid Laurier University. The following year, Terry and Mike Bechthold published the first issue of *Canadian Military History*, a journal that serves both an academic and a popular audience. In 1994, Terry and Mike began a series of battlefield guides for Canadians travelling to France and Northwest Europe. (Eric McGeer and Matt Symes have continued with volumes that explore the Canadian contribution to the Mediterranean Theatre.) In November 2010, with Matt Symes and Nick Lachance, Terry Copp co-authored *Canadian Battlefields 1915–1918: A Visitor's Guide*. Terry contributed the first of an ongoing series of articles to

Legion Magazine's "Canadian Military History in Perspective" in September 1995. All of these initiatives continue.

From the start of his military studies in the early 1980s, Terry insisted that one could not draw meaningful conclusions about the Canadian military efforts in Northwest Europe or the Mediterranean without having studied the ground. In 1995, he led the first tour of university students to Northwest Europe with the support of the Canadian Battle of Normandy Foundation. For over fifteen years the foundation (now the Canadian Battlefields Foundation) has helped fund at least twelve students yearly to explore Canada's contributions to both world wars. In more recent years, Terry and Michel Fortmann, with the support of a former Chancellor of Wilfrid Laurier University, John Cleghorn and his wife Pattie, have invited students from Wilfrid Laurier University and Université de Montréal to consider Canada's wartime experience from both French and English language perspectives. With the help of the Historica/Dominion Institute and Veterans Affairs Canada, Terry and Blake Seward, a remarkable teacher and principal organizer of the "Lest We Forget" project, organized tours for English- and French-speaking high school history teachers. These teachers soon discovered that the First and Second World Wars remain some of the few common subjects taught in classrooms across the country.

Many participants in these battlefield study tours have played an important role in extending an interest in Canadian military history at all levels. Ron Haycock's survey of eighteen Canadian universities in 1993 found 129 courses devoted to military history. They represented just 5.4 percent of the total number of history courses on offer. Only twelve of those courses dealt with the Canadian military experience in some form.[1] Serge Bernier formerly of the Directorate of History and Heritage, Department of National Defence, organized a more extensive survey of fifty-three Canadian universities in 2009. The 465 military history courses he found made up 6.8 percent of the total history courses taught. Sixty-one courses were devoted to Canadian military history, of which seventeen were devoted to Canada and the Second World War. An interest in military history under the wider rubric of War and Society extends further to the graduate level. In 2004, some forty-nine master's theses or doctoral dissertations were in progress or completed in Canada on a topic related to Canadian military history. Almost half of those focused on Canada and the Second World War.[2] Add to this a very successful run of annual conferences started by Copp in 1991 that rotates annually between Wilfrid Laurier University, the University of Waterloo, and the University of Western Ontario, and one may conclude that the study of Canada's military experience is very healthy indeed.

The continued health of any field of study comes by asking new questions of the evidence. As Mark Humphries notes, "evidence-based history" has served Copp well as both a social and a military historian. Readers may be surprised that Copp continues to find inspiration in R.G. Collingwood's *The Idea of History*. As a scholar, Terry was skeptical of the influence of Marx, Clausewitz, and a host of Canadian "national" historians, and he felt liberated by Collingwood's notion that a careful reading of the evidence could help a historian "imagine" a past that was complex, nuanced, and inclusive. The authors here share Copp's vision of the past.

The Home Front

The Canadian home front has long brought up associations with William Lyon Mackenzie King, conscription, the treatment of Italian and Japanese Canadians, and the contested role of women in the Second World War.[3] These remain important, but as Jeffrey Keshen explored in *Saints, Sinners, and Soldiers: Canada's Second World War* (2004), the wartime experience affected Canada and Canadians in many different ways.[4] Cynthia Comacchio's detailed portrait of Canada's youth considers how the war formed a "generational marker" that cut across divisions of gender, class, and culture. Young people responded to the war's demands (and later remembered their experience) in complex ways. Those who lived through the Great Depression often associated the war with the first steady work for themselves or for their parents. The war also marked a rite of passage for many men and women, who tried to enlist in the armed forces or participate in any way they could. Scores of school activities, from cadet training to model airplane building to farm work, reinforced messages of citizenship, responsibility, and sacrifice. But like the girls who hung out near military bases or boys who donned zoot suits, young people also remained objects of suspicion. There was nothing simple about this "generational" response.

The wartime actions of Aboriginal communities in Canada were equally complex. Scott Sheffield argues that Canadians at the time, and historians much later, profoundly misunderstood the motives of First Nations communities during the war. Native people volunteered in significant numbers, though enlistment rates varied dramatically across the country. They also donated land and money to the wartime cause. Through these gestures, Native people tried to display their loyalty, but on their own terms. Through council resolutions, personal letters, petitions, court challenges, and occasionally violence, Native people across the country opposed being conscripted into military service. As one B.C. native chief maintained in a 1940 letter to a government official, "We think your government has no right to compel us to become soldiers unless you first give us the same rights and privileges as our white brothers have." Sheffield's work reveals that Native people responded to the war with diverse but articulate voices that not only declared "their right to belong" but also "their right to be."

Long ago a CBC journalist maintained in the series *The Valour and the Horror* that his wartime predecessors were merely "cheerleaders for a cause."[5] Mark Bourrie is a journalist as well as a historian whose study of wartime censorship offers a more nuanced view. Bourrie argues that appointing professional journalists as press censors, rather than government officials or military officers, was far from ideal. As one would expect, the censors battled the editorial stance of the nationalist journal *Le Devoir* in Quebec, but the *Globe and Mail* showed equal disdain for the press censors in Toronto. Canadian politicians tried to take advantage of the censors at times. Some journalists, such as Bruce Hutchison, occasionally "crossed the line and became government agents" worked to convince American reporters to write more sympathetically about Canada's position. But the censors also resisted political demands that information be suppressed, especially during the Quebec provincial election campaign of 1939 and the conscription crises of 1942 and 1944. Bourrie concludes that overall, the system of voluntary self-censorship employed during the war sought a middle ground that balanced security concerns with the public's right to know.

Andrew Iarocci begins his study on the home front in the cavernous LeBreton Gallery of the Canadian War Museum, where Canadian Military Pattern (CMP) trucks of the Second World War loom over horse-drawn wagons of a generation before. Iarocci admits that the scale of motorized transport changed dramatically between the two wars: the number of wheeled vehicles in just one division after 1939 represented half the vehicles available to the entire Canadian Expeditionary Force in 1918. Yet numbers tell only part of the story. Iarocci argues that the human element—the need for well-trained drivers and mechanics—made the experience of the two wars far more similar than we might otherwise expect. Canadian soldiers in both wars had to learn how to drive, maintain, refuel, and repair a remarkable range of vehicles. Mechanization may have helped bring victory, but not before Canadian soldiers overcame imposing logistical challenges that historians too often overlook.

Roger Sarty provides here a careful study of the young Charles Stacey, later the official historian of the wartime Canadian Army and the dean of Canadian military historians. Stacey enjoyed few prospects when he graduated from the University of Toronto in 1927, eager to embark on a career teaching British history. After a stint at Oxford, Stacey headed to Princeton, where a lack of funding limited his research to North American history. There was pragmatism in Stacey's turn to Canadian military subjects, but his work was well timed, for as Sarty shows so well, it caught the attention of influential academics, public servants, and military officers like H.D.G. "Harry" Crerar. The two met while Stacey was on his honeymoon, on 3 September 1939, the day Britain went to war with Germany. Despite Stacey's heavy teaching commitments at Princeton, Crerar encouraged him to complete a draft of *The Military Problems of Canada* for the Canadian Institute of International Affairs. The war delayed its publication, and extensive editorial suggestions caused Stacey considerable angst. But Stacey's hard work, professionalism, and diplomacy won the day. Soon after the book went to the printer in the fall of 1940, General Crerar appointed Major Stacey as Historical Officer, General Staff, at Canadian Headquarters in England.

The War of the Scientists

Recent studies of Canadian generals A.G.L. McNaughton and Harry Crerar affirm their belief that the scientific study of the battlefield held the key to Allied victory.[6] Terry Copp made his own contribution to this field when, in 2000, he published *Montgomery's Scientists*. In that work, Terry reproduced the studies and observations of scientists that fundamentally challenged what historians had thought happened on the battlefield. The OR scientists played a large role in all three services, but personalities and nationalities were often crucial factors in how the Allies understood the application of science on the battlefield.

As a scholar and military officer, Randall Wakelam is interested in both the scientific side of the Allied bombing campaign over Germany and the human side of decision making. Wakelam takes up his story in the aftermath of the infamous Butt Report of September 1941, which showed that just one bomber in three came within five miles of their target. Group Captain Sydney Bufton thought he had a solution, and in 1942 he tried to convince Arthur Harris, the head of Bomber Command, to employ a Path Finder Force (PFF) to lead bomber crews onto their targets. Harris did not like Bufton's methods, but he had to accept the PFF in August 1942 when Bufton subverted the chain of command. Interestingly, operational research found that the Path Finders were no panacea well into 1943. In exploring just who was right, Bufton or Harris, Wakelam highlights the complexities of both military command and operational research.

The human element also figures prominently in Jason Ridler's study of the wartime career of Omond Solandt, a Canadian who became superintendent of the British Army Operational Research Group (AORG). Ridler traces how OR grew from the development of radar and anti-aircraft defences to wider studies of weapons, equipment, and tactics. At each stage, personalities and connections mattered. Basil Schonland, a brilliant South African physicist with close ties to Prime Minister Jan Smuts, helped Solandt emerge as the first superintendent of AORG. Solandt understood the importance of connections, but Ridler describes how the young Canadian's remarkable intelligence, leadership, and drive made him Schonland's replacement in 1944. Not everyone liked his aggressive approach, but his views on the role of a scientific establishment in the postwar military drew the attention of Canadian officials, who invited him to be the first director of Canada's Defence Research Board (DRB).

Dr. Solandt's appointment to the DRB is the interest of another soldier/scholar, Andrew Godefroy. He details how the wartime government mobilized Canada's small scientific community through the National Research Council (NRC). Scientists became influential advisers to the government, but as victory grew closer, the future of Canadian defence research remained in doubt. A single meeting in C.D. Howe's office on 4 December 1945 established in principle the Defence Research Board, a body independent of the NRC that would coordinate defence research for the three military services. Solandt's name went forward as director general that same day.

Time was short, especially as research into atomic weapons generated such enormous concern in the early days of the Cold War. In the first four months of 1946, Solandt produced a budget and a policy paper for the DRB. The three services, especially the air force, did not like the idea of losing control over their research projects, so they found an uneasy compromise of sorts when the DRB was formally established in 1947. Solandt, with a position equal to that of the Chief of Staff, took over a number of existing defence establishments across the country; but he set his scientists to pursue pure rather than applied research. That decision may have helped justify the end of the DRB in 1974; even so, Godefroy argues that "the DRB clearly signalled Canada's intent to take its own defence and security requirements seriously."

The Mediterranean Theatre

We turn to the conduct of the Second World War on the ground, beginning with scholars who agree with Copp that we know far too little about the Mediterranean campaign. Few can match Lee Windsor's passion for understanding the Allied operations in this "forgotten" theatre. In this piece, Windsor takes aim at the persistent view that the British and Americans had no common commitment to a campaign in Sicily and Italy. Windsor revisits the claims of Field Marshal Sir Harold Alexander, the Commander of Allied Armies, Italy (AAI), who maintained that the dreadful fighting in the spring of 1944 at Cassino and Anzio kept large numbers of German formations from transferring to France in advance of the cross-Channel invasion. Says Windsor: "This policy was sound in ensuring Overlord would have the strength required to succeed, but it condemned those soldiers committed to secondary theatres to difficult, dangerous, and seemingly hopeless fighting to keep pinned down a German force of almost equal size." The Allied soldiers who fought in the Mediterranean have had good reason to feel forgotten. Windsor argues that historians should consider the role they played—with limited resources against a well-entrenched enemy—as vital to defeating the German armies in the west.

Among the many casualties of the Italian campaign were the soldiers of the First Special Service Force (FSSF) a Canadian–American commando unit first raised in 1942. James Wood details how its training in Montana to fight in the mountains of Europe paid off during the unit's perilous capture of Monte la Difensa in December 1943. In the face of mounting casualties, and with few reinforcements available, the FSSF's commanders were already questioning their force's viability when it was ordered in January 1944 to reinforce the fragile bridgehead at Anzio. The force reorganized under fire, drew upon Canadian volunteers and some disbanded US Ranger battalions, and prepared for the breakout on 23 May 1944 which ended in the capture of Rome on 4 June. The fierce fighting cost the FSSF nearly one-third of its total strength. Twenty days later, Brigadier-General Robert T. Frederick, the FSSF commanding officer and "the driving power behind the Force," announced his departure. On his recommendation, the force was disbanded in December 1944. As Wood so clearly shows, the reputation of the "Devil's Brigade" could not overcome the administrative hurdles put up by the two national armies from which it sprung.

Yves Tremblay's wide-ranging work focuses on the "lessons learned" from Operation Chesterfield, 1 Canadian Division's attack in the Liri Valley in May 1944. For him, this costly engagement reveals a persistent Canadian "tactical culture" that drew from the legacy of the First World War as well as the pervasive influences of the British Army. Articles in the *Canadian Army Training Memorandum* offered some chance to learn tactical lessons after 1941. But Tremblay argues that Canadian generals in the Mediterranean Theatre after July 1943 drew more from the experiences of the Western Front than from the lessons of the recent desert campaign. Tremblay's close reading of the "lessons learned" from Operation Chesterfield suggests that Canadian generals still had much to learn about operational tempo, reliable communications, and close infantry–tank cooperation.

Doug Delaney's work affirms the view that, with the exception perhaps of Andy McNaughton and Bert Hoffmeister, Canada's generals were not a very inspiring lot. Charles Foulkes was among the least likeable, and historians have faulted him for his handling of 2 Canadian Infantry Division through the summer and fall of 1944. Yet Foulkes rose to become I Canadian Corps commander in Italy in November 1944. Foulkes did not endear himself to his new staff, but Delaney concludes that in Operation Chuckle, the relentless battles over the sodden waterways in December 1944, Foulkes handled his two Canadian divisions surprisingly well. By that, Delaney means that Foulkes consulted rather than fought with his staff as he had done in Normandy. Hardly an innovator, Foulkes allowed his subordinates to get on with the ugly business of defeating the Germans in northern Italy. These lessons Charles

Foulkes brought home, for as unoriginal and prickly as he was, he became the Chairman of the Chiefs of Staff from 1951 to 1960.

Northwest Europe

"Military History Without Clausewitz" is the provocative opening chapter to Copp's *Fields of Fire: The Canadians in Normandy* (2003). In it Copp took aim at the long-held belief that it was largely through "numerical and material superiority" (to use Colonel Stacey's phrase) that the Allied "citizen" soldier defeated his superior German adversary.[7] Such judgments did not seem to jive with the ground that Copp walked or with the records he uncovered. Marc Milner, Mike Bechthold, and Angelo Caravaggio share Terry's passion for the Normandy campaign. They present here three battle studies drawn from a careful reading of the primary sources. Together they construct portraits of the Canadian performance in Normandy at its opening stages and in its dying days – portraits that question what we think we know about the Canadians in Normandy.

Milner's study of 9 Infantry Brigade Group on 7 June 1944 (D-Day + 1) challenges Colonel Stacey's assessment that it had "come off second-best" when its leading elements were "over-run" by the infamous 12 SS Panzer Division northwest of Caen. Milner's detailed and complex picture maintains that the Canadians gave a good account of themselves in a pitched battle against elements of three German divisions. But with no British support on the left flank, and with too few FOOs (Forward Observation Officers), who could not bring the guns to bear through most of the day, the Canadians withdrew to the only ground they could defend, Villons-les-Buissons. From there the field guns finally came on line late in the afternoon, working with the Canadian armour and infantry to smash a German counterattack. The youthful fanatics of 12 SS Panzer had little to boast about, and they took their grim revenge on Canadian prisoners captured near the villages of St-Contest, Authie, and Buron. It may have taken another month before the Canadians reached Carpiquet, their objective on 7 June 1944. But the Germans never reached the landing beaches.

Several kilometres west, the soldiers of 7 Canadian Infantry Brigade fought a series of equally important and difficult battles. Mike Bechthold focuses on the Royal Winnipeg Rifles, which lost over a quarter of its fighting strength storming "strongpoint Courseulles" on 6 June 1944. The next day it moved forward on the right of the brigade's advance to Putot-en-Bessin, a small walled Norman village that overlooks the rail line between Caen and Bayeux. The attacks by 12 SS Division that began in the early morning of 8 June forced the Winnipegs out of Putot, but quick action by Canadian and British forces prevented the Germans from outflanking the position. The Canadians were not "put to flight" as some have argued, for on the evening of 8 June, the Canadian Scottish Regiment retook Putot and held it against more German counterattacks the next day. He concludes that the Canadians showed careful leadership, planning, and coordination to retake an important position. In contrast, the attacks by 12 SS Panzer Division were badly coordinated, poorly led, and brutal: the Germans executed about fifty prisoners from the Royal Winnipeg Rifles.

From the beginning of the Normandy battles to the end, the discussion goes on about the role played by II Canadian Corps under Lieutenant-General Guy Simonds. Angelo Caravaggio's study takes us to mid-August 1944, when Allied forces converged on the ground east of Falaise that overlooked the final escape route of two German armies. Stacey, English, and Copp have looked to the dismissal of Major-General George Kitching, the General Officer Commanding (GOC) of 4 Canadian Armoured Division, as evidence that the Canadians faced difficulties of their own making as they fought to close the Falaise "gap" from the north. Caravaggio suggests otherwise. He details the workings of an inexperienced formation that faced three weeks of almost constant fighting. Kitching's regimental and brigade commanders seemed especially vulnerable; their replacements worked to fulfill orders that changed constantly after 16 August when the Germans went into full retreat. Operation Smash, Kitching's plan to move his armoured division through the winding countryside northeast of Falaise towards the town of Trun, was complex, but Caravaggio argues that it was extremely well conceived and executed. However, the battles that ended the Normandy campaign went beyond Trun, earning Major David Currie a Victoria Cross but costing General Kitching his command of 4 Division.

Then there is Lieutenant Jones, an anonymous young reinforcement officer whose story is told by Geoffrey Hayes through his personnel files, but which draws heavily upon Terry Copp's work. Jones was an ideal candidate to take the King's Commission. He was bright, athletic, and well educated. He had enlisted in the Canadian Officers Training Corps at his university before he took more formal officer training in early 1943. Finally overseas in 1944, he joined his unit, the Black Watch (Royal Highland Regiment) of Canada, in Belgium in late September 1944. His battlefield service lasted for not quite two weeks, ending at the horrendous battle for Woensdrecht on 13 October 1944. Soon after, Jones was diagnosed with a case of "psychoneurosis anxiety state." This chapter considers his service against several questions: By what assumptions were young Canadian men chosen as leaders? How well prepared were they for the battlefields on which they fought? And how well do we understand the experience of men like Lieutenant Jones?

The Aftermath

We end this collection by considering the legacy of the Second World War through several different lenses. Michelle Fowler traces the career of Ronald Balfour, a Cambridge-educated British officer attached to First Canadian Army as one of the "Monuments Men," a member of the Monuments, Fine Arts, and Archives Division at Supreme Headquarters Allied Expeditionary Force (SHAEF). Balfour was charged with protecting, preserving, repairing, and cataloguing the rich cultural heritage that the Canadians found throughout France, Belgium, the Netherlands, and Germany. Some have dismissed the work of the Monuments Men as a propaganda exercise, but Fowler's portrait of Balfour reveals an extraordinary intellect who did all he could to save Europe's rich cultural legacy.

Matt Symes is fascinated by the many kinds of informal commemorations he has come across throughout Normandy. In some places, simple street signs or roadside gardens recall passing Canadian units, or soldiers. Chance meetings between Canadian veterans and French civilians over the years have inspired more elaborate memorials, such as the private home that still sits on the beach where the Queen's Own Rifles of Canada came ashore on 6 June 1944. No similar memorial exists for the North Shore (New Brunswick) Regiment, which stormed the beaches just a short distance away. In trying to understand these shifts of memory, Symes explores the different ways that French civilians have memorialized the three infantry units of 8 Canadian Infantry Brigade. He maintains that these memorials have curious histories of their own, driven less by a clear understanding of events and more by the strength of personal relationships.

Finally, Jonathan Vance considers how Canadians remember the Second World War. A country of 11 million people had placed one million people in uniform and had suffered over 44,000 dead. That was a remarkable contribution, but Vance maintains that the memory of the Great War, when a country of 7 million people lost over 60,000 dead, overshadowed the Second. In the new cemeteries that so resembled those of the Great War, and in the "big words" that tied the dead of Dieppe to the dead of Flanders or Vimy, Vance notes, "one can only be struck by the degree to which the Second World War was passed over in favour of language and symbols from the First." Why was this so? The answer, he maintains, lies in the conditions of the peace. Unlike 1918, the victory of 1945 was unequivocal. Canada was relatively prosperous and stable. Reflecting this, the war memorials built after 1945 were not cenotaphs, but libraries, community centres, or hockey arenas. Through these "useful" memorials, Canadians looked not to the past, but to a better future.

In its thematic breadth, this collection offers an important contribution to our understanding of Canada and the Second World War, and it is a tribute to Terry Copp, a remarkable historian whose work continues to help us question, inform, and remember.

Notes

1. Ron Haycock and Serge Bernier, *Teaching Military History: Clio and Mars in Canada/ L'enseignement de l'histoire militaire: Clio et Mars au Canada* (Canada: Athabasca University, 1995), 151; Serge Bernier, "Canadian Military History: Must We Agree to Ignore a Lot?", unpublished manuscript, February 2009. The editors are most grateful to Dr. Bernier for making this second paper available to them.
2. Bernier, "Canadian Military History," 4.
3. J.L. Granatstein, *Canada's War: The Politics of the Mackenzie King Government, 1939–1945* (Oxford University Press, 1975); J.L. Granatstein, *Broken Promises: A History of Conscription in Canada* (Toronto: Oxford University Press, 1977); Franca Iacovetta and Roberto Perin, eds., *Enemies Within: Italian and Other Internees in Canada and Abroad* (Toronto: University of Toronto Press, 2000); Ken Adachi, *The Enemy That Never Was: A History of the Japanese Canadians* (Toronto: McClelland and Stewart, 1977); Ruth Roach Pierson, *"They're Still Women After All": The Second World War and Canadian Womanhood* (Toronto: McClelland and Stewart, 1986).
4. Jeff Keshen, *Saints, Sinners, and Soldiers: Canada's Second World War* (Vancouver: University of British Columbia Press, 2004).

5 Brian McKenna, *The Valour and the Horror: Episode Three, In Desperate Battle: Normandy 1944* (Montreal: National Film Board of Canada, 1992).
6 John Nelson Rickard, *The Politics of Command: Lieutenant-General A.G.L. McNaughton and the Canadian Army, 1939–1943* (Toronto: University of Toronto Press, 2010); Paul Douglas Dickson, *A Thoroughly Canadian General: A Biography of General H.D.G. Crerar* (Toronto: University of Toronto Press, 2007); Stephen John Harris, *Canadian Brass: The Making of a Professional Army, 1860–1939* (Toronto: University of Toronto Press, 1988).
7 Terry Copp, *Fields of Fire: The Canadians in Normandy* (Toronto: University of Toronto Press, 2003); Charles Stacey, *The Victory Campaign: The Operations in North-West Europe, 1944–1945* (Ottawa: Queen's Printer, 1960).

2

Terry Copp's Approach to History

Mark Osborne Humphries

Terry Copp has been teaching and writing history now for more than fifty years. During that time he has produced over a dozen books and numerous articles, but to his former students he is known best as a teacher. He is the type of academic who is as impactful in the classroom as he is prolific on the printed page. This makes it difficult to encapsulate the career of an historian that has ranged so widely across Canadian political, social, labour, and military history and that has had such a profound impact on so many academic lives. It is all the more difficult because I have only known Professor Copp during the most recent phase of his career—and I say *most* recent because it is a career that is still evolving.

I first met Terry—or rather, I first encountered him—on 11 September 2001 in the largest lecture hall in the Peters building at Wilfrid Laurier University. It was the first day of my second year at university, and that morning I had watched as the World Trade Center towers collapsed on live television. Copp was in a Board of Governors meeting. Nevertheless, he came to class that night and spent two hours talking to us about those events, what they meant politically, and what they would likely come to mean for our generation. Most of my professors that day had cancelled class. But as always, Terry wanted to talk to the students and help them understand what was happening at a very chaotic and confusing moment in history.

In his classes at Wilfrid Laurier, Professor Copp taught his students to ask questions and pursue their intellectual curiosity. He taught us to write narrative but analytical history based on thorough research into primary sources. The lucky few who were invited to continue their studies as graduate students at the Laurier Centre for Military Strategic and Disarmament Studies, were given the opportunity to learn the historian's craft by actively engaging in research, public outreach, teaching, and service. It was excellent training for aspiring academics and it changed the lives of all those who spent time at "the Centre." Terry has mentored dozens of young scholars over the years, both as a writer and as a teacher. Many have made contributions to this book. Although Terry is fond of saying that he is a simple, evidenced-based historian, he has consistently taught his students to employ a very specific theoretical and methodological approach—what many of his former students informally call the "Terry Copp School" or "Laurier Military History School"—that presents a coherent theoretical model for practicing and teaching history. It is the model he has used to bring the past alive for many readers and former students over the years.

It is now common to say that historians have found the methods and assumptions of their craft under attack from a postmodernist critique, which, at its most extreme, suggests that the discipline of history is based on the flawed and ultimately doomed foundation of scientific rationalism.[1] This critique has cast the historian's traditional pursuit of truth in documentary evidence as a logical impossibility—as an optimistic methodological construction born of an Enlightenment belief in scientific objectivity and the reification of singular, Western standards of knowledge and academic research.[2] In this analysis, documents (of all types) are texts that, as artifacts of language, must be viewed in relativistic terms and can only provide evidence of different discourses rather than objective truths, causalities, or explanations. The type of "truth seeking" advocated by E.H. Carr and Geoffrey Elton in the 1960s now looks profoundly naïve, and in 2012, no one should claim it as their objective.[3]

It is now safe to say that the fear and panic of the mid-1990s has subsided and that most historians have found a new *terra firma*, one that has been strengthened by the postmodernist approach rather than eroded by it. The new generation of historians finds the methodological and theoretical wars of the past strange and *passé*—who ever would have argued with the notion that fact is subjective and that "truth" is relative? New scholars only know the discipline that emerged from the history wars of the 1970s, 1980s, and

1990s. Jack Granatstein's claims that the discipline committed suicide by abandoning a Whiggish colony to nation (to colony) thesis in favour of exploring the experiences of ordinary Canadians—many of whom could not or would not relate to such a metanarrative—make little sense to our ears.[4] As Brian McKillop writes:

> Younger historians, with little deep commitment to the monarchy or the empire-commonwealth, and who did not share the anglophilic sensibilities of those who often taught and wrote within such frameworks, looked around them and began to write about the history of their own Canada: a multi-ethnic, multilingual, highly regionalized nation in which social and economic inequality was abundantly evident, entire groups within it were marginalized, and many voices remained silent.[5]

Narratives of nation building and national triumph that focus solely on the development of British Canadian institutions—assuming them to be the pinnacle in a progression that began at the Conquest—cannot exist unqualified, unrefined, and unchallenged in our world.

The new generation of historians has been taught to be self-critical and self-conscious, to see "race," gender, class, region, and other (sometimes "contested") theoretical categories of analysis as the lenses through which all structures of power and the experiences of ordinary Canadians—from the majority and the minority—must be viewed. We have been told, and we believe, that overarching truth in history does not exist, and that each historian can develop an interpretation of the past that may be internally coherent but that is only "true" for that historian at a particular time and in a particular context. We know and accept that in the discipline of historical analysis, the only constant is change. Perhaps most important, we know that objectivity in either research or analysis is impossible and can never be attained. This knowledge, we understand, must influence the questions we ask and the way in which we write history. All of these points, I think it safe to say, are now assumed to be true by the majority.

But it is important to point out, especially for younger scholars, that these ideas are not exactly new and that good historians have expressed them (and lived them) in one way or another since the advent of the new social history many decades ago. It is true that some once believed that a singular truth exists in the documents; but this has never been good history. In essence, this was the point of Herbert Butterfield's 1931 book, *The Whig Interpretation of History*, which pointed out the fallacy of seeing history as a progression towards a finite, singular, and empirically correct eventuality, in his case the supremacy of British constitutional democracy.[6] As Terry wrote in 1969, "Canadian historiography, pervaded by the sterility of what Herbert Butterfield has called 'Whig History,' has been made to seem irrelevant to the experience of the average citizen. Every man is, after all, his own historian, and a historiography which relates neither to experience nor aspiration is rightfully condemned to obscurity."[7]

Terry's approach to history, which he has taught since 1959 to countless students at Loyola College, Concordia University, McGill University, and Wilfrid Laurier University, embodies good history and good historical practice. For Terry, history is about posing questions of a body of evidence and seeking the answers through a combination of quantitative and qualitative research. He describes this approach as "evidence-based history," something that he claims is neither theoretical nor overly complicated. Both contentions are untrue.

Terry's approach to history draws heavily on R.G. Collingwood. In completing his undergraduate degree at Sir George Williams, Terry read Collingwood's *Idea of History*. As he writes in the preface to *Fields of Fire*, he never quite got over Collingwood's notion that the historian could rethink the processes behind past decisions.[8] For Collingwood, the problem facing historians was their distance from the evidence and their inherent lack of objectivity and the resulting subjectivity of historical analysis. Wrote Collingwood:

> The historian is not an eyewitness of the facts he desires to know. Nor does the historian fancy that he is; he knows quite well that his only possible knowledge of the past is mediate or inferential or indirect, never empirical. The second point is that this mediation cannot be effected by testimony. The historian does not know the past by simply believing a witness who saw the events in question and has left his evidence on record. That kind of mediation would give at most not knowledge but belief, and very ill-founded and improbable belief. And the historian, once more, knows very well that this is not the way in which he proceeds; he is aware that what he does to his so-called authorities is

not to believe them but to criticize them. If then the historian has no direct or empirical knowledge of his facts, and no transmitted or testimoniary knowledge of them, what kind of knowledge has he: in other words, what must the historian do in order that he may know them?[9]

For Collingwood, the only possible solution to the question was for the historian to "re-enact the past in his own mind."[10] In essence, Collingwood believed that

> when a man thinks historically, he has before him certain documents or relics of the past. His business is to discover what the past was which has left these relics behind it. For example, the relics are certain written words; and in that case he has to discover what the person who wrote those words meant by them. This means discovering the thought (in the widest sense of that word) which he expressed by them. To discover what this thought was, the historian must think it again for himself.[11]

For Collingwood, the historian's field of inquiry was narrowed to only that which could be re-enacted in the historian's mind.[12] "Of everything other than thought," he wrote, "there can be no history."[13] In practice, the historian would be required to examine constructs and objects that might not be "thoughts," but these, said Collingwood, would form only a bare skeletal structure and would not constitute proper history until they could be covered in flesh by the historian, able to grasp them within a coherent, ordered picture in his or her own mind. "This is only a way of saying," he wrote, "that the historian's thought must spring from the organic unity of his total experience, and be a function of his entire personality with its practical as well as its theoretical interests."[14]

Collingwood's *Idea of History*, written in the late 1930s but assembled and published after the author's death in 1946, presented a clear and prescriptive approach to history. For Collingwood, history was about problems that could be solved by reimagining the questions as they originally presented themselves to historical actors. The documents would function as signposts, allowing the historian to reconstitute the processes of history; but to go beyond simply reciting the script to understand why events had transpired as they had would require the historian to conceptualize the problem within a larger, coherent picture of the whole—a considerable feat of intellectual skill requiring a vast familiarity with all aspects of a particular period so as to enable her or him to engage with the sources. Collingwood's ideas about history were formed within a larger post-1918 cultural milieu influenced by moral and scientific relativism. Just as Einstein's *General Theory of Relativity* (1913) had suggested that the perspectives and relationship between object and subject changed as one moved through physical space and time, so too did it seem that written history could also only exist as subjective interpretation, always changing as the subject moved farther away from the object of study.[15] In other words, one's perspective was always changing. When Collingwood claimed that the only possible history was thus the history of thoughts, he was arguing from a relativist standpoint, agreeing with Benedetto Croce that "all history is contemporary history" while also providing a solution to the inherently subjective nature of textual sources.[16] Whereas the postmodern critique has argued that the meaning of language is entirely subjective and thus any reading of source materials can only result in new discourses, Collingwood solved a similar problem by arguing that one could indeed rethink the thoughts behind past actions and thus understand documents, so long as the historian was capable of reconstructing the problem addressed by the evidence in its proper historical contexts. While historians would surely still impose themselves on the sources through the process of selection—and the result would be interpretive rather than definitive—meaning could be derived from the texts once the past was reconstructed in whole in the mind of the historian. This would, necessarily, limit fields of inquiry to those areas where the thoughts behind identifiable actions as distinct from the ideas behind unknowable thoughts could be reconstituted.

It was these ideas about how to bridge the gap between object and subject and the process that the historian could use to overcome such obstacles to historical inquiry that Terry found so fascinating. "I found [Collingwood's] *The Idea of History* to be a liberating book," he says, "the idea that you could rethink the thoughts behind past actions as distinct from the thoughts behind past thoughts fascinated me. I still pull it out today and recommend it to my students because I feel it represents the best approach one can take towards primary material."[17] Like Collingwood, he views history as a series of problems that were addressed and solved in the past—for better or worse—and that it is the task of the historian to ask questions that allow us to reconstruct the decision making and thoughts behind the actions of the past. In reconstructing the thoughts and processes behind past actions, we can also understand why history developed as it did. But it is not a task that carries much possibility of objective success. "The task of the historian is to analyze events as they happened without the benefit of hindsight and independent of our own assumptions," Terry suggests. "But none of us ever succeed in this regard. We are inevitably drawn into imposing ourselves on the subject through our selection of events, regardless of how much we strive to avoid such an outcome." In this analysis, history becomes a process of asking questions and seeking answers—but in doing so the historian must be humbled by the knowledge that objectivity and definitiveness are impossible goals.

For Terry, the method of historical inquiry is inseparable from the purpose of studying history. In Terry's view, history explains the present and provides a laboratory in which past solutions to various problems can be studied and analyzed. It is in learning to reconstruct past decisions and actions in their proper context that trains the mind to see problems from a detached and relativistic point of view. It is his desire above all else to understand the past on its own terms—why things happened the way they did—as distinct from seeking solutions to contemporary problems or proofs for theoretical models, that provides historians with their *raison d'être*. "It is distressing," he says, "to face a room full of undergraduates, most of whom have no historical knowledge base. They are perfectly willing to discuss current events and problems at the level of the New York Times Op-Ed page, but they have no sense of the history behind current affairs nor the notion that others have faced similar problems in the past or asked similar questions."[18] Only through learning to rethink those past problems and to process questions within a known and visualized set of historical constraints can one be prepared to approach contemporary issues, be it the war in Afghanistan or the current economic crisis. In this sense, Terry believes that history provides lessons for the present, but only in terms of patterns of thinking and problem solving. The lessons of history can thus be found in the process and methods of historical inquiry, not the narratives or interpretations the inquiry generates.

Terry has adapted Collingwood's ideas to form his own approach to history. Although he believes that his metaphorical "evidence-based historian" is a simple, straightforward academic interested only in questioning and answering, he also believes that he must be restrained by an empirically rigorous and profoundly honest methodology. Says Terry:

> If you are, in fact, actually concerned with actions—things that actually happen and events that you can actually analyze, then you should be able to rethink the thoughts behind those past actions. You might not be able to rethink the motivations behind the actions, but you can reproduce the decision-making path. This is, of course, the essence of the coherence theory of truth. It describes the development of a logically compelling image—a picture or sketch of the past—that, in the end and at least for you, cannot look any different—you will, in essence, fail to reach any other conclusion. Now of course, very often the evidence is contradictory and you cannot actually reach such a conclusion—it is then the task of the historian to say just that.[19]

To attain this level of clarity, every historical research project must begin with a defined question posed of a body of evidence. For this reason, Terry instructs all of his students—as they will well remember—to begin each essay with two sentences. The first must begin: 'the purpose of this essay is ...' and the second must start: 'this paper argues ...' For him, clear questions lead to clear results. Clarity is impossible to achieve because of internal inconsistencies in the evidence, irreconcilable contradictions between documents, or a simple lack of evidence. But the historian must be equally clear about the impossibility of achieving a satisfactory answer to their question. For him, the greatest historical crime is to massage or explain away inconsistencies so as to produce a satisfactory conclusion to the second sentence above. In so doing, the historian would be abandoning the purpose that prompted the inquiry in the first place.

Terry's evidence-based historian must then, above all else, be true to the source material. This does not imply that there is an objective truth buried in the documents waiting to be uncovered, nor does it suggest that the evidence or documents speaks for themselves. Instead, it means that the documents must be viewed as fragments of a past that existed once and was internally coherent, which means that each fragment of the past must be taken into account by historians as they answer their questions. This being true, that documents—be they textual, photographic, material, or oral—are evidence of a real lived past, it is possible for the historian to reassemble them and thus reconstruct an approximation of the larger past of which they were a part—what Terry metaphorically describes as a *picture* or *sketch* of the past. Beginning from the evidence, then, in his view the historian's task is to re-create and reframe the problems of history in their original context. If successful, the historian should then be able to envision the decision-making paths that allowed events to unfold as they did.

If history is about explanation, it is no surprise that externalized theoretical models of causality in history appear counterproductive for Terry's evidenced-based approach. "I think [theory] gets in the way of real inquiry," he says.[20] It is not that understanding various theoretical models is unimportant, but for Terry, one must not approach the past looking to apply a theory to a historical problem or seeking evidence to support a particular model. In military history, as one example, it is common to begin with various theories that explain events on the battlefield—why one general was successful or why the campaigns of another failed—but for Terry, "if Clausewitz—or any other theorist—had influenced the decision makers, it would be reflected in the source material" and need not be imposed artificially on the situation.

Here a distinction must be made between Terry's rejection of *a priori* theoretical models of causality and explanation in history as opposed to the use of theoretical categories of analysis that can explain experience and help bring order to complexity. He rejects the former because in his view they reduce human agency and the human capacity for change by ascribing all causality to large, impersonal forces, regardless of the evidence the historian might uncover in the archive or through oral history. Such models, in his view, impose a superstructure on the past that the documentary evidence must then be made to fit. This, he argues, is bad history.

This does not mean that Terry rejects gender, class, ethnicity, region, and other categories of analysis—all of which are theoretical lenses too. Instead, he sees them as bringing clarity to the analysis and explanation of what happened to ordinary people in the past because they can be used to explain human experience. In this sense theoretical models of causality are also useful, but only insofar as they serve to make sense of the evidence uncovered by the historian.

On its face, this perspective invites some just criticism in the postmodern era. It can, of course, be argued that the sources themselves—textual documents written predominantly by literate men often for an official purpose—already distort the historian's picture of the past and provide their own patriarchal, European, privileged framework on which historians are then forced to hang their evidence. But on this point, Terry would probably agree. This is because his rejection of theoretical constructs is more of a linguistic argument, constituting a rejection of all kinds of *a priori* assumptions about the nature of truth in history, than it is a statement about how he perceives history in practice.

Terry began writing history by challenging the larger political-economic narratives because they failed to address or explain the experiences of ordinary Canadians. He wrote:

> The "covert whiggery" of the economic determinists [Donald Creighton, Harold Innis, Ferdinand Ouellet] has been kinder to tories and conversely more critical of liberals who believed in liberalism. But it has banished the west, the Maritimes and minority parties, as well as French Canada, from participation in the essential tasks of nation building ... Of even greater concern [is] the need for sensitive social and ideological enquiries, based upon a recognition of regional differences as well as on long overdue studies in labour history, urbanization, immigration, and business history.[21]

For Terry, history was (and is) about complexity rather than simple explanation—about a diversity of experiences and meanings in Canadian history rather than a simple narrative describing a positive evolution of the nation-state from British colony to English Canadian nation. "The utility of history," he concluded in 1969, "lies in its ability to reveal only one inevitability: change. History indicates complexity rather than pattern, the uniqueness of events rather than their similarity, the importance of chance rather than of probability. History deals in time, not timelessness."[22] History, he writes, is about experience.[23]

This approach to history—choosing to privilege the experiences and the lives of ordinary Canadians over the "great men" of history, using these to challenge metanarratives of nation building and progress—is evident in Terry's first monograph, *The Anatomy of Poverty: The Condition of the Working-Class in Montreal, 1897–1929*.[24] It was the first book to be published in the now prestigious Canadian Social History Series, originally produced by McClelland and Stewart and later taken over by Oxford University Press and then the University of Toronto Press. At the time, the editors of the series, S.F. Wise and Michael Cross, were able to explain to a public used to political history that "social history is about people ... [and] Canadian social history is still in its infancy."[25] Terry has always been most intrigued by new fields, barely touched by the secondary literature. The purpose of *Anatomy of Poverty* was "to examine the economic and social conditions of the lower-middle-class / working class population of Montreal during a period which is commonly regarded as a time of national expansion and prosperity."[26] True to form, its real purpose was to test assumptions about the success of the urban progressive movement in improving the lives of Canadians during the Laurier boom and postwar years by examining the hard evidence of how the lives of the working class changed over time.

Terry grew up in Montreal in a lower-middle-class / working-class craftsman neighbourhood, and he knew the area and the people he was writing about. Copp holds that dual narratives of urban progress led by elites from above as well as Marxist ideas about the importance of working-class associations in improving the lives of their members from the bottom did not hold true to his own experiences:

> My brothers and I were the first ones to go to university as my father had a grade 7 education and had immigrated to Canada from Ireland when he was sixteen in 1924. He worked at Dominion Textile while my mother's father had been a Grand Trunk Railway carpenter and tradesman. We all went to West Hill High School and lived in a rented flat below Sherbrooke. When the family allowance came in 1946, my mother was fond of saying that it paid for the groceries for one week a month. It was a significant change in our domestic economy, and I think most people care to forget how important it was to working families at the time as a means of income redistribution. I guess this means that I came from a typical aspiring self-made working-class family in which my father took night classes to move from a low-paying job greasing machinery at Dominion Textile to being a draftsman for Bell Canada. For me the reality of working-class life was that every wage earner I knew wanted a job that provided a steady income and little else. No one was interested in celebrating the glories of having dirty fingernails at the end of the day.[27]

In Terry's view, the lives of the working class did not materially improve, except perhaps in the area of public health, and they did not share in the fruits of the economic boom that the rest of Canada experienced during those years.[28]

The Anatomy of Poverty was a difficult book because it posed more questions than it answered. Its ultimate conclusion begged further study rather than closure:

> While it is true that all societies undergoing rapid economic growth have developed one method or another of forcing capital accumulation, it is important to recognize that in Canada, as in other countries, the working-class was required to pay the price for industrial growth without receiving much in the way of benefits, at least in the years before World War II.[29]

In the early 1970s, this was an important statement about the future direction that research in working-class and labour history would have to take, but it was also a direct challenge to the broad metanarratives that had been written about the evolution of the Canadian state and economy by previous generations.

The Anatomy of Poverty provides an excellent example of the methods used by Terry's metaphorical, evidence-based historian—an early result of what his students would come to call "the Laurier School." It is a local case study in urban history that examines the experiences of the working class. It illustrates the point that while Terry derides theory, he uses the categories of analysis typical to social history as a lens through which to view past experiences. Its chapters explore the real incomes of the working-class; women and children in the labour force; formal education as a tool of elite power; class conflict; the health of working people; and the failure of official social policies to materially alter the lives of Montreal's working citizens. All became important themes of the new social history.

After examining industrial unionism in Montreal and beginning a book on the emergence of the welfare state in the 1940s, Terry chose to abandon the field of labour history. As a subdiscipline, Terry felt that it was moving in a different direction, away from the type of history that he was increasingly interested in writing. When he turned to military history in the 1980s, he transposed his method and approach to examine the problems of the ordinary Canadian soldier on the battlefield. In the preface to *Fields of Fire*, he writes that "I began to study the experience of the Canadian army in the Second World War without benefit of training or extensive reading in military history."[30] But in his view, it was the type of wide-open field of study that would allow him to pose questions and seek answers without becoming bogged down in ideological debates. He recalls:

> I remember flying on a plane to Europe on an SDF [Security and Defence Forum] postdoctoral grant. In those days they let you fly for free on military planes so I was sitting with some important officer and explaining what I was going to do—go to the archives in London and then on to the battlefields to walk the ground—he asked me questions about my background and I told him I'd been an officer cadet in the 1950s but had not stayed with it. He probably asked me questions about Clausewitz and others, but I said to him, "No, I really don't want to read that stuff." I'[d] had enough contact with 19th century theorists in labour history to be suspicious. I was not going to go in that direction. I wanted to find out what happened by reading the primary sources ... I am really struck by the way in which historians romanticize the story of valour and honour. I want[ed] to go back to the basic sources, not the narrative sources.[31]

For Terry, this was the appeal of military history: it offered the type of source base and wealth of evidence that made it possible to pose specific questions and achieve specific answers.

As A.M.J. Hyatt once told a class of senior undergraduates, "when Copp became a military historian the workers became the soldiers and the bosses became the generals."[32] He had read the official narrative account by C.P. Stacey, but for Terry it was similar to the top-down histories that he had challenged in *Anatomy of Poverty*. Stacey's was a history of elite generals and their decisions, an admirable work of official history that did nothing to explain or give voice to the experiences of the working-class and middle-class soldiers who had actually done the fighting. He recalls:

> I remember standing at the Leopold Canal. [Robert Vogel and I] had brought copies of Stacey with us as well as the maps and I was standing there at the pillbox and I remember looking across at the canal and then back down at the pages in my hand and thinking, "This does nothing to explain what went on

here over the course of several days of what must have been intense fighting for the men involved."[33]

This visit to the battlefields, where he walked the ground where ordinary Canadian soldiers had fought only a few decades before, woke new questions in Terry's mind. Just as he had set out to analyze and describe the real condition of the working class in Montreal, he now became interested in writing a history of ordinary Canadian soldiers and their accomplishments in the Second World War—"bottom-up" history as he described it.

Over the next seven years, Terry worked with his mentor and colleague Robert Vogel to produce the five volumes of *Maple Leaf Route*.[34] They were a critical and eventually a commercial success, and they marked the beginning of a new type of military history in Canada focused on the ordinary soldier in battle—a school of scholarship that had been inspired by John Keegan's *Face of Battle* and Dennis Winter's *Death's Men*. In *Maple Leaf Route*, Terry used oral histories taken from ordinary soldiers to explore their experiences in battle and refight the war on paper from their perspective. Gone were arbitrary lines on maps and discussions that relied solely on generalship and logistics to explain why events had transpired as they did. Instead he constructed a narrative that placed the common infantry soldier and their decisions at the centre of both the story and the explanation.

This interest in the social experience of war naturally led Terry to examine what would today be called Operational Stress Injuries (OSI)—the modern equivalent of First World War shell shock. In *Battle Exhaustion: Soldiers and Psychiatrists in the Canadian Army, 1939–1945*, Terry and his co-author Bill McAndrew explored how war destroyed minds and how doctors attempted to diagnose and treat traumatized soldiers.[35] Again he drew heavily upon oral history, privileging the voices of the men themselves and their psychiatrists (as well as extensive archival research) over imposed theoretical explanations. Books on operational research, 5th Canadian Infantry Brigade, and the Regina Rifles followed.[36] His monographs, *Fields of Fire* and *Cinderella Army*, are regarded as definitive statements on the ordinary soldier's experience at war in Northwest Europe.[37]

At the same time, some have accused Terry of writing "maple syrup history"—of being overly nationalistic and pro-Canadian—and of constructing nation-building metanarratives of the type he began his career tearing down. He would counter that he simply follows the evidence and that he is critical of the Canadian soldier where warranted. His interpretations, he points out, sometimes fail to fit into accepted theoretical models of or notions about tactical or doctrinal progress. Therein lies the real problem. In writing both social and operational military history, Terry has sought to explain events and actions in the context in which they happened, preferring to ignore the theoretical impositions and paradigms that are now as common in military history as they once were in labour history:

> There is far too much hindsight in military history. People are always writing operational military history from the point of view that there is a single right answer—that if only the generals had done things in such a way or the supplies had been allocated differently then they would have found the solution. Of course military history is not the only variant of history that applies theoretical precepts to it and then works from hindsight, but it is certainly prone to it.[38]

It is for this reason—as an antidote to theoretical impositions—that Terry so strongly advocates that his students walk the battlefields. Once you have seen folds in the ground from the point of view of the common infantry soldier, lines on a map drawn by generals behind the lines inevitably change their meaning. In his view, by walking the ground and realizing that orders given from above must be accomplished at the tactical level, students learn to re-create military problems in the mind and thus re-enact the decision-making process. This same line of reasoning led him in 1969 to call on historians to explore the experiences of common Canadians rather than to elaborate national narratives focused on the experiences and ideas of a few elites.

The battlefield tour is, in essence, Terry's teaching method and philosophy of history distilled to its constituent and raw elements. In the classroom, he is a provocateur and a role model. He designs each class around a particular question, which is then examined and dissected throughout the lecture. "If students leave feeling like there are more questions than there are answers," he says, "then I know I have been doing my job."[39] He wants his students to ask their own questions, to learn what other historians have said on a subject, but so that they can ask their own questions rather than recite the views of others. His classes in this way re-create and model the historical methods he uses in his own research. Questions are posed, context is sought, documents and evidence are examined, and conclusions are reached about why events transpired as they did. The student groups he has led since the early 1990s go through the same process on the battlefield. The ground, for Terry, is the physical context that defined and restricted actions during battle, so it is the duty of the historian to read the ground like a document, using it to re-create the world and context in which past decisions were made.

Terry Copp's evidence-based historian is someone who asks questions and allows—as much as possible—the evidence to dictate the answers. In his view, she or he must seek to re-create the constraints and possibilities that faced decision makers in the past and rework historical questions within a Collingwoodian framework that is both demanding and rigorous. He or she requires a clarity of purpose as well as defined research questions that are answerable given the available evidence. From this theoretical position, he argues that historians should accept the relativity of their position to the past and try to overcome that gap through a thorough and holistic reading of the sources. This approach suggests that the historian can gain insight into the past from a close reading of texts when they are understood in their proper contexts. But it also demands that they plead ignorance if definitive pictures fail to emerge from the archive. This methodology embraces all forms of evidence and can be taught in the classroom—traditional or metaphorical. It is the approach to history that Terry has been modelling to his students ever since he edited the *Problems in Canadian History* series in the mid-1960s, and he continues to teach it to students at Wilfrid Laurier University today.

Notes

The author would like to thank Geoffrey Hayes, Kellen Kurchinski, Geoffrey Keelan, and Lianne Leddy for their comments on the paper. Terry Copp agreed to conduct several hours of interviews for this piece. He and his wife Linda read drafts of the paper.

1 For an overview of the postmodern critique and its implications for history, see Ernst Breisach, *On the Future of History: The Postmodernist Challenge and Its Aftermath* (Chicago: University of Chicago Press, 2003), 1–26. A more succinct overview is John Tosh with Sean Lang, *The Pursuit of History: Aims, Methods, and New Directions in*

the Study of History, 4th ed. (Harlow: Pearson Education, 2006), 194–205. A sustained refutation of the postmodern critique is provided in Richard J. Evans, *In Defence of History* (New York: Norton, 2000).
2 Breisach, *On the Future of History,* 1–26.
3 See E.H. Carr, *What Is History?* (Cambridge: Cambridge University Press, 1961); and Geoffrey Elton, *The Practice of History* (London: Thomas Crowell, 1967).
4 See J.L. Granatstein, *Who Killed Canadian History?* (Toronto: HarperCollins, 1998).
5 A.B. McKillop, "Who Killed Canadian History? A View from the Trenches," *Canadian Historical Review* 80, no.2 (June 1999), 284.
6 Herbert Butterfield, *The Whig Interpretation of History* (London: G. Bell and Sons, 1931).
7 Terry Copp, "The Whig Interpretation of Canadian History," *Canadian Dimension* 6 (April–May 1969), 23.
8 Terry Copp, *Fields of Fire: The Canadians in Normandy* (Toronto: University of Toronto Press, 2004), xii–xiii.
9 R.G. Collingwood, *The Idea of History* (Oxford: Oxford University of Press, 1966), 282.
10 Ibid.
11 Ibid., 282–3.
12 Ibid., 302.
13 Ibid., 304.
14 Ibid., 305.
15 Evans, 30–1.
16 Ibid.
17 Interview between author and Terry Copp, 28 January 2011.
18 Interview between author and Terry Copp, 1 February 2011.
19 Interview between author and Terry Copp, 28 January 2011.
20 Interview between author and Terry Copp, 1 Feb 2011.
21 Copp, "The Whig Interpretation of Canadian History," 23–4.
22 Ibid., 33.
23 Ibid., 23.
24 Terry Copp, *The Anatomy of Poverty: The Condition of the Working-Class in Montreal, 1897–1929* (Toronto: McClelland and Stewart, 1974).
25 Ibid., 7.
26 Ibid., 9.
27 Interview between author and Terry Copp, 28 January 2011.
28 Copp, *Anatomy of Poverty,* 140.
29 Ibid., 148.
30 Copp, *Fields of Fire,* xi.
31 Interview between author and Terry Copp, 28 January 2011.
32 Interview between author and Terry Copp, 28 January 2011.
33 Ibid.
34 Terry Copp and Robert Vogel, *Maple Leaf Route,* 5 vols. (Alma: Maple Leaf Route Publications, 1983–88).

35 Terry Copp and Bill McAndrew, *Battle Exhaustion: Soldiers and Psychiatrists in the Canadian Army, 1939–1945* (Montreal and Kingston: McGill–Queen's University Press, 1990).

36 Terry Copp, *The Brigade: The Fifth Canadian Infantry Brigade, 1939–1945* (Stoney Creek, ON: Fortress Publications, 1992); Terry Copp, ed., *Montgomery's Scientists: Operational Research in Northwest Europe* (Waterloo: Laurier Centre for Military Strategic and Disarmament Studies, 2000); Gordon Brown and Terry Copp, *Look to Your Front—Regina Rifles: A Regiment at War, 1944–1945* (Waterloo: Laurier Centre for Military Strategic and Disarmament Studies, 2001).

37 Terry Copp, *Cinderella Army: The Canadians in Northwest Europe, 1944–45* (Toronto: University of Toronto Press, 2006).

38 Ibid.

39 Interview between author and Terry Copp, 1 February 2011.

3
"To Hold on High the Torch of Liberty"
Canadian Youth and the Second World War

Cynthia Comacchio

For many young Canadians, the national call to arms that sounded in September 1939, scarcely more than a generation after the "war to end all wars," signalled a personal obligation to be "taken seriously by the whole population, not just those who rushed to join the colours." As one woman recalled, although "terrified" at the prospect of war, "All of us, of all ages, accepted that we must do something, no matter how little."[1] Another member of the generation that came of age during the Second World War—famously dubbed "The Greatest Generation" by American journalist Tom Brokaw—affirmed that young Canadians "believed that we were fighting for our survival, and for the survival of civilization ... I would have volunteered proudly, if I had not been too young to fight."[2] Still others recall their sense of adventure and excited anticipation: writer Budge Wilson, a Halifax teenager at the time, was secretly thrilled to be experiencing the war in a city "on the edge" of warfare while herself poised "on the edge of childhood and very close to adulthood."[3]

What is important about being young in the midst of world-historic events such as war, what connects the multitude of personal and often divergent experiences, what imprints individual and collective memory, is not the universality of experience so much as the fundamental elements of age and life stage. Age profoundly mediates the experience of world events, making them "historic" on myriad levels. The sense of belonging to a "wartime generation" shaped a particular generational consciousness, both among peers and in relation to those younger and older. Whether enlisted or participating in homefront activities, rural or urban-based, in school or earning wages, male or female—and despite variations in class, race, culture—for many Canadians, the Second World War was distinguished by the simple fact of belonging to a certain age cohort and sharing its life stage perspectives, challenges, and opportunities at that precise historical moment.

It is not the veracity or accuracy of what is remembered about coming of age in wartime that reveals the generational stamp of war, but the ways in which that experience is framed, both by contemporaries and by those looking backward.[4] Personal recollections and contemporary commentaries alike testify to its generational impact. While this naturally applies to all ages and life stages, it could be argued that those "on the edge of childhood"—the adolescents who, by the 1940s, were becoming popularly known as "teenagers"—were in many ways the most affected of the wartime generations.[5] At least officially, many were too young to fight or to take on authoritative homefront roles. Yet, more aware than their younger siblings of the meaning of war, they were very much "in the midst" of the tumult, challenge, and opportunity presented by both their adolescent condition and the historic situation that served as its context.

War necessarily focuses attention on the population, the essential resource for its successful prosecution, and especially on those who are young, healthy, and male. The public discourses of the time recognized that youth embody both the dread and the promise of war. Young Canadians were both strongly urged to participate in the war effort and especially commended for it, in public acknowledgment that the greatest burden of war is shouldered by the young. Just as Depression youth had paid a steep price in deferred ambitions for a "normal" life, so would wartime adolescents, some of whom would sacrifice life itself. Thus the Second World War constituted an "even bigger challenge" to youth than had the economic crisis that it effectively ended, for "the children of a depression and its handicaps" had become "the adolescents of another war era and the hazards that accompany it."[6] Among such hazards were the vulnerability of "latch-key" children obliged to fend for themselves in empty homes; the impulsive curtailing of education in favour of well-paying jobs; the "running off" to enlist of under-age boys and even girls; and the promiscuity and delinquency evidently encouraged by the failure of adult supervision in the urgent atmosphere of wartime.[7] As well, like those who had come of age during the Depression, wartime adolescents were shaken by their insecure prospects. The Young Women's Christian Association reported that, among young women, "the uncertainty of the future often looms large"; requests for their counselling services had increased greatly as the "normally perplexing problems of youth" were aggravated by the "unsettling influences of a war-torn world."[8] The YMCA was also mindful of its "continuing responsibilities" to young men, the "leaders of tomorrow, on whose shoulders must ultimately fall the responsibility of preserving and maintaining in Canada those very principles and freedoms for which we now fight."[9]

Enlistment was the most self-evident of youthful contributions. The age qualifications in themselves—between 18 and 40 years—demonstrate that, at least ideally, the armed forces relied on young men. Most voluntary enlistment was at the lower end of that span, among those too young to have major family or work commitments or health impediments. It is difficult to know precisely how many under-aged men succeeded in signing up for duty, since their very success in doing so ensures that their actual number remains obscured. Yet stories in the daily press, then and now, memoirs and oral histories and anecdotal evidence about those turned away for being too young and those who served nonetheless, as well as the discharge records of those who were "caught," suggest their significant participation.[10] One man remembers that during his high school years in Saskatchewan, "boys were all mad keen to join up, though only 16. Any time a guy was absent, nine times out of ten he was down at some recruiting desk in town trying to sneak his way in ... these guys kept trying, even to using false identification."[11]

We need not be cynical about the heartfelt patriotism of past times. Yet historians are obliged to acknowledge that there may be, alongside the tricky workings of memory, a measure of nostalgia affecting such personal recollections. Certainly no claim can be made that all Canadians, of all ages and backgrounds, experienced "the good war" in the same manner—or even that they shared in that conceptualization of it. And certainly there is ample reason, beyond youthful patriotism and idealism, for those who came of age during the Second World War to remember it in a positive light. For many, fresh memories of a Depression childhood could not help but shape responses to the war: as writer Mordecai Richler, then a high school student in Montreal, attested, "I cannot remember it as a black time and I think it must be so for most boys of my generation. The truth is that for many of us

"They Enlisted Straight Out of School," These young men from the rural Alberta town of Edson went straight from the classroom to the armed services. [Glenbow Museum and Archives Collection, Edson, Alberta, 1941, NA-3240-84. Reprinted with permission of the Glenbow Museum, Calgary, AB.]

to look back on the war is to recall the first time our fathers earned a good living."[12]

For the generation of youth emerging from the Great Depression, the war also bestowed their first opportunity to be productively engaged, adequately clothed and fed, and earning wages.[13] Growing up in the economically ravaged mining town of Glace Bay, Nova Scotia, Bill McNeill remembered how

> that first wave of enlistment brought in the worst victims of the Depression, those poor lads who didn't know what it was like to have enough to eat or wear. I know, because many of them were my friends and neighbours. I would have been with them too, but in September 1939 I was only 15 years old, too young to fool the recruiting officer into thinking I was a mature man of 18. Not that I didn't try many times.[14]

McNeil was "crushed, devastated and jealous beyond belief" when his friends were accepted, although, at the age of seventeen, they were only slightly older than he. Shortly after shipping out, they were counted among the first wave of casualties from his hometown.

Others were more fortunate than McNeill's childhood friends, though no less courageous. Robert Skipper, a top student at Chatham Collegiate Institute, was obliged to leave school at the age of fourteen to help on his parents' farm. Without their approval or even a "goodbye or good luck," he persisted in trying to enlist. Though only seventeen and undersized, he was finally accepted by the Irish Regiment at Toronto's Fort York.[15] In Saskatchewan, Donald Tansley joined the Second (Reserve) Battalion of the Regina Rifles at the age of fifteen and enlisted in the Active Army on his eighteenth birthday, just a few weeks short of finishing grade twelve.[16] In late 1942, the astounding story of "Dieppe Tom Brown" captured newspaper headlines in Toronto. After enlisting at the age of sixteen, Brown had reluctantly returned to the city's Central Technical High School, "back from the edge of beyond" after fighting for six-and-a-half hours at Dieppe; he was one of two survivors in his section of eight men. Remarkably unaffected by the public amazement that his story inspired, he insisted that "Sure, I wanted to get in as soon as it started. My dad was wounded in France when he was 16. What's so wonderful about me wanting to get into this war as young as dad?" Discharged when his family reported him as under-aged, Brown was "just biding his time" until he could enlist legally.[17] Similarly, seventeen-year-old Bill Marshall went ashore with the 3rd Division at Juno Beach in June 1944, probably the youngest of his platoon in the Highland Light Infantry. He survived D-Day but was wounded in Buron a month later, just three days past his eighteenth birthday.[18]

Nor was under-age enlistment restricted to adventurous young men. In Kitchener, Number 10 Canadian Army Training Centre opened in Knollwood Park early in 1941. At the end of 1942 it was converted to train young women for the Canadian Women's Army Corps.[19] A woman who arrived there when she was sixteen was "scared to death they'd find out my age," only to discover a fourteen-year-old at the camp: "After that I felt brave." Two local girls also went together to the Kitchener recruiting office when they heard that "they were taking seventeen year olds ... and we begged them to take us. We were willing to do anything, but the ruling had not changed." They signed up when they turned eighteen. A seventeen-year-old francophone girl from Montreal, however, managed to enlist by lying about her age and telling the recruiters that her birth certificate was lost.[20]

CWACs in basic training at Knollwood Park, Kitchener, Ontario, 1944. [*The Dominion Institute, The Memory Project: Digital Archive*. http://66.241.252.164/digital-archive//]

There are doubtless many such stories of young Canadians who, in Skipper's words, "never got to be a teenager" due to their determination to enlist; there are countless more, however, male and female, who did not see battle but nonetheless experienced the war as a "shortcut to adulthood."[21] Blackouts and air raid testing, ration books and first-aid courses, "precautions" and "preparations," were integral to the homefront experience for all ages. While none escaped the war news that saturated the media, teenagers were more conscious of the meaning of that news than their younger siblings, and perhaps more continually exposed to it in classroom radio broadcasts and "social studies" discussions. The young also regularly took in the ubiquitous newsreels preceding the movies that were the principal adolescent pastime. These featured shocking actual footage from overseas, and often the National Film Board's "Canada Carries On" series that documented what was happening at training camps.[22] By the 1940s, radio broadcasts had become part of the evening routine for many Canadians. They solemnly attended to CBC news reports delivered by a young Lorne Greene, remembered by some as "the Voice of Doom": "Walk down any city street on a summer's night at 9 o'clock and you could pick up his voice from house to house," intoning the latest from the battlefields.[23]

Modern technology delivered the sights and sounds of war, the violence and human suffering, the chaos and destruction, the true sense of emergency, more profoundly and immediately than ever before in history. There were also unrelenting government poster and advertising campaigns urging all to "do their bit," and sending strong recruitment messages for "Canada's New Mechanized Army," as witnessed in a friendly "High School Students Wanted!" pitch published in newspapers across Canada in 1943.[24] As one man recalled, "We were steeped in propaganda up to here. They seemed to direct an awful lot of it at the kids."[25] During "Reconsecration Week," held annually to honour the anniversary of the Canadian declaration of war in September 1939, public ceremonies included "pleas to the youth of Canada" from such parliamentarians as Justice Minister Erneste Lapointe. In a CBC radio broadcast on the occasion in 1941, Lapointe asked that "young men of my native land" make their "own individual choice between freedom and slavery, between the path of duty and the road of selfishness."[26] The very notion of "taking up the torch," immortalized in John McCrae's emblematic poem of the Great War, was a generational premise used in any number of exhortations to motivate Canadians—especially the young who embodied the nation's future—to support the war effort.

Representing a ready supply of young people ostensibly dedicated to social service and national welfare, youth organizations played an important role in the war effort. As during the Great War, the Girl Guides were reminded that the "service of youth" was a "vital service for the nation." They answered the call enthusiastically with a wartime program that emphasized emergency preparedness, physical fitness, homecraft, nursing, and first aid. The Guides also participated in the customary feminine voluntary homefront activities: they were "quietly but busily knitting, sewing, making bandages, acting as messengers, typists

World War II poster featuring "The Torch." [Library and Archives Canada C-087137]

or chauffeurs and otherwise assisting local war agencies" across the land.[27] A fourteen-year-old patrol leader from Alberta reported to the *Free Press Prairie Farmer* that "the companies in our town have sent one shipment of clothes for the homeless victims in bomb-shattered Great Britain and they are busily making more." She reminded the newspaper's young readers that "the future queen, Princess Elizabeth, is a Girl Guide."[28] The Boy Scouts followed suit: they collected salvage, shipped hundreds of pounds of seeds to Britain, promoted and grew Victory Gardens. They served as messengers, telegraph operators, and first aid attendants, and took active part in Victory Loan campaigns.[29] In Preston, Ontario, the First Preston Troop's Scout House Band made its debut public performance in 1940, marching the Galt-based members of the Women's Reserve of the Canadian Naval Service, the Wrens, to Sunday morning church services.[30]

In Canadian high schools, the war's effects on the structure, the organization, and even the content of secondary education were direct and immediate. During the interwar years, the age of school-leaving was raised to sixteen years in most provinces, prompting the expansion or construction of many new secondary schools. Although the majority of young Canadians were working full-time by the age of seventeen, modern adolescence was gradually becoming characterized by some measure of high school attendance.[31] Citizenship training came to figure strongly in both the curriculum and the newly important extracurriculum; not surprisingly, this emphasis on the social formation of ideal citizens through schooling drew new strength from the exigencies of war.[32]

With equal emphasis on individual sacrifice and the importance of collective effort, the messages disseminated through state and quasi-state agencies, through voluntary and professional organizations, and through schools, churches, and the media, reinforced certain expectations about what young Canadians could and should do for their nation. The fascist regimes were quick to channel youthful passion toward their vision of a new world order; just as they had "recognized and exploited the potential power for social change which youth possesses," the Allies had to do likewise among their own to avert that horrific end.[33] Thus the schools constituted the front line of battle. As one educator observed, the war had "caused people to realize the place of education as fundamental to the working of democracy and as the agency for developing those attitudes and ideals which must permeate nations if they are to live together in a normal human way." In November 1940, New Brunswick's education minister initiated a meeting in Ottawa of all provincial education officials to consider ways and means of delivering a citizenship education that would best serve both present and postwar needs. The outcome was the formation of the Canadian Council for Education in Citizenship, which was charged with developing relevant materials and procedures toward its stated end, "the teaching of democratic citizenship" in order to ensure "a finer type of Canadian citizen."[34] The efforts of youth "for the duration" were vital, but so too was their education for the roles that they would one day shoulder as adult citizens. "We must not think of ourselves as merely onlookers in the tremendous drama which unfolds itself from day to day," one principal admonished his students:

> We are participants and a realization of this is very important. Spectators have no responsibility in the way a game is played; the players have. The tumult of the tanks, bursting bombs from warring aircraft and all the other awful machinery of war is not a part of a show presented for our entertainment...We must feel that we are a part of these events; that in the shaping of the future, the much heralded post war world, we have a much greater share of responsibility than we realize at present...We do matter; we are of tremendous importance. Let us not forsake our responsibility.[35]

Despite such grand objectives, the diversion of funds and government energies to the war effort after many years of Depression restraints and cuts quickly made its impact felt in the nation's high schools. Courses were cut; facilities were crowded; supplies were lacking; equipment was in need of repair and refurbishing. Classes were bigger as "one of the most important effects" on the schools was the enlistment of teachers, ensuring that most high school classes would be taught by women or—at least in the eyes of students—"much older men."[36] Notwithstanding the complications for public education, these teachers were seen to be "an inspiring example" whose sacrifice exemplified to the young how "devotion to freedom, loyalty to throne and native land come before all other things."[37] Likewise, in the higher grades the enlistment of male students meant an increasingly female senior class. To some of the younger students, their departure to serve "looked glamorous and worldly."[38]

Student publications showed the stamp of war in the tone and nature of their content, which resonated with a generational concept of idealism, patriotism, and sacrifice for a larger cause. Yearbooks were dedicated to teachers, students, and alumni who had enlisted. Honour rolls of those on active service, those returned, and, later, of the "missing" and the casualties, came to fill the front pages. Sombre promises were made to "take up the torch," in oblique reference to the generational imagery of the famed McCrae poem. At Sangudo High School in rural Alberta, the 1943 yearbook was dedicated to those who had "left all to face your seeming destiny ... When a threat had neared our land ... left your youth and trust to us / To carry on." Their peers pledged "to hold on high the torch of liberty ... for the life you left behind, / That now we live and love anew."[39]

As noted in provincial education department annual reports across Canada, the curriculum was modified to meet the ideals, goals, and day-to-day exigencies of wartime. Essays, poetry, and composition were dedicated to war themes, the defence of democracy, the evils of fascism, and support for Canadian participation.[40] In British Columbia, there were discussions about the place of "modern foreign languages" in the high school curriculum, in both present and future. As the provincial school inspector wondered, "Will students care to study German in order to read the works of Germans of former times? One may doubt it." He also considered that, although French might continue to be important due to the "French fact" in Canada, the "same processes of intellectual decay" were afflicting France as well as Germany.[41]

Technical courses were frequently "slanted ... to the grim necessities of today," with lessons based on the needs of war production. At Toronto's Central Technical High School, the largest and oldest of the province's "Techs," seven hundred students were trained for war industry at special evening and night classes. At the Ford of Canada Trade School in Windsor, Ontario, teenage apprentices, the "craftsmen of tomorrow," acquired skills that were seen as essential to the "growing strength" of Canada and the Empire.[42] Under the aegis of the Dominion-Provincial War Training Program, itself an outgrowth of the shared youth training program devised in 1937, students at Hamilton's Westdale Technical High School began training in machine shop practice, motor mechanics, radio, and drafting for war industry and the armed forces during a special summer school session in July–August 1940. Westdale was also the only school in Ontario selected to train toolroom improvers in a six-month course that required a $30,000 investment in toolroom equipment.[43]

One of the largest in-class wartime projects involved 40,000 boys in high schools across Canada who worked on the production of scale models of ninety different fighting aircraft from both the Allied nations and the Axis. Fifty thousand models were urgently needed to help pilots, observers, and gunners in the British Commonwealth Air Training Plan identify aircraft instantly from any angle. *Saturday Night* magazine remarked that knitting, "once supposed to be the chief wartime occupation" among high school girls, had been changed by the "all-out slacks and bandannas of this war." In some schools, the girls had reportedly "ganged up" and insisted that they too be admitted into the Commonwealth model airplane plan: "In these cases the knitting needles are idle while the young ladies cut patterns and paint up the finished models." Their participation, however, clearly stayed within the domain of traditional feminine skills. Every boy who completed an acceptable model as part of his war effort earned an official certificate from the RCAF; no mention is made of recognition for the girls' efforts.[44]

This gendered participation of youth in the war effort proved enduring, however much women were pressed to take on "men's work" for the duration. When the hulls were laid for the corvettes HMCS *Kitchener* and HMCS *Galt* in 1941, local girls formed the Sister Susie Club to raise funds, principally by means of such traditional feminine production as knitting afghans and making quilts for raffling. Local girls and women also worked to supply the "domestic" needs of HMCS *Prestonian* and HMCS *Hespeler*, commissioned in 1944. Once the labour shortage became acute, however, a number of the community's young women quickly surmounted the gendered expectations of homefront duty to enroll in the machinist and material inspection courses held at Kitchener–Waterloo Collegiate.[45]

Another of the pressing concerns of the wartime economy was the shortage of agricultural labour. Rural youth had long worked on family and neighbouring farms, but by 1940, a growing number were also attending high school for longer periods. An Albertan remembered how his high school in the Lethbridge area stopped taking attendance because farm help was so scarce that absentees were assumed to be legitimately working on family or neighbouring farms. In Waterloo County, on average, every other farm was missing the vital labour of a family member just as farmers were obliged to expand production to meet war needs.⁴⁶ The war also brought farm youth early attainment of one of the coveted rights of adulthood: "Becoming fourteen years old then was as big a deal as becoming twenty-one today because during the war they'd give driving licenses to fourteen year olds, and that meant you could drive the farm truck or go to town for your father … I can remember going down the highway in our old car with only my eyes showing above the windshield."⁴⁷

Urban and other non-farm youth, especially high school students, would serve as a critical source of agricultural labour as enlistment left many farmers without help at a time of tremendous need. In 1940, in a program replicated across the nation, the Hepburn Liberal government instigated the Ontario Farm Service Forces to organize the enrolment of "farm cadets." Initially these were high school boys fifteen years old and over, but the age was quickly lowered to recruit those between the ages of twelve and seventeen. Admonished to "remember you are serving not only the farmer but your country's needs," young volunteers would spend the summer at special camps, going out to work where needed on a daily basis, for a $25 monthly wage.⁴⁸ By 1941 the Ontario provincial government had implemented the corollary "Easter Scheme," taken up by at least 6,000 students that year, which granted students their full year's credit if they left school in the spring to assist farmers.⁴⁹ Not all Ontarians were enthusiastic about the program; the president of the Trades and Labour Congress decried it as a return to "the dark ages" of child labour, while education officials were displeased by their lack of control over the "full year's credit" and also by proposals to delay the school year to accommodate those working on the harvest.⁵⁰

Eventually, as boys went into war industry, the farm brigades became largely female. By 1944, newspapers were reporting that six hundred boys had enlisted in the Ontario Farm Service Forces, "but between 1,500 and 2,000 more could be placed at once." At the same time, 1,800 high school girls were at the camps, with the number "slowly increasing" toward an expectation of 4,000 "farmerettes" by summer's end.⁵¹ Even after V-E day in the summer of 1945, the demand for teenage farm labour remained high. Haligonian Budge Wilson joined an Ontario farmerette camp near St. Catharines that summer. Sixty female high school students went out to work on neighbouring farms each day under the supervision of five older teens: "What we did was keep the place clean and prepare the food for the other sixty kids … At that camp I

"Farmerettes" picking cucumbers at a farm service camp, ca. 1941. [Ministry of Agriculture, RG 16-20-0-3, Archives of Ontario, I0006635]

discovered what hard work could really be like, putting in a twelve hour day, then sometimes going out to work in the orchards when the trees were loaded down with overripe fruit."[52]

War also brought back one of the more traditional rites of passage for the young, the introduction to full-time wage labour. During the Depression, soaring youth unemployment had forced many to spend more time in high school. Under the provisions of National Selective Service (NSS) in the interests of "total manpower" for total war, as enacted in August 1942, young people were urged to register for summer or regular placement in war industry and homefront services. Enticed by the war economy's opportunities, the 3,911 teenagers who left Toronto high schools before senior matriculation in 1943–44 were immediately absorbed into full-time work.[53] According to the Toronto manager of the NSS, the majority of these were not interested in non-essential jobs: "Rather, they want to be able to tell their older buddies, brothers and fathers they are doing their share. And the jobs they have or are taking aren't soft, either." A representative of the John Inglis Company declared that "there is no doubt about the willingness of the youngsters, for we frequently have line-ups outside the plant with boys anxious to get jobs," while a Massey-Harris manager confirmed that the "youngsters ... work hard and are conscientious."[54] A Wellesley (Ontario) Township farm girl, sixteen when the war began, joined her sister at the Sunshine Company plant in

Waterloo, soldering land mines initially and then working in the smoke bomb department; she joined the Wrens in April 1943.[55] As a Regina high school student, Donald Tansley found that "as a direct result of the War ... suddenly there was a shortage of young people to fill all sorts of menial, but paying, tasks." At fourteen, he landed a choice sales job at a men's store that lasted him through high school, and spent summers building a highway from the new Commonwealth Air Training Centre at Mossbank to Assiniboia, where the pay, at $3.50 for each ten-hour day "plus mattress and meals ... was great."[56]

While boys "of the football player type" were much in demand for war industry, those of slighter physique, and young women, became increasingly important in various aspects of homefront service as labour shortages threatened. Canadian National Railways trained and employed hundreds of teenage boys as telegraph operators at its National Telegraph Office in Edmonton, as well as in secondary offices.[57]

Girls as young as fifteen were much in demand for general office, switchboard, and clerical duties, and also served as bicycle-riding "messengerettes," particularly for the armed forces and various provincial and federal government agencies. Fifteen-year-old Rita was recruited to do messenger service for various federal agencies in Ottawa, one of about thirty young people working for the Consumer Branch of the federal government.

Sixteen-year-old telegraph operators in the Canadian National Telegraph office, Edmonton, Alberta. [CN Images of Canada Gallery, CN001976; Canadian Science and Technology Museum, Ottawa, www.imagescn.technomuses.ca.]

Although anaemic and diabetic, she worked from 9:00 to 5:30, attended night school three nights per week to learn typing and shorthand, and "in her spare time, she sings, plays the piano and tap dances." According to *Chatelaine* magazine, her hard work and energy ensured that "Rita has a future."[58]

For all the service, sacrifice, duty, and atmosphere of necessary restraint, the young did not entirely relinquish their hard-earned fun. In a time when youthful frivolity could hardly be seen to receive adult encouragement, homefront participation, closely entwined with ideals of citizenship, often became the purpose for even ostensibly "recreational" activities. The extracurriculum that had become a vital element of modern high schools during the interwar years was pared down, the remaining activities largely refashioned to serve the cause. While there was some discussion about the propriety of continuing with school dances and "socials," most schools did not do away with them entirely; rather, the favourite pastimes of high school youth were made to serve the war effort. War savings stamps drives were carried out with intense competition between forms and schools. At an Alberta high school, the winners of the "spot dance" for "most romantic couple" were subjected to a "mock wedding," with the principal playing the piano while "the bride carried a beautiful bouquet of war savings stamps."[59] The students also staged a war savings stamps competition between junior and senior forms; at the end of a week's drive, the boys of the losing form would wear their socks over their pant legs and the girls would wear their hair in pigtails. The junior form lost, but felt vindicated because "before the week was over, all the townfolk knew about the campaign."[60] Boxes passed around the classroom each week to collect war savings stamps was a ritual repeated across the nation in both elementary and secondary schools: in 1941 students at Ottawa's Glebe Collegiate bought over $4,000 in stamps.[61] Sixteen stamps purchased one $4.00 certificate, which could be redeemed for $5.00 after seven-and-a-half years. Young Patricia Galloway invested most of her babysitting money in the stamps that her school sold every Friday afternoon.[62]

At tiny Alexandra High School in rural Alberta, an Ice Carnival to support the local Red Cross campaign had a "united nations on ice" theme, in which all the Allies were represented, with four of the senior girls costumed as America, Canada, Russia, and Britannia.[63] Students at Montreal High School produced a show featuring student talent to raise money for a mobile canteen to send overseas. The city's teenage girls joined such groups as Hilda Galt's

Dance for Defence and the Evans Sisters Revue, travelling to camps on buses in the evenings and on weekends to entertain servicemen.[64] At Vancouver's Magee High School, girls were reportedly "given their choice of [training and participation in] two of the following: knitting, sewing, rivet sorting, home nursing and cadets."[65]

The war revived high school cadet corps across the nation, after a long hiatus in some locations where public feeling had turned against the use of school time and facilities to promote a "militarism" associated with the horrors of the Great War.[66] Supporters of mandatory cadet training, or at least physical drill, argued that "the state owes to each boy that he be instructed mentally, morally and physically, that he may be fitted to compete in the business world for a livelihood and bear his share of the burdens of the state." Military drill was not only important for reasons of citizenship and national defence, but also, and not least, because it protected boys against effeminacy: "without drill or [physical] culture, the first thing that we will be seeing in Canada will be afternoon classes for boys in crochet work and knitting." Others observed that:

> Certain effects of the training are already apparent elsewhere than upon the parade ground. The manners of the boys have improved and a slouchiness of bearing which developed when cadet training was abolished is disappearing, or has disappeared. Parents make pleased comment upon the improvement in their offspring. In schools where cadet corps have not been formed, the compulsory squad and platoon drill is having similar effect … This should not be forgotten after the war has been won.[67]

An estimated 230,000 former sea, army, and air cadets served during the Second World War.[68] In June 1944, all male students who had reached their eighteenth birthday were required to register for training in the reserve army, with an officer training corps, or otherwise to "come in some way under military control as designated persons."[69]

A number of high schools inaugurated marching, drills and shooting practice for girls as an adjunct to the boy's cadet corps. They were sometimes awkwardly called "cadet-ettes" to accentuate or perhaps "protect" their femininity. The Barrie Collegiate cadet corps, with a membership of two hundred boys in 1940, initiated marching and drills for girls that year. At

Ottawa's Lisgar Collegiate, the Lisgar Girls' Rifle Club was established in 1941 on the girls' own initiative as an adjunct to the school's cadet corps. As the city's *Evening Citizen* described their training sessions, in a typically gender-typed manner, "Friday is the day that the comely young misses, dressed in warm ski slacks, gather during the lunch hour ... to lend their feminine charms to the firing of the cadet corps' BSAs [air rifles] at targets some 20 yards away, instructed by 'a lady teacher.'"[70] Contrast this depiction to the view of one member who declared enthusiastically, "We'll be able to lick the Hun if he ever comes."[71] Vancouver's Magee High School started organizing young women in cadet corps in 1942, two years after mandatory cadet training was reinstituted at the school. A senior male cadet trained the school's female Air Cadets, who were said to be "trying their best ... to bring their standards up to those that the boys have set."[72]

Several such unofficial "flights" of girl air cadets were established, including one at Kitchener–Waterloo Collegiate in Ontario, where the "Airettes" came together in 1942. Local air cadet officers gave their support to city resident and chief organizer Margaret Long, and some eighty to one hundred girls signed on before the war's end. Betty Ruppel joined at the beginning; with three older brothers in the RCAF, one of whom had been killed, she professed "a deep interest in flying" and in aircraft identification. In addition to drills and marching, the Airettes were given lessons about internal combustion engines, first aid, and Morse code. Male officers lectured them on aircraft recognition. As one member expressed it, "Girls felt important. They were doing their part and might enlist if the war went on."[73] On the national scene, the Canadian Auxiliary Service Corps established a cadet corps for girls twelve years old and over in 1943, evidently also popularly referred to in the diminutive and "cute" feminine form as "Army-ette-Cadets." Considered "the little sister" of CWAC, they were "on the verge" of official recognition by National Defence Headquarters in early 1945, which would have placed them on equal footing with male cadet corps in the high schools. The war ended before the goal was achieved.[74]

As more of the older boys enlisted, their departure created a vacuum in the traditional senior male leadership in student government and team sports, thereby opening the way for senior girls to assume student council positions aside from the customary secretarial ones, and also newspaper and yearbook editorships.[75] At the same time, this meant a shortage of eligible older boys for mixed-sex social activities, especially dances, which many students considered the best part of the extracurriculum. Mary Peate, a Montreal teenager at the time, remembered that by the midwar years, "the disappearance of boys and young men" from the city's streets and venues made her feel "as if an invisible Pied Piper had traversed the land, spiriting them away." The Catholic high school girls of her acquaintance took to praying to St. Ann, patron of single girls, with a certain mock sincerity: "Dear Saint Ann / get me a man / quick as you can." [76] High school girls lamented the absence of eligible men even as the war ended, as reflected in one such plaint from Toronto's Northern Vocational High School yearbook, thought to be so revealing of the sad situation that it was reprinted in the Toronto *Star*:

> The war of wars is over and our boys are coming back.
> The bands they play, the people shout but we poor girls—
>   alack,
> Are lonely still and smitten by the scarcity of males.
> For thirty-two poor Northern girls the shortage still
>   prevails.[77]

Syndicated columnist and popular youth adviser George Antheil, known to his young readers as "Uncle George," was well-positioned to observe that "the more patriotic the boys become ... the more romantic the womenfolk of the land become ... The young people are carried away with this talk of war and bravery."[78]

Others likewise remember the early years, before war ennui set in, as "rather romantic, really. The magazines were full of stories about lovers parting on train station platforms or being reunited on docksides, or sometimes never reunited. There were also hundreds of movies with the same kinds of scenes. And there were songs."[79] The "big band" sound, with its requisite jitterbug dance style, continued into the war years, popularized in countless dance halls and high school gyms by recordings of the American Glenn Miller Band and tours by Guy Lombardo and the Royal Canadians. Robert Collins remembered his wartime adolescence as

> a time of young men swirling young women through the intricate weaving patterns of the jitterbug, skirts planing out like saucers with a tantalizing flash

of thigh. Of music forever linked to that war, wistful ballads of love and parting: "I'll Be Seeing You" and "White Cliffs of Dover" and "When the Lights Go On Again." A thousand pianists with a single accomplishment–a nimble left hand that could coax out the rippling, rumbling eight-to-the-bar of boogie-woogie. And the World War II anthem, Glenn Miller's "In the Mood", soaring ...[80]

Advertisers were quick to exploit this youthful romanticism, at once fanning both patriotism and postwar hopes for the resumption of interrupted relationships. A full-page, full-colour silverware advertisement in the *Canadian Home Journal* pictured a young woman in passionate embrace with a soldier. "Today," the ad acknowledged, "he has a war on his hands," but "there'll come a day" when, by strong implication, love, marriage, and family would become "his" foremost objectives, as they were unwaveringly hers. In the meantime, young women should invest in both silverware and Victory Bonds, the latter in order to "Speed the Day."[81]

For the generation of young Canadians who came of age during the Second World War, both the young men who enlisted and the young women "left behind," history might well pre-empt the "dating" and "going steady" that were, by the 1940s, the typical—or at least normative—experience of modern adolescence. In some instances, suspicion of those of "enemy heritage" impeded courtship, as for one sixteen-year-old German Canadian girl in Calgary, whose Navy boyfriend was advised by the RCMP that her family was "under surveillance" and "did he think it wise to go with a girl like me."[82] But the young were reminded that patience, sacrifice, and virtue would

Full-page advertisement, Community Distinctive Silverplate, [*Canadian Home Journal*, December 1944.]

see both victory and a return to the traditional domesticity classified as "normalcy" after the Great War.[83]

The paradoxical nature of ideas about "modern youth" constituting both hope and fear, the best of modernity and its worst elements, meant that public discourses during the anxious years of the war were both commendatory and disapproving, often at the same time. For every acknowledgment, even glorification, of youthful sacrifice for the greater good, there were any number of charges that the young were immature, frivolous, unreliable, and even delinquent. There was considerable "scolding and yelping" in the press, in the juvenile courts, and among "those who deal with the youth of the country" about how teenagers were "letting the boys in service down." Another of the worries about youth recirculated from the Great War years concerned the "loosening" of sexual morality and its foremost repercussions: increasing rates of venereal disease, prostitution, and unwed pregnancy. Manitoba's Director of Venereal Disease Control noted the "alarming fact" that the increase was chiefly in the younger age group, many of whom were only in their teens. These were the "khaki kids," young women known to "hang around barracks and railway stations or go soldier hunting in juke joints and dance halls," all too often caught up in "the vast social dislocation of a country at war and without any organized constructive part to play in that country's war effort."[84]

A Winnipeg juvenile court judge reported that girls ranging in age from twelve to seventeen were "regular hangers-on at military camps or railway stations, picking up soldiers and spending day or night at one of the hotels." There was evidently a "serious increase" in the numbers aged thirteen to fifteen reported missing from home, while the proportion of infected girls between fourteen and seventeen had apparently risen 50 percent over the year 1941–42. Victoria's welfare officer announced that the number of unmarried mothers in that city had increased from 70 in 1941 to 114 in 1942; 49 of the latter were under twenty-one, the youngest a child of twelve. Citing medical and government reports, the media inflamed a veritable moral panic about the wartime degeneration of youth, especially girls, whose participation in a seeming wave of juvenile delinquency was largely related to sexual misdemeanours.[85]

If fears about promiscuity and its ill effects were largely focused on young women, among young men, the generationally defined, countercultural, and oppositional posture was adopted by the emerging brotherhood of "zoots" or "zoot suiters." They represented only a tiny fraction of young men; nonetheless, they caused all manner of moral panic. Zoot suits made the news in the United States and Canada in the early summer of 1943. Put simply, a "jive-set" of young urban men, "the boys with the reat pleats," adopted this attire as a counter to the military uniform on display on the streets of wartime Canada. The anti-zoot contingent was irked by this defiantly unconventional apparel, fundamentally a caricature of respectable male business and "Sunday best" attire. They were also annoyed by their wearers' defiance of the Wartime Prices and Trade Board regulations that actually prohibited the manufacture of zoot suits. These suits were not simply unmanly, unpatriotic, and immoral; in the context of wartime rationing, they were illegal.[86]

The zoot suit, in sum, was the outfit of the urban dandy, a suit for lolling about street corners and smoky billiard halls, for drinking and "cutting a rug" in dance halls, for "mashing" and seducing and worse, but not for working, fighting, or carrying out the activities that respectable adult men were supposed to carry out during the war. In Toronto, an adolescent zoot suiter told a *Globe and Mail* reporter that he wore the suit because "it looks very good. It's in style, and if I want to wear it, why should I be stopped?" His five male companions, however, evidently thought him "nuts" and declared that they "wouldn't be found dead wearing one of those outfits." One expressed sympathy for the servicemen, who had "exchanged their civilian clothes for a uniform of which they are very proud. They feel a lot of these kids wearing the funny clothes should be either in the army, navy or air force." The city's tailors contended that the zoot suit's end was in sight, "not by violence but by sheer ridicule," because Canadian boys were "too conscious of their strength, they like hard-fighting games too much, to go for such attire." So explained one tailor.[87] There were sporadic reports of zoot suit-wearing youths perpetrating various forms of public mischief, as in Victoria Park in Kitchener, Ontario, where a group was caught pushing young children off swings.[88] A Brantford, Ontario, family was affronted when, on their way home from the cinema, a "car full of zoot-suiters ... of foreign ancestry" yelled "sarcastic remarks" at them.[89]

Because of "strong feelings toward the rug-cutters" expressed by Toronto-based servicemen, the city's police removed the jukeboxes from two popular beaches, Sunnyside and Hanlan's Point, but not before sailors and servicemen had "heaved zoot suiters into the lake or torn the clothing from them."[90] The fight was on between servicemen of all ages and the "slackers" in zoot suits, a significant proportion of whom were not even of military age.[91] In late May 1943, an hour-long battle took place between "boys" from the St. Lambert suburb and other youths "said to be zoot suiters from Montreal," involving an estimated two hundred young rioters.[92] Further clashes, mostly between the standard enemy sides of zoot suiters and servicemen, were reported through the fall of 1943 and the winter of 1944. The apex was reached almost exactly a year after the St. Lambert fracas, in late May and early June 1944, when the Montreal area was again the scene of street fighting between zoot suiters and servicemen, primarily sailors. Initially, the city press identified the zoot suiters as mainly of Italian background, with some francophones among them, while the soldiers and civilian non-zooters were declared to be mostly English-speaking "Canadians." In Verdun early in June, several hundred servicemen sought out zooters at nightclubs, poolrooms, and dance halls, beating them, stripping them, and shredding their despised suits. Dozens were injured, and more than forty—of whom thirty-seven were sailors—were arrested.[93]

The zoot suit controversy stirred public anxiety, again focused squarely on youth, in an especially anxious time. It was obviously not so much about apparel as about the apparent desire of modern youth—though chiefly those who were male, urban, and often depicted as (if not actually) "non-Canadian" or even "non-anglophone"—to set themselves apart in provocative subcultures at precisely the moment when the citizen-soldier represented the ideal man. Yet the two—the seeming anti-soldier and the citizen-soldier—were not irreconcilable, at least not in the adolescent world view, as one man's memories testify: "Young fellows, sixteen, seventeen, eighteen ... We dressed in these outlandish clothes ... We were a wolf pack ... We were against soldiers, people in uniform, but I don't think it was because we were against the war or anything like that. They were just somebody to beat up on." After he and nine fellow zoots were unceremoniously tossed from a Greek restaurant in Toronto by three policemen, he was so ashamed that "when I got home I took off that silly uniform and I never wore it again."[94] And then there is the famous case of "Dieppe Tom Brown," whose story compelled a *Toronto Star* reporter to declare that "it is a strange thing to hear a 16-year-old kid in a leather jacket, with zoot-suit pants rolled up over pointed yellow shoes and a tie hanging out over a sports sweater, talk like that. But after he has told you what he has been through for you and me, and for his right to wear zoot-suits if he wants to, you know he also has the right to fight this war of his whatever way is best for him."[95] For their part, the younger generation saw the anti-zoot campaign, backed by state, police, and military force, as "persecution of a minority," meaning "teenagers in general."[96]

In response to the kind of public misapprobation that teenagers often attracted during the war years, three young women, aged seventeen to nineteen, tried to make a case for their generation and their gender. As they saw it,

> we the teen-age girls are the ones who are feeling this war most. Our brothers and fathers are away. Our mothers are working nights in munitions plants. We had to curtail our education in order to feel that we were doing our part in the war effort. We took jobs to help out. You accuse us of being asleep, of not knowing that there is such a serious thing as a war going on because you don't approve of the type of dancing we like or the things that stir us, as you put it. We would honestly like someone to tell us what is wrong with jitterbug dancing that makes you feel called upon to classify it with crime and juvenile delinquency ... why pick on our generation?[97]

Their sense of injustice had translated into generational animosity, fuelled by the frustrations of youth at being constrained by historical circumstances. They were making extraordinary sacrifices in extraordinary times, yet they still were not measuring up to the older generation's expectations—simply because they were young people behaving, at times, in the ways that defined their generation of youth.

The Second World War made youth a valued resource and a worthy investment for the brave new postwar world for which Canadians of all ages were struggling. For the first time in history, the Canadian government became committed to finding out about, and giving due consideration to, the needs and desires of the young with respect to how they would like to see that world manifest. The Royal Commission on Dominion–Provincial Relations (1937–40) heard from a number of youth organizations supporting the YMCA's recommendation that a "Dominion Youth Bureau" be established to research the needs of youth and make policy for their "protection and development" as "our most valuable national resource."[98]

The Canadian Youth Commission was created in 1940 under the Y's auspices, with support and assistance from the federal government to ensure that youth participated in reconstruction plans. Through national surveys on the subjects of jobs, health, recreation, organization, marriage and family, and especially citizenship, the commission heard from youth groups across Canada.[99] If little in the way of permanence or policy ensued from its recommendations, the commission's very existence demonstrated a new understanding that age marked a socio-political group and a particular class of citizens that was becoming a recognized collective force in national life.

Whatever the experiences of individual youth, the war at once pre-empted or postponed certain aspects of the adolescent experience and accelerated others on the path to maturity. Reflecting in her 1944 high school yearbook on the meaning of youth in a time of global emergency, an Ottawa student plaintively noted that "we are forced to become men and women when we are confronted with big issues, big responsibilities."[100] But the war also inspired generational solidarity, first in the cause of victory and finally in its celebration. On V-E Day in May 1945, many students, like those at Vancouver's Magee High School, doubtless found themselves "intoxicated with joy," having known only war for their entire high school stay. Magee students "swarmed" into the auditorium amid wild yells and hoots of pleasure" as the principal suspended classes. The whole school was "awarded a dance," and "students and teachers kicked up their heels on the long-awaited V-E Day."[101] As a member of the graduating class of 1945, whose schooling ended just as the war did, one woman remembered her peers' strong sense that "the traditional system was not to be challenged and we were not conflicted by value choices … We saw ourselves as 'decent people.' We were not trained for uncertainty … Succeeding within the system was approved and the unconventional or the strivers were viewed as interlopers."[102]

For each generation that shares a historic moment, the "same time" is also a different time, constituting a generationally distinct experience. Events such as war take on primacy in individual lives in different ways and for different reasons. Ultimately, however, such events function as generational markers, distinguishing the culture of specific age groups, imprinting collective memory, and shaping lifelong impressions of personal, social, and political issues and relations.[103] Particular memories form patterns that denote the generational effects of certain events. From these can be discerned personal meanings that take on collective or generational significance, depending on the age of the individual at the time of the event. Age and historic location, where personal and national history intersect, form the basis of generational consciousness.[104] The Second World War shadowed everyday life for young Canadians who came of age in its midst, whether they enlisted, spent the duration in the classroom, left school early to work in war industry and essential services, participated in the cadet corps, or volunteered in a host of homefront campaigns. Accident of birth and historical circumstance made the war their generational marker, the signal "coming of age" experience. However much Tom Brokaw's "greatest generation" label may simplify the complex historical situation of Second World War Canadian youth, it is the very complexity of that situation that makes it ring true.

Notes

Thanks are due to the Social Sciences and Humanities Research Council for a research grant that supported the larger project from which this article is in part derived; and especially to Terry Copp, mentor, colleague, friend, and continuing inspiration to generations of historians.

1 Dorothy B. Inglis quoted in Bill McNeil, ed., *Voices of a War Remembered: An Oral History of Canadians in World War II* (Toronto: Doubleday Canada, 1991), 120-1. Inglis was employed as a clerk for the Ontario civil service in Toronto during the war.
2 Priscilla Galloway quoted in Priscilla Galloway, ed., *Too Young to Fight: Memories from Our Youth During World War II* (Toronto: Stoddart, 1999), 30. Brokaw applied the classification to his elders in light of their having endured a Depression childhood only to be called upon to fight Nazi tyranny as they came of age in the 1940s. See Tom Brokaw, *The Greatest Generation* (New York: Random House, 1998). Although the book and its various related collections were North American bestsellers, Brokaw's view that this was "the greatest generation any society has ever produced" (xxxviii) has been decried as simplistic by some critics; see, for example, Paul Duke, "The Greatest Generation?," *Virginia Quarterly* (Winter 2002), 19-25. Others have embraced Brokaw's classification: see Kriste Lindemeyer, *The Greatest Generation Grows Up: American Childhood in the 1930s* (Chicago: Ivan R. Dee, 2005).
3 Budge Wilson, cited in Galloway, *Too Young to Fight*, 187.
4 Here I am once again indebted to Neil Sutherland; see Sutherland, *Growing Up: Childhood in English Canada from the Great War to the Age of Television* (Toronto: University of Toronto Press, 1997), especially Chapter 1, "Listening to the Winds of Childhood," 7-12.

5   In their examination of cohort memories of historic world events, American sociologists Howard Schuman and Jacqueline Scott found that all their subjects spoke of the Great War, the Depression, and World War II as the formative events of their youth; see Howard Schumann and Jacqueline Scott, "Generations and Collective Memories," *American Sociological Review* 54 (1989), 359–60; see also N. Ryder, "The Cohort as a Concept in the Study of Social Change," *American Sociological Review* 30 (1965), 843–61. Historical sociologist Bryan S. Turner contends that "war and its social consequences have been a particularly important lever for the formation of generational consciousness and leadership"; see Turner, "Strategic Generations," in Bryan S. Turner and J. Edmunds, eds. *Generational Consciousness, Narrative, and Politics* (Lanham: Rowman and Littlefield, 2002), 14. John Ayto, *Twentieth Century Words* (London: Oxford University Press, 1999), 181 & 309, locates the use of "teenage" as an adjective as early as 1921, but finds "teenager" to have emerged in the popular press only in 1941.

6   Public Archives of Ontario, YWCA Toronto, Annual Reports, F794 ACC 9844; box 11, B-1, MU 3527, *Annual Report* 1941, A.E. Robinson, General Secretary, Big Sister Association of Toronto, "Memo on Big Sisters," 7 February 1941. Similar views are expressed in G.E. Millard, Principal, Havergal College, Toronto, "The Psychiatry of the Older Girl," *Canadian Guider* 9, no.2 (March 1940), 5.

7   On delinquency fears during the Second World War, see Jeff Keshen, *Saints, Sinners, and Soldiers: Canada's Second World War* (Vancouver: University of British Columbia Press, 2004), especially Chapter 8, "The Children's War: Youth Run Wild"; and Mariana Valverde, "Building Anti-Delinquent Communities; Morality, Gender, and Generation in the City," in Joy Parr, ed. *A Diversity of Women: Ontario, 1945-80*, (Toronto: University of Toronto Press, 1995), 25–31.

8   Public Archives of Ontario, YWCA Toronto, Annual Reports, F794 ACC 9844; box 11, B-1, MU 3527, *Annual Report* 1939, 11; also *Annual Report* 1941, 4–5, Public Archives of Ontario, YWCA Toronto, Annual Reports, F794 ACC 9844; box 11, B-1, MU 3527, *Annual Report* 1943, 9; *Annual Report* 1946, 10.

9   Pamphlet, *First Year: A War Service Record of the Canadian YMCA from the Outbreak of the War* (Ottawa: National YMCA War Services Board, 1941), 6.

10 The subject of "boy soldiers" is as yet undeveloped for the Second World War; on the Great War experience, see Tim Cook, "'He Was Determined to Go': Underage Soldiers in the Canadian Expeditionary Force," *Histoire Sociale / Social History* 41, no.81 (2008), 41–74.

11 Cited in Barry Broadfoot, ed., *Six War Years, 1939–1945: Memories of Canadians at Home and Abroad* (Toronto: Doubleday Canada, 1974), 127. Regrettably, Broadfoot's fascinating collection of memories does not consistently indicate age, location, or even gender of the anonymous subjects.

12 Mordecai Richler, *The Street* (Toronto: McClelland and Stewart, 1969), 69.

13 Robert Collins, *You Had to Be There: An Intimate Portrait of the Generation That Survived the Depression, Won the War, and Re-Invented Canada* (Toronto: McClelland

and Stewart, 1997), 3. Collin's book contextualizes the memories of the wartime generation.
14 McNeil, *Voices of a War Remembered*, 2–3.
15 Robert C. Skipper, *I Never Got to Be a Teenager: Up the Irish and All Army Volunteers in World War II* (Tilbury: R.C. Skipper, 1996), 3–5; 9–10.
16 Donald D. Tansley, *Growing Up and Going to War, 1925–1945* (Waterloo: Laurier Centre for Military Strategic and Disarmament Studies, 2005), 20–21.
17 Allan May, "Zoot Pants 'n' All, Dieppe Tom Brown Is Back at School," *Toronto Star*, 5 December 1942.
18 Joe Friesen, "Facing German Guns, Soldier Knew He Had to Kill," *Globe and Mail*, 1 June 2004.
19 Geoffrey Hayes, *Waterloo County: An Illustrated History* (Waterloo: Waterloo Historical Society, 1997), 166. See also the recollections of Margeurite Moncrief Nelson of Peterborough, who also signed on at the age of 18 and completed basic training in Kitchener: Dominion Institute, Memory Project Digital Archive, http://66.241.252.164/digital-archive.
20 Cited in Carolyn Gossage, *Great Coats and Glamour Boots: Canadian Women at War, 1939–1945* (Toronto: Dundurn, 1991), 54–55; 66.
21 Skipper, *I Never Got to Be a Teenager*; Collins, *You Had to Be There*, 6; Budge Wilson, in Galloway, ed., *Too Young to Fight*, 181. See also the memories discussed in Emilie Montgomery, "'The War Was a Very Vivid Part of My Life': The Second World War and the Lives of British Columbia Children," in *Children, Teachers and Schools in the History of British Columbia*, ed. Jean Barman, Neil Sutherland, and J. Donald Wilson (Calgary: Detselig, 1995), 162–64.
22 Montgomery, "The War Was a Very Vivid Part of My Life," 162; Tansley, *Growing Up and Going to War*, 20.
23 Cited in Broadfoot, *Six War Years*, 124.
24 Advertisement, "High School Students Wanted!," *Summerside Journal*, 27 May 1943.
25 Cited in Broadfoot, *Six War Years*, 124.
26 Ernest Lapointe, quoted in "Directs Plea to Youth of Canada," *Hamilton Spectator*, 11 September 1941.
27 Public Archives of Nova Scotia, MG 898, Girl Guides of Canada, Nova Scotia Council, Canadian Council of the Girl Guides Association, *Annual Report Ending April 1940*, 10.
28 Letter of Mary Kett, from Marshall, Saskatchewan, published in "Pathfinders," a regular column for young people in the *Free Press Prairie Farmer*, 3 June 1943; cited in Norah Lewis, ed., *"I Want to Join Your Club": Letters from Rural Children, 1900–1920* (Waterloo: Wilfrid Laurier University Press, 1996), 98–99.
29 "Boy Scout Week," Pathfinders page, *Free Press Prairie Farmer*, 16 February 1944, in Lewis, ed. *"I Want to Join Your Club,"* 100–101.
30 The renowned First Preston troop's Scout House Band was formed by Wilf Blum in late 1938; see http://www.prestonscouthouse.com.

31 Leonard Marsh, *Canadians In and Out of Work: A Survey of Economic Classes and Their Relation to the Labour Market* (Toronto: Oxford University Press, 1940), 162–63; Paul Axelrod, *The Promise of Schooling: Education in Canada* (Toronto: University of Toronto Press, 1997), 68. See also John Modell and J. Trent Alexander, "High School in Transition: Community, School, and Peer Group in Abilene, Kansas, 1939," *History of Education Quarterly* 37, no.1 (Spring 1997), 1–2.

32 Ontario, Department of Education, Report of the Inspectors of High Schools, 1919, 32–33; ibid., 1922, 45–46; Richard Ueda, *Avenues to Adulthood: The Origins of the High School and Social Mobility in an American Suburb* (Cambridge, MA: Cambridge University Press, 1987), 141.

33 On German youth, see Derek Linton, *Who Has the Youth, Has the Future: The Campaign to Save Young Workers in Imperial Germany* (Cambridge, MA: Harvard University Press, 1990). Contemporary Canadian views include M. McLeachy, "The Effect upon Young People of the Economic Depression and Unemployment," *Child and Family Welfare* (November 1935), 15; and E. Muncaster, "Strengthening Family Ties Through Recreation," *Child and Family Welfare* (November 1933), 47. See also Library and Archives Canada [LAC] Canadian Welfare Council papers, Canadian Council on Child and Family Welfare, Division on Leisure Time and Educative Activities, "Relief Is Not Enough: The Idle Time of Compulsorily Idle Canadians," *Bulletin No.1* (25 September 1933), 1–4; "Will Canada Have a Youth Movement?" *Canadian Doctor* (January 1939), 17–18.

34 H.B. King, PhD, Chief Inspector of Schools, *Seventieth Annual Report of the Public Schools of the Province of British Columbia, 1940–41* (Victoria: Charles F. Banfield, 1942), 38.

35 R.A. Morton, "Principal's Message," *Wings*, 1944–45, 4. This is the yearbook of Sangudo High School in Sangudo, Alberta. The principal makes much of the fact that this is the "invasion year" of 1944.

36 Dorothy Joan Harris, cited in Galloway, *Too Young to Fight*, 58.

37 King, *Seventieth Annual Report*, 40.

38 Tansley, *Growing Up and Going to War*, 15.

39 "Dedication," *Wings*, 1942, 5.

40 Serge Marc Durflinger, *Fighting from Home: The Second World War in Verdun, Quebec* (Vancouver: UBC Press, 2006), 123. This seems to have been the case in Regina classrooms: see Tansley, *Growing Up and Going to War*, 14–15; and also, regarding Vancouver, see Montgomery, "The War Was a Very Vivid Part of My Life," 160–2.

41 King, *Seventieth Annual Report*, 40.

42 Ford Motor Company, "War Comes to a Classroom," *Saturday Night* (10 October 1942), 9. This is a full-page advertisement showing a young man with goggles working on a lathe, other boys at their books, and the [male] teacher writing on a blackboard.

43 "Westdale Training Adds Skilled Workers to Rapidly Growing War Industry Ranks," *Hamilton Spectator*, 21 November 1944.

44 R.B. Matthews, "The Air Force Needs 50,000 Model Planes … 40,000 Schoolboys Will See It Gets Them!" *Saturday Night* (19 December 1942), 4–6. See also Bernice

Coffey, "Canada's Children Look Forward to the Future in the Skies," *Saturday Night* (5 February 1944), 19.
45 Hayes, *Waterloo County*, 169–70.
46 Ibid., 168.
47 Cited in Broadfoot, *Six War Years*, 128–9.
48 Pamphlet, Ontario Farm Service Branch, *Farm Cadet Program* (Toronto: Government of Ontario, 1941).
49 Canadian Youth Congress, *Report on Education*, Toronto, April 1941, 4.
50 There was considerable discussion over the delayed opening of schools in the southern Ontario press; see, for example, "Farm 'Child Labor' Scored as Return to "Dark Ages": Delay In Reopening Schools Held Definitely Retrograde Step," *Toronto Star*, 3 August 1940; Editorial, "Purpose Good, Procedure Wrong," *Toronto Star*, 15 August 1940; "Many Students Have Signed Up for Farm Work," *Hamilton Spectator*, 3 June 1942.
51 "Large Force of Girls Going to Farm Service Camps," *Globe and Mail*, 12 April 1944. "Boys Respond to Appeal for Help on Farms," *Hamilton Spectator*, 4 July 1944.
52 Budge Wilson, in Galloway, ed., *Too Young to Fight*, 183–184.
53 Editorial, *Toronto Star*, 9 May 1946. The NSS call for "total manpower" was issued by Mackenzie King in a CBC Radio broadcast on 19 August 1942. See William Lyon Mackenzie King, *Canada and the War: Manpower and a Total War Effort* (Ottawa: Edmond Cloutier, 1942). Available online at http://www.collectionscanada.gc.ca: First Among Equals: The Prime Minister in Canadian Life and Politics: Right Honourable William Lyon Mackenzie King: Speeches. See also Jennifer Stephen, "Canada's Greatest Wartime Muddle: National Selective Service and the Mobilization of Human Resources during World War II," *Canadian Historical Review* 85, no.4 (December 2004), 841–43.
54 "Pupils Scorn Placing by NSS in Soft Jobs," *Globe and Mail*, 4 July 1944.
55 A number of such stories are detailed in Hayes, *Waterloo County*, 167–170.
56 Tansley, *Growing Up and Going to War*, 17.
57 CN Images of Canada Gallery, CN001976, Canadian Science and Technology Museum, Ottawa, Ontario.
58 Mary Ewart Jukes, "Who Is Rita?", *Saturday Night* (27 March 1943), 29.
59 Sangudo High School, Alberta, *Wings*, 1944–45: 12.
60 Dorothy Williams, "Social Chit-chat," Alexandra High School, Alberta, *En Avant*, 1945: 17; see also John Oliver High School, Vancouver, *The Souvenir*, 1945–46: 30.
61 Christine Hamelin, "A Sense of Purpose: Ottawa Students and the Second World War," *Canadian Military History* 6, no.1 (Spring 1997), 35–36.
62 Priscilla Galloway, in Galloway, ed., *Too Young to Fight*, 26.
63 Jack Kent, "Ice Carnival," *En Avant*, 1945, 5.
64 Mary Peate, *Girl in a Sloppy Joe Sweater: Life on the Canadian Home Front during World War II* (Montreal: Optimum, 1988), 96.
65 Magee High School, Vancouver, *Adventure*, 1944, 46, 54.
66 By the early 1930s, many school boards, including the nation's largest, that of Toronto, had suspended their high school cadet training, much of it instigated under the auspices of the Strathcona Fund established in 1909; see "Citizens Join in Discussing

Cadet Problem," *Edmonton Journal*, 18 March 1927. See also Public Archives of Ontario, Pamphlet no.22, 1943, *History of the Barrie Collegiate Institute, 1843-1943*, 60-62, and Public Archives of Ontario, Pamphlet no.31, 1957, Riverdale Collegiate Institute, *Golden Anniversary, 1907-57*, 42.

67 "Westdale Training Adds Skilled Workers to Rapidly Growing War Industry Ranks," *Hamilton Spectator*, 21 November 1944.

68 Editorial, "Drill vs. Culture," *Guelph Mercury*, 12 April 1939. This was regarding a motion before the Toronto Board of Education to revive cadet training in high schools. See also "Cadet Training Viewed as One of Most Essential Preparations for Ultimate Victory," *Hamilton Spectator*, 30 January 1942. See the Department of National Defence website, http://www.dnd.ca, for information on the development of cadet programs in Canada.

69 "High School Boys, 18 1/2, Must Train Part-Time," *Globe and Mail*, 11 March 1945; also "Callup Upsets School System," *Ottawa Citizen*, 10 April 1945.

70 Cited in Hamelin, "A Sense of Purpose," 40. The "BSAs" were probably Lee-Enfield rifles produced by the Birmingham Small Arms Company of Birmingham, UK, which the British Ministry of Munitions contracted to supply rifles, ammunition, bicycles, and motorcycles for the British and Allied forces during both the Great War and the Second World War. The BSA Company produced 1.25 million Lee Enfield rifles, 568,100 Browning machine guns, and 60,000 'BESA' machine guns during the Second World War. For a brief history of the company to the First World War, see *BSA History From the Days of the Crimea*, pamphlet published by the Birmingham Small Arms Company (Birmingham-Redditch-Coventry: 1918), reprinted in its entirety at http://www.rifleman.org.uk; for the Second World War, see http://www.bsaguns.co.uk/chronology.php.

71 Hamelin, "A Sense of Purpose," 40.

72 Public Archives of Ontario, Pamphlet no.22, 1943, *History of the Barrie Collegiate Institute, 1843-1943*, 60-62; *Adventure*, 1944: 46, 54.

73 Stephanie Walker, "K-W Airettes," *Annual Volume of the Waterloo Historical Society* 92 (2004), 103.

74 Bobbie Rosenfeld, "Army-ette Cadets Thrill as Ottawa Recognition Due," *Globe and Mail*, 6 January 1945. Not until the mid-1970s were young women officially accepted into the cadet corps in Canada; see Walker, "Airettes," 109.

75 Cynthia Comacchio, *The Dominion of Youth: Adolescence and the Making of Modern Canada* (Waterloo: Wilfrid Laurier University Press, 2006), 116-17.

76 Peate, *Girl in a Sloppy Joe Sweater*, 136. Peate notes that "the situation spawned a social phenomenon called the 'hen party.'"

77 "No Men in Their Lives," *Toronto Star*, 27 April 1946. Described as "brighter than the average of topical verse in school magazines," the poem by student Mona Van Ark was originally printed in *The Norvoc*, yearbook of Toronto's Northern Vocational High School.

78 George Antheil, "A Man Talks to Women," *Toronto Star*, 1 October 1940.

79 Dorothy Joan Harris, cited in Galloway, *Too Young to Fight*, 58.

80 Collins, *You Had to Be There*, 61.
81 Advertisement, Community Distinctive Silverplate, *Canadian Home Journal*, December 1944.
82 Broadfoot, *Six War Years*, 35.
83 A number of interviewees, male and female, recalled the "romantic" aspects of the war in Montgomery, "The War Was a Very Vivid Part of My Life," 162.
84 Dr. W. Clarke, Director, American Social Hygiene Association, "They Are in Danger," *Health* (March 1941), 12–14. Clarke was speaking before the Vancouver Social Hygiene Council on the event of "Social Hygiene Day."
85 C. Smith, "Teen Age Tragedy," *Health* (Autumn 1945), 10–14. See also Christabelle Sethna, "'Wait Till Your Father Gets Home': Absent Fathers, Working Mother, and Delinquent Daughters in Ontario During World War II," in *Family Matters: Papers in Post-Confederation Canadian Family History*, ed. E.A. Montigny and Lori Chambers (Toronto: Canadian Scholars' Press, 1998), especially 22–23. In reality, the distribution of illegitimate births by age did not change to any considerable extent between 1931 and 1951: during those twenty years, it actually declined for the group under age 20. See *The Liberty Study of Young Canada* (Toronto: Canadian Marketing Analysis, 1955), 17, Chart 13. The percentage of mothers under 20 in 1931 was 38.8; for 1941, 29.9; for 1951, 33.
86 The zoot suit comprised pants "with the ankles so tight they can hardly be pulled over the feet" and a knee-length "Prince Albert-type" jacket featuring exaggerated shoulder padding. Accessories included suede shoes, often in unusual colours, a wide-brimmed hat, usually of brown straw with a wide and "noisy" hat-band, and, "zootiest of all," a watch chain descending to the shoes in a wide loop; see "Zoot Suit's Day Wanes, In Opinion of Tailors," *Globe and Mail*, 12 June 1943.
87 "Zoots in Uniform," *Globe and Mail*, 19 June 1943. The report tells how John R. MacNicol, Progressive Conservative, Toronto-Davenport, mentioned in the House of Commons a "new life-saving suit" for the navy and another member interjected "a zoot suit," to which Navy Minister Macdonald responded, "The Navy is VERY much against the zoot variety" (his capitals).
88 "Zoot Suiters Push Kids Off Swings," *Globe and Mail*,4 July 1944, 5. "Rough older boys" were "monopolizing swings and other play facilities" at Victoria Park in Kitchener, Ontario.
89 Letter to the Editor, from Brantford, Ontario, *Globe and Mail*, 3 July 1943.
90 Editorial, *Globe and Mail*, 19 June 1943.
91 Mauricio Mazon, *The Zoot-Suit Riots: The Psychology of Symbolic Annihilation* (Austin: University of Texas Press, 1984), 6–8, contends that most American zoot-suiters were more likely rejecting adult ways than government policy; they were more a social than a political grouping. Robin D.G. Kelley, in "The Riddle of the Zoot: Malcolm Little and Black Cultural Politics During World War II," in *Generations of Youth: Youth Culture and History in 20th Century America*, ed. Joe Austin and Michael Nevin Willard (New York: NYU Press, 1998), 137, sees the zoot suit's adoption by young male African Americans as a "signifier of a culture of opposition," 137. On the Montreal situation,

see Serge Marc Durflinger, "The Montreal and Verdun Zoot-Suit Disturbances of June 1944: Language Conflict, A Problem of Civil–Military Relations or Youthful Over-Exuberance?," in Serge Bernier, ed., *L'Impact de la Deuxième Guerre mondiale sur les sociétés canadienne et québécoise*, (Montreal et Ottawa: Université du Québec à Montréal et la Direction Histoire et patrimoine de la Défense nationale, Ottawa, 1998); see also Durflinger, *Fighting from Home*, 160–64, 168. Montreal's famed zoot suit disturbances are also mentioned in William Weintraub, *City Unique* (Toronto: McClelland and Stewart, 1996), 50–52. See also Keshen, *Saints, Sinners, and Soldiers*, 207–8.

92   "Zoot Suit Wearers of Montreal Start Riot in St. Lambert Suburb," *Globe and Mail*, 30 May 1944. The newspaper reported one arrest, five injured.

93   This was reported in the *Verdun Messager* and cited in Durflinger, "The Montreal and Verdun Zoot-Suit Disturbances," 225. The subject was discussed at the highest military and political levels. An inquiry ordered by the navy produced the predictable verdict that the zooters were a "definite sect or clan of a subversive nature who aim at sabotaging the war effort by unwarranted attacks on service personnel." Their alleged "Italian ancestry" was evidence of their ill will, disloyalty, and absence of patriotism; allegations that they were primarily francophone were cast in the same manner. Five of the eight witnesses described the zooters as being of Italian background; two believed that they were francophone; several described some as "Jewish" or "Syrian," and most agreed that they were predominantly English speaking; see Durflinger, 225–26.

94   Broadfoot, *Six War Years*, 164.

95   May, "Zoot Pants 'n' All," *Toronto Star*, 5 December 1942.

96   Peate, *Girl in a Sloppy Joe Sweater*, 122.

97   "Three Teen-Age Girls," letter to George Antheil ("Uncle George"), *Toronto Star*, 15 April 1944, 8. Antheil's weekly column, "A Man Talks to Women," featured letters from young people seeking his advice on conduct, relationships, and all manner of adolescent concerns.

98   National Council of Young Men's Christian Associations of Canada, Young Men's Committee, Submission to the Royal Commission on Dominion–Provincial Relations, Toronto, April 1938, 3.

99   Each was published by the late 1940s; their findings are summarized in Blodwen Davies, *Youth Speaks Its Mind* (Toronto: Ryerson, 1948). See also Canadian Youth Commission, *Youth Speaks Out on Citizenship* (Ottawa: Queen's Printer, 1948); and *Youth in Your Town* (Ottawa: Queen's Printer, 1950).

100 Joan Finnigan, "Youth Styled in 1944," *Vox Lycet* 1943–44; cited in Hamelin, "A Sense of Purpose," 35–36.

101 Magee High School, Vancouver, *Adventure*, 1945, 6.

102 Susan Crawford, "Magee 1945, A Class Portrait: Memoir of a Homecoming," *Vancouver Sun*, 18 September 1999.

103 This is what sociologist and generational theorist Karl Mannheim refers to as "the non-contemporaneity of the contemporaneous" in relation to generations; Karl Mannheim, "The Problem of Generations," in Mannheim, *Essays on the Sociology of Knowledge*

(London: Routledge and Kegan Paul; 1972; originally published 1927), 288–89. See also Paul Kecskemeti, "Introduction," in Mannheim, *Essays on the Sociology of Knowledge*, 23.

104 Harvey Graff, *Conflicting Paths: Growing Up in America* (Cambridge, MA: Harvard University Press, 1995), 302; Schuman and Scott, "Generations and Collective Memories," 359–60. See also Norman Brown, Steven Shevell, Lance Rips, "Public Memories and Their Personal Context," in David C. Rubin, ed., *Autobiographical Memory* (Cambridge: Cambridge University Press, 1986), 137–58; David C Rubin, Scott Wetzler, and Robert Nebes, "Autobiographical Memory Across the Lifespan," in *Autobiographical Memory*, 202–21; and Mark Freeman, *Rewriting the Self: History, Memory, Narrative* (London: Routledge, 1993). See also Bryan Turner, "Strategic Generations," 19.

4

Fighting a White Man's War?
First Nations Participation in the Canadian War Effort, 1939–1945

Scott Sheffield

Canada's First Nations added their weight to the national war effort against the Axis powers in a remarkable range of ways.[1] On the homefront, they lent their vocal support, time, labour, and limited financial resources; at the same time, young Native men and women volunteered in the thousands for service with the armed forces. Many others found themselves conscripted, called to report for medical exams and compulsory training under the National Resources Mobilization Act of 1940.[2]

Canadians were surprised and pleased by First Nations' sacrifices and contributions, which gained significant media attention.[3] The dominant society interpreted Indian actions as admirable patriotism and loyalty and as an attempt to prove themselves capable and worthy of inclusion in the mainstream of national life. Canadians viewed this as achievable solely via assimilation. Postwar efforts to reform Canadian Indian policy reflected these concerns and aspirations and succeeded in recasting Indian assimilation in liberal democratic garb. But this white man's war was not the one that First Nations people were fighting.[4]

The subject of indigenous contributions to Canada's wars of the twentieth century has emerged from obscurity to a relative degree of prominence over the past thirty years. Beginning in the 1970s, First Nations and Metis veterans' groups drove the burgeoning awareness of the issues, concerned that their service had been forgotten and angered at their unequal access to veterans' benefits after the Second World War and Korea. A growing number of scholars and graduate students began resurrecting First Nations' wartime experiences with the goal of achieving the recognition and remembrance that indigenous veterans deserved. Fred Gaffen's *Forgotten Soldiers*, published in 1985, became a catalyst for a number of master's theses in 1988, 1992, and 1995 that were shaped and inspired by similar themes of historical resurrection and commemoration.[5] Veterans Affairs Canada published another laudatory example of this genre in 1993.[6] Importantly, veterans' political efforts began to bear fruit in the 1990s when the Standing Senate Committee on Aboriginal Peoples produced a report on Aboriginal veterans in 1994–95.[7] This was soon followed by extensive attention given to indigenous veterans' experiences in the mammoth first volume of the Royal Commission on Aboriginal Peoples (RCAP).[8] These studies formed an evolving orthodoxy that had conjured enough attention by the late 1990s that a National Round Table on First Nations Veterans' Issues was established to examine the historical experience of Status Indian veterans.[9] The final report from that process concluded that First Nations veterans had been systemically disadvantaged. Based on these findings, the government made an offer of compensation in 2003.

Such developments reflected the predominance of what some have called the 'forgotten warrior' interpretation of the Indians' Second World War experience.[10] This approach emphasized the injustice of conscripting Status Indians, as well as the disadvantages faced by First Nations veterans after the war, juxtaposed with claims of phenomenally high enlistment rates and of heartfelt and unrequited loyalty to treaties and the Crown. The impression created conveyed a tragic irony of Status Indians fighting bravely and ably in Europe for rights they were denied at home. The weight of such claims was politically potent, even if not always grounded in sufficient evidence. However, political exigencies of the 1980s and 1990s sometimes inhibited other lines of scholarly inquiry. It was difficult to question claims that Status Indian enlistment rates were higher than for any other segment of Canadian society, or to imply that not all indigenous recruits were uniformly courageous and natural soldiers, or to suggest that not all First Nations veterans were welcomed home as heroes.[11] While such questions were legitimate, they at times seemed to threaten political agendas and to impugn the memory and sacrifice of those soldiers. Thankfully, the trend has begun to change in the past decade, during which scholars have moved in new directions unfettered by the 'forgotten warrior.'[12]

This chapter assesses the broad national patterns of First Nations' responses to the Second World War, building on both the actions and the words of Status Indian people during the war. It will look at the broad spectrum of ways in which First Nations communities and individuals contributed to the war effort, as well as at those occasions when they resisted the dominant society's demands and sought to constrain Indian contributions. In addition, First Nations' peoples spoke out on a wide variety of topics throughout the war, both in newspapers and in correspondence with the Indian Affairs Branch (IAB). These expressions ranged from band council resolutions proclaiming support for the war effort to mothers writing to have enlisted sons returned, to native rights activists challenging conscription laws, to young men seeking to enlist. Together, these resources suggest to us whose war the First Nations were fighting and what it looked like to them. Fundamentally, First Nations people fought, not to prove their capacity and readiness for assimilation, but to stake a claim to a legitimate inclusion in Canadian society and the right to remain indigenous peoples.

When Europe finally erupted into open war in September 1939, First Nations men were among the thousands who presented themselves at recruiting depots across the country. In Cardston, Alberta, the first man to enlist was from the neighbouring Blood Reserve.[13] But while voluntary enlistment remains an important measure of First Nations commitment to the war, by itself it is not an adequate yardstick. The decisions of individual young Cree or Mohawk or Mi'k maq might have had more to do with youthful enthusiasm than with expressing their communities' political will or cultural imperatives. We must look beyond military service if we are to gain a more complete portrait of First Nations' contributions and intentions.

Archival records and newspapers amply demonstrate the diversity of First Nations' activities connected to the war. The *Regina Leader-Post*, for instance, recognized Saskatchewan Indian enlistment but also recognised that "those who must stay home are also serving. Generous donations to the Red Cross, purchase of war savings stamps, money for the purchase of an ambulance; band funds diverted to the war cause; sports days and bazaars; socials and teas; donations even of cows; knitting of socks and sweaters. All war work."[14]

Indian public statements, as well as demonstrations of loyalty and support for the war effort, were widespread, persistent, and eagerly reported by the nation's media.[15] In late June 1940, the Stoney First Nation prayed for Allied victory during a Sun Dance—a ritual officially banned under the Indian Act. The ceremony expressed the community's desire to avoid killing and its determination to help in the war effort.[16] In northern Manitoba, one remote Cree community decided to forgo their annual treaty payments, a gesture warmly applauded in the *Winnipeg Free Press*:

> It is a long trip ... to The Pas, two hundred miles ... [but] the Chief of the Nelson House Indian band and his councillor ... made it by dog and carriole. Nelson House band had got word that the King needed their help. Canada was at war. So there was talk around the lodges and out on the trap lines. Finally the decision was reached and the Chief got ready for the visit out to consult with The Pas Agent. His band was prepared to go without relief this year and asked that the Government be not concerned about the problems of the Red Man.[17]

In southern Ontario, the Six Nations offered a portion of their reserve known as the Glebe Property for the use of Canada's military, and refused to accept anything but a nominal one dollar in rent, though the market value of the property would have been a lucrative addition for their band funds.[18]

First Nations people did much more than just enlist in the military services.[19] They also offered their meagre financial resources through donations to humanitarian organizations such as the Red Cross or to patriotic funds.[20] Sometimes these were targeted to a specific cause, such as the Mi'kmaq's large gift of $2,000 in 1941 to "aid the suffering children of Scotland."[21] In addition, the Status Indian population purchased Victory Bonds and War Savings Certificates, officially contributing $26,493 through Indian Affairs channels.[22] Canadians warmly appreciated these generous actions. For instance, in 1941, local dignitaries in Cardston, Alberta, feted Blood chiefs after their $200 contribution pushed the regional Victory Bond quota over the top.[23] So prolific were community offers of money from band funds that Indian Affairs officials took steps to curtail the drain on this finite source.[24] The majority of First Nations giving was in this way pushed outside the official channels of the Indian Affairs Branch, making it difficult to quantify accurately, but officials estimated that contributions of all types in 1943 exceeded $400,000.[25]

Such vast sums, so communally gathered, certainly imply a broad base of support for the war effort.

First Nations' contributions came from a cross-section of the community. Children, such as Sto:lo pupils at the Colqueleetza Residential School in Chilliwack, B.C., sewed and knitted goods suitable for wartime causes.[26] Women not only kept home and community functioning in the absence of many of their menfolk but also dedicated their energies to a variety of wartime activities, often through homemakers' and other women's organizations.[27] Community elders, too, found ways to participate, often in creative ways: Blackfoot elders in southern Alberta pointed out old buffalo jumps so that the bones might be unearthed for the war effort.[28] On the Cape Croker Reserve in Ontario, where every able-bodied man and a number of the women enlisted, the women and children sustained the community's substantial role in the lake trout fishery on Lake Huron.[29] Taken in sum, the homefront evidence suggests that First Nations people chose to engage in the war effort in ways that were meaningful to them.

Domestic activities were important, but the voluntary enlistment of Status Indian men and some women has gained the most attention and developed the strongest mythology. Most pronounced has been the debate about the extent and significance of Status Indian enlistment rates. Military records took no note of ethnicity, and IAB records of 3,090 Indian enlistments were woefully incomplete. In lieu of any hard figures, speculation blossomed. Olive Dickason claims in her survey that "Amerindians, despite the fact that they were not citizens, enlisted in proportionately higher numbers than did any other segment of the general population; it has been estimated that they numbered up to 6000."[30] Dickason's unsubstantiated estimate pales in the face of the more profligate claims of Allen Andrews, who estimates "that 30,000 Natives and persons with some Indian ancestry" served during the war.[31]

The widely expressed confidence in the extraordinary enlistment rates of the First Nations does not hold up to even the most casual scrutiny. Even 6,000 First Nations voluntary enlistments represents about 5 percent of Canada's Status Indian population, which was listed at 118,378 in 1939 and at 125,946 by war's end.[32] The most accurate statistics available put the figure closer to 4,300, roughly one-third of the national rates.[33] By comparison, roughly 10 percent of Canada's 11 million people served during the Second World War, the overwhelming majority of them volunteers. This picture of voluntary enlistment should be modified somewhat, however, by consideration of those who offered their services and were rejected on medical, educational, racial, or other grounds; and there are reasons to believe that the rejection rates for First Nations were significantly higher than the national average.[34] Saying this in no way denigrates the service and sacrifices of First Nations veterans and their families; it is simply an accurate assessment shorn of the 'forgotten warrior' mystique.

Moreover, the gross national statistics by themselves disguise a tremendously varied picture. At the provincial level, the per capita rates of enlistment for Status Indians vary from 10 percent among the Mi'kmaq and Maliseet populations of P.E.I. and New Brunswick to just over 1 percent in Manitoba, Alberta, and B.C.[35] Some First Nations or specific communities do demonstrate rates of enlistment of the sort claimed by the 'forgotten warrior' school. In Saskatchewan, many Plains Cree communities had high levels of enlistment, including the Mistawasis Band, where 20 men out of a population of 225 had volunteered by early October 1939.[36] The Indian Agent from the Kootenay Agency in B.C. recorded over 50 enlistments and no deferrals from a population of 435.[37] The Ojibwa community at Cape Croker may well have had the most extraordinary record of enlistment of all: from a population of 471 in 1943, 53 men and women had volunteered for active service, 3 more were rejected for medical reasons, and 9 had joined the Veterans' Guard.[38]

Other communities present a different image. According to admittedly incomplete IAB figures for January 1945, the Peigan Reserve had recorded only four voluntary recruits, while the neighbouring Sarcee and Stoney Reserves recorded only two each: lower even than the 1.1 percent that was the provincial average.[39] In the case of many northern First Nations, numbers were low due to the difficulties in reaching recruitment offices and the army's reluctance to accept recruits from remote regions, though some disinterest in events so far away may also have been evident.[40] On B.C.'s Pacific coast, there were many examples of low enlistment such as that reported by the Indian Agent for the Kwawkewlth Agency in March 1944. From a population of 1,270, only one man was serving overseas, four were in General Service in Canada, two were NRMA conscripts serving in Canada, and 106 had requested and gained deferment from compulsory training due to essential service in the Pacific fishing fleet.[41] In this case, though, lest his superiors misinterpret these figures, the Agent hastened to add that

Indians are very loyal. At the outbreak of the war many Indians tried to enlist in the Naval Service, as they felt that ... they were best suited to serve in this Branch of the Service. A great many of them volunteered their services, spent considerable sums of money going to recruiting offices only to be turned down ... To this date no Registered [Status] Indian has ever been allowed to enter the Canadian Navy ... It is this discrimination against the B.C. Indian that has made them oppose being called up and put in the army, a Branch ... in which they do not wish to serve ... Since the beginning of the war the Indians of this Agency have supported the war effort to the best of their ability. They have purchased Thousands of Dollars of Victory Bonds, given freely to the Red Cross cause, and many have joined the Pacific Coast Rangers for home defence ... Each village has its own officers and equipment, and stand ready to serve in any emergency.

The Agent concluded that as a result of their off-reserve employment in the fishing fleet and canneries, First Nations men and women were paying substantial income tax and had become "a national asset and ... deserve credit and consideration for their efforts."[42] In this instance, then, lack of recruits was not a manifestation of opposition to the war effort per se, but a product of the cultural preferences, practical experience, and economic reality of the local communities, as well as their frustrated desires to enlist in the Royal Canadian Navy.

The words of First Nations people can help clarify our understanding of the war that First Nations people were fighting. Some of the statements that Indian leaders made were stridently supportive of the war effort. For example, on 30 November 1939, the *Toronto Star* quoted Ambrose Reid, a delegate to a conference of the Native Brotherhood of British Columbia (NBBC). He claimed that it was "our duty as patriotic citizens to put aside our personal claims or the claims of our brotherhood and aid our country in this time of stress ... Our country is at war, so we, the Native Brotherhood, are also at war."[43] Ted Yellowfly made a similarly vigorous pronouncement at a council meeting of the Blackfoot in June 1940:

In this hour when our country is faced with extreme difficulties and trying moments, we the Blackfoot Tribe of Indians, desire to show out [sic] loyalty to Canada and the Empire, by doing our humble bit to help in the struggle for freedom from tyranny. Canada has, and always shall be, our home; the outlook of the Indian is purely Canadian in its nature and character, and therefore we ask that a sum of $850.00 representing $1.00 from each Blackfoot soul, be donated to the Red Cross of Southern Alberta from the Blackfoot Band Funds.

The Indian Agent, G.H. Gooderham, quoted Yellowfly, noting afterwards that the council unanimously passed this motion, "with many patriotic assertions."[44] In their words, both Reid and Yellowfly were making declarations of belonging. In claiming the status of "patriotic citizens" or trumpeting the "purely Canadian" outlook of the Indian, they were expressing not only a desire for their people to take part in the national war effort but also their right to do so. Such pronouncements may have played to the ear of the dominant society in the tense atmosphere of wartime Canada. Many non-English Canadians felt intense pressure to proclaim their loyalty to King and country, and the First Nations were no different.[45] Indian leaders recognized the potential utility of their contributions to the cause, and some professions of support and loyalty were undoubtedly employed, or amplified, for this purpose. When the people of Alert Bay, B.C., sought help in reducing alcohol availability in their community, they phrased the request in the following terms:

> We Indian people have always had the greatest respect for the King's uniform, and ... are doing everything we can to assist the Government in the war effort; at this very moment the third Victory Loan is taking place, and in Alert Bay alone we are told the Indians have to date subscribed half the total subscriptions, but this liquor traffic which is increasing all the time is undermining our young people.[46]

Others sought to leverage loyalty and wartime contributions into more favourable postwar support for their long-standing grievances with the government. The Nishga Land Committee expressly made this connection when they sent a letter to the prime minister "to show our loyalty to our country contributing $25 ... To protect our tribal rights and to strengthen his Majesties [sic] Forces."[47] Such efforts generated moral capital for First Nations people to press for Indian policy reforms. However, it would be a disservice to write off their expressions of loyalty, patriotism (for lack of a better word), and enthusiasm for the war effort as merely crass or clever means to gain advantage and positive attention from the dominant society. The extent of actions described earlier demonstrates that these words were not disingenuous, but substantial and genuine.

A poignant case, reported in an unidentified and undated news clipping in the Indian Affairs files, drives the point home. The news story quoted at length a letter in uncertain English sent by Peter Gladue, from Lac la Biche, Alberta, to the recruiting sergeant who had turned down Gladue's enlistment on medical grounds. While the writing is not always clear, the sincerity and level of concern are unmistakable.

> Here today arrived with a deeply worrying how can I save my children and my land. As I know and we all know and see, that when we relations die, we cry for him or her and we couldn't see no how to save his or her life. Today and on is our chance to save our children their lives is beyond to help of winning this big flame of fire coming toward us in a world war. Today every stitch of everything is needed. And beyond, all Indian of Canada of all points should now look in future if they love their children and their lands, to help winning this terrible war. A man is fit for war should now go and stop this big flame of fire coming to burn our children their lives. And any one not fit to go should help on every penny to help those people are fighting for us all.[48]

First Nations people were deeply moved by the loss of life, the widespread devastation, and the human hardship brought on by the war, as well as by a desire to join in the effort to stop the Axis powers and defend their country and/or traditional territories.

First Nations peoples considered the decision to enter military service as a personal choice, made only after consultation with one's family, one's conscience, and one's spiritual guides. While the Canadian armed forces overseas were raised almost solely through voluntary recruitment, most Status Indian communities supported their young men enlisting. But their support was not unconditional. In the spring of 1940, the German conquest of Norway, Denmark, the Low Countries and finally France left Canada as Britain's ranking ally. With defeat a very real possibility, Canada began gearing up for a total war effort. The National Resources Mobilization Act, passed in June, introduced national registration for all men and women over the age of sixteen as well as conscription for home defence only. Having their young men compelled to take training for military service provoked a very different response from First Nations communities. From one end of the country to the other, chiefs, band councils, indigenous rights advocates, parents, and young men protested their liability to conscription.[49]

Most communities expressed their concerns about compulsory service in the context of their willingness to volunteer. For instance, the Pas Band filed a protest over conscription, but concluded by saying that they "wish to be understood that we are not disloyal. Any Treaty Indian who wishes to join the Army can do so. We will not stop him. We will be glad to see him go help our King and Country."[50] Mi'kmaq leaders, likewise, passed a unanimous resolution at Wycocomaugh, N.S., in August 1942, seeking an exemption from conscription, but reassured the government that "when this is granted, the Nova Scotia Micmacs, through their leaders, will be urged more than ever, to serve through voluntary enlistment and otherwise."[51] Others wished to be of use to the country but felt they could be so more effectively through other avenues. Robert Yidlan articulated this well in a letter to Indian Affairs requesting information and help in locating a job:

> Although I am an Indian, I am willing to help as much as any one else with the defence of our country. And if I am not obliged to join the Army unless voluntarily, I think that I would be helping the Defence [sic] of our country just the same if I could get employment in some of the war industrial plants here in the city.[52]

Most First Nations people who wrote on the issue wanted to choose how they might best contribute.

Opposition to conscription took many forms. Most common and widespread were band council resolutions, petitions, and letters written by indigenous people from every walk of life, and from many different communities, to express their views and pressure the government to change its stance.[53] When their letters prompted the official IAB response that "Indians are in the same position as white people with regard to military service," First Nations people wrote to or met anyone they believed might be able to address their concerns.[54] The increasingly frustrated Six Nations sent delegations to Ottawa in the spring and fall of 1943 and subsequently in

March of 1944 and 1945, though without success.[55] Despite such protests, Six Nations people continued to volunteer.[56]

In some instances, the opposition to conscription emerged at high-profile political and legal forums. In 1943, dozens of First Nations leaders gathered in Ottawa in meetings that led to the formation of the North American Indian Brotherhood. They garnered substantial media attention for their grievances, which included conscription.[57] That same year, a Mohawk named Harris Smallfence tested the legalities of conscripting Status Indians before the Supreme Court of Quebec.[58] The judge decided against Smallfence and he was led away to begin his military training. The strongest opposition arose on the Caughnawaga Reserve in November 1943, where RCMP attempts to apprehend draft dodgers twice provoked skirmishes with hostile crowds, resulting in three Mohawks being shot before the Mounties withdrew with their captives.[59]

Such violence, however, was exceedingly rare. More common was passive resistance at an individual, family, or community level. Many refused to appear for medical examination upon receiving their call-up notice from the Department of National War Services. Indian Agents reported such incidents among the Squamish in Vancouver in September 1940; the Stoney Nation of Alberta in April 1941; the Mohawks at Caughnawaga throughout the war; and the Micmac of Nova Scotia in October 1942.[60] The men's reticence to report may have reflected their communities' opposition to conscription. In some cases, elders sanctioned young men's refusal and helped them avoid the reach of the RMCP.[61] Some crossed the border and took refuge in the United States, while members of more isolated communities could simply vanish into their hunting territories. The problems became so prevalent that the Director of Indian Affairs, Harold McGill, finally issued a circular letter to his field personnel on 31 July 1943, in which he stated:

> The National Selective Service authorities have now advised that some difficulty is being experienced in the call up of Indians under the Mobilization Regulations. Please do everything within your power to see that the Indians comply with the regulations and report circumstances to the department requiring attention.[62]

While such resistance was pervasive, the majority of First Nations who were called up complied with the law, reported for their medical exam, and performed their military service if they could not gain deferment under the NRMA regulations.

The reasons behind First Nations' opposition to conscription were diverse. For millennia, the decision to participate in a military venture had been a voluntary one in indigenous societies across northern North America. Thus, at a fundamental cultural level, forcing young First Nations men into military service during the Second World War appeared especially abhorrent. While this visceral response lurked beneath Indian reactions, the protests were usually framed around other issues. One of the most common objections stemmed from verbal promises made by Crown treaty negotiators in the nineteenth century, especially in some of the Numbered Treaties encompassing the southern plains and the North. For example, in 1873, Commissioner Alexander Morris guaranteed the Saulteaux at the negotiation of the North-West Angle Treaty (Treaty 3) that the "English never call the Indians out of the country to fight their battles."[63] Many First Nations communities recalled these words during the Second World War when conscription of their young men inspired understandable anger. Mrs. Paul Noon alluded to treaties in a letter to Indian Affairs in 1940 requesting papers of exemption "for my 2 sons as I don't want them to be Soldiers. Queen Victoria had made a promise to all the Indians here in Canada that Indians shall never go and fight again."[64] Treaties rested at the centre of the First Nations' relationship with the state and the Crown, and it proved a difficult argument for the government to ignore. During the conscription crisis in 1944, it was the existence of verbal treaty promises in the written record of the negotiations of Treaties 3, 6, 8, and 11 that forced the government to grant a limited exemption from overseas conscription for Status Indian conscripts covered under those treaties.[65] Concern about conscription was partly pragmatic in nature: could the small First Nations population afford to sacrifice so many of its men, even temporarily? One letter to the Governor General, from Walpole Island, Ontario, requested exemption from military service for a son, arguing in part, "We are descendants of the diminishing, original inhabitants of this country which was ours before the white race came."[66] Alfred Adams, President of the NBBC, made his request based on labour availability in February 1944, when he wrote the Indian Commissioner for B.C. to "most earnestly ask that you ask the authorities to order that no more Indians be called into the army as the man power supply is depleted, and because those that remain are engaged in an essential war industry."⁶⁷ Some struggled to comprehend the government's persistence, given the relatively few First Nations men still available. The communities of White Fish Lake and Saddle Lake, B.C., protested against compulsory service, but also claimed that if "our numerical strength were a factor and we were invaded then the situation might be different and in such case we would not wait to be asked to help."⁶⁸ For Indian Affairs officials, however, the relatively small numbers were irrelevant. Their insistence on Status Indian liability to conscription was to prevent any real or perceived distinction between Indians and other British subjects that might jeopardize their assimilation agenda in future.⁶⁹

The most prevalent issue raised by First Nations opponents of conscription, however, was the marginalized place of Status Indians in the social and legal landscape of Canada. A number of people questioned why they should feel obliged to serve for a racist society that denied their people acceptance. Percy Ross, Chief of the Songhees Reserve in Victoria, pointed out the racial inconsistencies in Canada's conscription policies: "The Indians do not seem to understand why Chinamen are exempt from compulsory military service and the Indians who originally owned the country be called up under the Selective Service Act."⁷⁰ One Indian soldier saw his forced service as an injustice, noting that he had not been accepted into a high school "because I was an Indian. If I am not good enough to have an [sic] schooling in the white school I am not good enough to fight."⁷¹ A petition from Burns Lake, B.C., spoke passionately about the burdens of the war, especially taxation and military service, being shouldered by the First Nations equally,

> yet they never even let us allowed [sic] in the hotel or in the beer parlor [sic] and so forth. If you are not going to give us the same privileges as the white people, then we want you to bring the Indian boys back to Canada ... If the Indian boys are going to stay overseas then we want to be mix with the white people like one, don't matter we stay on reserve or not.⁷²

While many letters and petitions took aim at racism, not all were so open to amalgamating First Nations people into the mainstream and forgoing their reserves. Chief Gamble of Kitlakatla succinctly made this point in a letter in March 1945: "also Natives be Franchised [sic] is not agreed upon by the Native people, we were born Indians and always will stay as Indians."⁷³

Alongside the treaty issue, however, the most damning criticism of conscription was over the government demanding the most onerous and dangerous duties of citizenship from people expressly denied its freedoms and privileges. For Canadians fully engaged in a war against totalitarianism and in defence of democracy, equality, and freedom, such an injustice was morally and philosophically troubling. First Nations opponents of conscription tried to leverage this point to seek exemption from conscription, as did an Indian conscript who said that if the "Canadian Indian had full citizenship in the country, I don't mind fighting for it."[74] Similarly, one community's leaders wrote that as "wards of the government ... we submit the ward should not be asked to fight for the guardian."[75] Other communities took their protests in another direction, seeking to parley their liability for conscription into greater rights. Few stated this as eloquently as the chiefs of the Blood Reserve in southern Alberta:

> why should we be asked to go when we only live in the empire and are not a part of it. We are only wards of the government and have no voice in controlling the affairs of government but are asked to submit like children and take full responsibility with those who are fortunate to be full citizens and subjects of the King ... Surely if our young men are good enough to wear the King's uniform and take their place with others, they should have full right to say with the others when and where Canada should fight.[76]

Several, like the community at Fort Fraser, B.C., were more equivocal about the outcome, so long as the untenable situation in which they found themselves changed:

> We Indians want to help defend our country, we are ready and willing to fight, but we can only do so effectively if we have the same civil rights and privileges as our white brothers have. We think your government has no right to compel us to become soldiers unless you first give us the same rights and privileges as our white brothers have; otherwise you must leave it to us to decide whether we want to fight for our country in your army or not.[77]

The strident indigenous voices raised on rights and conscription make it clear how viscerally the First Nations felt about their distinct status, while also emphasizing their legal and constitutional reality beyond the pale of the Canadian norm.

Examining both the actions and the voices of the First Nations during the Second World War enables a clearer understanding of what the conflict meant to them, as well as the purposes behind Indian communities' participation and opposition. The response was varied and enormously complex, involving virtually all segments and age groups in many communities. Collective actions on the homefront, including generous donations to humanitarian and patriotic causes, large-scale purchases of Victory Bonds and War Savings Certificates, and enthusiastic public acts and words of patriotism, confirm that First Nations people were deeply moved by the human suffering and threat presented by the war. First Nations engagement in the war effort was meaningful, and their commitment—not only to the defence of their country and traditional territories, but also to Allied victory—was genuine.

While the significance of First Nations prosecution of the war effort is readily apparent, what of the motivation behind it? And what, if any, message was being conveyed to the dominant society? The national patterns of actions and voices show their desire to belong, to be included in a great collective endeavour, to win respect and prove their worth. Many First Nations shared the feelings of the most famous indigenous soldier of the war, Sergeant Tommy Prince, who volunteered in 1940 because he had always "wanted to do something to help my people recover their good name. I wanted to show they were as good as any white man."[78] First Nations saw contributions to the war effort as a way to gain the attention and appreciation of the dominant society and to begin overturning the pervasive racism in Canadian society, as well as excise the lingering feelings of inferiority within their own population. Many also hoped that wartime efforts would lead to greater rights, usually conceptualized as citizenship rights—the only rights paradigm widely accepted at that time.[79] Only after the Second World War would developing regimes in human rights and Aboriginal rights provide First Nations people with other conceptual tools to further their aspirations. The desire for recognition, acceptance, and status shaped First Nations efforts during the Second World War along primarily cooperative avenues. This is in striking contrast with contemporary Indigenous–state/society relations, which are often marked by litigiousness, antagonism, and even violence.

The second part of the motivation and message for First Nations was a declaration of being—of their determination to make their own choices and live as culturally distinct communities. While First Nations populations were generally supportive of the war, their support was not sycophantic, nor was it unqualified or unlimited; theirs was a measured and thoughtful response. When necessary, many communities opted to disengage from the war effort: to reshape their role, to protest, and to resist the state's employment of Status Indians and resources in its prosecution of the war. The diversity of disengagement strategies demonstrated the resolve of each First Nation, of each band, and of each family to achieve self-determination.

Both engagement and disengagement garnered some success by war's end. The sympathy that engagement won from the dominant society generated a public campaign for Indian policy reform, and the subsequent government review process from 1946 to 1948. First Nations' desires to reduce legal limitations and wardship status resonated with Canadians. The Special Joint Parliamentary Committee on the Indian Act even recommended the granting of the federal franchise without having to surrender Indian Status.[80] But First Nations critiques about societal racism and lack of acceptance found less fertile soil. Though many Canadians were discomforted by First Nations criticisms of their racism, social attitudes on the ground had changed little from the prewar years.[81] This particularly struck First Nations veterans, who had anticapted, on their return, the respectful treatment they had enjoyed in the military.

When First Nations people reached certain limits, they opted for strategies of disengagement. Efforts to moderate their involvement were circumscribed by the Indians' marginal social status and political disenfranchisement, by an unsympathetic bureaucracy, and by the constraints on dissent in wartime Canada. Interestingly, the resistance and anger over conscription was not generalized to broad withdrawal of support for the national war effort by most First Nations communities. Total disengagement, while plausibly an option, could have carried too high a cost to be considered viable, and arguably did not satisfy First Nations determination to play a role in bringing the war to a successful close. Nevertheless, in some ways, First Nations disengagement, protest, and resistance did force the government to take note of their views. The eventual decision to offer exemption to some Treaty Indians was, though limited, a victory for this approach.

Reflecting on this double-barrelled motivation and meaning, First Nations people in Canada were declaring their right to belong. But fundamentally, their contributions to winning the war were also declarations of their right to be. They wished to be accepted, but not according to the assimilationist terms offered and expected by the state and the dominant society. The efforts to define, constrain, and ideally control the nature of their contributions amounted to a rejection of the profoundly conformist demands of wartime Canada. Yet the war also generated substantial moral capital that offered First Nations leaders and Native rights organizations opportunities to win concessions from the state at war's end. In the wake of the Second World War, Canadians struggled to acknowledge First Nations actions and to accommodate the implications within the still dominant ethos of assimilation. Most Canadians felt they had laid the groundwork for the accelerated movement of First Nations into the Canadian body politic, through the vehicles of the Special Joint Committee and the new Indian Act, passed in 1951. But this white man's war to prove Indians' readiness and suitability for assimilation into the mainstream was not the war that First Nations people had fought. Their war was a fight for acceptance of their culturally distinct and vibrant communities, and of their desire to determine their own future.

Notes

1. A note on terminology: I have generally used First Nations in describing Status Indian peoples, though the term "Indian" is used as well, a reflection of the time period under discussion. The terms "Aboriginal" and "indigenous" have been inserted where appropriate to denote references to Métis and Inuit peoples as well.
2. Michael Stevenson, "The Mobilisation of Native Canadians During the Second World War," *Journal of the Canadian Historical Association* 7 (1996), 205–26.
3. The issues raised in this paragraph have been explored thoroughly in R. Scott Sheffield, *The Red Man's on the Warpath: The Image of the "Indian" and the Second World War* (Vancouver: University of British Columbia Press, 2004).
4. Tom Holm has argued that this was how Native Americans' service was interpreted in the United States, where Americans presumed that Native Americans' extraordinary support and enlistment numbers were proof that the time had come to get the government off the back of the Indian. The result would be the disastrous policy of termination initiated in the early 1950s. Tom Holm, "Fighting a White Man's War: The Extent and Legacy of American Indian Participation in World War II," *Journal of Ethnic Studies* 9, no.2 (1981), 69–81.

5   Fred Gaffen, *Forgotten Soldiers* (Penticton: Theytus, 1985). James Dempsey was the author of the first of these graduate theses, and later published his work as *Warriors of the King: Prairie Indians in World War I* (Regina: Canadian Plains Research Centre, 1999). The second was Janet F. Davison, "We Shall Remember Them: Canadian Indians and World War II" (MA thesis, Trent University, 1992), whose wide-ranging coverage and at times polemical style would later be much in evidence in the RCAP sections on veterans that she helped draft. The last of these is my own MA thesis, which was partly inspired by the "forgotten warrior" interpretation and which repeated many of its myths, though the approach and analysis differ: "'In the same manner as other people": Government Policy and the Military Service of Canada's First Nations People, 1939-45" (MA thesis, University of Victoria, 1995).

6   Janice Summerby, *Native Soldiers, Foreign Battlefields* (Ottawa: Ministry of Supply and Services Canada, 1993).

7   Canada, *The Aboriginal Soldier After the Wars*, report of the Standing Senate Committee on Aboriginal Peoples, 1995.

8   Canada, *Report of the Royal Commission on Aboriginal Peoples*, vol. I, *Looking Forward, Looking Back* (Ottawa: Canada Communication Group, 1996).

9   At the National Round Table were the Assembly of First Nations, First Nations veterans' organizations, and the Departments of Indian and Northern Affairs, National Defence, and Veterans Affairs; all came together to seek a consensus interpretation of what happened to Indian veterans' benefits. See the final report: R. Scott Sheffield, *A Search for Equity: A Study of the Treatment Accorded to First Nations Veterans and Dependents of the Second World War and Korea* (Ottawa: Final Report of the National Round Table on First Nations Veterans' Issues, May 2000).

10 R. Scott Sheffield and P. Whitney Lackenbauer developed the concept of the "Forgotten Warrior" in the historiographical essay "Moving Beyond Forgotten: The Historiography of Canadian Native Peoples and the World Wars," in Whitney Lackenbauer and Craig Mantle, eds., *Aboriginal Peoples and the Canadian Military: Historical Perspectives* (Kingston: Canadian Forces Leadership Institute, 2007).

11 This is the author's own impression of writing and working in this field during the period, particularly during the National Round Table process in 2000-1. Conversations and briefings I had with Indigenous participants and political leaders made clear their discomfort with any such lines of inquiry. That was a consensus document and took heed of indigenous stakeholders' perspectives.

12 Those interested in this increasingly rich and varied field can refer to the sources listed in this essay's notes as well as to excellent starting points such as the following: Lackenbauer and Mantle, eds., *Aboriginal Peoples and the Canadian Military: Historical Perspectives* (Kingston: Canadian Forces Leadership Institute, 2007); P. Whitney Lackenbauer, R. Scott Sheffield, and Craig Mantle, eds., *Aboriginal Peoples and the Military: Canadian and International Perspectives* (Kingston: CDI Press, 2007); Whitney Lackenbauer, *Battle Grounds: The Canadian Military and Aboriginal Lands* (Vancouver: UBC Press, 2007); Robert A. Innes, "'I'm on Home Ground Now. I'm

Safe': Saskatchewan Aboriginal Veterans in the Immediate Postwar Years, 1945–1946," *American Indian Quarterly* 28, nos. 3–4 (2004), 685–718.
13   "First Local Volunteers for Army Service Leave Here for Training," *Cardston News*, 14 September 1939, 1.
14   "Saskatchewan Indians Respond Well," *Regina Leader-Post*, 24 July 1940.
15   Media reporting of indigenous subjects during these years, and the implications for English Canadians' collective image of the "Indian," have been more extensively examined in Sheffield, *The Red Man's on the Warpath*, Chapters 3 and 4.
16   "Tom-Toms of Stonies Beat Time for Tribesmen's Sun Dance Ritual," *Calgary Herald*, 20 June 1940, 1. While this public display of loyalty and patriotism was likely heartfelt, the inclusion of such elements in the traditional ceremonies may also have helped the Nakoda avoid prosecution from Indian Affairs officials, who would have been loath to undermine such a gesture.
17   "Honor Where Due," *Winnipeg Free Press*, 18 January 1940, 11.
18   Lackenbauer, *Battle Grounds*, 99; "Reveal Indians Most Generous," *Hamilton Spectator*, 31 December 1941.
19   Probably the most comprehensive coverage of home front contributions by First Nations communities is Roy Toomey, "Canadian Indians and the Second World War: The Pivotal Event of the 20th Century for Canadian Indians and Canadian Indian Policy?," MA thesis, University of Northern British Columbia, 2006, 65–71, who provides literally dozens of examples from coast to coast.
20   See, for instance, "Aid from Indians: Residents of Manitoba Do Bit in Filling Red Cross Coffers," *Winnipeg Free Press*, 7 August 1940; Harold McGill to Deputy Minister, 26 June 1940, Library and Archives Canada [LAC] RG 10, vol. 6763, file 452-5, pt. 2; "Indians Display Loyalty in Gift of Treaty Money," *Saskatoon Star-Phoenix*, 17 June 1940; "Natives Value Civilization, Aid War Fund," *Globe and Mail*, 8 July 1941; and "Indian Generous to War Causes," *Saturday Night*, 10 August 1940.
21   Gabriel Holliboy and John Googas to Secretary of Indian Affairs, 6 June 1941, LAC RG 10, vol. 6763, file 452-5.
22   This number is mentioned by Davison, "We Shall Remember Them," 83; and Toomey, "Canadian Indians and the Second World War," 65. Media mention of such contributions are numberless, but include "Indian Trappers Buy Certificates," *Brantford Expositor*, 28 January 1941, and "Indian Women First to Buy War Bond," *Vancouver Sun*, 31 May 1941.
23   "Blood Indians Generous to War Service Fund," *Cardston News*, 29 April 1941, 1, 2.
24   Davison mentions IAB obstruction to some band efforts to draw on their band funds in "We Shall Remember Them," 20, as does Toomey in "Canadian Indians and the Second World War," 68–69. The official records of this are in Harold McGill to Deputy Minister, 26 June 1940, LAC RG 10, vol. 6763, file 452-5, pt.2; Harold McGill Circular Letter, 12 July 1940, LAC RG 10, vol. 6763, file 452-5, pt. 2.
25   Gaffen, *Forgotten Soldiers*; Toomey, "Canadian Indians and the Second World War," 66; and Annual Report of IAB for 1943, 157.
26   "Indian Children Assist Red Cross," *Vancouver Sun*, 6 July 1940, 16.

27 "Indian Girls Help Park Spitfire Fund," *Calgary Herald*, 30 May 1941.
28 "Canada's Indians Are Helping with Tons of Old Buffalo Bones," *Saturday Night*, 10 June 1944.
29 "Their Braves Gone to War, Cape Croker's Indian Women and Children Carry On," photo collection, *Globe and Mail*, 23 October 1943; "Bruce Peninsula Reserve Does Bit to Put Every Victory Loan over Top," *Globe and Mail*, 23 October 1943. An undated list of the recruits is available in IAB records, "Indians Enlisted in Armed Forces from Cape Croker," LAC RG 10, vol. 6765, file #452-6X, pt. 3.
30 Olive Patricia Dickason, *Canada's First Nations: A History of Founding Peoples from Earliest Times*, 2nd ed. (Toronto: Oxford University Press, 1997), 304.
31 Allen Andrews, "Canada's Indian Warriors: Volunteers to a Man," in *Brave Soldiers, Proud Regiments: Canada's Military Heritage* (Vancouver: Ronsdale Press, 1997), 326.
32 The first figure can be found in the Annual Report of the Department of Indian Affairs, 1940, 22; and the second in the report for 1945, 4.
33 The National Round Table was a coming together of the Assembly of First Nations, First Nations veterans' groups, and the Departments of National Defence, Veteran Affairs, and Indian and Northern Affairs, with the purpose of determining what happened to First Nations veterans after the Second World War and Korean War. The National Round Table statistics were generated by cross-referencing personnel files at Veterans Affairs Canada and Indian and Northern Affairs. The process was not quite completed during my involvement in the NRT, hence there is not a hard final figure, but this double-check provides the most convincing empirical foundation for an estimate. There may still be some Status Indian soldiers who fell through the cracks, but it is unlikely that the number of those would be in the hundreds, let alone thousands.
34 Rejection rates varied widely across the country and through the duration of the war based on many criteria. Most Status Indians rejected from military service ran afoul of racial barriers or stringent health and educational standards in the recruitment policies of the three branches of the armed forces. These are examined more fully in R. Scott Sheffield, "'Of Pure European Descent and of the White Race': Recruitment Policy and Aboriginal Canadians, 1939–1945," *Canadian Military History* 5, no.1 (Spring 1996), 8–15. See also Stevenson, "The Mobilisation of Native Canadians," 212.
35 Toomey, "Canadian Indians and the Second World War," 22.
36 "Eighteen Mistawasis Indians Join Infantry," *Saskatoon Star-Phoenix* (14 October 1939), 3.
37 J. Colman to Indian Affairs Branch, 3 May 1945, LAC RG 10 vol. 6769, file 452-20-3.
38 "Their Braves Gone to War," photo collection, *Globe and Mail*, 23 October 1943; "Bruce Peninsula Reserve Does Bit," *Globe and Mail*, 23 October 1943. By war's end, Cape Croker had recorded a total of seventy-eight voluntary enlistments according to the IAB, Voluntary Enlistments by province and reserve as of 15 January 1945; see LAC RG10, vol. 6764, file 452-6, pt. 2. There are records of a number of indigenous women who served in the women's auxiliaries of the various military branches during the war; see Grace Poulin, "Invisible Women: Aboriginal Servicewomen in Canada's Second World

War Military," in Lackenbauer and Mantle, eds., *Aboriginal Peoples and the Canadian Military*.
39 This is based on figures from Voluntary Enlistments by province and reserve as of 15 January 1945; see LAC RG 10 , vol. 6764, file 452-6, pt. 2; and the Annual Report of the Department of Indian Affairs, 1946, 5.
40 Only seven recruits were recorded from Yukon, and none from the Northwest Territories; see Annual Report of the Department of Indian Affairs, 1946, 5. These issues are addressed effectively in Stevenson, "The Mobilisation of Native Canadians," who explores in detail the patchwork quilt of administrative practices developed by the mobilization authorities with regard to indigenous populations in remote regions. The Indian Affairs perspectives on this issue are covered in Sheffield, "'In the same manner as other people,'" especially in connection to National Registration and conscription in Chapters 3 and 4.
41 Agency Report for Kwawkewlth Agency, March 1944, LAC RG 10, vol. 6769, file #452-20-3.
42 Ibid.
43 "Indians to Assist as Canada at War," *Toronto Star*, 30 November 1939, LAC RG 10, vol. 6764, file 452-6, pt. 2.
44 Blackfoot Minutes of Council Meeting, 19 June 1940, LAC RG 10, vol. 6763, file 452-5, Alta. The Indian Agent in this case may have embellished the patriotism of the occasion to some degree, but the words of Yellowfly were (atypically) recorded in quotation marks, and it seems likely that they may have been quoted from a prepared statement. Similar contributions were recorded from the Blood and Peigan Nations as well, with the latter being to the government for war purposes rather than to the Red Cross; see Band Fund Release, Blood Band, 21 June 1940, LAC RG 10, vol. 6763, file 452-5, Alta.; and Band Fund Release, Peigan Band, 27 June 1940, LAC RG 10, vol. 6763, file 452-5, Alta.
45 For discussion of war on various minorities, see Thomas M. Prymak, *Maple Leaf and Trident: The Ukrainian Canadians During the Second World War* (Toronto: Multicultural History Society of Ontario, 1988); Peter Lorenz Neufeld, *Mennonites at War, a Double-Edged Sword: Canadian Mennonites in World War Two* (Deloraine: DTS, 1997); Marjorie Wong, *The Dragon and the Maple Leaf: Chinese Canadians in World War II* (London: Pirie, 1994); Simon Theobold, "A False Sense of Equality: The Black Canadian Experience of the Second World War," MA thesis, University of Ottawa, 2008; and Patricia E. Roy, "The Soldiers Canada Didn't Want: Her Chinese and Japanese Citizens," *Canadian Historical Review* 59, no.3 (1978), 341–58.
46 Petition to the Secretary, Indian Affairs Branch, 27 October 1942, LAC RG 10, vol. 6770, file 452-26, pt. 3.
47 Peter Calder to McKenzie [sic] King, 6 March 1941, LAC RG 10, vol. 6763, file 452-5, B.C. The Nishga persisted in their campaign for recognition of their rights to their traditional territory for over a century.
48 "Indian Says All Should Help in War to End "Flame of Fire,'" undated news clipping, LAC RG 10, vol. 6764, file 452-6, pt. 2.

49 For an example, see an unaddressed letter presumably to Indian Affairs from Chief Joe Myream, Russell Bill, and Dan Assiniboine of Long Plain, 22 January 1943, LAC RG 10, vol. 6768, file 452-20-3.

50 Chief of the Pas Band and Antoine Constant to the Department of Indian Affairs, 26 November 1942, LAC RG 10, vol. 6769, file 452-20, pt. 5.

51 Unsigned to Matthew MacLean, 24 August 1942, LAC RG 10, vol. 6769, file 452-20, pt. 5; similar was a letter from Lake of Two Mountains, Quebec, by Clan Chief Angus Aroniahwente to the Governor General, 27 March 1945, LAC RG 10, vol. 6769, file 452-20, pt. 6.

52 Robert Yidlan to the Indian Affairs Branch, 2 June 1941, LAC RG 10, vol. 6765, file 452-6-17. Similar sentiments were asserted by John Norton in a letter to the Indian Department, 28 August 1942, LAC RG 10, vol. 6769, file 452-20, pt. 5; and Andrew Paul in a letter to the minister, Crerar, on behalf of another family who hoped to get their son discharged, arguing that he "would be of more service to the war effort as a fisherman." Andrew Paul to T.A. Crerar, 23 June 1944, LAC RG 10, vol. 6768, file 452-20-3.

53 There are many such letters scattered throughout Indian Affairs records, but they are most prolific in LAC RG 10, vol. 6768, file 452-20, pt. 4; as well as vol. 6769, files #452-20-3 and 452-20 pts. 5 and 6. For examples, see Resolution, River Desert Band, Maniwaki, 6 June 1942, from J.E. Gendron, LAC RG 10, vol. 6769, file 452-20, pt. 5; Minutes of Council Meeting, Resolution No.1083, Caughnawaga, 18 June 1942, LAC RG 10, vol. 6768, file 452-20, pt. 5; and Mrs. Paul Noon to the Department of Indian Affairs, 19 November 1940, LAC RG 10, vol. 6768, file 452-20, pt. 4; unaddressed letter presumably to Indian Affairs from Chief Joe Myream, Russell Bill, and Dan Assiniboine of Long Plain, 22 January 1943, LAC RG 10, vol. 6768, file 452-20-3; and Petition from Native Brotherhood of BC to Mackenzie King, (n.d. but likely March 1945, LAC RG 10, vol. 6769, file 452-20, pt. 6.

54 Quote from T.R.L. MacInnes to N.P. L'Heureux, 14 August 1942, LAC RG 10, vol. 6769, file 452-20, pt. 5. For instance, one delegation from St. Regis, Quebec, arrived in the fall of 1940 without official permission to discuss their concerns regarding compulsory military training; T.R.L. MacInnes to D.P. McNaughton, 30 October 1940, LAC RG 10, vol. 6768, file 452-20, pt. 4. Examples of writing outside official channels include the following: Shot Both Sides, Frank Red Crow, Percy Creighton, Fred T. Feathers, and Cross Child to the Minister of National Defence, 3 September 1942, LAC RG 10, vol. 6769, file 452-20, pt. 5; Chief Reuben Bull to the Honourable William Mackenzie King, 1 October 1941, LAC RG 10, vol. 6768, file 452-20, pt. 4; and Jules Sioui to the Ministers of the Cabinet, 30 November 1943, LAC RG 10, vol. 6769, file 452-20-10.

55 For information on these various visits, see Charles Camsell to E.P. Varcoe, 15 May 1943, LAC RG 10, vol. 6769, file 452-20, pt. 6; Crerar to Louis St. Laurent, 26 February 1944, LAC RG 10, vol. 6769, file 452-20, pt. 6; Hoey to Gamble, 17 March 1945, LAC RG 10, vol. 6769, file 452-20, pt. 6.

56 *Warriors: A Resource Guide* (Brantford: Woodland Indian Cultural Education Centre, 1986), 26, notes approximately 225 members of the Six Nations of the Grand River who served in either Canadian or American forces during the Second World War.
57 The North American Indian Brotherhood, which arose from these wartime meetings in Ottawa, would become one of the more prominent of many associations arising among First Nations' communities. The meetings received extensive coverage, such as the following: "Indians Ask Exemptions," *Prince Albert Daily Herald*, 23 October 1943, 8; *Vancouver Sun*, 21 October 1943, 11; "Indians Ask Tax, Army Exemptions," *Vancouver Sun*, 22 October 1943, 25; "Indian Petition Was Presented," *Brantford Expositor*, 23 October 1943, 4; "Indians Press Gov't To Grant Exemptions," *Calgary Herald*, 23 October 1943, 7; "Indians Ask For Army, Tax Exemptions," *Globe and Mail*, 22 October 1943, 7. For discussion of the coverage, see Sheffield, *Red Man's on the Warpath*, 89–90.
58 Le Roi vs. Harris Smallfence, Notes du Juge, 21 June 1943, LAC RG 10, vol. 6769, file 452-20-10, pt. 2. This case and its context are explored fully in R. Scott Sheffield and Hamar Foster, "Fighting the King's War: Harris Smallfence, Verbal Treaty Promises, and the Conscription of Indian Men, 1944," *University of British Columbia Law Review* 33, no.1 (1999), 53–74.
59 Brisebois to McGill, 2 December 1943, LAC RG 10, vol. 6769, file 452-20-10, pt. 2. This incident involved two altercations on the night of 26 November 1943. The first involved an assault on two constables at a restaurant on the reserve by a larger number of Mohawks, during which one of the constables was wounded and both retreated under a hail of rocks and bottles. The two returned some hours later with six reinforcements from Montreal. They raided the restaurant and arrested several draft dodgers, but were forced to retreat by a large, hostile crowd that slashed their tires and threw rocks and bottles. One of the officers was separated from his fellows and assaulted; during the scuffle that followed, the officer shot three of his attackers. The incident drew significant media attention.
60 Agent's Report for September, F.J.C. Ball, September 1940, NAC, RG 10, vol. 6770, file 452-26, pt. 2; J.H.R. Iredale to Schmidt, 21 April 1941, LAC RG 10, vol. 6768, file 452-20, pt. 4; Director of Mobilization to MacInnes, 21 October 1942, LAC RG 10, vol. 6769, file 452-20, pt. 5; RCMP Division File 41 M 172-302, Montreal Detachment, 18 August 1941, LAC RG 10, vol. 6768, file 452-20, pt. 4. Many other examples of the Caughnawaga, not to mention a large number of other First Nations groups, could also be provided.
61 Iredale to Schmidt, 21 April 1941, Brisebois to Secretary, 19 February 1942, LAC RG 10, vol. 6768, file 452-20, pt. 4.
62 McGill to all Indian Agents, Inspectors, and the Indian Commissioner for B.C., 31 July 1943, LAC RG 10, vol. 6768, file 452-20, pt. 4.
63 Memorandum to T.R.L. MacInnes, by R. Grenier, 13 June 1941 LAC RG 10, vol. 8594, file 1/1-11, pt. 1. Grenier was quoting from Morris, *The Treaties of Canada with the Indians of Manitoba, the North West Territories, and Kee-wa-tin* (Saskatoon: Fifth House, 1880), 69.

64 Mrs Paul Noon to Department of Indian Affairs, 19 November 1940, LAC RG 10, vol. 6768, file 452-20, pt. 4.

65 Conscription for home defence from 1940 to 1944 was not considered equal to the conscription discussed in the treaty negotiations, and this issue thus only emerged in full when the conscription crisis erupted in the fall of 1944. Once overseas service was a possibility, Indian Affairs officials could no longer dodge the relevance of the treaty promises. Nevertheless, the exemption was only limited to Status Indian conscripts who hailed from those specific treaty regions; all others still found themselves liable to be sent overseas; Sheffield and Foster, "Fighting the King's War."

66 Chas. K. Johnson to the Governor General, 12 August 1941, LAC RG 10, vol. 6768, file 452-20, pt. 4. Similar sentiments were expressed in Chief Isador to the Director, 25 October 1943, LAC RG 10, vol. 6768, file 452-20-3; and Chief A.E. Prince and Council of Hogson, 15th (no month) 1943, LAC RG 10, vol. 6768, file 452-20-4.

67 Alfred Adams to Major D.M. MacKay, 10 February 1944, LAC RG 10, vol. 6769, file 452-20, pt. 6.

68 Chief Reuben Bull to William Mackenzie King, 1 October 1941, LAC RG 10, vol. 6768, file 452-20, pt. 4.

69 See Sheffield, *The Red Man's on the Warpath*, Chapter 2.

70 Percy Ross to Harold McGill, 10 February 1944, LAC RG 10, vol. 6768, file 452-20-3.

71 Samuel [last name indecipherable] to Department of Indian Affairs, 2 July 1943, LAC RG 10, vol. 6768, file 452-20-3.

72 Chief Tibbetts and Paddy Isaac to the Department of Indian Affairs, 7 February 1944, LAC RG 10, vol. 6768, file 452-20-3. This discussion of prejudice against indigenous people seems to have been a consistent thread in letters and petitions from British Columbia. The Homalco Band on Vancouver Island noted that they were "always disliked by white people ... sometimes get kicked out [of] places we go." Chief Tommy Paul, unaddressed and undated, LAC RG 10, Vol. 6763, file 452-5, B.C.

73 Chief E.H. Gamble to the Honourable Premier of Canada, 9 March 1945, LAC RG 10, vol. 6769, file 452-20, pt. 6.

74 Samuel [last name indecipherable] to Department of Indian Affairs, 2 July 1943, LAC RG 10, vol. 6768, file 452-20-3.

75 Reuben Bull Chief to W.M. King, 29 September 1941, LAC RG 10, vol. 6768, file 452-20, pt. 4.

76 Chief Shot Both Sides, et al, to the Minister of Defence, 3 September 1942, LAC RG 10, vol. 6769, file 452-20, pt. 5.

77 Chief [illegible] George to T.A. Crerar, 5 April 1940, LAC RG 10, vol. 6769, file 4452-20, pt. 5.

78 Mackenzie Porter, "Warrior: Tommy Prince," *Maclean's* 65, no.17 (1 September 1952), cited in P. Whitney Lackenbauer, "'A Hell of a Warrior': Remembering Sergeant Thomas George Prince," *Journal of Historical Biography* 1 (Spring 2007), 31.

79 I am indebted to Australian historian Russell MacGregor for this insight. It is discussed in his excellent book, *Imagined Destinies: Aboriginal Australians and the Doomed Race Theory, 1880–1939* (Melbourne: Melbourne University Press, 1997), 249–60, as well

as in Russell McGregor, "Protest and Progress: Aboriginal Activism in the 1930s," *Australian Historical Studies* 25, no.101 (October 1993), 555–68.

80 Canada, Parliament, *Special Joint Committee of the Senate and the House of Commons appointed to examine and consider the Indian Act*, Minutes and Proceedings no.5, 13 April to 21 June 1948, 181–84. This recommendation did not survive the revisions process that led up to the new Indian Act in 1951, and it would be another decade before the federal vote was finally extended to First Nations people without prejudice to their Indian status.

81 Jim Walker's monograph makes this point: *"Race," Rights and the Law in the Supreme Court of Canada: Historical Case Studies* (Waterloo and Toronto: Wilfrid Laurier University Press and the Osgoode Society, 1997).

5

Harnessing Journalists to the War Machine
Canada's Domestic Press Censors in the Second World War

Mark Bourrie

It was a quiet afternoon at the Social Credit Party's national convention at Toronto's Royal York Hotel on 16 April 1944 when Dr. Joshua Haldimand, a Regina chiropractor, took the podium. The war seemed quite far away as Dr. Haldimand looked over the crowd in the hotel ballroom. A few reporters from Toronto's daily newspapers, along with some western Canadian journalists, were sprinkled among about seven hundred delegates. Dr. Haldimand had an interesting story to tell: scientists in the United States were working on a bomb fuelled by the splitting of uranium atoms that would be capable of destroying an entire city. Dr. Haldimand had picked up the story from some of his patients who were working on the Eldorado uranium mine in northern Saskatchewan. A physics buff, he had correlated the information from the miners with studies he had read in academic journals through the years and had come up with this startling bit of news, and now he wanted to share it.

The physics seems to have gone over the heads of the *Toronto Star* and *Toronto Telegram* reporters who were in the hall, but a *Regina Leader-Post* correspondent knew a good story when he heard one. The Regina reporter called the Toronto censorship office asking for clearance of his story on Dr. Haldimand's remarks. Toronto regional press censor Bert Perry very quickly killed the *Leader-Post* story, then called the *Star* and the *Telegram* and warned the papers to stop any mention of atomic research. Worried that a reporter for a small-town weekly paper or a Social Credit publication might write a story or that it might spread by word of mouth, Perry tracked down Dr. Haldimand at the convention and asked him to make an announcement to the gathering warning delegates and press from repeating the information.[1]

This was one of the more dramatic episodes in the story of Canada's wartime domestic press censorship system. For nearly six years, a small group of censors from across the country tried to suppress stories on troop movements, submarine attacks, captured spies, Japanese fire balloons, and new technology. The censors had no power to keep news out of the press, but journalists who did not heed their advice and printed information that threatened Canada's war effort faced sanctions enumerated in the Defence of Canada Regulations of the War Measures Act. In peacetime, all of the front-line censors were respected reporters and editors, but like many of their colleagues in the media, they became part of the country's war effort.

William Lyon Mackenzie King, the only Canadian prime minister ever to hold a permanent job in the newsroom of a daily paper, believed that journalists understood their colleagues' attitudes, work environment, professional culture, and competitive instincts and that they would make censorship decisions that their peers would accept.[2] Unlike Robert Borden, whose government operated a harsh, intrusive censorship system from August 1914 until the end of 1919,[3] King was a serious student of media and public relations techniques. He took a personal interest in the press censorship system and was determined to maintain it as a voluntary system under civilian control, despite pressure throughout the war from the military for pre-censorship of domestic military news by the armed forces.[4]

A survey of the newspaper coverage of the domestic press censorship system shows that the print media in Canada reacted very positively to the decision to use their colleagues as censors. Even at the end of the war, after years of government news control, newspaper editors and reporters still supported the censorship system, with editors explaining in postwar editorials that the use of journalists as censors had given the system credibility with members of the media.

Defiance of censorship, especially in English Canada, was very rare. Some working members of the media had very quickly changed from adversaries and critics to eager participants in the war effort and had become conduits of official news. On 1 September 1939, Robert Keyserlingk, who had spent the previous eight years as a journalist in central Europe and had returned to Canada as manager of the British United Press wire service, told a group of editors and reporters gathered at the Canadian National Exhibition Press Day luncheon: "No matter what conditions of censorship become necessary, it shall not be by official decree but through a sense of responsibility to assisting the public toward the goal of maintaining liberties and peace."[5] Keyserlingk's opinion of the patriotism of journalists was shared by war planners, who had decided more than a decade earlier to harness this patriotism if war broke out again.

Planning for a media-staffed censorship system began in a series of meetings of senior federal officials and media managers in the late 1920s. During the Bennett administration, censorship planning was shelved, but it was revived when King returned to office in 1935. The Interdepartmental Committee on Press Censorship suggested an advisory press censorship system that would rely on newspapers to self-censor. Those periodicals that did not "voluntarily" submit to censorship's directives would be showing themselves to be unpatriotic and leaving themselves open to prosecution and suspension of publication.[6] The committee suggested the censorship system that was, for the most part, adopted:

> It is proposed that a War Press Bureau, staffed by experienced newspapermen, should be formed, the role of which would be almost wholly advisory in character, the actual censorship being carried out by the editors themselves in the light of the Bureau's advice. It is not intended that the Press Bureau should possess the power to prohibit publication but if a system of voluntary censorship is to be effective, and if those newspapers which loyally observe the regulations which would be issued are not to be penalized, it follows that power should be taken to control others which might fail to accept the advice of the War Press Bureau and willfully publish information contravening the underlying principles of censorship.[7]

The power to enforce censorship existed under the provisions of the War Measures Act of 1914. Then Lieutenant-Colonel Maurice Pope, who handled much of the Department of National Defence war planning in the late 1930s, asked executives of the Canadian Press (CP) in 1938 to supply a list of names of people to run the Directorate of Censorship in time of war.[8] On 19 August 1939, twelve days before the war broke out, Canadian Press's general manager, E.J. Archibald (who had previously been involved with censorship planning in 1936 when he was employed by the *Montreal Star*), gave Pope a list of twenty names of likely candidates.⁹ Censorship rules were included in the Defence of Canada Regulations passed on 3 September 1939.

Policy for censorship was set by the federal cabinet, but administration of press censorship stayed in the hands of journalists through two reorganizations and five managers. Wilfrid Eggleston, who supervised the English press censorship system from the outbreak of the war until the end of 1944, was an Ottawa syndicated columnist and author who had been president of the Parliamentary Press Gallery in 1933–34. Eggleston was at his home in Aylmer, Quebec, when news of the German invasion of Poland reached Canada's capital. He went immediately to the Press Gallery suite in the Centre Block at Parliament Hill.¹⁰ A few minutes later, the *Winnipeg Free Press*'s Grant Dexter, a confidante of the prime minister, ushered reporters into King's office in the East Block, where King and senior External Affairs official O.D. Skelton briefed the correspondents on the unfolding crisis. Eggleston had a visceral reaction to Hitler's assault on Poland, writing later that "my first reaction to the devastation of Poland was a sort of impotent rage."¹¹

Very soon after Eggleston's meeting with King, Eggleston received a telephone call at the Press Gallery from Clare Moyer, the Clerk of the Senate. Moyer had been seconded to the new Censorship Branch to be Press Censor for Canada (English).¹² Moyer invited Eggleston to his office and offered him a position as censor of the Press Gallery.¹³ Eggleston struggled with the idea. "The word censor called up in my mind the usual stereotype," he wrote in his memoires. "For a philosophical liberal like myself, a John Stuart Mill follower, a censor was a necessary evil at best. I was intelligent enough to know that in time of war censors were essential, but of all the wartime tasks I had considered, not one had been as obnoxious as this." If, Canada was directly threatened, Eggleston was willing to serve, but until that time, he told Moyer, he would prefer some other kind of war work.¹⁴

Eggleston was invited to a meeting the following day with Director of Censorship Walter Thompson, who was in charge of press censorship, mail openings, telephone taps, and telegram censorship. Thompson tried to assuage Eggleston's distaste for censorship work and held out the prospect of a job writing propaganda at the Bureau of Public Information, which, Thompson said, was to be established by the end of the year. Eggleston was hired at a rate of $12 a week, with the job beginning 1 November.[15] (Eggleston was disappointed that the job with the Bureau of Public Information never materialized.)

Less than two months into the job, Eggleston explained to one of his old high school teachers that he had come to see censorship as "more than a negative thing." But he struggled against pressure to "let censorship be employed to stifle legitimate criticism of the government or a realistic approach to the reporting of current history."[16]

In his memoirs, Eggleston said he continued holding those views, even during the "black days of 1940," when bad news "became worse every week." Support came from Mackenzie King, who had instructed the censors to "preserve and foster the freedom of the press in Canada so far as was consistent with winning the war."[17]

Eggleston replaced Clair Moyer as chief English press censor just as the Germans launched their offensive in the West in the spring of 1940. The collapse of France and the death of Defence Minister Norman Rogers in an airplane crash in May shook the capital. The mood of the media and the public was "bordering on panic and hysteria ... As the bad news poured in and the foundations of life were shaken, reason gave way to passion and tolerance to blind fury." The institutions of a democratic state, including a free press, were tested as Hitler's forces crushed Denmark, Norway, the Low Countries, and France. Eggleston credited King and his close advisers with preserving press rights from actions by cabinet ministers and senior civil servants who wanted a crackdown on information. He wrote in his diary: "The onset of total war greatly added to the weight and tension of censorship work. From apathy to a state of nerves is the swing of the pendulum, and people are in a mood to ban everything, even when the net effect of such a step would be highly detrimental."[18]

The collapse of France caused panic in much of official Ottawa. The end of "Phoney War" complacency brought problems for the censorship system, which was still dealing with a rapid turnover of much of its senior management and was struggling to make organizational changes to spin off a propaganda and information department, the Bureau of Public Information (later the Wartime Information Board).

The censors could not hide the bad news of the collapse of France and the smaller countries and the new threat to Britain from German bombers. Fairly accurate news came from media in the United States and German shortwave radio. The censors tried to keep out the more blatant propaganda stories, recognizing that "bad news might conceivably spur on our efforts; but bad news doctored up as enemy propaganda might sap our will to continue by making the enemy seem irresistible and the outcome foreordained ... Trying to insulate Canada from the propaganda circulating in the United States was, as Walter Thompson said, like trying to heat a Canadian house in winter if it had only three walls." Eggleston had to resist pressure from his minister to ban mainstream publications like the *Saturday Evening Post* for publishing an accurate description of the forces available to Hitler and an article on the roots of Irish discontent with England.[19]

Until 1941, Canada's censors had to deal with the flow of vast quantities of news and opinion from the United States. Before Pearl Harbor, most of the American media supported the Allied war effort, or at least, they did little to deliberately undermine it. Still, enough problematic material found its way into Canada to raise the ire of politicians and military officers.[20]

Through the year, Eggleston had to defend the work of his censors against critics in the media and the military. Writing in the *Canadian Journal of Economics and Political Science* in August 1941, Eggleston explained:

> The principles of military censorship are simple. The essence of successful warfare is secrecy. "Let us learn what we can from the enemy; let us teach him only what we must," was the rule laid down by Lord Balfour in the last war. Surprise is still the most valuable "secret weapon" of war; and the ideal state of affairs from the narrow viewpoint of military operations is a complete black-out on all information regarding such matters as the strength of military forces, the disposition of units, the nature of defences, the stocks of war supplies, the rate of growth of the armed forces, the rate of production of war weapons, and so on. In modern wars, these desirable military secrets must be extended to facts concerning the economic, financial, and psychological strength of the nation at war.[21]

This "ideal state of affairs," from the Department of National Defence's point of view, clashed with "other vital considerations." The military believed in censorship of information at the source, believing that secrets could only be kept from the enemy if the people of the home country were also denied access to them. Eggleston disagreed, arguing that a complete blackout of information was a threat to democracy itself:

> Complete acceptance of the military philosophy of censorship would raise grave problems in a democracy, which relies so largely on an informed public, and on voluntary effort. It would be a farce to retain parliamentary institutions, and to rely upon voluntary enlistment and voluntary war loans, if the public were to be kept completely in the dark as to the course of the war, the size of the armed forces, the progress of defensive and offensive preparations. A compromise is inevitable, expressed in some such vague phrase as this: "The public must be told the facts; the enemy must be kept guessing."[22]

In the end, Eggleston was not sure that press censorship of domestic news was an effective way of keeping secrets and maintaining morale. He cited a *Collier's* magazine article written by George Creel, chairman of the U.S. Committee on Public Information in the First World War, in which Creel expressed his belief "that press censorship as practiced in the United States in the last war was a farce." Information, wrote Creel, needed to be controlled at key points, with monitors at communications facilities such as cable offices.[23] Bad news should be disclosed, but in measured ways, by domestic authorities: "Better for bad news to be disclosed by our authorities themselves, if possible immediately after the disaster, and for enemy propaganda rumours to be invalidated or decontaminated by official refutation or modification. Action of some sort may be imperative."[24]

In Eggleston's view, censorship had more value as a weapon to fight enemy propaganda that was slipped into the Canadian media or that arrived in Canada in foreign publications, photographs, and films. In the Second World War, the Germans were engaged in psychological warfare that was designed to break down the will of the Allies, undermine their war effort, confuse and disunite them, and even soften their resistance to a military invasion. Some sort of information control system was needed to prevent this contagion from entering the country. "And while censorship may not be the only or even the most effective weapon of reply, it is a useful element of our psychological arsenal."[25]

The censors were opposed by military intelligence officers who believed that censorship should be taken from the hands of journalists and given to professional army, navy, and air force officers. During a committee meeting in August 1941, Eggleston and T.A. Stone, an External Affairs official who, at the time, was Acting Chairman of the Censorship Coordination Committee, had an argument over the extent to which the press in Canada should be censored.[26] Stone and military intelligence officers on the committee accused Canada's media of being one of Germany's most valuable intelligence sources. They claimed to have intercepted instructions to Nazi agents telling them that practically all of the information needed by Germany could be obtained from Canadian newspapers, radio broadcasts, and copies of *Hansard*. Eggleston was prompted to write a four-page letter to explain his view on the value of a free press in wartime. He quoted three paragraphs from an article in the June 1941 issue of *Fortune* magazine. Censorship, *Fortune* argued, can help cover up important problems and "lead to false optimism with consequent reaction of despair" when the truth eventually comes out. And the press had an important role in the functioning of a democratic state:

> The press in a democracy is still the fourth estate; it is almost a fourth branch of government. It is not, as in Germany or the U.S.S.R., a branch of the government, but a part of our constitutional system. There is the legislative, the executive, and the judicial branch—and there is the press. It is impossible to imagine governmental processes in the U.S. without a press. Its first function is to inform, its second to criticize. Censorship is a direct threat to both functions and hence a direct threat to effective democracy. Without information there is no basis for criticism and without criticism there is, as the saying goes, tyranny.[27]

Eggleston said that some reporters, including Grant Dexter of the *Winnipeg Free Press*, had performed an important public service by carefully analyzing manpower figures from the 1930s, even though Dexter's work might well be valuable to the Nazis. Canadian morale problems would also be of interest to an enemy country, but Eggleston could see no way to limit the debate on political issues without undermining Canadian democracy: "How can conscription vs. voluntary enlistment be discussed and settled by democratic means if the press is not free to inform the public? Or, how can our leaders cope with disunity if every sign of it is suppressed? They may never even hear of it." Press censors, he wrote, should not be seen to be "in the middle," as balancing the interests of military security against the information needs of the press. Censorship had an obligation to analyze from more than just a security standpoint whether an article violated the Defence of Canada Regulations' prohibition of "information of value to the enemy." Fierce censorship of the press and the suppression of all information of potential use to the enemy would generate a clampdown on *Hansard* and reports from the Bank of Canada, and the "Bureau of Statistics will pretty well close up its printing plant." That was "the absurd extreme," Eggleston told Stone. In reality, the press censors had to find some middle ground between information needed for healthy political discourse and factual material that was useful to the enemy. Censors should focus on this question: "On balance, will the publication of this item aid or impede Canada's war effort?" In the end, the censors could never satisfy everyone. "And wherever we draw the line those interested in security are likely to think that we went too far one way and those interested in publicity think we went too far the other way."[28]

The chief censors of the English and French press maintained that a relationship of trust developed between the censors and the Canadian press: "More and more security officers came to the realization that the newspapers themselves were as intent on winning the war as the Army, Navy and Air Force, and that in the Censor they had an ally ready to take any necessary action for suppression once he was convinced that the interests of security necessitated such action. Further than this, the services learned not only that a censor could be trusted with very secret information but that hundreds of newspapermen could safely be taken into their confidence."

They pointed to the secrecy that was maintained in the early spring of 1945 when I Canadian Corps was moved from Italy to Northwest Europe. "Information which was then classified by the Army as 'top secret' was given to the Censors for transmission to every newspaper and radio station in Canada. This move, sponsored by the Director of Military Intelligence, shocked many a senior officer but it worked. From coast to coast of Canada the Army had enlisted some 1,500 allies who concentrated their efforts on suppression of any hint of the move."[29] (In fact, Canadian war correspondents had willingly contributed to the fake "noise" of radio traffic and newspaper stories that was generated at the Italian Front to disguise the movement of I Corps.)[30]

The system did face some political abuse. The opposition parties believed that press censorship, along with mail openings by postal censors, had been used against them. Conservative Party leaders argued that the press censors were, in their journalistic careers, supportive of the Liberal Party and its policies—an accusation that had some truth to it. The Conservatives advocated a censorship system operated by lawyers, with judges determining policy and making the most important decisions.[31]

Eggleston, in his postwar writings about his career as a censor, denied being a government shill. But he did believe that he had sometimes been manipulated by members of King's cabinet, especially Minister of Naval Affairs Angus Macdonald, who early in the war had asked for the suppression of an item of naval information (probably news of the May 1942 U-boat attacks in the St. Lawrence River). "I enlisted the cooperation of the press only to find that the only reason behind the request was to give the Minister of Naval Affairs a scoop when he announced it in the House."[32] Eggleston believed that the press censors deserved some of the political and editorial criticism levelled at them during the war. In many cases, he admitted, the censors' hands were tied: they had no more right than any other public servant to impose their views on cabinet ministers. At most, they could try to persuade politicians, and Eggleston staved off several bizarre policy changes "by persuading my minister (Secretary of State Norman McLarty) that they were unsound; and at least once I was prepared to turn in my resignation if my protest was unacceptable." He had just two requests from the prime minister. One, Eggleston believed, was "eminently reasonable" and was carried out at once. The other was for a severe tightening of censorship during the 1944 Conscription Crisis. "This I opposed as strongly as I knew how, and it was never followed up."[33]

French-language press censorship was handled by Fulgence Charpentier, a Parliament Hill journalist who had previously been appointed head of the Senate's journal branch. Charpentier went on to a brief diplomatic career before returning to journalism. He wrote a political column until 2000, when he retired at the age of 101. Charpentier spent most of his career in censorship waging his own war with *Le Devoir*. He believed that the influential political daily opposed Canadian participation in the war; also, that after the fall of France, it had supported Marshal Petain's Vichy regime and republished French fascist propaganda in its news and editorial pages. Through most of the war, Charpentier lobbied to have *Le Devoir* suspended or suppressed, but the King government refused to act against the newspaper. Charpentier also went after Quebec City's *L'Evenement Journal* for its fake "letters from Adolf Hitler to his sister," a series of articles that ran almost every day in the first two months of the war and that advocated a Quebec boycott of the war effort. He tried to suppress the weekly journal *L'Oeil* for its anti-Semitic editorials, and fringe papers like the Social Credit mouthpiece *Vers Demain*. In the end, only one paper, Quebec City's *Le Soleil*, was prosecuted, and the charges were laid for its breach of the news blackout of the sinking of SS *Cornwallis*, not for any isolationist articles.

The censorship system was decentralized, with local censors, all of them journalists, headquartered in Canada's larger cities. They were given power to make immediate decisions on most of the stories submitted to them. Most of the censors were seconded from the Canadian Press or from editorial departments of major local newspapers in the region where they acted as censors. Toronto censor Bert Perry had worked as an editor of the *London Advertiser*, which was owned by *Toronto Star* publisher Joseph Atkinson. In charge of all the newspapers in Ontario west of Kingston, for the Canadian Press and British United Press wire service newsrooms in Toronto, and for books and magazines published in the city, Perry came to the job with a great hatred of Germans. He had spent most of the First World War as a prisoner of war working as a slave labourer in a German coal mine. Perry was the most rigid of the regional press censors. His suppression of news of the departure of troops from Toronto was so extreme that he forced newspaper photographers to airbrush tears from the faces of people who gathered to cheer the departure of members of the 1 Canadian Division. Later, he instituted a complete news blackout on the POW riot at Camp 30 in Bowmanville on the Thanksgiving weekend of 1942.[34]

The Halifax press censor, H. Bruce Jefferson, was given the responsibility for censoring the news of the Battle of the Atlantic and U-boat incursions into the Gulf of St. Lawrence. Jefferson had bounced around Nova Scotia journalism for three decades and had just taken a job as an editorial writer on the *Halifax Chronicle* when he was recruited for war work. He suppressed most of the U-boat attack stories and articles on convoy sailings by ruling that they contained material useful to the enemy. On domestic stories and critical analyses of government policy, however, Jefferson tended to side with journalists. Jefferson let reporters print everything they had on the VE-Day riot in Halifax, and he intervened with his superiors to prevent the suppression of a newspaper in Sydney, Nova Scotia, printed by a Marxist publisher.

The Vancouver censorship office was operated by Lew Gordon, the city editor of the *Vancouver Province*. Along with a young reporter, John Graham (who later went on to a career at the *Vancouver Sun*), Gordon protested the suppression of the province's three Japanese-language newspapers in 1941 and intervened to protect Tommy Shoyama, editor of the *New Canadian*, from politicians and members of the mainstream media who wanted the *New Canadian* shut down and the editor jailed. In this, Gordon and Graham were supported by Eggleston and the Undersecretary of State for External Affairs, Norman Robertson. Gordon sometimes helped Shoyama get the newspaper out on time and also helped ensure that it continued to publish when Shoyama was forced to leave Vancouver for relocation in Kaslo, British Columbia.

At the same time, the two censors tried to dampen the more extreme racist news stories that were published in the Vancouver dailies. Rather than force editors and reporters to cut stories aimed at whipping up hatred of Japanese Canadians, the two censors visited senior editors in the province to try to persuade them not to quote the more vocal racist politicians in British Columbia. When this effort failed, they sent letters of protest to publishers and collected newspaper clippings for Eggleston and Robertson.[35] While the Vancouver's *Sun*, *Province*, and *Herald* and the Victoria's *Times* and *Colonist* did not tone down their rhetoric, Shoyama's paper did survive, and the editor eventually went on to a spectacular career in the Saskatchewan and federal public service after a brief stint in the army at the end of the war.

In Montreal, press censorship was in the hands of Claude Melançon, a member of the Canadian National Railway's public relations team, but most of the work was done by Charpentier, who was aided until 1943 by *Le Canada* journalist Willie Chevalier. Chevalier watched *Le Devoir* very closely and wrote a series of memoranda demanding the closure of the paper. Even before the German attack on Poland, *Le Devoir* and other nationalist papers and magazines had come out against Canadian participation in a war against Hitler.[36] A signed editorial by Georges Pelletier that ran in *Le Devoir* on 16 September 1939 laid the blame for the war on Britain, which it claimed had had the power early in Hitler's reign to nip Nazism in the bud. Had war come because "for centuries the cities of Poland have harboured thousands of Jews whom England does not want to be dispersed?" he asked. England had never fought for Quebec, except in 1759, "and that was to take us over."[37]

That fall's provincial election in Quebec was fought partly on the issue of censorship. Normally, CBC news managers screened the content of newscast and radio talks to determine whether they breached the Defence of Canada Regulations. During the Quebec election campaign, Ernest Lapointe, the federal Minister of Justice, did not trust journalist-censors to handle this sensitive work. Instead, he seconded federal lawyers to work as broadcast censors in Quebec, placing them in Montreal, Quebec City, Rimouski, and New Carlisle. These lawyer-censors did not stop Premier Maurice Duplessis and his Union Nationale party from getting its message onto the airwaves. Duplessis's people simply ignored the censors' decisions and denounced them over the air. On election night, when Liberal Adelard Godbout defeated Duplessis, there were no interviews of candidates or broadcasts of the victory and concession speeches of the candidates, and announcers were told to stick to pre-censored scripts.

In English Canada, the most serious criticism of the system came from senior reporters on some of the country's better newspapers. In December 1939, the editors of the *Financial Post* argued that "some newspapers—so fervently loyal in Canada and the Empire as any newspapers we have—have reserved the right of constructive criticism. Other newspapers have surrendered it. One, at least, of the country's leading daily newspapers will not even run news reports of criticism of the Government made by other people."[38]

The *Globe and Mail* was a consistent opponent of censorship through the war. Backed by her publisher, the mercurial George McCullagh, columnist Judith Robinson was the earliest serious critic of the wartime censorship system in a series of columns run through the fall of 1939.[39] Robinson first took issue with the government's treatment of soldiers' dependents. Initially, the Toronto censors defended Robinson's right to publish her opinion, but in early December 1939 she submitted a column to the censors containing a paragraph with the statement that "Canadian boys are deserting from their units" and mentioning in passing that they were "leaving for overseas." These two sentences were cut, but the following day the same phrases ran in the lead paragraph of Robinson's column and reached the streets in the first edition of the newspaper. Later, when Robinson took up the cause of a Communist convicted and jailed under the War Measures Act, Toronto censor Bert Perry wrote to his colleagues that she had "made an extreme attack on constituted authority."[40]

In the federal election campaign of 1940, the *Globe and Mail* attacked the King government for its tight control of the radio airwaves. The *Globe and Mail* took the position that the majority of the Quebec press had embraced the previous fall: censorship of opinion had no place in an election campaign. In an editorial titled "Democracy Under Test" published on 30 January 1940, the paper's editors argued: "If censorship is imposed on speakers, there is no electoral freedom; if it is relaxed, the war effort may suffer. Must democracy be sacrificed in deciding which political party is to hold office in the coming five years?" It asked whether censors employed by the government could be truly objective. The censor

> will be less than human if he lets the Opposition leaders get rough with the government to which he owes his position, and it will not be hard to find an excuse that the criticism is detrimental to Canada's defence ... We have no hesitation in saying that because a political party is in power it should not be [in] a position to interfere with the effort of the Opposition to throw it out. There should be no suspicion of unfair advantage.[41]

The paper returned to that theme the following day in an editorial titled "Call Off the Censors." The *Globe* accused the Liberal government of using censorship to gag opposition candidates:

> Before broadcasting, these men must submit their speeches to appointees of the Government of the day, for which some are campaigning and others are criticizing. Leaving aside the possibilities of unfair discrimination, the immediate inference is that the candidates are not trustworthy. They are all tarred with the brush of suspicion or too ignorant to know how to behave themselves, although they will make up Canada's Parliament after March 26.

The *Globe* warned of "a radio Gestapo" that was "an insult, not only to the candidates, but to the people who nominate them." The newspaper asked whether the Censorship Committee and the censors, and the government to which they are responsible, have a monopoly on loyalty and intelligence; if they are the only ones concerned with keeping useful information from the enemy and furthering the war effort, why an election at all? ... Why not go the full way with a dictatorship, as with a blacked-out Parliament, and have it over with?[42]

The *Globe and Mail* continued its assault on the censorship system in the conscription referendum campaign of 1942 and maintained it through the summer, when it supported Ontario Conservative leader (and Opposition Counsel of the Royal Commission on the Canadian Expeditionary Force to the Crown Colony of Hong Kong) George Drew's demands that his criticism of the failures of the Hong Kong deployment be made public. For once, the *Globe and Mail* was joined in its criticism of censorship by Conservative papers across the country, which waged an unsuccessful campaign to have the letter tabled in Parliament, where they would be free from censure from Supreme Court of Canada Chief Justice Sir Lyman Duff, the Royal Commissioner of the Hong Kong inquiry.

Still, the great bulk of the country's newspapers and magazines deferred to the censors. The Halifax dailies, especially the *Herald*, pushed for greater freedom to cover the Battle of the Atlantic but were thwarted through the entire war by censor H. Bruce Jefferson. Despite some verbal brawls between Jefferson and the editors of the *Herald*, most of the details of sub attack stories were suppressed. Except for a flare-up over the publication of Camillien Houde's controversial statement opposing the use of Montreal municipal offices for manpower registration in 1940, Montreal's Conservative *Gazette* and that city's smaller English periodicals, the *Herald* and the *Standard*, were barely noticed by the censors. Toronto's *Star* and *Telegram* complained privately about censorship, but they, like most newspapers in English Canada, were outwardly supportive of the system.

After the war, Charpentier had advice for anyone who might some day hold his job. In his final report to cabinet, he wrote that in times of war, censors and journalists needed from the beginning to develop "mutual confidence and understanding." The press and radio of Canada "must feel that Censorship is being administered in a manner which, while it takes adequate account of security, is not unduly or unnecessarily restrictive, and does not worship suppression as an end rather than a means." Censorship needs to be clean of any sign of "political taint," and censors must give advice that is seen by journalists as "honest and realistic." Charpentier was not sure that the government had made the right decision, during its information management planning when it split the censorship and propaganda systems into two independent agencies: the Directorate of Censorship and the Wartime Information Board. Perhaps, he argued, censorship and propaganda were part of the same information management system and should be handled by one department. That way, people within the same department could argue for and against releasing information.[43]

"Censorship of Publications in the early stages of the war lacked adequate representation of the case for publicity," Charpentier wrote in the censors' final report. During the war, the censors had found themselves arguing for the publication of facts that were not real military secrets. "The danger of such a one-sided arrangement," he wrote, "is the growth of an unimaginative and rigid policy of suppression whenever the matter is in any doubt as against an intelligent, well-balanced policy of considering the effect of any move upon the total prosecution of the war." And he argued that if future press censorship was part of a ministry of information, the case for publication would presumably always be voiced when decisions were being made.[44]

Censorship ended on VJ-Day. Most of the editors of the major newspapers (with the exception of the *Globe and Mail*, which buried the news of the end of censorship in a brief item on its comics page) had kind words for their colleagues in censorship: "The press censors were evidently well chosen," the *Saint John Telegraph-Journal* editorialized. "Most were trained newspapermen and it must have irked them grievously when they had to suppress news. They were men whom the newspapers respected, even if there was not in all cases complete agreement." The censorship system worked because of the patriotism of journalists on both sides of the censorship divide, the *Telegraph-Journal* editors argued. "We know of no serious or deliberate breach of regulations by any Canadian newspaper during the war. Every newspaper many times has sat on war secrets, sometimes for months, which would greatly have interested its readers, but always they were held until the public interest permitted their publication." The papers praised the censors for being "sources of information when clarification was needed."[45]

The *Windsor Star* praised the "spirit of co-operation" between the censors and the media and called Eggleston "a good newspaperman with sound judgment." In the *Star*'s view, "any difficulty they had with editors was due to stipulation of army, navy, or air force intelligence which kept certain news from being published. The censors had their own difficulties with these other officials."[46]

The war was as disruptive to the news media as it was to the rest of society. Almost half of the reporting staff of the Canadian Press wire service—a cooperative that collected news from member papers and its own bureaus in major cities and distributed it across the country—had enlisted in the first year of the war. Nine of them died in action.[47] Others in the organization found other kinds of war work. The general superintendent, Gil Purcell, took leave from CP in 1940 to serve as Press Relations Officer for the 1 Canadian Division. In 1941, he lost his left leg above the knee during a manoeuvre in Sussex when a supply canister dropped from an aircraft tore loose from its parachute and struck him. After convalescing in Britain, he returned to his job with the wire service. Media executives found their way into the wartime bureaucracy: Victor Sifton, owner of the *Winnipeg Free Press* and *Regina Leader-Post*, joined the industrial managers and technocrats who went to Ottawa as "dollar-a-year men" or who joined the writing and photography staff of the Bureau of Public Information, the propaganda agency that after May 1942 became the Wartime Information Board.

War correspondents for the major newspapers, Canadian Press, and the CBC donned the uniform of Canadian army majors, were given support staff, including vehicles and drivers, and depended on the military for communications with their home offices.[48] Some became frustrated with the military's censorship system, but unless they returned to Canada, they were unable to tell their readers about how their coverage was being distorted.[49] Peter Stursberg, who covered the war for the CBC, later argued that there was no point struggling against censorship. An outright breach of the rules would bring down "disaccreditation, disgrace, even imprisonment" upon a journalist.[50] Richard Malone, a journalist turned Army Public Affairs officer, wrote after the war that a correspondent who travelled with the Canadian forces "began to see that he himself was part of the show."[51]

A few working journalists crossed the line and became government agents. Bruce Hutchison, then a *Winnipeg Free Press* reporter in the Parliamentary Press Gallery, eagerly accepted two invitations to do secret work. In the summer of 1940, his bureau chief, Grant Dexter, ordered him to break off his vacation in British Columbia and return to Ottawa as quickly as possible. Hutchison caught a flight to Toronto, where a telegram from Dexter awaited him, ordering him to hurry to Barrie to meet a special train. There, Hutchison found parked on a siding, a lavish government-chartered train carrying reporters from important American publications. The train, with two dining cars, gourmet food, and ample liquor, took the journalists through Ontario, Quebec and the Maritimes, ostensibly to visit arms factories and military bases. The trip was simply a junket meant to develop social links between the journalists and Canadian officials, but Hutchison was asked to spy on his American colleagues. In Halifax, he and Dexter were told to track one American reporter through the city, but their target managed to shake off the Winnipeg journalists and board a ship to the United States. That fall, Hutchison went undercover on the campaign of Republican presidential candidate Wendell Willkie. Having been armed with $5,000 in cash provided by "a group of five leading Canadian newspapers," he was told to try to sway journalists on the tour away from Willkie's isolationist policies and to visit newspaper editors along Willkie's campaign route.[52]

In Quebec, *Le Canada* reporter Willie Chevalier, who worked part-time for the Directorate of Censorship, was one of a group of francophone reporters recruited by British military intelligence for espionage work in French North Africa in 1943.[53] Even Tommy Shoyama, who had endured four years under the press censors' thumb as editor of the country's sole surviving Japanese Canadian newspaper, *The New Canadian*, took a job in Canadian military intelligence in the last weeks of the war, when the Canadian government finally relented and let ethnic Japanese into the armed forces as translators.

The Canadian journalists who had covered the war returned home to good media jobs, and military public relations officers like Malone and Purcell easily slipped back into news media management. Most of the censors, though, never worked in the media again. Charpentier, after some attempts to land a parliamentary reporting job with Quebec newspapers, eventually accepted a federal appointment to a diplomatic post in French Africa. Jefferson, in Halifax, took a job with the Nova Scotia government, though he did try to start a weekly newspaper in New Brunswick in the 1960s after he retired from his public service job. Lou Gordon, the senior B.C. censor, left the media and started a mink farm in the Fraser Valley. Bert Perry, the Toronto censor, left the media. Only John Graham, the junior Vancouver censor, and Warren

Baldwin, who handled censorship of the Parliamentary Press Gallery, found steady work, Graham with the *Vancouver Sun* and Baldwin with the censors' old sparring partner, the *Globe and Mail*.

Censorship changed Eggleston's views on journalism. He had no trouble resuming his freelance career, selling articles to major newspapers and magazines in Canada, the United States, and the United Kingdom. He had come away from his experience with the censorship system with a new appreciation of the value of the media in a healthy political system. "One curious result of my four years in press censorship was a heightened awareness of the basic and fundamental importance of a free press in a parliamentary democracy," he later wrote.[54] Nagging doubts about the quality of Canadian journalism motivated him to accept an offer from Carleton University to become the first director of its new journalism department. There he designed a program that integrated studies in political science, history, and economics with courses in media theory and practice.

Had they clung to the misconception that journalists place their craft ahead of their country, Canada's war planners probably would not have employed journalists as press censors and military press relations officers. Wisely, they realized that some journalists would be attracted to war work and that the advice of senior members of the media would be respected by their colleagues. While the military and the Conservative opposition wanted to put censorship in the hands of soldiers or lawyers, war planner Maurice Pope and the King government crafted and protected a censorship system that successfully harnessed journalists to the war effort. The censors could not anticipate Dr. Haldimand spilling the secret of the atomic bomb to a crowded convention, but the system did prevent any mention of his speech from being published. The censorship system also kept news of convoy and troopship sailings out of the media and guarded numerous other secrets, such as details of the mysterious Japanese fire balloons that drifted over western Canada in late 1944 and early 1945. Only in Quebec, where censorship was focused on political opposition to participation in the war, and at the *Globe and Mail*, which sought to inflict harm on the King government by criticizing Ottawa's information control system, did opponents of the federal government inflict real damage on the censors' credibility and effectiveness.

Notes

1. Library and Archives Canada [LAC] RG 2, Privy Council Office, (Records of the Directorate of Censorship), Vol. 5967, File: general-1. Memorandum, B.B. Perry, 16 April 1944.
2. King was employed by the *Toronto Globe* and the *Toronto Star* before beginning graduate school.
3. See Jeff Keshen, *Propaganda and Censorship during the Great War* (Edmonton: University of Alberta Press, 1996).
4. Military Officials urged that news be censored of the Terrace, B.C. "mutiny" of conscripted soldiers in the fall of 1944.
5. "Place of press in nerves war is emphasized," *Globe and Mail*, 3 September 1939, 3.
6. LAC RG 2, Privy Council Office (Records of the Directorate of Censorship), Vol. 5945, File: 1-A-3. First Interim Report, Committee on Censorship (C.C. 1 Draft).
7. Ibid.
8. See above, as well as Gillis Purcell, "Wartime Press Censorship in Canada," (Unpublished MA thesis, University of Toronto, 1946), 11.
9. M.E. Nichols, *The Story of the Canadian Press* (Toronto: Ryerson Press, 1948), 251.
10. The Press Gallery operated out of a newsroom at Rm. 350 North, Centre Block, on the northeast side of the building. Wilfrid Eggleston, *While I Still Remember* (Toronto: Ryerson Press, 1968), 244.
11. Eggleston, *While I Still Remember*, 254.
12. Claude Melancon, a Canadian National Railways public relations officer, was Moyer's French-language counterpart. Both were quickly replaced by Wilfrid Eggleston and Fulgence Charpentier, former members of the Parliamentary Press Gallery.
13. In the end, this position was never created and national reporters submitted their copy to Warren Baldwin or Wilfrid Eggleston at the Ottawa censorship offices or to censors in their home cities.
14. Eggleston, *While I Still Remember*, 256.
15. The Bureau of Public Information became the Wartime Information Board after 9 September 1942.
16. Eggleston, *While I Still Remember*, 260.
17. Ibid., 262.
18. Ibid.
19. Ibid., 263.
20. Ibid., 319.
21. Wilfrid Eggleston, "Press Censorship," *The Canadian Journal of Economics and Political Science* Vol.7, no.3 (August 1941), 313.
22. Ibid., 315.
23. Ibid., 316.
24. Ibid., 321.
25. Ibid., 317.
26. The dispute might have been caused by Eggleston's article in the *Canadian Journal of Economics and Political Science*, which was published that month.

27 LAC RG 2, Privy Council Office, (Records of the Directorate of Censorship), Vol.5982, file: 2A-G (External Affairs). Wilfrid Eggleston to T.A. Stone, 13 August 1941.
28 LAC RG 2, Privy Council Office, (Records of the Directorate of Censorship), Vol.5982, file 2A-G (Memoranda re: Meetings of Various Committees.) W.E. Eggleston to T.A. Stone, 13 August 1941.
29 LAC RG 2, Privy Council Office, (Records of the Directorate of Censorship), Vol.5941, Final Report of the Directorate of Censorship, (Fall, 1945).
30 A.E. Powley, *Broadcasting from the Front* (Toronto: Hakkert, 1975), 165.
31 Hanson, Richard B. (Conservative MP, York-Sunbury), Parliamentary Debates, 12 May 1944, 2859.
32 Eggleston, *While I Still Remember*, 264.
33 Ibid., 265.
34 For details on Perry's attitudes to Germans and POWs, as well as the black-out of the Bowmanville Riot, see LAC RG 2 (Records of the Directorate of Censorship), Vol.5983, File: Bowmanville Incident.
35 Gordon and Graham's memoranda on *The New Canadian* and their attempts to tone down anti-Japanese material in West Coast newspapers can be found in LAC RG 2, Privy Council Office, (Records of the Directorate of Censorship), Vol.5960, File: Japanese.
36 LAC RG 2, Privy Council Office, (Records of the Directorate of Censorship), Vol.5974 File: *Le Devoir* 1. Telegram, Pelletier to Thompson 6 September 1939.
37 Ibid., The English text is from the Government Translation Office. Memorandum for Walter Thompson Esq. Chief Censor Re: Editorial signed by Georges Pelletier. 16 September 1939.
38 *Financial Post*, 9 December 1939.
39 Robinson was one of the first women to win a National Newspaper Award. She was fired from the *Globe* in 1941, supposedly because of a witty come-back she made during an editorial board meeting. McCullagh told the writers he could easily talk Franklin Roosevelt into bringing the US into the war, to which Robinson answered "on whose side?" The story was told by Robert Fulford in "George McCullagh," *The Globe and Mail*, 15 April 1998, 7.
40 LAC RG 2, Privy Council Office, (Records of the Directorate of Censorship), Vol.5968 File: *The Globe and Mail*. Memorandum, Perry, 8 December 1939.
41 "Democracy Under Test," *The Globe and Mail*, 30 January 1940, 6.
42 "Call Off the Censors," *The Globe and Mail*, 31 January 1940, 6.
43 LAC RG 2, Privy Council Office, (Records of the Directorate of Censorship), Vol.5941 (NF). Final Report of the Directorate of Censorship (Fall 1945).
44 Ibid.
45 Editorial, *Saint John Telegraph-Journal*, 16 August 1945.
46 Editorial, *Windsor Star*, 16 August 1945.
47 M.E. Nicholls, *The Story of the Canadian Press*, 230.
48 For an outstanding analysis of this relationship, see Timothy Balzer, *The Information Front: The Canadian Army and News Management During the Second World War*

(Vancouver: University of British Columbia Press, 2011). For an interesting point of view by a journalist working for the military, see Richard Malone, *Missing from the Record* (Toronto: Collins, 1946).

49 Ralph Allen, "How Do You Cover a War?" *Globe and Mail*, 16 January 1944, 4.
50 Peter Stursberg, *The Sound of War* (Toronto: University of Toronto Press, 1993), 57.
51 Malone, *Missing from the Record*, 164.
52 Bruce Hutchison, *The Far Side of the Street* (Toronto: Macmillan, 1976), 145–52.
53 Final Report of the Directorate of Censorship.
54 Eggleston, *While I Still Remember*, 264.

6

Dangerous Curves
Canadian Drivers and Mechanical Transport in Two World Wars

Andrew Iarocci

Inside the Canadian War Museum there is a cavernous open-concept exhibition space called the LeBreton Gallery. Flanked by floor-to-ceiling windows that look across the LeBreton Flats to Parliament Hill, the gallery has been described as "a lens into the museum."[1] LeBreton is also home to the national collection of military transportation and artillery artifacts. In addition to an impressive line of tanks, the heaviest of which weighs well over 50 tons, visitors can inspect a variety of lighter wheeled or tracked transport vehicles dating principally from the Second World War and Cold War periods. The Second World War machines, including variants of the flat-nosed Canadian Military Pattern (CMP) truck and the squat universal carrier, seem quaintly primitive by today's standards, but in their day they represented the cutting edge of automotive technology and production. Nestled among these trucks and cross-country vehicles is a humbler artifact from an earlier conflict. It is a 1916 general service (GS) horse-drawn wagon, a simple wooden vehicle that took on every kind of burden during the First World War. The museum visitor who compares the nineteenth-century technology of the GS wagon with the modern angular sheet metal of a CMP truck can reasonably conclude that the nature of forward supply and transport underwent a profound shift between the two world wars.

Certainly the numbers of mechanized supply and transport vehicles in the field increased dramatically between the First and Second World Wars.

Draught and pack animals outnumbered mechanical transport (MT) vehicles by a significant margin throughout the First World War. While the number of MT vehicles in service across the British armies grew from fewer than 100 in August 1914 to more than 119,000 four years later, there were still more than six horses for every motor vehicle in British military service in 1918.[2] Among Canada's overseas forces there were about 1,300 lorries, cars, and ambulances operating in England and France in early 1918—a modest fleet compared to the nearly 23,000 draught and pack animals under Canadian control at the time.[3] Moving forward to the early years of the Second World War, a Canadian infantry division had not a single horse in its establishment. Moreover, the number of wheeled vehicles on that division's order of battle approached seven hundred, about three times as many as a First World War division and fully 50 percent of the *total* MT strength of the entire Canadian Expeditionary Force in 1918.[4]

These contrasts were profound, but technological transformation does not tell the whole story of people and machines at war. To focus only on improvements in transportation technology or enormous increases in fleets is to overlook threads of continuity that have more to do with people than machines. Closer study of human factors such as manpower allocation, driver training, vehicle maintenance, and approaches to procurement underscores the similarities between the two war experiences. LeBreton Gallery visitors can be forgiven for being unaware of the practical limits to mechanization that we will explore in this chapter. Laid bare in the exhibition space, the artifacts cannot speak for themselves. And during the world wars, they could have done little but break down and rust without the trained hand of a human master at the wheel.

The Birth of MT and the First World War

With the notable exception of the tank, the important mechanical technology operating on the battlefields of 1918 predated the outbreak of the First World War. Four-wheeled MT vehicles powered by internal combustion engines had been on the roads for ten to fifteen years before 1914. During that last stretch of peace, military theorists appreciated that it was time for mechanical transport to complement, if not fully replace, animal power as a vital link between supply railheads and combat units.[5] In practice, British Royal Engineers had employed steam-powered traction engines with limited success during the South African War at the turn of the century. The War Office, meanwhile, established the Mechanical Transport Committee in 1900 to oversee trials for lighter, more capable vehicles. A year later, the British Army hosted competitive trials at Aldershot for special-purpose military trucks of three-ton capacity. Although just one competitor used an internal combustion engine (with the rest driven by steam), officers at the trials recognized "the great possibilities for military purposes of the internal combustion lorry."[6] The benefits of MT were clear: a single three-ton lorry could carry the same cargo as a pair of four-horsed wagons, yet it took up less road space. The lorry could travel two to four times faster than the wagons over good roads. Lorry fleets also escaped the perennial sanitation problems that high concentrations of horses caused on thoroughfares.[7]

Two years after the Aldershot competition, junior officers who shared an interest in mechanics formed the Motor Volunteer Corps (MVC).[8] The MVC counted among its members wealthy gentlemen who placed their personal cars and drivers at the disposal of British General Staff officers for annual manoeuvres. Soon after, the War Office drafted mobilization plans for nine hundred motor vehicles by arranging for civilian owners to register their machines for emergency national service in exchange for an annual government subsidy. By 1912 there were 1,000 registered vehicles in Britain, with each owner receiving £110 per year from the Crown—a significant sum, considering that a new lorry cost as much as £600 in 1911–12.[9] At the outset of the coming war, Britain relied in large part on repurposed civilian vehicles for military transport.

Canada's MT procurement plans before 1914 were even more basic than in Great Britain. There was simply not enough commercial motor transport on Canadian roads to follow the British example. A 1913 Militia census of cargo vehicles across southwestern Ontario revealed just four three-ton lorries, twelve two-tonners, and a smattering of lighter models—not even enough to fill out a single division's supply column of thirty-eight three-ton lorries.[10] With no precedent whatever for a mechanical transport fleet, Minister of Militia and Defence Sam Hughes instructed T.A. Russell, an automotive entrepreneur and fellow Conservative, to buy up enough cars and trucks to outfit the first overseas contingent (soon known as the 1st Division) upon the outbreak of war. Russell purchased several makes and models, some through his own company.[11] Amidst Liberal allegations of patronage and profiteering,

Hughes and his overseas representative, John Wallace Carson, struggled to find enough suitable MT for an expanding Canadian Expeditionary Force (CEF).[12]

The result was that each of Canada's four overseas divisions arrived in England and embarked for France badly short of MT equipment. Canadian agents ordering models from American factories ran into numerous shipping delays and Imperial defence agreements that decreed that all Canadian military formations operating in France were to be supplied and supported through British logistical channels. This meant that the cars, trucks, or motorcycles the Canadians lacked when they set foot on French soil would be issued from British Expeditionary Force (BEF) army-level parks. Such a state of affairs frustrated Sam Hughes to no end. The Minister wanted Canadian boys to fight the Hun with "Canadian" equipment, be it boots or rifles or lorries—even if the lorries came from the United States.[13] Canadian Army Service Corps (CASC) transport officers in France were scarcely more satisfied. Unlike Hughes, their frustration stemmed from pragmatic rather than nationalistic considerations: newly arrived Canadian divisions in France often had to make do with worn out British trucks issued from the parks. Meanwhile, brand new trucks that Ottawa had purchased from American suppliers arrived in England too late for issue to Canadian troops. Instead they were often turned over to the Imperial Army Service Corps as repayment

A column of Kelly-Springfield 3-ton trucks pauses in a Belgian town, June 1916. The faintly visible club-shaped marking on the cargo box of the first vehicle suggests that these trucks belong to a divisional supply column. [PA 000025]

in kind for the vehicles that the Canadians had earlier borrowed. Perhaps this was not a fair practice, but if Ottawa could not get its contracts filled in a more timely fashion, there was no alternative except to do without.[14] Given that each infantry division required 218 motor vehicles in 1916, the Canadian divisions had to accept what was available and serviceable if they were going to fight the Germans.[15]

Finding skilled drivers and mechanics to keep these vehicles rolling was an equally complex matter. Canadian soldiers of the period were not especially familiar with automotive technology. The car, wrote one contemporary auto enthusiast who had driven across Canada shortly before the war, had yet to "transform the village blacksmith's into a garage and repair shop, nor turn the rural grocery store into a motor-fuel emporium."[16] The CASC had little choice but to turn to the Dominion's nascent automotive industry for skilled men. Early in the war, Captain Fred Eaton, a Permanent Force CASC officer, travelled to Windsor to recruit several hundred such men from the city's auto factories and workshops.[17] Eaton's recruiting of civilian specialists continued throughout the war, but a chronic shortage of skilled men persisted—there were only so many auto workers to poach from Windsor's shops. The reinforcement crisis of 1916–17 made matters worse, for as the number of volunteers tapered off, all physically fit men, no matter their technical or mechanical skills, were liable for transfer to infantry units. CASC officers resorted to tampering with medical boards in a desperate effort to hold on to their best motormen. The gambit worked at first, but the Quartermaster General at the Headquarters of the Overseas Military Forces of Canada (OMFC) caught on to the ruse when driver-mechanics once declared fit for active service were suddenly relegated to lower medical categories—a circumstance engineered to block their transfer to combat battalions.[18] With the implementation of the Military Service Act (MSA) in 1918, scores of young Canadian men with supposed driving or mechanical experience suddenly felt the urge to volunteer for MT service, no doubt hoping that a stint in the CASC would spare them the hardships and risks of infantry service. This new wave of volunteerism was little help to the CASC, since men called up under the MSA were not permitted to serve as drivers. Even though the CEF needed several hundred MT men for overseas service in the early months of 1918, infantrymen and gunners were in much higher demand.[19]

Since MT units lacked complete establishments of experienced tradesmen and drivers, raw recruits had to be trained from scratch to make up the difference. Military authorities recognized early on that they needed a formal syllabus of instruction for MT personnel, but the output of drivers from MT training depots in Winnipeg and Toronto varied in quality as there was rarely enough time to train new drafts before they sailed for England.[20] Moreover, some volunteers who claimed to possess mechanical skills were sent to England without proper testing or verification.[21] These self-professed mechanics often needed remedial instruction in training schools that were already oversubscribed.

Overseas with the CEF, Lieutenant-Colonel Charles Spittal, a prewar militia officer with CASC experience, was the first to take charge of ad hoc MT training, maintenance programs, and general organization. Spittal admitted privately in May 1915 that he knew very little about this aspect of army service corps duties. In fact he did not know of

> any Canadian officer who is really qualified to take practical charge of general Mechanical Transport. [The] Canadian Army Service Corps has not had any training in this branch, in fact we have never had a lorry in any of our training camps, and up to the outbreak of war, MT was unknown to us, as horse transport was used exclusively.[22]

Spittal turned for help to "Major" Gordon Watney, a British ex-officer who ran a large automobile garage at Weybridge, southwest of London. In early 1915, Spittal and Carson agreed to have Watney's outfit overhaul more than fifty of the CEF's American-built trucks, many of which had proven unserviceable even at low mileages. Spittal's men participated in the overhaul program, both to reduce Watney's labour costs and to give the Canadians some hands-on maintenance training with heavy transport vehicles. The scheme seemed to work well enough at first, but plans quickly unravelled as Spittal grew to resent Watney's expertise. Watney also experienced disciplinary problems with restless Canadian soldiers and some of their junior officers. Carson ultimately grew so frustrated with the slapdash scheme that he threatened to "take these damned lorries away from Weybridge and chuck them into a ditch. Between the all round gossip that is going around, the fault finding and interfering of all sorts from every standpoint," lamented Carson, "I am getting pretty well tired of the whole thing."[23] Most of the lorries stranded at Weybridge were eventually repaired, but assigning Canadian soldiers to work for a British civilian firm proved less than satisfactory. So did Spittal's leadership as a key MT officer. He lacked the organizational and technical ability required to keep a mechanized force running smoothly.

Charles Spittal had been a Hughes appointee, but the minister was flexible enough to find a new and better man by mid-1915. Lieutenant-Colonel Alexander Duncan McRae was a Vancouver millionaire who had been serving as Director of Remounts (horses) for Western Canada when Hughes asked him go to England to take up the new post of Director of Supplies and Transport for the overseas forces.[24] When McRae assumed his appointment later that year, he inherited a largely dysfunctional system from the likes of Spittal and Watney. "As soon as we get matters in hand," McRae wrote to the QMG in Ottawa in October 1915, "I will make you a report on the mechanical transport. Owing to neglect it is in very bad shape at the present time, about one-third of it being in the shops."[25] McRae's job was not an easy one, but he managed to bring a good deal of order out of chaos, and his administrative abilities came to notice. In late 1916 he was named Quartermaster General at OMFC Headquarters.[26]

Even under McRae's improved regime, Canadian MT training courses left much to be desired. They consisted mainly of classroom lectures, for at times there were no vehicles available for practical instruction in driving, repairs, or maintenance.[27] Time was also an enemy. As late in the war as mid-1917, the Deputy Director of Transport admitted that "it is impossible to train a man in the time specified in the syllabus of training."[28] Mechanical breakdowns, careless driving, and accidents were the unhappy consequences of slipshod instruction. Mishaps were so frequent that transport officials at the War Office branded Canadians as chronic speeders. Civilians, their lawyers in tow, complained loudly when they or their children were run over, a not uncommon occurrence. In an especially pitiable but not atypical case, a Canadian ambulance alleged to have been travelling at a "furious pace" struck and crippled a thirteen-year-old girl.[29] At the Shorncliffe training area, military courts of inquiry reviewed more than 140 accident cases during the first six months of 1917. A few of these involved horse-drawn wagons, but many were single- or two-vehicle motor accidents.[30] Transport officers responded with ever longer lists of directives and regulations for MT drivers, such as speed limits ranging from 10 to 20 miles per hour.[31] Rules were easy to issue, but motivating soldiers to follow them was another matter. Civilian police officers and military provost personnel could not be everywhere at once.

Poor driver training and rough handling of vehicles only exacerbated the limited degree of standardization within the CEF vehicle fleet and between Canadian-purchased and British-supplied vehicles. The dozens of makes and models in service complicated maintenance, as well as the inventory of spare parts. This was especially problematic for Canadian units running handfuls of Canadian-supplied vehicles at the front, where British-supplied machines were in the majority. Maintenance channels in France functioned by British War Office standards. Consequently, a Canadian officer whose unit operated small lots of non-standard vehicles (supplied by the Canadian government) often could not get spare parts for them through normal Imperial channels. In one such case, a Lozier car assigned to Lieutenant-Colonel G.G. Nasmith, commander of the 5th Canadian Mobile Laboratory in France, needed new tires that were unavailable through the British supply chain. Carson arranged for the tires to be purchased in England and sent over to France, but only at the risk of incurring the wrath of War Office authorities, who objected to "anyone 'shipping coal into Newcastle' and refused to have anything shipped into France that can possibly be secured there [in France]."[32] British authorities were right to object to Carson's short-circuiting. Canadian officials also disliked shipping parts directly to Canadian units in France, since Ottawa was already paying a per diem to the War Office for the upkeep of the Canadian Corps. Yet with so many non-standard types of MT, there was often little choice but to work around the rules.

It should be said that the challenges of a poorly standardized fleet were not unique to the Canadian or British forces; at one point the Americans operated nearly three hundred varieties of lorries before settling on a common military pattern in 1918.[33] Not until very late in the war, in September 1918, did the Allied Supreme Command organize a standard pool of motor transport for inter-Allied use.[34] The lessons of standardization were well remembered by the British, Canadian, and American forces in time for the next war, even if not always fully implemented. Other nations, most notably Germany, failed to take much heed and suffered accordingly.

To be fair, the practical application of First World War MT was not limited solely by manpower issues or organizational difficulties. Automotive technology was itself part of the problem, as civilian-pattern vehicles were pressed into highly demanding military service for which they were never intended. Ford cars, for example, proved wholly unsuited to the rigours of field service. In 1915, Major-General Sam Steele complained about the Fords in his 2nd Canadian Division:

> I would like to point out that so far this division has only received Ford cars with the exception of the Cadillac, and it [is] very questionable whether it is advisable to supply these Fords for units going abroad as it is understood that these cars will not stand the wear and tear of the roads which shakes them to pieces, and in my opinion it would be desirable that a stronger and heavier car be supplied.[35]

Yet even the sturdier vehicles could only stand so much wear and tear, a reality that was all too evident during the high-intensity operations of the Hundred Days campaign in 1918. Hard pressed MT drivers, along with horse drivers and tactical railway troops, kept the armies moving forward, but had the war lasted for another six months, the situation would likely have grown more desperate. After several years of trench warfare, transport officers and engineers were accustomed to relatively short advances punctuated by long pauses. The comparatively rapid tempo of the Hundred Days fighting pushed transport capacity to the limits of human and mechanical endurance.[36]

After four years of struggle to organize and maintain a mechanized transport infrastructure, the CEF's motor fleet was unceremoniously disbanded and discarded in 1919. The OMFC auctioned off motor vehicles and related equipment in England as the Canadian Corps demobilized. Every spare penny counted, so even the Rolls-Royce staff cars used by Lieutenant-General Arthur Currie and Lieutenant-General Richard Turner had to go under the auctioneer's hammer.[37] Between May and August 1919, British buyers eager to escape the strictures of wartime shortages purchased more than £100,000 in motor vehicles and parts from the Canadians, leaving only about 170 vehicles in the CEF motor pools.[38] The *Canadian Military Gazette* reported later that autumn that vehicles sold during the previous few weeks totalled nearly £60,000, but asked rhetorically: "How much [did] they originally cost?"[39] Actually, the Canadian government did rather well at the MT auction sales, given that most of the vehicles were well worn, if not verging on obsolescence. Shipping these tortured machines back to Canada would hardly have been the best way to equip Canada's postwar military forces. The handful of professional soldiers who stayed in uniform after 1919 soon turned to the question of postwar equipment. A satisfactory answer was a long time coming, and it almost came too late.

Interwar Design and Procurement in Canada

Although Canada's interwar soldiers continued to rely on horses for artillery and logistical applications, domestic military vehicle development during the 1920s and 1930s was never completely dormant.[40] Veteran officers who had served in the Great War wanted their forces to be better equipped for the next war than they had been in 1914. In terms of transport, their first priority was to develop sturdy mass-produced vehicles with good off-road capabilities.[41] To this end, Canadians not only watched the latest British and American trials but also conducted their own.[42] Good intentions notwithstanding, peacetime budget constraints repeatedly stalled the development of modern vehicles that could be built in Canadian factories. Only at the eleventh hour, when a major war with Germany could not be avoided, did the government find funds for new military vehicles.

As long as war seemed unlikely, which it did in the 1920s, the government counted on automobile manufacturers to sustain the costs of military research and development. In 1927, Canadian military authorities invited manufacturers—in this case the F.W.D. Motor Company and the Ford Motor Company—to demonstrate wheeled and tracked vehicles to pull Great War–vintage guns and howitzers. The manufacturers paid for the entire demonstration, with no obligation on the part of the Department of National Defence (DND) to purchase even a single spark plug or wheel nut.[43]

Such corporate goodwill had its limits, especially after the Depression began. The 1935 saga of producing a pair of six-wheeled Ford and General Motors armoured car prototypes speaks to the risks incurred by manufacturers at a time when Canada's soldiers could afford to look but not to buy. Military funds were so tight during the Ford and GM trials that Lieutenant-Colonel N.O. Carr, chair of the Standing Arms Committee, considered the purchase of such essential accessories as crash helmets and a special heavy-duty grease gun as impossible extravagances.[44]

Both car prototypes performed quite well under rigorous field testing. Lieutenant-Colonel N.C. Sherman, the Chief Ordnance Mechanical Engineer of the Royal Canadian Ordnance Corps (RCOC),[45] suggested that additional examples be purchased, not only because the army needed the vehicles, but also to maintain a functional working relationship between the DND, Ford, and General Motors.[46] Although the government decided to procure one additional car of each type, L.R. LaFleche, the Deputy Minister of Defence, hoped that the second set of vehicles could be supplied along the same lines as the first pair: largely at the two manufacturers' expense.[47] Both companies were eager for further orders, but General Motors suggested politely yet firmly that the public should be willing to shoulder a more equitable share of the fiscal burden. GM comptroller W.J. Smith wrote to LaFleche from Oshawa:

> It was quite well understood when we produced the [first] car that subsequent deliveries would be made on a more reasonable basis. We would be very glad to reveal our costs, which were far in excess of the amount that was billed to your Department. We do not intend to intimate that on this particular order any profit should be made, but we hope to convince you to accept a billing which will come closer to our actual costs than on the previous transaction.[48]

Representatives from Ford expressed similar concerns, but the issue was mooted in early 1936 when the $21,000 set aside for the two additional pilot models was reallocated to an entirely different series of cargo trucks (mostly Ford V8 models) and six-wheeled gun tractors needed for Militia training.[49] With war on the horizon, serious development of a new transport fleet was only just getting under way.

By 1936, the rearmament of Nazi Germany was fostering a closer working relationship between Canadian industry and the DND, as well as a spirit of cooperation among competing manufacturers, who probably realized that there would be plenty of contracts to go around if war broke out. Late that year, Colonel Carr, then the Director of Mechanization and Artillery at National Defence Headquarters (NDHQ), asked Ford and General Motors to co-develop prototype 15-cwt general-purpose trucks, the forerunners of the famous Canadian Military Pattern (CMP) designs. In contrast to mismatched First World War–era MT that caused so many headaches in the search for spare parts, Canadian military transport experts wanted the new designs to

The CMP truck at left is a Chevrolet C15A. It is parked next to an American-built Ford GPA amphibious truck, also known as a 'seep' (perhaps for 'seagoing jeep'). Both vehicles belong to the 17th Duke of York's Royal Canadian Hussars. [LAC 3230150]

conform to British War Office patterns and standards from the outset. These Ford and GM pilot projects would also measure the capacity of Canadian manufacturers to produce effective war material.[50] Both companies were enthusiastic about participating, though representatives of each requested that the government compensate them more fairly than had been the case for the abortive armoured car project of 1935. Ottawa obliged, providing $4,500 for each pilot model.[51]

Sid Swallow was a young engineer who had joined Ford in 1935 and was heavily involved in the joint 15-cwt pilot project. He later recalled how these early designs evolved into CMP trucks—Canadian vehicles built largely to War Office specifications and driven by Allied forces in virtually every theatre of war. Canadian manufacturers went on to produce some 800,000 military vehicles of all types during the Second World War.[52] This high volume of automotive manufacturing reflected key trends in other sectors of Canadian war production, with surplus output being exported to Allied nations. Only about one-third of Canadian-produced war material was actually used by Canadian forces.[53] It took several years, however, for the new models like the CMPs to reach full-scale production. In the meantime, during the dark days of 1940–41, automakers supplied a selection of "modified conventional" civilian trucks to British Empire forces.[54] Fortunately perhaps, Canadian troops did not participate in extended operations until 1943, well after shortfalls in production had been made good.

Armies on Wheels and Tracks

Few popular commentators and military theorists doubted that the war would be a mechanized war. In its early years, many feared that Germany had all but won it. A 1942 US Army technical manual on driver selection and training emphasized the war of movement: "It is a war of machines. The Army's system of motorized transportation is the backbone of our whole military system."[55] Another military writer in 1942 was not alone as he accused allegedly backward-thinking Allied commanders of failing to exploit mechanization, while the supposedly more inventive Germans had mastered it.[56]

Thanks in part to Germany's resourceful war propagandists, contemporary observers overlooked the fact that German ground forces still very much depended on the horse for front-line supply and transport duties. Consider, for example, that just one in four German divisions in the Polish campaign was mechanized or motorized to a significant degree.[57] In reality, only the British Empire forces (and after December 1941, the Americans) relied exclusively on mechanical transport at all echelons of supply and transport. Given the impressive level of North America's wartime industrial output, it is tempting to dismiss Germany's defeat as the inevitable consequence of Allied "brute force" and material superiority.[58] Such a conclusion is far too simplistic, in part because extensive mechanization was a mixed blessing for the Allied armies. Mechanical transport enhanced the speed and mobility of ground forces, but these benefits were offset by the challenges of driver training, road discipline, maintenance, and, to no small degree, eleventh-hour procurement policies.

With Canada's Second World War forces entirely dependent on motor vehicles, drivers had to know how to operate their machines safely and efficiently in all conditions. In certain respects, the armies of the 1940s enjoyed clear advantages over their Great War predecessors. By 1939, motor vehicle culture was more intricately woven into the social and economic fabric than it had been in 1914.[59] But, as with the previous war, speeding, accidents, blackout conditions, fatigue, and sloppy driving habits claimed too many victims and ruined precious equipment. Canadian military hospitals in

England early in the conflict treated a disproportionate number of motorcycle accident victims, sometimes more than twenty per day. "Give the Canadians more motorcycles," people joked at the time, "and the Germans won't need to worry about them."[60] As late as 1943, high rates of serious injuries and fatalities on the powerful Harley-Davidson WLC motorcycle prompted Lieutenant-General Harry Crerar to favour less aggressive British models for general issue to Canadian forces.[61]

Four-wheeled vehicles were not much safer than motorcycles. A 1944 Canadian advertisement lamented the "20,000 gas casualties" suffered the previous year. The wrecked car in the poster's background hinted that the losses resulted not from chemical warfare, but from 3,000 traffic accidents involving gasoline-powered military vehicles.[62] The scourge of accidents was not limited to the Canadian Army. A famous Bill Mauldin cartoon shows a pair of American GIs surrounded by mountains of wrecked vehicles in an

A soldier of The Royal Canadian Regiment makes field repairs to his Norton motorcycle in Italy, August 1943. Canadian forces used British motorcycles, such as the Norton, as well as American models. [LAC 3228779]

ordnance salvage yard. "'I'll be darned!' says one of the soldiers, 'Here's one wot wuz wrecked in combat.'"[63]

Accidents caused only a proportion of vehicle damage. Poor driving technique and haphazard preventative maintenance also accounted for mechanical breakdowns. *Dangerous Curves*, a pamphlet published by the Ford Motor Company, explained that "Ford vehicles are designed and built to withstand hard service and will take rough handling, but this is no reason why their serviceability and life should be reduced by imposing unnecessarily high stresses through bad handling due either to carelessness or to mechanical ignorance."[64] In late 1943, at a time when too many vehicles were out of action thanks to negligence or outright abuse, the Directorate of Mechanical Maintenance at NDHQ published the first volume of *CAM*, a monthly periodical dedicated to the Canadian Army's Preventative Maintenance System (CPMS). In contrast to the long lists of terse maintenance orders, regulations, and directives of the First World War–era CASC, the *CAM* magazines were designed to be read and enjoyed by the average soldier with limited formal education. Key lessons in driving, maintenance, and repair work were cleverly woven into humorous anecdotes and cartoon illustrations. Articles written in friendly vernacular encouraged men to be aware of technical priorities. The pedagogy of the *CAM* series was also applied to the maintenance and repair manuals that came with each military vehicle. As the *Driving Instructions and Workshop Manual* for the Mark III Canadian Scout Car stated on the first page, knowledge was always better than guesswork: "There's no reason to guess when it's so easy to know!"[65]

Due to high demand for skilled technicians among the three armed services, army officials found that good drivers and mechanics could not be plucked from civilian life and put behind the wheel of a truck or the levers of an armoured vehicle. With large numbers of men being mobilized, it was not easy to shuttle skilled tradesmen into appropriate military trades and specialities. The British Army on the whole faced similar challenges. In 1941 Sir William Beveridge's Committee on the Use of Skilled Men in the Services recommended that the army allocate its manpower resources more carefully, train its technical personnel more thoroughly, and rationalize its maintenance infrastructure.[66] Beveridge's report had far-reaching consequences, for it prompted the British Army to create the Royal Electrical and Mechanical Engineers (REME) in October 1942.[67] Personnel assigned to REME assumed much of the responsibility for repair and maintenance of mechanical transport, duties that had previously been shared inefficiently by the Royal Army Service Corps (RASC), the Royal Army Ordnance Corps (RAOC), and other elements in the army.[68]

After much debate among senior officers and with the experience of the Italian campaign, First Canadian Army followed suit in 1944, regrouping technical tradesmen from the service and ordnance corps together into a new corps: the Royal Canadian Electrical and Mechanical Engineers (RCEME). RCEME units were responsible for maintaining the Army's vehicles, artillery, small arms, and all manner of electrical equipment; recovering damaged vehicles and guns from the battlefield; investigating design defects; and providing advice and insight during the developmental stages of new vehicles and equipment.[69] Drivers, cooks, and storekeepers generally continued to wear the Royal Canadian Army Service Corps (RCASC) or RCOC cap badges, while mechanics, armourers, and other engineering technicians were concentrated in RCEME units.[70]

Mechanics and tradesmen in RCEME had their work cut out for them. Despite the lessons of the First World War, the Army operated a mixture of Canadian, British, and American equipment. We have already seen that Lieutenant-General Crerar had yet to decide whether to use American or British motorcycles for general issue as late as 1943. In Normandy, Canadian artillery regiments used both the American M7 Priest and the Canadian-manufactured Sexton as self-propelled gun platforms. Canadian armoured divisions operated American Shermans and Canadian Rams together in the same formations. The Rams, which served as mobile artillery observation posts rather than gun tanks, were all too easy for German anti-tank gunners to spot and destroy.[71] In addition to a range of wheeled transport vehicles from the CMP family, Canadian forces used nearly 14,000 of the ubiquitous American 1/4-ton truck ("jeep"), known in Canadian and British English as the "car, 5-cwt."[72] Canadian- and American-supplied vehicles had little in common with respect to parts and design. Even the Canadian-built CMP trucks varied according to manufacturer. Ford trucks used different components from the General Motors models. Every minor variation further complicated a huge supply and maintenance infrastructure.

Some Canadian officers who played key roles in the design, development, and procurement of military vehicles during the war later believed that they had come up short. Plans for standardization had not been followed through. Thanks to interwar budgetary constraints, new models of trucks and armoured vehicles were rushed into production during 1940–42 without the chance to eliminate design flaws. Too many different types of vehicles, some of questionable value, were manufactured in Canadian plants. Writing in late 1945, Colonel E.D. James, the Director of Mechanization, hoped that "such hermaphroditic equipment" would never have to be produced again.[73] In the early postwar period, Canadian officers like Edmonds and Carr planned for a family of tactical transport vehicles known as the standard military pattern (SMP). These trucks were designed in the United States for the US Army but built under licence in Canadian factories beginning in 1951–52. The SMP trucks continued in service throughout the Cold War into our own day.[74]

RCEME craftsmen have their work cut out for them. It is impossible to say if this truck, photographed in Italy, was damaged in an accident or by enemy action. [LAC 3526000]

As Terry Copp's students and readers know all too well, logistics was a tough business for the Canadian overseas forces throughout the Second World War. While this chapter has largely explored procurement, training, discipline, and maintenance, it is useful to look briefly at some of the practical conditions on the ground. In 1943 the men of the Canadian divisions and armoured formations who fought in Sicily and Italy quickly discovered that the Italian peninsula was not intended for mechanized warfare. Poor roads, inclement weather, and a stubborn opponent with a penchant for blowing up bridges and culverts often slowed progress to less than a walking pace. Terrain conditions were so difficult in some places that Canadian soldiers relied on mules to carry vital supplies. In the summer of 1943, the RCASC companies of First Canadian Division requisitioned pack animals, known to the Canadians as the "Sons of Satan," for mountain resupply work. The newly minted First Canadian Division Mule Transport Company took charge of more than two hundred such animals, a throwback to the pack animal transport of the First World War.[75]

Animal power occasionally supplemented mechanical transport in Canada's Second World War Army. In this instance, soldiers transfer equipment from a universal carrier over to pack mules in the difficult terrain of the Italian peninsula, October 1943. [LAC 3582752]

The fighting in Normandy and Northwest Europe posed its own logistical challenges, even in moments of victory. As Terry Copp's scholarship emphasizes, a well-equipped mechanized army attempting to pursue an agile and lightly equipped enemy encountered certain difficulties, as

> the pursuing army expends great amounts of energy creating long lines of communication along which the desired amounts of fuel, ammunition, and supplies may flow. The retreating army ... simply keeps going: without transportation, it marches; without food, it does not eat.[76]

In the pursuit from France through the Low Countries in 1944, Allied mechanized forces had been unable to trap large German remnants on heavily broken ground. In spite of its mechanized force structure, First Canadian Army suffered from acute shortages of ammunition during crucial operations, such as the agonizing struggle to open the inland water approaches to Antwerp in October 1944.[77] It is easy to compare these circumstances with the transport dilemma that the Allies confronted during the victory offensives of August to November 1918. In both instances, the farther the winning armies advanced, the more difficult it became to sustain the troops through tortuous lines of communication. If Allied units lacked fuel or ammunition, it really made little difference how dire the enemy's predicament happened to be.

Motor vehicles played central roles in both of Canada's world wars. The state of the art improved significantly during the interwar years, as did the capacity to manufacture and deliver large fleets to military forces. Some of the artifacts preserved in the Canadian War Museum's LeBreton Gallery bear witness to dramatic technological change between 1918 and 1939. Yet the implicit themes we have considered in this chapter—training, road discipline, maintenance procedures, and procurement trends—tell a different story, one more concerned with humans than machines. Shifting our gaze from the artifacts to the people who operated, maintained, and procured them, we have identified some of the limits of technology in modern warfare. Perhaps further research in these areas will bring soldiers and machines closer together in our collective understanding of Canada's twentieth-century military experience.

Notes

The author is grateful to Doug Knight and Andrew Burtch for reviewing and commenting on this chapter.

1 Raymond Moriyama, *In Search of a Soul: Designing and Realizing the New Canadian War Museum* (Vancouver: Douglas and McIntyre, 2006), 90.
2 See *Statistics of the Military Effort of the British Empire during the Great War, 1914–1920* (London: Stamp Exchange, 1992), 595, 852, 878.
3 See full breakdowns in "Horses and Vehicles with the Canadian Contingent, 27 April 1918," Library and Archives Canada [LAC] RG 9 III-A-1, Vol.69, file 10-5-3.
4 The Second World War establishment for the First Canadian Division has been calculated based on a table of equipment and organization from Mark Bevis, *British and Commonwealth Armies, 1939–43: Helion Order of Battle*, Vol.I (Solihull: Helion and Company, 2001), 7–8.
5 This chapter considers the Canadian and British Empire experience. For an early German perspective on MT, see Lieutenant-Colonel Otfried Layriz, *Mechanical Traction in War for Road Transport* (London: Sampson Low, Marston and Company), 1900.
6 *Report on Trials of Self-Propelled Lorries*, Aldershot, 4–19 December 1901, Canadian War Museum.
7 For a detailed cost–benefit analysis of MT versus animal transport from immediately prior to the First World War, see *Army Service Corps Training. Part IV. Mechanical Transport* (London: HMSO, 1912), 2–6.
8 David Fletcher, *Staff Cars* (Haverfordwest: C.I. Thomas, 1990), 3.
9 John Sutton, *Wait for the Waggon: The Story of the Royal Corps of Transport and Its Predecessors, 1794–1993* (Barnsley: Leo Cooper, 1998), 48–54.
10 *War Establishments, Part I: Expeditionary Force* (London: HMSO, 1914), 208, 215.
11 On Russell's role as a purchasing agent, see Jaroslav Petryshyn, *"Made Up to a Standard": Thomas Alexander Russell and the Russell Motor Car Company* (Burnstown: General Store Publishing, 2000), 113–18.
12 For the Liberal viewpoint, see *War Contract Scandals* (Ottawa: Central Information Office of the Canadian Liberal Party, 1915), 26–30.
13 Ward to Carson, 22 May 1915, LAC RG 9 III-A-1, Vol.15, file 4-7-25; Carson to Hughes, 15 March 1915, LAC MG 27, II-D-23, file 1-18, Vol.1.
14 Correspondence detailing the experience of the 2nd Division is found in LAC RG 9 III-A-1, Vol.14, file 4-7-12.
15 "MT Equipment Required for a Division in the Field," May 1916, LAC RG 9 III-A-1, Vol.15, file 4-7-46C. This figure includes cars, lorries, ambulances, and motorcycles.
16 Thomas W. Wilby, *A Motor Tour Through Canada* (London: John Lane, 1914), x.
17 Arnold Warren, *Wait for the Waggon: The Story of the Royal Canadian Army Service Corps* (Toronto: McClelland and Stewart, 1961), 67. Captain Eaton commanded No.4 CASC Depot overseas in 1914.
18 QMG to AG, 9 July 1917, LAC RG 9 III-B-1, T-17-42, Vol.3240.

19 Adjutant-General to QMG, 14 March 1918; DST to W. Gibbons regarding Julius Miller, 16 July 1918, LAC RG 24, Vol.1445, file 593-8-3, (Vol.10).
20 QMG to MD No.2, 19 March 1917, LAC RG 24, Vol.1443, file 593-8-3 (Vol.4).
21 Memorandum on CASC Mechanical Transport Men, 18 September 1918, LAC RG 24, Vol.1446, file 593-8-3 (Vol.11).
22 Spittal to Carson, 27 May 1915, LAC RG 9 III-A-1, Vol.14, file 4-7-12.
23 Carson to Reid, 24 June 1915, LAC RG 9 III-A-1, Vol.17, file 4-7-54.
24 Carson to Dowie, 23 July 1915, LAC RG 9 III-A-1, Vol.17, file 4-7-47A.
25 McRae to MacDonald, 4 October 1915, LAC RG 24, Vol.786, file 54-21-8-16.
26 When Sir George Perley arrived in England to assume the post of minister of Canada's overseas forces, Lieutenant-General Richard Turner considered nominating McRae deputy minister. Because no other capable officer was then available to fill the post of QMG, McRae was instead given that important office. He was later seconded to the British government to set up the Ministry of Information. See Betty O'Keefe and Ian Macdonald, *Merchant Prince: The Story of Alexander Duncan McRae* (Surrey: Heritage House, 2001).
27 OC CASC Shorncliffe Area to Canadian Headquarters, 21 February 1917, LAC RG 9, III-B-1, Vol.3268, file T-44-42.
28 "Training of Mechanical Transport Officers and Men," 12 June 1917, LAC RG 9 III-B-1, Vol.3268, file T-44-42.
29 "Mabel Curd & Amb 23280K," 17-18-23, LAC RG 9 III-B-1, Vol.3217, file A-102-42, Vol.3217.
30 For details of the Shorncliffe accidents, see Standing Court of Inquiry to OC CASC, 11 July 1917, LAC RG 9 III-B-1, Vol.3268, file T-46-42 (Vol.II).
31 For examples, see "General Road Discipline," LAC RG 9 III-B-1, Vol.3228, file D-23-42.
32 Carson to Jones, 7 July 1915, LAC RG 9 III-A-1, Vol.14, file 4-7-8.
33 James A. Huston, *The Sinews of War: Army Logistics, 1775–1953* (Washington: Office of the Chief of Military History, 1966), 324–25.
34 See Memoranda on Inter-Allied Reserve of Motor Transport, September 1918, LAC RG 9 III-A-1, Vol.4474.
35 Steele to Carson, 11 August 1915, LAC RG 9 III-A-1, Vol.14, file 4-7-12A.
36 *Short Memoirs of the Third Canadian Divisional Mechanical Transport Company*, a copy of which survives in the Canadian War Museum's Military History Research Centre, gives some sense of the intensive duty cycles endured by MT units in the final months of the war.
37 LAC RG 9 III-A-1, Vol.69, File 10-5-4.
38 *Memorandum showing the progress in disposal of Government stores*, 19 August 1919, LAC RG 9 III-A-1, Vol.69, file 10-4-31; *Overseas Disposal Board, OMFC: Statement of Auction Sales*, LAC RG 9 III-A-1, Vol.104.
39 "Sale of War Equipment," *Canadian Military Gazette* 34, no.22 (25 November 1919), 6.
40 In a 1932 article, Lieutenant-Colonel R.S. Timmis of the Royal Canadian Dragoons argued that just as horses had survived the steam age, so they would continue to thrive

in tandem with the internal combustion engine: "The man who thinks the horse is doomed to extinction is not even original; our ancestors declared the same thing when steam was first utilized, and no sane person would let this matter cause serious mental anxiety, so let us go on breeding, but breed only the best." See "The Breeding of Light Horses," *Canadian Defence Quarterly* 9, no.4 (July 1932), 542. Captain E.L.M. Burns disagreed with Timmis's general view of the horse, arguing as early as 1924 that it was a "weapon that had had its day." See "The Mechanization of Cavalry," *Canadian Defence Quarterly* 1, no.3 (April 1924), 3.

41 Major L.C. Goodeve, "Mechanization," *Canadian Defence Quarterly* 5, no.4 (July 1928).
42 For a summary of developments up to 1927, see Lieutenant N.G. Duckett, "A Brief Outline of the Development of Mechanical Transport Wheeled Vehicles," *Canadian Defence Quarterly* 4, no.4 (July 1927), 432–41.
43 Lieutenant N.G. Duckett, "Trials of Mechanical Transport Vehicles at Petawawa Camp, June 6th to 19th, 1927," *Canadian Defence Quarterly* 5, no.1 (October 1927), 79–84.
44 Carr acknowledged that test crews should probably be equipped with crash helmets, but since none were on hand in quartermaster stores, football helmets had to suffice. Even this modest purchase was ultimately delayed. Memorandum, 7 June 1935, Hagarty to QMG, 24 July 1935, LAC RG 24, Vol.6294, file 38-72-261 (Vol.2).
45 On Sherman's military engineering career, see Murray C. Johnston, *Canada's Craftsmen at 50: The Story of Electrical and Mechanical Engineering in the Canadian Forces* (Borden: EME Officers' Fund, 1997), 21.
46 Sherman to Camp Commandant, Petawawa, 5 August 1935, LAC RG 24, Vol.6294, file 38-72-261 (Vol.2).
47 LaFleche to Ford Motor Company and General Motors of Canada, 14 August 1935, LAC RG 24, Vol.6294, file 38-72-261 (Vol.3).
48 Smith to LaFleche, 21 August 1935, LAC RG 24, Vol.6294, file 38-72-261 (Vol.3).
49 Memorandum, 28 December 1935, LAC RG 24, Vol.6294, file 38-72-261 (Vol.3).
50 LaFleche to Motor Vehicle Committee, 30 January 1937, LAC RG 24, Vol.6297, file 58-72-335 (Vol.1).
51 Memorandum, 12 December 1936, LaFleche to Motor Vehicle Committee, LAC RG 24, Vol.6297, file 38-42-335 (Vol.1).
52 By the end of September 1941, Canada had shipped more than 15,000 vehicles of all types overseas, including over 1,000 15-cwt and nearly 5,000 30-cwt CMP trucks. One year later, the number of shipments reached 27,495 units; as of October 1943, 67,106 vehicles had reached foreign shores, not including 9,629 motorcycles. See *Vehicles Shipped Overseas from 1939–1945* (Ottawa: 1945), Canadian War Museum.
53 By official accounts, Canadian forces received 34 percent of Canadian output; British Empire forces received 53 percent; American forces received 12 percent; other nations, presumably the USSR and China, received 1 percent. See C.P. Stacey, *Arms, Men, and Government: The War Policies of Canada, 1939–1945* (Ottawa: Queen's Printer, 1970), 488.
54 See William Gregg, *Blueprint for Victory* (Rockwood: Canadian Military Historical Society, 1981), 16–17.

55 TM 21-300, *Driver Selection and Training* (Washington: War Department, 1942), 29.
56 C.R. Kutz, *War on Wheels: The Evolution of an Idea* (London: Scientific Book Club, 1942), 9.
57 On the fact and fiction of German armour in the Polish campaign, see Major Robert M. Kennedy, *The German Campaign in Poland (1939)* (Washington: Department of the Army, 1956), 130–35; and Patrick Wright, *Tank: The Progress of a Monstrous War Machine* (New York: Viking, 2000), 231–37. Martin Van Creveld discusses the semimotorized state of the Wehrmacht in *Supplying War: Logistics from Wallenstein to Patton* (Cambridge: Cambridge University Press, 1977), 142–47. On Germany's war preparations more generally, see Wilhelm Deist, "'Blitzkrieg' or Total War? War Preparations in Nazi Germany," in Roger Chickering and Stig Förster, eds., *The Shadows of Total War: Europe, East Asia, and the United States, 1919–1939* (Cambridge: Cambridge University Press, 2003), 271–83. For a comparative view of France's preparations, see Talbot Imlay, "Preparing for Total War: The Conseil Supérieur de la Defense Nationale and France's Industrial and Economic Preparations for War after 1918," *War in History* 15, no.1 (2008), 43–71.
58 On the brute force thesis, see John Ellis, *Brute Force: Allied Strategy and Tactics in the Second World War* (New York: Viking, 1990).
59 Although horses had far from disappeared from the streetscapes of interwar Canada, the automobile population had expanded significantly. Canadian motor vehicle registrations grew from 21,873 in 1911 (one vehicle for every 330 people) to 464,805 in 1921 (one vehicle for every 18 people). By 1941, there were 1,572,784 vehicles registered nationwide (one vehicle for every 7 people)—a proportionately higher number than in the United States or Germany. See *Historical Statistics of Canada*, Transport and Communication, Series T147-194, Motor vehicle registrations, by province, 1903 to 1975. By way of comparison, there was one vehicle for every ten Americans and one for every seventy Germans in 1939. See Van Creveld, *Supplying War*, 144.
60 G.W.L. Nicholson, *Seventy Years of Service: A History of the Royal Canadian Army Medical Corps* (Ottawa: Borealis Press, 1977), 145.
61 Clive M. Law, *The Canadian Military Motorcycle* (Ottawa: Service Publications, 2010), 55–56.
62 The poster appears on the back cover of the January 1944 issue of *CAM* 1, no. 4.
63 Bill Mauldin, *Up Front* (New York: Henry Holt, 1945), 109. Mauldin, only half in jest, claimed that jeep accidents probably claimed more lives than any weapon during the war; on this comment and the genesis of the ordnance salvage yard cartoon, see Mauldin, *The Brass Ring: A Sort of a Memoir* (New York: W.W. Norton, 1971), 211–12.
64 *Dangerous Curves* (Dagenham: Ford Motor Company, 1942), Canadian War Museum.
65 *Driving Instructions and Workshop Manual, Car Scout Mark III (Canadian)* (Windsor: Ford Motor Company of Canada, 1942), Canadian War Museum.
66 On the state of technical training in the British Army as of 1940–41, see *Engines of War: The Mechanised Army in Action* (London: Adam & Charles Black, 1941), 83–86. On Beveridge's report and manpower allocation, see Jeremy Crang, "The British Army

as a Social Institution, 1939–45," in Hew Strachan, ed., *The British Army, Manpower and Society: Towards 2000* (Frank Cass, 2000), 16–35.

67   B.B. Kennett and J.A. Tatman, eds., *Craftsmen of the Army: The Story of the Royal Electrical and Mechanical Engineers* (London: Leo Cooper, 1970), 150. Strictly speaking, Beveridge's committee was not the first to examine the matter of maintaining the army's technical equipment. The foundations of REME can be traced back at last as far as 1928. See Colonel R.H. Hodgson, *A History of RCEME to 1946, Part 3: The Formation of RCEME* (unpublished regimental history, compiled by the EME Guild Charitable Trust, 2007).

68   On the duties of the RCOC prior to the creation of RCEME, see T.H. Turner, *Mechanics of Mars: The Story of the Canadian Ordnance Corps Training Center at Barriefield* (Barriefield: Canadian Ordnance Corps Training Centre), Canadian War Museum.

69   'RCEME: The Corps of Royal Canadian Electrical and Mechanical Engineers,' *CAM* 1, no.9 (June 1944), 141.

70   See, for example, J.C. Farrell, ed., *Memoirs: 4 Canadian Armoured Troops Workshop, RCEME, 1945–1945* (Enschede: 1st Canadian Mobile Printing Section, 1945), 6. For details on organization and maintenance responsibilities, see Hodgson, *A History of RCEME to 1946, Part 4A: Organisational Development*.

71   See Andrew Iarocci, "Close Fire Support: Sexton Self-Propelled Guns of the 23rd Field Regiment, 1942–1945," *Canadian Military History* 16, no.4 (Autumn 2007), 51–52.

72   Eric Booth, *The WW II Jeep in Canadian Service* (Ottawa: Service Publications, 2007), 8.

73   Quoted in Gregg, *Blueprint for Victory*. Edmonds referred to trucks as well as armoured vehicles such as the Ram tank.

74   On postwar developments, see Andrew Iarocci, *The M38A1 1/4-Ton Truck in Canadian Service* (Ottawa: Service Publications, 2008), and *The 3/4-Ton SMP Truck in Canadian Service* (Ottawa: Service Publications, 2009).

75   Historical Officer, Canadian Military Headquarters, *With Truck, Jeep, and Mule*, April 1944, 9–10, LAC RG 24, C-2, Vol.12750, file 24/episodes/6. The legacy of the Mule Transport Company lived on in Afghanistan, where Canada's heavily mechanized forces included the Kandahar Light Logistics Platoon, a pack-animal transport unit equipped with donkeys. See Major C.R. Jansen, "The Kandahar Light Logistics Platoon," *Canadian Army Journal* 12, no.3 (Winter 2010), 32–44.

76   Terry Copp, *Cinderella Army: The Canadians in Northwest Europe, 1944–1945* (Toronto: University of Toronto Press, 2006), 56.

77   This was not the only instance where the Canadians were starved for resources. The fighting for the Channel ports in September had also been carried out on a shoestring, as Operation Market Garden required vast resources. See Copp, *Cinderalla Army*, 65.

7

How C.P. Stacey Became the Army's Official Historian
The Writing of *The Military Problems of Canada,* 1937–1940

Roger Sarty

The Canadian Institute of International Affairs commissioned Charles Stacey's second book in 1938 to stimulate informed discussion about current Canadian defence policy at a time of international crisis.[1] Stacey mentions the book only briefly in his memoirs,[2] but his papers show that he was passionately committed to the project. He was engaged in nothing less than a campaign to preserve Canada's ties to Great Britain, including participation in war at Britain's side should tensions with Japan and Germany result in armed conflict. Many academic commentators, recoiling against the horrors of the First World War or enamoured with the League of Nations, urged a policy of isolation from overseas military commitments, and some urged closer ties with the United States. Much as Stacey welcomed defence cooperation with the United States that was just beginning in the late 1930s, he underscored its newness and Canada's lack of influence in Washington as compared to London. Canada's relations with Britain, especially its military relations, were the key to Canada's existence as a sovereign nation, historically and into the foreseeable future.

The writing of *The Military Problems of Canada*, the present paper argues, led directly to Stacey's selection as the historian of the overseas army in 1940. The considerable difficulties he faced in producing the book, moreover, foreshadowed in some detail those he would encounter as an official historian: the CIIA project was nothing less than a training exercise for the army histories. The book also focused Stacey's research on the twentieth century. Although his graduate research dealt with the Confederation era in Canadian history, he always had had an intense interest in current military and diplomatic events. In *The Military Problems of Canada* he combined those interests, but with the emphasis on the present and the recent past.

Stacey's papers reveal that his early career was much more the result of happenstance in a scramble to make a living than he relates in the generally candid account of his struggles in the memoirs.[3] When he graduated with honours from the University of Toronto in the spring of 1927, shortly before his twenty-first birthday, his ambition was to return there as a professor of British history. At that time the emphasis in the Toronto history department was on teaching, not research. He therefore went to Oxford University from 1927 to 1929 to take a second bachelor's degree; this involved an intensive reading program mainly in British history from medieval times to the present. When he began to hunt for jobs in 1928, he learned that there were no positions at Toronto, any other Canadian university, or in Britain. The advice he received was to take a research degree, the PhD, then something of an innovation for Canadian academics, and begin to publish. He had exhausted his fellowship for study in the UK, and the death of Stacey's father in 1927 had left his family in straitened circumstances. Hence his application to rich American schools. Only Princeton, not his first choice, offered financial support, and it was so modest that he realized he could afford only enough travel to do research solely in North American history, which had never attracted him.

Stacey had a lifelong interest in the military. He had joined the Officers Training Corps at the University of Toronto, and then become an officer in the signals corps of the militia. While in Britain he had arranged to be seconded to the Officers Training Corps at Oxford, and with it participated in the annual manoeuvres of the British Army. Curiously, his papers show no inclination towards a military career. He did, however, consider journalism as a fallback to his academic ambitions. Soon after he entered Princeton in the fall of 1929, he tried his hand by producing two articles on current military issues, one of them on Canadian defence policy for the *Canadian Defence Quarterly*'s 1930 essay contest. The essay shared first prize with a paper by

Major Maurice Pope, one of the most intellectual and politically astute members of the regular officer corps.[4]

Stacey's graduate research evolved into a study of British and Canadian defence policy in the face of the grave threat posed by the United States during the nineteenth century. He focused on the British government's efforts to shift the responsibility and steep costs of border defence onto the British North American colonies as the price of increased self-government and autonomy, and ultimately as one of the principal conditions for British support for Confederation. Published in 1936 as *Canada and the British Army, 1846–1871: A Study in the Practice of Responsible Government*,[5] Stacey's work was scrupulous in its scholarship. There was also a strong subtext. In the almost unwavering refusal of early Canadian governments to build and sustain armed forces that bore any relation to the country's defence needs, he discovered the roots of the government's virtual dismantling of the armed forces following the First World War. Canada, largely for domestic political reasons, had disarmed more completely than any other industrialized nation. The central point of his 1930 article on defence policy was the glaring disconnect between Canada's determined campaign for complete legal and political autonomy from Great Britain in the 1920s at the very time the country remained dependent on Britain for protection. On reading this first article, it is not difficult to see how, after an initial false start, Stacey found the thread of his thesis subject. *Canada and the British Army* is in this respect a "presentist" book.

C.P. Stacey at Princeton University in the early to mid 1930s. [University of Toronto Archives, B2008-0005/001P]

Stacey was lucky in his timing, and fortunate in the support of family and friends. In January 1934, Stacey's brother-in-law, Hartley Brown, then teaching at Brooklyn College, ran into his friend and fellow expatriate Canadian James T. Shotwell, who was director of the Division of Economics and History of the Carnegie Endowment for International Peace. Shotwell mentioned that he was launching a major new series of books on Canadian–American relations for the Carnegie Endowment. Brown described Stacey's thesis and arranged for his brother-in-law to meet with Shotwell—a rare opportunity for a young academic (at that time the only employment Stacey could find was a personal research contract from one of the senior faculty members at Princeton). It turned out that Shotwell's assistant in editing the series was Bartlett Brebner, then at Columbia University but previously one of Stacey's instructors at the University of Toronto. Shotwell and Brebner, impressed by Stacey's thesis, gave him a commission to write a volume on military relations for the Canada–U.S. series. They allowed him to draw on the large advance for that volume to assist in the publication of his thesis, which had been accepted for a British series whose budget allowed only a partial subsidy. Shotwell and Brebner also urged upon Stacey the necessity to get on the circuit of professional conferences to raise his profile. They had him attend the annual meeting of the American Historical Association in December 1934, and at a session chaired by Shotwell, he called upon Stacey for a comment. The Carnegie Endowment sponsored a series of large conferences on Canada–US relations that brought together business leaders, journalists, government officials, and academics, and Shotwell and Brebner arranged for Stacey to attend. The first was held at St. Lawrence University in Canton, New York, in 1935, the second at Queen's University in Kingston in 1937, and the third, in July 1939, which featured Stacey as a speaker, was once more in Canton.[6]

Thanks to the Carnegie funding, Stacey's *Canada and the British Army* appeared at precisely the right time, in the spring of 1936. In Canada, Mackenzie King's Liberals had been returned to office in the general election of October 1935, which took place against the backdrop of the international crisis created by the Italian invasion of Ethiopia. King, despite the deep cuts he had imposed on the defence budget during his first administration in the early 1920s, took up the question of rearmament. For one of the very few times in Canadian history, defence had become a relatively hot topic in political and academic circles. Reviewers quickly recognized the relevance of Stacey's book for current defence issues. It says much for Stacey's scholarship that critics from both ends of the wide spectrum of divided opinion in Canada, ranging from isolationists to supporters of military solidarity with Britain, commended the book. In Stacey's words, "anything even remotely resembling a 'military expert' was rare in the Canadian community in those days, and suddenly I found myself in some demand."[7]

Mackenzie King introduced the new defence policy during the opening of the parliamentary session in January 1937, with estimates that nearly doubled the budget of the defence department to $35 million a year (about $500 million in current dollars). It was a carefully crafted compromise; King privately confessed that he was caught "between the devil and the deep blue sea in having to steer between Imperialism [calls for direct military support to Britain] and Nationalism [isolationism in the 1930s context] in extreme forms."[8] The Chiefs of Staff Committee had advised that $70 million a year or more would be necessary to rebuild the forces within a five-year program, the longest that might bear any relation to the accelerating crises in Europe and the Far East. That level of expenditure would have allowed the provision of defences against "hit-and-run" raids by submarines, surface warships, and long-range aircraft on the Atlantic and Pacific coasts, as well as a land force of two divisions, with supporting air force squadrons, that would be available to reinforce any point on either coast threatened by serious attack or for operations overseas. King gave priority to home defence—and, for the first time in history, to the air force and the navy, the services principally responsible for coastal defence—over the militia, as the army was then known. The prime minister, who was especially concerned about resistance in his own party's stronghold of French-speaking Quebec to participation in war at Britain's side, promoted the program as the barest minimum for the protection of national sovereignty; dependence on Britain and the United States for the local protection of the Canadian coasts and adjacent waters would result in the country losing control over its own sea frontiers. The program did not, he underscored, look to intervention in overseas wars. In an appeal to supporters of direct military support to Britain, he marched out Sir Wilfrid Laurier's argument that improved Canadian national defences would strengthen the whole of the Empire, not least by relieving Britain of residual responsibilities for the defence of Canada.[9]

In May 1937 the annual conference of the Canadian Institute of International Affairs (held at McMaster University in Hamilton that year) featured the new defence policy as a topic for discussion by members. These "round tables," whose summary proceedings were printed, were one of the CIIA's principal activities; they were modelled on the conferences held by Britain's Royal Institute of International Affairs, and were a means to disseminate accurate information and a wide range of opinion on international affairs. Stacey, though not a CIIA member, participated by special invitation, probably from George Glazebrook, a professor of history at the University of Toronto, who knew of Stacey's expertise.[10]

Glazebrook was one of the most active members of the CIIA's research committee, which ran the publications program. This program was the creation of Escott Reid, who, after attending Oxford University as an Ontario Rhodes scholar, became the CIIA's national secretary in 1932. Reid obtained a generous multiyear grant from the Rockefeller Foundation in New York specifically to fund publications.[11] N.A.M. Mackenzie, a professor of international law at the University of Toronto, chaired the committee. The research committee's membership was a *Who's Who* of English Canadian academics. Those who attended the national meeting in Hamilton in May 1937 included H.F. Angus and F.H. Soward from the University of British Columbia; Vincent Bladen, Alexander Brady, and F.H. Underhill from the University of Toronto; and F.R. Scott, from McGill University in Montreal. Some of the members wanted to sponsor a "short book" on defence policy, but Glazebrook scotched the idea as impractical, in part because security issues severely limited the information the government could release. Finally the committee agreed that Glazebrook might produce a "factual article for public consumption."[12]

Glazebrook completed the conference report for the membership in October 1937,[13] and then had the research committee commission Stacey to write the longer article. Stacey completed a substantial draft of seventeen single-spaced typed pages, which in July 1938 was published as "New Trends in Canadian Defence Policy" in mimeograph form along with papers by other academics on Canadian external relations.[14] Stacey then revised and updated the paper, and Escott Reid arranged for it to be published in the *Canadian Journal of Economics and Political Science* in November 1938.[15]

In writing the paper, Stacey became something of an intermediary between the Department of National Defence and the several academics and others (like Reid) in the CIIA who had grave suspicions of the military in general and of military relations with Great Britain in particular.[16] Stacey approached the Deputy Minister of National Defence and received prompt responses to his questions about details of the defence program.[17] As the work continued, Reid was in regular touch with the DND on behalf of the CIIA, for additional information and later for a factual review of the manuscript. Reid, whose university studies were in political science and economics, applied himself to compiling tables that showed the full extent of defence expenditure, including funds expended by other departments for defence projects. He had reservations about the government's—and Stacey's—emphasis on the impoverishment of the armed forces prior to 1936 and the limited nature of the rearmament program. Stacey in the end refused to burden the article with the tables, pointing out to Reid that the "MS as you now receive it incorporates not only your own suggestions but also a considerable number from the department of National Defence as well as their corrections."[18]

One of Reid's sources of information in the DND was Colonel H.D.G. Crerar. From 1929 to 1935, Crerar had been a senior staff officer in the Directorate of Military Operations and Intelligence, the part of the army staff responsible for policy and plans. In 1935 he became the director of that office until, in August 1938, he was promoted to temporary brigadier and appointed Commandant of the Royal Military College of Canada in Kingston. Crerar, in his efforts at self-education and to widen his circle of professional and personal contacts, became an active member of the Ottawa branch of the CIIA, and with his move to the Royal Military College then joined the Kingston branch. A skilled analyst with facts ready to hand, Crerar was a willing correspondent with CIIA officials. Such correspondence was all the more important in putting forward the military's case for preparedness, because the officer corps was under a gag order. In November 1936, Crerar's briefing to militia officers in Halifax about defence plans had leaked into the press with alarmist headlines about the imminence of war, and embarrassed the government.[19]

In May 1938, Crerar sent Stacey a personal note—the two men had never met—ostensibly as a follow-up to the department's factual review of the article manuscript. "It occurred to me ... that you might be interested in another article on this same subject which appears in the latest issue of the Canadian Defence Quarterly, and with that in mind, I am forwarding a copy herewith as a personal gesture."[20] Stacey understood immediately that the article, "The Problems of Canadian Defence," published under the *nom de plume* "'Canuck,'" was Crerar's own.[21] It was a cogent statement of the assessment of the international environment—the threat to Canada's coastal districts and the possible need for intervention overseas—that lay behind the full rearmament program recommended by the chiefs of staff in 1936, and subsequently cut back by the government. Stacey incorporated the piece into his own work, citing it as "authoritative and lucid."[22]

Stacey's article came out soon after the Sudetenland crisis of September–October 1938, which had seen Britain and France on the brink of war with Germany. It was likely those events that led the the CIIA's research committee at its meeting of 12 November 1938 to revive the idea of a monograph on "Canada's Defence Policy." The book should be "prepared at once," and Stacey was the first choice as author.[23]

John Baldwin, a young historian who had completed three years' study at Oxford as an Ontario Rhodes scholar and who had recently succeeded Reid as the National Secretary of the CIIA, conducted the negotiations with Stacey. He explained that the research committee wanted a short book, 20,000 to 40,000 words, that would essentially be an expansion of Stacey's article. The book should include an exploration of the main differing points of view on defence. Baldwin explained that he would be writing to a number of "outstanding leaders in military circles" for their advice, and he suggested that Stacey should too.[24]

Stacey, by now familiar with the potential for protracted round robins in CIIA editorial review, was firm in his response. "Dr. Stacey wished this study to be entirely his own work," Mackenzie explained to the research committee. "He was willing to consult other persons but was not favourable to the idea of including essays by other persons, or statements by other persons in the work." The committee accepted Stacey's terms and approved an honorarium of $150 and an additional $50 that Stacey had requested for expenses.[25]

Stacey's bluntness in the negotiations showed self-confidence, especially for a thirty-two-year-old academic in a job market that was still profoundly affected by the Great Depression. His career, in fact, had taken off. In September 1934 he had started a one-year teaching contract at Princeton, and as a result of his publication record and popularity with the students, the contract had been renewed for each subsequent academic year. The history department strongly supported him for a three-year contract, and in December 1938 he received that appointment, with effect from September 1939. Moreover, Stacey was hard at work on the volume on Canadian–American military relations for the prestigious Carnegie series. If the research committee did not like his proposals for the defence policy book, it was welcome to search out another author: "it will not hurt my feelings ... as I am tremendously busy already ... and would not even consider doing it if it were not one that especially appealed to me."[26]

Certainly the chiefs of staff of the Canadian forces welcomed Stacey's involvement. Baldwin had applied to the Minister of National Defence for assistance to the institute's defence volume. The minister's private secretary, C. Norman Senior, asked the advice of the chiefs and passed on a copy of Stacey's published article. Rear-Admiral Percy Nelles caught the sense of the chiefs' reaction: "Dr. Stacey's article is excellent and to my mind, only errs on the side of restraint. I do not know, however, how far the Hon. The Minister is prepared to enlist the assistance of Dr. Stacey to prepare public opinion in Canada for further increase in estimates."[27]

Stacey plunged into full-time drafting as soon as classes were over early in the spring of 1939. On 15 April he sent the first chapter to Baldwin, and in August a fifth chapter, as well as a twenty-five-page "Postscript" that brought the whole work to some three hundred pages of typescript. That was nearly a 100,000 words and more than double the maximum length originally planned.[28] With the first chapter he sent a warning to Baldwin that he had not had any chance to consult any experts or opinion leaders, and doubted whether he would have the time to do so, let alone rework the manuscript in response to divergent opinions ("I am up to my ears in other work"). "I feel," he concluded, "that on the controversial aspects it is best for me simply to form and express my own opinions, taking full responsibility for them."[29] "I quite agree," replied Baldwin: "I think the matter may fairly be left in your hands." He did explain, however, that the research committee, "following its usual procedure," had appointed a subcommittee of Mackenzie, Crerar, and Loring Christie, of the Department of External Affairs, "to ... advise the Committee in the matter of publication. In reading it they may make a few suggestions for revision."[30]

The comments from Mackenzie and Crerar—Christie does not appear to have responded—give good evidence of the gulf of opinion and leave no doubt as to where Stacey stood. Following are extracts from two memoranda by Mackenzie:

> 1. I think Stacey overlooks the probability that Canada's century of conflict with the U.S., 1775–1871, was due to the relations of Britain with the U.S.

> 2. I consider that he overlooks the possibility that if our security is due to Britain our dangers in part at least arise because of that connection. Compare the Argentine. I feel the two pretty well cancel each other out ... I suggest that the position of French Canada is not due to their [sic] having anti-military prejudices as stated on P. 53. Nothing in the history of the French race bears this out. It is due to their reluctance to fight ... wars in which they have no interest of any kind.[31]

> (1) The view that Canadian Defence Policy, 1919 to 1936, or even later, was unwise. Stacey takes what I term the militarist point of view in this matter, which starts from the premise that a relatively large "defence" force is always desirable. This at least is implied in his language.[32]

By contrast, after reading the final chapter, Crerar wrote: "I have come to the conclusion that I am a poor critic of your material because I think and reason very similarly to yourself on Canadian military problems. As a result I find myself so much in agreement with what you write that I have little else to say but that I am."[33]

Stacey gave discreet acknowledgment to the help and encouragement he had received from Crerar in naming the new book. "I had been thinking of 'Problems of Canadian Defence,'" Stacey wrote on 26 June, "but then I suddenly realized that this is almost the same as the title of 'Canuck's' article in C.D.Q. a few months ago. Do you think Canuck would object to my using it? Or could you perhaps suggest something else?"[34] "'The Military Problems of Canada,'" Crerar responded, "might fill the bill."[35]

The two men finally met during the last week of August 1939. In Toronto on 26 August, Stacey married Doris Shiell, who had been a fellow undergraduate at the University of Toronto. In what must have been a true busman's holiday for the bride, who already had had some difficulty accommodating Stacey's nearly compulsive academic schedule, the first stop in the honeymoon was Kingston. They visited Fort Henry, watched the 3rd (Anti-Aircraft) Battery of the permanent force mobilize for the move to its war station at Halifax, and had lunch with Brigadier Crerar and his wife. When, on 3 September, Britain and France went to war with Germany, the couple cut their trip short and returned to Toronto. Stacey offered his services to his old militia unit and to Military District No. 2. Neither needed him, and he wrote to Crerar for advice on military employment. Crerar responded that large-scale expansion of the land forces was unlikely to happen quickly; Stacey should return to Princeton to begin the academic year, which he and Doris did.[36] It is rare indeed for a very junior militia officer long on the inactive list to seek help in an appointment from one of the most influential senior staff officers at National Defence Headquarters. Certainly Stacey was ambitious; he would maintain the link he had made with Crerar, and it would bring important results that would transform his career.

On 6 September the research committee of the CIIA decided to delay publication of Stacey's book and two others that bore on the international crisis. The United States had already declared its neutrality in the

Marriage of C.P. Stacey to Doris Shiell, Toronto, 26 August 1939. [University of Toronto Archives, B90-0020/001P(13)]

European war. The King government, however, had authorized the Canadian forces to mobilize, ostensibly as a precaution, though it was clear that Canada's formal entry into the conflict would take place within days, when Parliament reconvened. This created difficulties for the publication program, funded as it was by an American foundation. Anything produced with Rockefeller money must be "free from suspicion of any unfairness"—astonishingly, the context makes it clear the reference was to Germany or Japan—to ensure that the CIIA could not be charged with funnelling American money into pro-Allied propaganda.[37] Baldwin in fact hoped to carry on the program, but cautiously, as a compromise between two factions in the institute that had quickly developed with the onset of war. Some wanted to support the war effort fully; others were convinced that that would make the institute nothing more than a government mouthpiece, and that the institute should all but cease operations until the return of peace in order to preserve its integrity as a free forum for opinion.[38]

On 22 September, Baldwin wrote to Stacey with proposals for substantial changes in the manuscript. Chapter Five and the Postscript, which analyzed the government's defence program in light of requirements in the event of a major war breaking out, should go; that eliminated about one-third of the manuscript. He also wanted to recommend to the research committee that Chapters One to Four—an analysis of the country's geographical and strategic situation, followed by three chapters that gave a narrative history of Canadian defence from 1775 to 1939—should be published. Stacey agreed that the last third of the manuscript had been overtaken by events, and suggested it be replaced by a short, mainly descriptive account of the country's initial war effort.[39]

Baldwin had told Stacey only part of the story. On 6 October, Baldwin reported to the committee that Stacey's manuscript would require "considerable editorial work" and that Baldwin himself had already completed about half of the task. The committee raised no objections and directed that Baldwin's work be reviewed by Mackenzie and Glazebrook.[40]

When in November Stacey received the revised manuscript, he was aghast. "None of your letters," he replied to Baldwin, "had prepared me for the degree of mutilation which this manuscript has suffered":

> The most important class of alterations ... consists of a censorship of opinion and interpretation which appears to be systematic throughout the manuscript, and which far from confining itself to questions relating to the present war extends to the earliest periods of history covered in the study. This censorship has very decidedly altered the book's general interpretation of Canadian military development ...
>
> Page 164, 165 The only passages on the Bren gun affair marked for deletion are those favourable to the government. The opinion on the need for Bren guns is deleted.
>
> ... 59 Large deletions in interpretative remarks on War of 1812, all relating to the large degree of aid received from Britain.
>
> 44 Deletion of two sentences referring to Canadian desire to buy security and self-respect at too cheap a rate ... One thing that interests me is the fact that though this manuscript was read by a distinguished soldier, Brigadier Crerar, I have failed to find any trace of *his* criticisms in the revision ... I had assumed that the various comments sent me from time to time from readers were for my guidance when the time for revision came; I had counted on taking them all into account and making use of those which I thought forceful; I had not anticipated that some one in the Institute's office would undertake to make these decisions for me.

"Publication of the manuscript in its present state is out of the question," he concluded. "I could not consider allowing my name to be attached to it."[41] Stacey sent a copy of this letter to George Glazebrook, whom he clearly regarded as a friend on the research committee:

> I don't know how much knowledge you may have of what has been happening to this manuscript, but its condition when returned was a real shock to me. It has to be seen to be believed, and I cannot help being very much upset about it.
>
> My impulse is to ascribe the whole thing to Baldwin's inexperience and excess of zeal, but it really seems a pity that he should have had to acquire his experience at my expense. I may be wrong (as Mr. King would say) but I feel that there are some important principles at stake here—involving not only the Institute's intellectual integrity but also its common honesty.[42]

Stacey, though still a very junior academic, was equally tough and precise in his response to a long, conciliatory letter from Mackenzie, a senior and influential scholar. Mackenzie confirmed what Baldwin had already told Stacey: that the revisions were all subject to Stacey's approval. Interestingly, no one from the research committee mentioned the real reasons for the changes, which were, the fear of misusing the Rockefeller money and a reluctance to turn the institute into a pro-Allied mouthpiece of the government. Mackenzie only underscored the necessity that CIIA publications be "scientific and objective, rather than propagandist."[43]

The outcome reflected credit on everyone involved. Glazebrook and R.G. Trotter of Queen's, a member of the research committee who shared Stacey's views,[44] interceded as peacemakers. Baldwin took responsibility for the miscommunication and the excessive editing, and travelled to Princeton, where for a full day he went through the manuscript with Stacey change by change.[45] Stacey showed his confidence as a writer by admitting, even in his initial strong letter of protest, that in matters of organization and style "some of the suggestions are sound and valuable." In April 1940, Stacey sent the four revised chapters to Baldwin and reported: "I have worked with your suggested revisions beside me. In a good many cases I have accepted them, or made rather similar changes ... On the other hand in numerous instances, after careful consideration I have allowed my original version to stand."[46] Through the spring and summer, while Baldwin copy edited the manuscript, Stacey drafted the new postscript, a short account of the developments since the outbreak of the war. He would continue to make adjustments in light of the dramatic and rapid developments in the war in August and September, when the book was already in the printer's hands.[47]

By then Stacey was on tenterhooks. Crerar, after duty overseas to establish Canadian Military Headquarters in London, returned to Ottawa late in July 1940 and shortly thereafter became Chief of the General Staff. On 24 August he replied to a personal note from Stacey with the exciting, if cryptic, news that "since the outbreak of the war I have had hopes of seeing you employed in a service capacity for which you are so particularly suited." Stacey telegraphed that he was immediately available, but Crerar replied by telegraph that the appointment was not yet "assured."[48] As Stacey's letters to his mother show, he was in an agony of anticipation, until on 15 October he wrote to her with elation, only slightly disguised by his habitual understatement of good news:

Our letter from Crerar has come at last, and is something of a surprise. I am being appointed Historical Officer, General Staff, at Canadian Headquarters in England. This gives me the rank of Major and very good pay—$10 a day plus large allowances. The job entails collecting and preparing material for the history of the war, and should be a very interesting one ... This is really a flattering appointment ...

I have the last galley proofs of the book, and am trying to get that job finished.[49]

Finish he did before he left for Ottawa a few days later.

Crerar did not make the appointment lightly. As he told Stacey, he had been pushing for it for "ten months" before he got approval, which he ultimately sought and obtained from the minister himself.[50] Crerar had gone to bat for someone he had met only once, so this confidence arose mainly from Stacey's writings, and in particular from the drafts of *The Military Problems of Canada* that Crerar reviewed. Stacey had captured, in profound depth, the thinking of Canada's top professional military officers. This was in part a tribute to Stacey's scholarship. *The Military Problems of Canada* was the only book Stacey wrote that was not based on comprehensive research in primary sources; he had access only to published documents, and received little inside information. Yet Stacey was so careful and shrewd that the book still stands as an account of Canadian rearmament, especially the contradictory pressures on the government and the challenges faced by the military; anyone reading the full government and political

C.P. Stacey, left, in uniform on Parliament Hill in Ottawa, possibly in December 1940, just before he went to the United Kingdom as the historical officer for the overseas army. [University of Toronto Archives, B90-0020/001P(25)]

archives available today will find little to dispute Stacey's interpretation and facts. It is a superb example of contemporary history and a convincing demonstration of his ability to capture "on the run" the development and operations of the army overseas.

Certainly Stacey was the obvious choice as the historian of the new overseas army, being one of the first Canadian scholars to publish substantial work in military history. He was also one of the very few academics who published on international relations to show anything other than suspicion towards the military, and the British connection that was still the foundation of the Canadian forces. At the same time, such was the quality of his scholarship that he had won widespread professional respect, not least from the research committee of the CIIA, whose members included some of the most radical critics of the military and Canada's ties to Britain.

Crerar perhaps selected better than he realized. One of the keys to the successful completion of *The Military Problems of Canada* was that Stacey brought to his professional relationships the same meticulousness as was evident in his scholarship. Stacey was scrupulous in creating a written record of the terms under which he accepted the project, and in seeking specific approval for changes in the terms that proved necessary in the course of research and writing. He built his response to Baldwin's revisions on this written record, citing chapter and verse to show exactly where and how the editing violated the terms for the project. Reliance on the written record also moderated his response. Angry as he was, he could see the instances where Baldwin's changes fulfilled the stated expectations of the research committee. The near compulsion to create precise, comprehensive written records, be it for drafting historical accounts, or for overcoming bureaucratic obstacles in the army and government, would become the bedrock of Stacey's success in all phases of the army's official history program. So too would be his pursuit of fairness in scholarship and administration alike.

Above all, the making of *The Military Problems of Canada* shows Stacey's extraordinary drive to get the job done, and the satisfaction he found in getting the job done. When the initial task of drafting proved bigger than he had anticipated, he pushed on to produce three hundred pages of manuscript in five months. When the outbreak of the war instantly rendered one-third of that work obsolete, he did not hesitate in acknowledging that fact and moved on. In the dispute with the research committee, he sought quick resolution and again moved on, drawing the best he could from Baldwin's work rather than letting acrimony hinder progress. This creative drive grew from the depth of his commitment to the project. Aside from his sense of duty to put forth views all but absent from academic discussion, he had also found his métier. The subject of the book, and the perspective he brought to it, grew directly from one of his earliest published pieces, in the *Canadian Defence Quarterly*, written when he had scarcely embarked upon his PhD. *The Military Problems of Canada* in turn found for Stacey a career he had never considered, but for which the book project proved him ideally suited.

Notes

1. The author gratefully acknowledges the support of the Social Sciences and Humanities Research Council of Canada, which funded research for this study. Work at the University of Toronto Archives, which holds Stacey's papers, was as pleasurable as it was profitable; Harold Averill, assistant university archivist, shared his matchless knowledge of the papers and his own memories of Stacey. Professor Jennifer Brown shed new light on her uncle with her vivid memories of him, and has otherwise given every encouragement and assistance to this project, including a gift of offprints of Stacey's numerous articles and other short pieces.
2. C.P. Stacey, *A Date with History: Memoirs of a Canadian Historian* (Ottawa: Deneau, 1983), 59.
3. The details concerning Stacey's early career are drawn from Roger Sarty, "Canada and the British Army: The Early Career of Charles P. Stacey," paper presented at 17th Military History Colloquium, University of Western Ontario, May 2006.
4. "Canadian Defence Quarterly Essay Competition, 1930 Prize Essay," *Canadian Defence Quarterly* 8 (April 1931), 304–22.
5. C.P. Stacey, *Canada and the British Army, 1846–1871: A Study in the Practice of Responsible Government* (London: Royal Empire Society and Longmans, Green and Co., 1936).
6. On the conferences, see Frederick W. Gibson and Jonathan G. Rossie, *The Road to Ogdensburg: the Queen's/St. Lawrence Conferences on Canadian-American Affairs, 1935–1941* (East Lansing: Michigan State University Press, 1993).
7. Stacey, *A Date with History*, 58.
8. William Lyon Mackenzie King diary, 11 February 1937, Library and Archives Canada [LAC], MG 26 J 13.
9. Roger Sarty, *The Maritime Defence of Canada* (Toronto: Canadian Institute of Strategic Studies, 1996), 90–104, 110–37, includes analyses of the archives and published literature.
10. CIIA executive committee (with Glazebrook present), 6 May 1937, LAC, MG 28 I 250, vol. 3, "Minutes, 1937–1938," reel M4618. Glazebrook started teaching at

Toronto in 1924, when Stacey was an undergraduate there. They might have renewed their acquaintance in 1935 at the Carnegie conference in Canton, New York, which Glazebrook attended and, where, as Stacey reported to his mother, "I have met a lot [of] old friends." Stacey to Mrs. C.E. Stacey (his mother), 21 June 1935, University of Toronto Archives [UTA], Accession B93-0021, box 1, file 2; Walter W. McLaren, Albert B. Corey, and Reginald G. Trotter, eds., *Conference on Canadian-American Affairs Held at the St. Lawrence University, Canton, New York, June 17-25, 1935* (Boston: Carnegie Endowment for International Peace and Ginn and Company, 1936), 288.

11 J.L. Granatstein, "Becoming Difficult: Escott Reid's Early Years," in Greg Donaghy and Stéphane Roussel, eds., *Escott Reid: Diplomat and Scholar* (Montreal and Kingston: McGill-Queen's University Press, 2004), 11–22; Escott Reid, *Radical Mandarin: The Memoirs of Escott Reid* (Toronto: University of Toronto Press, 1989), Chapter 6; "Memorandum on Research Policy," 13 December 1939, p. 2, reported the Rockefeller Foundation grant for publications was $3,000 a year from 1 July 1936 to 30 June 1939, and thereafter $5,000 a year, LAC, MG 28 I 250, box 1, "Edgar Tarr 1939–41."

12 "Minutes of the Annual Meeting of the Research Committee, McMaster University … 23 May 1937," (filed as appendix "A" to executive committee, 18 June 1937), LAC, MG 28 I 250, vol. 3, reel M4618.

13 G.P. DeT. Glazebrook and Winslow Benson, *Canada's Defence Policy: Report of Round Tables of the Fourth Annual Conference of the Canadian Institute of International Affairs, Hamilton, Ontario, May 1937* (Toronto: CIIA and University of Toronto Press, 1937).

14 *Canadian Papers 1938*, Supplementary Papers, Series A., nos. 1–7, prepared for the British Commonwealth Relations Conference, 1938 (Toronto: CIIA, 1938), 55–72; see also R.W.G. Mackay, review of *The British Commonwealth and the Future: Proceedings of the Second Unofficial Conference on British Commonwealth Relations … September 1938*, in *International Affairs* 18 (March–April 1939), 276–78.

15 C.P. Stacey, "Canadian Defence Policy," *Canadian Journal of Economics and Political Science* 4, no.4 (November 1938), 490–504.

16 Reid, *Radical Mandarin*, Chapters 7–10; see also James Eayrs, *In Defence of Canada: From the Great War to the Great Depression* (Toronto: University of Toronto Press, 1964), 89–90, 98–100.

17 Stacey to Deputy Minister of National Defence, 10 January 1938, LaFlèche to Stacey, 18 January 1938, UTA, Accession B91-0013, box 5, "CIIA" (hereafter, CIIA file).

18 Stacey to Reid, 14 June 1938 (quoted) and 22 June 1938, CIIA file; Baldwin to Stacey, 16 November 1939, ibid., refers to Reid's suspicions about hidden defence expenditures.

19 J.L. Granatstein, *The Generals: The Canadian Army's Senior Commanders in the Second World War* (Toronto: Stoddart, 1993), 87–90; Paul Douglas Dickson, *A Thoroughly Canadian General: A Biography of General H.D.G. Crerar* (Toronto: University of Toronto Press, 2007), 91–3, 101–6.

20 Crerar to Stacey, 25 May 1938, CIIA file.

21 *Canadian Defence Quarterly* (April 1938), 264–73. Stacey refers to it as Crerar's article in Stacey to Reid, 14 June 1938, CIIA file.

22 "New Trends in Canadian Defence Policy," 66n16; "Canadian Defence Policy," 490n14.
23 Research committee, 12 November 1938, LAC, MG 28 I 250, vol. 4, reel M4618.
24 Baldwin to Stacey, 16 November 1938, CIIA file.
25 Research committee, 10 December 1938, LAC, MG 28 I 250, vol. 3, reel M4618.
26 Stacey to Baldwin, 24 November 1938, CIIA file.
27 Deputy Minister of National Defence to minister's personal secretary, 29 March 1939, NS 1017-10-1 pt. 2, LAC, RG 24, vol. 3832.
28 The only extant copy of this initial draft appears to be that in LAC, MG 30 E 157, Box 15, file 3.4.
29 Stacey to Baldwin, 15 April 1939, CIIA file.
30 Baldwin to Stacey, 20 April 1939, CIIA file.
31 Mackenzie, n.d., forwarded by Baldwin to Stacey, 19 July 1939, CIIA file.
32 Mackenzie to Baldwin, 8 August 1939, forwarded by Baldwin to Stacey, 10 August 1939, CIIA file.
33 Crerar to Stacey, 24 August 1939, CIIA file. See also Stacey to Crerar, 5 July 1939, and Crerar to Stacey, 10 July 1939, ibid.
34 Stacey to Crerar, 26 June 1939, LAC, MG 30 E 157, Box 15, file 3.4.
35 Crerar to Stacey, 10 July 1939, CIIA file.
36 Stacey, *Date with History*, 59-60; Doris Shiell to Stacey, 13 November 1938, UTA, Accession B93-0021, Box 1, file 10; Stacey to mother, 27 August 1939, UTA, Accession B 93-0032, Box 1, file 1; Stacey to Crerar, 4 September 1939, CIIA file.
37 Research committee, 6 September 1939, LAC, MG 28 I 250, vol. 4, reel M4619.
38 Baldwin to Tarr, two letters, 5 and 7 September 1939, LAC, MG 28 I 250, vol. 1, "Edgar Tarr 1939–41."
39 Baldwin to Stacey, 22 September, 1939, Stacey to Baldwin, 27 September 1939, CIIA file.
40 Research committee, 6 October 1939, LAC, MG 38 I 250, vol. 4, reel M4619.
41 Stacey to Baldwin, 23 November 1939, CIIA file.
42 Stacey to Glazebrook, 24 November 1939, CIIA file.
43 Baldwin to Stacey, 12 December 1939, Mackenzie to Stacey, 20 December 1939 (quoted), Stacey to Baldwin, 26 December 1939, Stacey to Mackenzie, 3 January 1940, CIIA file.
44 E.g., *Road to Ogdensburg*, 152–55. See also Stacey to Crerar, 5 July 1939, CIIA file.
45 Research committee, 15 December 1939, 11 January 1940, LAC, MG 28 I 250, vol. 4, reel M4619; Glazebrook to Stacey, 27 November 1939, Baldwin to Stacey, two letters, 12 and 27 December 1939, Trotter to Stacey, 18 April 1940, CIIA file.
46 Stacey to Baldwin, 12 April 1940, CIIA file.
47 Stacey to Baldwin, three letters, 9 June, 5 August, 12 September 1940, CIIA file.
48 UTA, Accession B90-0020, Box 10, 'D.H.Appt.'
49 Stacey to mother, 15 October 1940, UTA, Accession B 93-0032, Box 1, file 1.
50 Crerar to Stacey, 11 October 1940, UTA, Accession B90-0020, vol. 10, "D.H. Appt"; Stacey to mother, 22 October 1940, UTA, Accession B 93-0032, Box 1, file 1 (quoted).

8

"Strike Hard, Strike Sure"
Bomber Harris, Precision Bombing, and Decision Making in RAF Bomber Command

Randall Wakelam

At the outbreak of the Second World War, staff of RAF Bomber Command believed it had the doctrine, technology and procedures that would allow it to conduct daylight precision strategic bombing against Germany. Heavy losses, however, forced a switch to night bombing by early 1940, from which point evidence began to show that crews were failing to find and hit their targets. A statistical analysis, conducted at the behest of Churchill's scientific adviser in the summer of 1941 and known as the Butt Report after its author, confirmed this problem.

Flyers and junior commanders had by this time developed some ideas on how to mitigate the situation; their proposals centred on the creation of a "fire raising force" that, by hitting a target accurately with incendiaries, would draw other crews to the target area. When these proposals were put before Sir Arthur "Bomber" Harris, Air Officer Commanding in Chief of Bomber Command, and his group commanders in the spring of 1942, Harris rejected the concept. Only through the intervention and direction of the Chief of the Air Staff, Harris's superior, was a target-finding force created.

Subsequently Harris would be critical of the role played by a number of younger officers who pestered him with their brilliant ideas, leaving readers of his *Bomber Offensive*[1] and *Despatch on War Operations*[2] with the conclusion that they were, at best, a pain in the side. But this is a hasty conclusion, for in fact the small staff within the Directorate of Bomber Operations at the Air

Ministry had made a detailed study of the matter, collecting data and opinions from a large number of experienced flyers and COs, and their proposals were sound. Rebuffed by Harris, they did not give up. The chief instigator, Group Captain Sydney Bufton, used office politics to convince the CAS of their scheme. Once in place, however, the Pathfinder Force (PFF), a name Harris picked in the end, would not prove the panacea that its promoters had thought.

In examining the specifics of this case, the paragraphs that follow attempt to do a number of things, all of them related in many ways to the teaching and research of Professor Terry Copp. First, this study reviews the facts surrounding the target-finding challenges of Bomber Command; it does this using primary sources. Second, it reviews the debate around the creation of the actual Pathfinder force and its subsequent performance. And finally, the paper analyzes the decision making around the PFF debate using contemporary Canadian military leadership theories and concepts, for as Terry will often say, the purpose of his teaching is to examine the past with a view to understanding some aspect of current thinking. It is hoped that the story that follows will illuminate the nature of decision making and staff interactions in complex military organizations.

Some might think that the formation of the PFF has, like all Bomber Command topics, been studied ad nauseam. Such is not the case. While there is sufficient information about the circumstances leading to the creation of the PFF in the RAF official history, the Canadian companion study gives it just a few paragraphs.[3] Some mention is made in a number of biographies and memoirs, including those of Bomber Harris and Donald Bennett, the flyer who would form and command the force, and in the more recent biography of Air Chief Marshal (ACM) Wilfrid Freeman, the Vice Chief of the Air Staff.[4] Only the latter lays bare some of the institutional politics of the affair. These matters and more are to be found in the personal papers of both Harris and his chief antagonist Bufton, but these have not been broadly reported.[5]

The British official history does a decent job of describing how Bomber Command stumbled from a would-be daylight precision force into a disorganized collection of aircraft groping across Germany in the dead of night. Even by the closing days of 1939 there were those, including Air Commodore Arthur Coningham, the AOC of 4 Group and later the commander of the Desert Air Force, who felt that the problems were more than could be surmounted. "'The real constant battle,' the 4 Group Commander pointed out, 'is the weather ... The constant struggle at night is to get light on the target" and he foresaw 'a never ending struggle to circumvent the law that we cannot see in the dark.'"[6]

The evidence was clear and unequivocal. Daylight post-raid photo reconnaissance of targets that crews claimed to have hit hard the previous night showed no bomb strikes whatsoever. Earlier data underscored the nature of the problem: between 1936 and 1938 some 478 bomber crews lost their way over the UK at night or when flying in cloud.[7] If experienced flyers could not find their way across their own small island in peacetime, then who would imagine that new flyers could do better over Germany given blackout conditions, smog, poor weather, and active defences seeking to kill them?

In the summer of 1941 the extent of the problem became better understood when Mr. D.M. Butt of the War Cabinet Secretariat examined 650 bomb release photos taken between 2 June and 25 July. Butt found that "of those aircraft attacking their target, only one in three got within five miles."[8] Accurate targeting was lower in the smog-ridden Ruhr. Many middle-ranked flyers, the COs and flight commanders of the operational squadrons, found nothing surprising in this.[9] They had long suspected, but had no evidence to confirm their belief, that targeting was not accurate. Now they did have evidence.

On 1 November 1941, Group Captain Sydney Bufton, former Commanding Officer of 10 and 76 Squadrons and a man with first-hand experience over Germany, assumed a staff appointment as Deputy Director of Bomber Operations at the Air Ministry in London; "Bomber Ops" was in effect Bomber Command's superior agency. Bufton immediately took it upon himself—a theme we shall come back to in a moment—to outline the problems of finding the target and what to do about it. He was aided by a member of the section, Wing Commander Arthur Morley. Both were well connected with squadron COs and station commanders, and it seemed clear to the two staff officers that a target-marking capability of some sort was required. They proposed nothing particularly sophisticated—certain crews could get to the target before the bulk of the raiders and then bomb precisely using incendiaries to create a fire of sufficient proportions to attract those coming immediately behind. As additional crews added to the fires, these would act as a visual beacons to all crews participating in the raid.

Just days before Bufton's arrival, Morley prepared an informal memo dealing with the state of strategic and tactical bombing. He reminded his readers that this new incendiary policy was under review and that Bomber Command had tested the technique on a failed raid against Nuremburg. A very inexperienced crew had led the raid and bombed a town fifteen miles from the target. The other air crews followed and compounded the error. The solution, Morley said, was "*the immediate formation of special fire-raising squadrons (2-3), … crews to include specially selected first-class navigators with operational experience … incendiary bombs must be dropped in salvo … within 20 minutes and preferably within 10-15 minutes* [of zero hour]" (his emphasis).[10]

As soon as he arrived in Bomber Ops, Bufton recommended using flares to illuminate and then mark the target in addition to a fire raising force.[11] In a memorandum he pulled no punches: "Most people will agree that Bomber Command is running smoothly in well oiled grooves, but that tactically it is dead." "I am convinced that the formation of target finding Squadrons, either directly under Bomber Command or say one in each Group, preferably the former, would revolutionize our tactics, and put new life into our bombing effort."[12] Whether Bufton was resorting to classic British understatement is uncertain, but by the very fact that he wrote three memos on the subject in the span of as many weeks says something about his concerns.

Bufton was not the only one thinking hard about these problems; Bomber Command senior staff had also been pondering the issues. A 3 November 1941 letter from Bomber Command's Senior Air Staff Officer (effectively the second in command) Air Vice-Marshal Robert Saundby to group commanders proposed the formation of "special target-locating squadrons." The response from the groups was evenly split: two firmly against and two open to the idea.[13]

Towards the end of the month these same or similar documents apparently made their way to Bomber Ops, for in early December the Director of Bomber Operations, Bufton's superior Air Commodore Baker, commented on a Bomber Command paper "Problem of navigating to, locating and bombing a target by night." Writing to both his own superior, the ACAS (T), and to Saundby, Baker underscored that average crews could get to within ten to twenty miles of the target but from there were in trouble. This dilemma could be resolved, he felt, by using clearly identifiable coloured flares to mark the target and then raising fires, "employing not only a special technique but, as found necessary, specialised units for the purpose."[14]

Just a few days later, Wing Commander Morley began to brief crews from some twenty squadrons as well as forty-seven senior officers, including three group commanders and three group Senior Air Staff Officers (the SASO was the equivalent at the group and command level to a chief of staff) on the incendiary tactics and the special crews Bufton had proposed in his memos. On return to the Air Ministry, Morley prepared a detailed report on the responses from the flyers. The majority of squadron COs were in favour of forming special squadrons, though many felt there would be "disadvantages" by "milking squadrons of trained and experienced crews." Weighing against these concerns was "a feeling of hopelessness and ineffectiveness ... creeping into some squadrons." In Morley's view, forming a target-finding force that would allow crews to bomb effectively would more than offset skimming the best crews.[15]

In the closing days of 1941 and through January and February 1942, operational research scientists, planners, and flyers collaborated on a new technique called "Shaker" that would see the fire-raising concept put into practice. While selected crews would use a new navigation device, code named "Gee," to find the target, they would not be designated as target-finding units.[16]

It took Arthur Harris only a week after taking over Bomber Command on 23 February 1942 to oppose the target force notion. In a letter on 2 March to the Chief of Air Staff, Sir Charles Portal, Harris noted that while he was rarely in disagreement with logical proposals, he did not support the notion of a target-finding force. His principal concern focused on the regrouping of the best crews from most units and the adverse effect this would have on the morale of those left back.[17]

Just days later, and almost certainly without Harris's knowledge, Morley took part in the first use of the new technique over Germany—a raid on Essen on 8–9 March.[18] He reported three days later that despite the use of both Gee and Shaker, the fire-raising crews had not received special training nor had the raid gone particularly well. Linking the two, Morley put the cause squarely on the absence of a specialized target-finding force.[19] One can only imagine the frustration of Bufton and Morley when the next day Harris met with his group commanders as well as Baker and Bufton to review the technical and tactical employment of Gee.[20] There was general agreement about the need to master the use of Gee and to employ marker bombs, but when it came to the formation of a target-finding force, Harris remained unconvinced, stating that to do so would "cream off" the best, leaving the squadrons bereft of tactical leaders who could help develop new crews.

Bufton returned to London and, apparently with the assistance of Morley, prepared a survey, which they sent straight to colleagues in the squadrons (short-circuiting the chain of command), and in which they explained the situation as they understood it and asked for feedback on the appropriateness and need for a target-finding force.

Their survey did not make reference to Harris's opposition, but did allude to his objections, even using the phrase "'creaming off' the best crews in operational squadrons." Additionally, the proposal criticized Harris's concerns about creating a "corps d'elite." After a short two pages of discussion, the readers were asked to answer the following questions: "Do you agree generally with the proposals set out in the attached paper"; "Do you consider that the objections raised are sufficiently sound and insuperable to warrant the dropping of the whole scheme." The second question was in effect a vote of non-confidence in the leadership of Bomber Command. Dozens of replies came back in the first week of April, all agreeing with Bufton's reasoning and offering considerable personal examples of why a TFF was needed.[21]

It bears mentioning that while the survey was circulating, Morley sent Bufton a most incredible memo that proposed that all AOCs, SASOs, and senior staff involved in the campaign take part in at least two raids over Germany to "personally inspect conditions." This may have been a fairly reasonable albeit risky proposal, but what followed was a recommendation to remove all group commanders and command senior staff who lacked operational experience in the current war.[22] There is no evidence that the memo went beyond Bufton: perhaps Morley only needed to vent.

Emboldened by the support and by a previous offer from Harris to discuss any ideas, Bufton sent the responses to his survey to Harris on 11 April.[23] In his covering letter, Bufton explained what he had done: "so entirely convinced of the soundness of the T.F.F. idea, and having been confirmed in this opinion through casual contacts with those engaged at the present time in operations ... I decided to write personally to my friends of great experience and whose opinion I value, and put the case to them."[24]

Harris replied six days later, thanking Bufton for the material which he had studied. "I have a fairly open mind on the subject of the Target Finding Force, but I am not yet convinced by the arguments which you put forward." Turning to the comments of Bufton's respondents, Harris, displaying what can only be seen as remarkable restraint, wrote: "Much as I appreciate and pay attention to the ideas of the lads who really do the work, they necessarily have a very circumscribed view on any particular subject and are not given to appreciating any factors outside those which affect their own comparatively narrow spheres." The AOCinC went on to say that he had passed the information to his AOCs and they to their direct subordinates, the station commanders, and the consensus was that the TFF was not an appropriate concept.[25]

Bufton was not done. He replied with five pages of tightly packed confrontational prose,[26] dissecting Harris's every thought and even offering up some personal criticism for good measure. Bufton was emotionally engaged in the debate; in one instance he emphasized that he knew "in my heart" that the TFF would have the immediate effect of quadrupling the effectiveness of the raids.[27] Here was a junior group captain telling the head of a command that he had it all wrong and was out of touch with the current operational realities. That Harris did not reply was not perhaps surprising.

Nothing happened for a full month. Then on Saturday, 12 June, as Bufton was manning the shop in Bomber Ops the VCAS, Wilfrid Freeman, stuck his nose into the office. After some general discussion, Freeman asked if there were any issues. Using this opening, Bufton, according to his own account of the situation, raised the problem of Harris and the TFF.[28] Freeman was not a supporter of Harris,[29] and he prepared a letter for Portal's signature that brought the issue to a head within days. Portal wanted a target-finding capability, and Harris was in no position to go against the decision of his superior.[30]

If Harris was to be directed on what to do, he would at least pick the name of the new force, the commander, and the squadrons.[31] The organization would be the Pathfinder Force (PFF), and Harris selected as its commander a young, brilliant flyer named Donald Bennett, whom Harris had seen in action during the 1930s.[32] Bennett had until recently been CO of 10 Squadron (ironically one of the squadrons that Bufton had earlier commanded), and Harris now promoted him to group captain, giving him command of five squadrons.[33]

According to Bennett, as well as the official history, Harris was not inclined to give the PFF much priority in people or resources. The force would not get the best aircraft, and the units assigned were not necessarily the best in the command.[34] When looked at from the perspective of managing critical resources, Harris's decisions made some sense. His job was to allot limited resources, so why would he give the PFF everything it wanted, especially if the organization was foisted upon him? And perhaps the contrary views were a bit biased: did not every commander, Bennett included, want the best crews and planes? At the same time, Harris did recognize the special nature of the force, giving every Pathfinder a unique badge and a one rank promotion. The PFF stood up on 11 August 1942 and flew its first operation one week later.[35]

It was not a good beginning. There had been no time to develop new tactics or equipment that could make pathfinding more effective. Many technologies were on the way, but these would not be available for several months. Worse, Gee, which had underpinned the Shaker technique, had been jammed by the Germans for the first time just days earlier.[36] As such, the PFF crews had gone into action with nothing better to use than the main force crews they were leading.

By Bennett's account these constraints did not deter the Pathfinders.[37] But the reality pointed to many limitations.[38] The official historians write that the most noticeable improvement was an enhancement in concentration. Between March and August 1942 some 35 percent of bomb releases were plotted within three miles of the aiming point. That figure rose to 50 percent from August 1942 to March 1943. On the other hand, accuracy was equally important, and here the PFF was less successful: from March to August 1942, just 32 percent of night photos were plotted within three miles of the aiming point. By March 1943, this value had risen to just 37 percent. Simply stated, when the Pathfinders marked the wrong location, any improvements in concentration were for naught. The spread between the two values (i.e., what could have been achieved given the actual concentration and what was achieved as a result of the accuracy error) became known as the systematic error.[39]

Once these problems were identified, vigorous action was initiated to find a way to ensure that the PFF could mark targets with greater accuracy. The same Bomber Command Operational Research Section scientists—the "boffins," as they were called—who had developed the Shaker technique began tracking and analyzing PFF performance by gathering extensive data from all raids.[40] By comparing what was intended with what had actually happened, they could see which procedures, tactics, and technologies were working. During the fall of 1942 the ORS was able to conduct two reviews of pathfinding activities. The first looked at the results of thirteen raids and found that six had yielded improvements in bombing accuracy while only two had been failures.[41] Later in the year a more detailed study of twenty-one raids focused on the causes of failure: inadequate numbers of finder aircraft, malfunctioning flares, and the inadequacy of visual marking devices underlined the need for coloured marker bombs. Overall, the report concluded that pathfinding had succeeded on one-third of the twenty-one raids over Germany and had partially succeeded during another third. Five had failed, and three had ended up over the wrong target. At the same time, however, the aggregated statistics from all twenty-one raids pointed to the fact that only 24 percent of attacks had been within three miles of the target, which gave "much scope for improvement, as [figures show] only about 5 % within 1 mile [of the aiming point]." Over Italy, which had fewer air defences, results showed success on seven of nine attacks.[42]

Improvement would come, but the inconsistency in marking detracted from the efficiency of the bombing offensive right through to the end of the war. After an attack against Hanover on 23 September 1943, Harris called the pathfinding a "complete flop," opining to Bennett that his crews must have "light-heartedly" disregarded their navigation.[43] How this might be the case can be readily understood if not happily accepted. The crews were made up of young men with limited training who had been sent into the night with rudimentary technology to carry the battle to Germany. That they did as well as they did is little short of incredible. In fact, pathfinding techniques would continue to evolve during the remaining years of the war, and the crews—both Pathfinder and Main Force—would become better at getting bombs on target. By 1945, accuracy was being measured in hundreds of yards rather than miles.

But the question remains: Who was right, Harris or Bufton? Arguably, both recognized that something needed to be done to improve the accuracy of the strategic bombing, which would in turn make the strategic bombing campaign more efficient and hopefully more effective. Bufton reckoned that his solution would work well and that he had the popular support of his peers regarding what changes needed to be made. In working around the chain of command to make recommendations, he was unquestionably a thorn in Harris's side. On the other hand, in providing advice to his direct superiors in the Air Ministry he was within his mandate. When we set aside this dichotomy of tactics and look at Bufton's motive, it is reasonable to say that he saw a problem, believed he had a solution, and was prepared to put ethical principles above military hierarchy in his attempts to ensure operational success.

When looking at the Harris–Bufton debate through the lens of command and leadership, it is important to place these circumstances in a contemporary framework. Over the past decade, Canadian researchers Dr. Ross Pigeau and Carol McCann, working out of Defence Research and Development Canada's Toronto labs, have examined the constituent elements of command.[44] They argue that effective commanders need three things: competency in the domain in which they exercise command; authority to make things happen; and an acceptance of the responsibility entrusted to them. Arguably both Harris and Bufton—and many others—had the technical competency to understand the issues of target finding. But from here the lines split. By virtue of his formal appointment as AOCinC of Bomber Command, Harris had the legal authority to operate his command as he saw fit and—of course within the norms of the RAF—to discharge the tasks assigned to him and to the command by the Chief of the Air Staff.

Bufton, on the other hand, was a staff officer. His role was to provide advice—and if necessary to point out to his seniors at the Air Ministry what things were going well or poorly in the bombing campaign. So while he could go to Baker and perhaps even to Freeman, for him to presume—as he seems to have done—that he could directly influence Harris was arguably presumptuous. Finally, only Harris carried the responsibility for the effectiveness of the command. Had the PFF concept failed, leading to a drop in effectiveness and an increase in losses, it was Harris, not Bufton, who would have been cashiered.

Writing after the war, Harris was very specific about the responsibility of command and the strains it placed on the commander:

> I wonder if the frightful mental strain of commanding a large air force in war can ever be realized except by the very few who experienced it. While a naval

commander may at the most be required to conduct a major action once or twice in the whole course of the war, and an army commander is engaged in one battle say once in six months or, in exceptional circumstances, as often as once a month, the commander of a bomber force has to commit the whole of it every twenty-four hours; even on those occasions when the weather forces him to cancel a projected operation, he has to lay on the whole plan for committing the force. Every one of those operations was a major battle, and as much depends on the outcome, such is as vital and disaster as grave, as on any other occasion when the whole of a force engages the enemy. In addition, there is a continuous and fearful apprehension about what the weather may do, especially in the climate of North-West Europe.

The whole of the responsibility, the final responsibility, for deciding whether or not to operate falls fair and square on the shoulders of the Commander-in-Chief, and falls on them every twenty-four hours. For all he knows he may lose the whole of a very large proportion of the force by weather alone, to say nothing of enemy action. It is best to leave to the imagination what such a daily strain amounts to when continued over the period of years.[45]

In Harris's dealings with Bufton, all three elements of command were in play, and Harris captured their essence in a communication to Portal a full two years after the events described here. To Portal, in April 1944, he wrote:

My complaint is that [Bufton's] ideas on Pathfinders, as on some other matters, have always been and still are rammed down our throats whether we like them or not. I have personally considerable regard for his ability and honesty of purpose and have time and again stressed … that he should come and discuss things with me and regard himself as a welcome critic here and a Bomber Command agent in the Air Ministry in addition to being your personal Bomber Operations Staff Officer, rather than a sort of shadow C.-in-C. of the Bomber Offensive. In practice he has been a thorn in our side and the personification of all that is un-understanding and unhelpful in our relations with the Air Staff … His name has become an anathema to me and my senior staff.

Harris's biographer provides more context from Harris's letter: "he did not dislike Bufton: it was his methods he could not stand and if Bufton could rid himself of his idée fixe that he could have the fun of running the bomber offensive his way while the C-in-C took the responsibility, it should be possible to put relations on a proper footing."[46]

The establishment of the PFF illuminates many important themes of command and leadership within that most technical of the services—the air force. We can see that there is no perfect science to predicting which equipment, processes, and tactics may or may not work in combat. Often commanders are faced with what we would today call "wicked problems" and must make the best possible decision in the circumstances. Part of the complexity of these challenges has much to do with which officers have the responsibility and the authority to apply solutions. The RAF has for many years published a professional journal called somewhat intriguingly *Air Clues*. In each issue there is a piece called "I learnt about flying from that" in which the usually anonymous author reveals a nasty circumstance that allowed him (or her) to develop some wisdom to be applied in future flying duties. We can only presume that had a parallel piece been in vogue during the war years— something called perhaps "I learnt about command and leadership from that"—Harris, Bufton, Portal, and others would each have had worthy—and different—perspectives on the formation of the PFF. That there would not be a common view of these circumstances should not surprise us: air forces like all the services are complex organizations, with all the warp and weft of the human dynamic.

Notes

1. Marshal of the RAF Sir Arthur Harris, *Bomber Offensive* (Toronto: Stoddart, 1947).
2. Air Chief Marshal Sir Arthur T. Harris, *Despatch on War Operations 23rd February, 1942, to 8th May, 1945*, ed., Sebastian Cox (London: Frank Cass, 1995).
3. Sir Charles Webster and Noble Frankland, *The Strategic Air Offensive Against Germany 1939-1945*, vol.I, *Preparation* (London: HMSO, 1961), 249, 309, 397, 431-32; Brereton Greenhous et al., *The Crucible of War, 1939-1945: The Official History of the Royal Canadian Air Force*, vol. III (Toronto: University of Toronto Press, 1994), 524, 611-13.
4. Air Vice-Marshal D.C.T. Bennett, *Pathfinder: A War Autobiography*, 2nd printing (Manchester: Crecy, 1983); Anthony Furse, *Wilfrid Freeman: The Genius Behind Allied Survival and Air Supremacy 1939-1945* (Staplehurst: Spellmount, 2000).
5. The Harris Papers are held in the archives of the RAF Museum in North London; the Bufton Papers are in the Churchill Archives, Churchill College, Cambridge.
6. Webster and Frankland, *Strategic Air Offensive*, vol. I, 202.

7   Ibid., 112 note 1.
8   John Terraine, *The Right of the Line: The Royal Air Force in the European War 1939–1945* (London: Hodder and Stoughton, 1985), 292–94.
9   Furse, *Wilfrid Freeman*, 200; Webster and Frankland, *Strategic Air Offensive*, vol.I, 419n; Letter Dewdney to Peirse, 1 February 1941.
10 Untitled Minute Sheet, original emphasis, Bufton Papers, Folder 3/50.
11 Memoranda G[rou]p Capt S.O. Bufton to DBOps 5, 20 and 29 November 1941, Bufton Papers 3/6.
12 Memo Bufton to DBOps 20 November 1941, Bufton Papers 3/6.
13 Letter SASO to Groups, 3 November 1941. AIR 14, 516. National Archives (NA), United Kingdom.
14 Memo Baker to ACAS (T) 5 December 1941, Bufton Papers 3/6.
15 "Report on Visit to Groups and Stations Bomber Command," 10 December 1941, Bufton Papers 3/12.
16 Webster and Frankland, *Strategic Air Offensive*, Vol.I, 387.
17 Letter Harris to Portal, 2 March 1942, Harris Papers, H 81.
18 Letter Bufton to Martin Middlebrook, 7 April 1983, Bufton Papers 5/13.
19 "Report on 1st Night Operation Employing T.R. 1335," 12 March 1942, Bufton Papers 3/16.
20 "Minutes of the Conference on T.R. 1335 Technique and Tactics Held at H.Q.B.C. on 13.3.42," Bufton Papers 3/7.
21 "The Target Finding Force" n.d., Bufton Papers 3/12, 3/18.
22 "Immediate and Necessary Steps that must be taken to ensure the effective employment of the Bomber Force," 31 March 1942, Bufton Papers, 3/7.
23 Bufton made reference to this offer in a letter to Harris on 17 March 1942; they had apparently spoken on the previous day; Bufton Papers, 3/18. See also Bufton to Middlebrook, 7 April 1983, Bufton Papers, 5/13.
24 Bufton to Harris, 11 April 1942, Bufton Papers, 3/18.
25 Harris to Bufton, 17 April 1942, Bufton Papers, 3/18.
26 Furse, *Wilfrid Freeman*, 206. Furse assesses Bufton's letter as "courteous and good mannered, but ruthlessly logical and well informed." Harris's lack of reply he deems to be a sign of capitulation.
27 Bufton to Harris, 8 May 1942, Bufton Papers, 3/18.
28 Bufton to Middlebrook, 7 April 1983, Bufton 5/13; see also Furse, *Wilfrid Freeman*, 206–7.
29 Ibid., 203.
30 Ibid., 206–8. See also Webster and Frankland, *Strategic Air Offensive*, Vol.I, 431–32; and Portal to Harris, 14 June 1942, Harris Papers, H 81.
31 Bennett, *Pathfinder*, 155.
32 Ibid., 135; Harris, *Bomber Offensive*, 25, 129.
33 Bennett, *Pathfinder*, 162.
34 Webster and Frankland, *Strategic Air Offensive*, Vol.I, 432.
35 Ibid., 432.

36 Ibid., 433.
37 Bennett, *Pathfinder*, 168–77.
38 Webster and Frankland, *Strategic Air Offensive*, Vol.I, 434.
39 Ibid., 434–36.
40 Reasonably one should be able to conclude that the figures cited from the official history are based on these ORS studies, but the source of the data in the official history is not in fact indicated.
41 2 OIC ORS to CinC, 22 September 1942 covering ORS loose memorandum, "An Assessment of the Success of Operations Led by the P.F.F.," 22 September 1942. UK National Archives AIR 14/1804 Minute.
42 ORS loose memorandum, "Notes on Effectiveness of P.F.F. Operations to 21/22 November," n.d., AIR 14/1804, NA.
43 Sir Henry Probert, *Bomber Harris: His Life and Times* (Toronto: Stoddart, 2001), 231. Probert quotes Harris to Bennett, 23 September 1943.
44 Ross Pigeau and Carol McCann, "Reconceptualizing Command and Control," *Canadian Military Journal* 3, no.1 (Spring 2002): 53–63.
45 Harris, *Bomber Offensive*, 72; Norman Longmate, *The Bombers: The RAF Offensive Against Germany, 1939–1945* (London: Hutchinson, 1983), 148.
46 Harris to Portal, 14 April 1944, in Probert, *Bomber Harris*, 267–68.

9

Leadership and Science at War
Colonel Omond Solandt and the British Army Operational Research Group, 1943–1945

Jason Ridler

In 2000, Terry Copp made a significant contribution to our understanding of science and its role in the Second World War by compiling and contextualizing the efforts of No. 2 Operational Research Section (No. 2 ORS) as it analyzed battle data as part of 21 Army Group in his fine work *Montgomery's Scientists*.[1] No. 2 ORS was part of a larger British effort to enlist science in war, beginning with radar work for the RAF Fighter Command and Anti Aircraft (AA) Command, leading to the development of a new applied science called "operational research" (OR). Scientists from a variety of backgrounds were employed to serve alongside all three services, both in training and, more controversially, in the field. By applying their skills of observation, measurement, and calculation to examine how the services conducted their business, teams of OR scientists were able to provide realistic and effective solutions to a range of problems, ranging from the tactical to the strategic. The most famous impacts of OR related to the increased efficiency and lethality of Fighter and AA Command and to the demonstrable though counterintuitive value of large convoys in surviving the Battle of the Atlantic. Given this importance, OR in the Royal Navy and Royal Air Force has received the most attention from historians examining OR and the Second World War.[2]

But the history of OR in the British Army does not rest solely on AA Command. By 1942 the British Army had consolidated its army-centric research assets into the British Army Operational Research Group (AORG). During the war, AORG was commanded by two unique individuals. The first was Brigadier Basil Schonland, the respected South African First World War veteran and physicist whose name was synonymous with his research on lightning and early radar work. Schonland was also a personal friend of Colonel Jan Smuts, the South African prime minister and one of Winston Churchill's inner circle. Schonland's deputy and successor was the young Canadian physiologist Colonel Omond Solandt.[3]

Unlike Schonland, Solandt entered the war with only an academic background, though it was a stellar one. The star pupil of Dr. Charles Best, the co-discover of insulin, Solandt had made a name for himself as a hotshot academic at the University of Toronto and Cambridge, and he entered the war ready to prove himself at any and every task at hand. He had succeeded in managing the Southwest London Blood Depot during the worst of the German bombings in 1940 and became an OR pioneer with the British Armoured Corps. His success at not only research but also leading and managing his innovative laboratory led to his selection to start a new section for AORG on tank gunnery and other concerns, but his management skills soon led him away from research. He became Schonland's deputy and then successor as Superintendent of AORG when Schonland became scientific adviser to General B.L. Montgomery at 21 Army Group.

Solandt's rise to replace Scholand and his role in leading AORG provides a useful window onto the fruits and frictions involved in managing a new wartime science organization under duress. Schonland's efforts in creating AORG have long been heralded.[4] Solandt's contribution—he turned AORG into an efficient and diverse organization, expanded its mandate, and championed the use of OR sections in the Normandy campaign—are less appreciated. Here, we describe Solandt's critical role in managing Army OR during the Second World War, as well as the organization's accomplishments, including Solandt's own personal research and analysis of British OR teams in India and Burma. That analysis provided an opportunity for Solandt to comment on AORG's successes and failures; and today it provides us insight into how a postwar defence research organization should be run.

However, Solandt's efforts as a pioneer in OR were not without friction. His aggressive approach to managing science led to a controversy with Schonland over the use of Army OR in the field; and this demonstrated the difficulties inherent in controlling the lines of responsibility when science went to war. Overall, however, Solandt's tenure as Superintendent of AORG was a net positive, not least for Canada. Soon after war's end, Solandt became chairman of Canada's Defence Research Board, the nation's first peacetime defence research organization. He brought to the job not just his incredible mind and skills but also the invaluable experience of leading a new and growing scientific organization at war—experience he had gathered at AORG.

Origins of Operational Research (OR)

Operational Research was a form of applied science that became a critical and innovative component of Britain's war effort. Its roots were in the 1935 Tizard Committee and in early radar work in the UK; its value became manifest in the wake of radar's success and the usefulness that OR teams demonstrated in the field. By 1941, Professor Patrick Blackett, a pioneer of OR as well as a noted physicist, then in charge of Coastal Command's OR Section (ORS), had written the first useful treatise on OR's purpose:

> The object of having scientists in close touch with operations is to enable operational staffs to obtain scientific advice on those matters which are not handled by the service technical establishments. Operational staffs provide the scientists with the operational outlook and data. The scientists apply scientific methods of analysis to these data, and are thus able to give useful advice. The main field of their activity is clearly the analysis of actual operations, using as data the material to be found in an operations room, e.g. all signals, track, charts, combat reports, meteorological information, etc. [I]t will be noted that these data are not, and on secrecy grounds cannot, be made available to the technical establishments. Thus such scientific analysis, if done at all, must be done in or near operations rooms. The work of an Operational Research Section should be carried out at Command, Group, Station or Squadron as circumstances dictate.[5]

OR within the British Army began with Blackett, who in August 1940 was made scientific adviser (SA) to General Frederick Pile, commander of Anti Aircraft Command. Here he formed an ORS named "Anti Aircraft Command

Research Group" (AACRG), but known as "Blackett's Circus." Blackett studied AA teams in action and deduced ways to improve their training and operations by using gun-laying radar, predictors, and searchlights. These innovations continued even after Blackett left AA Command in March 1941. This success led to OR sections being stationed at most command headquarters in Britain.[6] The "Circus" also worked with a radar school in Petersham on the edge of Richmond Park under the directorship of radar pioneer Dr. J.A. Ratcliffe.

Sir John Cockcroft, Superintendent of Air Defence Research and Development (ADRDE) in the British Ministry of Supply, had selected Ratcliffe for the radar school. The "Circus" and the radar school were amalgamated into Cockcroft's organization but under Ratcliffe's direction. In June 1940, the group was formally recognized as the Operational Research Group of the Air Defence Research and Development Establishment: ADRDE(ORG).[7]

In July 1941, Ratcliffe moved to join the Telecommunications Research Establishment (TRE) in Malvern. Cockroft then selected his friend, Lieutenant-Colonel (later Brigadier) Basil Schonland, an eminent South African physicist, to lead ADRDE(ORG). Cockroft would be Chief Superintendent of ADRDE, but Schonland would have direct access to key commanders such as Pile. Schonland's original mandate encompassed radar and the anti-aircraft needs of the army, including training and equipment, as well as general applications of science towards army needs. He inherited Ratcliffe's two OR sections: one, under Dr. Maurice Wilkes, was dedicated to radar; the other, under Dr. L.E. Bayliss, to gunnery fire-control problems. Major Patrick Johnson, a physics professor, friend of Schonland's, and future rival of Solandt's, led the radar school.[8]

By late 1942, ADRDE(ORG) had sections for a wide range of concerns beyond air defence. With active combat being encountered in North Africa, and with plans for a successful invasion of Europe now beginning to ferment, AORG looked beyond its initial mandate on AA issues, which were so tied with British survival. On 16 January 1943, Schonland and his staff were separated from ADRDE, and on 1 February, they were named the Army Operational Research Group (AORG). They maintained their equipment and facilities at Richmond Park but were then headquartered at Ibstock Place, Roehampton, with OR sections spread across England. AORG was now responsible to both the War Office and the Ministry of Supply. Schonland was responsible to the Scientific Advisor to the Army Council (SA/AC) in the War Office. Sir Charles Darwin was briefly SA/AC; then Sir Charles Ellis, a friend of Cockcroft and Schonland, was assigned the post and held it for the remainder of the war. Administration and technical efficiency rested with the Ministry of Supply and its Controller of Physical Research and Scientific Development (CPRSD), Dr. Paris.[9]

AORG's initial duties were strongly focused on technical issues and efficiency. They included the following:

1. to investigate the performance of selected types of service equipment under conditions obtained in field operations;
2. to collaborate with design establishments in studying the performance and use of early models of new equipment;
3. to investigate methods of using selected equipment;
4. to analyze statistically the results of selected tactical methods, whether they involve the use of technical equipment or not;
5. to advise the War Office and Commands upon the experimental planning of troop trials of equipment or not;
6. to be represented by observers at troop trials; and
7. to carry [out] any scientific investigations which may be approved by SA/AC or the CPRSD.[10]

But as the demands of war grew beyond the survival of the home island, AORG's needs would diversify. These changes would be overseen not by Schonland but by his successor. According to some who worked under both men, the organization benefited from the young successor's diverse intellect and dynamism.

Omond Solandt—Career Highlights, 1920–39

Like Schonland, Omond Solandt was a colonial, far from home, trying to contribute to Allied victory. Unlike Schonland, a Great War veteran, Solandt had come to military affairs by circumstance, not inclination. By the time the war started, he was one of the brightest minds of his generation in Canada, with a fierce intellect and self-professed "aggressive enthusiasm" for any subject that interested him. Born in Winnipeg in 1909, he was the son of the Reverend Donald and Edith Solandt, both educated at Queen's University, from which his father held two MAs. The unusual family surname had Protestant Swiss origins, via France. The Solandts settled in Quebec. Omond's unusual first name was taken from a beloved uncle. Like his older brother Don, young Omond excelled at school and technical training, and when the family moved to Toronto in 1920 he followed his brother to Central Technical School before finishing at Jarvis Collegiate. He relished that institution's technical as well as academic courses, and he worked as a radio telegraph operator and later as a flying observer for the Ontario government during his university summers. At the University of Toronto, he achieved Gold Medal standing as he studied arts and science under the tutelage of Dr. Charles Best, who supervised his master's thesis. Solandt's meticulous intellect aligned well with Best's firm conviction that all research required accurate data, and Solandt later attributed his success in OR—which often took the form of learning to measure and quantify things that had no previous metrics—to the lessons he had learned from Best and from the American physiologist Lawrence Irving. After surviving a near fatal attack of bulbar polio, Solandt, on Best's recommendation, pursued his final graduate work under Dr. Alan Drury at Cambridge. He returned to Canada to serve his internship at Toronto General during the worst outbreak of polio in Ontario's history, in 1937. Given his experience with the disease, Solandt was thought immune, and he ran the polio ward throughout the crisis, thus receiving a crash course in managing a medical environment under duress, which he did with aplomb.[11]

After passing the dreaded exams of the Royal College of Physicians, Solandt was set to begin a career in mammalian physiology when the Second World War broke out on 1 September 1939. He was soon assigned to run the Southwest London Blood Bank, where he made a name for himself as a relentlessly efficient manager and leader, one who championed hard work and maximized the efficiency of a vital civil defence network under wartime conditions. The British Medical Research Council was so impressed with his work that they assigned him an even more challenging task: helping the British Armoured Corps, whose tank crews were passing out during gun trials. At the Armoured Fighting Vehicle School at Lulworth, in Dorset, Solandt created a laboratory from scratch that examined the physiological and technical dimensions of tanks and their crews. He championed the use of actual battle data from North Africa to give his experiments at Lulworth more verity, sending his schoolfriend Major Laurie Chute to follow the

British Army as it fought through 1942. Chute's data became the bedrock of the laboratory's analysis. In this way, Solandt became a pioneer in OR, a field that suited his meticulous, pragmatic, and utterly scientific approach to investigating any phenomenon. It also impressed his superiors, and their allies. He was awarded the US Medal of Freedom (Bronze Palm) for his work on tank OR.[12]

Solandt also established himself as a first-class manager and an aggressive committee man on the Military Personnel Research Committee's Sub-Committee on Armoured Fighting Vehicles. In that venue, he argued his case for improved ventilation, night vision, and armaments for British tanks to maximize their effectiveness. By 1943, Solandt's research, leadership, and proven track record at Lulworth had impressed the War Office staff, who asked him to run a section of AORG dedicated to tank gunnery and mobility. Within a year, Solandt's obvious gift for managing diverse people and science organizations led to his selection as Deputy Superintendent and later full Superintendent of AORG with the rank of full colonel.

While in England in 1939, Solandt had tried to join the Royal Canadian Army Medical Corps, but he was told he would have to come back to Canada. Since the Canadian Army was on its way to England, he thought he would stay put and wait until they arrived. After 1940, however, the Canadian authorities made it difficult for him to join, as he was fully employed by the British government in his many jobs. Finally, Solandt spoke with General A.G.L. "Andy" McNaughton about this problem. McNaughton was a supporter of Solandt's tank research and told him that if he joined the Canadian Army he would likely be removed from his important position at Lulworth. By 1943, Solandt had convinced McNaughton that his work at AORG would be greatly advanced if he was in uniform; also, the change would reduce his payable tax and thus increase his salary. McNaughton agreed, and in 1943, Solandt became a captain. Within days he was made a lieutenant-colonel and, later, a full colonel.[13]

Solandt, Schonland, and the AORG

AORG was an even greater test than Lulworth on how to run a unique, varied, and dispersed government science operation. Solandt gave a good account of himself, learning by doing and building on his past successes. By the spring of 1943, Schonland was sufficiently impressed with Solandt's efforts to promote him to Deputy Superintendent of AORG. They were an odd duo: the South African physicist and the Canadian physiologist. Schonland, at forty-seven, was a senior statesman of science with a proud military record, a respected international reputation, and a patrician demeanour. Solandt, thirteen years younger, was an aggressive former wunderkind with no military experience whose scientific achievements had only just begun, first in research into "crush injuries" during the Blitz, and later in OR and tank design.

And here they were, two "colonials" running a new, unique, and complicated British wartime science establishment without a map. Tony Sargeaunt, a physicist with AORG who would succeed Solandt as superintendent, detected a mild tension between them because of Schonland's military bearing and Solandt's forceful attitude. This personality clash led to only one major confrontation, after Schonland left and Solandt became superintendent (see below). Otherwise it never interfered with their work.

Solandt worked with Schonland to establish new ORS sections 5, 6, and 7, the remaining two sections were formed entirely under Solandt (see Table 1). Schonland was a good boss, and Solandt respected his skills as well as his approach to leadership, which in many ways mirrored Solandt's own. Schonland discussed concerns and offered critical suggestions but left the implementation of solutions to the section chiefs.[14] Schonland provided the strategic vision for the organization, and Solandt kept the section heads in line. Being AORG's taskmaster likely made Solandt the less popular of the two.[15]

Table 1. The Operational Research Sections (ORS) of the British Army Operational Research Group (AORG)[16]

AORS1 Anti Aircraft Defence, Radar, and Searchlights
AORS2 Coastal Radar and Gunnery
AORS3 Signals in the Field
AORS4 Armoured Fighting Vehicles, Artillery, and Tank Gunnery
AORS5 Airborne Forces
AORS6 Infantry Weapons and Tactics
AORS7 Lethality of Weapons
AORS8 Mine Warfare, Assault Equipment, Tactics, and Flame-Throwers
AORS9 Time and Motion Studies
AORS10: Battle Analysis

As deputy, Solandt served in many other capacities, primarily administrative and diplomatic. He participated in the SA/AC "control meetings" where Sir Charles Ellis, SA/AC in the War Office, who was responsible for AORG, provided general direction for the group's research.[17] In Solandt's estimation, Ellis was a good man and a fine administrator but too easily dominated by others. Solandt attended meetings on diverse topics, from artillery doctrine to plans for sending OR teams into the field, though largely as an observer so that he could keep the sections on task.[18] His only criticism of Schonland was that he had an utter lack of interest in administration. Solandt was horrified when he discovered that the best civilian scientists at AORG were making peacetime university wages far below what many officers were drawing, though he knew they were working just as hard as their military counterparts. Solandt always made a point of increasing material support for his best team members, so to address this discrepancy, he visited the physicist C.P. Snow, who was in charge of scientific manpower at the Ministry of Labour. Snow had no knowledge of the salary situation. The two worked to improve the staff's wages, though Snow resisted Solandt's pressure to double his team's salaries within a year.[19] (One of Solandt's legacies at Canada's Defence Research Board—one that was largely rooted in his AORG experience—would be that the director of that organization controlled the hiring of staff as well as their salaries.[20])

Solandt also led a fact-finding and diplomatic mission to the United States and Canada. While on that trip, he made contacts and gathered data on a range of American and Canadian scientific efforts of interest to his organization. He also gave presentations on AORG work in all the sections, including AA artillery and radar. Solandt maintained an active interest in the entire AORG organization, not just in the armoured warfare research group, where he still had friends. He took great interest, for example, in the lethality-of-weapons studies being conducted by another South African expatriate, Frank Nabarro, whom Solandt ranked among the best scientists on the AORG's roster.

Becoming Superintendent of AORG

In February 1944, Ellis asked Schonland to join 21 Army Group as Scientific Advisor to General Montgomery for the Normandy invasion. Schonland agreed, and Solandt, only thirty-five, succeeded him in March as Superintendent of AORG.[21] Schonland's boots would be hard to fill. Solandt and Schonland were very different leaders. Everyone respected Brigadier Schonland for his service, his reputation, and his well-established scientific acumen. Solandt had to fight for respect, as his reputation could not match that of his predecessor. He was not a master of any one subject, but more a young renaissance man of science with a penetrating knowledge of diverse fields.

Solandt maintained Schonland's ethos that AORG's priorities were determined by the army's needs and that operational needs always came first. If problems arose in the deserts of North Africa, or with AA coastal gunnery, those problems became the priorities.[22] Almost all of AORG's research during the Solandt era followed the same general procedures. Observing came first: one must "never uncritically accept the users' diagnosis of the source of his problems," since he is often wrong. This was a double-edged sword: the military wanted to use the best available equipment and the best possible procedures, but they resisted anyone outside their profession telling them how to go about their business. Solandt, then, believed that one had to know the original reasons why the army used their equipment in the way that they did. Unless you knew that, they would resist any attempt at change.[23] The next step was collecting quantitative data, which often meant measuring things that had never been measured. Here, rough quantification was better than no numbers at all. The next step after that was experimenting to confirm or dismiss a hypothesis or to test a remedy. Solandt maintained his role as maestro with his section heads. He provided guidance and support but left them to decide the best way to proceed.

Solandt's team was a diverse lot, in both training and background. Most of the early OR pioneers were physicists like Cockcroft, Blackett, and Watson-Watt. When demand quickly dried up the supply of the country's physicists, more esoteric and diverse scientists were employed in OR work. Solandt was among a small cache of OR pioneers from the biological sciences, who included Solly Zuckerman, a zoologist who became famous for his bombing surveys, and Cecil Gordon, noted for his work on optimizing the RAF's air escort maintenance and deployment.[24]

While it did not lack physicists, AORG was home to an eclectic range of scientific and technical personnel. G.D. Kaye was an actuary who served as a living computational device for Neville Mott and Frank Nabarro's lethality-of-weapons studies.[25] Theo Fabergé, the grandson of the famous Russian jeweller Carl Fabergé, was one of Solandt's best machinists, despite a violent temper that raged in the soil analysis lab.[26] But of all his scientists, it was Nabarro whom Solandt held in the highest regard. Nabarro was one of Mott's best students, and his work on the lethality of weapons was among the best research AORG produced during the war. Solandt also had a soft spot for Nabarro's outsider status, in that he was both a South African and a Jew.[27] Indeed, Solandt championed outsiders and genuine eccentrics, who were nonconformists by nature. As he said in 1954, eccentrics were often the sources of innovation:

> One of the very real dangers to our North American civilization is our worship of conformity. In almost every walk of life the person who conforms most pliably [sic] to the accepted standards of dress and behaviour is most likely to succeed. We must recognize that this enforcement of conformity will finally result in universal mediocrity. New ideas, especially in human relations and often even in science, come from those who refuse to conform.[28]

This was an enlightened and useful position for a ruggedly non-eccentric man to take. Others might have found working with so many strange and interesting people akin to herding cats. Indeed, managing various scientists and assorted tinkerers required firm guidance and a flexible mind. Solandt provided both, even for those who did not care for him. Treadwell felt that this was Solandt's greatest gift. Few doubted the direction Solandt was taking them in.[29] Solandt also worked hard to get promotions and increased pay for those whom he felt were doing excellent work, often having to raise an "uproar" in the War Office to get his way.[30] Simply put, Solandt backed hard work, even if it meant having to confront his superiors.

Solandt took an active interest in every section, visiting the dispersed teams when he could and keeping abreast of their developments and needs. His wide interests and strong intellect were engaged across a spectrum of military concerns, from infantry battle analysis to continental air defence against modern rockets.

AA Command had done the best with Army OR. Years later, Solandt would say that AORS 1 and 2 had advantages the other sections did not: they had got in at the beginning; modern electronics had revolutionized every aspect of AA gunnery so that the need for scientists was clear to all; and in

General Pile they had a powerful supporter who had completely embraced the value of scientists in war. Solandt quipped later in life: "There is nothing more sobering for an advisor than to know that his advice is quite likely to be accepted and acted upon." It was Pile's support for science, more than anything else, that convinced Solandt of the need for direct access to the Minister of National Defence.[31]

AORG focused sharply on preparations for the Normandy invasion. Besides many other things, this included bombing analyses, weapons studies, and improvements in training exercises.[32] After September 1944, AORG also became involved defending against German V1 and V2 rockets. Before the V2 sites were overrun, Solandt recalled, "AORG had tested a system that anti-aircraft command was prepared to try that gave the same calculated probability of a kill against the V2 as the best that the anti-aircraft could do with a slow flying bomber at 10,000 feet at the beginning of the war. Unfortunately permission to fire the guns against the V2s was never obtained."[33] Also by September 1944, Nabarro's team had done excellent analysis of minor battles in Italy. Now the War Office wanted the same done for OVERLORD.[34] Solandt also had high regard for Bayliss's AA work and that of his section, which was filled with scientists and civilians, both men and women, and often included a complete army survey regiment with recording vans under his command.[35]

The View from Below

For some, Solandt never matched up. Neville Mott, a physicist and future Nobel Laureate, worked under Solandt at 3 ORS and disliked him from the start. Lieutenant Michael Swann, later Lord Swann and head of the BBC, who worked at AORG and later joined an OR section in Normandy, found Brigadier Schonland a bit frightening but very approachable, tough yet fair, always engaging and charming. Swan recalled the young Solandt as less patient and more critical, even if he was usually right. Many believed that Solandt never had Schonland's "old firm hand" in the War Office over Ellis. Some believed he was easily coerced by Ministry of Supply mandarins like Lieutenant-Colonel Nigel Balchin, a rival of Solandt's and future novelist, and others.[36]

But Solandt's wide knowledge, aggressive support for good work, bottomless energy, and engaged personality earned him many supporters. Engineer E.A. Treadwell had worked with Solandt's brother in the 1930s and worked for both Schonland and Solandt at AORG's soil analysis lab. The differences between the inspections the two man conducted are revealing. When Schonland visited the soil lab, Treadwell recalled, they were given advance warning and cleaned things up so that it was fit for a brigadier's inspection. But they were often left uncertain what exactly he wanted from them, leaving the lab with little direction.

Solandt, by contrast, would arrive unannounced to see the lab in action. The staff found him a keen supporter of the lab's work, so long as the research was in step with AORG's strategic outlook as decided on at the control meetings. Solandt's approach meant that Treadwell and company always had to be on their toes and working at their best, since they never knew when the "boss" might drop in. Treadwell, like Sargeaunt, felt that Solandt's broad knowledge and appreciation of science and technology made him one of the best superintendents AORG ever had.[37] Sargeaunt argued that Solandt's great strength as Deputy Superintendent had been in administering and managing the growing sections of AORG. Indeed, he was better suited to this than Schonland, whose keenest interest was in radar and AA work. Solandt's wider interests and efficient management "tightened" AORG's scattered sections and provided him with insight into their research that was, as Treadwell described, personal and enthusiastic.[38] Solandt also had no illusions about the abilities or machinations of Balchin and other War Office mandarins. Perhaps Swann mistook his quiet Canadian demeanour for naïveté. Omond Solandt was many things, but he was rarely naïve.

For his subordinates, however, Solandt had one huge weakness compared to Schonland: he did not have access to Prime Minister Churchill and his cabinet.[39] Schonland was a friend of General Jan Smuts, the former South African prime minister, and Smuts was a good friend of Churchill. Many felt that this political patronage had helped gain support for AORG.[40] From working with Charles Best, Solandt knew the value of working with the policy "big shots" or "operators." So he cultivated powerful friendships and connections as best he could. Cockcroft, his old friend from Trinity Hall, was one ally. Solandt's friendship with Sir Robert Watson-Watt, Scientific Advisor to the Air Ministry, allowed him to cut bureaucratic red tape. Sargeaunt recalled Solandt's strong relationship with Colonel M. Bond and the Directorate of Armoured Fighting Vehicles, themselves powerful forces in the War Office.[41] Solandt also secured support from Brigadier Robertson,

Deputy Director of Research (DDR), who was interested in Nabarro's work on lethality of weapons.[42] Still, Solandt was outside the "inner ring" of power in Britain.

AORG and the OR Sections Abroad

Before leaving for 21 Army Group, Schonland had established OR sections that would be used during the coming battles in France. AORG provided most of the scientists. The exception was physics professor Major Patrick Johnson, who had been working at Petersham. Johnson, a friend of Schonland's, would lead No. 2 ORS. The teams were picked by Schonland after consultation with Johnson and Solandt.[43]

The relations between AORG and ORS after D-Day generated the only major controversy during Solandt's tenure as Superintendent.[44] Schonland had promised Solandt that AORG members would be allowed to conduct research in the field and that he would ask the Chiefs of Staff to invite the AORG members when the time was right. Solandt maintained close contact with Schonland throughout the Normandy campaign. He was happy to send any staff Schonland might require, knowing full well he might lose some of his best scientists.[45]

Months passed, and the Normandy campaign ran its course. No requests for AORG scientists arrived, and no ORS reports were being sent to Ibstock Place, Solandt's headquarters near Richmond Park. By August, Schonland was arguing that he did not have the authority to send the reports and that Ellis or a senior rank should be contacted to initiate any AORG staff heading to 21 Army Group.[46] By September, Nabarro and others were prodding Solandt and Schonland about getting data from the field. Solandt had learned at Lulworth that battlefield data were priceless to good OR. Ministers and colonels could dismiss field tests with some disdain; it was harder, if not impossible, to argue against data taken from the army's combat experience. Such data from the North African campaign had helped Solandt push the Ministry of Supply to take seriously his changes to tank design. They would likely prove even more valuable in the wake of the Normandy campaign, yet this critical source of data was flowing at a mere trickle. What limited information Solandt got from the battlefield came from personal correspondence with Tony Sargeaunt, who was in No. 2 ORS. All the while, the War Office was pressing Solandt to use more operational data at AORG.[47]

Feeling pressure from above and below, Solandt pushed Schonland to request that AORG staff visit France to study German long-range guns and fire control.⁴⁸ He also sent an uncharacteristically harsh letter to Schonland in early October 1944. No real OR had yet been done in 21 Army Group, Solandt claimed. That was a poor choice of words. Solandt's desire for operational data—the bedrock of OR, the kind that generals and politicians could not dismiss—got the better of his tact.⁴⁹

Schonland, fighting illness, was responsible for both OR sections in 21 Army Group. In fact, those sections had conducted large amounts of research that generated many reports ranging from casualty analyses and enemy firepower analyses to air power analyses and more.⁵⁰ Naturally, Schonland responded angrily to this jibe. "What the hell is biting you?" He then scolded Solandt, discussed all the positive work done by each OR section notwithstanding the difficulties that they and he had faced over the past two months in an army that did not want them, and stated that it was only now possible for him to summon an analytic team from AORG.⁵¹ Both Schonland and Solandt had faced resistance from British units regarding the need to send scientists to observe them either in training or in action. Solandt had sent Captain Laurie Chute to North Africa to collect battle data from the campaign, and Chute remembered well how he had been met with disdain by soldiers and officers, who viewed all scientists and other observers as "just another bloody tourist." But their minds changed when the results of their data collection and analysis, and subsequent policy changes, produced positive results for the front-line soldier. Schonland had seen first-hand the positive work done by the ORS teams in Normandy, and he found Solandt's comments distasteful and wrong.

Brian Austin's excellent biography of Schonland does not follow the dialogue beyond this point and thus leaves an unbalanced impression of Solandt.⁵² We know, however, that Solandt continued the dialogue, his own anger and frustration still evident though now kept in check. Schonland, Solandt reiterated, had told him that AORG would be "the direct servant" of 21 Army Group through him. Solandt was to visit every month, and most of the senior AORG people would be invited over for various jobs. "You personally told most of them this. I did not believe this ideal could be achieved for some time but some of the others did." Solandt's own patience was now being tried by scientists who expected him to fulfill Schonland's promises.⁵³

What little information AORG had received had been about Johnson's poor conduct and about interference with Schonland's attempts to support the ORS teams in the field. "Since then there has been no news from and no reply to an intervening letter asking if you would object to us trying to get [AORG scientist] Varley over to look at German coast guns," Solandt wrote. "Can you blame us for being a bit fed up?"[54] Solandt had managed to stay in the loop with Sargeaunt, though Swann had never returned his letters.[55] Then Solandt got to the heart of the matter—the increasing demand for battlefield data and its relevance to AORG:

> Briefly, it is just what always bit you so hard when you were here. The overseas people expect us to supply our best people on no notice at all for jobs that we know nothing about and we then hear nothing at all about anything that goes on. You know that if you were in my place you would be madder than I about the inefficiency and muddling of Sc.1., which blocks what little contact we might have with you e.g. Chapman says that you have written him telling about Sargeaunt's work and what he needs in the way of assistance. You did not mention this in your letters to me although you presumably want a person from AORG and, in fact, under the present scheme the man will remain on our staff on loan to you. You know from bitter experience that things do not pass through the WO with any speed or certainty.[56]

In the end, peace was restored between the two men. Solandt, once he finally received a large batch of ORS reports, was very impressed.[57] He revealed that his initial negative impressions of the teams were based on Schonland's own letters before any reports had been made available: "Maybe you did not realize how depressing your first letters were."[58] By March 1945, Solandt had established effective liaison with the ORS teams, but little else. For this, he blamed Johnson, who had replaced Schonland as SA at 21 Army Group when General Smuts requested Schonland's return to South Africa to begin critical scientific work. Johnson had really let AORG down, never forming a strong working relationship between the ORS and AORG.[59] Solandt hoped that the increase in AORG staff overseas might force Johnson's hand, though his opinion of Johnson never changed. For Solandt, Johnson was a charming man and a fine teacher, but also a poor leader and a worse evaluator of quality research, and he could be absolutely "pig headed and reactionary."[60] The feeling was mutual. According to Johnson, whenever Solandt visited, he "seemed more of a bore than ever."[61] Schonland became the repository for their mutual distaste, getting an earful from both men throughout his last days with the British Army in the field. Despite the cross words, Solandt and Schonland maintained a positive and collegial relationship long after the war, discussing defence research matters relevant to both Canada and South Africa, such as scientific personnel exchanges and possible job opportunities.[62]

India and Burma and the Future of Science and War

Solandt's time at AORG was not without career frustrations. Not only was he passed over for Schonland's position as Montgomery's Scientific Advisor, but he also failed to secure the position of Deputy Scientific Advisor to the Army Council, in part because illness prevented him from applying his full efforts against the near Byzantine intrigues of his rivals.[63] With the defeat of Germany imminent, however, he was soon tasked with a field assignment that would finally allow him the chance to do some "boots on the ground" research himself. In early 1945, convinced that the war in Europe would soon be over, Ellis and Paris decided to send joint representatives to India and Burma to work with South East Asia Command (SEAC). Solandt was the man for the job.[64]

He left on 1 May with Major Macklen of Ellis's staff and spent a month travelling through Egypt and India. Their primary task was to survey the OR sections in Asia and provide advice on expanding and improving them. Solandt also attended a conference on 20 May held by Brigadier Welch on the future work of ORS and user trial establishments (UTE) as well as on postwar plans. He witnessed trials by UTE on their method of work and experiment, then visited the Ordnance Laboratories at Awnpore on 21 and 22 May, then returned to various sections of GHQ in New Delhi before heading home on 29 May.[65] Solandt returned home with data on how OR and the UTEs operated in an environment so different from that of Europe.[66]

Two reports were produced. Solandt himself authored "Science in the Army in India"; and both he and Macklen contributed to the formal report "Army Operational Research in South East Asia." While generally positive about OR in India, Solandt's paper allowed him the opportunity to critique his own organization. The report is critical of AORG's structure—which had been a result of its ad hoc, wartime creation—and provides suggestions about future OR and other science organizations within the military. Clearly, Solandt had carefully thought-out ideas about wartime and postwar research organizations.[67]

According to the formal report by Solandt and Macklen, OR in SEAC should be organized to avoid the many organizational pitfalls in AORG. India should have an SA directly under the Commander in Chief and should have access to all branches of the army; furthermore, the SA should not focus his efforts on research. His main duties should be to stay in close contact with scientific progress in universities, industry, and the service; offer scientific advice to the CinC; develop a staff that included "forward thinkers" who could assess the feasibility of new scientific ideas; and maintain a staff of specialists in key scientific disciplines. He should also have an Army OR group as a self-contained organization under SA direction, similar in structure to AORG; this body would include field sections.[68]

The report emphasized any future organization's need for independence and freedom of thought. These themes reappear in Solandt's postwar science writings, so in the report they likely came from him. If independence was not achieved, their research would suffer from the same political ruin that Solandt had experienced on MRC committees and at the Ministry of Supply. So, the SA's organization should be responsible to an independent body such as the Privy Council. While these suggestions related to the army, "many of the problems affecting the future of the Army cannot be separated from those of other services. Close collaboration between the scientists in the three services should be championed. An inter-service research team to study problems of mutual interest should be formed. Personal contact between scientists in different services should be encouraged."[69]

The formal report outlined the history and structure of OR sections within the Allied Land Force South East Asia (ALFSEA). It praised the OR units, whose problems were particular to their theatre. Still, they suffered problems similar to those of other OR units in the field. For instance, Brigadier Welch had never met the Army Commander. There was little interservice work and too rigid control of the scientists. There was also an OR Division at HQ of Supreme Allied Commander South East Asia Command (SACSEA) under Mr. T.W.J. Taylor that coordinated OR and scientific advice on planning problems. Direct contact with senior commanders was crucial to the success of OR:

The division consists of a head with a small personal staff and attached representatives from the operational research organizations of the three services. The Division coordinates Operational Research in the three services and also acts as a means whereby the results of Operational Research are brought to bear on future planning. Through this division operational research has a direct channel of approach to the Supreme Commander which does not exist in any other theatre. This facilitates the effective use of the results of operational research.[70]

Though he did not know it at the time, Solandt's conclusions on the future use of science by the military paralleled the emerging vision in Canada for postwar defence research. When Solandt returned to Canada in 1945, he brought with him these conclusions, where they became the strategic and structural framework for the Defence Research Board.

From AORG to SEAC

While in India, Solandt met Lord Louis Mountbatten at South East Asia Command HQ Kandy[71] and his scientific adviser Dr. Taylor. Mountbatten "asked for me to go out to replace Taylor. I have agreed to go and hope to go out there about Sept. 1." The War Office agreed, and Solandt was to be made a brigadier.[72] Before leaving, Solandt contributed to discussions on the future of AORG, arguing against the various machinations of Dr. H.J. Gough and Ellis.[73] He "violently" opposed the splitting up of separate sections between the War Office and the Ministry of Supply, but to no avail. For this development, he blamed old rivals in the War Office.[74] Solandt also contributed reports on the postwar use of OR in the Directorate of Scientific and Industrial Research[75] and on creating an industrial physiology research group for the MRC. Both emphasized the need for OR-type teams to be able to quickly conduct research.[76]

During the final AORG "Conversazions" [sic],[77] Solandt led two tours of the establishments for "the common herd" as well as the elite. During the former, he made a "very unpopular speech emphasizing the need for independence in operational research." The arguments echoed those of his India report. The future organization needed the backing of top people, such as General Pile. They required young scientists full of enthusiasm "prepared to attempt the impossible and free from pre-conceived ideas and from the dogma of the army." All branches of science should be represented and encouraged. And they should foster an independent and impartial attitude. AORG had often acted as arbiter between weapons designer and user and had never been accused of having its own agenda. "Independence is absolutely essential to the maintenance of impartiality." This was due to the Ministry of Supply "allowing us freedom even to the point of criticizing other departments of the ministry and partly to vigorous ways in which Brigadier Schonland[78] repelled any attempts to encroach on our freedom."[79] Solandt summed up his thoughts of future army science management:

> I think that these three essentials must be maintained in any post-war organization. You can supply the first essential - support in high places. The second can be maintained by making arrangements for a steady flow of young scientists from the government research establishments, the universities, and from industry. The third can probably best be maintained by having the work of scientists guided by a committee appointed by some independent scientific body [such] as the Royal Society.[80]

As he knew it would, Solandt's speech upset his civilian masters so much that they made "mildly rude" comments about it. He was not concerned. After all, he thought he was right.[81]

For Solandt, the war ended with both disappointment and opportunity. While denied the position of Scientific Advisor to 21 Army Command, he led an investigative mission on the use of Operational Research in India and Burma. His report revealed many observations on science management that he would employ as Chairman of Canada's Defence Research Board after the war. While there, he was selected to become the SA to Lord Louis Mountbatten's South East Asian Command (SEAC) as soon as a replacement could be found for the commander's ailing scientific adviser. SEAC cabled him after VE-Day to depart for the Far East no later than 1 September 1945. On 31 August this order was cancelled. Atomic bombs had been dropped on Hiroshima (6 August) and Nagasaki (9 August), and by 15 August the formal war with Japan was over. Solandt had few regrets in his life, but failing to serve as Scientific Advisor to Mountbatten, a theatre commander who championed science, was one of them.[82]

This disappointment was fleeting. Ellis informed him that the War Office was sending a mission to Japan to investigate the effects of the atomic bomb. Solandt's experience and medical training made him an ideal candidate for the team. Would he like to join? He had also been contacted by the Canadian government regarding the possible opportunity of becoming scientific adviser to the new Chief of the General Staff in Ottawa, Lieutenant-General Charles Foulkes. Would he accept the job?

There was no question about Japan. It was a rare and important opportunity to witness the only atomic battlefield of the war. He was less certain about Canada. He wrote Schonland:

> If I go back to Canada I will be sorely tempted to give up Physiology and stay on the military or administrative side of science—what do you think of it? I have grave misgivings but feel that I will be better qualified for administration than for research after another year of it. I would very much value your advice on what sort of job you think that I should look for.[83]

Schonland's response is not known, but in the end, Solandt chose Canada. For six years he had applied his mind and energies to the challenge of directing science for war. His reward for this was a rise in prominence within British scientific, military, and government circles the likes of which he would not have not attained in his chosen profession of physiology. While his pioneering work in OR was heralded, his years at AORG solidified his reputation as a highly effective, if aggressive, manager of government science. It was in this role, rather than research, that his career would reach its apex. AORG had provided him with the means to excel at what would be his greatest endeavour: managing complex science organizations for military needs. But such experiences were not without the sting of failure. The difficulty in maintaining a clear and direct link with the OR sections in the field stayed with him long after the war, as did the limitations on his influence because of his outsider status as a Canadian and a civilian. He also did not have a firm and direct route to the corridors of power in London, as Schonland had.

Solandt would carry both his successes and his failures at AORG into his role as chairman of Canada's first peacetime defence research organization, the Defence Research Board. These lessons would become part of the structure of the organization and the style of his leadership. As chairman, he would be a full Chief of Staff with an equivalent rank of lieutenant-general and would have access to all the ministers, including the Minister of National Defence. When Solandt championed the sending of OR teams to Korea, he made sure the DRB did not fall out of the loop when the army sent the Canadian Army Operational Research Team (1—CAORT) into the field, and he maintained clear lines of communication between the team and the DRB.[84] In short, AORG, and indeed all of Solandt's wartime experiences, provided an excellent education for Canada's premier military science czar of the postwar era.

Notes

1. Terry Copp, ed., *Montgomery's Scientists: Operational Research in Northwest Europe, The Work of No.2 Operational Research Section with 21 Army Group, June 1944 to July 1945* (Waterloo: Laurier Centre for Military Strategic and Disarmament Studies, 2000).
2. Maurice Kirby, *Operational Research in War and Peace* (London: Imperial College Press, 2004), 86–184.
3. Brian Austin, *Schonland: Scientist and Soldier: From lightning on the veld to nuclear power at Harwell: the life of Field Marshal Montgomery's scientific adviser* (London: London Institute of Physics, 2003).
4. See Austin, *Schonland, passim.*
5. P.M.S. Blackett, "Scientists at the Operational Level" (1941), reprinted in 1948 in "Operational Research," *Advancement of Science* 17 (1948), collected in *Studies of War: Nuclear and Conventional* (Edinburgh and London: Oliver and Boyd, 1962), 169.
6. The original "circus" included such scientific luminaries as physiologists D.K. Hill, son of A.V. Hill, and A.F. Huxley, physicists A. Proter and F.R.N. Nabarro, astrophysicist H.E. Butler, general physicist I. Evans, and surveyor G.W. Raybould. Latecomers would include physiologist L.E. Bayliss and mathematicians A.J. Skinner and Miss M. Keast. Many of these would be critical members of Solandt's AORG team. Austin, *Schonland*, 212.
7. Ibid., 215.
8. Schonland's rise in operational research is well covered by Austin's biography. See ibid., 224–26.
9. Ibid., 251.
10. UK The National Archives [TNA], WO 291/22, "Reconstitution of Operational Research Group, Ministry of Supply," 26 January 1943.
11. Jason S. Ridler, "State Scientist: Omond McKillop Solandt and Government Science in War and Hostile Peace, 1939–1956," PhD diss., Royal Military College of Canada, 2009, 29–66.
12. Ibid., 98.

13 See Omond Solandt interview by David Grenville, 9 September 1985, Part IV. All Grenville interviews were provided by the author.
14 At the Defence Research Board, Dr. Cecil Law was always impressed with this approach. Solandt would always be interested and ask terrific questions, but he left it to the establishments to get the job done, and done well. Solandt had no tolerance for poor performances or sloppy research. Cecil Law interview by Jason Ridler, 27 May 2007.
15 Tony Sargeaunt interview by David Grenville, 4 December 1985.
16 From Austin, *Schonland*, 251.
17 The control meetings were important but infrequent affairs. Few of their minutes have been found. They were attended by representatives of the senior scientific organizations within the War Office and the Ministry of Supply. Among them was Cockcroft and Solandt's Cambridge friend Lieutenant-Colonel Owen Wansbrough Jones, representing the Directorate of Special Weapons and Vehicles, War Office. See TNA WO 233/22, Minutes of the Control Meeting, Army Operational Research Group, 9 September 1943.
18 The third meeting on 20 May 1943, where he announced he would work with Lieutenant-Colonel Nigel Balchin at the Directorate of Ballistics Research (DBR) on laying and firing of the 17-pounder gun. That day they also discussed the revised plan for sending OR sections abroad, likely music to Solandt's ears. TNA WO 233/22, Minutes of the Third Control Group Meeting, Army Operational Research Group, 20 May 1940.
19 Solandt interview by Grenville, 9 September 1985, Part IV.
20 Frank Nabarro, section head for AORS 7, was making the same salary as a graduate student in peacetime, roughly 600 pounds, despite the importance of his work and the size of his staff, often with military members receiving much higher salaries. With Solandt's intervention, wages improved, but never to Solandt's satisfaction. He blamed in part the "bastard" nature of AORG having two parents as much as Schonland for the state of affairs. Solandt interview by Grenville, 9 September 1985, Part IV.
21 L.E. Bayliss and Humby acted as his deputies, though it is unclear if this was an official position. Solandt only mentioned his deputies in September 1944, and there is no indication he had a deputy until then. Laurier Centre for Military Strategic and Disarmament Studies, Wilfrid Laurier University [LCMSDS], Ronnie Shephard Archives [RSA], Letter from Solandt to Schonland 25 September 1944; Imperial War Museum [IWM] Basil Schonland Papers, 86/63/01 draft of article "Some Recollections of my Time with 21st Army Group," n.d. OR scientist Dr. Ivor Evans believed Bayliss to have been deputy to Ratcliffe at Petersham, then to both Schonland and Solandt at AORG. IWM Ivor Evans Papers, Box P426, file A2/A2, letter from Evans to Mrs. J.B. Alton, 28 February 1978.
22 E.A. Treadwell interview by David Grenville, 8 December 1985, University of Toronto Archives [UT], Omond McKillop Solandt Fonds [OMS] B93-0041/31, file: UK AORG Correspondences and Reports, "Operational Research" written for the final AORG Coversations, 26–27 July 1945.

23 O.M. Solandt, "Observation, Experiment, and Measurement in Operational Research," *Journal of the Operational Research Society* 3, no. 1 (February 1955), 1–14.
24 See Solly Zuckerman, *From Apes to Warlords 1904-46. An Autobiography* (London: Hamish Hamilton, 1978), passim. J.G. Crowther and R. Whiddington, *Science at War* (London: HMSO, 1947; reprinted 1948), 99–113.
25 Kaye interview by David Grenville, 18 September 1985.
26 Treadwell interview by David Grenville, 8 December 1985, Part II.
27 Solandt interview by David Grenville, 8 September 1985, Part II.
28 UT OMS B93-0041/0031, Address to U of T Convocation, 1954.
29 E.A. Treadwell interview by David Grenville, 08 December 1985.
30 LCMSDS, WSA, Letter from Solandt to Schonland, 21 December 1944.
31 "Not only was this condition met but I was also made a full member of the Chiefs of Staff Committee so had no possible excuse for failure." UT OMS 0041/31, file: International Symposium on Military Operational Research. "Notes for an After Dinner Address by O.M. Solandt," 4 September 1986.
32 Austin, *Schonland*, 260–70.
33 UT OMS 0041/31, file: International Symposium on Military Operational Research, "Notes for an After Dinner Address by O.M. Solandt," 4 September 1986.
34 LCMSDS, RSA, Solandt to Schonland, 13 September 1944.
35 UT OMS 0041/31, file: International Symposium on Military Operational Research, "Notes for an After Dinner Address by O.M. Solandt," 4 September 1986.
36 LCMSDS, RSA, Transcription of interview with Lord Swann by Terry Copp, 1989. On Solandt's "weaker hand," see IWM, Basil Schonland Papers, 86/63/01, letter from DMZ Lewis to Schonland, 26 April 1946.
37 E.A. Treadwell interview by David Grenville, 8 December 1985.
38 H.A. Sargeaunt interview by David Grenville, 4 December 1985.
39 Churchill was both Prime Minister and Minister of Defence.
40 Treadwell interview by Grenville, 8 December 1985, Part II; Sargeaunt interview by Grenville, 4 December 1985, Part II; Solandt interview by David Grenville, 14 March 1990.
41 Solandt interview by Grenville, 13 November 1985.
42 LCMSDS, RSA, Letter from Solandt to Schonland, 12 August 1944.
43 IWM, Basil Schonland Papers, 86/63/01, draft of article "Some Recollections of my Time with 21st Army Group," n.d. For Solandt, Johnson was affable but a useless OR team leader. His team succeeded despite, not because, of his leadership. According to Solandt, Schonland agreed with him, but he could not remove Johnson unless he found him a position of equal significance. Omond Solandt interview by David Grenville, 8 September 1985, Part I.
44 Solandt interview by David Grenville, 8 September 1985, Part I.
45 Solandt said that while AORG set up an OR section for India, they lost three men to it that had only recently been recouped. LCMSDS, RSA, letter from Solandt to Schonland, 12 August 1944.
46 LCMSDS, RSA, letter from Schonland to Solandt, 13 August 1944.

47 UT, OMS, B93-0041/0031, file: UK AORG Solandt and OR in 21st Army Group. Sargeaunt to Solandt, 26 July 1944 and 25 September 1944.
48 LCMSDS, RSA Solandt to Schonland 6 September 1944.
49 He wrote to Johnson about the need to get Sargeaunt back to Lulworth so that the tank section could be put back on the right lines. LCMSDS, RSA, letter from Solandt to Johnson, 16 October 1944.
50 Copp, *Montgomery's Scientists*, passim.
51 This exchange is well described in Austin, *Schonland*, 289–90.
52 Austin also does not note that Schonland also apologized for having the AORG scientists waiting so long. LCMSDS, RSA, letter from Schonland to Solandt, 7 October 1944.
53 LCMSDS, RSA, letter from Solandt to Schonland, 25 September 1944.
54 Ibid.
55 Ibid.
56 Ibid.
57 LCMSDS, RSA, letter from Solandt to Johnson, 16 October 1944.
58 LCMSDS, RSA, letter from Solandt to Schonland, 12 October 1944.
59 UT OMS B93-0041/0031, file #11, letter from Solandt to Schonland, 4 March 1945.
60 UT OMS B93-0041/0031, file #11, letter from Solandt to Schonland, 26 March 1945.
61 LCMSDS, RSA, letter from Johnson to Schonland, 14 May 1945.
62 Solandt often sought his old boss's advice, including on whether or not he should accept Canada's initiative to run a peacetime defence research organization, and also attempted to secure Schonland work in Canada should he be interested. UT OMS B93-0041/0031, file #11, Letter from Solandt to Schonland, 5 September 1945.
63 Ridler, "State Scientist: Omond McKillop Solandt," 118.
64 UT OMS B93-0041/31, file: U.S. Army Tripartite Operations, "Army Operational Research in South East Asia," n.d.
65 Ibid.
66 The itinerary of the trip included visits to Q ALFSEA, Barrackpore, the OR sections at 14th Army HQ in Meiktilla, Burma (9 May), SEAC HQ, Kandy (15 May), GHQ I in New Delhi (May 16–17), and Dera Dun (May 19). He also attended a conference held by Brigadier Welch on future work of ORS and user trial establishments (UTE) as well as postwar plans (20 May). He witnessed trials by UTE on their method of work and experiment, then visited the Ordnance Laboratories at Awnpore (21–22 May), before returning to various sections of GHQ in New Delhi and then heading home (29 May). UT OMS B93-0041/31, file: U.S. Army Tripartite Operations, "Army Operational Research in South East Asia, Appendix B, Itinerary," n.d.
67 This included the SA not being a member of the Army Council, but being under the Deputy Chief of the Imperial General Staff; two different parent organizations for AORG; and the separation of the ORS teams in Europe from AORG.
68 UT OMS B93-0041/31, file: US Army Tripartite Operations. "Science in the Army in India," n.d.
69 Ibid.

70   UT OMS B93-0041/31, file: U.S. Army Tripartite Operations, "Army Operational Research in South East Asia."
71   Ibid.
72   LCMSDS, RSA, letter from Solandt to Schonland, 6 June 1945; letter from Sargeaunt to Solandt 2 February 1945.
73   UT OMS B93-0041/0031, file #11, Solandt to Schonland, 4 September 1945.
74   Balchin was amazingly competent, Solandt felt, but a "menace" in his own way, putting across things to Ellis that they had not fully considered. UT OMS B93-0041/0031, file #11, letter from Solandt to Schonland 4 September 1945.
75   UT OMS B93-0041/31, file: UK AORG Correspondence and Reports, letter from Solandt to Sir Edward Appeleton, 9 October 1945.
76   UT OMS B93-0041/31, file: UK AORG Correspondence and Reports, letter from Solandt to Lansborough Thomson, 9 October 1945.
77   These were annual get-togethers that included informal reports for AORG. Started by Schonland, the meetings were celebratory in nature but also dealt with highs and lows. The "Conversations" pamphlet included words from the Superintendent, jokes and songs, and observations on the organization and its goals for the next year.
78   Solandt apologized to Schonland for not putting 21 Army Group on a higher plateau but felt that Schonland had not been there long enough to make the same mark he had with AA command. UT OMS B93-0041/0031, File #11, letter from Solandt to Schonland, 4 September 1945.
79   UT OMS B93-0041/0031, file #11, letter from Solandt to Schonland, 4 September 1945.
80   UT OMS B93-0041/31, file: UK AORG Correspondence and Reports, "Operational Research" written for the final AORG Coversations, 26–27 July 1945.
81   UT OMS B93-0041/0031, file #11, letter from Solandt to Schonland, 4 September 1945.
82   Mountbatten was considered a pro-science theatre commander, having utilized scientists, both good and bad, while operating the Combined Operations Headquarters. See Zuckerman, *From Apes to Warlords*, 150–71.
83   UT OMS B93-0041/0031, file #11, letter from Solandt to Schonland, 5 September 1945.
84   Ridler, "State Scientist: Omond McKillop Solandt." Passim.

10
Wartime Military Innovation and the Creation of Canada's Defence Research Board

Andrew Godefroy

No one can foresee how history will judge this century but it is not too difficult to put down on paper some of the things for which we shall be remembered. Among the more important of these the men and women of the future will, I am sure, record that our generation were the first to apply science to warfare on an organized basis.

—Dr. J.J. Green, Defence Research Board[1]

During the Second World War, Canada's defence scientists and engineers played a central role in some of the most secret and advanced research and development programs in modern history. These projects included, but were not limited to, the development of guided weapons systems, jet propulsion, radar, atomic energy, and chemical and biological warfare.[2] Appreciating the value of having such military capabilities as well as advancing them further in the postwar era, the Canadian federal government began to put in place a permanent Defence Research Board (DRB) capable of making salient contributions to ongoing Western alliance security requirements.

The decision by the Canadian government to pursue what had become commonly referred to as "big science and technology" during the war and afterwards permanently displaced the traditional scientific and engineering communities in the country, shifting them from relative isolation to, in some cases, the very centre of Canadian politics and security. Such moves demonstrated the country's emerging innovation and modernity, which affected traditional representations of the Dominion as capable of producing only raw resources and simple materials. It also signalled the resolve of the country's defence organizations to remain a salient actor in the postwar era, capable of engaging in all aspects of modern warfare to defend Canada and its interests. But before that could happen, the Department of National Defence (DND) first had to weigh its options and consider how exactly it would organize for postwar defence research and development.

Organizing National Science Programs

At the end of the First World War, Canada's national science program remained largely undeveloped. The annual expenditure on government laboratory research was approximately $1 million; of nearly 2,400 leading Canadian firms, fewer than forty had dedicated research laboratories. Industry spent less than $150,000 annually on research and development.[3] The National Research Council (NRC) had been founded in 1916 to direct national scientific research and development, but its early postwar years were plagued with political rivalries and with competition from Canadian universities for whatever scarce government funding existed at the time.[4] The situation improved somewhat during the interwar years, however, with a notable but limited increase in dedicated federal funding and scholarships tendered through Canadian universities by the NRC.[5] Scientific human resources also increased slowly during this period, though a number of Canadian scientists continued to travel to the United States in search of new ideas, research challenges, and gainful employment. Though interested in scientific development, the federal government remained reluctant to devote significant resources or support to research beyond that already ascribed to the NRC in the NRC Act of 1924.

The detached relationship between science and government in Canada was drastically altered during the Second World War. The National Resources Mobilization Act (NRMA) of June 1940, designed to concentrate all of Canada's resources on the defeat of the Axis powers, collected nearly all of the country's scientists within the NRC and its ancillary departments. There, they were provided with funding and resources unlike any previous assistance ever received from the federal government, giving them the ability to expand rapidly the country's scientific capabilities and potential for defence research. Between 1938 and 1945, federal government research and development expenditure increased sevenfold, from $4.9 million to $34.5 million, or roughly 0.3 percent of the gross national expenditure.[6] This investment decreased somewhat after the hostilities ended, but by then the massive influx of wartime funding and effort into centralized research and development had forever altered, thanks to defence, the traditional relationship between science and government in Canada.[7]

As well, the war created an environment that allowed prominent scientists, such as NRC president Dr. Chalmers Jack Mackenzie, to join the upper ranks of decision makers in Ottawa.[8] A close personal friend of the Minister of Trade and Commerce, Clarence Decatur Howe, Dr. Mackenzie exerted an influence over the direction of Canada's national science efforts during and after the war that his profession had never previously enjoyed. Though this relationship was not comparable to the one between British Prime Minister Winston Churchill and his wartime science adviser, Dr. Frederick Alexander Lindemann, Dr. Mackenzie's personal access to C.D. Howe and the innermost circles of the wartime government allowed him and his fellow scientists and engineers to enjoy unprecedented power and status within Canada's scientific community.[9] One example of this status may be found in the NRC annual report of 1944–45. Almost twenty years after its inception, the organization explicitly noted for the first time that among its major functions was to act as "advisor to the various departments of government, particularly those of National Defence, Munitions and Supply and Reconstruction."[10] Such was the result of gaining access to the inner ring of science and government.

Mackenzie was not the only technocrat to emerge from the scientific shadows during this period. Other notable scientists and engineers advising government at the time were John Cockcroft, scientific director of the Anglo-Canadian atomic projects at Montreal and Chalk River; Everitt George Dunne Murray, director of Canada's biological warfare program between 1941 and 1945; Omond Solandt, a leading expert in Second World War operational research and the first director general of Canada's post-war DRB; and George Wright, a prominent influence in Canada's wartime explosives and propellants programs.

Yet as the tide of the Second World War turned in favour of Canada and its allies, it remained uncertain whether the end of the conflict would return Canadian scientists into isolation from the government, or if they would remain heavily involved in postwar nation building. Any longevity for national scientific research would depend greatly on the creation of a solid postwar policy for science in Canada. Realizing this necessity, the government, the military, scientists, and industrial leaders met even before the end of hostilities to consider the potential options. The main concerns were policy, program development, human resources, and funding.

In February 1944, Mackenzie presented a paper to the Engineering Institute of Canada (EIC) that outlined the basic requirements for a successful future national science program.[11] First, he argued that it was essential to retain the best Canadian scientific personnel in Canada after the war. Second, the government would have to continue expanding its financial support for national research programs; for example, salaries for scientists, engineers, and technicians would need to be increased and restructured in order for scientific research to remain a competitive career path. As well, industrial research needed to be encouraged, perhaps through liberal tax policies and reimbursements for technological developments made available to the public. Third, in order for the above to succeed, the various government branches and departments focused on Canadian research and development would have to be better coordinated. Finally, Canadian research needed to be refocused at war's end from a program of purely military application to a balanced peacetime program that encompassed both defence and civilian interests. If all this could be accomplished, Mackenzie argued, then Canada might see itself become a world leader in science and technology.[12]

In mid-1944 the senior leadership within the DND also began meeting to consider the issue of postwar defence research in Canada. It was obvious that once the war ended, a large portion of the military scientific corps would request their release from uniformed service and seek civilian employment elsewhere. To ensure that some form of defence research program continued, Air Vice-Marshal Ernest W. Stedman, the Director General of Air Research (DGAR), recommended that a permanent cabinet committee on research for defence be formed under a chair nominated by the government. The idea was endorsed by the Cabinet War Committee and later approved by Cabinet on 3 October 1944. The committee would be chaired by C.D. Howe and would include the three armed service chiefs of staff, the NRC's president, two representatives from industry, and two other civilian members. Cabinet again concurred on the composition as recommended and approved the terms of reference for the defence research committee on 10 August 1945, one day after the atomic bombing of Nagasaki.[13]

Ten days after the committee's terms of reference were approved, Lieutenant-General Charles Foulkes was appointed the Chief of the General Staff (CGS).[14] General Foulkes had commanded the 2nd Canadian Division in Normandy and the 1st Canadian Corps in Italy, and he appreciated how much new technologies had changed the nature of war. Foulkes required no convincing that peacetime defence R&D would be crucial to Canadian defence planning. Just over a week after he assumed office, he directed his staff to prepare an appreciation of the organization required for defence research. His immediate concern was that if defence research were left to the three services, then the duplication of effort, interservice political rivalries, and reduced postwar defence budgets would together seriously impede the advancement of any capability. Simply put, he felt that Canada's military scientific effort was too vital a thing to be influenced and squandered by the three services.[15]

The committee considered many options for organizing postwar defence research. One suggestion was to remove all activities and resources from the army, navy, and air force and use them to create a military division within the NRC under the executive oversight of a Director of Defence Research. Foulkes discussed this option with Mackenzie, but the NRC president was reluctant to accept any oversight for Canada's postwar defence research programs. Although the NRC had assumed this responsibility in wartime, Mackenzie was anxious to return the NRC to fundamental research activities applicable largely to the civilian sector.[16] Mackenzie also argued that even though the NRC had substantial resources, the financial and administrative responsibility for defence research was large enough that it ultimately would require its own dedicated funding and staff. This decision proved later to be a blessing.[17]

The result of the meetings between Foulkes and Mackenzie was the realization that neither the armed forces nor the NRC was the appropriate vehicle for directing Canada's postwar defence research. Another solution was needed instead. Further analyses from within the DND produced a number of options, the most provocative of which were a series of recommendations from Colonel W.W. Goforth, head of the Directorate of Staff Duties (Weapons). He suggested that instead of attempting to wrap defence research activities around existing structures, DND should create a completely new defence research agency headed by a representative at the Chief of Staff level.

Colonel Goforth's proposal found immediate favour with the CGS, who in turned passed it on to the three service chiefs for their consideration. They too agreed to the concept in principle, and armed with that consensus, Foulkes's staff prepared a memorandum outlining the proposal for submission to the Cabinet Committee on Research for Defence.[18]

This committee met only once, at C.D. Howe's office on Parliament Hill on 4 December 1945. Among those present were the NRC president, C.J. Mackenzie; the CGS, Foulkes; the Minister of National Defence, the Honourable Douglas Charles Abbott; the Secretary of the Privy Council Office, Wing Commander A.M. Cameron; and a small number of Foulkes's military staff.[19] The committee reviewed Foulkes's memorandum in detail and agreed that research for the three services would be coordinated under a single Director General for Defence Research and that the person occupying the office should be a civilian with scientific training. Furthermore, since the suggested course of action only required some reorganization within the department, no cabinet approval was required to implement it. All that was needed was an order-in-council authorizing the appointment of a Director General of Defence Research. Then a subcommittee composed of Mackenzie and the chiefs of staff agreed on a list of potential appointees to the newly created position. The committee expected that the position would be filled in short order, and with that, the immediate future of defence research in Canada was all but determined. With nods and smiles all around the room, C.D. Howe adjourned the committee meeting.

In a show of efficiency that could hardly be repeated today, after the meeting had adjourned but before everyone had left Howe's office, someone put forward the idea that a suitable candidate might be Colonel Omond McKillop Solandt, a senior Canadian operational research analyst who had recently been appointed Chief Scientific Advisor to Lord Louis Mountbatten. A graduate of the University of Toronto, Colonel Solandt was both a scientist and a qualified medical doctor who had completed his graduate studies at Toronto's Banting and Best Department of Medical Research. In 1938 he had gone to Cambridge, where he worked under Sir Joseph Bancroft. When the war began, had Solandt held several senior appointments in medical research in England.

Later on, his work on physiological problems related to tank personnel led to his appointment as Deputy Director of the British Army's Operational

Research Group, which he went on to command in May 1944. In early 1945, Solandt was appointed to Lord Mountbatten's staff, but soon after was reassigned as a member of the Joint Military Mission sent to Japan to evaluate the effects of the atomic bombs used against Hiroshima and Nagasaki. He had returned to England later that year after completing his research, but not being a career soldier, it was expected that he would likely resign from military service and return to civilian employment. This, as well as his education, background, and experience both in administrative duties and in wartime operational research, made Solandt an excellent candidate for the position.[20]

The armed service chiefs, who were also still in the minister's office, concurred with the recommendation. Another conversation, this one between Foulkes and Dr. Charles Herbert Best at the University of Toronto later that afternoon, confirmed the nomination. Ten days later, on 14 December 1945, the Minister of National Defence submitted the draft order-in-council for the reorganization of research and the position of Director General of Defence Research. The Privy Council officially approved his request on 28 December. Colonel Solandt was then informed of his new assignment, and arrangements were made for his immediate repatriation to Canada. The first phase in the creation of the Defence Research Board was complete.

Science and Security

By the end of the Second World War, science had delivered to the Western allies, among others, the ultimate "winning weapon" in the form of the atomic bomb. Yet even before the end of hostilities, a supposed wartime ally, the USSR, had stolen the secret for this device along with many other Western technological advances that would undoubtedly have given the United States and the West an early strategic advantage.[21] The discovery of these activities would shape an increasingly cold relationship between the East and West for decades to follow.

More often than not, the Soviet weapon of choice in cultivating Western technological secrets for the Soviet Union was the scientist or engineer. Smart, innovative, and conscientious, many Western scientists and engineers working in wartime defence projects feared the potential destructive power they had developed. Soviet agents often encouraged these lamenters, already burdened by their conscience, to "share" their knowledge with the Soviet

Union in the false hope that by doing so they would help create a balance of power in the postwar world. In fact, such activities proved ineffective in creating a cooperative post-1945 scientific environment, were disastrous for Western security, all but eliminated the West's temporary military technological lead over the Soviets, and ultimately placed the entire Western allied scientific community under many years of close surveillance, suspicion, and prosecution by their own governments and security agencies.[22]

Canada's scientists were not immune from such pressures. The defection of cipher clerk Igor Gouzenko from the Soviet Embassy in Ottawa on 5 September 1945, and his subsequent detention and interrogation, revealed that a number of Canadian public servants, including several prominent scientists working with the National Research Council, may have been spying for the Soviet Union.[23] Canadian officials deemed the allegations so serious that Norman Robertson, the Under Secretary of State for External Affairs, immediately reported the defection directly to Prime Minister Mackenzie King.[24] Out of all the alleged security leaks revealed by Gouzenko, King took particular interest in those related to breaches in Canada's defence research. He noted in his diary on 7 September 1945:

> [Robertson reported] that everything was much worse than we could have believed ... In our Research Laboratories ... where we had been working on the atomic bomb there is a scientist who is a Russian agent. In the Research Laboratories in Montreal ... there is an English scientist who is ... acting as a Russian agent.[25]

Dr. C.J. Mackenzie was notified immediately of the spies in the laboratories, and security experts were brought in to further investigate suspects now under surveillance.[26] Arrests were made in February 1946; this was followed by the convening of a Royal Commission on Espionage. A series of treason trials followed in which the defendants were various individuals whose names had appeared in documents that Gouzenko had brought to Canadian authorities.[27] In addition, several other scientists not named in the Russian papers were placed under surveillance as distrust and paranoia swept through the Canadian scientific community.

Besides all of this, Canadian authorities investigated a number of related organizations, such as the Canadian Association of Scientific Workers

(CAScW). Defence scientists associated with such organizations often had their security clearances "temporarily" revoked, or they were simply denied any new clearance and access to restricted projects. Membership at the CAScW dropped dramatically, as did that of other unions working in or with the defence research community. Worse, perhaps, scientists and engineers who were not members of such organizations were encouraged not to join if they wished to retain their employment. The Gouzenko affair proved disastrous for organized scientific labour.

The history of these investigations and their outcomes has already been well explored in other academic literature. It is important to note here that the scientist spy scare and the potential theft of restricted technology emphasized two critical points for the Canadian government.[28] First, as historian Donald Avery noted, "By the summer of 1946 Canadian military planners no longer considered war with Russia a remote possibility." The side that had the better long-range bombers, rockets, and atomic bombs would likely win.[29] Second, given that this and other technology was very likely to be the key to victory in any future conflict, Canadian national security had to encompass the organization and protection of strategic research and development.[30]

Creating the Defence Research Board

Scientific and technological innovation would be crucial to Canada's postwar defence and security, but transforming this concept into reality would require a serious commitment to the objective. Such commitment did exist, interestingly, in two men who would be critical to the process: the man chosen to become Director General of Defence Research, Colonel Omond Solandt, and the incoming Minister of National Defence, the Honourable Brian Brooke Claxton.[31]

Both Claxton and Solandt understood that scientists and engineers would have little influence on Canada's Cold War military modernization unless DND created internal positions that would serve as advocates for new scientific concepts. Furthermore, the effective management of defence science would require leadership and authority similar to what was enjoyed by the admirals and generals who commanded the armed services. Despite orders from the prime minister to get tough with the department and begin the massive postwar reduction of Canada's armed forces, Claxton remained committed to ensuring that defence research had the proper leadership, was adequately organized and manned, and received proper support and funding. As discussed below, senior-level support would be critical to getting past the many obstacles placed in the way of the DRB's creation.

While the NRC struggled to extricate itself from the growing scientist espionage crisis, Solandt began organizing and activating the DRB. From very modest temporary accommodations on Slater Street in Ottawa, he and his tiny staff of four, including a First World War veteran from the Veteran's Guard of Canada, compiled initial budget and manpower estimates, as well as a plan for reviewing all existing and contemplated future defence research projects, from which recommendations would be made regarding the future research directions. In February 1946, Solandt submitted a request to the Treasury Board for an initial budget of $1 million for defence research within the War Appropriations of 1946–47, over and above the $14 million request already submitted by the R&D programs of the three services. The funds were to help create the initial facilities and staff with which to complete the survey of Canadian defence research during that year.[32]

As happens with any new organization, challenges and growing pains from all quarters beset the DRB as DND began shifting ownership of defence research towards it. Plans to use the entire year of 1946 to complete a survey and assess the status and future direction of defence research in Canada were abruptly curtailed when the Cabinet Committee on Defence made a hurried request to Solandt for a comprehensive policy paper on the subject no later than the end of April. The sudden announcement of an informal conference on Commonwealth defence science in London, England, in June 1946 demanded that Canada be prepared to table some form of policy during this event, but the government had not yet even agreed on the basic principles that such a policy might contain. Regardless, there was little time to spare, and after a concentrated effort, on 17 April 1946, Solandt produced a draft paper for review titled *Policy and Plans for Defence Research in Canada*. The document was discussed in detail at a meeting of the Chiefs of Staff Committee on 30 April.[33]

The first draft brought a generally cool reception from the committee, particularly from the Chief of the Air Staff, Air Marshal Robert Leckie.[34] Although he appreciated the advantages of having some form of centralized defence research organization, Leckie imagined it being more administrative in nature and less directly involved in specific projects than the policy suggested. He and his technical staff were concerned that the proposed organization for the DRB was too ambitious and that the suggested authority it would have over each service's research and development would be too much. The other service chiefs agreed: the DRB could be responsible for all defence research and development, but the services wanted control over their respective areas of expertise. This was particularly the case for the RCAF, which had a particular agenda and was already planning the development of jet engines and an all-Canadian designed and built fighter aircraft.[35]

The three service commanders gave no ground on the issue of agenda control, and for a moment it seemed that the DRB's future was in doubt. As the meeting concluded, the members concurred only that a revised draft agreeable to all parties should be prepared as soon as possible. Solandt returned the following week with a new version of the policy paper, but even with the revisions, only part of the new policy was unanimously approved.[36] A final version was approved and forwarded to the Cabinet Committee on Defence shortly after 14 May.[37]

Divided into three parts, the policy paper emphasized a number of key points that would shape the future of defence research in Canada. First, Solandt was firmly against any form of static organization that might rotate around Ottawa and its government bureaucracy. While acknowledging that Canadian efforts were not large enough to support separate establishments for research, for development, and for production, he did recommend that DRB facilities combining these functions be located throughout Canada to best take advantage of its geographical situation in support of research projects. The choice proved both very popular and successful. Solandt later reported: "When we were planning the Defence Research Board establishments after the war we definitely decided we were going to put them right across Canada, and looking back now it was a very wise decision."[38]

The DRB estimated that general war with the Soviet Union or its allies was at least a decade away, and as such it could focus on long-term research and development without concerning itself too greatly with immediate requirements. The intention was always to develop a completely independent defence research capability in Canada; the short-term plan for achieving this was to concentrate on those areas where Canada had important original ideas or special interests, facilities, or resources to devote to a research problem.[39] To retain access to information on research that the DRB was not directly engaged in, Canadian military and civilian personnel were attached to other defence research facilities in the United States and the United Kingdom, where they acted as liaison officers and observers. A final part of the policy paper, dealing with the scope of Canadian defence research, recommended that the DRB concentrate primarily on research while distancing itself from the engineering, design, and development stages of defence projects. The policy suggested that the actual design and construction of projects could even take place outside Canada. This point in particular upset the RCAF's senior leadership again, for they had every intention of strongly controlling the research and development of their next generation of aircraft, and were reticent to turn it over to a new Canadian defence research organization, let alone some foreign agency. Any thought of foreign control was anathema to every part of the RCAF agenda, and the air staff soon let its concerns be openly known.[40]

The official history of the DRB, published in 1958, suggests that the Air Staff were never comfortable with the idea of relinquishing control over their research and development organizations and facilities and that they continued to try to amend Canadian defence science policy so that they could retain some authority over their own integral assets. This attitude does not appear to have changed after the departure of Air Marshal Leckie in 1947; the Air Member for Technical Services, Air Vice-Marshal A.L. James, was likewise strongly focused on complete RCAF control over any future development of Canadian jet aircraft and weapon systems.

This highly contentious and politically sensitive issue, and its overall implications for the long-term health of the DRB, deserve further consideration. The DRB's official history and subsequent recorded interviews with Solandt suggest that his motive for pushing his particular policy was so that he could prevent defence researchers from becoming immersed in the administration and bureaucracy of seeing a research project through to completion. By allowing his scientists and engineers to focus on a small number of long-term projects that might take several years to reach the design stage, Solandt could help them pursue pure scientific research rather than military scientific applications. While such research programs provided scientists with a free environment to chase their own interests, later federal commissions studying government reorganization considered them irrelevant. Ultimately, the DRB's intent to restrict its efforts in application contributed to the untimely disbandment of the organization in the early 1970s. There simply was no political appetite to spend tax dollars on science for the sake of science. Taxpayers expected science for the sake of application.

The Commonwealth Conference on Defence Science, held in London in June 1946, marked the first public announcement of Canada's postwar defence science policy. Despite having been overtaken by events back home, Solandt and the Cabinet Committee on Defence had created a sound baseline document in a very short time that was well received by Canada's allies. At home, the new policy prepared the ground for a permanent DRB staff and for the transfer of army, navy, and air force R&D establishments to its authority. By the end of the year, the DRB had established its Personnel Selection Committee under the direction of Dr. Otto Maas and had made arrangements to retain the services of other valuable scientists already employed elsewhere within the DND.[41] Finally, the CGS initiated the legislation required to revise the 1927 National Defence Act (NDA) to include the Defence Research Board. Despite continued resistance from the RCAF on various details, the legislation went before the newly appointed Minister of National Defence, Brooke Claxton, on 20 January 1947. The bill went before the House of Commons on 7 February and proceeded through the required three readings without any great discussion or debate. On 28 March 1947, the amendment became law. The DRB had finally achieved legal status and authority.[42]

Getting Science Organized

The DRB's initial organization clearly reflected its mandate and intent to become the centre of gravity for defence science and technology in Canada. Under Solandt's chairmanship, it began as a loosely organized collection of advisers, laboratories, sections, stations, and research establishments scattered across the country. As an equal to the Chiefs of Staff and adjunct to the Deputy Minister of National Defence, Solandt had two deputies, a Deputy Director General and an administrative deputy directly supporting him. His immediate counsel also included a secretary of the board, scientific advisers from each of the three services, a project coordination section, and liaison offices in London and Washington. The DRB chairman also oversaw the Directorate of Research Personnel and the Directorate of General Services, each of which supported the many other similar organizations under his stewardship.

Under the aegis of the DRB were a number of highly focused organizations. Existing facilities transferred to the DRB included the Canadian Armament Research and Development Establishment (CARDE), the Suffield Experimental Station (SES), the Defence Research Chemical Laboratories in Ottawa, the Kingston (biological warfare) laboratory, the Radio Propagation Laboratory (RPL), the Defence Research Establishment at Churchill, Manitoba (renamed the Defence Research Northern Laboratory in 1947), and the Naval Research Establishment. Additional smaller cells also brought under DRB control included the Weapons Research Section, the Electrical Research Section, the Special Problems Research Section, the Biological Research Section, the Naval Research Section, and the Scientific Intelligence Section. Additionally, the DRB formed or co-chaired a number of advisory committees both in its own armed services as well as cooperatively with other Western allies.

At its formation, the DRB's various organizations employed roughly 1,000 personnel, including 200 scientists and engineers and between 30 and 40 technical officers. In 1947 and 1948, the government spent approximately $4 million on defence research and development, an amount that quadrupled in 1948–49 when materials, supplies, equipment, and salaries were added to the existing budget. Defence research expenditures continued to increase between $7 and $10 million a year through to 1956–57, a clear indication of the strong commitment made to defence science and technology by Canada during the early years of the Cold War. More important perhaps, the DRB's creation clearly signalled Canada's intent to take its own defence and security requirements seriously.[43]

The Role of Defence Science and Technology
Current scholarship on the strategy and security of the Cold War devotes considerable attention to the scientific and technological drivers that shaped its evolution, but only those actors and activities originating in the United States, Britain, and the Soviet Union are generally well known, studied, and popularized. The Cold War actions of other countries, such as Canada, are much less recognizable to the public and historians alike. This is disconcerting, especially as Canada's defence research establishments played a central if not altogether unique role in protecting the West from Soviet political and military technological aggression.

Canada worked aggressively to safeguard its postwar sovereignty through a robust and self-centred national security policy. While the country supported the ideals of multilateralism and collective security through the newly created United Nations, it also ensured that its own security interests were met through regional or bilateral security arrangements.[44] Canada joined other Western nations in the North Atlantic Treaty Organization (NATO) in 1949 and actively sought to strengthen its bilateral defence and production ties with the United States throughout the early 1950s. Even growing anti-American political rhetoric did not deter the government from solidifying a North American Air Defence (NORAD) agreement with the United States in 1957, or from allowing American-designed nuclear weapons into the country soon after. It is important to note as well that the success of many of these and other Cold War security arrangements depended on the active development and sharing of advanced defence science and technology between Canada and the United States.

Canadian strategic planners, like those of its allies, actively considered how science and technology might play a role in security. The DRB emphasized those research areas where Canada's military research was strong and where it could achieve and sustain success.[45] Those technologies and associated research included some if not all of the most dangerous elements of future Armageddon—namely rocketry, missiles, biological agents, chemicals, and even atomic weapons.

Given the potency of Canada's arsenal at the end of the Second World War and its considerable investment in postwar defence science, it is somewhat surprising that greater academic attention has not been paid to the subject. Historians James Eayrs, Jon McLin, Brian Cuthbertson, Joseph Jockel, Sean Maloney, and Andrew Richter have focused on the strategic, political, and policy aspects of some of these weapons of mass destruction, but they make little note of the scientific and technical aspects of the period.[46] Perhaps Canadian historian Carl Berger's assessment is largely correct when he notes that "literature on the history of science in Canada has concentrated on those features of it that were comprehensible to historians who lacked any formal training in the field."[47] Whatever the case, it is certain that political and diplomatic history rather than science and technological history has been the focus in analyses of Canadian Cold War national security. So besides the political and security assessments provided by the historians mentioned above, it is important to examine the defence research aspects of Canadian national security, with particular attention to the role played by the DRB, which served as the lead agency during the early Cold War.

Conclusion

Canada's senior military leadership appreciated before the end of the Second World War what impact that science would have on the future battlefield, and it acted quickly to put in place the required mechanisms for a sustained postwar defence research establishment. Though not initially palatable to the three services and though often clashing with their own agendas during its early stages, the DRB still managed to assert its place within the defence community as a valuable and at times vital partner in the security and defence of Canada. This article has attempted to capture those decisions that led to the creation of the DRB, while also proposing that much more inquiry is required to fully understand the influences and relationships between Canadian research and defence during the first decades of the coldest and potentially deadliest confrontation the globe had ever witnessed.

Notes

1. J.J. Green, "Science and Defence," *Canadian Aeronautical Journal*, April 1955, 3.
2. Current histories of Canadian science in the Second World War include Donald H. Avery, *The Science of War: Canadian Scientists and Allied Military Technology During the Second World War* (Toronto: University of Toronto Press, 1998); and John Bryden, *Deadly Allies: Canada's Secret War, 1937–1947* (Toronto: McClelland and Stewart, 1989).
3. D.J. Goodspeed, *A History of the Defence Research Board of Canada* (Ottawa: Queen's Printer, 1958), 6; see also Michel Girard, "The Commission of Conservation as a Forerunner to the National Research Council, 1909–1921," in Y. Gingras, and R. Jarrell, eds., *Building Canadian Science: The Role of the National Research Council. Scientia Canadensis* 15, no.2 (Ottawa: Canadian Science and Technology Historical Association, 1991), 19–40.
4. P. Enros, "'The Onery Council of Scientific and Industrial Pretence': Universities and the Early NRC's Plans for Industrial Research," in Y. Gingras, and R. Jarrell, eds., *Building Canadian Science: The Role of the National Research Council. Scientia Canadensis* 15, no.2 (Ottawa: Canadian Science and Technology Historical Association, 1991), 41–52.
5. Y. Gingras, *Physics and the Rise of Scientific Research in Canada* (Montreal and Kingston: McGill-Queen's University Press, 1991); for this period see also M. Thistle, *The Inner Ring: The Early History of the National Research Council of Canada* (Toronto:

University of Toronto Press, 1966); and W. Eggleston, *National Research in Canada: The NRC 1916-1966* (Toronto: Clarke Irwin, 1978).
6   A. King et al., *Reviews of National Science Policy: Canada* (Paris, OECD, 1969), 43. See also Department of Reconstruction and Supply, *Research and Scientific Activity: Canadian Federal Expenditures, 1938-1946* (Ottawa: King's Printer, 1947).
7   Ibid., 42-45.
8   C.J. Mackenzie CC, CMG, MC, FRSC (1888-1984) was an engineering graduate of Dalhousie University (1909) and a decorated veteran of the First World War.
9   The relationship between Churchill and Lindemann is described in C.P. Snow, *Science and Government* (Cambridge, MA: Harvard University Press, 1961). For details on relationship between Howe and Mackenzie and the rise of scientific influence in wartime Canada, see G. Bruce Doern, *Science and Politics in Canada* (Montreal and Kingston: McGill-Queen's University Press, 1972), 4-49.
10 NRC, *Annual Report: 1944-45* (Ottawa: King's Printer, 1945), 7.
11 C.J. Mackenzie, "Industrial Research in Post-War Canada," paper presented to the EIC at Quebec City, 11 February 1944.
12 Goodspeed, *A History of the Defence Research Board of Canada*, 12.
13 Ibid., 13-16.
14 Lieutenant-General Charles Foulkes C.B., C.B.E., D.S.O. (1903-1969). General Foulkes joined the Royal Canadian Regiment in 1926 and went on to command 2nd Canadian Infantry Division and, briefly, II Canadian Corps in Normandy. Later he commanded I Canadian Corps in Italy. In 1945 he was made Chief of the General Staff, a position many had assumed would go to General Guy Simonds.
15 Goodspeed, *A History of the Defence Research Board*, 19-22.
16 Ibid., 21.
17 Unknown to C.J. Mackenzie at the time (1944-45), the NRC was apparently riddled with a number of Soviet spies and other security leaks that might have proved disastrous for the success of Canadian postwar defence science. See Avery, *The Science of War*, 228-55.
18 Ibid., 28-41; see also A.M. Fordyce, "How It All Started: The Goforth Paper," *Canadian Defence Quarterly* 1, no.4 (Spring 1972), 15-16.
19 A complete list of those present is available in Government of Canada, *Minutes of the First Meeting of the Cabinet Committee on Research and Defence, 4 December, 1945*.
20 C.E. Law, G.R. Lindsey, and D.M. Grenville, eds., *Perspectives in Science and Technology: The Legacy of Omond Solandt* (Kingston: Queen's University Quarterly,1994); Goodspeed, *A History of the Defence Research Board*, 45-46; G.R. Lindsay, ed., *No Day Long Enough: Canadian Science in World War II* (Toronto: Canadian Institute of Strategic Studies, 1997), 264-66; and C.E. Law, "Omond McKillop Solandt: Operational Research Pioneer," *INFOR* 31, no. 2 (May 1993). Solandt's personal papers reside in the University of Toronto Archives.
21 Soviet espionage in the West is covered in numerous volumes. Of particular quality and interest to the topic discussed here is C. Andrew and V. Mitrokhin, *The Mitrokhin Archive: The KGB in Europe and the West* (Middlesex: Penguin, 2000).

22. Arguably, there was limited scientific cooperation between East and West in the years after the Second World War. However, scientific and technological intelligence—particularly that related to defence and national security—remained a closely guarded secret. For early Cold War Soviet espionage in the United States, see Alexsander Feklisov, *The Man Behind the Rosenbergs* (New York: Enigma Books, 2001); R. Radosh and J. Milton, *The Rosenberg File* (New Haven: Yale University Press, 1983); John Earl Haynes and Harvey Kehr, *Venona: Decoding Soviet Espionage in America* (New Haven: Yale University Press, 1999); and Mitrokhin, and Andrew, *The Mitrokhin Archive*.
23. For details on this subject, see J.L. Black and M. Rudner, eds., *The Gouzenko Affair: Canada and the Beginnings of Cold War Counter-Espionage* (Manotick: Penumbra, 2006).
24. J.L. Granatstein, *A Man of Influence: Norman A. Robertson and Canadian Statecraft, 1929-1968* (Toronto: Deneau, 1981), 172.
25. Library and Archives Canada [LAC], W.L.M. King Diary, 7 September 1945, cited in Granatstein, *A Man of Influence*, 172.
26. Ibid., 173-74.
27. Avery, *The Science of War*, 228-34.
28. The early Cold War arrests and trials of Canadian scientists have received considerable coverage in a number of publications. See also Reg Whitaker and Gary Marcuse, *Cold War Canada: The Making of a National Insecurity State, 1945-1957* (Toronto: University of Toronto Press, 1994); J.L. Granatstein and D. Stafford, *Spy Wars: Espionage and Canada from Gouzenko to Glasnost* (Toronto: Key Porter, 1990); and J. Sawatsky, *Men in the Shadows: The RCMP Security Service* (Toronto: Doubleday Canada, 1980).
29. Avery, *The Science of War*, 228. Even Norman Robertson and Prime Minister Mackenzie King conceded as early as 10 September 1945 that there was a grave possibility that any future war between the United States and the Soviet Union would likely come through Canada. See Granatstein, *A Man of Influence*, 174.
30. Further notes on early postwar Canadian assessments of the looming Soviet and technological threats may be found in J. Starnes, *Closely Guarded: A Life in Canadian Security and Intelligence* (Toronto: University of Toronto Press, 1998), 76-81. Starnes, who had a long and distinguished career both in Canada's intelligence service and in the Department of External Affairs, made numerous references to the role and importance of defence research in the Cold War.
31. Brian Brooke Claxton (1898-1960). A soldier in the First World War, he was practising law when elected to Parliament in 1940. He became Minister of National Defence on 12 December 1946 and served until 30 June 1954.
32. Goodspeed, *A History of the Defence Research Board of Canada*, 47-49. As previously stated, the intent is not to repeat *verbatim* that which is already well covered in Goodspeed's official history; however, its publication (1948) soon after its intended period of coverage (1945-1956) resulted in both a timely and comprehensive narrative of the DRB during these years and makes it an essential reference for any current discussion on the topic.
33. Ibid., 49.

34 Robert Leckie (1890–1975). A veteran of the First World War, Leckie was an experienced naval aviator with a good fighting record. He was made Director of Civil Flying Operations in Canada in 1919. He returned to the United Kingdom soon after but later came back to Canada to take charge of the Commonwealth Air Training Plan during the Second World War. He transferred to the RCAF in 1942 and became Chief of the Air Staff in 1944. He was succeed by Air Marshal Wilfred Curtis in 1947.
35 Goodspeed, *A History of the Defence Research Board of Canada*, 49.
36 LAC, DND, Chiefs of Staff Meeting, 7 May 1946. See also O.M. Solandt, *Policy and Plans for Defence Research in Canada*, Part II, dated May 1946.
37 LAC, Privy Council Office (PCO), Series A-5-a, vols. 2638, 2639, and 2640, Defence Research and Development—External Policy, Organization of Research for Defence, and Defence Research; Organization of Board, 1946–47. The cabinet decision papers summarize more lengthy memoranda and reports submitted by the Director General for Defence Research and the DRB for review and recommendation to the prime minister.
38 Senate of Canada, *Committee on Science Policy*, No.9 (1969), 1264–65.
39 Goodspeed, *A History of the Defence Research Board of Canada*, 50–51.
40 Ibid., 51n and 58–61.
41 Dr. Otto Maas (1890-1961). A graduate of McGill University, Maas studied in Germany and at Harvard before returning to McGill's Chemistry Department. During the Second World War he directed Canada's chemical warfare and explosives programs. In 1947 he was appointed Director of the Biological and Chemical Warfare Research Division of the DRB.
42 The final process to create the DRB is well covered in Goodspeed, *The History of the Defence Research Board of Canada*, 62–68.
43 Ibid., 109–10. General information on Canadian early postwar scientific research and development expenditures may also be found in A. King et al., *Reviews of National Science Policy: Canada* (Paris: OECD, 1969).
44 Traditional arguments about Canada's early postwar foreign and defence policy development are being actively challenged by new research and scholarship. See A. Chapnick, "Principle for Profit: The Functional Principle and the Development of Canadian Foreign Policy, 1943–1947," *Journal of Canadian Studies* 37, no.2 (Summer 2002), 68-85; and A. Chapnick, "The Canadian Middle Power Myth," *International Journal* 55, no.2 (Spring 2000), 188–206. See also A. Richter, *The Evolution of Strategic Thinking in the Canadian Department of National Defence* (Toronto: Centre for International and Strategic Studies, York University, 1996), 11–35.
45 LAC, RG 19, vol. 520, file 124-62, pt. 1, Defence Research Board, Annual Reports 1947–1949; and LAC, RG 24, Series E-1-b, vol. 5250, file 19-73-4, Defence Research Board—Minutes of Meetings, 1947–1951.
46 For example, James Eayrs' *In Defence of Canada* volumes covering 1945–1955 make only one or two mentions of the DRB, and do not consider the role of science and technology in the formation of national security strategy. Other authors tend to make similar omissions in their own work, including S. Maloney, *Learning to Love*

the Bomb (Washington, D.C.: Potomac Books, 2007); J. McLin, *Canada's Changing Defense Policy, 1957–1963* (Baltimore: Johns Hopkins Press, 1967); B. Cutherbertson, *Canadian Military Independence in the Age of the Superpowers* (Toronto: Fitzhenry & Whiteside, 1977); A. Richter, *Avoiding Armageddon* (Vancouver: UBC Press, 2002); and J. Jockel's numerous publications on Canadian defence policy during the Cold War.

47 C. Berger, *The Writing of Canadian History: Aspects of English Canadian Historical Writing Since 1900* (Toronto: University of Toronto Press, 1993), 212–14.

11

Overlord's Long Right Flank
The Battles for Cassino and Anzio, January–June 1944

Lee Windsor

Matthew Parker's 2004 popular history of the battles for Cassino reveals how deeply entrenched is the view that the Italian campaign made no strategic sense. Parker echoes a generation of writers who see no "unity of purpose driving the forces in Italy. With so many different national and ethnic groups from such radically different societies, it would have been an impossibility." He complains that the coalition of so-called "United Nations" was "riddled at the highest level with distrust and jealousy, with the inevitable consequences of misunderstandings and mistakes." Soldiers unlucky enough to be posted to the Italian theatre were thus "badly led and poorly equipped." Like many historians writing of the war in Italy, Parker's vitriol originates in the strategic decisions that led to Allied soldiers setting foot on the Italian peninsula in the first place—a process fraught with the "stormiest negotiations ever to occur between the western Allies" and that betrayed "serious disagreements about strategy." The final imperfect outcome was less a compromise and more a deception. Parker argues that the Americans were "duped, or led down the garden path" by the imperially minded British.[1]

For critics like Parker, the battles for Cassino symbolize all that was wrong with the Allied war effort in Italy. The bloody five-month struggle for the heights around the famous home of the Benedictine monastic order on Monte Cassino culminated in the liberation of Rome on 5 June 1944. But the city fell months behind schedule and only a day before the Normandy landings on

6 June 1944, after which the Allied armies in Italy faded from view. Parker concludes that "it is hard to reconcile the appalling cost of this diversion" with the arguments of some Allied generals and historians that fighting in the Mediterranean diverted German resources from the Normandy campaign.

It is not surprising that histories of the D-Day landings in Normandy make little mention of the killing grounds at Cassino and Anzio. Instead, the four attempts to break the German Gustav Line defences at Monte Cassino and to outflank them at Anzio from January through to May 1944 are depicted as separate Mediterranean "adventures" that were foiled by skillful and resolute German defenders. Even the final battle that forced the Germans to abandon Cassino in May and Rome in early June 1944 is portrayed as a great opportunity that was squandered through inter-Allied politics. The standard explanation is that the US Fifth Army's commander, General Mark Clark, abandoned Allied plans to encircle the German armies in Italy between Anzio and Cassino, instead turning north to ensure that American troops would be first to reach and enter Rome. Campaign veteran Field Marshal Lord Carver believes that Clark "was determined to get there ahead of the British, whom he suspected of trying to forestall him there."[2] Most histories of 1944 in Italy concur that the Allies failed to make the most of their hard-fought victory south of Rome in May of that year. John Strawson, another campaign veteran turned historian, lamented that as a result of Allied bungling "much of Tenth [German] Army got away to fight more battles" through a second bitter winter in Italy along the Gothic Line, thereby negating the campaign's strategic value in mid-1944.[3]

The view that Cassino and Anzio were German defensive triumphs and symbols of Allied folly resonates with veterans who made it out of those places with their lives. For them the "truth" of Cassino and Anzio was misery, death, and destruction for months on end where one futile assault in impossible winter conditions followed another. New Zealand platoon commander Lieutenant Clem Hollies remembers:

> Our days and nights there were absolute hell. Mortar bombs continued to rain down; we had a nebelwerfer rocket through our roof; and never ending smoke shells meant we lived in a world where there was no day. Our nerves were stretched to the breaking point, hands shaking so much cigarettes were hard to light. Hot meals were impossible, as was washing and shaving.[4]

CBC correspondent Peter Stursberg expressed the frustration of those soldiers he interviewed by describing "failed repeated attempts to take Cassino" as the story of how Mark Clark "frittered away division after division." The troops he interviewed thought that Anzio was "the only landing since Dieppe that had failed" and a ghastly SNAFU.[5]

Nonetheless, an alternative perspective—what could be called a parallel "truth"—exists alongside veterans' memories. Its lead proponent was Field Marshal Sir Harold Alexander, Commander of Allied Armies, Italy (AAI), the Army Group Headquarters responsible for ground and air operations. Alexander long maintained that the five-month struggle at Cassino–Anzio was intimately tied to Operation Overlord and that his troops accomplished their strategic mission of guaranteeing Allied victory in Normandy. Critics dismiss Alexander's description of events as post-mortem justification for poor Allied generalship and failure to reach Rome sooner with fewer casualties.[6] These same critics have judged Alexander to be an adequate diplomat but a less than stellar commander who lacked imagination and "grip" over his subordinates.[7]

In the 1980s newly declassified Ultra decrypts breathed life into Alexander's case. This long-secret signals intelligence source shaped Allied strategy throughout the war by providing information on German formation locations and sometimes their intentions. These documents laid bare how Allied plans for Italy and Normandy were based on understanding how enemy forces would react to any move. Ultra-decrypted intelligence and analysts' reports provide evidence connecting the bloody, water-filled trenches at Anzio and the rock shelters of Cassino to the Normandy beaches on the other side of Europe. In short, Ultra proved Alexander's case that Allied activity on the Italian Front was calculated to convince German decision makers to deploy large forces to southern Europe in 1943–44, away from the Normandy landing area.[8] That strategic mission did not include capturing Rome for its own sake. Indeed, during the fourth and final battle for Cassino, planned for the very eve of the Normandy landings, Allied armies in Italy attacked with the explicit mission of inflicting such severe losses on the Mediterranean Front that the Germans would have to reinforce it from forces gathering in Western Europe and Germany to meet the expected 1944 cross-Channel attack.[9]

The weight of evidence demonstrating how the battles for Anzio and Cassino contributed to victory collides with the brutal experiences of the Allied soldiers deployed there. Parker has little regard for Ultra evidence and instead reflects the collective memory of a generation of Italian campaign writers and veterans who remain unsure whether the blood shed at Cassino and Anzio under Great War-like conditions was worth it. These two interpretations need not be mutually exclusive. In the end, the available evidence suggests that Cassino and Anzio were integral to victory in Normandy, but with a heavy price in blood. Indeed, lining up the strategic benefits against the human costs of Cassino and Anzio may be the best way to understand the largest containment, deception, and attrition mission of the Second World War.

The Italian campaign's mission began to develop in January 1943, two months after the successful Operation Torch landings in French North Africa and four months before the Axis was finally defeated in Tunisia. Roosevelt, Churchill, their political advisers, and the Combined Chiefs of Staff met at Casablanca for a series of strategic planning conferences. The Combined Chiefs acknowledged that priority in early 1943 must be the defeat of the German U-boats. They also agreed to expand the bombing campaign against Germany through the Combined Bomber Offensive to win control of European airspace.

The third question resolved at Casablanca was where the Allies would strike once North Africa was liberated. Sicily was chosen for a variety of reasons tied closely to the primary aim, which was to launch a cross-Channel attack in 1944. The British Joint Intelligence Committee (JIC), the guardians of Ultra intelligence decrypted from intercepted German wireless messages, informed Allied planners at Casablanca that forty-one German divisions stood within range of the proposed Overlord landing area. The Combined Chiefs agreed that this was more German fighting power than they could handle in 1943, and they resolved to put off Overlord until 1944, after German reserve strength was reduced or dispersed. In early 1943, indications grew that Mussolini's Fascist government would likely collapse if one of the Italian home islands was captured in advance of a mainland occupation. If Italy was knocked out of the war, German units would have to replace thirty-four first-line Italian divisions guarding the Mediterranean coast as well as thirty more reserve divisions of uncertain quality. At the very least, such an extension of German strength would drastically limit the number of German formations that could react to Overlord.[10] At best, the Italians might turn en masse against the Germans, creating an even greater threat to the southern flank of Hitler's Reich.

The Sicilian campaign and the September 1943 invasion of Italy produced an effect somewhere in the middle, but still worked well enough that by late 1943, 20 percent of all German forces had been moved to the southern coast of Europe. This southward shift influenced the great battle of Kursk–Orel in the Soviet's favour. The drain on German human and material resources added to demands to feed the Russian Front, fight off the Allied bomber offensive, and maintain the U-boat campaign against Allied shipping. Such a diversion of strength to southern Europe represented a massive chunk of new and rebuilt forces that the Germans were mustering to meet the 1944 invasion of western Europe.[11]

Having drawn the Germans into battle in Italy, the Allies then had to give them cause to stay. The task was made more difficult because the Combined Chiefs of Staff had ruled that the forces in Italy must only be powerful enough to keep up the illusion of a threat to Germany through the south. The Allied armies in Italy could never be given enough men and weapons to ever break through the Alps to Vienna. Although the Americans were eventually convinced of the utility of Mediterranean diversionary operations, from the earliest planning sessions they insisted that sustaining those efforts could not jeopardize the buildup to Overlord.[12]

In modern military language, operations to contain the enemy with minimal resources are labelled "economy of force" tasks. This policy was sound in ensuring that Overlord would have the strength required to succeed, but it condemned those soldiers committed to secondary theatres to difficult, dangerous, and seemingly hopeless fighting to keep pinned down a German force of almost equal size. Italian terrain and weather conditions favoured the defender and helped drain the morale of Allied soldiers, who were convinced that higher powers and people back home had forgotten them. Such sentiments drip from the pages of postwar literature produced by campaign veterans like Canada's Farley Mowat, Fred Cederberg, and Strome Galloway.[13]

The remark of US Army Chief of Staff General George Marshall at Casablanca that he was "most anxious not to be committed to interminable operations in the Mediterranean" are often re-reprinted to show that the Americans were reluctant to commit to operations in Italy.[14] The popular American writer Rick Atkinson is the latest to make this case, stressing Marshall's fear that a campaign in Italy "would establish a vacuum in the

Mediterranean that would suck troops and material away from a cross Channel attack."[15]

Less well known is Marshall's concern that an Italian political collapse might prompt a German evacuation of Italy, leaving a major Allied force stranded in the southern Mediterranean in mid-1943 with no enemy to fight. He fully endorsed landing on the mainland to secure Italy's surrender and to attack German units.[16] Based on the Tunisian experience, Marshall's counterpart and Chair of the British Chiefs of Staff Committee, General Sir Alan Brooke, felt confident that the Germans would fill an Italian military vacuum.

The arrival of German reinforcements in Italy before, during, and after the Allied invasion of the Italian mainland in September 1943 belayed Marshall's concern and fulfilled General Brooke's strategic vision of drawing in and bleeding German reserve strength. During the September fighting around Salerno, thirteen Allied divisions pinned down eighteen German divisions both at the front and in coastal defence. By October 1943, after Hitler's order that his armies hold a line south of Rome, eleven Allied divisions had attracted the attention of twenty-five German divisions in Italy.[17] This figure did not include the two new army groups established to take over Italian defensive duties on the French Riviera and in the Balkans after Italy surrendered. The total German forces moved to the Mediterranean coast and Italian Front in the fall of 1943 rose above forty divisions, plus significant naval and air units to protect southern Europe's coast and airspace.[18]

The Allies had achieved their strategic aim. But the substantial German force in Italy made the most of the weather and the terrain to bring Allied operations to a standstill in the fall of 1943. This conundrum would plague the Italian campaign until its end. If at any point the Germans felt secure in Italy and southern Europe, the Allies ran the risk that enemy divisions might be moved to France to defend against the cross-Channel invasion expected the following spring. But at the same time, Allied senior planners understood that they could not send any reinforcements to the Italian Front in serious numbers because doing so would water down the force that was preparing for the coming decisive battle in Normandy. Nonetheless, the German High Command had to be convinced of the need to maintain large forces in the Mediterranean. On this matter, Marshall and Brooke differed. Brooke wrote in his diary on 27 October 1943 that "plans and preparations for Overlord must not be allowed to slow down operations in Italy which were themselves one of the most important preparations."[19] Marshall was not convinced during the autumn, believing that the limited Allied force in Italy was sufficient to its task to divert and attrit the enemy.

With few reinforcements forthcoming, the Allied armies in Italy had to keep the Germans guessing. Raids, elaborate counter-espionage, and support for French, Italian, and Yugoslav resistance units kept the Germans on guard along the northern coast of the Mediterranean. But Allied leaders also reasoned that they must continue attacking with the same tired and weakened formations, some of which, like the 1st Canadian Division, had been in the line with little respite since landing in Sicily in July.

By the end of 1943, vicious fighting between evenly matched forces in horrific conditions was conjuring up memories of Great War battlefields. In November and December 1943, Eighth Army's bloody offensive on the Adriatic carried it over the Sangro and Moro Rivers, culminating in the ferocious Canadian battle for Ortona. Alarming losses, impassable mud, the natural and man-made strength of the Gustav Line's Adriatic wing, and the absence of any material or numerical advantage for attacking forces convinced General Alexander and the British Eighth Army's commander, General Bernard Law Montgomery, that any large-scale flanking operation around Rome was impossible, at least until spring. At the Gustav Line, the Allies had engaged for the first time a contiguous defensive line echeloned in depth, and the Germans were prepared to hold it by launching immediate counterattacks to retake defensible features.[20] That German policy slowed the Allied advance and cost many Canadian and Commonwealth lives, but it fulfilled the Allies' strategic goal, which was to contain and bleed the Germans.

In the new year of 1944, Alexander switched the full Allied effort to the western portion of the Gustav Line, where the US Fifth Army had reached the last line of hills overlooking the Liri Valley, the invasion route to Rome. The approaches were well protected by strong German forces and by imposing natural barriers like the Rapido-Gari River. The Abbey of Monte Cassino loomed like an ominous sentinel over its opposite bank. As the Fifth Army had found out during the bitter fighting in front of the main battle positions in November and December 1943, the western end of the Gustav Line was every bit as strong and well defended as the Ortona Front. In fact, Allied commanders suspected that the natural and man-made defences and the lack of any appreciable Allied numerical advantage made the Gustav Line impregnable.[21]

The solution was to go around the Gustav Line with an amphibious landing at Anzio that, in combination with a broad attack across the Cassino front, would convince German commanders to withdraw from their prepared Gustav defences into more open terrain where Allied firepower could be brought to bear.[22] Unfortunately, in this shoestring campaign, the available amphibious lift in the Mediterranean was sufficient only to carry three divisions that were already in Italy. The hole left in the line was covered by squeezing the British Eighth Army west, leaving a tiny covering force, including the Canadians, at Ortona.

Plans also changed based on enemy reactions. In mid-January 1944, British forces on the Tyrrhenian coast and French colonial mountain troops in the central Apennines made attempts to outflank Cassino; these succeeded in penetrating the Gustav defences, which forced many of the best German mobile divisions in Italy to counterattack and restore the line.[23] Then on 22 January 1944, the amphibious assault began, during which one British and two American divisions landed in the Anzio-Nettuno area, 30 miles south of Rome. For its first three weeks, Operation Shingle seemed a disaster. The small invasion force could not penetrate beyond a narrow bridgehead, nor could it convince the Germans to abandon their permanent defence line on the Cassino Front, which offered the only permanently defensible space south of Rome. Instead, the Germans despatched reinforcements from elsewhere in Europe. Further British, French, and American attempts to link up with the beachhead were checked, with heavy losses.

Critics of Shingle, including Winston Churchill, suggest that the US corps commander and his subordinates lacked drive and as a result failed to exploit their initial advantage of surprise by driving inland to seize the Alban Hills and the approaches to Rome.[24] Events would spawn Churchill's now famous comment on Anzio: he had wanted a tiger thrown ashore and all he got "was a beached whale." American, British, and Canadian soldiers paid the price for what US official historian Martin Blumenson would call "the gamble that failed."[25]

The fighting around Anzio and Monte Cassino that winter inspired some of the most compelling literature of the Second World War, including Wynford Vaughan-Thomas's *Anzio*, Fred Sheehan's *Epic of Bravery,* and Fred

Majdalany's *Cassino: Portrait of a Battle*. Allied losses on the Anzio beachhead were the highest of the Italian campaign, with some divisions losing all of their front-line fighting strength in a single month.[26] It is no accident that the American Battle Monuments Commission selected Anzio as the site of the larger of the two US war cemeteries in Italy.

But the struggle for Anzio also cost the Germans greatly, for it played on Hitler's fear of an amphibious threat and induced his commanders, not to pull Tenth Army formations from the Gustav Line, but rather to draw south nine divisions from northern Italy, Germany, and western Europe. These forces included a number of first-class mobile panzer and panzer-grenadier formations controlled by Fourteenth Army Headquarters near Rome, which together with Tenth Army formed Army Group "C" under Field Marshal Albert Kesselring. Activated under Contingency Plan Marder I, Fourteenth Army's mission was to destroy the Anzio invasion force and to throw it "back into the sea."[27]

The new units of German Fourteenth Army were hurled into a piecemeal attack on the Anzio bridgehead. In February, Generals Brooke and Marshall grasped that even though Anzio had failed to achieve its original intent, which was to turn the Gustav Line, it had produced a strategic result of far greater import. As German units continued to pack themselves onto the Anzio plain, Brooke wrote in his diary that "ultimately we may score by not having an early easy success. Hitler has been determined to fight for Rome and may give us a better chance of inflicting heavy blows under the new conditions."[28] The German counteroffensive, Operation Fischfang, prevented Allied troops from advancing inland and made their lives worse than miserable. But it also allowed the Allies to coordinate ground, air, and naval firepower to kill vast numbers of the enemy, thereby committing a second German western reserve army to a battle that the Germans could neither afford nor stop. Put another way, Allied Armies Italy was able to hold a full German army group in close attritional combat. The German Fourteenth Army enjoyed none of the advantages found on the Gustav Line and was condemned to fight on a vast expanse of open, flat terrain within range of the large-calibre guns of British and American warships. German targets had often proved elusive during the Italian campaign, yet US logistics planners at Anzio were able to complain "that there were so many Germans to shoot at, and not enough artillery rounds to get them all."[29] Local Italians would come to know the flat open killing grounds north of Anzio as the *Campo di Carne*—Field of Meat.

The problem that Anzio presented for Germany was that its forces were becoming ever more dispersed to meet the demands of a global war. *Oberkommando der Wehrmacht* (OKW) had been building a strategic reserve in western Europe in preparation for the decisive channel battle they fully expected in the summer of 1944.[30] But the German decision to commit Fourteenth Army to destroy the small Anzio beachhead in February 1944, and the failure of that counteroffensive, shrank that reserve and left twenty German divisions locked into an attritional campaign that German strategic planners had sought to avoid. Even the Mediterranean skeptic, General Marshall, realized in early February 1944 that if the Germans were still engaged in large numbers on a broad front south of Rome in April 1944, then the planned invasion of southern France to support the Normandy landings would not be immediately necessary. His fear that the Germans would cut and run from Italy abated.

But at the same time, the commitment of another German army completely equalized the force ratio in Italy in infantry and artillery, thus removing any positional advantage created by landing a corps behind the Gustav Line. Once again the front was threatened with stalemate. General Marshall understood in March 1944 that it was not enough to tie German units to the terrain— they had to be attacked, engaged, and constantly held in action in Italy to keep them away from Normandy in the coming months. He realized that the Germans could recall formations from Italy that were not directly engaged.[31] So bitter fighting at Anzio and Cassino sputtered on through the first three battles at Cassino between January and March 1944.

While Allied riflemen trudged through the cold mud and cursed the Germans' increased resistance, General Alexander recognized the German reaction as something of a blessing for Overlord preparations.[32] In his postwar memoirs he wrote:

> The Führer Order to stand south of Rome proved of positive assistance in carrying out the Combined Chiefs of Staff Directive. If the Germans had adhered to their original intention, it would have been very difficult to carry out my mission of containing the maximum enemy forces; an orderly withdrawal up the peninsula would have required only a comparatively small force, aided

by the difficulties of terrain. Although we had the initiative in operations, the Germans had the initiative in deciding whether we should achieve our object: they were free to refuse to allow themselves to be contained in Italy.

All danger of such an alarming result was removed by Hitler's decision. From the moment of that decision the German Army undertook a commitment as damaging and debilitating as Napoleon's peninsular campaign, the final result of which was that it saw itself next summer [1944] under the deplorable necessity of pouring troops into Italy to retrieve disaster at the very moment when Allied invading forces were storming the breaches of the crumbling West Wall.[33]

On 12 March 1944 the staff at Allied Armies, Italy Headquarters in Caserta alerted the Combined Chiefs of Staff to their related concern that if a spring offensive in Italy forced German retirement too quickly, then the Germans might disengage behind a seven-division covering force, freeing nineteen German divisions either to man the Gothic Line defences in northern Italy or to redeploy to Normandy in the critical weeks prior to the *Overlord* landings.[34]

To address concerns that the Germans might still cut and run, Brooke and the British Chiefs of Staff proposed temporarily diverting French and US divisions in North Africa from their proposed invasion of southern France (Anvil) to Italy. The newly designated commander of the Overlord forces, US General Dwight D. Eisenhower, agreed. By March 1944 both Brooke and Eisenhower had convinced the US and British Combined Chiefs of Staff that Allied forces in the Mediterranean should be temporarily stood down from the invasion of southern France to "concentrate whole-heartedly on bleeding and burning Germans divisions where they had apparently determined to fight to the last."[35] Thus by March 1944, Allied commanders understood the renewed spring offensive in Italy not just as another "attrition and containment" offensive, but as a preliminary supporting attack for Overlord.

The offensive in Italy had been planned for April to allow the US and French divisions time to rest and refit before landing in southern France in late June or July. But weather, terrain, and thickening German resistance forced a postponement to May 1944. At first, the chiefs on both sides of the Atlantic were irritated at what they perceived to be a lack of drive in Alexander's headquarters. However, Alexander was able to convince the British chiefs in London that the sheer size of the German force arrayed against him was

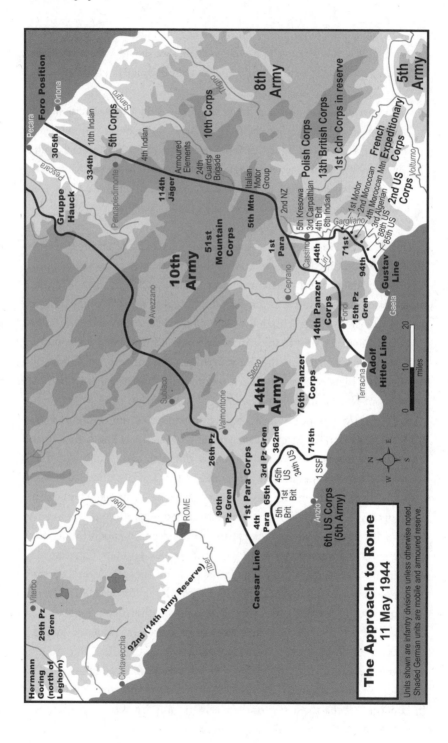

in fact proof of the diversionary success the Allies had achieved in the first three battles for Cassino and at Anzio. If Diadem, the assault on the Gustav Line, was launched with adequate preparations, resources, and dry weather, it would inflict greater damage on the enemy and for a more reasonable Allied blood price than if it were rushed. The larger the enemy casualty count, the greater the potential to lure in and destroy even more German strength.[36] Alexander was more than a dashing Guardsman—he clearly understood his strategic masters' intention to contain German forces in Italy.

The Combined Chiefs subsequently agreed that instead of Anvil, Diadem would serve to divert German strength and attention in the west as Overlord began in June. The Italian campaign was no longer a separate and distinct theatre from the one about to open in northwest Europe. Alexander recognized this synergy and wrestled with difficult morale problems resulting from the relentless challenges posed by the terrain, the weather, and the force ratio. He wanted to go so far as to issue an "order of the day" to his soldiers prior to Diadem outlining how their diversionary task was critical to Overlord's success. Unfortunately for the soldiers in Italy, security concerns kept Alexander's orders vague.[37]

The concept for Operation Diadem was laid down on 25 March 1944. It was to be the largest offensive of the Italian campaign, employing some twenty-seven American, British, Indian, Canadian, French, Polish, and Italian divisions. Its central purpose was to contain German ground, sea, and air strength along Europe's Mediterranean coast. That wider mission included coordinating and equipping resistance movements in southern France, northern Italy, and Yugoslavia in 1944 to stoke German fears of major Allied landings there. Second, Diadem was calculated to inflict so much damage on German armies in the field that the enemy's High Command would be forced to despatch to Italy reinforcements from the limited pool available in western and central Europe.[38] It was deemed so important to match the launch time to the Normandy invasion that documents relating to Diadem were stamped "BIGOT," the security classification reserved for top secret Overlord plans.

With such a purpose in mind, it was important that Rome not be captured too quickly. Before that was accomplished, a significant portion of enemy formations would have to be destroyed in a major battle south of the city, to ensure that they did not withdraw to the Gothic Line farther north. On 2 April 1944, Alexander and his staff outlined how Diadem, also known as the fourth battle for Cassino, would not break through the Gustav Line and make a lightning advance on Rome. Instead, there would likely be at least ten days hard fighting in the Liri Valley to destroy the German Tenth Army and to pull German units from Anzio. Only then would the main American weight strike out of Anzio to threaten the Germans with encirclement and put a smashed enemy to flight.[39]

Diadem opened on 11 May 1944. Even with the extra divisions originally committed to Anvil, the Allies barely mustered a force ratio of 1.5 to 1 in their favour. That compelled nearly a month of hard fighting before the Gustav and Hitler Lines were breached and the link-up made with the Anzio Front. The climactic battle was the largest of the campaign, employing troops from every participating Allied nation, including the 1st Canadian Corps. The encirclement of the main body of the German Fourteenth and Tenth Armies was almost completed, all but for US General Mark Clark's now famous decision to turn left and be the first to Rome rather than follow General Alexander's directive to cut off fugitive German survivors. Despite this notorious command misunderstanding, the offensive was a major strategic success. Rome was captured thirty-six hours before the start of the Normandy invasion.[40]

Vastly more important to Allied strategy than the fall of Rome were the disastrous losses inflicted on German Army Group C. It is worth noting that most German losses came not as they were blasted out of their Gustav and Hitler Line bunkers or Anzio trenches, but as they tried to restore buckling defence lines with repeated counterattacks. The Canadians found this as they fought their way into the midst of the Hitler Line between Pontecorvo and Aquino on 22 and 23 May.[41] Indeed, Alexander's plan for decimating German Army Group "C" depended on wiping out local counterattacks. In this manner, the fighting strength of twenty German divisions was reduced to the equivalent of six.

Ultra intelligence confirmed Brooke's prediction that the Germans were replenishing those losses from reserve strength that otherwise would have been capable of responding to Overlord. The German High Command was desperate to restore the front in Italy well before the Allies reached the unfinished Gothic Line defences, so they moved six divisions from Denmark, Hungary, the Ukraine, and Croatia in May and June 1944. OKW also released tens of thousands of trained soldiers and large quantities of heavy weapons and vehicles to rebuild divisions that had been gutted in the Liri Valley. Large-calibre anti-tank guns and heavy gun tractors were in particular demand to make good those destroyed in the fluid later phase of Diadem.[42] This reallocation came at the very moment that OKW was trying to cope with the Allied invasion of Normandy on 6 June 1944 and the Soviet summer offensive that began sixteen days later.

Recent German scholarship confirms what a minority of senior Allied planners and commanders knew through Ultra in the late spring of 1944. Hitler and his staff concluded in late 1943 that the Allied invasion of the Channel coast offered the only opportunity to concentrate superior force for a knockout blow. If the invasion was defeated in its early stages, the western Allies would be unable to mount another attempt soon, leaving Germany

A Churchill Armoured Recovery Vehicle tows away the wrecked hulks of German Stug III Assault Guns destroyed in a failed counter-attack against the 48th Highlanders of Canada midway between the Gustav and Hitler Lines. [LAC 169082a]

with a free hand to focus on the Soviet Union.⁴³ But this plan broke down. The reserves that Hitler had gathered under Field Marshal von Rundstedt in 1943–44 for a decisive battle against the cross-Channel invasion were repeatedly dispersed to "contain" the Allies in Italy. In this context, Allied operations in Italy may not have conquered territory quickly, but they succeeded brilliantly in furthering the success of Overlord.

Throughout Diadem, General Alexander understood the mission as an attritional battle. At the height of the destruction phase of battle, he wrote excitedly to Winston Churchill detailing the German divisions that had been broken since his assault began. At the end of May he wrote again: "you will have heard by now of the fresh enemy divisions on their way here [to Italy]." Such news was one of the successful conditions for Overlord.⁴⁴

In this context, Allied operations in Italy rarely conquered territory quickly. Except in the imagination of Winston Churchill, who sometimes harboured visions of penetrating the Balkans and reaching Vienna, the Allied mission was never to break out of Italy and reach Germany from the south. Rather, Italy amounted to the strongest piece in a game to convince the Germans that a southern breakthrough was imminent. In the final analysis, our understanding of what was achieved in Italy must change. Many astute soldiers understood that their goal was not to capture Rome and Venice and then Vienna but to destroy the enemy wherever they stood. It was cold and ugly duty that not all who fought there could understand. Nonetheless, Canadian and other Allied soldiers who served in Italy fulfilled their duty as part of a campaign to contain and destroy German forces, enabling their brothers-in-arms in Normandy and Northwest Europe to deliver more fatal blows that ultimately ended the war and German oppression in Europe.

The struggle at Cassino–Anzio is not part of the Normandy narrative. It should be. Histories of the Normandy campaign are incomplete without mention of the elaborate efforts to guarantee the success of Operation Overlord on 6 June 1944. Terry Copp has noted:

> First the Soviets would have to continue to engage the energies of two thirds of the German army. Nothing was more vital to the success of Overlord than a Soviet summer offensive. Second, the elaborate deception scheme code-named Fortitude, designed to reinforce the German army's belief that the real invasion

would take place in the Pas de Calais, had to work. Third, complete air and naval supremacy had to be established.[45]

It is time that history includes the battles of Cassino and Anzio as preconditions in paving the way for Overlord. Those Italian killing fields represented the long right flank for the invasion of Normandy.

Notes

1. Matthew Parker, *Monte Cassino: The Hardest-Fought Battle of World War II* (New York: Anchor Books, 2004), 1–4.
2. Field Marshal Lord Carver, *The Imperial War Museum Book of the War in Italy: 1943–1945* (London: Sidgwick & Jackson, 2001), 204.
3. John Strawson, *The Italian Campaign* (London: Secker & Warburg, 1987), 162.
4. Lt. Clem Hollies, 21st New Zealand Infantry Battalion, interviewed for Lord Carver, *The Imperial War Museum Book of the War in Italy*, 166.
5. Peter Stursberg, *The Sound of War: Memoirs of a CBC Correspondent* (Toronto: University of Toronto Press, 1993), 153–55.
6. General Sir William Jackson, et al., *The Mediterranean and the Middle East*, Volume VI, Part 1: *Victory in the Mediterranean, 1 April to 4 June 1944* (London: HMSO, 1984), 360–61; Strawson, *The Italian Campaign*, 171–72, 195–98; Douglas Porch, *The Path to Victory: The Mediterranean Theatre in World War II* (New York: Konecky & Konecky, 2004), 561.
7. The greatest proponent of this view is Alexander's own biographer. See Nigel Nicolson, *Alex: The Life of Field Marshal Earl Alexander of Tunis* (London: Konecky & Konecky, 1973); see also Matthew Jones, *Britain, The United States and the Mediterranean War, 1942—1944* (London: MacMillian, 1996), 165.
8. F.H. Hinsley, *British Intelligence in the Second World War: Its Influence on Strategy and Operations*, vol.III, pt.1 (London: HMSO, 1984), 198–207, and vol.III, pt.2 (London: HMSO 1988), 307–18.
9. The National Archives, UK [TNA] WO 214/33, Minutes of British COS(44) Meeting #118, "Future Operations in the Mediterranean Theatre," 12 April 1944.
10. Hinsley, *British Intelligence*, vol.III, pt.1, 69–70; Field Marshal Lord Alanbrooke, *War Diaries, 1939-1945*, eds. Alex Danchev and Daniel Todman (London: Weidenfeld & Nicolson, 2001), 281–82.
11. D.M. Glantz and J.M. House, *When Titans Clashed: How the Red Army Stopped Hitler* (Lawrence: University Press of Kansas, 1995), 150; Ralph Bennett, *Ultra and Mediterranean Strategy* (New York: Morrow, 1989), 239; Hinsley, *British Intelligence*, vol.III, pt.1, 103–7.
12. George Catlett Marshall, *The Papers of George Catlett Marshall*, vol.IV, *1 June 1943-31 December 1944: "Aggressive and determined leadership,"* Larry I. Bland, Sharon Ritenour

Stevens, eds., (Baltimore: John Hopkins University Press, 1996), 90; Maurice Matloff and Edwin M. Snell, *Strategic Planning for Coalition Warfare, 1941–1944* (Washington, DC: Department of the Army, 1959), 102.

13 See Farley Mowat, *And No Birds Sang* (Toronto: McClelland and Stewart, 1979); Fred Cederberg, *The Long Road Home* (Toronto: Stoddart, 1984); Strome Galloway, *The General Who Never Was* (Belleville: Mika Pub. Co., 1981).

14 A.N. Garland, *The United States Army in World War II: The Mediterranean Theatre of Operations, Sicily, and the Surrender of Italy* (Washington: Government Printing Office, 1965), 11.

15 Rick Atkinson, *Day of Battle: The War in Sicily and Italy, 1943–1944* (New York: Macmillan, 2007), 13.

16 Matloff, *Strategic Planning for Coalition Warfare*, 1941–44, 126.

17 Bennett, *Ultra and Mediterranean Strategy*, 253; John Ehrman, *Grand Strategy*, vol.V: *August 1943–September 1945* (London: HMSO, 1956) 344; Hinsley, *British Intelligence* vol. III, pt.2, 64.

18 Bennett, *Ultra and Mediterranean Strategy,* 239; Hinsley, *British Intelligence,* vol.III, pt.2, 103–7.

19 Alanbrooke, *War Diaries,* 464.

20 "Operations of 1 Cdn Inf Div and 1 Cdn Armd Bde in Italy, 25 Nov 43–4 Jan 44," CMHQ Report No.165, Historical Section, Canadian Military Headquarters, 27 November 1946, http://www.cmp-cpm.forces.gc.ca/dhh-dhp/his/rep-rap/cmhqrd-drqgmc-eng.asp?txtType=2&RfId=165.

21 US National Archives and Record Administration [NARA] APO 464, HQ US Fifth Army, Report on Cassino Operations, Operation Instructions #11, 24 Nov 1943; #12, 16 Dec 1943; #13, 10 Jan 1944.

22 NARA HQ US Fifth Army, Op Instr#13, 10 Jan. 1944.

23 C.J.C. Molony, *The History of the Second World War: The Mediterranean and Middle East,* vol.V, *The Campaign in Sicily 1943 and the Campaign in Italy 3rd September 1943 to 31st March 1944* (London: HMSO, 1973), 606–30.

24 Strawson, *The Italian Campaign,* 144.

25 See Martin Blumenson, *Anzio: The Gamble That Failed* (Philadelphia & New York: J.B. Lippincott Company, 1963).

26 H.G. Gee, *Battle Wastage Rates, British Army, 1940–1945: Army Operational Research Group, Report No.2/54* (Waterloo: Laurier Centre for Military Strategic and Disarmament Studies, 2010), 13, 42.

27 Hinsley, *British Intelligence*, vol.III, pt.2, 185; Historical Section, Army Headquarters, *The Italian Campaign Jan–June 1944: Information from German Military Documents Regarding Allied Operations,* AHQ Report No.20, 13, http://www.cmp-cpm.forces.gc.ca/dhh-dhp/his/rep-rap/ahqrd-drqga-eng.asp?txtType=3&RfId=209.

28 Alanbrooke, *War Diaries,* 14 February 1944, 521.

29 NARA, *US Fifth Army G-4 Report on Operations in the Anzio Beachhead,* March 1944.

30 Heinz Magenheimer, *Hitler's War: Germany's Key Strategic Decisions, 1940–1945* (Munich: Barnes & Noble Publishing, 1997), 255–71.

31 Marshall, *Papers*, 7 February 1944, 15 March 1944.
32 Bennett, *Ultra and Mediterranean Strategy*, 253.
33 Field Marshal Earl Alexander of Tunis, *The Alexander Memoirs: 1940–1945* (London: Cassell, 1962), 118.
34 TNA WO 214/33, AAI WD CGS Appreciation 12 March 1944.
35 Marshall, *Papers*, Radio 314, Marshall to Eisenhower, 16 March 44; Ehrman, *Grand Strategy*, vol.V, 242–47.
36 TNA WO 214/33, Minutes of British COS(44) Meeting #118, "Future Operations in the Mediterranean Theatre," 12 April 1944.
37 Ibid.
38 Ibid. Presentation by General Alexander to the British Chiefs of Staff Committee.
39 Ibid.
40 Some recent histories of the war in the Mediterranean continue to portray *Diadem* as a failure, but these are generally based on pre-Ultra mainstream narratives of the battle. See Mathew Jones, *Britain, The United States and the Mediterranean War*, 159–65; John Ellis, *Brute Force: Allied Strategy and Tactics in the Second World War* (New York: Viking, 1990) 337–38.
41 Charles Eddy, *Before They Were the D-Day Dodgers: 1st Canadian Infantry Division and Operation Chesterfield*, unpublished MA thesis, University of New Brunswick, 2009, 140–65.
42 OKW–1576 "Report on the Fight for the Apennine Position and the Improvement of the Western Alps Position, 15 August–31 December 1944." National Defence Headquarters, Directorate of History and Heritage, SGR II/255, 10; Alanbrooke, *War Diaries*, 584; Bennett, *Ultra and Mediterranean Strategy*, 294.
43 Magenhiemer, *Hitler's War*, 244–57.
44 TNA WO 214/15, Alexander Papers, Correspondence with Churchill and Alanbrooke, 24 May, 30 May, 6 June 1944.
45 Terry Copp, *Fields of Fire: The Canadians in Normandy* (Toronto: University of Toronto Press, 2003), 19.

12

A Sharp Tool Blunted
The First Special Service Force in the Breakout from Anzio

James A. Wood

On the morning of 30 January 1944, a US Fifth Army messenger tore into the First Special Service Force (FSSF) headquarters at Santa Maria, Italy. He reported that the situation at Anzio was taking a turn for the worse and that US VI Corps desperately needed reinforcements. The Force had been ordered in. As the unit began preparing for a move to the beachhead, the 1st and 3rd Battalions of Colonel William O. Darby's Ranger Force were being shot to pieces in the Pantano ditch, an irrigation canal leading towards the German-held town of Cisterna on the outskirts of the Anzio perimeter. Assigned to spearhead 3 US Division's attack on Cisterna, Darby's Rangers had attempted to infiltrate up the canal during the night, and at daybreak they had been caught in a German ambush. As the situation quickly worsened, the First Special Service Force boarded a small fleet of landing craft bound for the port of Anzio, where it was to take up defensive positions on the right flank of the newly established Allied beachhead. The Force disembarked on 1 February, with its three combat units proceeding to an assembly area overlooking the front lines. By the very next night the Force had taken up its position along the Mussolini Canal.

The First Special Service Force was an elite bi-national commando unit drawn from the armies of Canada and the United States. It arrived at Anzio buoyed by its reputation of recent successes at Monte la Difensa and the Majo line. Formed in 1942 to conduct raids in the alpine regions of occupied

Europe,[1] this elite US–Canadian infantry brigade established a remarkable combat record. Canadian and American soldiers wore the same uniforms, carried the same weapons, and answered to the same superiors; an American private took orders from a Canadian sergeant, who in turn answered to an American or Canadian lieutenant. Their reputation was built on the intensive training they had received at Fort William Henry Harrison in Helena, Montana, and on their remarkable battle success.

The Force was organized into a combat echelon of three regiments, each consisting of two battalions, which in turn were formed by six companies. Canadian and American soldiers were interspersed at all levels of these units. Meanwhile, service support was provided by a battalion with three companies: headquarters, maintenance, and service. The entire unit numbered approximately 2,500 men, with Canadians generally forming about one-third of the enlisted men and half the officers. The Force Commander, Lieutenant-Colonel Robert T. Frederick, was confident of their fighting potential. In a letter to the US Army's Deputy Chief of Staff in February 1943, Frederick boasted that they had "subjected themselves to a course of training more demanding and rigorous than has ever been attempted elsewhere, in order that they might be in top condition for combat [and be] able to withstand severe and difficult conditions."[2]

The FSSF had arrived in Italy on 17 November 1943, during a stalemate in the US Fifth Army's drive towards Rome. They were joining the Italian campaign, originally envisioned by British Prime Minister Winston Churchill as a second front to take the pressure off the Soviets until the Allies could launch their cross-Channel invasion. The Allies had crossed into Italy from Sicily in September 1943 but hopes were by then fading that the British Eighth Army on the east coast and the US Fifth Army on the west would be able to advance quickly to take Rome. For nearly a month, the Allied advance had been bogged down before a belt of fortifications known as the Winter Line, the western portion of the strongly fortified Gustav Line, which the Germans had built to stall the anticipated Allied advance. On 24 November, the Force received orders to capture the summit of Monte la Difensa, a mountain stronghold that had been frustrating the Allied advance since the first week of November. On the night of 1 December, the Force marched ten miles to the base of la Difensa; there they remained hidden throughout the following day. On the night of 2–3 December, the FSSF's

Second Regiment[3] began their six-hour, almost vertical ascent using ropes. After their daring assault up the cliffs on the north face of the mountain, which the enemy had believed to be impassable, the shooting started before dawn with a firefight to secure the summit. Although the German defenders, the veteran 104 Panzergrenadier Regiment, had every advantage of terrain, weather, and experience, the Force held its ground against repeated German counterattacks and artillery bombardments—a six-day effort that cost the Force some 511 casualties, or roughly one-quarter of its total strength.[4] A *New York Times* war correspondent portrayed the intensity of the la Difensa–Camino battle in his report as a "slow tortuous envelopment of numberless ridges and peaks ... The entire tone of the struggle is one of fierce will to resist. Despite severe losses, the German Tenth Army is setting a standard of savage defensive fighting that its opponents will never forget."[5] The capture of Monte la Difensa destroyed a key anchor of the Winter Line and earned high praise from Lieutenant-General Mark W. Clark, the commanding general of the US Fifth Army. Clark extended his congratulations to the Force in December:

> Capturing la Difensa ... was vital to our further advance in that sector. The mission was carried out at night in spite of adverse weather conditions and heavy enemy rifle, machine-gun, mortar, and artillery fire on the precipitous slopes over which it was necessary to attack. Furthermore, the position was maintained despite counterattacks and difficulties of communication and supply.[6]

Following its success at Monte la Difensa, the FSSF was assigned the right flank of the US II Corps advance as it rolled up the German defences in the mountains north of the Mignano Gap, which guarded the entrance to the Liri Valley and Highway 6 to Rome. The area was held by 15 Panzergrenadier Division, reinforced by 29 Panzergrenadier Division. The official *Fifth Army History* recounted: "Howitzers and long-range guns, often self-propelled and usually defiladed behind protecting crests, could reach nearly every area held by our troops. Peaks such as Mount Sammucro ... provided posts from which forward observers could see every movement made by our forces in daylight ... The enemy, safe behind the mountain barrier, could supply his troops with relative ease and could maneuver almost at will to reinforce the ... individual defenses."[7]

By the time the Force was withdrawn from the front on 17 January 1944 for rest and reorganization, casualties had reduced all three of its regiments to approximately half-strength. These losses were particularly devastating to the Canadian portion of the Force, for Canadian officials had decided in March 1943 that the 1st Canadian Special Service Battalion, as the Canadian element of the Force was known, would receive no reinforcements upon departure for overseas.[8] In light of this, and of the fact that the highly specialized unit was "acting in a straight infantry role as shock troops for the Fifth Army,"[9] the acting senior Canadian officer of the Force, Lieutenant-Colonel Thomas P. Gilday, recommended in January 1944 that the Canadians be withdrawn from the FSSF "while there is enough of it left to be of assistance to the Canadian Army."[10]

Thoughts of disbanding the FSSF quickly vanished with the developing emergency at Anzio. Two weeks after Gilday made his recommendations, the Fifth Army messenger rushed into FSSF headquarters at Santa Maria with news of VI Corps' urgent situation at Anzio. Operation Shingle, the Corps' amphibious landing on 22 January 1944, was intended to circumvent the German defences of the Gustav Line and open the way north to Rome. However, Fifth Army's offensive against the lower Gustav Line had stalled, leaving VI Corps at Anzio on its own. Two battalions of Darby's Rangers had been annihilated near the German-held town of Cisterna: of the 767 Rangers who set out on 29 January, only six had returned.[11] The German block of an advance out of the Anzio Front revealed that Italy was hardly "the soft underbelly of Fortress Europe" that Churchill had predicted. Instead, VI Corps had become mired down, trapped in the Anzio beachhead and surrounded by German forces holding the high ground.[12]

On 2 February, the FSSF joined British and American forces in the centre and left sectors of the Anzio perimeter. Its three combat regiments, reduced by high casualties and harsh fighting conditions to just over 1,200 men, relieved the US 39 Combat Engineer Regiment on a 12,000-yard stretch of the Mussolini Canal that represented roughly one-quarter of the beachhead perimeter. Stretched thin, the Force was directed to hold the canal, improve existing defence, and conduct nightly harassing and reconnaissance patrols to force the Germans back and take prisoners. Behind the front, the unit received attachments from the 160th Artillery Battalion, the 465th Parachute Field Artillery Battalion, and a company of tank destroyers to provide fire support. Opposing the Force were elements of the Hermann Göring Panzer Division.[13]

Even as it rose to meet the difficult tactical challenges of the Anzio beachhead, the Force was having difficulties recovering from its recent fighting in the mountains. In the five months between arriving at Anzio to its seizure of the bridges of Rome, the Force achieved legendary status as "the Devil's Brigade," but it had also moved closer to being disbanded. Ironically, the Anzio-to-Rome segment of the FSSF's history was about to make clear that the same elements that underlay its effectiveness would ultimately lead to its demise. A fierce but brilliant combat performance against stubborn enemy forces, combined with its legendary Canadian–American structure, was by the winter of 1944 creating both a reinforcement crisis and administrative entanglements. By the end of February, the Canadian element numbered only 27 officers and 339 other ranks—roughly half its assigned strength.[14] American replacements had come up in January and been trained at Santa Maria. Meanwhile, personnel recovering from injuries suffered in December and January were beginning to filter back to the unit from both Canadian and American hospitals, but they were only slightly in excess of the numbers being killed and wounded on the beachhead.[15]

Reports from this period recount an unending series of patrols into disputed territory on the far side of the canal—a war of reconnaissance, ambushes, and raids intended to gather information and keep the enemy off balance. On numerous occasions these patrols were punctuated by short, violent engagements fought by sections and platoons on both sides of the waterway as the Force infiltrated enemy positions. The Germans responded in kind. These actions in particular earned the FSSF its reputation as the "Black Devils" for their silent, ruthless, almost invisible attacks. The nature of the fighting at Anzio weighed heavily on the Force, as it did on every unit engaged in the struggle to hold the beachhead. Night patrols were a dangerous, nerve-wracking business. Having experienced first-hand the conditions now faced by the FSSF at Anzio, US war correspondent Ernie Pyle wrote: "On this beachhead, every inch of our territory is under German artillery fire. There is no rear area that is immune, as in most battle zones. They can reach us with their 88s, and they use everything from that on up."[16] After the war, Canadian Lieutenant-Colonel J.G. Bourne, commanding officer of the 2nd Battalion, Third Regiment, said the Force was "punch-drunk" at Anzio.

Worked beyond endurance during the earlier assault on the Winter Line, it never fully recovered from the experience.[17]

On 19 February 1944, newly promoted Brigadier-General Frederick addressed his concerns to US Fifth Army's General Clark with a detailed and rather blunt report of the difficulties facing the FSSF almost three weeks following its arrival at Anzio: "There is no existing source, either United States or Canadian, of trained replacements for the Force."[18] Frederick's force was exhausted, and if the unit survived Anzio intact, he believed it would require an extended period to reorganize. "To continue the force with its present characteristics is not possible under the existing conditions. The successes the force has achieved in combat have been the result of special training and the development of certain qualities and spirit in the officers and enlisted men."[19] Developing these certain qualities and the high standard of training, however, had required a comparably long period under favourable conditions at Helena.

Frederick further stated that if the Force was to remain an elite formation, rebuilding the unit after Anzio required its withdrawal from combat for four to six months. Frederick viewed the Canadian element as a brake on the

In early April 1944 the FSSF adopted a new tactic of daylight raids on the southern flank in order to apply more pressure against enemy outposts and mainline defences. Here a patrol is skirting a minefield along a barbed wire fence while advancing against a fortified German-held farmhouse. [Gallagher, US 163rd Signal Photo Co. NA-SP SC 189580-S]

general usefulness of the FSSF due to the lack of reinforcements. The situation was made worse by the Canadian Army's reliance on voluntary enlistment at the same time that it had expanded to five overseas divisions organized into two corps, one in Italy and the other preparing for the imminent invasion of France. Casualty rates for Canadian troops then fighting with the British Eighth Army in Italy were also very high, given that they had faced fierce German opposition in battles such as the Moro River and Ortona. Frederick recognized that the withdrawal of the Canadians would absolutely cripple the Force: "The elimination of Canadian personnel from the Force would deprive the unit of many of its key officers and men. When the Force was activated, the Canadian Army furnished, in general, better qualified officers and enlisted men than did the United States, and this has resulted in a large number of the positions being filled by Canadians."[20]

For all that its officers and men had accomplished in the field, the unit remained problematic and expensive for both armies. Frederick believed it was better to let it disappear while it was still a source of pride to Canada and the United States, rather than allow it to drain the resources and patience of both countries: "For the sake of United States and Canadian relations, it may be felt best to let this unit pass out of existence while it is still in its prime, rather than to sustain it through a period when it will be remembered only for its faults and defects."[21]

Until such time as the unit could be withdrawn from the Anzio beachhead, however, Frederick insisted that the problem of Canadian reinforcements required immediate attention. To date, the American element had received limited numbers of regular infantry replacements; the Canadians had received none at all. Neglecting to mention that Canada's National Defence Headquarters (NDHQ) had offered in December 1942 to establish a permanent quota of Canadian reinforcements for the unit, Frederick had turned down Ottawa's offer to create a Canadian reinforcement system,[22] as he felt certain that the Canadians in the unit would not require reinforcements upon commitment to combat.

Frederick's earlier decision was understandable given that the Force had originally been intended to conduct a single commando mission, a devastating attack on some vital point of the German war machine. Frederick's letter of February 1944 demonstrates that while the amalgamation of Canadian and American personnel had succeeded in establishing a fully integrated and

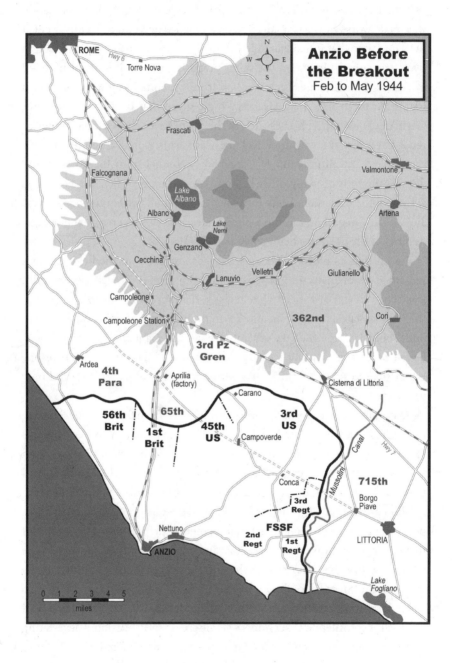

With a US 1st Armored Division Sherman tank burning in the background, Brigadier-General Robert T. Frederick discusses the results of a FSSF raid with Lieutenant-Colonel Robert S. Moore, commander of Second Regiment. Having earned a reputation for leading from the front, Frederick earned eight Purple Hearts for wounds sustained in combat. [NA-SP SC 437687]

effective military formation, the two countries had failed to coordinate a means of maintaining the unit in sustained combat. On the ground, relations between soldiers within the Force were highly satisfactory—the men served together with little or no regard for nationality; indeed, they were often unaware whether their comrades were American or Canadian. From the perspective of Washington and Ottawa, however, the arrangement seemed unnecessarily difficult and unwieldy.

By early February 1944, both Brigadier-General Frederick, the Force commander, and Lieutenant-Colonel Gilday, the acting senior Canadian officer, had considered disbandment of the First Special Service Force, although it is unclear whether they colluded in making the suggestion to their respective headquarters. Opposed to disbandment, however, were those commanders who remained more immediately concerned with the situation at Anzio, including Supreme Commander Dwight Eisenhower, US Fifth Army General Mark Clark, and British General Sir Harold Alexander, Deputy Supreme Commander—Mediterranean. By the first week of March, a decision had been reached: Clark's Fifth Army was to retain the First Special Service Force as a combined US–Canadian formation—at least temporarily.

While Allied planners were discussing the long-term future of the First Special Service Force, both Canadian and American officials considered short-term solutions to maintain it until it could be withdrawn from Anzio. For Fifth Army, arriving at a solution proved relatively simple. With the disaster outside Cisterna on 30 January having destroyed Darby's 1st and 3rd Battalions, leaving only the 4th Battalion intact, on 17 February Clark recommended that what remained of Ranger forces be inactivated to provide replacements for the FSSF.[23] The next month, Clark accepted Frederick's recommendation that the Force be rebuilt "to increase its strength, revise its organization and equipment, and re-orient its mission to encompass essentially Ranger actions and, at least in part, paratroop capabilities."[24]

On 4 March 1944, the Canadian Army began to bring the 1st Canadian Special Service Battalion back up to strength by drawing volunteers from the existing infantry reinforcement pools in the Mediterranean theatre, thus restoring the Canadian element of 47 officers and 583 other ranks.[25] With the German 735 Grenadier Regiment moving into position on 6 March, the FSSF now faced enemy strength of 3000 to 5000 men.[26] On 8 March, Fifth Army permanently attached the 456th Parachute Field Artillery Battalion that had

Soldiers from Second Regiment FSSF are shown firing 2.36-inch bazookas during a raid southwest of Littoria. The Force also carried M1941 Johnson .30 cal. automatic rifles and M1 Thompson .45 cal. submachine guns. [NA-SP SC 189581-S]

been fighting alongside the Force in Anzio. General Clark also ordered the US 4th Ranger Battalion to disband and provide roughly 20 officer and 500 enlisted man replacements.[27] In doing so, Clark intended to reorganize the Force and expand its strength of 2,000 men to as many as 3,500. Such an organization would, he explained, "combine the best of Fifth Army's special troops into a hard-hitting, well-led unit which will be of even greater value to the Army Commander than its very excellent component parts."[28]

This was easier said than done. In March 1944, the officers and men of both the Ranger battalions and FSSF were equally convinced that *their own* unit was the most elite formation of the United States Army. This created some tension when Fifth Army opted to combine them into an expanded FSSF. Many of the former Rangers resented being assigned to the Force. One recalled that "we were amazed by the apparent lack of organization in the Force—we were also the outsiders coming into a new unit."[29] On the night of 21 March, the Rangers arrived as replacements for the Force, with the largest portion of the newcomers being assigned to First Regiment. It was not an easy integration.

The Canadian replacements from units serving with the 1st Canadian Corps in Italy had literally lined up to volunteer for the Force, drawn by the unit's reputation and the promise of higher pay. For every vacancy there were three volunteers. In April, the Canadian Army provided the FSSF with 15 officers and 240 other ranks, though the officer responsible for the Canadian reinforcement stream in Italy had to intervene to prevent these men from being sent to Anzio without proper training. Brigadier-General Ernest Weeks, officer commanding Canadian General Headquarters, wrote at the time: "With the Canadian reinforcements totally unacquainted with American weapons, customs and methods of fighting, I am somewhat concerned that in the event of these troops being involved in combat, there is a possibility of loss of life because of unfamiliarity with weapons."[30] Seeing the point, Frederick agreed to provide the Canadians with two weeks of instruction by Force officers and NCOs before they were sent to the beachhead. Arriving at the port of Anzio on 27 April, the Canadian replacements were divided among the three regiments of the Force.[31]

The long period of training at Helena had established "an exceptional example of complete integration of personnel of two armies into a single unit," with an *esprit de corps* that Frederick regarded as absolutely critical to the combat effectiveness of the FSSF.[32] At Anzio, two different replacement systems were being put into place. Fifth Army adopted the expedient of attaching the remnants of other elite units to the Force, reasoning that Rangers were already highly trained and could be integrated into the Force with a minimum of inconvenience. Canadian reinforcements, on the other hand, were selected individually and then sent for special training in American weapons and operating procedures. Among separate groups of elite soldiers there was bound to be a clash of unit personalities, although such antagonism was also likely to fade in the face of battle.

While integrating American and Canadian replacement personnel, the Force began preparing for its role with US VI Corps, which would be to fight its way out of the Anzio beachhead and rejoin the Fifth Army for an advance on Rome. Although the FSSF had gained extensive experience working with artillery, tank–infantry cooperation remained a relatively new concept, as the unit's rigorous training in Montana had stressed operating alone in mountainous terrain. Perhaps the most serious obstacle encountered during the "reorganization under fire" at Anzio was that the entire beachhead was exposed to German artillery from the surrounding hills. Training on the beachhead itself did offer a few advantages, however, including the possibility of conducting "live-fire" training exercises under extremely realistic conditions. By rotating units off the front line during the day, the Force was able to conduct some fifteen exercises in tank–infantry cooperation in preparation for the breakout.[33]

There was a sense of optimism within the Force in April 1944 as the unit prepared for its role in the breakout. The weather had begun to improve, and on the far side of the Mussolini Canal the Germans had been relatively quiet for some time. The arrival of replacements from the 1st Canadian Corps indicated to the Canadians of the Force that they had not been abandoned after all. By 30 April, these reinforcements had brought the effective strength of the Canadian element back to its authorized level of 49 officers and 595 other ranks. The Americans in the combat echelon, particularly for enlisted men, still greatly outnumbered the Canadians, with 56 officers and 1,361 other ranks.[34]

After ninety-eight days on the Anzio Front, the FSSF was relieved on 9 May by the 36th Combat Engineer Regiment. It spent the next eleven days working with the tanks and training the reinforcements. On the eve of the impending breakout, Frederick addressed his men, offering a special greeting to those who had recently joined the unit: "We welcome you to our ranks knowing that you are the kind of soldiers who will fight with only the thought of victory in mind. We know that you will take the same pride in successful accomplishment of the mission as do the men you have joined." Frederick then gave a similar welcome to the unit's supporting attachments and closed with a final encouragement: "Our superior officers expect us to succeed as before. We shall prove to them that their confidence is not misplaced. The eyes of Canada and the United States are upon us. Let them see that, as in the past, we move only forward."[35]

The breakout from Anzio over the twenty-two-mile route to Rome began at 0630 hours on 23 May 1944, with more than 150,000 Allied soldiers advancing out of the perimeter in which they had been trapped for four months. The FSSF moved on the right of the VI Corps advance, guarding the flank of US 3 Division's attack on Cisterna. As the FSSF First Regiment led the attack with two companies of tanks and a battalion of tank destroyers in support, German machine guns were quickly overcome by the rifle sections. By 0815 hours, First Regiment had advanced some 2,000 yards beyond its line of departure and was approximately halfway to Highway 7, its initial objective.[36] Small-arms fire began to die down as the Germans launched mortar and artillery attacks. Caught in the barrage, First Regiment suffered a great loss when the commanding officer of its 2nd Battalion, Lieutenant-Colonel Walt Gray, was killed along with several others as the regiment charged through the curtain of shrapnel.[37] Upon reaching the far side of this artillery barrage, however, they found German resistance beginning to collapse.

By 1000 hours, First Regiment had secured Highway 7 and one of its battalions had advanced to the railway. Recalled William Sheldon, a platoon commander who a few days later would rise to 4th Company commander by virtue of his being the sole surviving officer in the bitter fighting of the breakout:

> We advanced again, the tanks giving us great support and several Jerries surrendering to them. I felt confident—ever so confident then. We had cracked Jerry's main line of resistance. With the tanks, it seemed easy ... We crossed the highway without opposition, and 200 yards beyond came to a high railroad bank

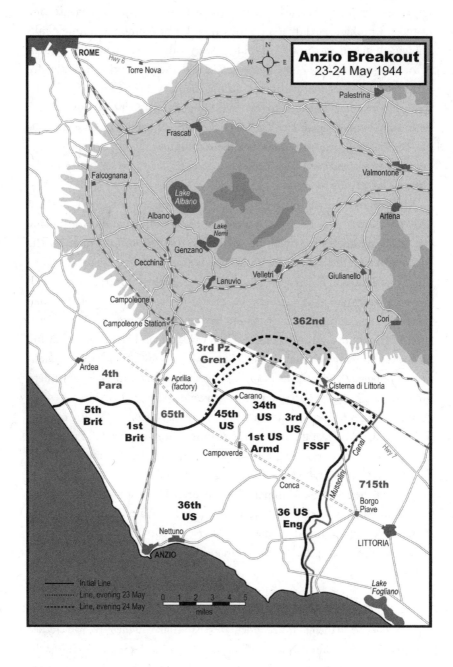

where our company set up a defensive line—our final objective. It all seemed too terribly easy. I couldn't believe it.[38]

Indeed, cutting the highway and railway had been too easy. That is when real trouble began. By advancing beyond Highway 7, First Regiment had created a salient that exposed its soldiers to a crossfire of German 88s in Cisterna and Littoria. Captain Thomas Zabski, later awarded the Distinguished Service Cross, remembered the lightning speed with which the situation changed: "We got out into the plains of high grass beyond Highway 7 and ran into heavy artillery fire from 88s and German tanks causing terrific casualties. When we looked back, we saw a dozen of our Shermans, all of them burning and with smoke pouring out. It was a terrible feeling … Our losses were 'hell.'"[39] To make matters worse, Paulick Force, the provisional company-sized unit formed to close the gap and maintain contact between the Force and US 3 Division, had been stalled by German small-arms fire, leaving the Force's left flank exposed. "Doesn't look good around canal," radioed First Regiment. "Two companies cut off on [far] side of Highway by heavy concentration of artillery coming from Cisterna."[40]

At noon on 23 May 1944 an enemy counterattack formed in the woods east of the Mussolini Canal. At 1230 hours, the two forward companies that were dug in along the railway line reported seeing five Tiger tanks coming down the Ninfa road and another three from Littoria.[41] The Tigers launched a violent counterattack, inflicting terrible losses, while the supporting Allied artillery radioed that they were unable to see what was going on beyond the highway. First Regiment fell back to Highway 7. Warrant Officer D.W. Libby of Winnipeg described a scene of complete chaos:

> Suddenly the whole front was filled with advancing tanks. Rather than be captured, I turned and started to run toward our own lines … Each time I looked back, I could see them gaining on me and the long 88 mm looked like telegraph poles. Just as they were about to run over me, I heard our guns open up and the sound of shells approaching. I threw myself on the ground and the shells exploded amongst the tanks … I was up and on my way again [as] the tank attack was broken up by the artillery barrage.[42]

The ruins of Cisterna di Littoria in May 1944 show the intensity of the fighting in the region over the two preceding days. First Regiment bore the brunt of the battle near the railway, with 39 dead. Advancing on the right flank of VI Corps' Operation Buffalo during the breakout to Rome, the FSSF captured some 400 prisoners in the Cisterna area. [NA-SP SC 190732]

Allied air and artillery were coming in with observed fire, but this did not prevent the much more powerful Tigers from destroying much of what remained of the Force's tanks and tank destroyers. One veteran recalled seeing the shell fired from a tank destroyer bounce off a Tiger, while Intelligence Officer Robert D. Burhans reported a Tiger shell that went through a house, then a Sherman, and continued another thousand yards beyond the destroyed tank.[43] The line held briefly at Highway 7, but according to Lieutenant Sheldon, "the big German tanks began moving in closer and then machine-gunning us ... Finally, the order came to withdraw and it was truly a wise move."[44]

The Force pulled back 500 to 600 yards short of the highway, where it linked up with Paulick Force and closed the gap. The two forward companies tried to withdraw but were pinned down. First Regiment was bearing the brunt of the battle; only half of 1st Company made it back and 3rd Company was badly shot up. Although some had been able to withdraw to the line south of Highway 7, suffering heavy casualties in doing so, others remained cut off for two days before linking up with attacking elements of US 34 Division.[45] Steady air and artillery support, along with the arrival of reinforcements in tanks and tank destroyers, had broken up the German counterattack by 2100 hours. The Force thus avoided the fate of Darby's Rangers in almost the same location the previous January. Once the situation had been stabilized, the US 133 Infantry Regiment relieved the Force on the front line, allowing the unit to prepare for a renewed drive against Monte Arrestino the next day.

General Frederick would always maintain that the Force never took a step back in battle. When official historian Sidney T. Matthews asked him later about the orders to withdraw south of Highway 7, he replied: "No withdrawal order was given on the 23rd of May, or any other time. Units were extended on the left flank as an expedient to gain lateral communication and contact. Units moved back to protect the flanks, after which regrouping, they continued on in the attack to the front and Monte Arrestino."[46] From the perspective of the Force commander, we can say that the Force did not withdraw, but rather "regrouped," or advanced to the rear. However, the contemporary reports tell a very different story—the word "withdrawal" is found in all three US reports of action, as well as in the Canadian record of that day in May 1944. G.W.L. Nicholson's official history, *The Canadians in Italy*, also refers to the action as a "temporary withdrawal," while Burhans's operational history uses language that more closely resembles Frederick's. Burhans, as the unit's intelligence officer, was more likely concerned about maintaining the reputation of the Force when he recorded that First Regiment merely "pulled its line back."[47] If the recollections of Sheldon, Zabski, and others are at all representative, the Force had indeed withdrawn, and for good reason.

On 25 May the Force occupied Monte Arrestino and reorganized for the next phase of the attack in support of 3 Division's push towards Cori. All across the VI Corps front the Germans were pulling their forces back in the direction of Rome. Determined to be "the liberator of Rome," General Clark directed the main body of his forces northward, leaving the monumental task of blocking the German Tenth Army's withdrawal up Highway 6 to the FSSF and units of 3 Division and 1 Armored Division already in the valley.[48] On 28 May the breakout towards Rome continued as the Force set out from the high ground above Artena, advancing northeast towards Valmontone in an attempt to sever Highway 6, the enemy's main east–west line of communication in the area. To counter the threat to their escape route, the Germans sent every man available to defend this vital point. "The Jerries … brought up some high class troops and equipment," recalled John Dawson, a machine gunner from Illinois. "When we moved out of [Artena] to the plain below, I believe the small arms fire was the heaviest I have ever encountered … It was touch and go."[49] The fighting outside Artena lasted for five hours as the Germans rolled Tigers, self-propelled guns, and flak wagons into the fight, inflicting heavy casualties before the forward companies of the Force could report that all objectives had been secured.[50]

Consolidating its defences in the last days of May, the Force suffered heavy casualties as the Germans kept up their shelling on the town of Artena and on the Force's front lines. Burhans's history of the Force echoes gunner Dawson's battle perspective, recording that "[e]nemy resistance to the attack from Artena to the railroad was probably the heaviest a Force attack ever faced."[51] On the night of 29–30 May, a German battalion reinforced with tanks launched an attack to regain lost ground but was driven back by field guns attached to the Force. Supporting artillery broke up a second German counterattack the next night. On 1 June the Third Regiment held against one final attempt by the Germans, inflicting heavy casualties on the enemy. Colleferro fell next to an attack by Second Regiment. With Highway 6 now in Allied hands, the Force withdrew to Artena to join the final stages of Fifth Army's advance into Rome.

On the morning of 3 June 1944 the tanks of Task Force Howze were attached to the FSSF as it moved to secure six bridges across the Tiber River. Rearguard elements of the German Tenth Army remained to delay the Allied advance while their retreating troops escaped. On 4 June the Force encountered strong resistance on the outskirts of the city through most of the day. The Force operations summary recorded: "Entrance of our troops into the city was made at approximately 1600 … the first permanent entrance of Allied troops into Rome. The six bridges were all secured by 2300 after further bitter street fighting."[52]

The Force lost many good men taking the Tiber bridges, including the First Regiment's commander, Colonel A.C. Marshall, who was shot by a sniper just outside the city. Within Rome itself the fighting became somewhat confused, as described by Colonel J.G. Bourne:

> It was indeed thrilling to receive such a tumultuous welcome from the Romans. The cheering and happiness was quite moving. Every now and then, the crowds on the street would suddenly disappear and some die-hard Germans in an armoured car would turn a corner and start shooting. It was rather

uncomfortable, as there was no cover to be taken—but skillful use of bazookas, grenades, and machine-gun fire quickly disposed of the enemy—then the crowd would reappear again.[53]

Sporadic battle continued throughout the day as elements of the Force moved cautiously through civilian-lined streets, scouted unguarded routes, cleared resistance, and posted traffic signs for the Fifth Army to follow into the city. By the evening of 5 June 1944, Rome was in Allied hands. The next day, the Allied landing went ashore in Normandy, diverting much of the world's attention from the victory in Rome.

Reports indicate that the morale of the Force was high throughout the fighting in late May, reaching its peak during the entry into Rome.[54] Beginning with the training period at Helena and continuing into 1944, differences in nationality, experience and training had created a unique spirit that complemented the unit's fighting abilities. Reinforced and reorganized for the breakout, the men fought tenaciously in operations leading from Anzio to Rome, earning the Force a position in the lead of Fifth Army's advance into the Eternal City. Victory came at a high cost, however: in two weeks of fighting, the unit suffered an enormous number of casualties. From 23 May to 4 June 1944, the FSSF suffered 749 casualties in a combat echelon of 2,061

When the "Anzio breakout" became the "road to Rome," FSSF troops became the first to enter the city. Shown here, troops of Second Regiment leave the protective cover of a burning Mark IV tank to move deeper into the city. After fighting all day against Hermann Göring Division rearguards, by nightfall on 5 June 1944 the Force controlled all bridges over the Tiber. [NA-SP SC 191061]

soldiers. Nine officers were killed or missing, 24 had been wounded. Among enlisted men, 156 were killed or missing and 560 wounded.[55] The Canadian element was left with only slightly more officers and men than there had been before the arrival of the replacements in April. Once again, the 1st Canadian Special Service Battalion needed reinforcements, prompting senior Canadian officer Lieutenant-Colonel Jack Akehurst to include a request in his monthly report to Canadian Military Headquarters in London: "The last reinforcements proved to be excellent men. We hope the next group will be just as good."[56]

The Force, meanwhile, had adapted to Fifth Army's new vision of its assault infantry role, reorienting towards what Clark described as "Ranger actions": intense, rapid strikes against the most persistent targets. At Anzio, the Force's specialty had been close-quarter combat against numerically superior forces. During the breakout, however, one would have been hard pressed to differentiate Force operations from those regularly assigned to a conventional infantry formation. In the fighting from Anzio to Rome, success depended more on attachments of tanks, armoured vehicles, mortars, and especially artillery than it ever had in the past.

With the Force transferred to a nearby rest area on the shores of Lake Albano, Frederick considered the "lessons learned" on the road from Anzio to Rome. First, just as he had warned back in February, it had not been possible to train FSSF replacements to the standard of the original personnel in just one month. No amount of enthusiasm on the part of these volunteers could equal the full year of intense training provided at Helena, Montana. Second, it was immediately apparent that armoured and artillery support had been absolutely critical to the success of recent operations—just as it would be for any conventional US infantry regiment conducting standard infantry battles. When the supporting armour was destroyed during the breakout from Anzio, the advance faltered and two forward companies of the Force were overrun. Five days later, at Artena, supporting artillery had been essential, both in preparing the ground over which the Force would advance and in repelling the German counterattacks that followed. With these lessons in mind, Frederick recommended to Lieutenant-General Clark "that the First Special Service Force be organized and equipped in accordance with the Tables of Organization and Equipment for an Infantry Regiment, with the addition of one (1) battalion of light Field Artillery."[57]

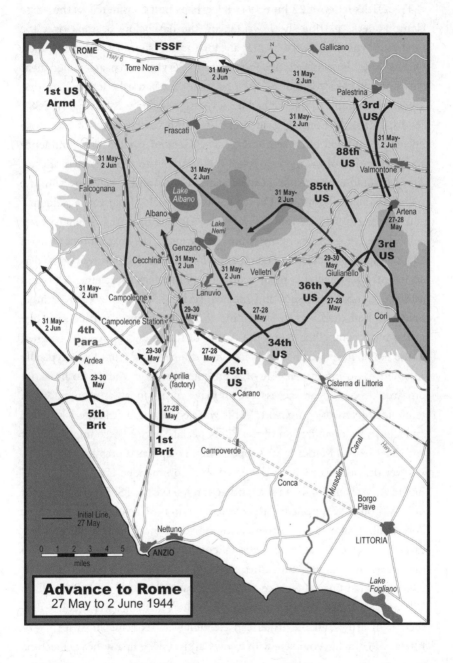

Frederick's letter of 22 June 1944 is perhaps best considered as the Force Commander's "parting shot," written on the day before he took over the First Airborne Task Force to prepare for the invasion of southern France. On 23 June, he ordered the First Special Service Force assembled near the shore of Lake Albano for the presentation of awards. It was here that Frederick announced that he had been reassigned and was leaving the FSSF. "A discernable, protesting gasp broke the hush in the ranks of men who normally withheld such sentiments. The General carried the confidence and admiration of his men ... From the first fight to the last, memories of combat would evoke visions of the General up forward somewhere with the men who did the fighting."[58] On the day of Frederick's departure, a saddened entry in the Canadian war diary reads: "He has been the driving power behind the Force and its future is now in the air."[59] The next month, General Clark endorsed Frederick's recommendation that the FSSF be reorganized as an infantry regimental combat team with permanent complements of field artillery, combat engineers, and medical services.[60] In his letter of 22 June, Frederick had cited several overriding reasons why this was necessary, one of the most compelling being the nature of the missions recently assigned to the Force. Recent combat missions had differed little from those typically assigned to an infantry regiment. Consequently, from the Anzio breakout onwards it had been necessary to make provisional attachments and temporary loans of equipment.[61] This was something that Frederick hoped an extensive reorganization of the First Special Service Force might correct and that General Mark Clark's support would help make a reality.

Over the next six months, the new Force Commander, US Army Colonel Edwin A. Walker, fought a rearguard action to save the FSSF as a specialized unit. Although he repeatedly attempted to retain the Canadian element of the Force, both Canadian and American authorities now agreed with Frederick's earlier assessment that the bi-national composition of the Force introduced unnecessarily complex difficulties for both parties.[62] Thus on 5 December 1944, the First Special Service Force was disbanded after a final parade in Villeneuve-Loubet, France, at which time the Canadians were returned to their own army and the American element was reorganized to form 474 Infantry Regiment, complete with its own anti-tank company, heavy machine guns, mortars, and vehicles—all the things that Frederick had been asking for since Anzio.

The men of the First Special Service Force could look back with a great sense of pride at their string of victories from La Difensa to Anzio to Rome. The breakout from the Anzio beachhead, however, demonstrated how the bi-national composition of the Force made it so difficult to solve the reinforcement crisis. It was at the higher levels and in communications between the national military bureaucracies that the Force suffered its most significant setbacks. From the earliest days at Helena, relations between Canadians and Americans in the unit had always been good, but the Force was bogged down by administrative complexities, as evidenced by a continuing exchange of telegrams and letters between various headquarters and by a multitude of discussions among American, British, and Canadian planners over the Force's future. Due to the international nature of the Force, bureaucratic difficulties were encountered in legion. Solutions came too late to save it from disbandment.

In his letter of 19 February 1944, General Frederick had suggested that the time had come to let the Force "pass out of existence while it is still in its prime, rather than to sustain it through a period when it will be remembered only for its faults and defects."[63] In hindsight, this warning seems depressingly exaggerated. On the ground, the FSSF proved repeatedly that Canadians and Americans could be moulded into an extremely effective fighting unit. Viewed from above, however, the special status and international character of the Force introduced unique difficulties that were never fully resolved before the unit was disbanded in December 1944. It must be said, however, that at least one of Frederick's stated objectives had been achieved: when the Force was allowed to "pass out of existence," it was definitely *before* its faults and defects overshadowed its achievements. Instead, the predominant image of the First Special Service Force stands as it was portrayed at Anzio by a war correspondent: "The Force has two armies behind it, two governments, two peoples ... Wherever it is known it must be an inspiration in international goodwill ... If it continues in the same brilliant way, it may become a legend of this war that will exert its influence in peace to no small advantage."[64] Sholto Watt's rhetoric captured the enthusiasm of an eyewitness to the Force's action at Monte la Difensa and the Winter Line. Its potential then seemed unlimited. Ironically, army censors would delay the publication of Watt's article until April 1944, by which time casualties and a continuing reinforcement crisis had blunted the Force's fighting effectiveness.

The First Special Service Force had earned a remarkable combat reputation, but both the Canadian and American leadership had come to believe that it could not produce the same impressive results without a major overhaul, particularly in its casualty replacement scheme. Both Gilday and Frederick believed that the Force should be disbanded and were arguing forcefully to that effect at the time the unit was called into Anzio. Once again, as on the Winter Line, the harsh tactical realities of combat in the Italian theatre reduced the Force to half its assigned strength. By year's end, senior officials from both countries agreed that its personnel should be reassigned to more conventional infantry formations.

Neither before nor since have Canadian soldiers served in such close association with the US Army. During its brief existence, the Force established an enviable combat record—and it did so despite the difficulties encountered in meeting reinforcement needs. Today, the First Special Service Force is remembered both in Canada and the United States for its outstanding achievements in combat as well as its unique, bi-national composition. They are known as "the Devil's Brigade," the North Americans who broke the Winter Line atop Monte la Difensa and who went on to become the first Allied formation to enter Rome. The Force is not, as Frederick once predicted it would be, remembered for its faults and defects. Nor should it be.

Notes

1. Memorandum, Lieutenant-General Ken Stuart to the Minister of National Defence, 11 July 1942, DND Directorate of History and Heritage, Ottawa (hereafter DHH), 112.3S2009 (D255), file: Org & Mob, 1st SS Bn, June—Dec. 42.
2. Letter, Robert T. Frederick to Deputy Chief of Staff, US Army, 3 February 1943, National Archives at College Park [NA-CP], RG 165, Entry 418, Box 830, Stack 390/36/30/6, Folder OPD 3222.9.
3. For more detailed information on the goals, formation, Table of Organization, training, administration, and combat record of the Force, see James A. Wood, *We Move Only Forward: Canada, the United States, and the First Special Service Force 1942–1944* (St. Catharines: Vanwell, 2006).
4. Robert D. Burhans, *The First Special Service Force: A War History of the North Americans, 1942–1944* (Washington: Infantry Journal Press, 1947), 124. Lieutenant-Colonel Burhans was the S-2 Intelligence Officer of the FSSF and his book is the classic operational reference for the force's training and combat activities. The 400 German troops atop Monte la Difensa consisted of the 3rd Battalion, 104 Panzergrenadier

Regiment, alongside half the 3rd Battalion, 129 Panzergrenadier Regiment of 15 Division. The 115 Reconnaissance Division was in reserve, and the Hermann Göring Division in the rear. Burhans, *The First Special Service Force*, 96.

5   Milton Bracker, "Battling in Italy—3 More Camino Peaks Are Taken Despite Fierce Resistance," *New York Times*, 7 December 1943, 1. There were 114 pieces of enemy artillery in the area, largely *nebelwerfers* and 170 mm heavy guns firing 150-pound shells at a range of up to 32,000 yards. German high-volume 20 mm guns had a maximum ceiling of 4000 yards while the 88s threw a 22-pound shell to a height of 12,000 yards. Continual German artillery fire disrupted Allied field lines and made communication most difficult and hazardous (Fifth United States Army, *Fifth Army History*, vol. 3, *The Winter Line* (Wilmington: Scholarly Resources, 1980), 7–8 and 29.

6   Letter, Lieutenant-General Mark W. Clark to Commanding Officer, First Special Service Force, 10 December 1943, LAC, RG 24, vol. 12,540.

7   *Fifth Army History*, 6.

8   Telegram, CGS, Ottawa, to Cdn Army Staff, Washington, 23 March 1943, DHH file: Org & Mob, Jan 43/Feb 45.

9   Letter, Lieutenant-Colonel T.P. Gilday to Brigadier-General A.W. Beament, 15 January 1944, DHH, 145.3009 (D3), file: Instructions and Directives, 1 Cdn Spec Serv Bn.

10 Ibid. In Ottawa, National Defence Headquarters refused to act on Gilday's recommendation, citing the FSSF not only as being in a theatre of operations, but also as engaged against the enemy. While the FSSF was not actually "engaged against the enemy" at the time, the situation would soon change. Reorganizing the Force would create a severe burden for Fifth Army at a time when VI Corps was already fighting for its life at Anzio.

11 Michael J. King, *Rangers: Selected Combat Missions in World War II* (Fort Leavenworth: Combat Studies Institute, 1985), 39.

12 Burhans, *The First Special Service Force*, 163, reported a "full new army being built" from more than half the strength of 29 Panzergrenadier Division, 1 Parachute Division, 26 Panzer Division of LXXVI Corps, and the Hermann Göring Panzer and Parachute Division as it swung northward from its reserve position at Cassino.

13 Burhans assessed the Hermann Göring Division as having such prestige in the field that it "operated more frequently as a corps than as a division headquarters." Its panzer regiment held twelve to fifteen Mark IV tanks in the FSSF sector. On February 6-7 two companies of its Luftwaffe Battalion, reorganized and retrained for ground combat, attacked FSSF patrols and were stopped short of their canal objectives. FSSF patrols thus succeeded in establishing a buffer zone on both sides of the Mussolini Canal. Burhans, *The First Special Service Force*, 170–72.

14 Activities of the First Canadian Special Service Battalion, "Summary of the Enemy's Actions," 1–29 February 1944, 3, BN, CA(A) DHH, 145.3009 (D7), file: Monthly Reports. The Allied position in flat, open tableland adjoining the canal was dominated by German artillery on the heights overlooking the beachhead. Along with towers at Littoria, the mountains provided the German troops with brutally effective observation points. The tactical difficulties of the Mediterranean also included the constant threat

of a seaborne assault on an open-water flank that was impossible for the undermanned FSSF to cover fully.
15　Ibid.
16　David Nichols, ed., *Ernie's War: The Best of Ernie Pyle's World War II Dispatches* (New York: Random House, 1986), 237. In his operational history, Robert Burhans also wrote of the constant shelling, explosions, and casualties, resulting in "Anzio having the highest psychoneurotic rate of any campaign in the war." Burhans, *The First Special Service Force*, 179.
17　Interview, J.G. Bourne, 30 September 1963, Hoover Institution Archives [HIA], Robert H. Adleman Papers, Box 12, file: Miscellaneous Interviews. In David Wolper's Hollywood film, *The Devil's Brigade*, the prototype Canadian commander played by Cliff Robertson was based largely on Bourne's real-life role in the FSSF. He was a gentlemanly "soldier's soldier" from Montreal, who at age twenty-five was one of the youngest Allied officers to hold the rank of lieutenant-colonel.
18　Letter, Robert T. Frederick to Commanding General, US Fifth Army, 19 February 1944, HIA, Robert D. Burhans Papers, Box 19, file: Table of Org.
19　Ibid.
20　Ibid.
21　Ibid. For a more detailed summary of Frederick's correspondence regarding the role and requirements of the FSSF, see James A. Wood, "'Matters Canadian' and the Problem with Being Special: Robert T. Frederick on the First Special Service Force," *Canadian Military History* 12, no.4 (Autumn 2003), 19–33.
22　Letter, CGS to McQueen, 9 December 1942, DHH file: Org & Mob June–Dec. 42. Frederick's decline of the Canadian offer to create a reinforcements system is found in Letter, Dir of Staff Duties to DCGS, 15 December 1942, DHH file: Org & Mob.
23　Memorandum, FSSF Supply Officer to Frederick, 27 February 1944, HIA, Robert D. Burhans Papers, Box 7, file: Secret Corresp.
24　Letter, Headquarters, US Fifth Army, to Commanding General, First Special Service Force, 8 March 1944, HIA, Robert D. Burhans Papers, Box 19, file: Table of Org.
25　Telegram, Stuart to Murchie, 4 March 1944, DHH, 112.3S2009 (D255), Org & Mob, 1 SS Bn, Jan 43/Feb 45.
26　Burhans, *The First Special Service Force*, 186. The Hermann Göring Division was replaced by 715 Division on 6 March and returned opposite the FSSF on 27 May.
27　Telegram, Stuart to B-Gen E.G. Weeks, 4 March 1944, LAC, RG 24, vol. 12,540, file: Rfts File#1. The reinforced Canadian contingent at 47 officers and 583 other ranks represented a significant increase over the previous month in February at 27 officers and 339 other ranks.
28　Letter, Headquarters US Fifth Army to CG, FSSF, 8 March 1944, Burhans Papers, Box 19, file: Table of Org.
29　Interview Questionnaire, George Sabine, HIA, Robert H. Adleman Papers, Box 8, file: 1st Regiment Interviews.
30　Letter, Brigadier-General E.G. Weeks to Fifth Army Headquarters, 3 April 1944, HIA, Robert T. Frederick Papers, Box 1, File: FSSF Miscellany.

31   Activities of the First Canadian Special Service Battalion, 1–30 April 1944, DHH, 145.3009 (D7), file: Monthly Reports.
32   Letter, Brigadier-General Robert T. Frederick to General Mark Clark, 19 February 1944.
33   FSSF Summary of Operations, 1–30 April 1944, NA-CP, RG 407, Entry 427, Stack 270/64/24/6-7, Box 23,274.
34   Activities of the First Canadian Special Service Battalion, 1–30 April 1944 and 1 May–10 June 1944. In keeping with Frederick's earlier recommendation that the FSSF be properly equipped for the type of operations in which it was to be employed, attachments to it for the upcoming mission were increased to include the 463rd Parachute Field Artillery Battalion; D Company, 39 Combat Engineer Regiment; two companies of the 645th Tank Destroyer Battalion; A Company, 191st Tank Battalion; the mortars of B Company, 84th Chemical Battalion; and a collecting company from the 52nd Medical Battalion.
35   Letter, Brigadier-General Robert T. Frederick, 22 May 1944, HIA, Robert T. Frederick Papers, Box 1, file: FSSF Miscellany.
36   FSSF G-3 Journal, 23 May 1944, NA-CP, RG 407, Entry 427, Stack 270/64/24/6-7, Box 23,280.
37   Burhans, *The First Special Service Force*, 216.
38   William Sheldon, "Battle—1944—Anzio to Rome," 6, HIA, Robert H. Adleman Papers, Box 8, file: 1st Regiment Interviews.
39   Interview, Thomas Zabski, 11, 15, HIA, Robert H. Adleman Papers, Box 12, file: Miscellaneous Interviews.
40   FSSF G-3 Journal, 23 May 1944.
41   Burhans, *The First Special Service Force*, 217.
42   Interview, D.W. Libby, 8, HIA, Robert H. Adleman Papers, Box 12, file: Miscellaneous Interviews.
43   Burhans, *The First Special Service Force*, 217.
44   Sheldon, "Battle," 7–8. Although 2nd Regiment had the most experience working with tanks, especially from the intense battles at Cerreto Alto, 15 April, 18 April, and 1 May 1944, this unit was held in reserve for the breakout battle of 23 May. The actual breakout was to be led by 1st Regiment—the same unit that had received the largest number of Ranger replacements and had spent much of April integrating these men, while also holding a sector of the front line. One battalion from 2nd Regiment did accompany the 1st during the breakout; however, it was to be, essentially, a 1st Regiment show.
45   FSSF Summary of Operations, May 1944, NA-CP, RG 407, Entry 427, Stack 270/64/24/6-7, Box 23,274.
46   Sidney T. Matthews, "Interview with Major General Robert T. Frederick," Historical Division, Special Staff—United States Army, 31 December, 1948, 3, HIA, Robert T. Frederick Papers, Box 3, file: First Special Service Force—History—Correspondence.
47   First Special Service Force S-3 Operations Summary, S-3 Operations Log, S-2 Intelligence Summary, May 1944, NA-CP, RG 407, Entry 427, Stack 270/64/24/6-7, Box 23,274. The question from the Matthews interview was: "Who gave the order to

withdraw 600 yards south of the Highway 6?" See also "Activities of the First Canadian Special Service Battalion," DHH 145.3009 (D7) file: Monthly Reports. G.W.L. Nicholson, *Official History of the Canadian Army in the Second World War*, vol. 2: *The Canadians in Italy, 1943–1945* (Ottawa: Queen's Printer, 1956), 456, refers to the action as a "temporary withdrawal south-west of the road"; Burhans, *The First Special Service Force*, 218, states that First Regiment had "pulled its line back of Highway 7 some 500 yards."

48   Nicholson, *The Canadians in Italy*, 399 and 437. Clark, determined to take Rome before the British Eighth Army could, and before the impending landings at Normandy would divert attention, ignored General Alexander's plans to create a roadblock on Highway 6 to check the retreat by Tenth Army and some divisions of Fourteenth Army by the only available modern road. Instead, Clark shifted the axis of the VI Corps advance to aim directly for Rome. Hence, a gap was created through which retreating Germans were allowed to escape and rebuild divisions to fight again. Once again the FSSF was vastly outnumbered; units of US Third and 1 Armored Divisions and the FSSF were left to accomplish the mission originally intended for VI Corps.

49   Interview, John R. Dawson, 16 October 1963, HIA, Adleman Papers, Box 13, file: 2nd Regiment.

50   FSSF Summary of Operations, May 1944.

51   Burhans, *The First Special Service Force*, 227. On 28 May the FSSF held back a platoon of the 751st Tank Battalion, a platoon of tank destroyers from the 601st, and came under heavy fire from the Hermann Göring Reconnaissance Battalion. Opposite the FSSF on the 3 Division flank between 29 May and 2 June were the German 29 Panzergrenadier Division, 26 Armoured Division, 725 and 735 Infantry Regiments, 7th Luftwaffe Battalion, 103rd Reconnaissance Battalion, 1st and 2nd Battalions of the 1028 Grenadier Regiment of 362 Division, and a battalion of pro-Axis Italian SS Infantry.

52   FSSF Summary of Operations, June 1944, NA-CP, RG 407, Entry 427, Stack 270/64/24/6-7, Box 23,274.

53   Interview, J.G. Bourne, 30 September 1963. Bourne is also cited earlier in the paper for his views on the exhaustion of the FSSF ("punch drunk" at Anzio).

54   Activities of the First Canadian Special Service Battalion, 1 May–10 June 1944.

55   FSSF Headquarters, Office of Personnel Officer, 8 Oct 1944, Burhans Papers, Box 1, file: Hist File, General.

56   Activities of the First Canadian Special Service Battalion, 1 May–10 June 1944.

57   Letter, Robert T. Frederick to Commanding General, US Fifth Army, 22 June 1944, HIA, Robert D. Burhans Papers, Box 7, file: Confidential.

58   Burhans, *The First Special Service Force*, 249. From the force's inception to the breakout from the Anzio perimeter, General Frederick had continued to earn the trust, devotion, and respect of his men by his near-constant presence on the front lines. Even after his promotion to brigadier-general in January 1944, Frederick received eight Purple Hearts for wounds sustained in combat, earning him the dubious distinction of being the most shot-at-and-hit general officer of the Second World War.

59 War Diary of 2nd Cdn Para Bn, 23 June 1944, LAC, RG 24, vol. 15,301.
60 Letter, Headquarters, US Fifth Army, to Commanding General, North African Theater of Operations, 3 July 1944, HIA, Robert D. Burhans Papers, Box 19, file: Table of Org.
61 Letter, Frederick to Clark, 22 June 1944.
62 Letter, Frederick to Clark, 19 February 1944.
63 Ibid.
64 Sholto Watt, "Crack Mixed Force Is Gradually Becoming American," *Montreal Star*, 9 April 1944.

13

La culture tactique canadienne
le cas de l'opération Chesterfield, 23 mai 1944

Yves Tremblay

Les armées sont souvent accusées d'être incapables d'apprendre. Si par bonheur certains de leurs membres montrent une capacité d'apprentissage au-dessus du commun, d'aucuns prétendent que l'institution les malmènerait parce qu'elle préfèrerait les solutions éprouvées. Il y a du vrai et du faux là-dedans.

Il y a surtout que cette explication n'en est pas une, car elle suppose que quelques hommes feraient la différence, alors que l'on devrait bien savoir qu'une société militaire, comme toute société, est un arrangement qu'on caricature si on ne l'étudie pas dans toute sa complexité. Pour prendre le cas de l'Armée canadienne en 1939-1945, il serait facile de montrer que plus qu'une simple machine de combat elle fut une grande école de guerre, et de paix à compter de 1944, car s'y donnait des centaines de cours différents à des centaines de milliers d'hommes, cours pouvant durer de quelques jours à cinq mois. On pourrait également remonter à l'avant-guerre et montrer que, du moins en ce qui concerne les officiers, les avancées théoriques était analysées, critiquées et débattues avec beaucoup d'ardeur. On pourrait enfin ajouter que les apprentissages étaient révisés en continu à travers un mécanisme de rétroaction dit de « leçons apprises », qui passaient soit par le renvoi d'officiers du front vers les écoles de l'arrière, soit à travers des publications largement distribuées.

Il est vrai que cela ne démontre pas la capacité d'adaptation de l'armée aux difficultés de la guerre moderne. En effet, ce n'est pas parce que l'on discute ou même donne un cours pertinent que la méthode réellement employée change pour le mieux. Il faudrait alors s'intéresser au rapport entre l'enseignement et les méthodes sur le terrain. C'est possible, car les formations opérationnelles – elles organisent des cours d'ailleurs – font rapport sur cette question. Et les troupes sont plus studieuses lorsque les choses vont mal.

Un cas intéressant est celui de la courte bataille du 23 mai 1944 sur la ligne Hitler, une victoire qui, parce que les généraux responsables l'ont trouvée coûteuse, déclenche une série d'études et de rapports (au moins huit[1]), plus trois études historiques officielles détaillées[2], dont l'une réalisées dès août 1944 était susceptible d'entrer dans le processus de rétroaction opérationnel. Pareille cascade d'analyses, sans compter les exercices des semaines suivantes pour intégrer les leçons tirées et qui provoquent la rédaction d'autres rapports, fait douter d'une proposition à l'effet que l'armée ne soit pas désireuse d'apprendre.

Comment parler de tradition quand les « vieux » comme les « jeunes » semblent avoir une attitude consensuelle ? Question de discipline ? Réponse facile qui revient à préférer la tautologie d'une armée bornée parce qu'elle est armée. Je crois plutôt qu'il y a quelque chose de plus profond qui limite la volonté de mieux faire la prochaine fois, car il ne faudrait pas oublier que la préparation d'une bataille est une série de décisions prises rapidement avec une information abondante mais contradictoire, ce qui implique que l'on doive avoir en tête des solutions schématiques adaptables aux circonstances.

L'accusation de traditionalisme excessif ne résout par conséquent rien. Il me semble qu'il faut lui préférer un concept scientifiquement plus neutre et plus à même de nous conduire vers une meilleure compréhension des difficultés connues en Italie, et probablement en Normandie et ailleurs en Europe : la culture tactique. Cette culture est un objet dynamique fait de traditions mais aussi d'adaptations, plus ou moins réussies, cela dans des cadres géographiques, comme la région au sud de Rome, et humains particuliers, y compris l'ennemi allemand. L'insistance sur la culture, parce qu'elle lie individus et institutions, a l'avantage d'éviter d'imputer trop facilement un échec à un seul responsable[3], ce qui paraît vraiment inappropriée lorsque l'on étudie une armée de plusieurs centaines de milliers d'individus dans laquelle pas même le commandant en chef n'a les mains libres.

De fait, il semble qu'il y ait parfois un monde entre l'expression d'une idée et sa traduction en gestes, et que cette traduction en gestes se fait selon des modalités qui sont particulières, dépendantes de traditions remontant à l'avant-guerre, d'habitudes acquises avant 1939, puis en 1940, 1941 et 1942 et d'adaptations encore plus récentes, disons depuis la Sicile en 1943. La fusion des trois couches que sont une tradition, l'acquisition de nouvelles habitudes et l'adaptation de dernière minute est inévitable, car la guerre moderne est une affaire complexe qui ne peut s'apprendre à partir de zéro. Le soldat est donc amené à un niveau de savoir suffisant, et il l'est efficacement, lorsque les méthodes reconnues depuis assez longtemps et toujours efficaces (les traditions), ce qu'il peut apprendre en quelques années sous l'uniforme (depuis le début de la Deuxième Guerre mondiale) et les changements introduits pour s'adapter au terrain et à l'ennemi après les premières rencontres s'intègrent bien. Les adaptations finiront par laisser quelque chose qui deviendra habitudes voire traditions, du moins dans une culture ouverte et dynamique. Tout ça forme une culture militaire particulière. Inversement, une culture peut être un facteur d'inadaptation relative ou totale si la rencontre avec la réalité conduit à une trop radicale remise en question, qui sera refusée ou mal intégrée. Dans l'affaire de la percée de la ligne Senger (vrai nom de la ligne « Hitler »), on voit bien cette dynamique traditions-habitudes-adaptations à l'œuvre. Le 1er Corps canadien en Italie fournit donc un bon échantillon de la culture tactique canadienne du moment.

Mais avant d'entrer dans le détail des leçons tirées de la fatale journée du 23 mai 1944, il faut comprendre les mécanismes par lesquels l'Armée canadienne apprend.

Les trois filières d'instruction de l'Armée canadienne

Deux éléments de contexte doivent être gardés à l'esprit : l'héritage de 1914-1918 et l'appartenance au Commonwealth britannique.

Toutes les armées occidentales ont ressenti profondément l'effet des hécatombes de la Grande Guerre. Il n'est donc pas nécessaire de s'étendre sur le sujet. Disons seulement qu'à cause de la petitesse de la force régulière de 1939 (4 000 hommes dont 400 officiers) et d'un avancement lent et limité à peu d'élus, l'Armée canadienne a dû absorber un concentré puissant des conséquences de la Grande Guerre, qu'aggravaient des difficultés budgétaires qui se firent sentir jusqu'à l'année de Munich. En outre, et malgré des pertes qui n'avaient rien à voir avec celles des armées européennes (61 000 pour l'armée de terre, pour une population de quelque 8 millions), les décideurs étaient obsédés par le souci d'éviter un nouvel engagement canadien sur terre. Du reste, le gouvernement de W.L. Mackenzie King était peu porté sur les affaires militaires, premier ministre en tête, craintif qu'une nouvelle conscription entraîne des difficultés politiques internes identiques à celles de 1917-1918. L'armée de terre fut donc peu choyée entre 1920 et 1939, les décideurs lui préférant la marine. En 1939, on verra même qu'ils accueilleront avec enthousiasme une formidable expansion de l'aviation, y compris une aviation de bombardement stratégique, à leur grand dam, car la RCAF sera proportionnellement le service armé le plus touché par les pertes en 1939–1945, parce qu'on n'avait pas compris les risques du bombardement à longue distance. Il n'y a aussi aucun doute que des considérations matérielles (un Canada arsenal du Commonwealth) servaient à justifier les limites imposées à un engagement significatif de l'armée de terre[4].

Le second élément est le lien impérial. Que l'Empire britannique s'appelle depuis peu Commonwealth des nations n'y change rien, car le Canada joue un rôle politique marginal dans la coalition alliée pour toute la durée de la guerre[5]. La planification stratégique relève donc exclusivement de Londres. Mais cela va plus loin, car l'Armée canadienne s'identifie à sa grande sœur britannique depuis toujours. Elle est organisée sur le modèle anglais, ce qui permet d'insérer facilement ses divisions dans l'ordre de bataille d'une force expéditionnaire britannique. La doctrine générale (*Field Service Regulations*) et la tactique des bataillons et régiments (les divers *training pamphlets*) sont rigoureusement identiques, les manuels britanniques étant repris tels quels au Canada, sauf pour la mention de l'imprimeur. Il faut donc prendre avec un grain de sel les affirmations que les Canadiens se battent autrement que les Britanniques, ce que beaucoup trop d'auteurs considèrent comme un truisme. Le matériel est de conception britannique jusqu'à 1940 au moins et lorsqu'il est manufacturé au Canada, il l'est souvent sous licence britannique. La ligne logistique britannique pourra donc servir sans hiatus une division canadienne. La parenté d'organisation et de matériel facilite aussi la substitution d'unités des dominions aux unités britanniques, ce qui pose un problème politique que les Britanniques ont tendance à sous-estimer. Plus important encore est le fait que les officiers supérieurs suivent leurs cours avancés dans les écoles de guerre britanniques durant tout l'entre-deux-guerres, favorisant des liens personnels étroits entre les états-majors canadien et britannique. À ce sujet, Steve Harris a montré que le général McNaughton préférait comme candidats aux écoles d'état-major des officiers d'artillerie ou du génie, ce qui a eu pour effet de conduire ce type de spécialistes au faîte de l'Armée canadienne au début de la Seconde Guerre mondiale[6] : les deux commandants de la 1ère Armée canadienne, McNaughton et Crerar, étaient artilleurs et les deux premiers commandants de corps à voir le feu, Burns et Simonds, respectivement ingénieur militaire et artilleur[7].

L'état-major canadien concevra pendant longtemps (toujours ?) l'offensive sur le modèle des *set piece attacks* des années 1916-1918, avec gestion scientifique de l'artillerie et passage successif d'unités élargissant la brèche (infanterie), ensuite d'unités d'exploitation (infanterie et artillerie de campagne) et finalement d'unités de poursuite (cavalerie et artillerie à cheval) à travers les lignes des bataillons ayant conduit l'assaut initial. McNaughton (chef de la contre-batterie canadienne en 1916-1918), Crerar (premier officier d'état-major de l'artillerie en 1918) et Burns (des transmissions, plus jeune officier d'état-major canadien en 1918, à 21 ans) firent leur réputation dans la préparation des attaques de rupture de la fin de 1916 à novembre 1918. Seul Simonds, trop jeune, ne fut pas personnellement marqué par ce type d'attaque. Il va se révéler le meilleur commandant de corps canadien en 1944-1945, notamment parce qu'il fut, jusqu'à un certain point, capable d'innover dans l'utilisation de l'artillerie automotrice et de l'infanterie montée sur des véhicules blindés spécialement adaptés. Reste que Simonds fut lui aussi fervent des plans sur-élaborés avec grosses préparations, phases multiples et minutage serré, et que sa solution opérationnelle consistait à écraser l'adversaire sous un déluge de feu, pour vaincre grâce à une série de batailles d'attrition[8].

J'ai montré ailleurs que la réflexion sur la guerre moderne était avancée dans l'Armée canadienne de 1939[9]. Mais elle restait asservie aux conceptions britanniques. Pour prendre un seul exemple, à l'instar du modèle britannique, les grandes formations canadiennes étaient des divisions d'infanterie sans chars et, lorsqu'on décidera de former un corps blindé, des divisions blindées faibles en infanterie. Comme l'on ne concevait tout de même pas que l'infanterie puisse triompher des mitrailleuses et des barbelés seule, existaient aussi des brigades de chars d'infanterie constituées aux fins d'appuyer les brigades d'infanterie en distribuant des escadrons de chars selon les besoins.

De la sorte, on évitait que les « cavaliers » d'une grande division blindée n'émoussent leur allant en coopérant avec des fantassins. Les deux types de formations de chars ayant des missions divergentes, il était prévu que chacune soit équipée de véhicules différents, des chars lourds d'infanterie lents, au blindage épais, armés d'obusiers à explosifs brisants, d'une part, et, d'autre part, des chars croiseurs rapides, mais au blindage mince et armés d'un *2-pounder* ne tirant que des obus perforants. Pis, jusqu'à 1941, on n'avait pas admis que les chars lourds puissent tirer des munitions perforantes et vice versa, avec les conséquences qu'on imagine. C'était suivre exactement la doctrine britannique.

Les deux types de formation de chars devaient être engagés dans des situations différentes, et en séquence, car s'impose dans les forces impériales une doctrine imaginée par Bernard Law Montgomery, d'abord publiée dans un article du *British Army Journal*, et repris dans le *Canadian Defence Quarterly* d'octobre 1937. Montgomery, alors général de brigade, y préconise la bataille séquencée, où la division reconnaît, entre en contact et livre un combat d'artillerie, puis fait pause car « il sera rarement avisé, et en fait impossible, de livrer un combat divisionnaire le jour même où le contact est établi[10] ». Mutatis mutandis, cette conceptualisation de la bataille ressemble à s'y méprendre aux grandes opérations anglo-canado-australiennes de 1918. Dans ce type d'opération, la succession des divisions alimente la bataille, et pour chaque phase la préparation d'artillerie est soigneuse. Les différences d'avec 1918 tiennent au fait qu'en 1937 la mécanisation totale des armées britanniques et canadiennes est en cours, ce facteur devenant apparemment le seul garant d'une vitesse supérieure. L'article est longuement commenté sur un mode louangeur par la rédaction du magazine canadien[11]. Par ailleurs, Montgomery est conscient que l'Armée britannique peut être tentée d'être conservatrice. En conséquence, il préconise l'attaque de nuit et le positionnement d'un PC de combat près du front d'attaque pour permettre au divisionnaire de sentir la bataille. Toutes ces caractéristiques se retrouveront à El Alamein en octobre 1942, PC avancés, attaque de nuit et séquences journalières. La méthode Montgomery deviendra la pratique standard britannique en Italie et en Normandie, comme l'ont montré David French et Niall Barr[12].

Une autre caractéristique de l'art de la guerre britannique est notable : c'est le manque d'autonomie des officiers subalternes, une caractéristique qu'on trouve aussi chez les Canadiens, lacune en grande partie attribuable à la faiblesse de leur instruction théorique et à la médiocrité de l'entraînement des subalternes et des pelotons, ce jusqu'en 1941[13]. Les cadres supérieurs sont un peu mieux lotis, car s'ils ont accès aux grandes écoles britanniques, mais l'on sait que celles-ci ont eu tendance à négliger la tactique au profit de la stratégie. De plus, à cause des restrictions budgétaires, aucunes manœuvres n'ont été tenues au Canada dans l'entre-deux-guerres sauf en 1938, et ici seulement entre bataillons. Les manœuvres de 1939 ont été annulées à cause de la mobilisation[14].

Tout cela fait que l'état-major canadien a une conception linéaire des opérations, que l'artillerie lui paraît essentielle en tout, de la plus grande opération au plus modeste raid, en défense comme en attaque, d'où de longs ordres écrits détaillés mais lents à produire.

Sans expérience, peu entraînée et faible dans l'enseignement tactique, l'Armée canadienne est prise de cours lorsqu'en mai 1940 elle se voit confrontée aux nouvelles tactiques allemandes[15]. La rapide défaite française et la chanceuse retraite britannique causent une crise à Ottawa, dans le gouvernement et dans l'armée. Il devient urgent d'apprendre. Un système est improvisé. On pourrait presque dire trois systèmes, car jusqu'à 1942—1943, il repose sur trois filières concurrentes : une filière en sol canadien, une filière autour du Quartier général canadien à Londres et une dans les divisions et corps d'armée. Les trois filières existent en parallèle, sans coordination dans les premières années de la guerre. Du reste, le désarroi tactique est si grand, l'autorité doctrinale si absente que des centres d'entraînement locaux et des unités, et jusqu'aux simples bataillons d'infanterie, improvisent des méthodes que les divers quartiers généraux peinent à superviser. L'innovation, qui conduira à infirmer l'idée du peu d'autonomie à laisser aux subalternes, vient du bas, et de plusieurs endroits, avec ce que cela a de vivifiant, mais avec le risque d'un manque de coordination entre unités d'armes différentes, entre unités de la même arme s'entraînant loin les unes des autres et entre grandes unités stationnées au Canada, en Grande-Bretagne ou en théâtre d'opérations[16].

Cette situation, que connaissaient les quartiers généraux à Ottawa et à Londres, ne pouvait durer. La rationalisation a lieu entre 1941 et 1943 : instruction de base au Canada seulement, en deux étapes (camps de recrues, premiers camps de spécialisation d'armes) ; instruction avancée au Canada et en Grande-Bretagne (tactique élémentaire et avancée) ; mise à niveau en Grande-Bretagne et en théâtre d'opérations (familiarisation avec les procédures locales et mises à jour selon les besoins). Malheureusement, la duplication demeurait dans les spécialisations et, pis, dans chacun de ces trois mondes il y avait une perception que l'on savait mieux y faire que dans les deux autres[17]. En plus, tous les chefs – d'armée, de corps, de divisions, de brigades et de régiments – avaient toujours assez de latitude pour qu'apparaissent des variations d'une unité à l'autre.

À peine moins anarchique fut le processus de rétroaction. Théoriquement, tout devait être validé par les services du War Office à Londres, puis par la Direction de l'Instruction à Ottawa, du moins pour les manuels relatifs aux cours élémentaires et avancés. En réalité, toutes les unités, et parfois même le bataillon, y allaient de leurs cours polycopiés si jamais un officier dynamique en décidait ainsi, d'un grade aussi peu élevé que capitaine. C'est ainsi que le plus important manuel tactique, le plus radical par les changements proposés et celui qui va susciter les réactions les plus vives, fut le résultat d'expériences menées par une poignée de chefs de pelotons et de commandants de compagnie des Calgary Highlanders[18].

Parce que l'approbation et la publication des manuels ne pouvaient s'effectuer assez rapidement, le War Office avait aussi lancé une série de notes du champ de bataille, y compris des documents allemands traduits, qu'il diffusait auprès de toutes les forces du Commonwealth. La Direction de l'Instruction canadienne, création récente, fit un pas de plus en publiant un mensuel – le *Mémorandum sur l'instruction dans l'Armée canadienne*. En page 2, on peut lire l'avertissement suivant : « Chaque officier de l'Armée au Canada doit recevoir un exemplaire de la publication mensuelle : *Mémorandum sur l'instruction de l'Armée canadienne*. S'il ne lui parvient pas, il doit en avertir son commandant. »

Logiquement, les rédacteurs ont d'abord proposé d'étudier la *blitzkrieg*.

L'emploi du mot « blitzkrieg » a fait croire au monde qu'il s'agissait d'une déviation des principes tactiques, quand, en réalité, il ne s'agissait que d'une application de deux principes reconnus dans tous les pays :

(a) Toutes les armes doivent coopérer pour permettre à l'infanterie d'en venir aux mains avec l'ennemi, pendant qu'elle a encore les moyens d'infléchir la situation.

(b) Toutes les armes doivent contribuer à la poursuite acharnée de l'ennemi une fois sa résistance brisée.

[…] Même si les véhicules blindés de combat, l'aviation et les troupes mobiles peuvent contribuer à faire d'un succès tactique une victoire stratégique, l'infanterie a son rôle à jouer, qui est de pousser en avant, au prix même de perdre contact sur ses flancs, pour empêcher l'ennemi d'établir une position de repli. Dans une telle situation, les chefs subordonnés, souvent laissés à leur propre initiative, doivent agir avec audace et être prêts à assumer des responsabilités[19].

Compte tenu des difficultés futures à coopérer des diverses unités canadiennes, les extraits suivants sont également intéressants :

Les Allemands ont organisé des unités d'armes combinées et, dans la vaste zone d'instruction de Luneberger Heide au nord de Berlin, ils ont développé la technique du tir et du déplacement de ces unités. Dès 1936, au cours d'une conversation avec von Schell, alors lieutenant-colonel, il m'a déclaré qu'ils étaient « convaincus d'avoir développé une méthode efficace d'attaque blindée ». Le bataillon d'armes combinées constituait alors, comme aujourd'hui, le fondement de leur organisation. […]

On peut résumer comme suit les principes tactiques enseignés :

1. il n'existe aucune règle en tactique ; […]
6. l'action offensive : les Allemands enseignent que l'attaque dérange les plans de l'ennemi, crée des occasions favorables aux chefs agressifs, permet d'apprécier l'effectif ennemi et conserve l'initiative[20].

En général on peut dire que dans le *Mémorandum* étaient publiées des informations en provenance du War Office, auxquelles s'ajoutait ce qu'on avait pu glaner d'autres sources, telle l'Armée américaine, plus des directives d'instruction émises au Canada. Parfois la rédaction tentait une timide synthèse dans les premières pages. C'est le mieux que put faire une armée finalement peu préparée à combattre les Allemands.

L'effet désert

Les publications ne sont qu'une facette du processus de rétroaction, dont on s'attend bien qu'il passe surtout par les affectations d'officiers revenant du champ de bataille. Dans le cas canadien, c'était une impossibilité avant la seconde moitié de 1943 ; peu de Canadiens avaient vu le combat et la majorité de ceux qui l'avaient connu, à Hong Kong et à Dieppe, ne sont pas revenus avant 1945. Pour pallier, des instructeurs britanniques ayant vu le feu furent prêtés à l'Armée canadienne, Crerar et Simonds firent de brefs séjours auprès de la 8ᵉ Armée en Égypte et 201 officiers supérieurs et subalternes et 147 sous-officiers et soldats furent affectés à des unités britanniques en Tunisie à l'hiver 1943[21]. Malgré cela, la Tunisie laisse peu de traces dans les documents sur le

Soldats canadiens au bivouac le 18 décembre 1943. [BAC PA-204299]

retour d'expérience, et les idées tactiques en vogue en 1943-1944 découlent plutôt de la guerre en Lybie en 1941-1942.

Les procédés développés en Lybie auront une influence jusqu'en Normandie, théâtre pourtant peu comparable. Tenons-nous en ici à la collaboration entre les chars et l'infanterie, ce que les grands chefs du Commonwealth appellent coopération, concept en retrait de la symbiose relevée dans les documents allemands. Ainsi, dans le numéro 2 des *Nouvelles des théâtres de guerre*, sur les combats en Cyrénaïque, on peut lire ceci :

> Le rôle de nos éléments blindés est ordinairement la destruction des opposants ennemis. Cette mission ne peut s'exécuter par des manœuvres d'attaque directe que si nos chars sont armés de canons meilleurs que ceux de l'ennemi ou si nous jouissons d'une grande supériorité numérique. Pour le moment, nos canons ne sont pas meilleurs et nous ne sommes pas assurés d'une supériorité numérique suffisante. Ce n'est qu'en donnant à nos éléments cuirassés le plus d'appui d'artillerie possible que nous pourrons remplir ce rôle. […]
>
> Sauf lorsqu'il s'agit de poursuivre un ennemi en déroute, *il est interdit* de faire avancer les chars une fois qu'on a pris contact avec l'ennemi, sans avoir quelques canons en batterie derrière soi. […]
>
> Il semble que nous avons infligé à l'ennemi ses pertes les plus sérieuses quand il a voulu attaquer nos canons en batterie. Nous devons donc chercher à attirer ses chars sur nos canons. C'est d'ailleurs la méthode *allemande*[22].

Clairement, l'auteur met en garde contre l'utilisation indépendante des chars et préfère la méthode « allemande », forme de trappe où les chars sont attirés sur les canons antichars. Tout cela est très bien, mais ce qui est déroutant, c'est l'absence d'infanterie. Dans le désert, elle a de la difficulté à suivre et souvent on peut limiter le nombre de fantassins. Mais en déduire que c'est le cas général est dangereux. C'est l'effet désert[23].

Il n'y a pas de coopération organique entre chars et infanterie. C'est encore plus évident dans la seconde partie de la note sur l'emploi des chars d'infanterie.

> Chronométrage de l'attaque. – Le succès de ces attaques dépend pour une bonne part du chronométrage précis des opérations et de l'appui mutuel des chars, de

l'infanterie et de l'artillerie. Les mesures préliminaires et le chronométrage sont d'une extrême importance.

L'expérience a encore une fois fait voir que l'infanterie ne doit accueillir qu'avec une extrême réserve les renseignements touchant le chronométrage de l'appui des autres armes. Cet avertissement est encore plus important lorsqu'on n'a pas eu souvent l'occasion de travailler avec les unités en cause.

Dans toutes les opérations où deux armes ou plus doivent collaborer, on doit prévoir de très larges tolérances dans le chronométrage. À cause d'un certain nombre de facteurs pouvant changer leur vitesse, cette précaution s'impose surtout à l'égard des chars d'infanterie dont la marche d'approche peut être fort longue et dont l'arrivée peut subir des retards si les routes sont mauvaises[24].

« Chronométrage » revient cinq fois dans l'extrait. Le mot est de fait continuellement utilisé dans les notes sur la Cyrénaïque. La première de celle-ci, publiée en novembre 1941 est claire sur le problème de la « collaboration de toutes les armes » (intitulé du premier alinéa après l'avant-propos) : « Quand on disposait de munitions de 25 [pour l'obusier *25-pounder*], l'emploi conjoint de barrages chronométrés, de chars, de chenillettes et d'un minimum d'infanterie eut un grand succès ». Cette leçon est le résultat de mauvaises expériences face à l'Afrikakorps opérant en Lybie depuis seulement six mois. Malgré que les méthodes allemandes soient décrites avec exactitude, jamais les auteurs britanniques ne conçoivent la coopération de leurs armes à eux en termes aussi organiques que ce qu'ils décrivent chez leurs adversaires.

Reste un point positif de l'expérience nord-africaine : c'est en Afrique du Nord que les Britanniques développent un système d'appui aérien en temps réel grâce à des camions radio et surtout grâce à la bonne attente entre quartiers généraux de l'armée et de l'aviation[25]. Avant l'Afrique du Nord, le corps d'armée coordonnait ; à partir de 1942, on réussit à décentraliser au niveau des brigades : « Une division d'infanterie à laquelle on accorde du support aérien sur le front aura normalement un "tentacule" d'écoute, en plus des "tentacules" qui sont confiés à ses brigades[26]. »

Traditions, héritage de 14-18 et effet désert ont pour résultat une doctrine canadienne caractéristique. Elle s'énonce en une série de directives publiées dans le *MIAC* en 1941, dont la plupart semblent venir du quartier général de McNaughton en Angleterre. Elles reprennent presque mot pour mot la doctrine britannique issue de la campagne de Lybie.

La Directive n° 2 expose les missions d'une brigade indépendante de chars d'infanterie, qui devrait procéder ainsi en attaque : « a) attaquer les postes de résistance solidement organisés, en collaboration étroite avec l'infanterie ; b) attaquer les postes de résistance organisés à la hâte ; c) exploiter les succès obtenus en agissant indépendamment ». Rappelons qu'il s'agit ici d'une unité opposée à des divisions d'infanterie ; or, l'idée d'exploitation sans infanterie y est bien vivante[27].

C'est encore plus vrai dans la Directive n° 3 sur la division blindée. À cette époque, le Corps blindé canadien vient tout juste d'être fondé et il est évident que sa doctrine reflète autant les débats d'avant-guerre que les leçons des combats en cours en Afrique du Nord, où de grands enveloppements par des forces blindées sont réalisés tant par les Britanniques contre les Italiens que par les Allemands contre les Britanniques. Les chars semblent être l'arme prépondérante et « [la] défaite [de l'ennemi] est de nature à produire un effet moral décisif ». On y formule une méthode directement opposés aux préceptes allemands publiés dans le *MIAC* de la même année et cités plus haut. Par exemple, l'alinéa 9 de cette troisième directive générale détaille la méthode d'attaque contre les formations d'infanterie. Les extraits suivants suffisent à en rendre l'esprit :

> (i) Les divisions blindées peuvent recevoir la tâche d'attaquer les divisions d'infanterie ennemies […] Si l'ennemi occupe une position défensive solidement organisée, la tâche ne convient pas à la division blindée. Voici les tâches appropriées : exploiter le succès obtenu par les autres troupes […], effectuer une brèche dans les lignes de l'arrière-garde au cours d'une poursuite, accomplir une poussée à travers un réseau protecteur d'avant-postes. […]
> (iii) […] Si l'on rencontre de la résistance dans un secteur inaccessible aux chars (c.-à-d. un village) mais qu'il faut détruire afin de débarrasser l'axe de progression, on a besoin de l'artillerie ou de l'aviation de bombardement en appui rapproché. Une fois bombardé, le secteur est nettoyé par l'infanterie du bataillon motorisé [élément organique de la division blindée]. Si la résistance

est ferme et qu'on a miné ou obstrué les voies d'accès, une attaque concertée minutieusement et livrée par le bataillon motorisé appuyé par tout le feu disponible s'impose.

Lorsqu'on exploite un succès ou qu'on poursuit un ennemi en déroute, la division blindée doit y aller hardiment [...] Les défilés et les obstacles antichars naturels doivent souvent être capturés afin de rendre aux blindés leur liberté de manœuvre. Dans ces tâches, la collaboration de toutes les armes et l'assistance de l'aviation en appui rapproché s'imposent. [...]
L'apparition soudaine et inattendue des chars provoque parfois l'écroulement de la défense entière[28].

Une logique apparemment sans faille ne masque pas le fait que l'infanterie est une reine qui s'efface devant le nouveau monarque, le char.

Entre 1941 et 1943 les procédés ont varié, de sorte que de temps à autre quelques lignes des directives font l'objet d'amendements, mais ceux-ci restent mineurs. Pis, le Quartier général de la Défense nationale peine à intégrer les nouveautés tactiques alors qu'il démêle l'écheveau des filières du retour d'expérience. Significativement, il ne publie sa première directive d'ensemble sur l'instruction tactique des troupes qu'en novembre 1943, quatre mois après la Sicile. Malgré cela, cette première vraie tentative de synthèse de la doctrine et des méthodes d'entraînement retarde sur l'expérience de Lybie, en restant à peu près aux procédés de 1916-1918. La section la plus importante est celle sur l'attaque d'une position principale. On y prescrit l'attaque sur un front étroit, la concentration de toute la puissance de feu disponible aux ordres du commandement supérieur et le principe de la saturation du feu[29].

Ajoutons qu'à la veille du débarquement de Sicile (14 juillet 1943), l'arrivée du Sherman américain, qui équipera bientôt toutes les formations blindées, met fin à la coûteuse distinction entre chars d'infanterie et chars croiseurs, du moins dans les formations canadiennes. Malheureusement, avec sa vitesse, sa fiabilité mécanique et son canon polyvalent, il accroît tellement la confiance des équipages qu'il aggrave la propension à agir de manière autonome, ce d'autant que sa réputation n'a pas encore souffert de rencontres avec les Panther et les Tiger.

Les Canadiens en Sicile et en Italie

C'est véritablement en Sicile que démarre un processus canadien de rétroaction. Sachant ce que l'on vient d'observer, on ne s'étonnera pas que les leçons paraissent parfois dangereusement primaires. Un compendium de « leçons apprises » en Sicile est publié dans le *MIAC* en janvier 1944. Parmi les quarante-trois mentionnées, retenons celles-ci :

> 3. En certains cas, on ne tenait pas assez compte du temps nécessaire à l'infanterie afin d'exécuter une manœuvre.
> 14. [...] On a constaté que, attaqué à l'arme blanche, l'ennemi, non seulement ne défend pas ses positions, mais, au contraire, se rend.
> 22. Les chars de combat étaient fortement secoués, apparemment par le feu des mortiers. On découvre alors que les détonations proviennent de l'explosion des mines. Avant cette découverte, neuf chars étaient hors d'usage, les chenilles complètement démolies.
> 23. Un chef de peloton en particulier fait rapport que les postes ennemis de mitrailleuses sont des chars de combat allemands, occupant d'excellentes positions défensives.
> 33. Notre mortier de 3 po. est aussi bon que le mortier allemand de 81 mm, sauf quant à la portée[30].

Sur la question de la collaboration des chars et des fantassins après la Sicile, où ne fut engagé qu'un seul des régiments blindés de la 1ère Brigade de chars d'infanterie, les historiens du Corps blindé sont plutôt critiques :

> [En Sicile, le Régiment de Trois-Rivières] fournissait le soutien de chars au bataillon d'infanterie de tête de la brigade qui était engagée. Ce changement continuel de brigades et de bataillons rendait la coopération chars-infanterie quelque peu difficile, du moins au début. Comme il n'y avait pas de procédures normalisées et imposées, les commandants ne se connaissaient pas ou ne se faisaient pas toujours confiance et ni les tankistes ni les fantassins ne savaient ce que voulaient ou ce qu'ils pouvaient obtenir de l'autre arme. Ceci était aggravé par les problèmes de communication avec l'infanterie, qui devenaient plus difficiles à mesure que le pays devenait plus montagneux. Ce problème fut exacerbé d'une part par les radios portatives de l'infanterie, de faible puissance, de courte portée

et souvent défectueuses, et d'autre part la non fiabilité des radios modèle n° 38 installées dans certains chars à atteindre les fréquences de l'infanterie[31].

Ces problèmes vont perdurer.

L'apparition du 1er Corps d'armée canadien sur le front italien a été controversée. D'une part, depuis 1939, les Canadiens terminaient leur entraînement au Royaume-Uni ; de l'impatience se manifestait tant chez les hommes que chez les officiers, et il devenait difficile de justifier une longue inaction auprès des opinions publiques[32]. D'autre part, en tant que nouvelle formation opérationnelle, le Corps canadien ne fut pas le bienvenu. Les Britanniques ne voulaient pas d'un autre corps national en Italie, prétextant les difficultés d'échanger les divisions entre corps d'armée conçus comme formations nationales. Pour les Canadiens, c'était l'inverse depuis le précédent de 1915 : afin que le Canada ait son mot à dire dans l'emploi de ses grandes unités, il fallait former un corps dans lequel les divisions canadiennes combattraient toujours ensemble. La thèse canadienne prévalut. La 1ère Division et la 1ère Brigade de chars d'infanterie engagées depuis la Sicile en juillet 1943 furent donc rejointes en février 1944 par la 5e Division blindée, l'artillerie d'un corps d'armée et les autres unités dépendantes de celui-ci. Le lieutenant-général H.D.G. Crerar, qui avait occupé un temps la fonction de chef d'état-major de l'Armée à Ottawa, prit le commandement du corps, mais pour seulement une saison, car il fut rappelé en Angleterre pour remplacer McNaughton, limogé pour incompétence après la faillite des manœuvres d'armée qu'il commandait[33]. Le major-général E.L.M. Burns, en dépit du fait qu'il n'avait pas combattu depuis 1918, est donc bombardé commandant du corps à la mi-mars 1944. Le major-général Simonds, qui commandait la 1ère Division, est lui aussi rappelé en Angleterre, car Montgomery l'a remarqué et lui fait confiance pour Overlord. Sauf pour le transfert de Simonds, ces nominations ont été faites contre la règle en vigueur dans la 8e Armée britannique (dont dépend le 1er Corps canadien) selon laquelle les généraux de brigade, de division et de corps d'armée doivent être tirés des formations inférieures en théâtre. Rien pour assurer une transmission bien huilée de l'expérience.

Non seulement les Britanniques s'opposèrent à la formation du corps canadien, mais ils étaient contre l'addition d'une division blindée. L'arrivée en Italie d'une division blindée supplémentaire, à une brigade de chars plus une brigade d'infanterie, se faisait alors qu'on jugeait que le terrain requérait plutôt des renforts d'infanterie. D'ailleurs, après seulement quelques jours de combat, du 23 mai au 3 juin 1944, le général Burns se rendit compte qu'il fallait augmenter la 5ᵉ Division d'une seconde brigade d'infanterie, car la 11ᵉ Brigade d'infanterie, brigade organique de la division blindée, était à bout de souffle. Des bataillons d'infanterie supplémentaires furent demandés au Canada, mais le War Office a opposé son veto, craignant que des unités canadiennes soient détournées de l'effort en cours en Normandie[34]. En conséquence, en juillet, une 12ᵉ Brigade d'infanterie fut improvisée avec des unités de reconnaissance et un bataillon antiaérien du corps.

Où en est alors la campagne d'Italie ? Débarqués à Reggio le 3 septembre 1943, la 8ᵉ Armée progresse rapidement vers les plaines de l'Italie centrale, autour de Foggia, d'où peuvent opérer des bombardiers lourds. Mais les mauvaises conditions climatiques diminuent l'effet de sa supériorité en chars, en artillerie et en avions et, lorsque les Alliés atteignent la ligne Gustav en décembre 1943, l'avance stoppe. L'infanterie est épuisée et le commandant en chef britannique, le général Montgomery, suspend les opérations à la fin de l'automne. Le 1ᵉʳ janvier 1944, en prévision de l'opération Overlord, il est relevé par l'un de ses commandants de corps, le lieutenant-général Oliver Leese. Crerar sera bientôt de la partie.

Pour débloquer la situation, un corps américain et un corps britannique débarquent le 22 janvier 1944 à Anzio, sur l'arrière de la ligne Gustav et du principal point d'appui, Cassino. Cinq jours auparavant, le 10ᵉ Corps d'armée britannique avait attaqué la ligne Gustav de front pour fixer les réserves allemandes. Malgré tout, les Allemands réagissent vite au débarquement, car ils avaient pris des dispositions au cas où les Alliés tenteraient justement de débarquer près de Rome. Ils arrivent à rétablir la situation en formant un périmètre serré autour d'Anzio, et en stoppant les autres forces alliées sur la ligne Gustav, sauf pour quelques reculs mineurs. Le mauvais temps se poursuivant, l'offensive générale est finalement reportée au printemps.

Les Canadiens sont alors à la toute droite du front, sur l'Adriatique. Avant le ralliement de la 5ᵉ Division, la 1ʳᵉ Division et la 1ʳᵉ Brigade de chars d'infanterie n'avaient somme toute pas été engagées souvent après la Sicile, si on fait exception des combats sur la Moro et autour d'Ortona en décembre

1943. De janvier à avril 1944, période de pluies fortes et continuelles, les troupes furent plutôt inactives. Le calme devait permettre le rodage des formations, particulièrement la planification d'une opération de corps, alors que de petites opérations devaient donner de l'expérience à la 5e Division blindée canadienne. L'offensive prévue pour le printemps 1944 serait donc la première grande opération pour le corps d'armée et ses unités auxiliaires (dont l'artillerie de corps et la police militaire, celle-ci chargée du trafic routier) et la première où toutes les formations canadiennes travailleraient réunies. Il fallait s'y préparer.

À ce stade de la guerre, le type d'opérations envisagées est la percée d'une ligne de fortifications de campagne, suivie d'une poursuite diligente afin d'empêcher l'ennemi de se rétablir. Dans ce but, le général Crerar organise une série de conférences et d'exercices d'états-majors du 3 au 12 février 1944. Sont invités des représentants de la 8e Armée britannique, dont le général Leese, qui arbitrera les exercices du premier après-midi, ceux du 13e Corps britannique et de sa 8e Division indienne d'infanterie, et évidemment des officiers du 1er Corps canadien et de ses deux divisions. Les sujets privilégiés sont assez limités : appui aérien avec présentation du tentacule Rover-David pour colonnes blindées en poursuite, lutte contre les mortiers, entraînement de l'infanterie et, plus que tous les autres sujets réunis, support de l'artillerie avant et pendant la percée.

Crerar, qui quittera le commandement du 1er Corps à la mi-mars, laisse pourtant son empreinte sur les méthodes tactiques. C'est lui qui prononce la conférence d'ouverture le 3 février. C'est un instantané extrêmement révélateur de l'art de la guerre canadien en cette fin de Deuxième Guerre mondiale. Puisque les Canadiens sont encore sur la côte est de l'Italie, les conférences et exercices de ces jours-là présupposent que la percée à effectuer se fera sur le front Ortona-Arielli. L'attaque réelle aura bien sûr lieu ailleurs, mais la méthode qui sera employée sur la Liri le 23 mai est identique à celle discutée en février, jusqu'au découpage en deux phases avec pause entre les deux. Crerar commence sa conférence en faisant preuve de fausse modestie :

> C'est non sans inquiétude que je me soumets aux ordres du commandant de notre armée qui m'a demandé de vous présenter mes vues sur le support d'artillerie d'un plan de percée sur notre front. Cette inquiétude n'a pas pour cause un manque de confiance dans la justesse de mes idées. Elle est le résultat

du fait que je suis un nouveau venu parmi vous, qui avez une réputation au feu que j'ai encore à acquérir[35].

La suite est passionnante, car Crerar se pose non pas en chef de corps exploitant la puissance de l'artillerie, mais purement en artilleur de 1918. Se limitant au connu, c'est presque avec soulagement qu'on peut l'entendre prononcer les phrases suivantes :

> Permettez-moi de commencer par des remarques plutôt déprimantes. Depuis mon arrivée il y a trois mois, je me suis promené sur le champ de bataille. J'en suis revenu avec l'idée très douloureuse que d'une certaine manière nous voilà à boucler le cercle tactique, que, sur ce terrain, les conditions et les circonstances auxquelles nous sommes confrontés nous placent à nouveau devant des problèmes tactiques typiques de la dernière grande guerre. Les tranchées continues et les barbelés en sont peut-être absents, mais en ce qui concerne ces derniers, les mines antichars et antipersonnel y ont été efficacement substituées. Pour le reste, le problème tactique est essentiellement le même[36].

Même s'il admet son manque d'expérience, Crerar a le souci que son message soit bien entendu dans les formations canadiennes. Pas question de laisser des doutes sur la tactique à employer. Il sollicite particulièrement l'approbation du commandant de la 1ère Division, plus expérimenté que lui et qui aurait pu être chef de corps à sa place, le major-général Chris Vokes. Il demande par écrit à Vokes son opinion, en prenant soin d'ajouter que « tes idées et les miennes coïncident généralement[37] », ce qui pose d'emblée des limites aux critiques du subordonné.

Vokes répond le lendemain midi. Il soumet très respectueusement que la bataille à venir se gagnera avec une infanterie qu'on devra mieux entraîner et qui devra apprendre à s'infiltrer, ce pour quoi il demande de retirer de la ligne deux de ses trois brigades pour une période de dix à quatorze jours[38]. On peut donc douter d'une totale coïncidence de vues. Dans ses Mémoires publiées en 1985, Vokes sera d'ailleurs cinglant lorsqu'il reviendra sur la conférence de son chef : « À un moment, Crerar nous a dit que les conditions étaient les mêmes que celles des Flandres durant la Première Guerre. Que nous devrions employer les tactiques d'alors. [...] Les pertes furent affreuses. Les conditions en Italie n'avaient rien à voir, sauf pour la boue. Tout le monde dans la salle a gardé un profond silence, y compris sir Oliver. J'étais plutôt embarrassé pour l'oncle Harry[39]. »

L'exercice de l'après-midi, arbitré par Leese, met à l'essai la solution tactique suivante : i) première phase, une attaque aux premières lueurs du jour sur un front de 3000 verges (un peu moins de 3000 mètres) avec deux brigades, sous couvert d'un barrage roulant avec pour premier objectif de dépasser les avant-postes et le cours d'eau (ici, l'Arielli) en face de la position principale allemande, installée plus loin à contre-pente ; ii) pause – on suggère une heure – pour permettre à la seconde vague d'infanterie d'approcher d'aussi près que possible cette position principale ; iii) deuxième phase, nouveau barrage roulant derrière lequel de l'infanterie fraîche avance et capture l'objectif final (ici, le village de Tollo, derrière la position) ; iv) ensuite faire avancer les moyens de soutien lourds incluant les chars pour qu'ils rejoignent l'infanterie, voire aillent plus loin ; v) finalement, début de l'exploitation sans délai[40]. L'exploitation même ne faisait pas partie des sujets étudiés en ce mois de février. Autrement dit, changer l'Arielli pour le rio San Martino et vous avez le plan qui sera employé le 23 mai.

Crerar répète cette conférence devant un parterre moins prestigieux d'artilleurs le 11 février. Le 14 février, dans une note à son chef d'état-major, il demande que le texte soit circulé en vingt exemplaires dans la 1ère Division, à quinze dans la 5e Division et à cinq dans la 1ère Brigade de chars d'infanterie, assurant ainsi que tous partagent la doctrine préconisée par leur chef [41]. Notons que le biographe de Crerar distingue les effets de l'influence de celui-ci, qui aurait été très grande sur l'état-major novice du Corps, mais plus faible au sein des formations combattantes[42].

En succédant à Crerar, Burns, qui n'a pas non plus d'expérience dans le maniement d'un corps d'armée, conservera ce canevas d'opération. Leurs principaux subordonnées, malgré des doutes exprimés ici ou là, s'y rallieront, y compris le commandant de la 5e Division blindée, le major-général Bert Hoffmeister[43]. Tous savaient, Vokes, Hoffmeister et Burns également, que c'est l'ancienneté dans la force régulière qui avait valu à Burns le commandement du corps. Terry Copp écrit de cette situation bizarre que « Vokes et Hoffmeister sont au combat depuis le débarquement de Sicile et ils sont hésitants et même hostiles envers un nouvel arrivé qui doit encore faire ses preuves. Ces relations difficiles ont peut-être poussé Vokes à tenter une attaque brusquée de la ligne Hitler les 21-22 mai plutôt que d'attendre l'assaut préparé prévu le 23 mai[44] ».

La plus importante opération menée pour dégourdir la 5ᵉ Division blindée a lieu le 17 janvier 1944, le jour où l'armée britannique monte à l'assaut de la ligne Gustav pour préparer Anzio. Les Canadiens attaquaient dans la vallée de l'Arielli, au sud-est de Pescara, une attaque de brigade (d'où le sujet d'études proposé par Crerar). L'affaire s'est mal passée malgré l'appui de neuf régiments d'artillerie canadiens et britanniques. Les leçons tirées de cet engagement sont, selon le colonel Nicholson, l'historien officiel : mauvais renseignements sur la progression des unités parce que la brigade et la division répugnent à utiliser les radios, même si les fils téléphoniques sont constamment coupés ; un problème aggravé par la perte du contact radio entre les compagnies de tête et le PC de bataillon lorsque les radios sont utilisées ; annulation du programme aérien à cause de la météo ; attaque en phases successives sur un secteur étroit, ce qui permet aux Allemands de détruire les vagues d'assauts les unes après les autres ; appui défectueux des chars, qui sautent sur des mines ou n'arrivent pas à franchir les ruisseaux.

Au moment où cette petite opération était montée, il semble que la troupe s'attendait à être relevée non seulement pour passer en réserve, mais pour un changement de front. En effet, la section de sécurité du 1ᵉʳ Corps canadien parle d'une rumeur répandue dans la 1ᵉʳᵉ Division à l'effet d'une relève arrivant de Grèce, ou d'Italiens montant en ligne du côté allié, ce qui « pourra raccourcir notre séjour sur ce front[45] ». Cet espoir fut déçu et on allait s'enfoncer dans une routine néfaste. En effet, selon le commandant de la 2ᵉ Brigade d'infanterie (1ᵉʳᵉ Division), l'entraînement a laissé à désirer jusqu'en avril 1944 : « La 2ᵉ Brigade canadienne d'infanterie a été relevée par la 25ᵉ Brigade indienne d'infanterie la nuit des 23-24 avril après un long hiver passé dans des conditions éprouvantes et des circonstances déprimantes. Les troupes n'étaient pas en bonne condition physique et leur entraînement s'est limité à tenir des positions défensives et à patrouiller. Il devenait évident que la brigade devrait subit un entraînement intensif à l'offensive avant d'être apte au combat pour la campagne estivale[46] ». Le brigadier Gibson écrit ceci après l'attaque sanglante du 23 mai, sur laquelle je vais m'attarder bientôt, mais il ne s'agit pas que d'une excuse. En effet, selon un autre rapport de la section de sécurité du corps, les semaines d'inactivité entre janvier et mai 1944 ont été vécues avec difficulté dans les rangs : « Le moral demeure généralement élevé quoique l'on grogne contre l'inactivité sur ce front[47] ». Inactivité évidemment

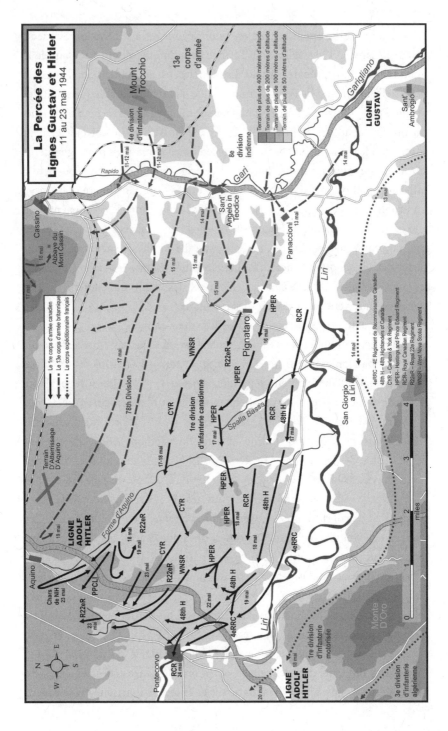

relative, puisque, on l'a vu, la période a été occupée par des études et des exercices.

Entre-temps, Rome est devenue l'enjeu. Outre l'importance symbolique, la grande attaque de mai 1944 a aussi un but stratégique : fixer le plus de forces allemandes possibles en Italie à la veille de l'opération Overlord. En prévision de l'attaque, le secteur de l'Adriatique devient passif, car les Alliés concentrent leurs efforts entre Cassino et la mer Tyrrhénienne. Cela explique le transfert de l'autre côté des Apennins du 1er Corps canadien entre le 20 avril et le 5 mai 1944[48]. Le corps est placé en réserve d'armée pour exploiter une percée à l'ouest de Cassino, secteur clef de la ligne Gustav, qui bloque l'un des axes principaux menant à Rome, la Route nationale 6.

L'assaut contre la ligne Gustav commence le 11 mai, mais les Canadiens n'y participent pas immédiatement, en-dehors de la 1ère Brigade de chars d'infanterie[49] qui soutient les brigades d'infanterie de la 8e Division indienne[50]. Ils sont maintenus en réserve par le commandant de la 8e Armée britannique, qui les engagera soit à droite du 13e Corps britannique, si Cassino est pris rapidement, soit à gauche, dans l'axe de la rivière Liri, si Cassino résiste et que la Nationale 6 demeure interdite. Dès avril 1944, Leese pensait que l'engagement des Canadiens avait toute chance de se faire à la gauche et il avait prévenu les commandants du corps et des divisions canadiennes de se préparer à cette éventualité[51]. Comme Cassino, dont le monastère n'est plus qu'un amas de décombres, tient encore une semaine, les Canadiens feront mouvement le long de la rive gauche de la Liri.

L'avance dans la vallée de la Liri

Le 11 mai, le front s'ébranle donc autour de Monte Cassino, mais pendant quelques jours encore se poursuit l'instruction, car tel que noté dans le journal de campagne de la 1ère Division le 10 mai 1944, « nous savons bien que nous jouerons les seconds violons dans la première phase » de l'offensive. Les permissions ne sont pas supprimées et les visites guidées autour de Naples, et en particulier à Pompéi, sont toujours fort courues[52]. Comme la division est presque certaine qu'elle sera engagée dans la vallée de la Liri[53], les exercices de ces jours-là sont conçus dans l'esprit de se préparer à l'exploitation d'une percée vers Rome, dans l'axe de la vallée. Une grande attention est à nouveau accordée à la sempiternelle difficulté de coopération entre les chars et l'infanterie. La 3e Brigade suggère de doter les pelotons d'infanterie d'un autre pistolet à fusées Verey, pour indiquer aux chars d'accompagnement les obstacles que l'infanterie veut voir neutraliser par les blindés[54]. Autre sujet d'un débat jamais terminé, la question des performances respectives du mortier de 3 pouces canadien versus le mortier allemand de 81 mm. La portée est ici en cause et, étrangement, des expériences conduites par les Britanniques montrent que les charges supplémentaires de poudre propulsive du mortier allemand augmentent la portée du mortier anglais de 2750 verges à 4000 verges[55].

Il est apparent que le niveau tactique de l'infanterie n'est pas ce qu'il devrait être à cette période tardive de la guerre. Prenons encore l'exemple de la 2e Brigade d'infanterie, qui fera l'effort le plus exigeant le 23 mai. Dans la suite du rapport cité plus tôt, le brigadier Gibson explique comment la forme physique a été regagnée à partir de la fin avril 1944 et ensuite comment l'entraînement a repris avec intensité, en insistant sur le rôle des subalternes et l'emploi de leurs compagnies. Plusieurs problèmes avec les armes de support ont été travaillés, notamment la montée au front des canons antichars. Puis la coopération avec les chars Churchill des North Irish Horse (puisque les chars de la 1ère Brigade canadienne travaillent avec les Indiens) est devenue l'enjeu de trois jours d'exercices du 8 au 10 mai. Au final, Gibson se dit satisfait de l'entraînement, même si le fait que l'on touche encore et toujours les mêmes sujets laisse croire que les solutions envisagées n'ont toujours pas données les résultats espérés[56].

Pendant qu'on tente de rectifier ces lacunes, les nouvelles du front sont plutôt bonnes. Si le Corps polonais a encore de la difficulté à prendre Cassino, la 8e Division indienne progresse, et plus encore les Français sur la rive opposée de la Liri.

Le 13 mai, les PC tactiques et les unités de reconnaissance sont prévenus d'un mouvement prochain. Les unités d'avant-garde de la 1ère Division partent le lendemain en vue de s'insérer dans la ligne entre le 13e Corps britannique et le Corps expéditionnaire français. Ce jour-là, on apprend que la division « sera engagée plus tôt qu'on l'avait anticipé, et que les Français vont si bien sur la gauche que l'on devrait être assuré d'être couvert sur ce flanc[57] ». Le gros de la 1ère Division fait mouvement dans la nuit du 15 au 16 mai avec deux brigades de front, 1ère à gauche, la 3e à droite. La 2e brigade et la 5[e]

Division blindée demeurent en réserve. L'avance se révèle difficile à cause de l'encombrement des routes, de l'absence de signalisation et d'une répartition confuse des responsabilités entre la 1ère Division canadienne et la 8e Division indienne[58].

Dans les jours précédant la bataille, il devient évident que les Allemands conduisent des combats d'arrière-garde aux fins de s'installer sur la position de repli préparée en prévision de la chute de Cassino et des autres positions de la ligne Gustav. Les rapports de renseignements concordent à cet effet, suscitant un optimisme modéré[59].

Deux incidents assombrissent pourtant ces jours de victoire. Dans l'après-midi du 15 mai, une jeep de l'état-major de la 1ère Division saute sur une mine, tuant l'aide-de-camp de Vokes et blessant grièvement le GSO2. Cet incident aura des conséquences en ce que Vokes ordonne que tous les planchers des jeeps du PC divisionnaire soient renforcés à l'aide de sac de sable[60]. Malgré cette mesure, le PC échappe de peu à une autre catastrophe, car les mines sont un danger omniprésent. Les ordonnances de l'officier de liaison français tout juste arrivées reculent leur jeep entre deux tentes où est installé l'officier des opérations de la division. La jeep « explose avec un grand bang, les deux Français sont chanceux et s'en sortent avec des écorchures ; les officiers d'état-major, y voyant une invite, déplacent leurs tentes[61] ».

Vokes remarque le 16 mai que le camouflage du PC et des échelons arrière est inadéquat. Il est vrai que l'aviation ennemie est peu active, mais elle continue à conduire des raids la nuit. Justement, dans la nuit du 17 au 18 mai, elle lâche quelques bombes sur cet arrière canadien si peu discret. Un camion d'essence explose, une ambulance est touchée, six patients sont blessés de nouveaux (dont trois prisonniers), alors qu'un autre camion de prisonniers a son chauffeur tué. Malgré les pertes somme toute faibles causées par le raid, « l'effet sur le moral de dix milles carrés de troupes est considérable[62] ! »

Le 17 mai, des éléments avancés de la 1ère Division canadienne connaissent des difficultés à progresser, avant d'être stoppés et contre-attaqués[63]. Sur la gauche, le 48th Highlanders a perdu l'appui des chars d'armée du 142th RAC, des Churchill, qui ont de la difficulté à franchir un petit cours d'eau (la Spalla Bassa) aux berges minées. C'est évidemment une embuscade : les Allemands détruisent cinq Churchill à coup de *Faustpatronen*. Mais le bataillon canadien poursuit néanmoins, détruisant ou capturant quatre 75 mm AC sur la hauteur dominante 1500 m plus loin. Vers 23h00, l'habituelle contre-attaque survient. Heureusement, si les chars n'ont pu suivre, le bataillon a ses *6-pounder* AC avec lui et les Allemands sont repoussés avec fortes pertes. En dehors d'escarmouches à l'arme légère avec des arrière-gardes, ce sera cependant la seule contre-attaque de ce côté du front canadien avant les défenses de la ligne Senger[64]. Sur la droite de la division, la 3e Brigade avait progressé avec célérité les 17 et 18 mai. Aussi, elle attaque avec deux bataillons appuyés par des Churchill du 51st RTR, un assaut sans préparation d'artillerie sophistiquée. Mais la brigade est stoppée, car les Allemands résistent. Les Canadiens n'insistent pas. L'avance canadienne s'arrête donc le 18 mai. Burns et Leese conviennent alors qu'il faut un assaut en règle[65]. Pourtant, rapporte-t-on dans le journal de la 2e Brigade tard le 18 mai « durant cette journée, nous n'étions pas au contact de l'ennemi, mais seulement au contact d'arrière-gardes nous harcelant. Le gros ennemi est sur la ligne Hitler[66]. » Les Français constatent quant à eux que la 8e Armée peine à suivre le rythme. Le général de Montsabert, patron de la 3e Division d'infanterie algérienne, fulmine : « C'est du véritable sabotage [...] C'est, paraît-il, la méthode Montgomery, qui lui a réussi à El Alamein. Elle ne lui a pas réussi à Enfidaville [nord tunisien], et ici, elle est fausse[67]. »

Néanmoins, Vokes reste attentif sur tout son front et lance tôt le 19 mai son bataillon de reconnaissance (19th Princess Louise Dragoon Guards) sur la même route qu'avait emprunté le 48th Highlanders trente-six heures plus tôt. Le bataillon de reconnaissance approche à moins de 1000 m de la ligne Senger, ne rencontrant que des retardataires et des tireurs d'élite avant d'être stoppé par des tirs de mortiers. Les PLDG connaissent quelques moments d'inquiétude lorsque des troupes non identifiées franchissent la Liri juste sur leur arrière, comme pour les encercler. Heureusement, ce ne sont pas des Allemands, mais des Français. La limite du corps à gauche, entre les Canadiens et les Français du général Juin, c'était la rivière. Des officiers de liaison sont échangés pour éviter toute nouvelle confusion[68].

Le soir du 19 mai, les troupes de Vokes sont sur une parallèle à environ 1000 m des défenses ennemies. La progression dans l'axe d'une vallée très étroite ne saurait se poursuivre sans pouvoir interdire aux Allemands les points d'observation en hauteur. Or, le corps polonais s'est enfin emparé du monastère de Cassino le 18 mai et on sait que les Français sont bien placés de l'autre côté. Il y aurait donc lieu de croire que les Canadiens seront bientôt en mesure de progresser sans entraves.

Le PDLG parvient à se donner une vue sur la localité de Pontecorvo tôt le 20 mai. Il y découvre une automitrailleuse allemande, ce qui laisse croire à un retrait prochain, « parce que l'on emploie souvent un bataillon de reconnaissance pour couvrir un tel genre de mouvement[69] ». La *set piece attack*, l'opération Chesterfield, est pourtant maintenue. Il semble que ce soit la décision de Burns. En effet, Vokes fait porter au journal de campagne de sa division l'entrée suivante le 19 mai : « Nos avant-gardes ont atteints les limites de la ligne ADOLPH HITLER. Nos renseignements sont d'avis que l'ennemi n'y est pas pour le moment en force et qu'un assaut déterminé permettrait de percer. Notre commandant est plutôt de cet avis, mais le Corps favorise une approche plus prudente. En conséquence, une attaque en règle sera préparée, conduite par la 2e Brigade d'infanterie. Elle aura probablement lieu le 21 mai[70]. »

À vrai dire, Vokes semble avoir des doutes à la veille de la grande bataille. L'image qu'il a laissé de lui-même d'un homme confiant, rude avec ses subalternes, usant d'un langage coloré avec tous, masque ici de l'indécision. Alors que nous sommes menés tambour battant dans ses Mémoires écrites quarante ans après les événements[71], le journal officiel de la campagne, qui ressemble à une dictée de Vokes – c'est semble-t-il le cas d'une bonne proportion des entrées du journal de la 1ère Division –, est empreint de plus de retenue. Dans la longue entrée du 20 mai, on peut lire ceci : « En fait, si l'on excepte la 1ère Brigade de chars d'infanterie, qui a fait un travail splendide de support à la 78e Division [britannique] et à la 8e Division indienne, nous avons fait peu jusqu'à maintenant [c'est-à-dire depuis l'offensive déclenchée le 11 mai]. Mais dans les prochains jours, ce sera à notre tour de subir le test[72]. »

La candeur des remarques de Vokes est tout à son honneur, mais parfois il va très loin. Les 19 et 20 mai, il fait deux critiques assez décourageantes. D'abord sur l'appui tactique aérien : « Depuis le début de cette bataille [le 11 mai], le support aérien a une curieuse histoire. La 1ère Brigade d'infanterie canadienne et le bataillon de reconnaissance ont souvent signalé des cibles à la division, tout en requérant directement ce support à travers leur tentacule lorsqu'ils en sentaient la nécessité pour les missions qu'on leur avait confiées, tandis que la 3e Brigade n'a jamais rien demandé jusqu'à maintenant, et ne s'en ressent pas plus mal pour autant[73] ! » (Les doutes de l'état-major de la

1ère Division sur l'efficacité de l'aviation tactique referont surface le 23 mai. Alors que la bataille est gagnée et que les chars de la 5e Division blindée roulent, le quartier général du corps canadien, et le PC arrière, pas le PC tactique, reçoit une bombe « lâché par un de nos avions ». Heureusement, elle n'explose pas[74].) L'appui aérien est fourni par la Desert Air Force, 239 (Fighter-Bomber) Wing, de la RAF, dont le propre rapport donne un tout autre écho, à l'effet de l'efficacité indiscutée de son rôle d'interdiction du champ de bataille[75]. Vokes s'en prend ensuite à l'artillerie : « Plusieurs fois aujourd'hui [20 mai], nous avons bombardé Pontecorvo, interdit plusieurs zones en périphérie ainsi que les casernements au nord. Impossible de dire combien d'obus ont touché la localité. Leur plus grande réussite est probablement d'avoir encombré les rues de débris. De toute façon, l'ennemi occupe rarement les zones bâties au cours d'une bataille, sauf lorsqu'il y est obligé, comme à Cassino et à Ortona[76]. »

Doutes aussi parce que même si les états-majors de la 8e Armée britannique, du 1er Corps canadien et de la 1ère Division canadienne viennent de s'entendre sur un plan avec effort sur la droite canadienne, Vokes se garde l'option d'une avancée sur sa gauche. Là, plutôt que d'attaquer de front les Allemands défendant leur route de retraite, on profiterait de l'avance du Corps expéditionnaire français, qui dépend de la 5e Armée US, pour s'emparer de la rocade entre Pontecorvo et la Nationale 6 (voir la carte 13 de l'histoire officielle de Nicholson en annexe). Au lieu d'un direct, on frapperait d'un crochet de gauche. Cette ambivalence sur le lieu de l'effort à faire est présente tout au long des jours précédant l'assaut du 23, et encore la veille, car les Français continuent d'envoyer des rapports encourageants. Du reste, Vokes s'étend sur les progrès des Français :

> Les Français avancent à grande vitesse sur la rive sud de la Liri. Ils ont nettement dépassé les positions de gauche de la ligne Hitler et ont poussé vers le nord sur la rivière même et Pontecorvo. La formation française sur notre flanc est la 1ère Division motorisée d'infanterie. C'est une division gaulliste, en fait la plus ancienne d'obédience gaulliste. Ses hommes sont du meilleur type, plus grand que les soldats français habituels, et très distingués. Nous avons deux officiers de liaison (opération et artillerie) venant de cette formation depuis le franchissement de la Gari[77].

Les nouvelles reçues le 21 mai sont tout aussi encourageantes, mais en même temps elle dérange le plan tout juste agréé. En effet, la situation est fluide dans le secteur français les 21 et 22 mai[78]. Les Allemands semblent déstabilisés par la rapidité de l'avance des troupes de montagne françaises. Leurs défenses sont maintenant sommaires et même s'ils contre-attaquent furieusement, ils ne repoussent pas les Français[79]. Aussi Vokes en vient-il à penser qu'il y a peut-être là une occasion, d'autant que l'honneur des armées du Commonwealth ne le laisse pas indifférent. Tôt le lendemain, Vokes reçoit un rapport de ces officiers de liaison à l'effet que les Français veulent pénétrer dans Pontecorvo, qui est pourtant en secteur de la 8e Armée, ce qui le conduit à ajouter ceci à ses remarques du jour précédent : « Les Français nous font pour le moins rougir un peu, même si nous avons nos raisons de faire une pause. [...] Ils nous préviennent de leur intention d'envoyer des patrouilles dans Pontecorvo ce soir. Il nous faut admirer leur audace, quoi qu'ils nous rendent un peu inconfortables[80]. » En un autre sens, le succès français perturbe la préparation de Chesterfield, car le général Burns est très pris par des visites à partir du 16 mai – il rencontre Juin et de Gaulle alors en tournée auprès du Corps expéditionnaire français –, ainsi que par des conférences de presse au cours desquelles il annonce ses intentions pour la bataille à venir[81].

Tout cela explique que, peu convaincu par la pause opérationnelle du 18 mai, Vokes s'essaye à une dernière attaque brusquée. Parce que les préparatifs de Chesterfield sont en cours, qu'en particulier sa brigade fraîche, la 2e Brigade, a le rôle principal le 23 mai, il ordonne à la 1ère Brigade et au bataillon de reconnaissance, qui ont beaucoup donné depuis une semaine, de faire une nouvelle tentative, avec encore une fois un appui blindé limité. Si jamais la localité est prise, la 2e Brigade poursuivra l'attaque, avant de passer le relais à la 5e Division blindée. Mais le 22, c'est la veille du jour J pour Chesterfield, ce qui fait que la 2e Brigade, au lieu de se placer à droite pour relever la 3e Brigade qui fera un pas de côté vers le centre du dispositif divisionnaire, que la 2e Brigade donc reste en réserve prête à se diriger sur la gauche. L'avance de la 1ère Brigade est d'abord satisfaisante, mais l'ennemi réagit. À sa gauche, la 3e Brigade qui tentait aussi d'avancer, rencontre les mêmes signes de résistance[82]. Vokes n'insiste pas, mais cette autre tentative improvisée a un effet pervers : elle repousse la relève de la 3e Brigade par la 2e Brigade à 17h00 le soir du 22 mai. Il fera sombre avant que l'infanterie de la 2e Brigade, chargée d'attaquer aux petites heures du matin, soit installée.

Bref, si l'on suit attentivement le journal de campagne et le relevé des transmissions téléphoniques/radio, on a l'impression que Vokes a de la difficulté à localiser son *schwerpunkt*.

Dans la première version du plan, Vokes prévoyait l'attaque par une brigade (la 2e) sur la droite de sa division, menaçant de la sorte la Nationale 6. Sur la gauche de la 1ère Division, il devait y avoir une feinte des 1ère et 3e Brigades vers Pontecorvo. Le secteur à percer par la 2e Brigade n'avait que 2000 verges. Un front d'attaque si étroit était dicté en partie par la largeur de la vallée de la Liri, mais aussi par les limites de corps d'armée. Du côté gauche, la sécurité est assurée et l'appui de l'artillerie française garantie (on l'a vue, il y a des officiers de liaison français depuis quelques jours[83]). Côté droit, le 13e Corps britannique (78e Division) doit occuper les Allemands dans le secteur d'Aquino. Vokes se plaindra amèrement dans ses Mémoires que les Britanniques furent trop passifs le matin du 23 mai[84]. Certains diront que Burns aurait dû obtenir pour son attaque le rattachement temporaire de la 78e Division à son corps, mais que cela fut refusé par Leese parce que celui-ci n'avait voulu ni du corps canadien comme formation indépendante ni de Burns, trop inexpérimenté[85].

Appelé à commenter cette première mouture du plan, Leese a objecté qu'un assaut contre une position préparée sur un front si étroit échouerait. Il a exigé l'élargissement du front à deux brigades[86]. C'est ce qui fait que dans le plan final un bataillon de la 3e Brigade attaque immédiatement à gauche de la 2e Brigade, qui elle a deux bataillons en tête. L'attaque doit être appuyée par les chars d'infanterie du North Irish Horse et du 51st Tank Regiment britanniques. Le plan de feu prévoit 810 canons provenant de 58 batteries canadiennes, britanniques, polonaises et françaises, dont 18 lourdes. En réserve de division se trouvent trois bataillons d'infanterie, plus le Régiment de Trois-Rivières de la 1ère Brigade de chars d'infanterie. La 5e Division blindée fournit la réserve d'exploitation. Pendant l'assaut de ses voisines de droite, la 1ère Brigade d'infanterie maintiendra la pression sur Pontecorvo.

L'attaque est déclenchée à 05h57, ce qui n'a malheureusement rien pour surprendre les Allemands. Elle est rapidement enrayée à droite, où l'on est dans le secteur le plus fort de la ligne Senger. Un champ de mines non repéré bloque les chars et des tourelles enterrées de Panther détruisent 41 des

58 chars britanniques engagés. Des compagnies d'infanterie de la 2ᵉ Brigade d'infanterie, qui ont progressé malgré tout, sont abandonnées et subissent de grosses pertes. Le barrage roulant de la deuxième phase doit être reporté une dizaine de fois entre 07h45 et 12h45, car les bataillons de la 2ᵉ Brigade sont enlisés sur leur premier objectif. Puis, en milieu d'après-midi, l'attention de l'artillerie est détournée vers les secteurs d'où l'ennemi préparerait des contre-attaques[87]. Durant tout ce temps, le contact radio est perdu avec les compagnies d'avant de la 2ᵉ Brigade. Comme l'avance de la 3ᵉ Brigade se déroule conformément au plan, celle-ci se retrouve avec son flanc droit en l'air. L'exploitation aussi est reportée en entendant que les deux brigades d'infanterie arrivent à la même hauteur.

Vokes peut bien se préoccuper du flanc découvert de la 3ᵉ Brigade, mais son chef de corps a un autre souci : la lenteur de l'avance cause un embouteillage dans la zone de la 5ᵉ Division. Burns et Vokes arrivent à la conclusion qu'il faut engager la réserve divisionnaire pour profiter du succès au centre, à savoir le 22ᵉ Régiment canadien-français, les West Nova Scotia Highlanders et les chars du Trois-Rivières.

Cette nouvelle attaque décolle à 17h00. Coup de chance, la visibilité est réduite par une forte averse, alors que les Allemands sont à préparer une autre contre-attaque. C'est ce qui fait qu'ils sont pris à découvert par le barrage canadien[88]. Le nouvel assaut réussit et peu après la tombée du jour les fantassins canadiens occupent le revers de la ligne Senger. Les chars du Trois-Rivières, qui n'ont pu suivre à cause de la difficulté à franchir le rio San Martino, petit cours d'eau, rallient à la tombée de la nuit. Non sans hésitation. Le caporal Prieur, du Régiment de Trois-Rivières, explique que tout de suite après que les « vandoos » [22ᵉ Régiment] et les escadrons A et C du Régiment de Trois-Rivières eurent percés dans leur secteur de la ligne Hitler, ils se trouvèrent vulnérables en raison de l'éparpillement. Ils s'étaient battus en contournant des chars Churchill britanniques en flammes, en passant sur des positions retranchées [de l'ennemi] qui s'étaient affaissées, de même qu'à travers des champs de mines et des barbelés. Le commandant de l'escadron C demanda alors la permission, qui semblait raisonnable, de se replier en vue d'un regroupement. « Avancez, avancez », répondit notre commandant, le lieutenant-colonel Fernand Caron, avec mauvaise humeur. « Vous les avez chassez, continuez de leur donner la chasse[89] ».

L'infanterie peut compter cette fois sur l'appui de chars en cas de contre-attaque. Ce succès soulage les compagnies isolées dans le secteur de la 2ᵉ Brigade. Mais d'autres contre-attaques ne viendront plus, car le 24 mai au matin les Allemands retraitent, la perte de Cassino, la sortie de la poche d'Anzio du 6ᵉ Corps US et la progression française des jours précédents les forçant à reculer. Pontecorvo est enfin pris par les Canadiens.

La 5ᵉ Division blindée débute l'exploitation et la 1ʳᵉ Division termine le nettoyage de la ligne Senger. La route de Rome s'ouvre aux Canadiens. Malheureusement, Leese décide de lancer la 6ᵉ Division blindée britannique sur la même route que la 5ᵉ canadienne. Mêlés aux deux divisions blindées se trouvent des éléments de combat de la 1ʳᵉ Division d'infanterie canadienne, ainsi que les colonnes logistiques de ces divisions. Cela pour une seule grande route, la Nationale 6…

C'est une victoire coûteuse : 949 morts, blessés et prisonniers dans la 1ʳᵉ Division canadienne le 23 mai 1944, dont 543 dans la seule 2ᵉ Brigade d'infanterie. C'est le plus important total pour une brigade canadienne en une seule journée durant la campagne d'Italie. Ce bilan désastreux conduit à la recherche de leçons.

Les leçons de la Liri selon Burns, Vokes et Gibson

À cause de ce bilan désastreux, la victoire du 23 mai est à certains égards une défaite. L'historien officiel, le colonel Nicholson, cite d'ailleurs longuement les rapports sur les fautes commises, donnant l'impression que les pertes sont bien trop importantes pour une opération qui visait à déloger un ennemi dont on savait qu'il battait en retraite et qu'il était débordé sur ces deux flancs[90]. Les principaux responsables, Burns, Vokes et Gibson, ne se bercent pas d'illusions, et au contraire des rapports faits à la presse, la journée du 23 mai est représentée en couleur sombre dans les documents officiels.

Burns et Vokes ordonnent que des comités se penchent sur l'attaque du 23 mai et sur l'exploitation qui suit immédiatement, celle-ci ayant également été perçue comme ratée par les officiers du corps canadien[91]. À vrai dire, Burns s'intéresse d'abord à la poursuite, mais Vokes, qui a commandé le PPCLI après la Sicile puis la 2ᵉ Brigade, cherche à cerner les raisons expliquant l'échec de cette 2ᵉ Brigade, de sorte que la question de la poursuite ne sera finalement étudiée en détail qu'au mois de juin[92]. De ces études, il ressortira en particulier que le « mariage » entre infanterie et chars, malgré tout ce qu'on peut trouver ailleurs dans les journaux de campagne de mai et juin 1944 sur la bonne collaboration des deux armes, que ce mariage souffre de mauvaises communications, ce que l'on savait déjà.

Plus intéressantes sont de brèves remarques sur l'emploi de l'artillerie. Celle-ci a fait du bon travail le 23 mai, les jours avant et les jours après. Pourtant, pour une fois, les documents soulèvent le problème qui peut sembler paradoxal des effets des bonnes performances de l'artillerie canadienne, et alliée aussi, puisque c'est devenu pratique courante de placer temporairement l'artillerie des corps voisins sous l'autorité du corps attaquant, cela grâce aux bonnes communications entre batteries, PC d'artillerie et QG des corps, peu importe les nationalités. La question posée est formulée ainsi : « Est-ce qu'un barrage lourd ne rend pas la coopération des chars avec l'infanterie plus difficile, à cause de la fumée, de la poussière et ainsi de suite[93] ? » Dans la réponse, le rédacteur fait plus que répondre à la question, car il suggère que le contrôle centralisé, merveilleux lorsqu'il s'agit d'accumuler la puissance de feu avant l'attaque, soit dévolu aux brigades dans l'avance et la poursuite, les automoteurs d'artillerie accompagnant les chars et les canons tractées l'infanterie[94]. Question et réponse portent la signature du brigadier J.D.B. Smith, le chef d'état-major de Burns.

La 2e Brigade d'infanterie étant la plus éprouvée, Nicholson cite d'abord son commandant, le brigadier Gibson : « [l]a leçon suprême de la bataille est qu'en un terrain comme celui-ci, où la direction et la reconnaissance sont difficiles, il faut garder bien à l'arrière les réserves de compagnie, de bataillon et de brigade et les engager selon le déroulement des combats […] Le PC doit rester bien en arrière de la ligne de contact ». Remarquant que la majorité des chars des brigades de chars d'infanterie ont été touchés avant que l'on ait découvert le meilleur axe de progression, Gibson insiste sur la nécessité de ne pas lancer le gros des forces cuirassées en une zone aussi couverte et fortement défendue, cela jusqu'à ce que des détachements d'infanterie et de sapeurs aient effectué plusieurs passages dans les champs de mines et aient réduit au silence une partie de l'artillerie antichar. Il attribue les pannes de sans-fil et la perte consécutive de la direction de la bataille au fait que « tous les PC de bataillon étaient trop à l'avant », les officiers de ces PC ne s'étant en outre pas assez servi des autres moyens de communication offerts par l'artillerie, les pièces antichars et les mortiers lourds, qui auraient pu transmettre des renseignements à l'arrière[95].

Toujours selon l'historien officiel, le divisionnaire Vokes estime quant à lui qu'il est difficile de s'en tenir à un horaire rigoureux, qu'il est dangereux de lier la progression au barrage d'artillerie, théorie qu'il qualifie de « forme la plus inflexible du soutien d'artillerie que puisse fournir le canonnier, […] elle n'a jamais convenu à la mentalité du soldat canadien en Italie ». Nicholson ajoute ceci au commentaire de Vokes : « Il ne voulait pas nier par là que le volume de feu requis pour la percée était si énorme qu'il exigeait un réglage assujetti à une mise en œuvre soigneusement préparée d'avance ; cependant, […] avant que la [1ère] Division livre ses combats à l'automne, on avait inventé une méthode plus souple de tir d'appui[96] ». Cet ajout est d'autant significatif que l'historien officiel de la campagne entreprendra au début des années 1960 une histoire régimentaire de l'Artillerie royale du Canada. La clause restrictive n'a pas dû déplaire à l'association régimentaire. Dans cette histoire régimentaire, Nicholson rapporte d'autres critiques de l'opération Chesterfield, dont le sibyllin « échec du QG de la RCA à fonctionner efficacement », évitant je crois à dessein de questionner l'idée qu'un plan de feu élaboré nécessite au

Éléments blindés canadiens le 24 mai 1944, [BAC, PA-140208]

moins une couple de jours de travail, alors qu'il admet que « la victoire a été moins décisive qu'elle aurait pu l'être, que la lenteur de l'avance de la 8ᵉ Armée a permis à l'ennemi de battre en retraite à son propre rythme, de fait à rompre le contact » avec nos forces avancées[97].

Dans le journal de campagne de la division, Vokes résume les leçons apprises, cinq, en quelques mots : ne pas engager sa réserve trop tôt, c'est-à-dire pas avant qu'on ait la certitude que la percée existe et pas avant d'avoir déterminé où se trouve le meilleur axe pour l'avance ; maintenir une réserve divisionnaire pour conduire cette avance ; avoir une infanterie agressive qui n'a pas peur d'en découdre ; artillerie mise à la disposition de la division attaquante lorsqu'il s'agit d'un assaut divisionnaire ; et ne pas assumer que le plan se déroulera selon les prévisions, car « rarement les arrangements préliminaires adviennent exactement comme on l'avait prévu. Le plan doit être suffisamment flexible et le commandant doit être rapide à exploiter toutes les occasions[98] ».

Il y a aussi que Vokes semble soucieux de justifier ses décisions depuis sa prise de commandement en novembre 1943. C'est patent dans le paragraphe qui précède la conclusion : « Pour la période d'entraînement de l'infanterie après la relève du secteur Adriatique, la politique que j'ai suivie était d'endurcir la troupe physiquement et mentalement et de se concentrer sur la tactique des compagnies. Il y a eu suffisamment de temps, trois jours, pour que toutes les unités s'entraînent à la coopération infanterie-chars, encore une fois au niveau compagnie-escadron. Tous ont bien travaillé et les résultats de la bataille le montre[99]. »

L'originalité n'est évidemment pas le seul critère à considérer, mais il reste que la méthode préconisée par Vokes diffère moins qu'il ne le laisse entendre des propositions de Crerar au mois de février précédent. En effet, Vokes écrit ce qui suit dans son récit des préparatifs pour l'offensive du printemps : « J'ai longuement réfléchi à la question d'une attaque de la ligne Hitler et en suis arrivé à la conclusion que du point de vue des possibilités offertes par le terrain, une attaque dans un corridor de 2000 verges avec la droite adossée à la *Forme d'Aquino* présentait les meilleures chances de succès. Une telle attaque demandera au moins 48 heures de préparation et préférablement plus parce qu'une grande quantité d'artillerie et des reconnaissances et une préparation des plus soigneuses seront nécessaires. »

Burns prend le contrepied de Vokes. Le commandant du corps déplore que les circonstances aient empêché les bataillons de la 2ᵉ Brigade de procéder aux reconnaissances nécessaires : le fait de « n'être pas en possession du secteur d'attaque constituait un sérieux handicap. Lorsqu'ils vinrent à la fin relever la 3ᵉ Brigade d'infanterie canadienne vers 1700 heures le 22 mai, ils ne disposaient pas d'un temps suffisant pour effecteur toutes les reconnaissances et les patrouilles requises ». Selon Burns, le front étroit sur lequel la division a attaqué a permis à l'adversaire de concentrer son artillerie et ses mortiers sur l'infanterie canadienne, les Allemands disposant de surcroît de points d'observation sur les hauteurs dominant le nord de la vallée. On aurait dû masquer l'attaque avec plus de fumée[100].

Il est étonnant que les trois généraux fassent des remarques sur la tactique en-deçà de leur niveau de commandement, ce qui indique il me semble qu'ils jugent que les tactiques de base, quatre ans et demie après le début de la guerre, sont toujours peu maîtrisées. Quant à l'exploitation, c'est en soi un objet d'analyse que je ne peux aborder ici, sauf pour dire que là également le cafouillage fut apparent, car les progrès demeurèrent en-deçà des attentes, certainement de celles de Leese. Est-ce pour cette raison que Leese a lancé dans les pattes du corps canadien la 6ᵉ Division blindée britannique ou était-ce pour assurer le prestige britannique lors de la prise de la capitale italienne ? Quoi qu'il en soit, Burns fut blâmé par Leese[101]. Pour rester bref, on peut aussi dire que l'état-major de la 5ᵉ Division blindée a aussi son opinion. Comme l'ennemi en retraite a toujours été une menace pour les chars, mais qu'en même temps il faut aller vite sinon la résistance s'accroîtra, il reste nécessaire de perfectionner les méthodes de reconnaissance (maintenir le contact avec l'ennemi) et assurer une meilleure coopération des chars avec l'infanterie pour réduire la menace antichar ennemie. Il faudra aussi mieux gérer le trafic routier. Tout cela pour accélérer le tempo. À cette fin seront tenus des exercices d'unités (jusqu'au niveau des escadrons) et des manœuvres divisionnaires dans la seconde moitié de juillet[102]. Même si les deux divisions avaient des missions successives et différentes, les leçons sont étonnamment interchangeables d'une grande formation à l'autre, nouvelle indication qu'il y a quelque chose de général, de semblable, à corriger dans l'ensemble des procédés opérationnels canadiens.

Tempo. Le temps justement mis à préparer Chesterfield est probablement le facteur explicatif le plus important des difficultés du 23 mai, car les

Allemands auront les journées du 20, 21 et 22 pour s'installer sur la ligne Senger. C'est d'ailleurs le reproche le plus explicite de Nicholson dans l'histoire officielle : « Le temps d'arrêt nécessaire aux Canadiens en vue de préparer un assaut d'importance avait donné à l'ennemi tout le loisir d'améliorer ses propres positions[103]. » Cela permettra aussi à l'état-major de la 10e Armée allemande de ramener des troupes aguerries dans le secteur critique, car il ne fallait pas être devin pour comprendre que la vallée de la Liri et la Nationale 6 qui la longe étaient de bonnes voies vers Rome une fois Cassino neutralisé[104]. Les synthèses du renseignement sur l'état de la ligne Senger et des troupes la défendant montrent que les unités qui la défendaient sont plus médiocres sur la gauche (des troupes *ersatz*), mais excellentes au centre, des *Panzergrenadiers*, et encore plus à droite, des hommes de la 1ère Division parachutiste rencontrés durant l'hiver sur l'Adriatique, probablement 700 fusiliers en tout, plus vingt-cinq chars devant les Canadiens. Les chars sont tous des Mk IV et il y a aussi plusieurs automoteurs armés de 75 mm mais très peu de 88 mm, et on n'a pas identifié de chars Mk V (Panther) devant le front canadien, même si la présence de ceux-ci est connue dans des régiments de chars qui pourraient contre-attaquer. On aura cependant la surprise de découvrir le 24 mai des tourelles de ce char (armé d'un 75 mm long) montées sur des abris bétonnés. Côté mortiers les Allemands semblaient vraiment bien pourvus, y compris en mortiers lourds, et les canons antichars de 50 mm et 75 mm ne sont pas rares[105]. En somme, on savait que l'on attaquait une ligne mal défendue dont le secteur le plus solide était sur la droite, couvrant la Nationale 6.

La réitération des mêmes problèmes tactiques laisse sceptique sur la capacité du haut commandement à changer de méthodes. Depuis 1940, les documents d'instruction des formations et des unités, du peloton à la division, reviennent continuellement sur les mêmes sujets. Il est difficile de ne pas voir dans ces leçons difficiles à apprendre un problème « culturel » de l'état-major canadien, et peut-être aussi britannique, mais exacerbé chez les Canadiens, lorsque l'on compare les succès du Corps expéditionnaire français à l'insuccès relatif du 1er Corps canadien.

Une comparaison d'historien aurait ici une valeur réduite. Mais lorsque la comparaison est faite par un contemporain, en l'occurrence un Canadien plutôt britannique qui a commandé le PPCLI en Sicile mais a dû rejoindre l'état-major après une blessure sérieuse, que cet officier compare le corps canadien au CEF et que cette comparaison est favorable aux méthodes françaises, on est en droit de se poser des questions. Surtout que le lieutenant-colonel lord Tweedsmuir (le fils du gouverneur général du Canada décédé en 1941) insiste sur les différences de méthode entre le CEF et le 1er Corps pour dire que la méthode canadienne semble inappropriée au terrain italien, que des erreurs de planification, spécialement la gestion du trafic routier, ont été préjudiciables à l'exploitation, que l'on ne maîtrise pas l'usage des noms de code sur les ondes et qu'en général l'information circule mal de l'avant vers l'arrière, que l'on commet des fautes tactiques assez navrantes, notamment que l'infanterie craint d'avancer sans l'appui des autres armes et que l'on formule mal ce qu'on attend des sapeurs, avec lesquels on adopte trop une attitude de « laissons-leur ce travail… », que les démolitions entraînées par le mode opératoire canadien entravent la poursuite, et que s'il y a tant de démolitions, c'est à cause des délais de préparation, forcément long avec cette méthode. À propos des communications, Tweedsmuir remarque que les Français ont posé leurs dernières lignes téléphoniques à D+2, soit le 13 mai, et qu'après ils ont seulement utilisé les radios[106]. Tweedsmuir pense qu'une journée a été perdue à cause d'une mésentente entre le 1er Corps et le CEF, les hésitations des 21-22 mai à propos d'un coup de main sur Pontecorvo[107]. Il ne s'agit bien sûr que de l'opinion d'un seul officier, mais vu ces antécédents et vu son rôle de liaison auprès du CEF, on doit probablement attacher de l'importance à ses critiques.

Du reste, Tweedsmuir n'est pas le seul à utiliser cette comparaison défavorable. On a vu combien embarrassante l'avance française était pour Vokes. Pour Burns aussi, qui ouvre la conférence du 16 juin sur les leçons à tirer des « break-in », « break-through » et de la poursuite en insistant sur la vitesse. Si les Français ont su maintenir leur élan, c'est qu'il ne comptait pas que sur les routes. Il prend une grande part du blâme en pointant « son QG », responsable d'avoir commis la faute de surestimer l'adversaire au moment où celui-ci venait d'être délogé de la ligne Gustav[108].

Pour les poursuites aussi l'état-major du corps veut que divisions et brigades retiennent que le « mariage » infanterie-char n'est pas suffisant et que, par exemple, il n'y rien de mal à placer un bataillon d'infanterie supplémentaire auprès d'une brigade blindée tant et aussi longtemps que l'avance est rapide. Il n'est pas nécessaire de faire de longue pause pour laisser passer une brigade d'infanterie à travers la brigade blindée à chaque fois qu'un obstacle est rencontré. Les antichars sont mal utilisés, trop en arrière, trop défensivement. Si en défense la centralisation fonctionne, en poursuite il faut décentraliser lorsque le terrain le requiert. Et sur le plan des communications (Burns vient des transmissions, il faut s'en souvenir), l'état-major du corps a remarqué que les pannes étaient trop nombreuses, celles-ci causées quatre fois sur cinq par le mouvement d'un char. Il faut donc s'efforcer de poser les fils en-dehors des axes utilisés par les chars. De plus, la radio haute-puissance n'est pas assez utilisée[109]. L'usage de lignes téléphoniques dans une opération avec du mouvement laisse songeur. En fait, on craint trop l'écoute de l'adversaire que permet la radio et l'on ne se rend pas compte que cela a peu d'importance si on ne lui donne pas le temps de réagir.

La Liri fut un épisode relativement court dans l'histoire du 1er Corps, mais violent. Le relevé des pertes journalières entre le 11 mai, début de l'offensive (seule la 1ère Brigade de chars est engagée avant le 15 mai), jusqu'à la prise de Rome le 4 juin 1944 fait état d'un total de 3353 morts, blessés et prisonniers dont 924 pour la seule journée du 23 mai, et sur ces 924, 865 pour la seule 1ère Division. Les deux jours suivants, les 24 et 25 mai, suivent avec 384 et 369 pertes pour l'ensemble du corps, la 5e Division blindée étant cette fois la plus éprouvée[110]. À titre comparatif, les pertes de la 1ère Division au complet pour la prise d'Ortona (du 20 au 27 décembre 1943) furent de 650 hommes[111]. C'est dire l'importance de l'échec de la 2e Brigade et les difficultés des premiers moments de la poursuite. Le chiffre des pertes correspond bien aux soucis des chefs canadiens.

Il est donc justifié de reprendre à notre compte la conclusion que Terry Copp tire de son analyse des campagnes de Normandie et de l'Europe du nord-ouest entre juin 1944 et mai 1945 : on est en présence d'une « armée qui continue de connaître tant succès qu'échecs, dans son commandement, ses états-majors et ses unités de combat. L'idée est bien enracinée dans l'historiographie militaire qu'il existe une courbe d'apprentissage ascendante, mais une analyse des opérations alliées comme allemandes de 1944-1945 ne permet pas de soutenir ce point de vue[112] ».

Conclusion

Le concept de « leçons apprises », si prégnant dans les armées depuis 150 ans, n'a aucune valeur herméneutique sans compréhension de la culture tactique dans lesquels ces leçons sont tirées. Par exemple, les délais nécessaires à la confection d'un plan de feu complexe annulent bien des leçons apprises sur la poursuite avant même qu'une implantation soit tentée. Il faut donc faire appel à une notion comme la culture tactique pour bien comprendre les limites du processus de rétroaction. Le déséquilibre entre nombre de fantassins et de chars, ou encore l'incapacité à faire travailler ensemble ces deux armes pour des raisons techniques (les radios notamment) ou organisationnelles (les régiments de chars et l'esprit cavalier prégnant dans ce type d'unité, renforcé par l'effet désert), rendent la coopération difficile malgré toutes les bonnes volontés. Une leçon petite ou grande doit avoir un terreau fertile pour être retenue avec succès.

Ce terreau est un objet protéiforme et intéressant en soi. Bien des problèmes rencontrés en Italie par le 1er Corps feront surface dans le 2e Corps en Normandie. Est-ce seulement à cause de la nomination de Simonds et de l'attachement aux méthodes de Montgomery, tous deux en provenance d'Italie ? Ce serait accorder à deux grands chefs beaucoup trop de mérite lorsqu'ils remportent la victoire, et trop les blâmer lorsqu'ils mènent leurs formations à des échecs. La culture tactique dans laquelle ils évoluent ne donne pas toute latitude[113].

Chez le simple soldat, la Liri laisse de mauvais souvenirs, d'autant que cette bataille a quelque chose de futile, car tous savaient depuis les premiers jours de mai, avant la montée en ligne vers la Liri donc, qu'un « second front » serait bientôt ouvert en France[114]. Pas étonnant alors qu'au lendemain des combats sanglants du 23 mai et des jours suivants les troupiers canadiens sentent qu'ils ont accompli leur devoir sur le front italien, d'où une autre rumeur qui se répand ces jours-là dans la 1ère Division à l'effet que l'on retournera en Angleterre dès la prise de Rome[115]…

Caricature illustrant la lassitude des troupes en Italie parue originellement dans le journal de l'armée pour la troupe, le Maple Leaf [republiée dans le Mémorandum sur l'instruction de l'Armée canadienne, avril 1945]

Notes

1. Du 1ᵉʳ Corps, de la 1ᵉʳᵉ Division, de la 2ᵉ Brigade, de ses trois bataillons d'infanterie et du régiment antichar qui y était rattaché, ainsi que le rapport de lord Tweedsmuir de l'équipe de liaison du corps.
2. L'étude préliminaire de J.B. Conacher (août 1944), l'étude finale de E.A. Haines (juillet 1947) et l'histoire officielle de G.W.L. Nicholson (1ᵉʳᵉ éd. 1956). À ces récits officiels, on peut ajouter les Mémoires de Chris Vokes, le commandant de la 1ère Division et auteur du plan de la bataille du 23 mai. Pour le ratage de la poursuite, voir aussi la biographie du commandant de la 5ᵉ Division par Doug Delaney, *The Soldiers' General : Bert Hoffmeister at War* (Vancouver, UBC Press), 2005, chap 8.
3. On aura une bonne idée de ce que je veux dire en lisant Delaney, *The Soldiers' General*, p.144, 155 et surtout p.162.
4. Résumé du contexte politique canadien dans C.P. Stacey, *Armes, hommes et gouvernements : les politiques de guerre du Canada 1939-1945* (Ottawa, ministère de la Défense nationale, 1970), p.1-7.
5. Andrew Roberts, dans son *Masters and Commanders : The Military Geniuses Who Led the West to Victory in World War II* (Londres, Penguin Books, 2009 (2008)), p.273 et 449, s'en étonne encore en 2008.
6. Stephen J. Harris, *Canadian Brass: The Making of a Professional Army, 1860-1939* (Toronto: University of Toronto Press, 1988), p.207 et suiv.
7. Pour des portraits de ces quatre grands chefs, voir J.L. Granatstein, *The Generals : The Canadian Army's Senior Commanders in the Second World War* (Toronto, Stoddart, 1993), chap.3, 4, 5 et 6. En outre, avant d'intégrer l'armée en 1914, McNaughton enseignait l'ingénierie à l'Université McGill.
8. Granatstein, *The Generals*, op. cit., p.164-165 ; Terry Copp, *Cinderella Army : The Canadians in Northwest Europe, 1944-1945* (Toronto, University of Toronto Press, 2006), p.5 et 10. Voir aussi le résumé des convictions doctrinales de Simonds et de la plupart des généraux britanniques et canadiens dans Terry Copp, *Fields of Fire : The Canadians in Normandy* (Toronto, University of Toronto Press, 2004 (2003)), p.26-30.
9. Yves Tremblay, *Instruire une armée : les officiers canadiens et la guerre moderne, 1919-1944* (Montréal, Athéna éditions, 2007), chap.2.
10. B.L. Montgomery, « The Problem of the Encounter Battle as Affected by Modern British War Establishment », *Canadian Defence Quarterly*, 15, 1 (oct. 1937) : 13-25. Citation (trad. libre) p.23.
11. *Ibid.*, p.1-2. La *Canadian Defence Quarterly*, trimestrielle, est la seule revue canadienne discutant de théorie militaire avant 1939.
12. David French, *Raising Churchill's Army : the British Army and the War Against Germany 1919-1945* (Oxford, Oxford University Press, 2001 (2000)), p.240-285, présente sous un jour positif les innovations d'un Montgomery qui « stage-manage » ses batailles (p.251). Niall Barr, *The Pendulum of War : The Three Battles of El Alamein* (Londres, Pimlico, 2005 (2004)), p.407-412, est plus critique.
13. Timothy Harrison Place, *Military Training in the British Army, 1940-1944 : From Dunkirk to D-Day* (Londres, Frank Cass, 2000), p.40 et suiv.

14 *Instruire une armée, op. cit.*, chap.1.
15 Yves Tremblay, « L'instruction des officiers canadiens après mai 1940 », dans *Guerres mondiales et conflits contemporains*, n° 229 (mars 2008) : 79-102.
16 Même problème chez les Anglais (French, *Raising Churchill's Army, op. cit.*, p.279-281).
17 Y. Tremblay, *Instruire une armée, op. cit.*, chap.4-7.
18 Polycopie dans les archives du ministère de la Défense, Direction Histoire et patrimoine, Ottawa, sous la cote 367.064(D1) : Canadian Battle Drill School, « Battle Drill – Lectures and Précis », 5e éd., Vernon (Colombie-Britannique), 27 janv. 1943, dactylographié, 244 p.Analyse favorable de ce cours dans Harrison Place, *Military training in the British Army, op. cit.*, chap.4 et Y. Tremblay, *Instruire une armée, op. cit.*, chap.5. Vue contraire dans John A. English, *Failure in High Command : The Canadian Army and the Normandy Campaign* (Ottawa, The Golden Dog Press, 1995 (1991)), chap.5.
19 Citation d'un document allemand « semi-officiel » non spécifié, *MIAC*, n° 4 (juillet 1941), p.3.
20 « Quelques principes essentiels des opérations militaires allemandes », extraits d'un rapport américain publié dans le *MIAC*, n° 7 (octobre 1941), appendice XI.
21 C.P. Stacey, *Histoire officielle de la participation de l'armée canadienne à la Seconde Guerre mondiale, volume I. Six années de guerre : l'Armée au Canada, en Grande-Bretagne et dans le Pacifique*, 2e éd. (Ottawa, Imprimeur de la Reine, 1966), p.259-260 et 433-435.
22 *Nouvelles des théâtres de la guerre*, n° 2, « Cyrénaïque, novembre-décembre 1941 », reproduit dans *MIAC*, n° 16 (juillet 1942), appendice IV, partie I, § 1, 2.2 et 2.3. Souligné par les rédacteurs.
23 Voir John Buckley, « Tackling the Tiger : The Development of British Armoured Doctrine for Normandy 1944 », *The Journal of Military History*, 74, 4 (oct. 2010) : 1161-1184. Buckley note le même effet dans une étude dont j'ai pris connaissance après la rédaction de cet article. Lui aussi parle de culture militaire et reconnaît une capacité d'innover, mais entravée. Contrairement à nous, il est toutefois positif dans ces conclusions, à savoir que le flou tactique favorisait l'adoption de solutions nouvelles.
24 *Ibid.*, partie II, § 4.3 et 6.2.
25 John Terraine, *The Right of the Line : The Royal Air Force in the European War 1939-1945* (Ware (Hertfordshire), Wordsworth Editions, 1998 (1985)), p.337-352. Terraine reproduit le diagramme de liaison armée/aviation, dont plusieurs versions se trouvent dans les *MIAC* de janvier, août et septembre 1942.
26 *MIAC*, n° 10 (janvier 1942), p.31.
27 *MIAC*, n° 5 (août 1941), p.27-43.
28 *Ibid.*, p.44-58.
29 « Directive d'instruction n° 1 », art. 31 dans *MIAC*, n° 32 (nov. 1943), p.13-34.
30 *MIAC*, n° 34 (janvier 1944), p.23-27.

31 John Marteinson et Michael R. McNorgan, *Le Corps blindé royal canadien: une histoire illustrée* (Toronto, Robin Brass Studio, 2001), p.148.
32 G.W.L. Nicholson, *Histoire officielle de la participation de l'Armée canadienne à la Seconde Guerre mondiale, volume II. Les Canadiens en Italie, 1943-1945* (Ottawa, Imprimeur de la Reine, 1960), p.20-27.
33 Officiellement, McNaughton fut remplacé pour raison de santé, mais il n'y a aucun doute que le vrai motif est l'incompétence, comme l'explique J.L. Granatstein, *The generals, op. cit.*, p.66-79.
34 G.W.L. Nicholson, *Les Canadiens en Italie, op. cit.*, p.499.
35 H.D.G. Crerar, « Address on the principles of effective fire support in the "break-in" battle, by Commander, 1 Canadian Corps », 3 février 1944, §1, dans Bibliothèque et Archives Canada (BAC), RG24, vol. 10785, dossier 224C1.036(D3), des conférences et des syllabus rassemblés par l'historien attaché au 1er Corps, le capitaine W.E.C. Harrison. Trad. libre comme pour toutes les citations qui suivent.
36 *Ibid.*, §3.
37 Dossier cité, lettre dactylographiée « PERSONAL & MOST SECRET » adressée à « Dear Chris », 4 février 1944.
38 Lettre manuscrite adressée à « My Dear General » et signée « Chris », 5 février 1944, 13h00, dossier cité.
39 Chris Vokes et John P. Maclean, *Vokes : My Story* (Ottawa, Gallery Publishing, 1985), p.155. Ce commentaire est relevé par le biographe autorisé de Crerar, Paul Douglas Dickson, *A Thoroughly Canadian Feneral : a Biography of General H.D.G. Crerar* (Toronto, University of Toronto Press, 2007), p.233-234.
40 Dossier cité, « I Canadian Corps study period », 3 février 1944, 3 p.
41 Voir les listes de distribution contenues dans le dossier 224C1. 036(D3).
42 Dickson, *A Thoroughly Canadian General, op. cit.*, p.234.
43 Delaney, *The Soldier's General, op. cit.*, p.137.
44 Terry Copp, « Breaching the Hitler », *Legion Magazine*, 83, 2 (mars-avril 2008) : 41-43. On le verra, l'intuition de Copp est confirmée par une lecture attentive du journal de campagne de la 1ère Division. Le journal du Corps étant plus laconique, il est impossible de savoir ce que Burns pensait avant ou pendant Chesterfield. C'est seulement après l'opération que Burns fait sentir sa marque.
45 GSI(b), 1 Cdn Corps, « Security Intelligence Report No 30. Period 1 Jan 45 to 15 Jan 45 », 27 janvier 1945, p.4, dans BAC, RG 24, dossier 224C1.023(D14).
46 « 2 Cdn Inf Bde in the Liri valley battle by Comd 2 Cdn Inf Bde », annexe 20 du journal de campagne de la 2e Brigade pour mai 1944, § 1-3 (BAC, bobine T-11075, image 000267.).
47 « GSI (b) HQ 1 Cdn Corps – Security Intelligence Report No. 12, period from 29 Apr to 5 May 44 », journal de campagne du 1er Corps canadien, mai 1944, app.13 (BAC, bobine T-7113, image 000539).
48 Nicholson, *Les Canadiens en Italie, op. cit.*, p.400-401.
49 Unité mal aimée des historiens militaires, alors qu'elle était probablement l'une des plus capables de la 8e Armée dans sa spécialité. Pour un compte rendu récent de cette

expérience particulière, en même temps qu'un appel à une étude sérieuse de son travail, voir Terry Copp, « Hard-hitting armour », *Legion Magazine*, 83, 5 (septembre-octobre 2008) : 37-39, dernier d'une série de cinq articles sur la bataille de Rome. Copp avait déjà exprimé une idée semblable en 2006 : Copp, *Cinderella Army, op. cit.*, p.294.
50   Terry Copp, « Breaking the Gustav Line », *Legion Magazine*, 81, 1 (déc. 2007) : 49-51. Premier d'une série d'articles sur la campagne d'Italie qui s'est conclue dans le numéro de juillet-août 2010.
51   Nicholson, *Les Canadiens en Italie, op. cit.*, p.416.
52   Journal de campagne de la 1ère Division, 10 mai 1944 (BAC, bobine T-1877, image 001275).
53   *Ibid.*, 9 mai 1944 (BAC, bobine T-1877, image 001275).
54   *Ibid.*, 11 mai 1944, image 001276.
55   *Ibid.*, 12 mai 1944.
56   « 2 Cdn Inf Bde in the Liri Valley Battle by Comd 2 CDN INF Bde », p.1-2, app.20 du journal de campagne de la 2e Brigade, mai 1944 (BAC, bobine T-11075, images 00267-00268).
57   JC de la 1ère Division, 13 et 14 mai 1944 (BAC, bobine T-1877, images 001277-001278).
58   *Ibid.*, 15 mai 1944, (BAC, bobine T-1877, images 001278-001280).
59   *Ibid.*, 17 mai 1944, images 001280-001281.
60   *Ibid.*, 15 mai 1944 et 18 mai 1944, images 001279 et 001281.
61   *Ibid.*, 18 mai 1944, image 001285.
62   *Ibid.*, image 001281. Le point d'exclamation est dans l'original.
63   2e Brigade d'infanterie, journal de campagne, 18 mai 1944 (BAC, bobine T-11075, image 000011). La 2e Brigade suit attentivement l'avance vers la ligne Senger même si elle n'est pas encore engagée.
64   Nicholson, *Les Canadiens en Italie, op. cit.*, p.425. On a ici l'exemple de pelotons canadiens se débrouillant sans les chars supposés les accompagner. Le point de vue des fantassins est décrit dans Copp, « Advancing on the Hitler Line », *Legion Magazine*, 83, 1 (janvier-février 2008) : 45-57.
65   Nicholson, *Les Canadiens en Italie, op. cit.*, p.428.
66   JC de la 2e Brigade, (BAC, bobine T-11075, image 000011).
67   Jean-Christophe Notin, *La campagne d'Italie 1943-1945 : les victoires oubliées de la France*, Paris, Éditions Perrin, coll. « Tempus », 2007 (2002), p.500. Notin cite le journal personnel de Montsabert.
68   JC de la 2e Brigade, (BAC, bobine T-11075, image 000012).
69   *Ibid.*
70   JC de la 1ère Division, 19 mai 1944, (BAC, bobine T-1877, image 001282).
71   *Vokes : My Story, op. cit.*
72   JC de la 1ère Division, mai 1944, (BAC, bobine T-1877, image 001283).
73   *Ibid.*, image 001282.
74   JC du 1er Corps, « G Log », 23 mai 1944, 20h20, bobine T-7113, image 000736.
75   J.B. Conacher, « Canadians Operations in the Liri Valley (Italy) May-June 1944 », Canadian Military Headquarters (Londres), rapport n° 121, app.D-II.

76 JC de la 1ère Division, mai 1944, (BAC, bobine T-1877, image 001283).
77 *Ibid.*
78 JC de la 1ère Division, mai 1944, compte rendu des renseignements de 09h00 dans « Telephone or message log » du 21 mai (BAC, bobine T1877, image 001587), et téléphone du même jour à 10h10 en provenance du 1er Corps canadien (image 001588).
79 J.-F. Notin, *La campagne d'Italie, op. cit.*, p.504-510.
80 JC de la 1ère Division, 21 mai 1944, (BAC, bobine T-1877, image 001284).
81 JC du 1er Corps, 16, 18, 21 et 22 mai 1944, (BAC, bobine T-7113, images 000496, 000497 et 000499).
82 JC de la 1ère Division, 22 mai 1944, (BAC, bobine T-1877, images 001284-001285).
83 Voir aussi la lettre d'introduction du général d'armée Juin à « M. le Général Cdt le VIe Corps Canadien », 16 mai 1944, dans JC du 1er Corps canadien, mai 1944, app.25 (BAC, bobine T-7113, image 000570). La mission de liaison française est menée par le chef d'escadron de Kersaudon. On remarque que l'état-major de Juin ne connaît ni le nom de Burns ni le numéro du corps canadien.
84 Vokes et Maclean, *Vokes : My Story, op. cit.*, p.159.
85 Copp, « Advancing on the Hitler Line », *op. cit.*, p.45-46.
86 Nicholson, *Les Canadiens en Italie, op. cit*, p.428.
87 Pour les reports à répétition, voir le JC du 1er Corps, registre des communications, (BAC, bobine T-7113, images 000727-000731). Récit du point de vue de l'artillerie dans G.W.L. Nicholson, *The Gunners of Canada : The History of the Royal Regiment of Canadian Artillery, volume II, 1919-1967* (Toronto, McClelland and Stewart, 1972), p.201-204.
88 Nicholson, *Les Canadiens en Italie, op. cit.*, p.438.
89 Charles Prieur, *Chroniques de guerre 1939-1945 du Three Rivers Regiment (Tank)*, [Trois-Rivières], Association du 12e Régiment blindé du Canada, [2005], p.245.
90 Nicholson, *Les Canadiens en Italie, op. cit.*, p.439-440.
91 Par exemple, voir l'ordre du 24 mai figurant à l'app.35 du JC de la 1ère Division, (BAC, bobine T-1877, image 001340).
92 JC du 1er Corps, juin 1944, app.30, ordre signé par le chef d'état-major du corps le 5 juin 1944 (BAC, bobine T-7113, image 001193) ; app.38, syllabus de la conférence d'entraînement à la poursuite, 10 juin 1944 (images 001208-001209) ; et addendum du 12 juin (image 001213) ; JC de la 1ère Division, mai 1944, app.35, formation d'un comité d'études sur la ligne Hitler, 24 mai 1944 (BAC, bobine T-1877, image 001340).
93 Question posée avec quelques autres dans JC du 1er Corps, juin 1944, app.38, convocation datée du 10 juin pour la conférence du 16 juin (BAC, bobine T-7113, images 001208-001209).
94 App.62, « Explanatory Notes on 1 Cdn Corps Training Instruction No. 4 : THE PURSUIT », (BAC, bobine T-7113, images 001310-001311).
95 Nicholson, *Les Canadiens en Italie, op. cit.*, p.439-440.
96 *Ibid.*, p.440.
97 Nicholson, *The gunners of Canada, op. cit.*, p.210-211.

98 « The Liri Vallley 15-28 May 44 by GOC 1 Cdn Inf Div », p.9, app.49 au journal de campagne de la 1ère Division, *op. cit.*, (BAC, bobine T-1877, image 001920). Vokes signe le document.
99 *Ibid.*, p.8.
100 Nicholson, *Les Canadiens en Italie*, *op. cit.*, p.430 pour la citation et p.440 pour d'autres commentaires de Burns.
101 Le plus récent commentaire des incidents entre généraux qui ont suivi la percée de la ligne Hitler se trouve dans Terry Copp, « Clash among Generals », *Legion Magazine*, 84, 4 (juillet-août 2008) : 25-27.
102 Delaney, *The soldiers' general*, *op.cit.*, p.159-160. Contrairement à Vokes, Hoffmeister brille par son absence dans le post-mortem de Chesterfield, car il est en repos médical à partir du 12 juin.
103 Nicholson, *Les Canadiens en Italie*, *op. cit.*, p.431.
104 E.A. Haines, « Canadian Operations in the Liri Valley May-June 1944 », Historical Section, Canadian Military Headquarters (Londres), rapport n° 179, p.52.
105 Voir en particulier les *Intelligence Summary* du 1er Corps nos 61, 62 et 63 des 23, 24 et 25 mai 1944 (BAC, bobine T-7113, images 916-937) et n° 62 de la 1ère Division (BAC, bobine T-1877, images 001337-001339). Le dispositif allemand est illustré dans G.W.L. Nicholson, *Les Canadiens en Italie*, *op. cit.*, croquis 7, p.432.
106 « Report on the factors which slowed up the Eight Army's advance in the Liri valley from D day to the capture of Anagui », 2 p. de résumé et conclusions + annexes A-G (BAC, RG24, vol. 10785, dossier 224C1.036(D3)). Résumé dans E.A. Haines, CMHQ, rapport n° 179, *op. cit.*, p.75-76.
107 Extraits d'un autre rapport de Tweedsmuir dans J.B. Conacher, CMHQ Report n° 121, *op.cit.*, app.D-I. L'original est le « Report on a visit to the French Expeditionary Corps », n.d., dactylographié, 2 p.+ annexes (dossier cité, BAC, RG24, vol. 10785).
108 « Memorandum on trg conference held at HQ 1 Cdn Corps 0900 hrs 16 Jun 44 », 7 p., app.48 au journal de campagne du 1er Corps, juin 1944 (BAC, bobine T-7113, image 001234). Blâme assumé dès la p.1. Les renseignements s'aperçoivent le soir du 23 mai qu'ils ont surestimés la ligne Senger (« 1 Cdn Div Intelligence Summary No. 62 », 23 mai 1944, § 1 et 7, annexe 34 du JC de la 1ère Division, (BAC, bobine T-1877, images 001337-001338).
109 « Memorandum on trg conference held at HQ 1 Cdn Corps 0900 hrs 16 Jun 44 », *op. cit.*, p.7.
110 « Summary of daily casualties, 1 Cdn Corps, Italy, 11 May – 4 Jun 44 » dans CMHQ, « Report No. 179 », *op. cit.*, app.C.
111 Nicholson, *Les Canadiens en Italie*, *op. cit.*, p.346.
112 Copp, *Cinderalla army*, *op.cit.*, p.287. Trad. libre.
113 Le biographe de Montgomery utilise une explication culturelle pour justifier le mode d'opération de son héros : Nigel Hamilton, *The Full Monty, Volume I : Montgomery of Alamein, 1887-1942* (Londres, Allen Lane, 2001), p.310 sq.

114 Interprétation des rumeurs dans le « Security Intelligence Report No. 12 : Period from 29 Apr to 5 May 44 », 9 mai 1944, app.13 au JC du 1er Corps canadien pour mai 1944 (BAC, bobine T-7113, image 000539).

115 « Security Intelligence Report No. 15 : Period from 20 May to 26 May 44 », 30 mai 1944, app.47 au JC du 1er Corps pour mai 1944 (BAC, bobine T-7113, image 000619)

14

Knowing Enough Not to Interfere
Lieutenant-General Charles Foulkes at the Lamone River, December 1944

Douglas E. Delaney

It is hard to find anything nice to say about Charles Foulkes as a battlefield commander. He possessed no great technical skill. None of his confidential reports during the interwar period identified him as anything better than an "above average" talent in the Permanent Force,[1] and his directing staff at Camberley pegged him as only "[a]verage ... a critic rather than a creator."[2] His control of the 2nd Canadian Division in July 1944 was so shaky that his corps commander at the time, Guy Simonds, had to be talked out of firing him.[3] Terry Copp agreed with Simonds and quite correctly criticized Foulkes's performance during Operation Spring (25 July 1944), wondering why Foulkes had not been fired for his foolish tactical decisions in the Forêt de la Londe battle at the end of August 1944.[4] His human skills were nothing to brag about either. He had few friends in the army and even fewer admirers, most of his contemporaries believing him to be little more than a master bureaucrat and an accomplished careerist who owed much of his rise in rank to his connection with General H.D.G. Crerar, Commander First Canadian Army.[5] He got into shouting matches with brigadiers,[6] and some openly questioned his orders. If he did try to secure the loyalty of his subordinates at all, Foulkes usually did it by generating fear rather than affection. He fired enough people to send a potent message that anyone could be next, and he often embarrassed people in public. While acting commander of the 2nd Canadian Corps during the battles of the Scheldt (October–November 1944), he made no friends or followers in the corps headquarters. Brigadier Elliot Rodger, the Corps Chief of Staff, stated plainly that he had "no respect" for Foulkes and "simply ... blocked out" from memory the period that Foulkes had been in temporary command.[7] Foulkes also drank too much on occasion and had several embarrassing incidents because of it. Yet owing to a dearth of senior command talent in the Canadian Army at the time, Foulkes ascended to command the 1st Canadian Corps, both in Italy and in Northwest Europe during 1944–45. Given his ignominious record to that point, one might have expected that his battles as a corps commander would have gone poorly.

But that was not really the case, particularly with Operation Chuckle, the so-called Battle of the Rivers in northern Italy during December 1944. Over the course of eighteen miserable and rain-drenched days, the 1st Canadian Corps slogged across fourteen miles of flat farmland, crossing five diked water obstacles and liberating the city of Ravenna in the process, all of this against a determined and well-posted enemy. The Canadians had planned to go farther, but the advance from the Montone bridgehead to the Senio River was a remarkable tactical accomplishment in itself, and it achieved its operational purpose. Chuckle was part of a larger Allied effort to capture Bologna. General Sir Harold Alexander had hoped that a strong thrust by the

Left to right: Major-General Charles Foulkes, Field Marshal Bernard Montgomery, and Major-General Dan Spry, 24 October 1944. [LAC 142115]

British Eighth Army, which included the 1st Canadian Corps, would draw German reserves to the Ravenna sector, leaving Bologna weakened and ripe for attack by the Fifth US Army. In fact, the Canadian attacks caused so much consternation in the German Tenth Army that the German commander committed more than a division to the Canadians' sector. That the Fifth US Army's attack never materialized takes nothing away from the Canadian battlefield accomplishments of Operation Chuckle; it just means that they were sadly squandered by strategic-level failures.

The Canadians succeeded in the tasks given them, but how much of that success can be credited to Foulkes? A closer look at the battle reveals that Foulkes the corps commander was pretty much the same as Foulkes the division commander. He had experienced no catharsis between Northwest Europe and Italy, had no change of heart or perspective. He did not bring much to the 1st Canadian Corps, which was an experienced and well-functioning formation by the autumn of 1944. What he did in Italy that he did not do in Northwest Europe was listen to his subordinate commanders and staff and resist the impulse to interfere. That way, despite his own limited abilities, he was able to get help from a lot of good subordinates, even though they did not like him.

As might have been expected, Foulkes did not get off to a good start as a corps commander, almost immediately putting everyone off when he arrived in November 1944. At a gathering of every officer in the corps at the rank of lieutenant-colonel and above, Foulkes imprudently denigrated how things had been done to that point in the Italian theatre of operations:

> [H]e implied that the tactics used by the formations in Italy were a little out of date and would have to change to make use of the new equipment which the divisions in Belgium and Holland were using and which would be made available shortly in Italy. He remarked that we were crossing the same rivers that Caesar had crossed and were using the same equipment as he had.[8]

Brigadier George Kitching, the corps chief of staff, "watched the faces of his audience as he spoke and it was obvious to me that he had failed to win their enthusiastic support ... [T]here was little interest in the eyes of his audience. He missed a great opportunity."[9] This was Charles Foulkes at his insecure worst. Any commander coming to a new theatre and a new command would have had concerns. Foulkes had all of them and more. It did not help that, earlier that day, his aircraft had landed at the wrong airfield, where no one from the 1st Canadian Corps was there to greet him, and from which he had to hitch a ride with a military policeman to Eighth Army Headquarters.[10] He took it as a slight. He also knew his own limitations as a tactician, but instead of acknowledging the experience and expertise of his audience, even asking for their assistance, he adopted a haughty and superior attitude that fell entirely flat. Montgomery had gotten away with that sort of thing in the desert, because he was so highly skilled. Foulkes, whose technical skills were wobbly at best, did not. Kitching was right. The new corps commander had missed an excellent opportunity to use some human skills and win over staff officers and commanders who could help compensate for his deficiencies, but by his actions Foulkes won few hearts. Brigadier William Ziegler, Commander Corps Royal Artillery (CCRA) of the 1st Canadian Corps, remembered that he too held "no respect" for the new corps commander and "never heard a good word about him."[11] To say that Foulkes had poor people skills would be an understatement.

Still, Foulkes did improve with the help of some talented subordinates such as George Kitching. Kitching had experienced difficulties as a divisional commander, but he was an exceptional staff officer.[12] He had been General Staff Officer 1st Grade (GSO 1) for the 1st Canadian Division during Operation Husky and the one most responsible for that formation's successful preparation for, and deployment to, Sicily in the summer of 1943. Kitching arrived at the 1st Canadian Corps on 10 November and fully assumed his duties four days later, which was a week before Foulkes's arrival on 20 November.[13] With the acting corps commander, Major-General Chris Vokes, Kitching started planning the Corps' part in a much larger army group effort to capture Bologna (See map opposite page). General Sir Richard McCreery, the Eighth Army's commander, issued formal orders to his corps commanders on 18 November.[14] McCreery wanted the Polish Corps and the British V Corps to cross the Montone River and secure jumping-off points for the 1st Canadian Corps, which would then drive hard "along the axis RUSSI... LUGO ... MASSA LOMBARDA."[15] Kitching took the direction and steered the staff planning for Operation Chuckle with skill. At this early planning stage, he saw three possibilities for which there had to be plans: that V Corps failed to gain a crossing over the Montone River; that V Corps succeeded in

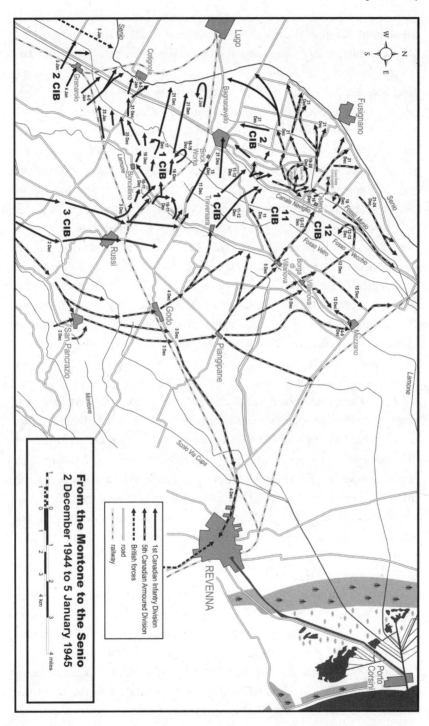

crossing the Montone River and forced the enemy back to the Lamone River; or that flooding put V Corps operations completely on hold. Later that day, at a planning conference attended by the key corps staff, the CCRA, and the chief engineer (CE), Kitching and Vokes passed on the planning parameters. By 20 November, Kitching had received the CCRA's planning notes for the three contingencies and a verbal briefing from the CE.[16] With those appreciations in hand, and with the assistance of other staff members, he now prepared an outline plan, which he presented to Foulkes just before the corps commander's 21 November conference.[17] Foulkes made a few minor ink amendments to the document, but in essence, he accepted the plan as it had been devised by Kitching. It was to be a four-phase operation to advance along the Highway 9 axis towards Massa Lombard and Argenta, with the 1st Canadian Division on the left and the 5th Canadian Armoured Division on the right. In Phase 1, the Canadians would relieve the 10th Indian Division and cross the Montone River with both divisions. The corps would then cross the Lamone River in Phase 2, capturing Bagnacavallo with the 1st Canadian Division and seizing Ravenna with the 5th Canadian Armoured Division. Phase 3 would see the capture of both Lugo and Cotingola. Finally, in Phase 4, the corps would exploit as far as possible towards Argenta. To ensure that the defending Germans would have little opportunity to recover, the outline plan emphasized that the operation would be "continuous day and night" and that brigades and battalions would be "stepped up, but not passed through until [the lead] f[or]m[atio]n or unit [was] completely tired out." On 28 November, Foulkes presented a "Revised Outline Plan," the only change being the elimination of the Phase 1 task to cross the Montone, because the 10th Indian Division had done that on 24 November and was currently cleaning up the start line for the Canadian attack.[18] In essence, Foulkes inherited the plan for Operation Chuckle and did little to interfere with the staff planning or the administrative preparations.

The attack out of the 10th Indian Division's bridgehead on 2 December went well—that is, until the 1st Canadian Division reached the Lamone River. The Canadians struck hard at the boundary between 356 German Infantry Division and the 114 Jaeger Division, both formations belonging to 73 Korps.[19] After some hard fighting, Russi fell to the 1st Canadian Division on 3 December, forcing a withdrawal of German delaying forces across the Lamone River, and the 5th Canadian Armoured Division seized a crossing of the Montone at San Pancrazio before sweeping east (to cut off Ravenna) and north (to close up to the Lamone River). Brigadier J.D.B. Smith, the acting GOC of the 1st Canadian Division until the arrival of Major-General Harry Foster on 9 December, had planned to break out of the 10th Indian Division's bridgehead, seize the initial crossings of the Lamone with the 3rd Canadian Infantry Brigade, then drive to Bagnacavallo with the 2nd Brigade, and finally capture Lugo with the 1st Brigade. But the 3rd Canadian Brigade had taken 106 casualties and a full forty-eight hours for its battalions just to reach the Lamone.[20] Here Smith made a judgment call. Because he was sure that any crossing of the Lamone would face a German counterattack, he thought it best to bring up fresh troops from the 1st Canadian Brigade to cross the river, instead of having the 3rd Canadian Brigade execute the crossing as originally planned. Unfortunately, bad tactical decisions at the brigade and battalion level exacerbated a difficult transition. Brigadier J.A. Calder, the 1st Canadian Brigade's commander, had been planning to attack out of Bagnacavallo and capture Lugo in accordance with Smith's original plan. Now, in haste, he prepared to cross the Lamone River quickly and without the benefit of detailed reconnaissance. His first attempt with the Hastings and Prince Edward Regiment (H & PER) during the afternoon of 4 December met a storm of machine-gun bullets from the twenty-five-foot-high flood embankments that lined the forty-foot-wide river. At 0100 hours the next morning, following the return of evening reconnaissance patrols that had crossed the river hours earlier, he tried again. His second attempt, on a two-battalion front, did not fare much better. The attack, with the Royal Canadian Regiment (RCR) left and the H & PER right, took place between the railway line and the Godo-Bagnacavallo road. With the support of four medium artillery regiments, his battalions managed to gain a very tenuous foothold on the west bank.

Holding that ground proved to be a problem. Sometime around 0300 hours on 5 December, Kitching advised Foulkes of the RCR bridgehead. Although satisfied with the good news of the crossing, Foulkes rightly worried that the infantry would be vulnerable to German counterattack. Through Kitching, Foulkes directed Smith to ensure the obvious—"that six-pounder anti-tank guns were rafted or dragged across to give the infantry the necessary support in case of a German counter-attack."[21] But the situation was worse than Foulkes had realized. The railway embankment was twenty to twenty-five feet high, and it dominated the flat and open ground around it. The RCR never gained control of it even though they had penetrated 1,000 yards beyond the river. They were therefore blind to the well-planned and well-rehearsed counterattack that was coming. The Germans hurled their strongly reinforced 356th Reconnaissance Battalion at the bridgehead.[22] Enemy assault guns fired through gaps in the embankment while machine guns fired unmolested from its heights. The official historian of the Canadians in the Italian campaign was unnecessarily kind in accepting that "the obscuring fog prevented effective use of the battalion PIATs."[23] If German machine gunners could engage their targets, Canadian PIAT gunners and machine gunners should have been able to do the same. The problem was that no one had been tasked to take and hold the railway embankment—a fatal error in both planning and execution.

Foulkes acted in the way that he normally did when faced with a setback—he fired people—but in this instance he was entirely justified. Smith's decision to replace the 3rd Brigade with the 1st Brigade for the Lamone crossing had forced Brigadier Calder and Lieutenant-Colonel J.W. Ritchie, the RCR commanding officer, to cobble together an unplanned action in fairly short order. Nevertheless, they both showed breathtakingly bad tactical judgment in not realizing the importance of the railway. Attacking on only one side of the embankment was an extremely precarious undertaking because it more or less surrendered to the enemy both the approaches on the west side of the railway and the embankment's heights. Calder and to a lesser extent Smith should have realized this. Calder made a bad oversight worse by not tasking the RCR to put someone on the embankment, either to observe what might be coming or to engage it with direct or indirect fire.[24] It also should have been obvious to Ritchie, whose patrols had seen the embankment only hours earlier. What should have been a battle for the railway embankment instead became a barrel-shoot for the 356th Reconnaissance Battalion and its attachments.[25] More than half the 205 RCR soldiers who crossed the river were killed, wounded, or captured.[26] The H & PER added another 58 casualties to the total, most of them the result of their own artillery fire landing on lead companies that had mistakenly formed up ahead of their start line. Calder had to go. So did Ritchie. Foulkes later claimed that he "should have also replaced Brigadier Smith,"[27] but Smith's questionable decision to substitute the battered 3rd Brigade with the 1st Brigade for the crossing was understandable, especially considering that the predictable German counterattacks meant that the bridgehead battle would likely be fought for a day or two more than the forty-eight hours that the 3rd Brigade had already been fighting. But Smith was only an acting GOC and due to be replaced in a matter of days, and his battle record as the commander of the 5th Canadian Armoured Brigade had been good to that point.[28] In the end, Foulkes sent Smith to the 1st Brigade to replace Calder. This was a good decision too, because Smith fought the 1st Brigade well for the remainder of the war.

Foulkes's first instinct after the Lamone setback was to regroup and attempt another crossing as quickly as possible, but the weather forced delays that, ironically, proved beneficial. By midday on 6 December, the 1st Canadian Division had issued orders for a renewed attack, this one with the 3rd Brigade "three b[attalio]ns up" astride both the railway embankment and the Godo-Bagnacavallo road.[29] And the 5th Canadian Armoured Division planned a silent attack (with no preparatory bombardment) by the 11th Canadian Infantry Brigade at Borgo di Villanova and Villanova, while the 12th Brigade on their left and the 5th Canadian Armoured Brigade on their right created distractions with whatever mortars, machine guns and anti-tank weapons they could muster. Unfortunately, heavy rains continued to threaten the Montone bridges and, by extension, the ability to reinforce any planned gains over the Lamone. Foulkes postponed the operation by twenty-four hours although he was anxious to get on with it. He was not alone in believing that an attack was better done sooner than later, because the rain forecasted for the next week or so would only make matters worse. On 7 December, even with a reported eight inches of water on the road near the main Montone crossing site south of Russi, Foulkes and his divisional commanders were still willing to attempt the attack.[30] The army commander was more cautious. Concerned that the Canadians could lose the bridges behind them during the attack, McCreery visited Foulkes on the morning of 7 December "to discuss the advisability of staging the attack across the F[osso] LAMONE tonight in view of the probability of continued bad weather."[31] Later that afternoon, he and Foulkes met with the two division commanders to garner their thoughts. The forecast of "ten more days of intermittent rain" brought a now-or-never haste to the deliberations. McCreery relented and "decided to put in the attack tonight."[32] As it turned out, though, that decision was short-lived: flooding of the Lamone later that day forced yet another postponement. The on-again-off-again nature of the preparations annoyed the troops, but the time waiting was not time wasted. All across the Corps front, Canadian patrols reconnoitred bridges and crossing sites, snapped up prisoners, conducted small raids, and laid ambushes behind the enemy's front line.[33] By the time they launched themselves across the Lamone on 10 December, the attackers had a very clear picture of where they were going and what they had to do.

The 1st Canadian Corps staff did well, considering that the ground to be crossed presented so many problems. In the seven kilometres that separated the Lamone from the Senio River, four diked waterways, each about eight feet in height, cut across flat and fairly drenched farmland. These waterways impeded vehicle movement, and the flat open ground meant that any enemy defenders perched on an embankment could observe and shoot any would-be attackers at will—at least in daylight. If the Germans decided to stand on any of these water obstacles, nothing short of a deliberate, set-piece attack would push them back. The 10 December attack went in much as it had been planned in the preceding five days and was very successful in the initial stages. The Corps achieved complete tactical surprise on the enemy with a silent attack that started at 2130 hours. On the 5th Canadian Armoured Division front, the 11th Canadian Infantry Brigade with the Westminster Regiment under command slipped across the Lamone in assault boats at Villa Nova and Borgo di Villanova while the two neighbouring brigades made as much noise as possible. Once across, the Westminsters had to fend off a very determined counterattack by two battalions—one from each of 278 and 98 Infantry Divisions—and at least fifteen tanks. Using their PIATs and their supporting artillery, the Westminsters held their little bridgehead at Villanova, allowing the 12th Canadian Infantry Brigade and the 5th Canadian Armoured Brigade to push out to the Fosso Vechio and Highway 16.[34]

On the 1st Canadian Division front, the 3rd Canadian Infantry Brigade, with the 48th Highlanders under command, executed a similarly stealthy assault at the site of the 1st Canadian Brigade failure of 5 December. This time, however, the attackers assaulted both sides of the railway embankment without announcing their arrival with a preparatory bombardment. Foulkes also arranged a diversionary attack by the 43rd Indian Brigade along the Via Emilia to the south, where the Germans had counterattacked with 90 Panzergrenadier Division on 8 December.[35] All the reconnaissance, staff work, and preparation paid off. The supporting guns began to fire approximately thirty minutes after H-Hour, and the 1st and 4th Field Companies of engineers managed to raft anti-tank guns to the three assaulting battalions before first light. From this foothold, the Royal 22e Régiment advanced towards the Fosso Vechio until it encountered fire from enemy positions just south of Bagnacavallo. Any approach to the walled and well-fortified town from the south and from the southwest exposed attackers to observation and fire from Bagnacavallo itself, from the enemy in the dry Canale Naviglio, and from the dominating twenty-five-foot embankments of the Senio.

In deciding what to do next, Foulkes consulted with his subordinate commanders and staff. Things happened quickly. During daylight hours, he moved around the battlefield continuously to confer with his divisional commanders and to view the ground for himself. The 1st Canadian Corps Log shows that, for the period 11–12 December, he visited the headquarters of both his divisions three times each. This was fairly typical for Foulkes during Operation Chuckle.[36] From these discussions, and those with Kitching and the Corps staff in the evenings, he worked out a plan whereby both divisions would attack simultaneously across the Naviglio—the 1st Canadian Division 1 kilometre northeast of Bagnacavallo, the 5th Canadian Armoured Division between Osteria and the road 1.5 kilometres to the northeast. In other words, instead of taking Bagnacavallo head on, Foulkes would focus on breaking the new line northeast of town.

Unfortunately, this was precisely the area that the German 98 Division was in the process of reinforcing. The Canadian attacks since 2 December had worn down 73 Korps to such a precarious state that the Tenth Army commander, Colonel-General Heinrich von Vietinghoff, had no choice but to reinforce the chewed-up Corps.[37] In spite of this, the Canadians still made it across the Canale Naviglio in yet another night assault. Hoffmeister attacked over the Fosso Vecchio with Brigadier J.S. Lind's 12th Brigade, and the 4th Princess Louise's Dragoon Guards actually made it over the Canale Naviglio, but very determined German counterattacks drove them back to the Fosso Vecchio with eighty-eight casualties, twenty-one of them fatal. The Lanark and Renfrew Scottish made it to the east bank of the Vecchio, but no farther.

The 5th Division's attack had failed, but in the 1st Canadian Division's sector, the 1st Canadian Infantry Brigade carved out a crossing two kilometres northeast of Bagnacavallo. Following an artillery bombardment of the Naviglio positions, Brigadier Smith sent the Carleton and Yorks across and then quickly reinforced their initial success with the H & PER.

On hearing that a counterattack by 190 Reconnaissance Battalion was imminent, Smith ordered the two battalions to stop and hold firm while he brought forward the RCR and arranged for air support at first light. When the expected counterattack came at 0800 hours on 13 December, German tanks and infantry very nearly overran the H & PER and forced the bridgehead back to a small perimeter near the crossing site. The Carleton and Yorks also faced a tank–infantry counterattack, barely holding on with towed anti-tank guns and artillery fire. But the situation soon improved. Shortly after midday, 13 December, the supporting engineers had completed tank crossing sites over the Vecchio and the Naviglio, allowing the British Columbia Dragoons to pour into the beleaguered bridgehead and save it. That evening, Smith used the Loyal Edmonton Regiment, which Foster had just placed under his command, to attack and expand the bridgehead. Smith had performed exceptionally well during this gruelling contest, vindicating Foulkes's decision not to fire him.

Other subordinates came through for Foulkes as well. The 5th Canadian Armoured Division commander, Major-General Bert Hoffmeister, who saw no chance of crossing the Naviglio in his sector without very heavy casualties, thought that he might instead use the bridgehead that Smith had made. While the battle to keep the 1st Brigade's foothold still raged, Hoffmeister proposed to Foulkes that he could send the Westminster Regiment through that bridgehead, provided it held, and have them sweep north along the Naviglio to Osteria.[38] This was an extremely risky manoeuvre, moving parallel to the line of enemy defences, but Foulkes agreed and directed that the 5th Canadian Armoured Division have a "combat g[rou]p ... prepared to pass through the 1 Cdn Inf Div br[idge]head [and] strike N[orth]W[est]."[39] The Westminsters and a squadron of tanks executed this well-orchestrated manoeuvre on 14 December, while Desert Air Force Spitbombers attacked enemy defences on the Westminster's left flank. It worked. For a cost of four killed and sixteen wounded, the Westminsters took 106 prisoners and so weakened enemy defences around Osteria that the Lanark and Renfrew Scottish were able to cross the Naviglio with very little difficulty.[40] The 4th Princess Louise's Dragoon Guards did the same farther north.

After this remarkable accomplishment, in appalling conditions and against a freshly reinforced enemy, the Canadians found themselves facing yet another well-defended obstacle at the Fosso Munio on the right and the still-strong defences of Bagnacavallo on the left. Calculating that Bagnacavallo was the vital ground of the German line, Foulkes set about trying to capture it. His first attempt—a one-two punch on either side of the city on 16–18 December—failed. A 1st Canadian Infantry Brigade attack between Boncellino and Bagnacavallo had faltered when enemy counterattacks drove the RCR and the H & PER back across the Fosso Vecchio, so Foulkes cancelled the second "punch," which would have been an assault across the Foss Munio by the 11th Canadian Infantry Brigade. Foulkes changed his plan. At 1000 hours on the morning of 18 December, he held an orders group attended by both divisional commanders, his CCRA, his CE, and two key brigade commanders, Lieutenant-Colonel Pat Bogert of the 2nd Canadian Infantry Brigade and Brigadier Ian Johnston of the 11th Canadian Infantry Brigade.[41] The Corps would now put in a two-division attack centred on Osteria, again in the darkness and again without any preparatory bombardment to announce it. On 19 December, the assaulting battalions of the 11th Brigade pushed over the Munio while the 2nd Brigade's battalions advanced across the open ground towards Casa Argelli and Casa Peli. The fight against 98 Division was difficult—it could hardly have been anything but difficult—but the troops of the 1st Canadian Corps succeeded. There were a few close calls as the Canadian engineers struggled to bring forward tanks and anti-tank guns to help the infantry against German counterattacks, but the guns and tanks got to where they were needed. In fact, the breakthrough in the centre of the Corps front so threatened the defences around Bagnacavallo that the enemy had started to thin out in the south, making the advance of the 1st Canadian Infantry Brigade across the Naviglio a fairly simple affair. By 22 December, the Canadians had reached the Senio across the Corps front. This was short of their phase 3 objectives for Operation Chuckle—just short—but, given the conditions of the terrain and the reaction of the enemy, they had done very well to make it that far. And they had succeeded in drawing away from the Bologna sector both 98 Division and the Field Marshal Kesselring Machine Gun Battalion, which was what McCreery had wanted. Unfortunately, the planned US Fifth Army drive on Bologna never happened, even though the Eighth Army offensive had drawn a total of three divisions away from Bologna. Fifth Army General Lucian Truscott believed his army to be too short on ammunition to capture Bologna, and Field Marshal Alexander,

Supreme Commander Mediterranean since 12 December, agreed to cancel the planned offensive until the spring.[42]

So how much of the hard-won 1st Canadian Corps successes during the miserable Battle of the Rivers can be credited to Foulkes? Not much, because not many of the tactical ideas for the offensive originated with him. He relied heavily on his staff, particularly Kitching, and this was consistent with how he had done business in Northwest Europe. Brigadier W.J. Megill, who had commanded the 5th Canadian Brigade under Foulkes in Normandy, recalled that Foulkes "got all his advice from his staff."[43] There was certainly some of that in Operation Chuckle. He more or less accepted Kitching's outline plan, and his faith in Kitching and the 1st Corps staff was well placed. They reacted well to the many readjustments and plan changes during Operation Chuckle, ensuring that fighting troops, ammunition, bridging equipment, and supplies got to where they were needed when they were needed. He was lucky in a way. The outcome of Chuckle might have been very different indeed had he been forced to fight it with the green Corps staff that had struggled in the Liri Valley battles only six months earlier. He was also lucky in that he had very capable subordinate commanders on whom he could lean, and lean on them he did. This was a change for Foulkes. Whereas, in Northwest Europe he had quarrelled with his subordinates, in Italy he conferred constantly with Hoffmeister and Foster. He accepted Hoffmeister's risky scheme to send the Westminsters through the 1st Canadian Brigade's bridgehead on 14 December, and he agreed to several "silent" attacks, which was something that had been rare in Northwest Europe but fairly common in Italy by the autumn of 1944. Hoffmeister and Foster may have found Foulkes a "vain egotistical man,"[44] even a "fraud,"[45] but at least the corps commander let them fight their battles as they wanted to fight them. They could live with that. With the exception of his awkward arrival in Italy, Foulkes adjusted fairly well to his new environment and found a way to make things work. So even if most of the plans or tactical decisions of Operation Chuckle did not originate with him, the Canadian success in appalling conditions suggests that he had at least improved at harnessing the talent of the people under him—which for Foulkes meant taking their advice and interfering as little as possible.

Notes

This chapter is based largely on portions of a chapter titled "The Master Bureaucrat: Charles Foulkes," in Douglas E. Delaney, *Corps Commanders: Five British and Canadian Generals at War* (Vancouver: University of British Columbia Press, 2011), 255-95. Reprinted with permission of UBC Press.

1. Library and Archives Canada [LAC], Personnel Records Unit [PRU], Personnel File, Charles Foulkes. Foulkes's personnel file contains confidential reports for the years 1926-27 and 1929-39. It also includes his course report from the British Army Staff College at Camberley (1938).
2. LAC, PRU, Foulkes Personnel File, Staff College Final Report, Senior Wing (Captain C. Foulkes), dated 20 December 1938.
3. National Defence Headquarters, Directorate of History and Heritage (DHH), J.L. Granatstein Interviews, General Robert Moncel Interview, Mahone Bay, NS, 6 October 1991; and George Kitching, *Mud and Green Fields: The Memoirs of Major-General George Kitching* (St. Catharines: Vanwell, 1993), 189.
4. Terry Copp, *Fields of Fire: The Canadians in Normandy* (Toronto: University of Toronto Press, 2003), 180-82; and *Cinderella Army: The Canadians in Northwest Europe, 1944-1945* (Toronto: University of Toronto Press, 2006), 35.
5. DHH, Granatstein Interviews, Brigadier G.E. Beament interview, Old Chelsea, 24 May 1991; Brigadier R.T. Bennett interview, Ottawa, 22 May 1991; General Robert Moncel Interview, Mahone Bay, 6 October 1991; General A. Bruce Matthews Interview, 25 April 1991, Toronto; Major-General W.J. Megill Interview, Kingston, 18 January 1992; J.W. Pickersgill Interview, Ottawa, 21 May 1991; Brigadier Beverly Matthews Interview, 16 October 1991, Toronto; General N. Elliot Rodger Interview, Ottawa, 21 May 1991.
6. Copp, *Fields of Fire*, 182.
7. DHH, Granatstein Interviews, General N. Elliot Rodger Interview, Ottawa, 21 May 1991.
8. Kitching, *Mud and Green Fields*, 214.
9. Ibid.
10. Ibid., 211-13.
11. DHH, Granatstein Interviews, Brigadier William Ziegler, Edmonton, 23 October 1991.
12. On Kitching's removal from command of 4th Canadian Armoured Division, see Copp, *Fields of Fire*, 248-50.
13. LAC, RG 24, Vol.13688, WD HQ 1st Cdn Corps (G Branch), November 1944.
14. General Sir William Jackson, *The Mediterranean and the Middle East*, Vol.VI, Part III (Uckfield: Naval and Military Press, 2004), 48-49.
15. LAC, RG 24, Vol.13688, WD HQ 1st Cdn Corps (G Branch), November 1944, Exercise "CHUCKLE" Notes on Corps Comd's Conference 18 November 1944.
16. DHH, Foulkes Papers, 72/1223, Series 6, Box 123, Final Operations 1 Cdn Corps Italy, "Operation Chuckle," Operation CHUCKLE RCA 1 Cdn Corps Planning Notes No. 1,

20 November 1944; and Appreciation of the Engr Situation Confronting 1 Cdn Corps by Chief Engineer, 24 November 1944.
17 DHH, Foulkes Papers, 72/1223, Series 6, Box 123, Final Operations 1 Cdn Corps Italy, "Operation Chuckle", OP "CHUCKLE" – OUTLINE PLAN, dated 21 November 1944.
18 DHH, Foulkes Papers, 72/1223, Series 6, Box 123, Final Operations 1 Cdn Corps Italy, "Operation Chuckle", Exercise "CHUCKLE" – Revised Outline Plan, 27 November 44; and LAC, RG 24, Vol.13688, HQ 1st Cdn Corps (G Branch), November 1944, Notes on Corps Comd's Co-ord Conference held at 'A' Mess HQ 1 Cdn Corps At 281130A hrs.
19 Jackson, *The Mediterranean and the Middle East*, 116–20.
20 G.W.L. Nicholson, *The Canadians in Italy, 1943–1945* (Ottawa: Queen's Printer, 1966), 616.
21 Kitching, *Mud and Green Fields*, 214.
22 The reinforcements included assault guns and a company from the 741st Regiment.
23 Nicholson, *The Canadians in Italy*, 618.
24 In a 1992 interview, Calder speculated that his sacking had to do with Foulkes being embarrassed about a drunken incident at Calder's headquarters, but this was obviously not the case. DHH, Granatstein Interviews, Col. J. Allan ("ding") Calder, Montreal, 4 May 1992.
25 The regimental history of the Royal Canadian Regiment is very frank about individual failings during this battle. See G.R. Stevens, *The Royal Canadian Regiment*, Vol. II, *1933–1966* (London, Ontario: London Printing & Lithographing, 1967), 171–78.
26 Nicholson, *The Canadians in Italy*, 618.
27 Kitching, *Mud and Green Fields*, 215.
28 See Douglas E. Delaney, *The Soldiers' General: Bert Hoffmeister at War* (Vancouver: UBC Press, 2005), 140–48.
29 LAC, RG 24, Vol.13,689, HQ 1st Cdn Corps (G Branch), HQ 1 Cdn Corps GS Branch Log, 6 December 1944, 1315 hours, Serial 158.
30 LAC, RG 24, Vol.13,689, HQ 1st Cdn Corps (G Branch), HQ 1 Cdn Corps GS Branch Log, 7 December 1944, 103 hours, Serial 514.
31 LAC, RG 24, Vol.13,689, HQ 1st Cdn Corps (G Branch), 7 December 1944.
32 LAC, RG 24, Vol.13,689, HQ 1st Cdn Corps (G Branch), 7 December 1944.
33 See 1 Cdn Corps Last Light Sitreps 6–10 December 1944. LAC, RG 24, Vol.13,689, HQ 1st Cdn Corps (G Branch), December 1944.
34 Nicholson, *Canadians in Italy*, 626.
35 Foulkes had first arranged the diversionary attack on 7 December. LAC, RG 24, Vol.13,689, HQ 1st Cdn Corps (G Branch), HQ 1 Cdn Corps GS Branch Log, 7 December 1944, 1550 hours, Serial 533.
36 LAC, RG 24, Vol.13,689, HQ 1st Cdn Corps (G Branch), HQ 1 Cdn Corps GS Branch Log, Serials 846, 915, 949, 954, and 956.
37 On the depleted strength of the 73rd *Korps*, see Georg Tessin, *Verbande und Truppen der deutschen Wehrmacht und Waffen-SS im Zweiten Weltkrieg1939-1945. Band 6: Die Landstreitkrafte Nrm. 71-120* (Osnabruck, 1979), 14.

38 LAC, RG 24, Vol.13,798, WD 5th Canadian Armoured Division (G Staff), 13 December 1944.
39 LAC, RG 24, Vol.13,689, HQ 1st Cdn Corps (G Branch), Intentions 1 Cdn Corps night 13/14 December 1944 and day 14 December 1944, 140040A December 1944.
40 Nicholson, *Canadians in Italy*, 631.
41 LAC, RG 24, Vol.13,689, HQ 1st Cdn Corps (G Branch), HQ 1 Cdn Corps GS Branch Log, 18 December 1944, Serial 648.
42 When General Sir Henry Maitland Wilson left the Mediterranean to lead the British Joint Staff Mission in Washington, Alexander took over as Supreme Commander Mediterranean, Clark became C-in-C Allied Armies Italy, and Truscott assumed command of Fifth US Army.
43 DHH, Granatstein Interviews, Major-General W.J. Megill Interview, Kingston, 18 January 1992.
44 DHH, Granatstein Interviews, General Bert Hoffmeister Interview, Vancouver, 2 March 1992.
45 This was the recollection of Tony Foster, Major-General Harry Foster's son, who also said that Foulkes was "the only senior officer of whom Gen. Foster spoke ill." See DHH, Granatstein Interviews, Tony Foster Interview, Halifax, 2 October 1991.

15

No Ambush, No Defeat
The Advance of the Vanguard of the 9th Canadian Infantry Brigade, 7 June 1944

Marc Milner

It is virtually an article of faith in the Normandy campaign literature that the vanguard of the 9th Canadian Infantry Brigade (hereafter 9 Brigade) was ambushed and defeated by 12 SS Hitler Youth Panzer Division on D+1. These young Nazi fanatics, led by battle-hardened Eastern Front veterans, took the naïve Canadians by surprise, denied them their ultimate objective and sent them packing.[1] For many historians, the defeat of 9 Brigade is also evidence of the flawed nature of Allied leadership and combat capability, and yet more proof of the superior fighting skill of German forces.[2] These ideas have proven powerfully enduring.

Ironically, the Canadian Army's own official history is largely to blame for the very negative interpretation of 9 Brigade's battle on 7 June. Charles Stacey's *The Victory Campaign* devoted seven pages to the battle: four and a half setting it up, and most of two analyzing why the brigade "had been caught off balance and defeated in detail."[3] In Stacey's view, the brigade fought with "courage and spirit, but somewhat clumsily" against "an unusually efficient German force of about its own strength, it had come off second best." The result was a "severe local reverse" that—in words that damned all Canadian efforts in the days after D-Day—"helped to ensure that Caen remained in German hands."[4] In fact, Stacey never did a full work-up on the battle. His account of the actual battle with 12 SS on D+1 consists of one eighteen-line paragraph, and six of those lines are devoted to the brigade consolidation at the end of the day. His entire description of the struggle for Authie is eleven words: the vanguard "fought hard but were overrun: only a few men got away."[5] Given this assessment by the Canadian official historian, it is hard to blame others for picking up the tone.

A closer look at the events of D+1 tells quite a different story. It reveals that the vanguard of 9 Brigade fought an enemy at least three times its size to a standstill, and did so largely without the crucial component of Anglo-Canadian doctrine: artillery support. Stacey admitted the latter point but claimed that the guns were simply out of range.[6] He was wrong: at least three Canadian field regiments were within range for much of the battle. In the event, the outcome of the battle resulted in the establishment of the 9 Brigade fortress on the only ground suitable under the circumstances. The brigade's ultimate objective of Carpiquet, and its alternate position between Buron and Authie,[7] were untenable without the 3rd British Division in line on their left. Finally, in the process 9 Brigade met and defeated a portion of the panzer forces that the 3rd Canadian Division had been tasked with destroying. So maybe 9 Brigade did all right on D+1 after all.

The task for the 3rd Canadian Infantry Division on D+1 was clear: it was to establish brigade fortress positions astride the Caen–Bayeux highway on either side of the Mue River "to meet the anticipated counter attack."[8] This was in keeping with the Allied expectation that German panzer formations, located generally east of Caen, would launch their counteroffensive against the landings across the excellent tank country north and west of the city. As a COSSAC appreciation of 22 October 1943 observed: "The country NORTH-WEST of CAEN is very suited to tank action, and it is therefore in this area that the panzer battle should be staged in order that the landing forces may be driven into the sea."[9] A SHAEF estimate completed on the eve of D-Day echoed that concern, noting that the armoured division now believed to be around Argentan (actually 21 Pz near Falaise) "would be employed in battlegroups in direct attack on the Allied bridgehead and might advance either EAST of the R. MUE … or attempt to seize the high ground NORTH of the R. SEULLES in the area BANVILLE-CREPON-BAZENVILLE."[10] The latter was most easily reached by moving up the west side of the Mue River. So the Canadians did not "push boldly" inland on D+1 "despite" the danger of powerful panzer forces moving towards them—as Russell Hart alleges[11]—but in *anticipation* of them.

The Germans were well aware of the value of this terrain. While units of 716 Division manned the coastal zone, the only German armoured formation near the beach on D-Day, 21 Panzer Division, deployed several of its key units north and west of Caen on 6 June, primarily its towed guns. This included the division's 200 Heavy Anti-Tank Battalion at St-Croix, Camilly, and Putot. These twenty-four towed 88mm Pak 43/41 guns (on an interim artillery-style carriage) had a lethal range of 3,500 yards.[12] The heavy anti-tank platoon (1 Zug) of 8 Company of 192 Panzergrenadier Regiment—three Pak 75mm self-propelled guns, with supporting anti-aircraft and mortars—was garrisoned at Cairon.[13] Astride what is now route D7 between Caen and Langrune-sur-mer, 21 PZ deployed I Battalion of 155 Panzer Artillery Regiment with its twelve towed guns. II Battalion of 192 Panzergrenadier Regiment was garrisoned in the area as support. The ground occupied by these advanced units of 21 Panzer was precisely where the Germans would try to orchestrate a major panzer attack in the days following the landing.[14]

To capture and hold this ground the Canadians were assigned an exceptional amount of firepower. A normal British Commonwealth infantry division had three regiments of field artillery totalling 72 guns. For the beachhead battles, the 3rd Canadian Division was assigned twice that number—six regiments totalling 144 guns—plus a medium regiment (4.5 inch) and two batteries of Royal Marine self-propelled 95mm howitzers. It is clear from the Operational Order for the artillery of the 3rd Canadian Division that these guns were under Canadian control for the forthcoming battle (though they could and did help along the entire British front).[15] More telling still of what planners anticipated in the Canadian zone was the assignment of the 1st British Corps' anti-tank regiment, the 62nd RA, to the Canadians for the initial phase of the Normandy operation. The 62nd's four batteries (each of three troops of four guns) were all equipped with 17-pounder guns, half of them on self-propelled M-10 chassis. This gave the Canadians an additional forty-eight of the most powerful anti-tank guns then in service among Anglo-American forces.[16]

The Canadians organized the field and medium guns into two powerful Field Artillery Groups. The 14th Artillery Group, composed of the 14th and 19th Field Regiments, Royal Canadian Artillery (RCA), the 191th Field Regiment, Royal Artillery (RA), and the 79th Medium Regiment, RA (4.5 inch), was to occupy positions between Authie–Franqueville and the Mue River valley once 9 Brigade was secure at Carpiquet. The 12th Artillery Group, composed of the 12th and 13th RCA and the 6th RA, was to deploy behind 7 Brigade (holding Bretteville–Putot) around the hamlet of Bray. The Canadian regiments were to land on D-Day, the 6th RA and 79th Medium on D+2, and the 191th RA on D+3. By D+1 each of the Artillery Groups was to be supported by a battery (of sixteen guns) of 95mm self-propelled howitzers of the 2nd Royal Marine Armoured Support (RMAS) Regiment in Centaur tanks to provide countermortar fire.[17]

All of the 240 field guns landed by the Anglo-Canadians on 6 June were self-propelled (SP): 168 American-built M-7 Priests equipped with a 105mm gun-howitzer and the rest (which landed with the 50th British Division) Canadian-built Sextons equipped with 25-pounders. Field regiments had been converted to SPs in part because of a conclusion reached in the spring of 1943 by British Home Forces that delay and confusion on assault beaches were the result of too many towed guns getting stuck. But the "Artillery Policy" of Second British Army also relied on "a speedy build up of guns in order to assist in the defence of the beach-head against the heavy enemy counter-attacks which were expected."[18] To deal with the expected panzer thrust in Normandy, the British also ensured that at least some portion of the anti-tank artillery landed on D-Day was SPs as well.

In the event, Canadian artillery got ashore largely unscathed on D-Day. Only six of their ninety-seven M-7s were lost, leaving the division with ninety 105mm guns for the beachhead battles. The towed 25-pounders of the 6th RA and 191th RA were delayed and missed the initial battles, as did most of the RM Centaurs, which were tied up in the battle to link Juno and Sword Beaches. The trade-off for mobility and protection in a fluid environment was loss of range. The 105mm threw a larger shell (33 pounds) than the British 25-pounder and consequently had a shorter range: 11,400 yards versus 13,400.[19] That difference is claimed to have had a profound impact on the fate of 9 Brigade on D+1.

The Canadian assault on Juno Beach went well, but the friction of war set in motion events that would shape the battle on D+1. The two assault brigades broke the beach defences quickly, and troops were moving inland by mid-

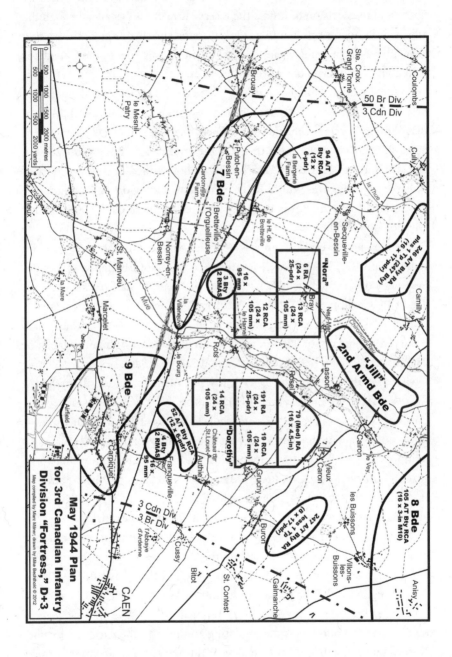

morning. However, the storm surge on 6 June had narrowed the beach by noon, and the decision to funnel the reserve brigade, 9 Brigade, through the village of Bernières resulted in a colossal traffic jam. By the time the leading elements of the brigade began to move inland, it was late, so the Canadians halted on their interim objective for the night.

As the Canadians fought their way inland on D-Day through the defences held by 716 Division, 21 Panzer Division responded to the invasion. Most of that division's forces north and west of Caen, including three Pak 43/41 88mm guns, shifted east to check the thrust of the 3rd British Division towards the city. The rest of 200 Heavy Anti-Tank Battalion shifted northwest, most of it deploying along the Seulles River by midday in support of 729 Battalion of 716 Division, which was trying to stem the landing of the 50th British Division on Gold Beach.[20]

The area northwest of Caen was occupied on the afternoon of 6 June by Kampgruppe (KG) Rauch of 21 Panzer. It consisted of I Battalion of 192 PG Regiment (Oberstleutnant Rauch's unit) mounted in half-tracks, eighteen SPs of II Battalion of 155 Panzer Artillery Regiment (on converted French chassis, "Schutzwagen Lorraine-Schleppers"), and the 2nd (half-track mounted) Company of 220 Panzer Pioneer Battalion.[21] While the tanks of 21 PZ launched the high-profile attack on the west flank of the 3rd British Division on the afternoon of D-Day, it was Rauch's formation that reached the sea at Lyon-sur-mer at about 1900 hours on D-Day.[22] When it looked like they might be cut off, KG Rauch—less a few destroyed SPs and half-tracks—retreated to St-Contest-Cussy, leaving the infantry of 1/192 Regiment to reinforce the garrison of the Douvres radar station. With his diminished force (later reinforced by 3 [Armoured] Company of 220 Panzer Pioneer Battalion from Cruelly), Rauch was ordered to hold the line from Cairon to Cambes. His headquarters was still in place at Cussy at noon the next day.[23]

After an unsettled night of mortar attacks, Luftwaffe bombing, and random clashes with small groups of the enemy, the Canadians set off on the morning of 7 June to occupy their "divisional covering position"[24] astride the Caen–Bayeux highway. The 7th Canadian Infantry Brigade (7 Brigade), advancing down the west side of the Mue River, reached its objective without serious opposition. By noon it was consolidating around La Villeneuve, Bretteville, Norrey, and Putot. The 12th Canadian Field Artillery Group covered them in bounds and then settled in around the little hamlet of Bray, about 1,500

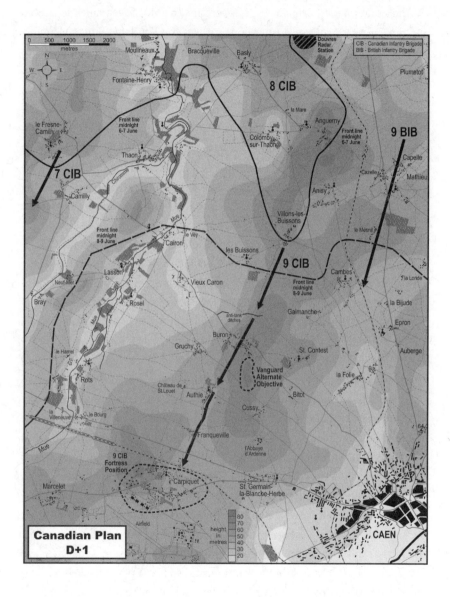

yards from the front, by 1600 hours. By mid-afternoon of D+1 the 7 Brigade fortress was in place, right where the Operational Plan had stipulated.[25]

The situation for 9 Brigade was less certain. The Mue River valley separated it from 7 Brigade, but of greater concern was the left flank, where elements of 21 Panzer were known to be operating. British 9 Brigade was supposed to be on the Canadians' left, but it was miles away. On 6 June it had been drawn into the British struggle to reach Caen and by D+1 was near the bridges over the Caen canal at Benouville. On D+1 there were only Germans on the Canadians' left flank. So Brigadier D.G. Cunningham was forced to echelon his battalions forward, guarding his eastern flank as he moved. Inevitably that meant, as Stacey observed, that the brigade was strung out and that the battalions were not able to support each other properly. Nonetheless, the orders were clear: 9 Brigade was to get onto its D-Day objective of the village of Carpiquet and dig in astride the Caen–Bayeux highway and rail line.[26]

At 0740 hours on 7 June the brigade vanguard moved south from Villons-les-Buissons down the D220 towards Carpiquet. The force consisted of the North Nova Scotia Highlanders (a battalion), supported by the Sherman tanks of the Sherbrooke Fusiliers, four Vickers machine guns of No. 11 Platoon of the Cameron Highlanders of Ottawa,[27] and a troop of M-10 tank destroyers of the 3rd Anti-Tank Regiment, RCA. The vanguard deployed in a wide arrow formation, led by the Sherbrookes' recce troop of Stuart light tanks. Behind them came C Company of the Novas borne by the battalion's Bren gun carrier platoon, supported by the Camerons and anti-tank guns. The Novas' B Company moved across the open ground to the left on the tanks of the Sherbrookes' B Squadron, while A Company did the same with A Squadron on the right. D Company and C Squadron of the armoured regiment, as well as the Novas' support company and battalion HQ, brought up the rear.

The 14th Field Regiment, RCA, was assigned to provide fire support. These gunners and the Novas had trained together, and the two units knew each other well. But the gunners had not participated in the final pre-D-Day exercise for vanguard's advance, Pedal II in mid-April. On that occasion 14th RCA was away doing its final amphibious training, and so fire support for Pedal II was provided by the two towed RA regiments attached to the division's artillery.[28] How this affected events on D+1 remains unclear. The 14th RCA's twenty-one remaining 105mm self-propelled guns, in position near Beny-sur-Mer at 0745 hours, were to move forward in stages (with at least one battery on the ground and ready to fire) to a new gun position at La Mare, northwest of Anguerney, by noon. According to the Operational Order, the Novas ought to have picked up four Forward Observation Officers (FOOs) of the 14th RCA as they moved through 8 Brigade: one for each company.[29] In the event, they received just two, who travelled with the battalion HQ. This meant that the vanguard operated according to the normal Anglo-Canadian fire support practice, not in accordance with the artillery-heavy doctrine adopted for the beachhead battles, which called for a FOO with every company.

In light of the rather cavalier dismissal of the vanguard's efforts by subsequent historians, including Stacey, it is important to record that it fought its way forward from the start. Obersharführer Bernhard Meitzel, the ordnance officer of 12 SS, would testify in 1945 that remnants of 716 Division, reorganized into a battalion,[30] held Buron, Authie, and Franqueville.[31] As well, 21 Panzer's 200 Heavy Anti-Tank Battalion remained in the area under command of 12 SS "throughout the first days of the invasion," though it is not clear how many guns they had left. Meitzel also claimed that "Battlegroup Rauch" of 21 Panzer operated northwest of Caen in the first days of the Normandy campaign,[32] while Luftwaffe troops continued to man their anti-aircraft positions near Franqueville.[33] These German units did not constitute a well-organized and coordinated force, but the vanguard had to fight them nonetheless. At a minimum, the 9 Brigade vanguard found itself confronted by a well-armed force about its own size even before 12 SS intervened.

The 9 Brigade vanguard advanced along a secondary road across a wide, rolling plain dotted with agricultural villages composed of stone houses and barns, with farmyards and homes surrounded by high stone walls and orchards. The ground south of Villons-les-Buisson is flat and open to the east towards Cambes and Galmanche, and slopes down towards the Mue River to the west. It also rises gently for about 1.5 kilometres towards a broad, flat crest north of Buron. In 1944, nothing of Buron, barely 1 kilometre away over open ground, could be seen from Villons-les-Buisson, though rooftops of St-Contest off to the southeast were visible. Buron only came into view when the crest was reached, about 600 metres south of Villons-les-Buisson. Just beyond that point the Germans had dug an anti-tank ditch for 100 yards on either side of the road.

South of Buron the road runs straight, across flat fields for 1 kilometre to Authie. This whole area is easily monitored from the slight rise at St-Contest, and even more so from the towers of the Abbey d'Ardennes, 1500 metres to the east. In 1944, Authie straggled along either side of the road for about 500 metres in the middle of an essentially flat plain. The road then dipped slightly in front of Francqueville before reaching the lip of the plain overlooking Carpiquet. The edge of the plain is not well reflected on the 1944 Ordnance Survey maps but is clearly visible on the ground and runs right around the northern perimeter of Caen. To the west of Authie, where the ground rises out of the Mue River valley, lay the village of Gruchy. The 4 or 5 square kilometres of open farmland that slopes gently down to the Mue River west of Authie were designated for the 14th Field Artillery Group's deployment once Carpiquet was secured. In sum, 9 Brigade's vanguard advanced across a gently rolling but open plain over which the Germans had excellent observation and fields of fire, a plain that ended abruptly in superb dead ground where the Germans could deploy their artillery and hide their counterattack force.[34]

The first task of the vanguard was to fight its way through elements of 21 Panzer holding the hamlet of Villons-les-Buisson.[35] The presence of at least one 88mm gun of 200 Heavy Anti-Tank Battalion was revealed when a Sherbrooke recce tank was hit. The infantry of the Novas' C Company dismounted while the carrier platoon, supported by 3-inch mortars, did a flanking move. The 88mm gun was taken out in a shower of grenades, and three half-tracks—one equipped with a rocket projector, which suggests the presence of the 3rd Company of 220 Panzer Pioneer Battalion—were also destroyed.[36] With orders to "leave the heavy mopping up to others,"[37] Villons-les-Buisson was reported secure by 0900 hours.[38]

C Company then remounted its carriers and, led by Shermans of the Sherbrookes' No. 2 Troop, C Squadron, set off for Buron. According to Sergeant T.C. Reid, the troop leader, Canadian tanks destroyed another 88mm gun and two "hornets"—a euphemism for enemy tanks, but probably SP guns—as they entered the village, and then waited for the infantry to follow.[39] The Novas arrived to find Buron "alive with snipers and machine guns and it took some time to get a foothold in the place."[40] Many prisoners were captured and another SP gun destroyed before Buron was declared "secure" at 1200 hours. About that time, the Novas' commanding officer, Lt.-Col. Charles Petch, arrived with the HQ company, the FOOs, and five Sherbrooke tanks of the regimental headquarters. They had been delayed by the need to fight through Villon-les-Buisson again.

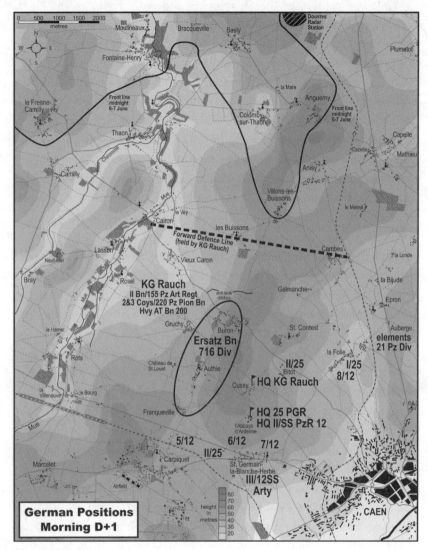

German Forces
KG Rauch — Kampfgruppe Rauch
II Bn/155 Pz Art Regt — 2 Battalion, 155 Panzer Artillery Regiment
2&3 Coys/220 Pz Pion Bn — 2 & 3 Companies, 220 Panzer Pioneer Battalion
Hvy AT Bn 200 — 200 Heavy Anti-Tank Battalion
25 PGR — 25 Panzer Grenadier Regiment
I/25, II/25, III/25 — 1st, 2nd & 3rd Battalions, 25 SS Panzer Grenadier Regiment
II/SS PzR 12 — 2nd Battalion, 12 SS Panzer Regiment
5/12, 6/12, 7/12, 8/12 — 5, 6, 7 & 8 Companies, 2nd Battalion, 12 SS Panzer Regiment
III/12SS Arty — 3rd Battalion, 12 SS Artillery Regiment

While A Squadron of the Sherbrookes and A Company of the Novas (which had dismounted in Villon-les-Buisson) moved towards Buron on the right without incident, B Company and B Squadron on the left drew fire from St-Contest and Galmanche to the east. This was a portend. Both villages lay in the British sector, but the British 9th Brigade did not begin to move from its positions near the Orne until 1400 hours (and it never did get anywhere near Galmanche and St-Contest on D+1). Both villages were heavily garrisoned by 21 Panzer, who knew their business. The infantry of B Company were initially forced to dismount the Sherbrookes' tanks by fire from St-Contest. When that shooting stopped, the Novas remounted the tanks and started moving again. That drew another hail of shell and mortar fire, driving the infantry to ground again, inflicting casualties and scattering one of the platoons. B Company then made its way into Buron on foot.[41]

Goaded especially by the firing from Galmanche, and spurred by the tanks, half-tracks, 88mm guns, and other vehicles they could see around the village, B Squadron moved to attack. Within minutes, three Shermans—including Maj. G.S. Mahon's—had been knocked out by an 88mm gun. By the time B Squadron disengaged, it was down to ten tanks and under command of Captain Bateman.[42] The Sherbrookes' attack on Galmanche did nothing to abate the fire coming from the eastern flank of the vanguard. When Lt.-Col. Petch arrived in Buron at roughly noon, B Company officers petitioned him to put artillery fire down on St-Contest.[43] This request roughly coincided with the initial deployment of the 14th RCA guns at La Mare, where they came under mortar, machine gun, and anti-tank gunfire from the radar station at Douvres.[44] The latter was a 10-hectare site with more than thirty concrete works, as well as minefields, barbed wire, anti-tank, flak, and field guns, and scores of machine guns all built around a five-storey-deep underground complex. Taking it on D+1 was a task of the North Shore (New Brunswick) Regiment (NSR), supported by the 19th Field Regiment, RCA. So half the artillery fire—and more crucially half the FOOs—designated in the Overlord plan to support the vanguard of 9 Brigade had been diverted. The 105mm shells sof 19th RCA's guns simply bounced off the steel-reinforced concrete of the radar station, and the NSR never got close to capturing it — it fell two weeks later to a British brigade.

According to conventional wisdom, harassing fire from the Douvres radar station prevented the 14th RCA from deploying forward to help the 9 Brigade vanguard. Actually, the 14th RCA was on its gun position around La Mare at noon on D+1, and according to veterans, harassing fire from the radar station had little serious effect.[45] In any event, the guns were supposed to move forward in bounds with at least one battery on call for immediate fire. But when, at noon, Petch asked that artillery be brought down on St-Contest, his FOO said that the guns were unavailable. According to Malcolm Langille, the Novas' intelligence sergeant, radio problems plagued the vanguard throughout the day. Since we know that the two FOOs from the 14th Field were with the battalion HQ, in this instance the lack of artillery support may well have been due to a failure of the radios. So Petch turned to his naval "Forward Officer Bombardment" (FBO), who was in contact with HMS *Belfast* offshore, which was standing by with nine 6-inch guns, to put fire down on St-Contest (and Gruchy to the right of Buron). The FBO was unable to contact the cruiser, and as he cried in frustration over the communications failure fire from St-Contest and Gruchy continued unabated.

This incident in Buron at noon seems to have become the iconic moment in the whole story of the failure of indirect fire support for the vanguard. There was no way that Petch could have known that he and his men would have to fight for the next seven hours without artillery support. All that could be managed at the moment was suppression of the enemy fire coming from St-Contest by direct fire from the 37mm guns of the Sherbrookes' three remaining Stuart recce tanks and from the 3rd A/T Regiment's M-10s.[46]

By noon the vanguard had concentrated three of its four infantry companies in Buron. C and B were preparing to make the next move to Authie, while D was clearing the village again—which produced more prisoners but failed to get them all.[47] From this point on Buron was under constant shell and mortar fire.[48] Meanwhile, A Company remained deployed in the open ground to the west. The support company, battalion anti-tank guns, and Vickers platoon of the Cameron Highlanders closed up on the anti-tank ditch between Buron and Villons-les-Buisson.

The push towards Authie began with a probe by three Bren carriers, which returned after taking small arms and machine-gun fire from the orchard north of the village. Petch ordered B Company and the Sherbrookes' B Squadron to make the first move. They advanced to the crossroads halfway to Authie, from where the tanks destroyed the machine-gunning positions on the northern outskirts of the village.[49] Using this suppressing fire, two carrier-mounted platoons of the Novas' C Company raced to Authie, dismounted on the outskirts, and began clearing the village. One section of carriers then flanked Authie to the left to meet the infantry as they emerged at the south end, while the other carrier section probed as far as Franqueville. When the third carrier section with the rest of C Company arrived (it had missed the movement order in Buron), the infantry dismounted and deployed on the road north of Authie, and these carriers too were sent south towards Franqueville. All the Bren carriers were driven back by mortar fire, and soon reassembled north of Authie.[50]

Meanwhile, two platoons of the Novas worked their way through Authie: Lt. J.H. Langley's on the right side of the road, and Lt. Jack Veness's on the left. Many of the enemy was driven from Authie into the fire of the tanks of B Squadron, which had moved east of the village "potting groups of the enemy in all directions."[51] Lieutenant Davies noted in his after-action summary that B Squadron had "lots of fun as we kept going."[52] About the same time, Maj. E.W.L. Arnold's A Squadron swept west of Authie and Franqueville, to a point where they could see the hangars at Carpiquet airfield and "bring fire to bear on them."[53] At roughly 1330 hours the infantry platoons reached the southern end of Authie, where they stopped for lunch.[54] Shortly afterwards, enemy tanks were seen 800 yards east of Authie by B Squadron and south of Authie by A Squadron. This was followed a few minutes later by tanks to the west of Franqueville, which engaged A Squadron[55] just as the whole area around Authie came under intense enemy artillery fire.

Canadian senior staff were well aware on the morning of 7 June that the situation was fluid, that the 3rd British Division was not keeping pace on the left, and that German armoured formations were in the area. Until the late afternoon, none of this warranted abandoning the D-Day objective of Carpiquet. Indeed, as the vanguard reached Authie, Petch expected to see some evidence of either the British on their left or 7 Brigade on the right.[56] What no one on the Allied side knew was that Authie was virtually surrounded by Germans and that German armoured forces besides 21 Panzer were already on the battlefield.

Late on the afternoon of D-Day, I SS Panzer Corps ordered a major attack by three Panzer divisions in the Caen sector. The 21 Panzer Division, primarily committed to holding the 3rd British Division north of Caen and trying to destroy the airborne bridgehead east of the Orne, was to consolidate north

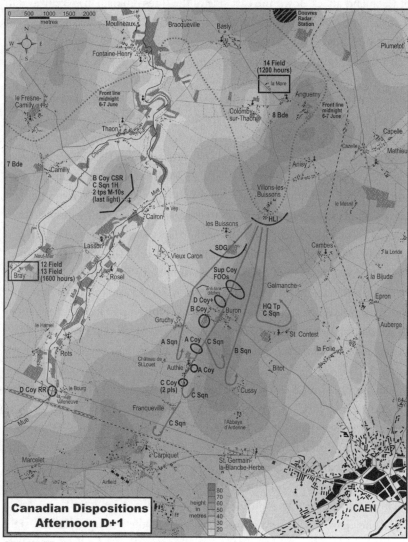

Canadian Dispositions Afternoon D+1

Canadian Forces
A, B, C & D Coy — Companies of the North Nova Scotia Highlanders
A, B & C Sqn — Squadrons of the Sherbrooke Fusiliers Regiment
1H — First Hussars
12, 13 & 14 Field — Field Regiments, Royal Canadian Artillery
CSR — Canadian Scottish Regiment
HLI — Highland Light Infantry of Canada
RR — Regina Rifle Regiment
FOO — Forward Observation Officer

of Caen and attack down the east side of the Caen-Luc-sur-mer railway. On their left, 12 SS Panzer Division (Hitler Youth) was to attack down the west side of the railway. The axis of both attacks lay across broad, largely flat plains that rolled unobstructed to the sea. Panzer Lehr was to join in to the west of the Mue River as it arrived. The attack was scheduled for 1600 hours on 7 June, with instructions to "drive the enemy … into the sea and destroy him."[57]

The 12 SS Hitler Youth Panzer Division was the most powerful German armoured formation in the west. It was composed of youthful fanatics, seventeen to nineteen years old, and led by veterans from 1 SS Panzer Division, Liebstandarte Adolph Hitler. At nearly 21,000 strong, it was equipped with some five hundred tanks and armoured fighting vehicles.[58] Even its engineer and reconnaissance battalions were larger and more powerfully equipped than normal SS or Wehrmacht units. Its field artillery included sixty 105mm and eighteen 150mm guns—more and heavier guns than the standard Allied or German division. And, of course, the division had a regiment (12 SS Panzer) of tanks: ninety-eight Mk IVs and sixty-six Mark V Panthers. On 6 June only the division's jagdpanzer battalion was not yet fully equipped, and its battery of six 280mm nebelwerfers had not yet appeared. In all other respects, 12 SS was an elite division even among elites, right down to its camouflage pattern uniforms.[59]

Having been freed to move by 0500 hours on 6 June from lodgements around Lisieux, fifty kilometres east of Caen, the first 12 SS units to arrive at the front were 25 Panzergrenadier Regiment (PGR), and twelve 150mm and four 105mm guns of III Battalion, 12 SS Artillery Regiment. This battle group, led by Sturmbanführer Kurt Meyer, deployed around the Abbey d'Ardennes in the early hours of 7 June. By mid-morning (0900 hours German time) the infantry and artillery were in place. The location was superb. The towers of the Abbey gave a full and unobstructed view of the whole battlefield, right back to the beaches, including the entire area of the Canadian vanguard's advance. About an hour later, fifty Mk IVs of II Panzer Battalion rolled in.

Meyer found the front loosely held by Kampgruppe Rauch, which was headquartered at Cussy. When Rauch's officers could not provide him with a clear picture of the situation, Meyer did his own reconnaissance towards Buron. Before he could get to the village he was fired on by tanks of the Sherbrookes' B Squadron. He beat a hasty retreat to the Abbey and climbed one of its towers to get a better view of things. He arrived just in time to see the Canadian vanguard move on Authie.⁶⁰ In an instant, Meyer realized that the planned attack with 21 Panzer towards the beach would have to wait for another day. It was probably at this point (1330 hours for the Canadians) that the sixteen guns of III/12 SS artillery, deployed on dead ground behind the abbey around the village of St-Germain-la-Blanche-Herbe, opened fire on Authie.

While the Canadians were being softened up by artillery fire, Meyer made the rounds of his battalions, passing orders. I Battalion, with only five tanks but reinforced by the 16 Pioneer Company, was waiting to the east of the abbey. It was pointed at Le Cambes and the leading elements of the 3rd British Division. Meyer's II Battalion was north of the abbey in the hamlet of Bitot with about twenty Mk IV tanks. His III Battalion, with about twenty tanks, was echeloned to the left rear as a flank guard. It was deployed on the dead ground south of Franqueville.⁶¹

Historians have uncritically accepted Meyer's view of what happened next: an opportunistic strike on an enemy carelessly strung out along the road. Russell Hart calls it an ambush, in which the Canadians were quickly overrun. Stacey implies as much. But Meyer's view is self-serving and wrong. His counterattack towards the sea was slated for 1600 hours, but now his III Battalion and its supporting armour were engaged by the Canadian vanguard. What followed was anything but an ambush: it was the commencement of six hours of intense and often brutal fighting.

Moreover, 12 SS was hardly the only German force on the battlefield. The Sherbrookes' pincer operation towards Franqueville was about to close when, according to Capt. Gray of the Novas' carrier platoon, "intense shelling and mortaring began to break loose on AUTHIE." Petch clearly recalled in testimony given in both 1944 and 1945 that the fire came in from both flanks and the front, which means that it came from more than the batteries of 12 SS at St-Germain-la-Blanch-Herbe.⁶² Canadian sources also indicate that what followed next was a tank-on-tank battle that lasted for about two hours.⁶³ The Sherbrookes' A Squadron duelled with tanks west of Authie, destroying three Mk IVs in the first exchange of fire, before the Germans began to hit, too. Meanwhile B Squadron fought east of Authie, destroying several tanks until the weight of German artillery and a "tank trap" laid with anti-tank guns (probably more of 21 PZ's 88mm) drove B Squadron off.⁶⁴

As the tanks squared off for their fight, Petch ordered the two platoons of C Company at the southern end of Authie to dig in, and consolidated B Company, the carrier platoon, and Lt. Graves' platoon of C Company in Buron. Maj. Don Learment came back to Buron with the carriers to consult with Petch, and then found himself along with Graves' platoon stranded there by the heavy shelling. Meanwhile, the shelling and the sudden appearance of German tanks did nothing to unsettle the vanguard. In fact, "the picture had its bright side," Captain Gray later recalled.[65] The Sherbrookes were moving up, a section of Vickers machine guns from the Camerons went forward into Authie. Flail tanks and pioneers—delayed by a traffic jam in Buron—were also on their way.

So, too, was A Company. Maj. L.M. Rhodenizer's men had just swept through Buron, clearing it yet again, and were taking position west of the village when the bombardment of Authie commenced. Rhodenizer held two of his platoons at crossroads west of Buron and sent Lt. Sutherland's platoon on the backs of Lt. Fitzpatrick's troop from C Squadron towards Authie to help. Sutherland's men took up positions just east of Authie, on the road to Cussy. Shortly after Sutherland's platoon was delivered, two of Fitzpatrick's three tanks were destroyed within sixty seconds by an 88mm gun firing from St-Contest. Now on his own, Fitzpatrick moved his Sherman Firefly to the southern end of Authie and joined C Company. Meanwhile, the rest of A Company (apparently unseen by the Germans) moved to a large, rectangular, hedged area halfway between Buron and Authie and dug in.

The brigade plan called for the vanguard to press on to Carpiquet only if there was "no serious opposition." According to Stacey, "if there was heavy opposition the North Novas were to consolidate on high ground between Buron and Authie as a base for further attacks on the objective."[66] The so-called high ground between Buron and Authie is simply an 80 metre contour line on the map in the middle of the open field due south of Buron. If it ever really existed, it is impossible to discern now. In any event, the whole area is directly overlooked from St-Contest. In the circumstances, the alternative position was utterly untenable.

By early afternoon, then, Petch was already in an impossible position, and his options were poor: reinforce Authie and try to hold it, or abandon it and try to hold farther back. His initial plan was to hold well forward, in Authie. However, when B Company tried to move up to a position on the east side of the road, near the so-called high ground, it was driven back by intense and accurate mortar fire. When Petch ordered B Company to try again, Capt. Wilson, now acting company commander, went forward to speak to Maj. Rhodenizer, who "was digging in and content to remain" in roughly the area of the "high ground." When Wilson got back he learned that Petch had now ordered his company to drive straight into Authie in the carrier platoon.

Now more than ever, Petch really needed help from the guns, but this was not to be had. Cruiser fire, which would have served well in a counterbattery role, was still offline. So, too, was the 14th RCA, but the problem at this stage was not radio failure. Rather, the FOOs, trapped in the traffic muddle of Buron's narrow streets under a shower of mortar and artillery fire, "withdrew [at 1400 hours] to get observation to the A/Tk ditch" north of Buron.[67] This effectively removed them from the battle, and even from contact with the Novas' HQ. While the 14th RCA's gunners stuck resolutely to their embattled position at La Mare, no orders to fire reached them. Malcolm Langille, the Novas' intelligence sergeant at the time, recalled in 2003 that he tried repeatedly throughout the afternoon to contact the 14th RCA through various networks and failed.[68] He was not alone: the Glens at Villons-les-Buissons initially relied on the brigade radio net to get supporting artillery on 7 June.[69] So the Novas battlegroup—trained to rely on artillery as the key component of the fighting doctrine of Anglo-Canadian formations—fought on without artillery support while being pounded from three sides by unrelenting German mortar and artillery fire.

Petch later explained that initially he had no worries about the troops in Authie because they "had not been committed" at this stage.[70] "No one was worrying too much," the Nova's regimental history recorded, at least "none of those dug in at Authie." By the time German shells "began to scream overhead in salvoes"—a sign that the attack was imminent—C Company was secure in an orchard on the southern edge of the village. Unfortunately, the two-gun section of the Cameron Highlanders of Ottawa led by Lt. Couper had failed to reach them: Couper and his men were all killed or wounded before they could get through Authie. Lt. Jack Veness recovered one of their Vickers machine guns on its Bren carrier and drove it into the orchard.[71] Some 50 calibre machine guns removed from disabled tanks were also added to the infantry positions, and Lt. Fitzpatrick's Sherman—with a disabled 17-pounder— added its machine guns to the firepower, as did "several" other tanks and M-10s. Unfortunately, none of this additional firepower seems to have been available to Lt. Sutherland's platoon from A Company, which was dug in along the Authie-Cussy road.

Meanwhile, B Company made another attempt to get forward. Supported by four tanks, two of the company's platoons, some of Lt. Graves's men of the missing platoon of C Company, and a mortar section finally reached the hedge at the northern end of Authie. One tank was destroyed by 88mm fire from St-Contest, and the whole group was mortared intensely. Major Douglas then elected to retreat to the comparative shelter of a large orchard at the southwestern end of Buron and await events.

The vanguard was now in a perilous state, stretched out and pounded by a circle of German mortars and medium and heavy artillery, and sniped at by tanks and 88mm guns. C Company, supported by Lt. Sutherland's platoon from A Company, was dug in in Authie. The rest of A Company held a hedged area along the road halfway between Authie and Buron, and B Company, for the moment, sheltered in the orchard southwest of Buron. By all accounts, Buron itself had been abandoned. Major Learment's small group (largely Lt. Graves's platoon) eventually dug in just north of Buron to the east of the road. A little farther back, about halfway to the anti-tank ditch, was D Company, while the support company, 6-pounder anti-tank guns, a section of the Camerons' Vickers guns, and the two FOOs held the anti-tank trench itself. By 1400 the Glens had dug in at Villons-les-Buisson (which they had to clear again), while the Highland Light Infantry, the brigade's third battalion, held the left flank just south of Villons-les-Buissson. So Stacey's criticism that the vanguard and the brigade were strung out is correct: by mid-afternoon Petch's force was spread like a string of pearls for three kilometres along the road to Carpiquet. It is not clear, however, what either Petch or Brigadier Cunningham could have done about it.

Canadian accounts agree that a tank duel preceded the main counterattack with infantry by as much as two hours.[72] Petch would recall in 1945 that the main tank battle had been between Buron and Gruchy—a claim echoed in the Novas' regimental history, and that this had delayed the forward movement of B Company.[73] As the German tanks retreated towards Carpiquet, for the third time Petch ordered B Company to Authie—this time on the battalion's carriers. This move was pre-empted when A Company was attacked from Gruchy by an unknown force that included tanks and half-tracks.[74] This was followed by news that Authie was under attack by tanks and a battalion of infantry.

So at roughly 1530 hours the vanguard was simultaneously attacked on two flanks, an assault that spread as far north as Buron. According to Petch's testimony in 1945, "at this time the remainder of the battalion was attacked from the direction of Gruchy by armour and infantry who dismounted from half tracks."[75] Who this was remains a mystery. The attack on Buron may well have been launched by 25 SS PGR Reconnaissance Company, which had been probing up the highway towards Bayeux, or by elements of Kampgruppe Rauch.

The only attack that historians seem to note is the one on Authie by III/25 PGR and some twenty tanks from the dead ground south of Franqueville. The Germans had to cross about 1200 metres of open ground and they would never have done so had Canadian artillery been available. Had there been a FOO in Authie, he could have drawn not only on the 14th Field but also, by mid-afternoon, on both the 12th and the 13th RCA, which had settled into gun positions behind 7 Brigade in the little hamlet of Bray. That put them just 5000 metres away from Authie on the other side of the Mue River. So the Germans came forward largely unmolested. Lieutenant Fitzpatrick watched them come from the turret of his tank: "two waves of infantry and then the tanks moving forward slowly and with determination."[76]

Finally, as they closed in on Authie, the Hitler Youth were met by withering fire from everything the Canadians had mustered. "First groups of the enemy simply melted away before the murderous hail," Will Bird wrote. "Time and again the enemy seemed but yards from the hedge and then they were blown down or hurled back. It seemed incredible that so small a force could keep back such weight and strength, but it was being done."[77] Lieutenant Sutherland's platoon on the Authie–Cussy road was eventually "forced back by a tidal wave of the enemy too numerous to halt." Meanwhile, C Company's positions were gradually surrounded, casualties mounted, and ammunition ran low. After more than an hour of intense combat, survivors were ordered to slip away in small groups to make their escape. Captain F.C. Fraser and Lt. Langley's platoon remained behind as a rearguard, "taking a dreadful toll on the fanatical S.S. troops."[78]

While the battle for Authie raged, Petch had to deal with the attack on Buron and with the danger that he was being outflanked from the valley of the Mue River to the west. B Company was therefore sent back north of Buron. One platoon took up positions behind the village in a series of abandoned German trenches. These had been sited to defend Buron from the north and had very poor fields of fire to the south because of their proximity to the stone walls and buildings of the village. Nonetheless, it was felt that this position prevented the village from being outflanked from the west. Two other platoons of B Company under the acting company commander, Capt. A.J. Wilson, withdrew to the anti-tank ditch, where, along with the others there, they "made ready to fight to the finish."[79]

At 1730 hours a white flare rose up over Authie, which Maj. Learment interpreted as a signal that the village was now in German hands.[80] It had taken an SS battalion most of two hours to overwhelm three Canadian platoons and their supporting arms. With Authie now in enemy hands and with the rest of the vanguard now dig-in north of Buron, Rhodenizer's two platoons of A Company in the hedged area north of Authie were now isolated in the middle of a fire-swept field. When his radio was shot-up by a passing tank[81] Rhodenizer could not receive an order to retire, so his small force eventually succumbed to a cordon of tanks and infantry. When the barrage on the position suddenly ceased, Major Rhodenizer stood up to see what was happening. He was greeted by two Germans who simply said: "Come." Another German shouted "Surrender" as a group of SS with machine guns rose from a ditch thirty yards away. Exhausted, burdened by casualties and nearly out of ammunition, Rhodenizer's men complied. Just when this happened remains unclear. The Novas' history says it was "near sundown,"[82] but this seems unlikely. The remnant of A Company probably surrendered shortly after Authie fell.

Unfortunately for the survivors of A Company, their ordeal was not over. After the SS murdered two Canadians with a burst of machine gun fire, three more were shot as they were hustled into Authie. The carnage of the struggle for the village was evident. "The dust and smoke had settled," Will Bird wrote, "and German bodies were lying in alleys and in the street and in the fields, everywhere, especially by the entrance to the orchard." In the aftermath of the collapse of C Company's position, Canadian POWs had been marshaled along the main street to be searched. As Bird recounted, the lifting of the smoke of battle had "showed the casualties inflicted by C Company, and this so enraged the Germans that they crowded around and shot several prisoners in cold blood." Several were laying there dead when Rhodenizer's men arrived. Fortunately, Rhodenizer spoke fluent German and helped calm the situation, at least in Authie.[83]

While A Company was fighting its epic battle, 12 SS committed its II Battalion to the attack: Canadian POWs in Authie reported seeing "a fresh German battalion marching towards Buron in close formation."[84] They were supported by tanks, SPs and half-tracks. The first to feel the weight of the renewed attack was Maj. Learment's small group east of the road entrance at the north of the village. Learment's men were practically out of ammunition and were easily overcome, captured and marched into Buron to be searched—and in a few cases shot in cold blood. The collapse of Learment's position at roughly 1900 hours opened the back of the B Company platoons holding out on the other side of the road. There, Lt. Campbell's men had checked every German attempt to get around the west of Buron. Suddenly they were attacked in strength from the rear and forced to surrender, although in the confusion some later escaped.[85]

And so by about 1900 hours on the evening of 7 June 1944 what remained of the 9 Brigade vanguard stood-to north of Buron to meet the enemy. D Company and stragglers from the other companies held trenches in front of the anti-tank ditch, supported by two mortars, two Vickers of the Camerons, and the anti-tank platoon of the Novas with its two 6-pounders.[86] About a dozen surviving Shermans of the Sherbrookes backed them up.

Mortar and machine-gun fire laced the SS as they came forward out of Buron and up the gentle slope towards Villons-les-Buissons, while tanks and anti-tank guns, some from the Glens at Villons, struck at German tanks moving around the right flank. When the Camerons' machine guns ran out of ammunition, they withdrew, and so did a number of Novas. But D Company held on and finally—after a long day's wait—the first rounds of Canadian artillery landed in front of the vanguard's position.

These were not the first rounds fired by the 14th RCA, but it had waited a long time to become engaged. Their War Diary reports the first "Mike" targets—the whole regiment firing—at 1800 hours. As David Struther, then the Gun Position Officer for C Troop of the 14th RCA, recalled, these were "scale 50"—50 rounds per gun, more than 1,000 105mm shells on a single target.[87] The first Canadian shells the vanguard saw directly in front of their positions landed around 1900 hours.[88] The surviving Novas wanted to "stand

and cheer!" as the fire "routed the Germans." The 12 SS tanks, according to the Nova's history, "vanished at first sound of artillery on the scene and the enemy were hounded all the way back to Authie, dying in groups all over the field."[89] The twelve remaining tanks of the Sherbrookes joined in the counterattack by D Company, "in some instances the enemy being so numerous they were run over by them."[90] The survivors of the vanguard recaptured Buron and drove the remnants of 12 SS back to Authie, St-Contest, and Bitot.

The recapture of Buron was a signal victory for the remnants of the vanguard, but it could not be held. The British 9th Brigade, attacking west from the Orne bridgehead, only got as far as Cambes, from which it was driven by Meyer's I Battalion. The British contented themselves with crushing the SS using artillery and naval gunfire.[91] Cambes, Galmanche, and St-Contest remained in German hands. That meant that Buron, on a forward slope overlooked by the enemy, was untenable. So the Novas settled in around "Hellfire Corner" at Villons-les-Buisson for the night, with the Glens to the right and the HLI behind them. Meanwhile, the Hitler Youth—who took some time to discover that Buron had been abandoned—distracted themselves with a petulant shooting spree of Canadian wounded and POWs, raising the Canadian death toll.[92]

The Canadians' plan to resume the march to Carpiquet was soon abandoned. It was a very sensible decision. Carpiquet was untenable without the British in Caen, and so too was the fall-back position, the "high ground" between Buron and Authie, so long as St-Contest and the abbey were in German hands. Buron would have been a nightmare to hold. Instead, the Canadians built their brigade fortress on the reverse slope around Villons-les-Buisson, which provided excellent fields of fire against a clear skyline and little direct observation by the enemy. It is difficult to see how the Canadians could have done better.

A proper accounting of the role of 21 Panzer Division in the battle on 7 June has never been done, but its presence was highly significant. The artillery, mortars, anti-tank guns, SPs, and troops of 21 Panzer, backed by a battalion of 716 Division, shaped the battle long before 12 SS intervened. The Sherbrookes' claim that all their tank losses fell to 88mm guns is not "Tiger phobia":[93] the long-range killing power of 21 Panzer Division's Pak 43/41 guns was a significant factor on the battlefield. Similarly, their claims for enemy tanks destroyed, equally dismissed by historians (who only count 12

SS casualties) as inflated, probably included many SPs and half-tracks from 21 Panzer. In the end, 302 Canadians were killed, wounded, or missing in the battle, roughly the equivalent of the losses inflicted on 12 SS alone, which are recorded as 300.[94] But since no casualty returns have ever been published for 21 and 716 Divisions for this battle, the final German casualty figure is probably significantly higher than 300.

And while some historians have lauded 12 SS for their "spectacular combat debut,"[95] it was anything but. The Novas' history boasts of the A Company story that it took the Germans "a large part of an afternoon to overrun a position held by a fifth of their number."[96] It is also clear that it took perhaps as much as two hours for the Germans to overrun Authie. The vanguard was not "thrown back in confusion," as some claim. The initial advance reveals a high degree of skill and effective combined-arms training. The response to 12 SS's attack reveals the same qualities, and no want of bravery and determination. In fact, once supporting artillery fire arrived, the remnants of the vanguard supported by a dozen tanks drove the Germans from most of the battlefield. According to British historian Michael Reynolds, German command and control of the battle was poor. "It would seem," Reynolds wrote, "that just as there was a failure to coordinate on the Canadian side, [the Germans] failed to get their act together at this important time."[97] The 12 SS never got close to the sea on D+1: indeed, they never got much beyond their initial gains in the first hour or so.

The utter failure of Canadian artillery to support the vanguard was not a single incident, as some sources suggest: in reality, the vanguard fought virtually the whole action without evident Canadian artillery support. Nor was range the issue: the problem was communications and the absence of FOOs.[98] Brigadier PSA Todd, the Commander Royal Artillery of the 3rd Canadian Division, had landed on D-Day with his HQ and might well have "gripped" the battle, but he did not. In fact, he was precluded from doing so by the D-Day Op order, which specified that the 12th and 14th Field Artillery Groups were to fight their own battles until the final D-Day objective had been secured. However, in the absence of FOOs with the forward companies of the vanguard, it is not clear what Todd or anyone else could have done. Suffice it to say that had Canadian artillery or British naval gunfire been on line, this story would have unfolded much differently.

Finally, the Canadian official history's claim that the vanguard was defeated and thrown back by a force roughly its own size is a gross miscalculation of the odds faced by the vanguard of 9 Brigade on D+1. Before 12 SS entered the fray, the Novas' battle group was facing even odds: an ersatz battalion from 716 Division reinforced by the armour and artillery of Kampfgruppe Rauch from 21 Panzer. In the afternoon the vanguard was attacked by two battalions of 12 SS supported by tanks and at least one-third of the division's artillery. On the face of it, this put the Canadians up against at least three times their own strength and the equivalent of an entire British Commonwealth division's supporting artillery. But the odds were actually much worse than that. The infantry companies of 12 SS were over strength, probably numbering 225 officers and men.[99] On D+1, companies of I Battalion, 25 Panzergrenadier Regiment, were reinforced by the regiment's Pioneer Company, bringing company strength to about 245 all ranks. It would seem that the description in the Novas' history of waves of Germans attacking the vanguard of 9 Brigade on D+1 is not hyperbole. Indeed, in sharp contrast to what Charles Stacey would claim, the vanguard fought a force four or five times it own strength.

The result on D+1 did not reflect the incompetence of Allied leadership or tactical ineptness among the troops. The vanguard of 9 Brigade fought well on 7 June 1944: the petulant fury of 12 SS, who shot forty-six POWs immediately following the battle, is evidence of that.[100] At the end of the day, and given the British inability to capture Caen, the brigade was secure on the only ground suitable for defence of the beachhead. No ambush, no defeat.

Notes

1. Recently, two Canadian historians observed that the 9th Brigade "outran the range of supporting artillery and blindly moved from Buron to Authie straight into Meyer's hands." See Whitney Lackenbauer and Chris Madsen, eds., *Kurt Meyer on Trial (A Documentary Record)* (Kingston: Canadian Defence Academy Press, 2007), 10.
2. Evidence for this view is not hard to find. See, for example, the passage from Russell Hart's *Clash of Arms: How the Allies Won in Normandy* (Boulder: Lynne Rienner, 2001), 344, in which the Canadians "push boldly" inland on D+1 "despite" the danger of powerful German forces moving toward them. See p.344.
3. C.P. Stacey, *The Victory Campaign: The Operations in North-West Europe, 1944–45*, vol. III, *Official History of the Canadian Army in the Second World War* (Ottawa: Queen's Printer, 1960), 133.
4. Ibid., 133.

5   Ibid., 131.
6   Ibid., 128n.
7   Ibid., 79.
8   Ibid., 77. See also "Overlord Operational Order, HQ RCA, 3rd Canadian Division, 15 May 1944," Library and Archives Canada [LAC], RG 24, reel T-15455. The historian of 3rd British Division observed that "it had always been impossible to imagine D plus 1." Steve Badsey, "Culture, Controversy, Caen and Cherbourg: The First Week of the Battle," in John Buckley, ed., *The Normandy Campaign Sixty Years On* (London: Routledge, 2006), 48.
9   All COSSAC planning going back to the summer of 1943 postulated a panzer attack on the landing beaches from two general directions. The primary concern was German use of Bayeux as a "pivot" for mechanized attacks towards the sea, especially along the Sommervieu ridge towards Courseulles-sur-Mer, typically on D-Day or D+1. The likely D+1 or later option was either a panzer thrust down the Caen–Bayeux highway to secure Bayeux for the first option, or panzer thrusts down either side of the Mue River. Quote from "Appreciation of Ground in the 'Neptune' area from the German point of view," Appendix A to "Re-Examination of Rate of Reinforcement—Neptune," G-2 Int, COSSAC 22 October 1944. The National Archives (UK) [TNA], WO 219/1836.
10 "Timing of Counter-Attacks Against the Neptune Bridgehead," n.d., but based on British Joint Intelligence Committee (44) 66(0) (Final) estimate of German forces in France May-June 1944, TNA WO 219/1836.
11 Hart, *Clash of Arms*, 248.
12 Specifications for the Pak 43/41 can be found in Ian V. Hogg, *German Artillery of World War Two* (Mechanicsburg: Stackpole, 1998), 214–18.
13 Jean-Claude Perrigault, *21.Panzerdivison* (Bayeux: Heimdal, 2002), 232.
14 F.H. Hinsley, *British Intelligence in the Second World War: Abridged Edition* (New York: Cambridge University Press, 1993), 475.
15 See "Landing Tables," War Diary, HQ RA 2nd British Army, June 1944, TNA WO 171/234. The 3rd British Division was supported by five field regiments and one medium regiment. However, two of those field regiments were designated to support 6th Airborne Division until that division's guns arrived by D+7. See Brigadier A.L. Pemberton, *The Development of Artillery Tactics and Equipment* (London: War Office, 1950), 218–19. Quote and information on 62nd A/T Regiment from Tony Foulds, "In Support of the Canadians: A British Anti-Tank Regiment's First Five Weeks in Normandy," *Canadian Military History* 7, no.2 (Spring 1998), 71–78 at 71.
16 See Foulds's account.
17 Overlord Operational Order, HQ RCA 3 Canadian Infantry Division, 15 May 1944. See especially Trace "UU." For an account of the 248th Battery of the 62nd Anti-Tank Regiment, see Foulds.
18 See "Overlord Narrative. Part VI: Notes by Arms," TNA WO 219/901, which then explains that the adoption of SP artillery was a key to this mobility in the defensive battles. *The Development of Artillery Tactics and Equipment*, 218.
19 Stacey, *The Victory Campaign*, 128.

20 Perrigault, *21.Panzerdivison*, 254.
21 Ibid., 253. These units had been garrisoned just south of Caen around St-Andre-sur-Orne, St-Martin, and Fontenay.
22 For the best modern account of the attack by 21st Panzer on D-Day, see William F. Buckingham, *D-Day: The First 72 Hours* (Stroud: Tempus, 2004), 223–26.
23 Details of action from Perrigault, *21.Panzerdivison*, 505–7. Closing remarks made by the defence during the trial of Kurt Meyer put the HQ of Kampgruppe Rauch at Cussy during the battle on 7 June. Lackenbauer and Madsen, *Kurt Meyer on Trial*, 485.
24 Operational Order, RCA 3rd Canadian Division.
25 Much has been written on the 7th Brigade battles that followed, but for the role of artillery, see M. Milner, "The Guns of Bretteville: 13th Field Regiment, RCA, and the Defence of Bretteville-l'Orgueilleuse, 7–10 June 1944," *Canadian Military History* 16, no.4 (Autumn 2007), 5–24.
26 Terry Copp, *Fields of Fire: The Canadians in Normandy* (Toronto: University of Toronto Press, 2003), 65.
27 Lt.-Col. Richard M. Ross, O.B.E., *The History of the 1st Battalion Cameron Highlanders of Ottawa (MG)*, privately published, n.d., 42.
28 Major Don Learment, in command of the vanguard on 7 June, later recalled that 14th RCA were "practically one of us." Telephone interview with Don Learment by Doug Hope, ca. 2003. The Exercise Pedal II report is in LAC RG 24, reel T-12785.
29 Operational Order, RCA 3rd Canadian Division.
30 Lackenbauer and Madsen, *Kurt Meyer on Trial*, 483. The court's summary of evidence is more emphatic about this than the published version of Meitzell's testimony; see Lackenbauer and Madsen, *Kurt Meyer on Trial*, 440. Copp notes that they, and elements of 21st Panzer, were there, but he does not attempt to assess their dispositions and strength; see Copp, *Fields of Fire*, 65.
31 Perrigault, *21.Panzerdivison*, says that elements of the 716th Division held Buron (see p.261). Meitzell put them in Franqueville and Authie. See Lackenbauer and Madsen, *Kurt Meyer on Trial*, 440.
32 Lackenbauer and Madsen, *Kurt Meyer on Trial*, 440. Meitzell's claim is supported by Perrigault, *21.Panzerdivison*, 505.
33 Lackenbauer and Madsen, *Kurt Meyer on Trial*, 449.
34 This description of the battlefield is based on about a decade of leading battlefield study tours in the area.
35 Perrigault, *21.Panzerdivison*, 261.
36 Perrigault lists this unit as equipped with "Granatwerfer (8,14cm)." See ibid., 219. Lt. N. Davies of the Sherbrooke's B Squadron claimed that the rocket-equipped half-track was on the left side of the road. See the report of B Squadron's action by Lt. Davies in LAC RG 24, reel T-12758.
37 Will R. Bird, *No Retreating Footsteps: The Story of the North Nova Scotia Highlanders* (Hantsport: Lancelot Press, 1983), 77.
38 The Stormont, Dundas, and Glengarry Highlanders arrived at les Buisson about 1000 hours and had to clear it of snipers. See Lt.-Col. W. Boss and Brigadier-General W.J.

Patterson, *Up the Glens: Stormont, Dundas, and Glengarry Highlanders 1783–1994* (Cornwall: Old Book Store, 1995), 102.

39 Account of No.2 Troop, C Sqn Sherbrooke Fusiliers, by Sgt T.C. Reid, LAC, RG 24, reel T-12758.

40 Bird, *No Retreating Footsteps*, 77.

41 Ibid.

42 Lt. N. Davies's account of B Sqn on 7 June 1944, LAC RG 24, reel T-12758.

43 Mark Zuehlke, *Holding Juno: Canada's Heroic Defence of the D-Day Beaches: June 7–12, 1944* (Toronto: Douglas and McIntyre, 2005), 90.

44 War Diary, 14th RCA, 7 June 1944. See also Lt. G.E.M. Ruffee and L/Bdr J.B. Dickie, *The History of the 14 Field Regiment Royal Canadian Artillery 1940–1945* (Amsterdam: Wereldbibliotheek N.V., 1945), 28.

45 Telephone interviews with Col. David Struther, the Gun Position Officer of C Troop on that day, and Wes Alkenbrack, the commander of D4 (fourth gun of D Troop, and the only one to survive the incident at Bernières-sur-Mer on 6 June, when the other three guns of that troop were destroyed) with Doug Hope, n.d. Struther recalled that fire from the Douvre radar station "didn't bother us." Alkenbrack confirmed this, saying they were "not endangered on the 7th ... Some mortar fire ... Sporadic."

46 Zuehlke, *Holding Juno*, 90. The account of the Sherbrooke's recce troop for 7 June 1944 notes that at 1230 hours they were fighting near St-Contest. LAC RG 24, reel T-12758.

47 Bird, *No Retreating Footsteps*, 78.

48 12th SS artillery was not ordered to open fire until some time after 1300 hours.

49 Zuehlke, *Holding Juno*, 92.

50 This account is drawn from the interviews of Capt. J.A. Wilson and Capt. E.S. Gray, both NNSH, in late June 1944 by a historical officer. It remains the most cogent short account of events. Directorate of History and Heritage (DHH), NDHQ, Ottawa, 145.2N2011 (D3).

51 Bird, *No Retreating Footsteps*, 80.

52 Account of B Sqn by Lt. N. Davies, LAC, RG 24, reel T-12758.

53 Lt.-Col. H.M. Jackson, MBE, ED, *The Sherbrooke Regiment (12th Armoured Regiment)*, privately published, 1958, 124.

54 In his testimony to the Kurt Meyer trial, Lt.-Col. Petch recalled that he ordered the advance from Buron to Authie "about one o'clock." Lackenbauer and Madsen, *Kurt Meyer on Trial*, 141. The NNSH War Diary reported that the leading elements of the battalion reached Authie at 1230 hours; see the verbatim version reprinted in Terry Copp and Robert Vogel, *Maple Leaf Route: Caen* (Alma: Maple leaf Route, 1983), 70–72. The Novas' history says Authie was secure at 1330 hours; Bird, *No Retreating Footsteps*, 80.

55 Jackson, *The Sherbrooke Regiment*, 124.

56 Bird, *No Retreating Footsteps*, 51.

57 Hubert Meyer, *The 12th SS: The History of the Hitler Youth Panzer Division*, vol. I (Mechanicburg: Stackpole, 2005) 134. Kurt Meyer claimed in 1945 that the division

had 214 tanks in service and 22 Mk IV *Jagdpanzers* and that the division was at full personnel strength on 6 June 1944. Lackenbauer and Madsen, *Kurt Meyer on Trial*, 68.

58   12th SS had an operational strength on 6 June 1944 of roughly 16,000, since not all of its units were complete. Buckingham, *D-Day: The First 72 Hours*, 44.

59   I am grateful to my former graduate student Arthur Gullachsen for details on the operations of 12th SS during this phase. See his MA thesis, "The Defeat and Attrition of the 12th SS Panzer Division 'Hitlerjugend,' a Case Study: June 6th–July 12th, 1944," University of New Brunswick, 2005. The camo uniforms confused Canadians in the first few days ashore: they often reported parachutists in their War Diaries. It turns out that 21st Panzer troops also wore their camouflaged shelter-half as a smock, so that it was not always easy to distinguish 21st Panzer from 12th SS from a distance.

60   Lackenbauer and Madsen, *Kurt Meyer on Trial*, 141–42.

61   Meyer, *The 12th SS,* 138. See also Niklas Zetterling, *Normandy 1944: German Military Organization, Combat Power, and Organizational Effectiveness* (Winnipeg: J.J. Fedorowicz, 2000), for a discussion of 12th SS organization and equipment.

62   Testimony of Lt.-Col. Petch, in Lackenbauer and Madsen, *Kurt Meyer on Trial*, 141.

63   Testimony of Major Don Learment, in ibid., 161.

64   Copp, *Fields of Fire,* 66.

65   Interview with Capt. Gray.

66   Stacey, *The Victory Campaign,* 79.

67   WD 14th RCA, 7 June 1944. LAC RG 24, 14,471; Major L.F. Ellis, *Victory in the West*, vol. I: *The Battle of Normandy* (London: HMSO, 1962), 229.

68   Malcolm Langille interview with Doug Hope, ca. 2003.

69   Boss and Patterson, *Up the Glens,* 103.

70   Lackenbauer and Madsen, *Kurt Meyer on Trial*, 141.

71   Ross, *The History of the 1st Battalion Cameron Highlanders,* 42; Bird, *No Retreating Footsteps,* 84.

72   According to Kurt Meyer, he launched an immediate combined tank–infantry attack on the Canadians once he saw the vanguard in Authie, but this is hyperbole. Lackenbauer and Madsen, *Kurt Meyer on Trial*, 141.

73   Ibid., 142; Bird, *No Retreating Footsteps,* 87.

74   Lackenbauer and Madsen, *Kurt Meyer on Trial*, 142.

75   Testimony by Lt.-Col. Petch, in Lackenbauer and Madsen, *Kurt Meyer on Trial*, 142.

76   War Diary, Sherbrooke Fusiliers, 7 June 1944, LAC, RG 24, reel T-12758.

77   Bird, *No Retreating Footsteps,* 89.

78   Ibid., 90.

79   Ibid., 87.

80   Lackenbauer and Madsen, *Kurt Meyer on Trial*, 162.

81   The position was sprayed by gun and machine gun fire from six tanks on their way from Gruchy to Buron, damaging the radio so it could send but not receive. Bird, *No Retreating Footsteps,* 95.

82   Ibid., 95.

83   Ibid., 97.

84 Ibid., 97.
85 Ibid., 98; Lackenbauer and Madsen, *Kurt Meyer on Trial*, 162.
86 Bird, p. 98.
87 Interview with Colonel D. Struther, by Doug Hope, no date.
88 The Novas history is clear only that it happened after 1930 hours; see Bird, *No Retreating Footsteps*, 100. The war diary of 14th Field says that the first shells were fired at 1800 hours. The problem of artillery support for the 9 Brigade vanguard is the subject of ongoing research by the author and Doug Hope.
89 Bird, *No Retreating Footsteps*, 100–1.
90 Novas War Diary, in Copp and Vogel, *Maple Leaf Route*, 72–74.
91 Buckingham, *D-Day*, 258.
92 For an account of the war crimes committed during and after this battle by the 12th SS. see Howard Margolian, *Conduct Unbecoming: The Story of the Murder of Canadian Prisoners of War in Normandy* (Toronto: University of Toronto Press, 1998).
93 Buckingham, *D-Day*, 259.
94 Canadian figures from Copp, *Fields of Fire*, 66; 12th SS figures from Buckingham, *D-Day*, 259.
95 Buckingham, *D-Day*, 259.
96 Bird, *No Retreating Footsteps*, 97.
97 Michael Reynolds, *Steel Inferno: 1st SS Panzer Corps in Normandy* (New York: Sarpedon, 1997), 69.
98 Doug Hope was the first to notice and began interviewing survivors about a decade ago.
99 The order of battle for November 1943. A July 1944 order of battle for 12th SS lists strength at that point at 190 men per company, but this may be a reflection of losses in battle. I am grateful to Chris Kretzschmar for locating this information for me.
100 During the trial of Meyer, the defence claimed that forty-one POWs had been murdered, while the prosecution alleged that the number could be as high as forty-six (these figures include the murders at the Abbey for which Meyer was held responsible); Lackenbauer and Madsen, *Kurt Meyer on Trial*, 485 and 507.

16

Defending the Normandy Bridgehead
The Battles for Putot-en-Bessin, 7–9 June 1944

Mike Bechthold

By noon on 7 June 1944, the day after the D-Day landings, the Royal Winnipeg Rifles held the small Norman village of Putot-en-Bessin, just 8 kilometres from the beaches they had stormed the day before. Their orders were to hold their position and stop any German assault that could threaten the precarious hold the Allies maintained in France. A major German attack was launched on the morning of 8 June. During the course of the day, many of the Winnipegs' positions in and around Putot were overrun, creating the possibility of a major breach of the Allied perimeter. But the Winnipegs continued to deny the Germans a chance to consolidate their gains. A counterattack by a battlegroup led by the Canadian Scottish Regiment restored the situation before darkness fell.

John A. English argues that the Winnipegs were put to flight in this battle and uses this episode to highlight the apparent failings of First Canadian Army in Normandy, a force that he maintains did not live up to the high standards set by the Canadian Corps in the Great War.[1] A close examination of the battle, however, shows the skill and determination of the Canadian Army to deal with an adverse situation. The Winnipegs did not collapse when pressed by elements of 12 SS Panzer (Hitlerjugend) Division, but held on until Brigadier Harry Foster, commanding the 7th Canadian Infantry Brigade, could organize a well-coordinated counterattack utilizing infantry, armour, and artillery to recapture Putot. In a situation that imperilled the entire Allied bridgehead, Canadians held the village of Putot to deny the Germans the possibility of pushing through to the English Channel.

The army raised by Canada to liberate Europe from the tyranny of Nazi Germany was a volunteer citizen army that has been criticized for displaying a lack of professionalism during operations, particularly in Normandy.[2] C.P. Stacey, the official Canadian army historian, hinted that the Canadian Army demonstrated little tactical acumen in Normandy when he stated that "the Allies owe their victory [in Normandy] in great part to numerical and material superiority."[3] Overwhelming air and naval power are credited with being decisive in the Allied victory in Normandy, but this understates the importance of the American, British, and Canadian armies in defeating the Germans on the battlefield. John Ellis argues that Allied success in the Second World War was achieved through "brute force" rather than operational and tactical skill.[4] This thesis appears convincing at the strategic level, and indeed, deploying superior economic and industrial resources formed a cornerstone of Allied strategy in the struggle against the Axis. Did the Allied armies make use of their superior resources? Certainly, but it does not necessarily follow that their tactical skill on the battlefield was somehow lacking in comparison to that of their German adversaries.

The Canadians' opponents at Putot, 12 SS Division, are often considered an elite formation. Stacey argued that "the division was to show in action the characteristics which its composition might lead one to expect: reckless courage and determination combined with a degree of barbarity found perhaps in no other formation." English deemed it an "exceptional division," and Max Hastings viewed 12 SS as "perhaps the most formidable of all the German units now on their way to Normandy." Niklas Zetterling considered 12 SS "one of the best [German] divisions."[5]

The Canadian Army was viewed quite differently. In evaluating Canadian battlefield performance in Normandy, Stacey stated: "The German soldier and field commander showed themselves ... to be excellent practitioners of their trade. The German fighting soldier was courageous, tenacious and skillful ... Man for man and unit for unit, it cannot be said that it was by tactical superiority that we won the Battle of Normandy."[6] Major-General Charles Foulkes, Commander 2nd Canadian Infantry Division in Normandy, would tell Stacey that "[w]hen we went into battle at Falaise and Caen[,] we found that when we bumped into battle-experienced German troops we were no match for them. We would not have been successful had it not been for our air and artillery support."[7] Hastings argued that "[w]hile the Germans coordinated armour, infantry and artillery superbly, the Canadians did not."[8] A close look at the evidence does not support this conclusion.

Terry Copp has created a new paradigm for our understanding of the Canadian Army in the Second World War. Compared to the previous top-down approaches to the study of battle, Copp reconstructs the battle from the evidence contained in the message logs and war diaries.[9] This chapter will use this methodology to examine the role of the 7th Canadian Infantry Brigade—specifically, the Royal Winnipeg Rifles and the Canadian Scottish Regiment at Putot-en-Bessin—during its defence of the Normandy bridgehead from 7 to 9 June 1944. The positions held by 7 Brigade astride the Caen–Bayeux highway in the villages of Bretteville-l'Orgueilleuse, Norrey-en-Bessin, and Putot-en-Bessin were the focus of a series of major attacks launched by 12 SS Panzer Division to drive the Allies into the English Channel. Standartenführer Kurt Meyer, Commander 25 Panzergrenadier Regiment, believed this would not be difficult. About midnight on D-Day, Meyer met with Lt.-Gen. Edgar Feuchtinger, Commander 21 Panzer Division, who warned him of the strength of the Allied invasion forces. Meyer dismissed his evaluation, commenting, "Little fish! We'll throw them back into the sea."[10] Meyer was wrong. With one temporary exception, the attempts by 12 SS to push the "little fish" back into the sea were defeated with serious losses. How was it possible for the green units of the 3rd Canadian Infantry Division to defeat attacks by 12 SS, an elite unit led by battle-hardened officers and NCOs from the Eastern Front? This chapter will show that the Canadian accomplishments in the battles for Putot demonstrate a degree of tactical skill not generally accorded the Canadian Army. The German failure to capture and hold Putot was the direct result of prolonged resistance by the Royal Winnipeg Rifles and the timely and effective 7 Brigade counterattack.

The 7th Canadian Infantry Brigade of the 3rd Canadian Infantry Division was one of the Allied assault units on D-Day, 6 June 1944. The Royal Winnipeg Rifles, the Regina Rifle Regiment, and the 1st Battalion, Canadian Scottish Regiment, had trained for months for their role in the assault on the western sector of Juno Beach, at the village of Courseulles-sur-Mer. The western portion of 'Strongpoint Courseulles,' assaulted by the Winnipegs, was defended by one 75 mm gun and two 50 mm guns entrenched in concrete bunkers along with supporting machine gun and mortar defences.

The Winnipegs' war diary contains one of the classic descriptions of the task they faced:

> In spite of air bombardment failing to neutralize, RN [Royal Navy] bombardment spotty, the rockets falling short and the AVREs [Assault Vehicle Royal Engineers] and DDs [Duplex Drive Tanks] being late C Company Canadian Scottish Regiment and RWR companies landed all within seven minutes. The bombardment having failed to kill a single German soldier or silence one weapon these companies had to storm their positions cold and did so without hesitation ... Not one man flinched from his task.[11]

Captain Phillip Gower's B Company landed directly in front of the German strongpoint on the west side of the river. It suffered heavy losses as it started to clear the position without support. The Duplex Drive (DD) tanks from the First Hussars arrived after the infantry and were essential in knocking out the German gun emplacements. Major Lockie Fulton's D Company landed just to the west at the same time, so its task was eased by the enemy's attention on B Company. After leaving the beach it proceeded to roll up the German positions before moving inland. A and C Companies moved inland immediately after landing to secure the villages of Ste-Croix-sur-Mer and Banville. At the end of the day the entire battalion dug in south of Cruelly, nearly 8 kilometres from the coast. The Winnipegs suffered over 130 casualties on 6 June 1944. The cost had been especially high for B Company, which was among the hardest hit of the Canadian D-Day assault companies. Out of a full establishment of 120, Captain Gower's company was left with only twenty-six men after the day's fighting. That night all five reinforcement officers and seventy-eight other ranks were posted to B Company.[12]

The Winnipegs were reinforced to the west by C Company from the Canadian Scottish Regiment. The initial landings by the Can Scots were relatively easy, and they advanced off the beach in good order, securing a number of small Norman villages. The Can Scots ended the day about 9 kilometres inland near Cainet and le Fresne-Camilly. The battalion suffered eighty-seven casualties on 6 June.[13]

The night of 6–7 June was relatively quiet on the Canadian front. The Winnipegs repelled a small German counterattack, but nothing serious developed. Stacey later remarked that the Canadians did not make the most of their opportunities on D-Day.¹⁴ But the minor counterattack launched by 21 Panzer on the afternoon of D-Day led Lieutenant-General Miles Dempsey, Commander Second British Army, and Lieutenant-General G.C. Bucknall, Commander British XXX Corps, to order their troops, the Canadians included, to dig in as a result of slow British progress in front of Caen and in case further German attacks developed. It was a cautious decision, but justified.¹⁵ Early on D+1, 7 Brigade set out for their original D-Day objective, the Caen–Bayeux railway line, designated "Oak."

The historian of 12 SS, Hubert Meyer, stated that the Canadians advanced "hesitatingly" on 7 June and did not take advantage of the undefended gap between Rots and Audrieu as they were unaware of the presence of 12 SS.¹⁶ In fact, the Royal Winnipeg Rifles made rapid progress during the 8 kilometre advance on the morning of 7 June, meeting only isolated German resistance along the way. By noon the battalion had reached "Oak" and had quickly established defensive positions in Putot-en-Bessin after finding it undefended.¹⁷ The Regina Rifles had also made good progress, and its companies were positioned astride the rail line in Bretteville-l'Orgeuilleuse, Norrey-en-Bessin, and la Villeneuve. The Canadian Scottish moved to Secqueville-en-Bessin, where they remained as the brigade reserve.

Lieutenant-Colonel John M. Meldram, Commander Royal Winnipeg Rifles, deployed his unit to maximize the advantages of the position. Putot was built in the characteristic Norman style, with houses and farms built of Caen stone making each a potential stronghold against small arms and shrapnel. But Putot did not dominate the surrounding terrain; instead, it offered the defenders in the village limited fields of fire to the south, where the Caen–Bayeux rail line served as a substantial tank barrier. Meldram thus deployed his three strongest companies outside the village to secure a better view of the terrain to the south, even though the wheat in the surrounding fields still obscured the battlefield. Major Fred Hodge's A Company, supported by the battalion's 6-pounder anti-tank guns, covered the rail bridge between Putot and Brouay to the west. Hodge placed one of his platoons in Brouay, while the other two overlooked the bridge. Major Jimmy Jones' C Company was located along the railway line directly south of Putot to guard a level crossing of the rail line, while Fulton's D Company held the area outside the eastern wall of the village. Gower's B Company, which had taken such a battering on D-Day, was designated the battalion reserve and placed in an orchard north of Putot, close to the Battalion HQ. There were no Canadian troops in the village itself.

Meldram drew on additional forces to strengthen his position. Two Forward Observation Officers (FOOs) and a battery commander from the 12th Field Regiment coordinated artillery support for the battalion. The FOOs had immediate access to the twenty-four 25-pounder field guns and in an emergency could call on all the artillery in the Anglo-Canadian bridgehead. The Cameron Highlanders of Ottawa deployed a platoon of four medium machine guns, and the 3rd Canadian Anti-Tank Regiment supplied a troop of four M-10 self-propelled anti-tank guns. Meldram could also call on fire support from the heavy mortars of the Camerons.[18]

Allied plans called for the 69th Brigade of the 50th British Division to advance parallel to the 7th Canadian Brigade and occupy positions to the west along the rail line at Brouay. This did not happen on 7 June. German resistance held up the British advance, and aside from patrols, their lead infantry, the 7th Green Howards, only advanced as far as Ste-Croix-Grand-Tonne, some 2 kilometres north of 7 Brigade's forward positions. This exposed the right (western) flank of 7 Brigade and the Winnipegs. Late on the afternoon of 7 June, Brigadier Harry Foster deployed part of his reserve to cover this gap. In a small wood 500 metres northwest of la Bergerie Farm he placed D Company of the Canadian Scottish Regiment, two platoons from the Cameron Highlanders of Ottawa (four medium machine guns and four 4.2-inch mortars), four towed 17-pounder anti-tank guns from the 62nd British Anti-Tank Regiment, and four 6-pounder anti-tank guns from the 3rd Canadian Anti-Tank Regiment. This position enjoyed clear fields of fire, and its substantial firepower could cover the open ground between Brouay and Ste-Croix-Grand-Tonne.[19]

The advance of the Canadians' 9 Brigade to the east on 7 June met fierce German resistance. A series of pitched battles between the Canadians and units of 12 SS supported by a miscellany of other German units checked the Canadian advance towards Carpiquet airfield. At the end of a bloody day, 9 Brigade was dug in north of Villons-les-Buissons, some 5 kilometres short of the Caen–Bayeux railway and Carpiquet. This exposed the left (eastern) flank of 7 Brigade. Brigadier Foster deployed a small force of infantry and armour along the Mue River valley to cover this gap.[20]

The villages of Bretteville, Norrey, Putot, and Brouay occupied by the Winnipegs and Reginas were a necessary jumping-off point for the German Seventh Army's plans to eliminate the Allied bridgehead. Wilhelm Mohnke's 26 SS Panzergrenadier Regiment, one of three regiments of 12 SS Panzer Division, was ordered to attack the 7 Brigade area before first light on 8 June. The plan called for a three-battalion attack on the Canadian positions supported by tanks and artillery. Panzer Lehr Division was to launch a simultaneous attack farther to the west against the British. But Allied air attacks and their own caution delayed Mohnke's units, which arrived piecemeal. Rather than wait a few hours to mount a coordinated brigade-strength attack against the Canadians, Mohnke rushed into the attack, committing his battalions individually as they arrived at the front.

Mohnke's I Battalion directed the first German attack from St-Manvieu against the Regina Rifles in Norrey at 0300 hours, 8 June 1944. The Germans went in without artillery or tank support but soon lost surprise when the battalion bumped into a Canadian screening force from the Reginas on the high ground south of Norrey. Heavy concentrations of Canadian artillery forced two of the assault companies to ground in the open fields around Norrey while the third company found sanctuary in the unoccupied buildings of Cardonville farm. The Canadian guns again broke up a dawn attack, and Mohnke's I Battalion retreated to St-Manvieu.[21]

After small probing attacks on the western side of Putot were stopped, II Battalion of 26 SS Panzergrenadier Regiment launched a full assault on the village at 1000 hours, complete with armour and an artillery barrage.[22] On the eastern side of the village, Major Fulton and his D Company watched the Germans emerge from cover as they passed over the railway line. Fulton's men repulsed the attack with the help of the battalion's 3-inch mortars and artillery fire directed by his FOO, Captain Ben Nixon.[23] Against the other Winnipeg positions, the Germans took advantage of the trees and bushes and the steep railway ditch immediately south of Putot to advance onto the Canadian positions without detection. Farther to the west the Germans used the Canadians' open flank to get around Hodge's A Company at Brouay and the railway crossing. By shortly after noon on 8 June, direct enemy machine gun, mortar, and artillery fire had isolated the forward companies. By 1330 hours ammunition resupply became impossible. Elements of A and C Companies were overrun, and B Company behind the village was engaged.

374 Defending the Normandy Bridgehead

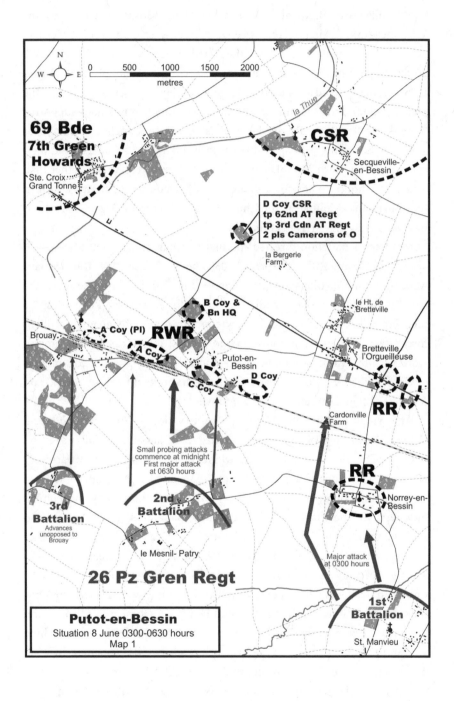

Meldram called for smoke to help extricate his companies, though few men made it back to Battalion HQ, which was located behind the town.[24] As late as 1420 hours, well after the forward companies had been surrounded, Battalion HQ reported to brigade that it "expected to handle the situation."[25] This report was likely made with the knowledge that D Company remained at full strength and had moved to the northeast corner of the village, where it had joined up with the Support Company, Battalion HQ, and other displaced elements of the battalion. The Germans then had control of Putot, but the Canadians checked all attempts to push beyond the village.

Numerous accounts capture the courage and resolve of the men of the Winnipegs. Sergeant-Major Charles Belton was with B Company in reserve when they were hit by the German assault. He realized the severity of the situation: "If this was allowed to continue, we were going to be pushed right back into the beach again." Lieutenant A.G. Bieber ordered Belton to seek help for the battalion. Belton had to run a gauntlet to escape. At one point he recalled that his carrier passed between two German self-propelled guns stopped on either side of the Caen–Bayeux highway. He passed them quickly enough that they never had time to get off a clean shot. Belton eventually reached 7 Brigade Headquarters, where he provided the staff with one of the first detailed reports of the situation in Putot.[26]

The inability of the 7th Green Howards to occupy Brouay had exposed the brigade's defences to the west, but a combination of factors saved the situation. During the main German assault on Putot, a large enemy force, reported as nine or ten tanks supported by infantry, was spotted north of Brouay trying to outflank the Canadians in Putot.[27] This force was engaged by the Canadian outpost in the woods northwest of la Bergerie farm. The initial shots from the Canadian and British guns knocked out four and possibly six German tanks. The German armour immediately returned accurate fire, and a heavy mortar and machine gun barrage on the woods caused some casualties. Lieutenant Blanchard, the commander of the British guns, called for reinforcements and moved in two guns to replace those knocked out. A troop of M-10s from the 62nd Anti-Tank Regiment arrived with two platoons of Canadian Scottish infantry, who brought the Vickers guns and mortars back into action. The battle around the wood lasted until approximately 1630 hours.[28] This stand in the woods behind Putot was pivotal to the outcome of the battle. The German advance to the west of Putot threatened to envelop the Winnipegs.

Later on the afternoon of 8 June a renewed thrust by a company from Mohnke's II Battalion again threatened to break the weakened Canadian perimeter around Putot. As the force approached the Caen–Bayeux highway it bumped into the reconnaissance troop of the 24th Lancers, the vanguard of a British armoured spearhead attempting to exploit south to Villers-Bocage.[29] A brief conference with Major Jones, the Winnipegs' C Company commander, produced a new plan to break back into Putot with two squadrons of Lancer tanks together with the Canadian infantry.[30] They failed, but the effort checked German attempts to move beyond Putot to the west. The force also inflicted heavy casualties and captured between forty and seventy-five German prisoners. The remaining German troops fell back into Putot.[31]

John A. English is the harshest critic of the Winnipegs' performance in Putot-en-Bessin on 8 June 1944, concluding that "three German companies put three defending Canadian companies to flight."[32] But the Germans deployed far more than just three companies of infantry that day. The initial attack by the three assault companies of Mohnke's II Battalion was supported by a fourth heavy weapons company. Elements of his III Battalion also supported the attack from Brouay, as did portions of Panzer Lehr Division.[33] It is also clear that German armour took part in the attack on Putot despite the denials by English and Hubert Meyer. There are too many reports of German armour in the Canadian and British war diaries and post-action interviews to discount its presence.[34] The Winnipegs faced an attack considerably stronger than just three companies from 12 SS.

It is also important to note that command and control did not break down for the Winnipegs on 8 June. Lieutenant-Colonel Meldram visited his forward companies on foot or in a Bren Gun carrier during the battle's early stages. When the battle became too fierce, Meldram rode in the FOO's tank until it was targeted by enemy anti-tank fire. He remained in contact with his forward companies until about 1230 hours on 8 June.[35] There was no panic in the battalion when it became apparent that the forward companies had been overrun. Rather, the remaining personnel dug in and prevented the Germans from bypassing Putot. To the east, Fulton's D Company withstood the initial German attack and, later on 8 June, "withdrew nearly intact to a defensive position around Battalion HQ."[36] The western side of Putot was secured by the resolute stand of the force in the woods northwest of la Bergerie Farm along with the timely intervention of the tanks of the 24th Lancers. Battalion HQ,

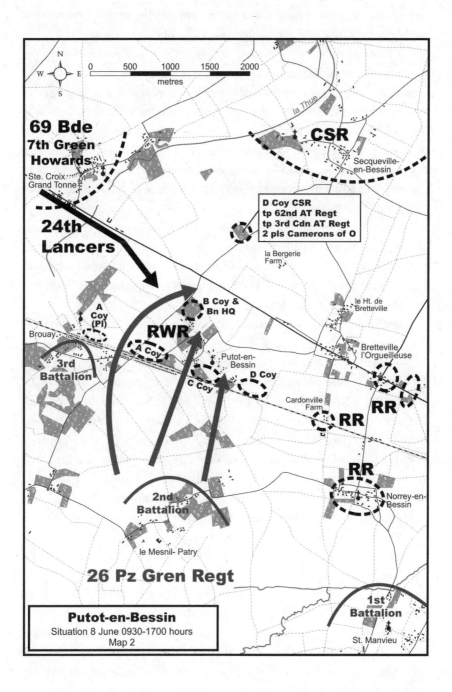

along with Support Company and stragglers from the overrun companies, maintained a strong position behind the village of Putot.

The importance of the Winnipegs' actions on 8 June cannot be overstated. A total collapse earlier in the day would have given the Germans time to consolidate their own defensive positions and continue the advance north. A German advance from Putot would have forced the Canadian Scottish at Secqueville into a defensive posture and would have delayed or prevented an immediate counterattack to regain Putot. A Winnipeg collapse would also have had dire consequences for the Reginas' position in Bretteville-Norrey to the east. This battle was not a victory for the Winnipegs, but neither was the battalion "put to flight."

Early in the afternoon of 8 June, Brigadier Foster warned Lt.-Col. Fred Cabeldu to have his Canadian Scottish Regiment, in reserve at Secqueville, to prepare for a possible German breakthrough. When that threat was checked, Foster ordered Cabeldu at 1830 hours to prepare a counterattack. He had just two hours to ready his battle group.

Cabeldu wrote after the battle, "My plan was simple."[37] Its execution speaks volumes about the skill and professionalism of the Canadian Army in Normandy. The startline for the attack was less than 1 kilometre from Putot in the small woods near la Bergerie Farm. The centreline for the attack was the Putot–Secqueville road. The assault was to be led by the Can Scots' D Company on the right and A Company on the left. C Company would follow D Company's axis. B Company had been detached on the previous day to help guard the open eastern flank of 7 Brigade, first at Bray and then farther east to Cairon. The company received its new orders while in the midst of a firefight with elements of 25 SS Panzergrenadier Regiment. It had to disentangle itself from one battle and then make a forced march of over 8 kilometres to take its place in the counterattack.[38]

Cabeldu commanded a strong all-arms battlegroup. He had eleven Sherman tanks from the First Hussars' composite squadron[39] as well as four 17-pounder M-10s from K Troop, 248 Battery of the 62nd Anti-Tank Regiment.[40] The First Hussars supported the right flank and the carrier platoon of the Canadian Scottish protected the left while the M-10s followed behind to provide additional fire support. The artillery plan called for a creeping barrage fired by the 12th and 13th Field Regiments to lead the troops onto their objective and to concentrate on known enemy positions

This composite air photograph, taken on 6 July 1944, shows the Royal Winnipeg Rifles (RWR) and Canadian Scottish Regiment (CSR) battlefield of 7-10 June 1944. The German attack came from the bottom left corner of the photo. The RWR were positioned along the railway. The wood in the top right corner was held by elements of the CSR and 62nd Anti-Tank Regiment and was crucial in stopping the German advance. The air photo clearly shows the open nature of the terrain which allowed machine gun and anti-tank fire from the small wood to dominate the fields outside Putot and prevent the RWR from getting cut off. [Air Photo Collection, Laurier Centre for Military Strategic and Disarmament Studies]

south of the railway line. Defensive fire tasks targeted select crossroads and other anticipated avenues for German counterattacks. The fireplan was complicated by the fact that nobody was sure of the exact positions of the remaining Winnipegs. The only information relayed to Cabeldu was that the Winnipegs' Battalion HQ was behind the village and that D Company remained on the left flank. Smoke from the Camerons' 4.2-inch mortars was to screen the advance. The Camerons would change to high-explosive shells once the Canadians were on their objective.[41]

Cabeldu briefed his company commanders before the plan was complete, stressing that there was no room for failure. As the battalion history emphasized, "The Canadian Scottish *must* capture and hold Putot. There was no other infantry battalion between Putot and the beaches."[42] Company commanders left the O Group and briefed their men as they moved to the startline. At 2030 hours, exactly two hours after receiving the warning order, the barrage opened and the infantry crossed the startline. The initial advance went undetected for approximately fifteen minutes before the Germans responded. The battalion's war diary continues the story:

> Enemy opposition consisting of all types of MG, Mortar and Shell-fire was bitter almost from the startline. The country was mainly flat wheatfields with orchards giving excellent concealment for the enemy. The men advanced without a falter into a veritable wall of fire, their courage was magnificent. Evidence of their feelings are well portrayed in the words of Cpl. Bob Mayfield of 8 Platoon who turned grinning to his section as they swung into the advance, "Boy, this is going to be one hell of a good scrap!" And this spirit was maintained throughout. The casualties were naturally heavy but never a wounded man whimpered.[43]

This account downplays the bitterness of the fighting. D Company suffered heavy losses during its advance to the Brouay crossing, including the company commander, Major G.T. MacEwan, who was severely wounded, and the second-in-command, Captain John Bryden, and the company sergeant-major, Charles Kilner, who were both killed. By the time it reached the bridge the company was down to twenty-six men. Not far behind, A Company fought its way through to the rail line, where the company commander, Major Plows, organized the remaining men of A and D Companies for defence. For a time the situation was so desperate, and ammunition running so low, that the men

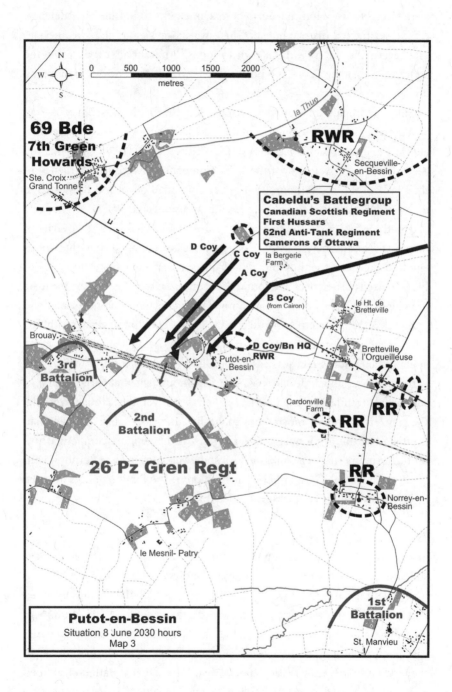

were forced to use captured German machine guns to bolster their defence. As the regimental history put it, "There was always an added sweetness to 'clobbering' the enemy with his own weapons." An hour after the start of the attack the Canadian Scottish reported to the brigade that they were mopping up.[44]

Putot was again in Canadian hands, but the battle was not yet over. Scattered resistance remained, and so did the threat of a renewed German attack. The men of the Canadian Scottish spent a sleepless night consolidating their defences. Private Roy Tutte of D Company conveyed the urgency of their task: "About 2230 [hours] things began to quiet down and we started to dig ... not like we used to on schemes, but what I mean is WE DUG! Badgers had nothing on us."[45] The Shermans and M-10s stayed forward overnight to provide additional security. No new attacks developed, but the troops endured constant shelling and mortaring. At first light on 9 June, Major Plows toured his defences and found the positions along the railway line to be too vulnerable. He received permission from Lieutenant-Colonel Cabeldu to pull back 50 to 100 metres and defend the approaches to the village with fire.

On 9 June, Mohnke attempted to regain Putot. The first small attack came at about 0800 hours and was easily repelled by small arms and mortar fire. A more serious attack developed about 1230 hours when at least nine tanks supported by infantry tried to force their way over the Brouay crossing. German artillery and mortar fire made life unpleasant for the Canadian Scottish, but the 6-pounder anti-tank guns of the support company drove off the armour. The German attack was renewed later in the afternoon with similar results. The Germans continued to probe the Putot defences over the next few days but did not pose a serious threat.[46]

The series of battles around Putot on 8 June had been costly. The Winnipegs suffered the most, with 256 casualties, including 150 men captured during the battle. Fifty prisoners were executed by the 12 SS after being disarmed and moved to the rear. Including these deaths, a total of 105 Winnipegs died during or shortly after the battle. The Canadian Scottish suffered 125 casualties, including 45 men killed in action.[47] Assessing German losses in the battle is more problematic. Hubert Meyer states that II Battalion suffered 19 killed, 58 wounded and 21 missing during the battle.[48] These numbers are almost certainly too low, for they do not include losses suffered by the other German units involved in the battle.

The German attack on Putot achieved a costly temporary success. Mohnke's II Battalion was exhausted by the battle and proved incapable of consolidating its gains. While III Battalion sat in Brouay, no reinforcements were brought forward and no anti-tank guns were deployed, nor was a comprehensive fireplan put in place. This battle was a defeat for the Germans. Their intention was to launch a major armoured counterattack to push the Allies into the sea. Possession of the area occupied by 7 Brigade was a necessary precursor to such an attack. The Germans failed to crack the Allied defensive perimeter on 8 June; not only that, but the disconnected employment of their forces precluded the type of large-scale, combined-arms attack that would have had the best chance of achieving their goal. As it turned out, 12 SS Division could do nothing to prevent the strengthening of the Allied foothold in France.

Between 7 and 10 June 1944, the 7th Canadian Infantry Brigade soundly defeated 12 SS Division.[49] This victory was the result of tactical skill rather than brute force. The numbers of troops involved in these battles was roughly even. Allied air power played no direct role. It was the skill of the Canadian commanders and their troops that made the difference. Terry Copp believes that 7 Brigade's battalion commanders were "simply outstanding."[50] Lieutenant-Colonels Meldram and Cabeldu exhibited calm, reasoned leadership throughout the battle. Meldram saw his battalion overrun, but neither he nor his men panicked. Rather, they continued to deal with the situation as their training had prepared them and they held on in Putot until rescued by the Canadian Scottish counterattack. Meldrum's initial troop positions have been criticized, but when asked to defend the Caen–Bayeux rail line, his options were limited. Confidence in Meldram's leadership of the Winnipegs was confirmed as he continued to command the battalion throughout the Normandy campaign.[51]

To the east of Putot, the Regina Rifles held the villages of Bretteville-l'Orgueilleuse and Norrey-en-Bessin. Beginning shortly after the Canadian Scottish recaptured Putot, Kurt Meyer's 25 Panzergrenadier Regiment attempted to wrest this ground from Canadian control. Over the next seventy-two hours, Meyer made four distinct attempts to break through the positions held by the Regina Rifles in Bretteville and Norrey. Each attempt was repulsed. Historian Michael Reynolds, generally dismissive of Allied combat capabilities, stated: "The Canadian defence of Norrey and Bretteville over the period 8th to 10th June must surely go down as one of the finest small unit actions of WWII."[52]

The Allies are often criticized for poor infantry–tank cooperation, but the successful defence of Putot was the result of close cooperation between the various fighting arms. Canadian success was derived from an effective working relationship between the infantry, armour, artillery, mortars, machine guns, and anti-tank units involved in the battle. This cooperation was displayed in the defence of Putot by the Winnipegs, but especially in the Canadian Scottish counterattack on the evening of 8 June. The ability of Lieutenant-Colonel Cabeldu to plan and carry out the attack in less than two hours is impressive. The counterattack involved a detailed artillery fireplan as well as careful coordination between the Canadian Scottish, the tanks of the First Hussars, and the M-10s of the 62nd British Anti-Tank Regiment as well as the mortars and machine guns of the Camerons of Ottawa. The success of the operation is a clear testament to the skill of First Canadian Army.

For an "elite" division, 12 SS performed poorly by any measure. The attacks launched by the division were not well coordinated. The Germans failed to apply overwhelming force to capture the Canadian positions; instead, their piecemeal attacks allowed the Canadians to use the full range of their ample artillery resources to deal with each. German cooperation between the various arms was either poor or lacking altogether. Max Hastings states that the Germans coordinated armour, infantry, and artillery superbly,[53] yet the opposite was true in these battles. Overall, 12 SS displayed a significant lack of skill, and as a result, by 10 June the Germans had been unable to launch a large-scale armoured counterattack against the Allied bridgehead and the Canadians still possessed the key territory the Germans wanted as a startline for that decisive counterattack.

The battle for Putot-en-Bessin was but one small piece of the battle for Normandy. Contrary to Stacey's contention, the Canadians displayed a clear tactical advantage over the Germans. The Canadians, with almost no battle experience, outfought an elite German division. There is still much to learn about the summer of 1944, and it is clear that historians need to re-examine some of the long-held "truths" about the Normandy campaign.

Notes

1. John A. English, *The Canadian Army and the Normandy Campaign: A Study of Failure in High Command* (New York: Praeger, 1991), 3 and 233n17. This was the title of the original edition of the book; subsequent reprints have reversed the title and subtitle to emphasize the aspect of failure: *Failure in High Command: The Canadian Army and the Normandy Campaign* (Ottawa: Golden Dog Press, 1995).
2. Canadians were first conscripted in 1942 for domestic service. A reinforcement crisis in the fall of 1944 saw conscripts sent overseas. There were no Canadian conscripts in Normandy. See David J. Bercuson and J.L. Granatstein, *Dictionary of Canadian Military History* (Toronto: Oxford University Press, 1992), pp.52—53.
3. C.P. Stacey, *The Victory Campaign: The Operations in North-West Europe 1944–1945— Official History of the Canadian Army in the Second World War*, vol.III (Ottawa: Queen's Printer, 1960), 271.
4. "Air power was the decisive factor in the Normandy campaign." John Terraine, *The Right of the Line: The Royal Air Force in the European War, 1939-1945* (London: Macmillan, 1985), 619; John Ellis, *Brute Force: Allied Strategy and Tactics in the Second World War* (New York: Viking, 1990).
5. Stacey, *The Victory Campaign*, 129; English, *The Canadian Army and the Normandy Campaign*, 212; Max Hastings, *Overlord: D-Day and the Battle for Normandy* (New York: Simon and Schuster, 1984), 118; Niklas Zetterling, *Normandy 1944: German Military Organization, Combat Power, and Organizational Effectiveness* (Winnipeg: J.J. Fedorowicz, 2000), 96.
6. Stacey, *The Victory Campaign*, 274.
7. Quoted in Stacey, *The Victory Campaign*, 276.
8. Hastings, *Overlord*, 124.
9. Terry Copp and Robert Vogel, *Maple Leaf Route*, 5 vols. (Alma: Maple Leaf Route, 1983–88); Terry Copp, *Fields of Fire: The Canadians in Normandy* (Toronto: University of Toronto Press, 2003).
10. Milton Shulman, *Defeat in the West* (London: Secker and Warburg, 1947), 105. Shulman was an intelligence officer with HQ First Canadian Army during the Second World War. In August 1945 he interviewed both Kurt Meyer and Edgar Feuchtinger. The transcripts of these interviews can be found in the war diary of the G Int HQ Canadian Forces in the Netherlands, October 1945, Library and Archives Canada [LAC] RG 24, C17, vol. 13,654. Shulman also used these interviews to write his book on the Northwest Europe campaign.
11. War Diary, Royal Winnipeg Rifles, 6 June 1944.
12. Ibid.; letter, Lieutenant-Colonel John Meldrum, CO RWR to 6 Cdn Armd Regt, 25 June 1944, reproduced in Copp and Vogel, *Maple Leaf Route: Caen*, 53; Bruce Tascona and Eric Wells, *Little Black Devils: A History of the Royal Winnipeg Rifles* (Winnipeg: Frye Publishing, 1983), 145–47.
13. R.H. Roy, *Ready for the Fray: The History of The Canadian Scottish Regiment (Princess Mary's) 1920–1955* (Vancouver: Evergreen Press, 1958), 209–27.
14. Stacey, *The Victory Campaign*, 118.

15 Copp, *Fields of Fire*, 56–57.
16 Hubert Meyer was a staff officer with 12 SS Panzer Division during the Normandy campaign. After the war he wrote the standard history of the division. Hubert Meyer, *The History of the 12. SS-Panzerdivision "Hitlerjugend,"* trans. H. Harri Henschler (Winnipeg: J.J. Fedorowicz, 1994), 48.
17 A recent article by Marc Milner contains a full discussion of the Allies' expectations of German armoured counterattacks early in the bridgehead battle and their plans to deal with them. Of note are two facts: the 3rd Canadian Infantry Division was substantially reinforced with artillery; and the brigade fortress positions assigned to the 7th and 9th Brigades were located to deal with such counterattacks. See Milner, "Stopping the Panzers: Reassessing the Role of 3rd Canadian Infantry Division in Normandy, 7–10 June 1944," *Journal of Military History* 74, no.2 (April 2010), 491–522.
18 War Diary, Royal Winnipeg Rifles, June 1944; Personal account by Major Lockie R. Fulton, DSO, 1989–1990, contained in Jean E. Portugal, *We Were There: The Army, A Record for Canada*, vol. 6 (Toronto: Royal Canadian Military Institute Heritage Society, 1998), 2917–18. Fulton is explicit in stating that on the night of 7 June a report was received that a German patrol had entered Putot. Lt.-Col. Meldram ordered Fulton to send a fighting patrol to investigate. Upon their return they reported finding no Germans in the village, but they also did not find any Canadians.
19 Tony Foulds, "In Support of the Canadians: A British Anti-Tank Regiment's First Five Weeks in Normandy," *Canadian Military History* 7, no.2 (Spring 1998), 73; and Roy, *Ready for the Fray*, 231.
20 This force was composed of a company of the Canadian Scottish Regiment, a squadron of tanks from the First Hussars, elements of the Camerons of Ottawa, and the 3rd Canadian and 62nd British Anti-Tank Regiments. See Stacey, *The Victory Campaign*, 126–132; Michael Reynolds, *Steel Inferno: I SS Panzer Corps in Normandy* (New York: Sarpedon Press, 1997), 65–69; English, *The Canadian Army and the Normandy Campaign*, 209; Craig W.H. Luther, *Blood and Honor: The History of 12th SS Panzer Division "Hitler Youth," 1943–1945* (San Jose: R. James Bender, 1987), 145–46, 151.
21 Lt.-Col. J.M. Meldram, CO The Royal Winnipeg Rifles, "Account for 21st Army Group Court of Inquiry re Shooting of Prisoners of War by German Forces at Chateau d'Audrieu, 8 June 1944. Exhibit 28 in report of 21st Army Group Court of Inquiry, Department of National Defence. Part of Report of No.1 Canadian War Crimes Investigation Unit re Shooting of Canadian Prisoners of War by the German Armed Forces near Fontenay-le-Pesnel, Normandy, France, 8 June 1944"; Fulton, personal account, in Portugal, *We Were There*, vol.6, 2918. Cardonville farm was not occupied by D Company (commanded by Major Gordon Brown) of the Regina Rifles until late on the afternoon of 8 June. Meyer, 50; War Diary, Regina Rifle Regiment, 7–8 June 1944.
22 The question of German armour in the attacks on Putot is contentious. Hubert Meyer is adamant that no tanks from 12 SS were involved, while Canadian accounts make numerous references to German tanks. The Winnipegs regimental history goes as far as to say that the attack was supported by "20-30 Panther and Tiger tanks." (151) While

this last statement is definitely an exaggeration, it is likely that both sides are correct. In the heat of battle, the Canadian troops were unlikely to differentiate between tanks and self-propelled guns (ie. Stug III), which to them were the same thing. There is also a possibility that armour (tanks or SPs) belonging to Panzer Lehr were involved in the fight.

23 Fulton, personal account, in Portugal, *We Were There*, vol. 6, 2918–19.
24 War Diary, Royal Winnipeg Rifles, 8 June 1944.
25 Stacey, *The Victory Campaign*, 135.
26 "Memo of interview and rept by CSM CA Belton, 'B' coy, R Wpg Rif re actions 6/8 Jun 44 Op 'Overlord' d/10 & 14 Jun 44," National Defence Headquarters, Directorate of History and Heritage [DHH] 145.2R20011 (D1) [Belton interview]. Another version of this is contained in Portugal, *We Were There*, vol.6, 3044–45.
27 The commanding officer of the British 62nd Anti-Tank Regiment reported that at 0945 hours a force of nine enemy tanks and supporting infantry crossed the railway line west of Putot, Appendix B, War Diary 62nd Anti-Tank Regiment, June 1944, The National Archives (UK) [TNA] WO 171/919. CSM Belton reported that at about 1400 hours, ten Mark IV tanks broke through on the right flank, where they were engaged by a troop of British 17-pounders, Belton interview; Captain Harold Gonder of the Cameron Highlanders of Ottawa reported that his position was attacked by nine Panther tanks, Gonder interview contained in War Diary, Camerons of Ottawa, June 1944.
28 Appendix B, War Diary 62nd Anti-Tank Regiment, June 1944; "Cdn Scottish Regt Battle narrative by Maj GT MacEwan on D Day & the counter attack on Putot-en-Bessin." DHH 145.2C4013(D3). The war diary of the 3rd Anti-Tank Regiment reported five killed, five missing, and eighteen wounded on 8 June. Most of these casualties would have been suffered in this fight.
29 Leonard Willis, *None Had Lances: The Story of the 24th Lancers* (Wiltshire: 24th Lancers Old Comrades Association, 1986), 85.
30 War Diary, HQ 7th Canadian Infantry Brigade, Battle Log, 8 June 1944.
31 War Diary, 24th Lancers, June 1944, TNA WO 171/849; Willis, *None Had Lances*, 86–88; Foulds, "In Support of the Canadians," 74; Meyer, *The History of the 12. SS-Panzerdivision "Hitlerjugend,"* 51; Simon Trew, *Battle Zone Normandy: Gold Beach* (Gloustershire: Sutton, 2004), 94–95; Meldram, "Account for 21st Army Group Court," in Portugal, *We Were There*, vol.6, 3115. The figure of forty prisoners is reported by the war diary of the 24th Lancers and by Hubert Meyer. Willis reports a figure of seventy prisoners. British losses in the attack were reported as nine killed and six wounded. "Putot-en-Bessin" was one of seven battle honours awarded to the 24th Lancers for their service in Normandy.
32 English, *The Canadian Army and the Normandy Campaign*, 233n.
33 Meyer, *The History of the 12. SS-Panzerdivision "Hitlerjugend,"* 50–52. German and Canadian troops both claimed to occupy Brouay prior to the battle. The nature of the village, which is bisected by the Caen–Bayeux rail line, makes it likely that this is true—the Germans south of the rail line, the Canadian to the north.

34 Repeated eyewitness accounts of tanks can be found in the war diaries of the Royal Winnipeg Rifles, Canadian Scottish Regiment, the 24th Lancers, and the 62nd British Anti-Tank Regiment. As well, separate mention of armour is made by men from these units as well as from the Cameron Highlanders and the 3rd Anti-tank Regiment. This is too much evidence to discount. The passage of time combined with the dearth of accurate surviving German records, especially those from Panzer Lehr Division, makes it extremely difficult to identify the specific German armoured units that participated in this battle. The existing records make it clear that the armour did not belong to the main tank battalions of either 12 SS or Panzer Lehr Divisions, which were not present at this point in the battle. It is most likely that the tanks were self-propelled anti-tank guns or self-propelled artillery guns. From a distance, these vehicles would look and sound like tanks, and as far as the defending Canadian infantry was concerned, were just as dangerous.

35 Meldram, "Account for 21st Army Group Court," in Portugal, *We Were There*, vol.6, 3114–15; War Diary, Royal Winnipeg Rifles, 8 June 1944.

36 War Diary, Royal Winnipeg Rifles, June 1944.

37 Letter, Lieutenant-Colonel F.N. Cabeldu to Colonel H.M. Urquhart, 22 June 1944, quoted in Portugal, *We Were There*, vol.6, 1949.

38 Roy, *Ready for the Fray*, 234.

39 Casualties to the First Hussars on D-Day were so high that A and C Squadrons were combined to form one composite squadron. On 7 June this force totalled eleven Sherman tanks. Michael R. McNorgan, *The Gallant Hussars: A History of the 1st Hussars Regiment 1856–2004* (London: The 1st Hussars Cavalry Fund, 2004), 125–27.

40 Foulds, "In Support of the Canadians," 74.

41 Cabeldu, quoted in Portugal, *We Were There*, vol. 6, 1949.

42 Roy, *Ready for the Fray*, 233.

43 War Diary, 1st Battalion, The Canadian Scottish Regiment, 8 June 1944.

44 Roy, *Ready for the Fray*, 245.

45 Personal account, Private Roy H. Tutte, contained in War Diary, 1st Battalion, The Canadian Scottish Regiment, June 1944.

46 Roy, *Ready for the Fray*, 239–40; personal account, Lieutenant Thomas W.H. Butters, contained in War Diary, 1st Battalion, The Canadian Scottish Regiment, June 1944.

47 Howard Margolian, *Conduct Unbecoming: The Story of the Murder of Canadian Prisoners of War in Normandy* (Toronto: University of Toronto Press, 1998), 80; Stacey, *The Victory Campaign*, 135–36.

48 Meyer, *The History of the 12. SS-Panzerdivision "Hitlerjugend,"* 51. Earlier in the chapter, Meyer states that the 24th Lancers captured forty prisoners, but later he says that only twenty-one men were reported missing. As well, he does not account for the other units that participated in the attack. It can safely be concluded that German casualties during the battle were higher than Meyer reported.

49 Reynolds, *Steel Inferno*, 85.

50 Copp singles out Cabeldu and F.M Matheson of the Reginas for particular praise, but goes on to say that "the miseries of the Winnipegs were ... beyond their control." Copp, *Fields of Fire*, 24.
51 Copp is critical of Meldram's initial dispositions but recognizes that he was faced with limited options. See Copp, *Fields of Fire*, 68 and 291n.
52 War Diary, Regina Rifle Regiment, June 1944: "Account of Operations of Regina Rif 6-8 Jun 44, by Lt-Col F.M. Matheson, O.C., given to Hist Offr, 3 Cdn Inf Div. 24 June 44"; Reynolds, *Steel Inferno*, 85.
53 Hastings, *Overlord*, 124.

17

Operation Smash and 4 Canadian Armoured Division's Drive to Trun

Angelo Caravaggio

In *Fields of Fire* (2003), Terry Copp concluded that historians had underrated the First Canadian Army's contribution to the Allied campaign in Normandy. He noted that Canadians "played a role all out of proportion to its relative strength among the Allied armies."[1] On Canadian generalship in the final stages of the Normandy campaign, Professor Copp maintained that it was not possible "to argue that any of the three Canadian divisional commanders passed the test of battle [near Falaise]," though he conceded that it was "not clear how much this failure of leadership at the divisional level mattered."[2] The command decisions of Generals B.L. Montgomery and Omar Bradley were more instrumental in the final outcome when the Allies failed to close off the final escape route of two German armies to the east of Falaise. Commenting on Major-General George Kitching, the General Officer Commanding (GOC) of the 4th Canadian Armoured Division, Copp stated that "assigning major responsibility for the events of 17–21 August to the senior commanders [Montgomery and Bradley] does not explain or excuse the command failures that marred the record of 4th Armoured Division during this crucial period."[3] In particular, Copp remains critical of Kitching's decision to advance "his entire division on a single axis to the Falaise–Trun road" during the push to Trun on 17 August.[4]

Copp's assessment reflects the current body of literature, which is critical of the performance of Maj.-Gen. Kitching and his division's drive to Trun. These assessments, however, have been made without a true understanding of the complex series of orders issued by the 2nd Canadian Corps[5] from 15 to 18 August 1944 that shaped the actions of the division. The 4th Armoured Division's drive to Trun, formally know as Operation Smash (Op Smash), was not a thrust along a single axis but a well-thought-out plan that had been devised and executed based on the best available tactical intelligence. This chapter will demonstrate that the leaders of the 4th Armoured Division were responsive, adaptive, and resilient in responding to the constantly changing tactical situation in their successful drive to Trun.

The 4th Division[6] entered the line south of Caen on 31 July 1944 as an untested combat formation. The division conducted a series of minor operations against Tilly-la-Campagne and La Hogue between 1 and 7 August 1944 before taking part in its first major operation, Operation Totalize, on 8 August. Totalize was a 2nd Canadian Corps operation designed to break through the German defences around Caen with the original intent of capturing Falaise. This operation was launched on the evening of 7 August. The 4th Division was tasked with participating in Phase II; its objective was to capture Point 195, a feature that dominated the Caen–Falaise highway located approximately 16 kilometres into German territory.

After three days of intense fighting, the division captured Point 195, but at great cost. The division went into Totalize at full strength, reporting a compliment of 328 tanks of all types, 869 officers, and 15,383 other ranks. Two days later, even with reinforcements in men and tanks, the division was down to 824 officers and 14,248 other ranks. One battle group, Worthington Force, had suffered significant casualties during the fight for Hill 140, losing 47 of their 55 tanks as well as 250 men.[7] Four other units—the Governor General's Foot Guards (GGFG), the Canadian Grenadier Guards (CGG), the Lincoln and Welland Regiment, and the Argyll and Sutherland Highlanders of Canada (Argylls)—after capturing and holding Point 195 for two days, were reporting effective strengths below 85 percent.

Of greater concern was that four of the division's eight regimental/battalion commanding officers were replaced or became casualties between 8 and 13 August. Major R.A. Keane took over command of the Lake Superior Regiment, Major W.T. Cromb was given the Lincoln and Welland Regiment, and Major R.A. Bradburn took over the Algonquin Regiment, while Major C.E. Parish commanded the British Columbia Regiment.[8] After one week of fighting, the 4th Division entered the next phase of operations with a new cadre of commanding officers whose time in command could be measured at best in days and sometimes in hours. Their performance, however, was to be extraordinary.

The division was launched into its second major operation in less than a week on 14 August. Operation Tractable was another 2nd Corps operation designed to continue the advance towards Falaise with the intent of capturing the important road network radiating from that city. Tractable was to be carried out in three phases. In Phase I the attacking forces were to cross the Laison River and seize the high ground area Point 118 as well as Point 103 southeast of Montboint. Phase II involved a push south and southwest to capture the high ground northeast of Falaise, and Phase III called for the capture of the bridges at Eraines and Damblainville before an advance southward on Trun to link up with US XV Corps. The specific tasks given to the 4th Division were to capture Point 159 approximately 2.5 kilometres northeast of Falaise, and also the bridges at Eraines and Damblainville, so as to exploit south and southeast to meet with the Americans.[9]

Intense fighting marked the launch of Tractable, but the 4th Division succeeded in breaking the forward German defensive zones, crossing the Laison River, and positioning itself for the drive to Point 159. The fighting, however, had been costly. Brigadier Eric Leslie Booth, Commander 4th Armoured Brigade, was killed along with key members of his tactical headquarters. Brigade command shifted to Lt.-Col. Murray Scott, the commander of the GGFGs. Scott had broken his ankle in a mine explosion that disabled his command tank; nevertheless, he accepted command, reorganized the armoured brigade, and made plans for the attack towards Falaise the following morning. The first day's operations had torn a 5 kilometre gap in the Germans' line, forcing them to withdraw to their rearward defensive positions.[10]

On the afternoon of 14 August, Lieutenant-General Harry Crerar, Commander First Canadian Army, received new instructions from Montgomery. First Canadian Army, and not Second British Army, was to capture Falaise with the least possible delay. According to Montgomery's direction, however, this new task was not to interfere with the larger and more important plan of driving southeast to capture Trun and linking up with the Americans who were now turning north.[11] Lieutenant-General Guy Simonds, Commander 2nd Canadian Corps, assigned the task of taking

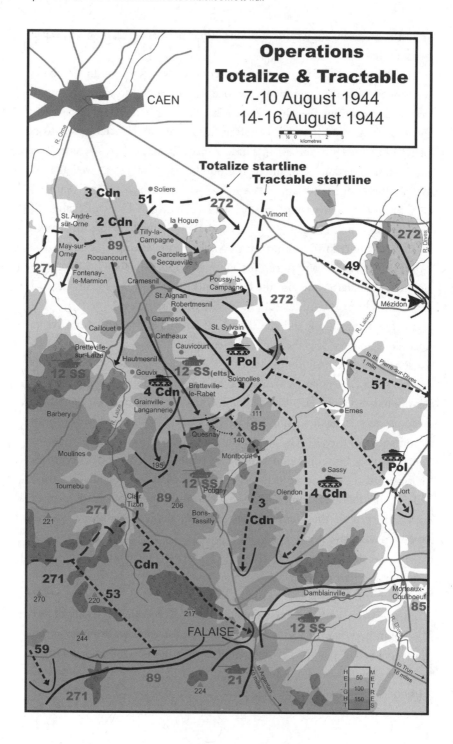

Falaise to Kitching without modifying or eliminating any of the original tasks assigned to the division in Tractable.

This new requirement to take Falaise forced Kitching to modify the intent of his plans for 15 August, which were still focused on taking Point 159 and the bridges at Eraines and Damblainville. Kitching tasked his infantry brigade to clear the Olendon–Epancy–Perrières area by first light; this would be followed by an advance by his armoured brigade to Point 159. These actions were to be followed by a thrust through to Falaise by the Lake Superior Regiment, the division's motorized battalion. The South Alberta Regiment (SAR) then had the task of securing the bridges at Eraines and Damblainville.[12] These orders were modified at 1200 hours, 15 August, since the SARs had been drawn into extensive fighting in the advance to Point 159. The 18th Canadian Armoured Car Regiment would now lead the attack on Falaise and capture the bridging at Eraines and Damblainville.[13]

Simonds's decision to task the 4th Division to take Falaise and not one of his two infantry divisions is confusing for two reasons: first, the armoured division had a smaller complement of infantry; and second, its tanks were vulnerable in the confined spaces of city streets. Capturing a town usually involved house-to-house fighting, an infantry-intensive operation, and was a task normally given to an infantry division, which had nine battalions in three infantry brigades compared to the one infantry brigade in an armoured division. But Simonds had to get to Trun quickly with enough combat power to seal the possible German escape routes out of Normandy. Ordering Kitching's division to fight on towards Falaise meant that it would encounter the strength of the remaining German defences while travelling in the opposite direction of Trun.[14]

During 15 August, Kitching's division made slow but steady progress towards the high ground above Versainville. Late in the afternoon Kitching was informed that Point 159 had been captured. Simonds was delighted, and he tasked Kitching to get his division into Falaise.[15] That evening, however, Kitching learned that his forces had withdrawn from Point 159 when confronted with enemy anti-tank guns and dug-in tanks.[16] Simonds was disappointed by the news, but Kitching assured him that new plans had already been prepared to attack again the next morning to take Point 159 and Falaise. Simonds cancelled the operation early the following morning, deciding instead to realign his forces with new objectives.[17]

Simonds's decisions were taking place within a strategic picture that was changing dramatically. Hitler gave orders to his armies in Normandy for a formal retreat to the Seine on 16 August 1944. That morning, the remnants of twenty-one German divisions, comprising 200,000 men, had been compressed into an area known as the Falaise Pocket, an area 56 kilometres deep and approximately 19 kilometres wide bordered by Falaise in the north and Argentan in the south.[18] Senior Germans commanders had concluded that they needed three nights to get the westernmost forces across the Orne River and one more night to complete the withdrawal behind the Dives River. The outcome of the operations to extricate the remaining German forces in Normandy would depend on keeping the Falaise Gap open for four days.[19]

Simonds's intent for the 2nd Canadian Corps on 16 August was to form a base with his two infantry divisions enclosing Falaise until relieved by Second British Army. Then his two armoured divisions were to capture Trun and the high ground dominating it to the southwest and northeast before the 2nd Corps advanced towards Lisieux to the northeast.[20] The 2nd Canadian Infantry Division was to take Falaise, while the 3rd Infantry Division was to widen its front to take over the area held by the 4th Division. The 2nd Canadian Armoured Brigade was to go into corps reserve.[21]

Simonds's orders are referred to extensively in current narratives of the Normandy campaign, but few have explored the specific tasks given to the 4th Division. That division was ordered to advance due south on the axis Eraines–Point 250–Point 252 and position itself to dominate the high ground at Moutabard; from there, it was to advance northeast when ordered in the direction of Trun to make contact with the Polish Armoured Division and at the same time link up with the Americans moving north from Argentan. The Polish Armoured Division was to advance on the axis Maizieres–Jort–Point 259 and was to dominate the area from Point 226 to Point 258. Simonds's strategy was designed to form a double-layered defensive line with his two armoured divisions on either side of the Dives River.[22]

These new orders significantly changed the plans that the 4th Division was ready to execute on the morning of 16 August. That division was still mentally and physically oriented to attack Falaise. The new orders were now directing it south of Falaise to deny the Germans the bridges, river crossings, and road junctions necessary for their escape out of Normandy.[23]

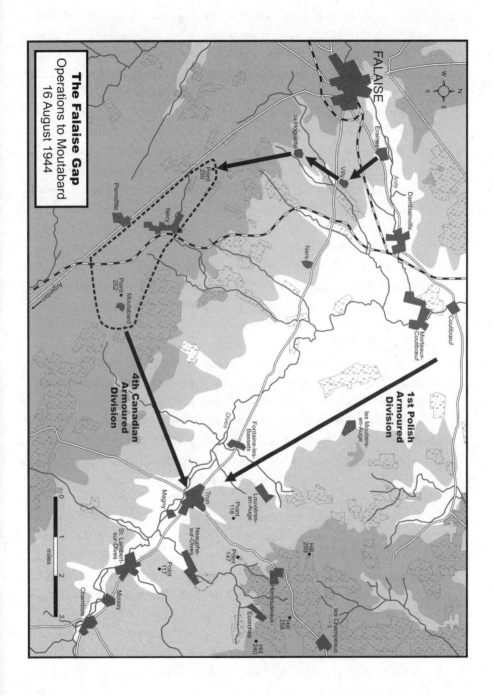

While some authors have described 16 August as a day of rest and rebuilding for the 4th Division, it was anything but for Kitching and his six new COs.[24] The number of Orders Groups (O Groups) recorded in the Lake Superior Regiment War Diary highlights this fact. The first 4th Brigade O Group occurred at 0030 hours on 16 August with orders for the renewed attack on Falaise. Lieutenant-Colonel Keane, the new CO of the Lake Superior Regiment, conducted his own O Group shortly thereafter, and the companies of the battalion reported themselves in position for the anticipated attack by early morning. The next O Group, at 1400 hours, detailed Simonds's new intent, which was the move south to Moutabard to link up with the Americans along the Falaise–Argentan road and with the Poles at Trun. The Lake Superior Regiment O Group to convey this change in orders was held at 1645 hours.[25] Kitching then held his third division O Group in less than twenty hours at 1700 hours; there, he outlined the details of a completely new plan called Operation Smash.[26] Smash was briefed to the 4th Armoured Brigade at 2000 hours, and Keane's O Group for this third change in orders took place at 0330 hours on 17 August.

Each of these divisional orders groups required the division to move in a different direction and attack towards different objectives. Each new plan required its own detailed intelligence, operational, and administrative planning in order to translate objectives into tasks for the various subunits of the division. One divisional O Group in a twenty-four-hour period was considered normal; having three with each successive plan ordering the division in a different direction created the potential for intellectual and operational chaos. Yet the division's commanders were able to respond and adapt.

Smash is poorly understood, but it was the one opportunity where George Kitching had the latitude to plan and execute an operation without direct influence from Simonds. Smash required the 10th Infantry Brigade to seize a bridgehead over the Ante and Train Rivers; the 4th Armoured Brigade would then pass through and advance towards Trun.[27] Kitching specified two routes for the advance: Route I (codenamed Irish) through Damblainville, and Route II (codenamed Japan) through Morteaux-Couliboeuf.[28] There would be three phases to the attack. The first was the capture of the dominating, partly wooded hill overlooking Damblainville; the second was the seizure of the village itself; and the third was the securing of yet another dominating

Angelo Caravaggio 399

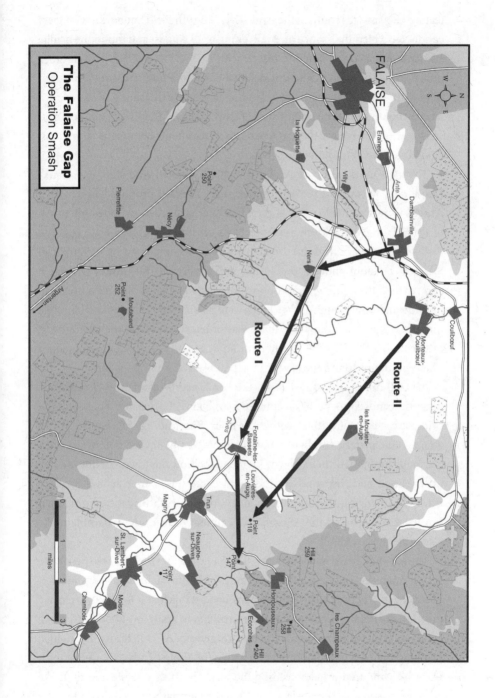

feature 1800 metres south of the Ante River. The 9th Field Squadron engineers conducted a reconnaissance on the evening of 16 August and found the bridge and crossing at Damblainville intact, with no Germans for at least another mile beyond the town.[29] Kitching decided to capture both crossing points but to go with Route I as the main axis of advance. The division would advance straight south to cut the main Falaise–Trun road and then southeast to Trun. The final objectives for the three armoured regiments lay northeast of Trun along the Trun–Vimoutiers highway.[30]

Advance units were deployed towards Damblainville and Morteaux-Couliboeuf to secure the river crossings for the two proposed routes. The Argylls were directed to move at once from Perrières to the wooded hill north of Damblainville and to be ready to press on into the village and cross the Ante.[31] Mounted in armoured half-tracks and accompanied by C Squadron SAR, the battalion moved southeast from Perrières at 1800 hours 16 August and reached their hill without opposition. Patrols reported Damblainville to be undefended, although enemy tanks were passing through it. A small mobile force from the Algonquin Regiment was ordered to capture the single-track bridge across the Dives at Couliboeuf, in accordance with Kitching's plan.[32] The Algonquins found the bridge intact and seized it unopposed.[33]

At 0730 hours, 17 August 1944, the combined force of Argylls and SAR tanks descended quickly and captured Damblainville, the river bank, and the bridge over the Ante River within an hour. The leading infantry advanced about 1000 metres south of the bridge at Damblainville before accurate German fire pinned them down. Elements behind the town tried to deploy off the road and disperse, but the town came under mortar and artillery fire and provided little room for manoeuvre. The 10th Brigade commander, Jim Jefferson, ordered the Algonquin Regiment to firm up in Damblainville alongside the Argylls.[34]

The advance guard of the armoured brigade tried several times to penetrate the German position, but the tanks came under immediate German fire.[35] It was clear to Kitching that the Germans had established a fortified defensive position during the night and were determined to resist any attempt to move south on Trun from the Damblainville bridgehead. At 1130 hours, 17 August, Kitching issued a warning order to change the route of advance to Route II, with the armoured brigade leading the way. The 10th Brigade and the Lake Superior Regiment were ordered to keep the Germans pinned down in their current position while the armour swept around their flank at Morteaux-Couliboeuf.[36]

In battle, tactical success cannot always be achieved without incurring appreciable risks. The significant danger involved in sending tanks into the attack without proper infantry support had been demonstrated many times during the war, most recently during Operation Goodwood, where the vulnerability of the Sherman tank and the killing power of German anti-tank guns cost the British over 400 tanks in three days of attacks against prepared German positions.[37] To attack with tanks alone went against Canadian doctrine on the employment of armoured forces in battle. The tactical situation on the morning of 17 August, however, demanded bold action. Kitching, understanding the risk, ordered his armoured regiments to attack, unsupported, towards Trun.

The shift to Route II involved an extraordinary effort by the division's staff.[38] Major M.R. Ware and Captain J.A. Berthiaume from Kitching's operations staff controlled the disengagement at Damblainville and the rerouting of the armoured brigade to Couliboeuf. According to the divisional war diary the move to the new bridge was made "if not in an orderly fashion, at least in control."[39] The division's operations officer Lt.-Col. Fred Wigle passed new instructions to the armoured brigade and went to the bridge at Couliboeuf, where he briefed the regimental commanders on the general situation as they passed through. Despite the initial setback at Damblainville, good staff planning allowed the division to continue the advance to Trun.[40]

The 4th Division war diary for 17 August records a conference between Kitching and Simonds at approximately 1100 hours. Some accounts argue that at this meeting Simonds gave Kitching orders to shift the advance through Couliboeuf. Others maintain that Kitching sought approval for the new plan.[41] Since Route II was always part of Kitching's original plan, it is more probable that the meeting allowed the two commanders to consider the implications of the division's new axis of advance. Route II followed secondary roads on the opposite side of the Dives River from that originally planned and in the area of operations allocated to the Poles. Kitching's tanks would have to travel through woods, rolling hills, and hamlets that provided excellent concealment for the Germans. Flanking the advance route were the hills on the western side of the Dives River, which were still in German hands. In addition, the tanks would have to traverse two additional water obstacles that bisected the line of advance. The conference between Kitching and Simonds helped establish the new boundaries between the Poles and the 4th Division; it was also an opportunity for the two men to consider whether new objectives needed to be identified.

Despite the obstacles presented by the switch to Route II, the 4th Division executed a coherent and successful advance over complex terrain into the heart of the Falaise Gap. By 1600 hours on 17 August the Grenadier Guards and Governor General's Foot Guards were across the bridge at Couliboeuf. The tanks then fanned out to the south and southeast. By early evening the Grenadier Guards had captured Point 118 on the outskirts of Trun.[42] Jefferson's infantry brigade was ordered to disengage at Damblainville, follow the armour across the river, and protect the division's right flank along the eastern bank of the Dives River from Morteaux-Couliboeuf to the area Fontaine-les-Bassels. This order placed the infantry brigade astride the high ground to Trun along the route of the Dives River.[43] The Lincoln and Welland Regiment was subsequently ordered to Point 104, about 7 kilometres northwest of Trun.

The tactical gamble to send the armoured regiments without infantry support had succeeded. The armoured brigade was in the German rear area without their knowledge, and the divisions' echelon forces were able to come forward on demand to resupply the tanks. Unfortunately, another regimental commander was lost when Maj H.R. Baker of the GGFG, who had taken over command only the previous day, was seriously wounded. Captain G.T. Baylay took over the regiment.[44]

On the afternoon of 17 August, Montgomery issued urgent new orders to First Canadian Army. The Polish Division was to "thrust on Chambois" while the 4th Division was to continue its "thrust" on Trun. "Essential to push on greatest possible speed regardless of losses in order to close the gap."[45] At 1945 hours, Simonds ordered the 4th Division to capture Trun that night.[46] Kitching assigned the 4th Armoured Brigade to capture Trun, but without infantry the attack could not proceed.

By the early morning of 18 August, the infantry of the Lake Superior Regiment had married up with their respective armoured regiments.[47] The BCR and C Company Lake Superiors pushed into Trun, but Canadian control of the town was not solidified until elements of the 10th Brigade arrived. In the meantime, Kitching's remaining armoured units swept eastwards, and by

1200 hours they had met up with a motor battalion of the Polish Armoured Division.[48]

Operation Smash was completed on the afternoon of 18 August 1944 when a combined force from the Grenadier Guards and the Lake Superior Regiment attacked south from Point 147 to cut off the approach to Trun from the southeast. The attack succeeded, and the infantry set up defensive positions while the tanks advanced to Trun from the south. There they met members of the Argylls who were already in the town. While the infantry solidified their hold on Trun, the Grenadier Guards repositioned themselves on the rising ground 1000 metres from the city's crossroads and began to engage targets of opportunity across and up the valley.[49] By 1500 hours on 18 August, Trun had become a Canadian strongpoint. By evening, the 4th Division had captured more than 500 prisoners as German columns continued into the town unaware that it was in Canadian hands.[50]

Earlier, at 1000 hours on 18 August, Kitching had outlined his plan to solidify the division's gains on the east bank of the Dives River and to prepare for anticipated German attacks.[51] The three infantry battalions of the 10th Brigade would hold the east bank of the river while his armoured regiments arrayed themselves on the high ground behind the infantry to deepen the defensive line and to counterattack any German breakthrough.[52] Kitching's plan, however, was altered significantly by new orders from Simonds.

By the end of the day the Canadians had set up a strong blocking position at Trun, but the Argentan–Chambois–Vimoutiers highway (D113–D16) was still open, as were the secondary roads and lanes through St-Lambert-sur-Dives and Moissy. The remnants of the Fifth Panzer Army and the Seventh Army were trying to escape along the valley of the Dives River, which led through Trun, St-Lambert-sur-Dives, and Chambois.[53] To the south, the highway leading from Falaise southeastward to Argentan was under American shellfire.[54] Clear skies further slowed the German withdrawal by allowing Allied air forces to engage ground targets at will.[55] The fate of the German armies depended on their ability to hold open the 7 kilometre stretch between Trun and Chambois.

On 18 August, Crerar ordered Simonds to seal off the front from Trun to Chambois. Anticipating that the German forces in the pocket would soon be destroyed, he also ordered Simonds to carry out active reconnaissance to the northeast in the direction of Vimoutiers. Simonds's plan was for the 2nd

Division to mop up Falaise, and for the 3rd Division to take over the east bank of the Dives River from Morteaux-Couliboeuf to Trun, while the 4th Division advanced southeast from Trun on Chambois. The Polish Division was to advance southwest from the area of Les Champeaux to Chambois and link up with the US forces.[56]

Kitching was to carry out his part of this operation the next day, 19 August, as soon as the division had cleared the enemy from the area north and northwest of Trun. To undertake this clearing task, Simonds ordered the 4th Armoured Brigade and the Algonquin Regiment, which were moving to solidify the defensive position along the Dives River, to deploy on the axis Trun–Vimoutiers, away from the Trun–St-Lambert line.[57] Opinions vary as to whether the splitting of the division was to counter an anticipated German attack from outside the Trun–Vimoutiers area or whether this was Simonds's attempt to pre-position the division for the drive to Lisieux as per the direction he issued on 16 August.[58] Simonds's orders entailed, as Kitching later recalled, changes to the orders Kitching had already issued to his brigades that morning, resulting in a significant redeployment of his forces.[59]

General Kitching remained concerned about how his division was disposed. The greater part of his division, including the three armoured regiments of the armoured brigade, the Lake Superior Regiment, and Algonquin Regiment, were sent largely unopposed to the northeast away from the Trun–St-Lambert–Moissy line. This left the three remaining units of the 10th Brigade (the Lincs, Argylls, and South Albertas) to carry out Simonds's orders to occupy the 7 kilometre line of the Dives River south of Trun, and to advance southeast towards Chambois.[60]

A battle group of South Alberta tanks and supporting infantry, under the command of Major David Vivian Currie of C Squadron SAR, had the task of taking Chambois. Rather than waiting for the next day, Currie's battle group had been tasked with seizing and holding Chambois the following day; instead it was ordered to do so before last light on 18 August.[61] Currie's squadron at this point was down to fifteen tanks. The battle group got under way at 1800 hours and reached St-Lambert-sur-Dives at dusk. Reports indicated that the town was strongly held by anti-tank guns and infantry. Currie was told, therefore, to wait until first light before clearing it. The remaining assets of the SAR were moved to Hill 117 above St-Lambert-sur-Dives to support Currie.[62]

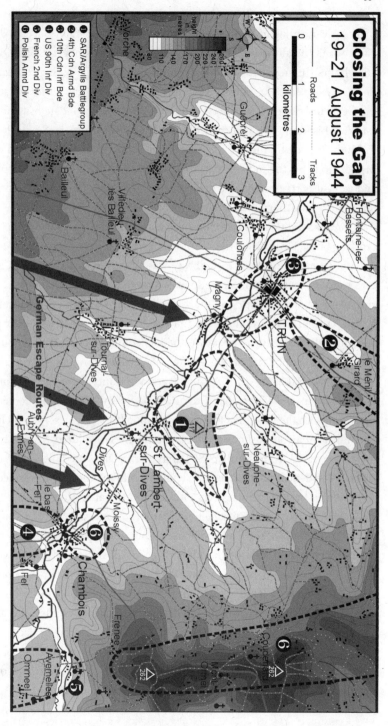

By early morning of 19 August, it was evident that the main German escape effort would be along the Dives River line Trun–St-Lambert–Chambois. At 0635 hours Currie's composite force attacked the village of St-Lambert. The force was able to clear half the town but was unable to go farther because of the Germans' superior numbers. Currie decided to consolidate his gains and establish his lines near the centre of town.[63] At 0845 hours the SAR informed the 10th Brigade that unless support arrived, Currie could be pushed out of his positions. As the morning wore on, Currie was forced from the southern and central parts of town. He now concentrated his infantry and remaining tanks at the northern end. Currie's force was saved in part by the fact that the Germans did not want to retake the village; they simply wanted to hold a crossing of the Dives River that would allow them to move east. Any German attempt to move up the D13 highway was effectively countered by Currie's force and by massive concentrations of Canadian artillery fire. There were simply not enough infantry on the ground between the 10th Brigade and the Polish Armoured Division to stop the German exodus or to seal the gaps in the Allied defensive line. The only Canadian counter was massive amounts of artillery and cannon fire on the avenues of German movement.[64]

Throughout the day of 19 August, German infantry kept surging forward between Trun and Chambois. Currie asked for infantry reinforcements to help cope with the prisoners that were flooding his PW cages. At 1400 hours, Kitching sent a composite force of two companies of soldiers from the Lincs and the Argyls from Trun to St-Lambert-sur-Dives to reinforce Currie's force.[65] The detachment reached St-Lambert on foot and was integrated into the defences by 2200 hours. Even with the additional reinforcements, Currie had to give up part of the village to tighten his defences.

As the intensity of the German breakout became apparent, Simonds finally realized the seriousness of the 10th Brigade's position and began placing formations under Kitching's command to thicken up the defences along the Trun–St-Lambert–Chambois corridor. Simonds's initial solution, however, was not to redeploy Kitching's 4th Brigade, which represented the closest units, but instead to commit the 2nd Canadian Armoured Brigade, which had to travel from the Morteaux-Couliboeuf area.[66] Simonds next helped Kitching by placing the 9th Infantry Brigade under his command on the evening of 19 August. But these two brigades arrived on 20 and 21 August, too late to be of any assistance. Kitching had no choice but to stop the flow of escaping Germans with his depleted 10th Brigade.[67]

The fighting in St-Lambert-sur-Dives lasted three days. By the time the SAR was officially relieved from its positions around St-Lambert, the regiment estimated that it had captured 7,000 prisoners, killed 2,000 men, and wounded another 3,000.[68] Major David Currie won the Victoria Cross for his leadership in defence of St-Lambert-sur-Dives, the first award of its kind to be won by a Canadian in Northwest Europe.

It took the 2nd Canadian Corps from 17 August to 22 August 1944 to close the Falaise Gap—a time frame that some considered unacceptable. Since he was the commander of the division spearheading the Canadian drive, the focus of attention landed on Kitching. Simonds assessed Kitching as ineffective and relieved him of his command at noon on 21 August 1944. Kitching was shocked and upset at that decision and made a number of points in his defence. The first involved the fact that it had taken five days for the designated replacement to command the armoured brigade, Brigadier Robert Moncel, to arrive to take command, even though Moncel was working only hours away. This delay meant that Kitching had had to appoint officers from his own armoured regiments to command the brigade until Moncel arrived. This in turn had robbed the armoured regiments of their senior leadership. Kitching also complained that the division had had too many changes in orders over a period of ten days and had taken very heavy casualties in commanders, soldiers, and tanks in its first battles.[69] The evidence heavily supports Kitching's claims. According to Kitching, Simonds had no rebuttal for any of these very valid points.[70]

The 4th Division entered Normandy as an untried, inexperienced formation and in the span of fourteen days of continuous combat became a mature fighting formation. The operations on 17 and 18 August demonstrated the flexibility, professional competence, and growing maturity of Kitching, his staff, and the formations within the 4th Division. The professional manner in which the division switched its axis of advance once Kitching realized that further attempts to advance through Damblainville would be costly is a testament to the training of the staff, who orchestrated the switch so that the armoured brigade could continue the attack late into the day of 17 August. The 4th Armoured Brigade attack was not simply a mad dash for ground, but a coherent advance where the echelon forces were able to advance and conduct resupply when called upon. The success of the advance is even more impressive when one considers that the officers leading the advance had been in command of their respective units for at best only a day or two. This successful advance is indicative of a division that was effectively commanded and controlled at all levels. Kitching's reputation as a commander has been defined by his dismissal, not by what he and his division accomplished. In the end, Major-General George Kitching proved himself an able commander in an almost impossible situation.

The combat operations associated with Operation Smash and the advance to Trun by the 4th Division were much more complex than previously understood. The evidence shows that the division and its leadership proved resilient to significant stresses, allowing them to function effectively in very difficult circumstances. All levels displayed effective and flexible leadership during this operation, especially the newly appointed commanders, who showed professionalism, expertise, leadership, and ingenuity. Given the enormous challenges during the unfolding battles of August 1944, Kitching and his 4th Canadian Armoured Division deserve greater credit for their actions than current histories have been willing to offer.

Notes

1. Terry Copp, *Fields of Fire: The Canadians in Normandy* (Toronto: University of Toronto Press, 2003), 267.
2. Ibid., 266.
3. Ibid., 236.
4. Ibid., 236.
5. The major formations of the 2nd Canadian Corps were the 2nd and 3rd Canadian Infantry Divisions, the 4th Canadian Armoured Division, the 1st Polish Armoured Division, and the 2nd Canadian Armoured Brigade.
6. The 4th Canadian Armoured Division was composed of one armoured and one infantry brigade. The 4th Armoured Brigade was composed of three armoured regiments, the Governor General's Foot Guards, The Canadian Grenadier Guards, the British Columbia Regiment, and the Lake Superior Regiment, a motorized infantry battalion. The 10th Canadian Infantry Brigade was made up of three infantry battalions: the Lincoln and Welland Regiment, the Argyll and Sutherland Highlanders of Canada, and the Algonquin Regiment, as well as one armoured reconnaissance regiment, the South Alberta Regiment. The division establishment on 2 August 1944 was 868 officers, 15,516 other ranks, and 333 tanks. War Diary, 4 Cdn Armd Div-AA&QMG, 1–31 Aug 1944, App 5 ADREP 2 August 1944.

7   Worthington Force was composed of the British Columbia Regiment and the Algonquin Regiment and commanded by Lieutenant-Colonel D. Worthington of the BCRs. Ops Log, 9 Aug 44 serial 61-65, War Diary, 4 Cdn Armd Bde, 1-31 Aug 44.
8   War Diary, British Columbia Regiment, 1–31 August 1944, entry 13 August.
9   Outline of Instructions Issued by GOC 4 Division 131230B Aug 44. OP TRACTABLE Dated 13 August 1944. War Diary, 4 Cdn Armd Div 1–31 August 1944, App 23.
10 Hubert Meyer, *The History of the 12.SS-Panzerdivision "Hitlerjugend"* (Winnipeg, J.J. Fedorowicz Publishing, 1994), 185.
11 Ops Log, 14 Aug 44, Serial 75. War Diary, First Canadian Army–General Staff, 1–31 August 1944, App 74.
12 Specifically, the 10th Canadian Infantry Brigade, less the Lincoln and Welland Regiment, was to clear the Olendon–Epancy–Perrières area while the 4th Canadian Armoured Brigade, with the Lincoln and Wellands under command and mounted in Priests, was to take the division's original objective, the contour feature 160 and Point 159. The Lincoln and Wellands were to form a firm base on the high ground that would facilitate the last phase of the operation, which was an advance by the Lake Superior Regiment passing through the Lincoln and Wellands to take Falaise. Ops Log 15 August serial 9, 42, 60. War Diary, First Canadian Army–General Staff, 1–31 August 1944, App 74.
13 Ops Log 15 August serial 62. War Diary, First Canadian Army–General Staff, 1–31 August 1944, App 74.
14 Copp, *Fields of Fire*, 232.
15 War Diary, 4 Cdn Armd Bde, 1–31 August 1944, entry 15 August.
16 Ops Log 16 August serial 4, War Diary, 2 Cdn Corps Main, 1–31 August 1944. An attack was attempted by the 4th Canadian Armoured Brigade late in the evening, which, as a minimum, advanced beyond Point 168 and reached the forward slopes of Point 159. Recce tanks were sent forward and overran southern portions of the feature before retiring. C.P. Stacey believes that a few tanks from the GGFG had worked their way forward under cover of smoke and had managed to reach the objective. He also states that withering fire from the line west of Eraines drove them off. *CMHQ Report No.169*, para 154.
17 News from the 3 Cdn Inf Div was also bad. They had advanced to Point 168 in a costly action that afternoon but the assaulting 7 Brigade troops were thrown out of Soulangy before dark. Meyer, *History of the 12th SS Panzer Division*, 186; Copp, *Fields of Fire*, 231.
18 Terry Copp, *A Canadian's Guide to the Battlefields of Normandy* (Waterloo: Laurier Centre for Military Strategic and Disarmament Studies, 1994), 140.
19 Martin Blumenson, *Breakout and Pursuit* (Washington, DC: Center of Military History, 1961), 528.
20 Memo GOC "Operations Following the Capture of Falaise" dated 15 August 1944. War Diary, HQ 2 Cdn Armd Bde, 1–31 August 1944, App 11.
21 Ibid.
22 Ibid.

23 Cassidy, *Warpath: the Story of the Algonquin Regiment, 1939–1945* (Cobalt: Highway Book Shop, 1990), 130.
24 In addition to the command changes already mentioned, Lt.-Col. Halpenny took over command of the 4th Brigade and Maj. H.R. Baker took over command of the GGFGs.
25 War Diary, The Lake Superior Regiment (Motor) 1–31 August 1944, entries 15–17 August.
26 War Diary, 4th Cdn Armd Div, 1–31 August 1944, entry 16 August.
27 War Diary, 4 Cdn Armd Div, 1–31 August 1944, entry 16 August.
28 Notes "Op Smash." War Diary, 4 Cdn Armd Bde, 1–31 August 1944, App 20.
29 M.O. Rollefson, *Green Route Up* (The Hague: Mouton and Cy, 1945), 33.
30 Notes "Op Smash." War Diary, 4 Cdn Armd Bde, 1–31 August 1944, App 20.
31 War Diary, 10 Cdn Inf Bde, 1–31 August 1944, entry 17 August; War Diary, 4 Cdn Armd Div, 1–31 August 1944, entry 16 August.
32 If the main attack was successful, the Algonquins were to clear the west side of the river and meet up with the Argylls south at Damblainville. Ops Log 17 August serial 47. War Diary, First Canadian Army–General Staff, 1–31 August 1944, App 74.
33 *CMHQ Report No. 169,* para 154.
34 War Diary, 10 Cdn Inf Bde, 1–31 August 1944, entry 17 August.
35 Meyer, *History of the 12th SS Panzer Division,* 192.
36 Op Log 17 August serials 41 & 53. War Diary, 4 Cdn Armd Bde, 1–31 August 1944, App 5.
37 Operation Goodwood ran from 18 to 20 July and involved the British 7th, 11th, and Guards armoured divisions.
38 War Diary, 4 Cdn Armd Div, 1–31 August 1944, entry 17 August.
39 War Diary, 4 Cdn Armd Div, 1–31 August 1944, entry 17 August.
40 Ibid.
41 See Copp, *Fields of Fire,* 237; and C.P. Stacey, *The Victory Campaign: The Operations in Northwest Europe, 1944–1945,* Volume 3: *Official History of the Canadian Army in the Second World War* (Ottawa: Queen's Printer, 1966), 252.
42 See the war diary entries for the three armoured regiments on 17 August.
43 War Diary, 10 Cdn Inf Bde, 1–31 August 1944, entry 17 June.
44 Major Ed Smith from the Grenadier Guards was ordered to take command of the Foot Guards the following day. War Diary, 4 Cdn Armd Bde, 1–31 August 1944, App 21.
45 Ops Log 17 August, serial 27, War Diary, First Canadian Army General Staff, 1–31 August 1944.
46 Ops Log 17 August, serial 144, Ibid.
47 A Coy under command GGFG, B Coy under command CGG, and C Coy under command of the BCR.
48 War Diary, 10 Cdn Inf Bde, 1–31 August 1944, entry 18 August.
49 A. Fortescue Duguid, *History of the Canadian Grenadier Guards, 1760–1964* (Montreal: Gazette Print Co., 1965), 279.
50 A Company was deployed on the road to Falaise, B Company on the road to Argentan, C Company on the road to St-Lambert-sur-Dives, and D Company covered the road

to Vimoutiers. Tanks and anti-tank guns were disposed to make strongpoints within the town and to cover the approaches to the Dives River from the east. War Diary, The Lincoln and Welland Regiment, 1–31 August 1944, entry 18 August. Robert Louis Rogers, *History of the Lincoln and Welland Regiment* (Montreal: Industrial Shops for the Deaf, 1954), 156.

51 The mission would expand once again on 19 August to capture Chambois. Ops Log 17 August, Appendix to Log—From 2 Cdn Corps 172315B, 17 Aug 44, War Diary, Main HQ 2nd Cdn Inf Div, 1–31 August 1944.

52 War Diary, 4 Cdn Armd Div, 1–31 August 1944, entry 18 August.

53 Reginald H. Roy, *1944: The Canadians in Normandy* (Toronto: Macmillan, 1984), 298.

54 This road would be completely cut on 19 August by American and French divisions.

55 Roy, *1944: The Canadians in Normandy*, 298.

56 The orders as recorded in the 4th Canadian Armoured Division war diary indicate that the entire division was to proceed south to Chambois. War Diary, 4 Cdn Armd Div, 1–31 August 1944, 18 August.

57 Duguid, *History of the Canadian Grenadier Guards*, 279.

58 Professor Terry Copp argues that the decision to place the 4th Armoured Brigade in defensive positions along the Trun–Vimoutiers highway instead of committing it to the closing of the gap between Trun and Chambois may have been the result of Ultra intelligence. "At 0916 18 August Ultra recipients were informed that 2nd SS Pz Corps had been ordered to clear up the situation resulting from the allied penetration northwest of Trun. This was to be accomplished by a concentric attack carried out by 2nd SS Pz Corps and two other panzer divisions directed on Trun from both inside and outside the pocket." Copp, *Fields of Fire*, 241.

59 Kitching's commanding officers had already given orders to execute his plan for the defence of the Dives River. Donald E. Graves, *South Albertas: A Canadian Regiment at War* (Toronto: Robin Brass Studio, 2004), 138.

60 Ibid., 143.

61 The battlegroup was composed of C Squadron SAR and a depleted B Company from the Argylls composed of fifty-five men. War Diary, Argyll & Sutherland Highlanders of Canada, 1–31 August 1944, entry 18 August.

62 This included his Regimental HQ of four tanks, recce troop, B Squadron, and 4 M-10 self-propelled anti-tank guns. Copp, *Fields of Fire*, 240.

63 Rooster was the codename for St-Lambert. Ops Log 19 August, serial 7. War Diary, 10 Cdn Inf Bde, 1–31 August 1944, War Diary, South Alberta Regiment, 1–31 August 1944, entry 19 August.

64 Graves, *South Albertas*, 154–58. Donald Graves provides a detailed account and analysis of the fighting in and around St–Lambert and in particular the actions of the SAR in *South Albertas*, 128–76.

65 The detachment came from the Lincoln and Welland Regiment, consisting of C Company plus one platoon from D Company and C Company from the A&SH/C. See the war diaries for the Lincoln and Wellands and A&SH/C entries for 19 August 1944.

66   The Sherbrooke Fusiliers were assigned Pt 259 and reached their objective at 2010 hours that night. The First Hussars were ordered to take over from the SAR in St-Lambert by 2000 hours 20 August. By the morning of 21 August, they were reporting their location as in the general area of Bois-de-Courcy and did not report themselves in position until 0900 hours. At 0745 hours 21 August, the Fort Garry Horse reported themselves on their objective at Pt 258 and reported everything quiet. Ops Log 20 August page 6. War Diary, HQ 2 Cdn Armd Bde, 1–31 August 1944.

67   The 2nd Canadian Armoured Brigade was placed under command of the 4th Canadian Armoured Division at 1300 hours and two regiments were ordered to thicken up the 10th Canadian Infantry Brigade's defences in the Chambois–Trun area. In addition, A Squadron of the 18th Canadian Armoured C Regiment was detached and placed under Kitching's command. While this squadron was under command of Kitching, it came with an assigned mission to recce the area from Trun to Vimoutiers. Kitching was left to deal with the unfolding tactical situation with armour units when what he actually needed was infantry to fill gaps in his lines. War Diary, 4 Cdn Armd Div, 1–31 August 1944, entry 19 August.

68   War Diary, South Alberta Regiment, 1–31 August 1944, entry 21 August.

69   According to the strength returns for the division for August, the 4th Canadian Armoured Brigade lost 65 percent of its majors and above between 1 and 21 August. Fifty-five percent of all division officers who began on 1 August were casualties by 21 August. War Diary, 4 Cdn Armd Div, 1–31 August 1944, strength returns August 1944.

70   George Kitching, *Mud and Green Fields: The Memoirs of Major-General George Kitching* (St. Catharines: Vanwell Publishing, 1992), 205.

18

A History of Lieutenant Jones

Geoffrey Hayes

The first volume of the Official History of the Canadian Army in the Second World War contains *The History of Private Jones*.[1] He was an anonymous soldier whose service offered a glimpse into how the Army selected, trained, treated, and finally discharged Canadians who volunteered for wartime military service. But what do we know about Lieutenant Jones? The Army's official historian, Colonel C.P. Stacey, understood the challenge of finding the army's 46,000 commissioned officers, but he only briefly summarized how they were selected and trained.[2] This chapter draws upon the personnel records of an anonymous young Canadian to consider his selection, training, and brief time in battle as an army reinforcement officer.

In 1945 a British officer defined the "officer quality" as a balance between the "technical equipment to lead" and the "moral equipment to inspire."[3] That army planners and trainers stressed an officer's technical training made sense in a war they anticipated would be won by those with scientific training and expertise. The moral side of the "officer quality" was more difficult to measure. While aging generals and politicians spoke of character, manliness, and a kind of noblesse oblige inspired by memories of the First World War, social scientists struggled to inventory the qualities of leadership. Within these discussions lay assumptions about the kind of leadership these young men were expected to give. As we will see, the case of Lieutenant Jones suggests that idealized notions of middle-class education and appearance offered only limited guidance to the leadership that young Canadians were expected to provide on the battlefields of Northwest Europe.

Lieutenant Jones was born in a small town south of Sherbrooke, Quebec, in late 1921.[4] There is little reason to think that his background and military training were all that different from those of thousands of other young Canadian men. Sickness kept him out of school for two years, but he remained robust enough to list rugby and hockey as his favourite sports. He collected stamps as a hobby. His attestation records tell us that he was an Anglican. When war broke out in September 1939, he was an eighteen-year-old high school student.

Such details mattered among Canadians who looked more to education rather than economic or social status as a way to choose their leaders. Jones was among the first generation that grew up in an era of widespread health, welfare, and educational reforms. Neil Sutherland tells us that Jones's generation worked less and was schooled longer than their parents. His teachers were better qualified to lead a "new" curriculum and his classmates were less likely to be physically punished (either by the school or the state) than were their parents.[5] Physical fitness grew in importance, particularly through team sports, which tested physical strength and taught lessons in teamwork. Still, social class and respectability remained important. Jones's family was not wealthy, but army examiners may have seen his membership in the Church of England as some evidence that Jones was part of an Anglo-Canadian social elite.

We may assume that Jones had at least some basic military training through his high school cadet corps, which remained a fixture across the country between the wars. Mark Moss has argued that such institutions, as well as newspapers, athletic clubs, and youth organizations, helped indoctrinate Ontario schoolboys before the First World War to accept notions of "patriotism, imperialism, manliness, and militarism, which, in effect, served to mirror the concerns of both official and elite culture."[6] No doubt family, school, and church framed Jones's behaviour as well as his world view. But the memory of the First World War was conflicted, and the effects of economic depression helped nurture a more cynical and less deferential generation than before. One Canadian veteran from Niagara Falls recalled how students spread Left-inspired rumours that the head of the high school cadet corps earned a dollar for each student he trained. These sentiments were common. Samuel Hynes believed that his generation of young American men carried an imagined "war-in-their-heads" inspired by the antiwar poetry of the

First World War. Some swore off taking part in any future war. Yet Hynes maintains that a more conservative collective memory won out. "And so," Hynes concluded, "when our war came, we enlisted." So it was in Canada. Three students in Niagara Falls who swore off the cadet corps in 1936 on philosophical grounds all served overseas when war came. Two of them were killed.[7]

In the fall of 1941 Jones began studying chemistry at Bishop's College in Lennoxville, Quebec. His university education certainly distinguished him from his peers. After four months he enrolled as a cadet in the college's Canadian Officer Training Corps (COTC). The first COTC contingents arrived on Canadian campuses in 1912. Their numbers declined after 1918, but they made a comeback in the 1930s, partly because Canada's tiny military establishment believed that an officer with a background in science and technology would help win the next war.[8] Jones seemed an ideal candidate. He attended COTC through the winter of 1942, completing his certification at a camp that summer. His COTC Commanding Officer noted with a touch of caution that "this candidate has not had much experience, but is of very good type, is smart and soldierly, has keenness and enthusiasm, and has displayed qualities of initiative and resourcefulness. I consider that he will develop rapidly with further training."[9]

Having set all of this against Jones's intelligence and classification test scores, an army examiner had every reason to be impressed when he interviewed the young man in July 1942 for service in the Active Army. Jones looked and acted like a young officer. He was then 6 feet, 1 inch, 168 pounds, well built, good-looking, and well educated. The examiner observed that Jones "has a very good personality, good approach and very serious manners." Jones was motivated, for he "hates to leave the College, but believes that now is the time to join and do his duty." The examiner detected some uncertainty, but also some naïve self-confidence: "[Jones] feels that he has not had much chance to test his leadership, but the few times that he was in charge of a Platoon at College, showed him that he could lead men anywhere." The examiner concluded: "Candidate seems very dependable, is very assured in his speech. His scores are high, schooling high. Leadership and background, good. Stability high. Candidate is *recommended* as officer material."[10]

In January 1943 Jones joined the Active Army with the rank of private. That was consistent with a policy laid down in late 1940 that a soldier had to first serve as an enlisted soldier before he could rise to commissioned rank. This was a nod to more democratic practice, but officials still considered time drilling with the COTC the equivalent of enlisted service. The next day Jones was promoted to the rank of acting sergeant.

The training regime Jones entered had changed dramatically when two officer training centres opened in the spring of 1941: one in Brockville, Ontario, the other in Gordon Head, British Columbia. Some regimental councils were suspicious of centralized officer selection and training. Experienced senior officers had long cast their "magic eye" on their potential officers, judging them by their appearance, attitude, and personal qualities.[11] The select few then often found themselves learning drill in a local armoury under the watchful gaze of a senior NCO.[12] The need for more wartime officers meant an end to regimental officer training, but Jones's case shows that the army had worked out a compromise with some militia units. Jones's name on the 35th officer training quota at Gordon Head showed that he had already been selected as a potential reinforcement officer for Montreal's Royal Highland Regiment of Canada (the Black Watch).

Jones spent twelve weeks training at Gordon Head through the winter of 1943. Four weeks were devoted to subjects common to all arms, then six focused on elementary subjects special to the infantry. A final two-week course in platoon tactics ensured that every officer could take over an area defensive scheme.[13] Physical fitness was important. All candidates at Gordon Head remembered the run from camp to Mount Tolmie and back. It appears that staffs, in the early going at least, emphasized the mechanical rather than the moral training of an officer. Of 180 training periods outlined in a 1941 syllabus, 20 each were devoted to drill, marching, and map reading. Field engineering took up 15 periods, while 12 periods each were given over to organization and administration, mechanical transport (cadets learned how to ride a motorcycle and drive a Bren gun carrier), protection against gas, and rifle training. Just four periods were devoted to leadership and morale.[14]

Certainly the officer training syllabus in Canada evolved constantly, so that by 1943 officer cadets spent a great deal more time in the field than on the parade square. Exercises continued regardless of weather.[15] These innovations most certainly reached Gordon Head by early 1943. Yet as much as Jones led fellow cadets on the parade square or in various schemes, there is little evidence that he had any chance during his training to lead real troops.

Yet when each class stood to graduate, the senior officers and politicians who addressed them spoke only of the importance of their moral qualities. General Victor Odlum nostalgically evoked the deep bonds between officers and men in the First World War when he told a class of officer cadets overseas in the spring of 1941:

> When I look for officers I look for three things—Character, Intelligence and Spirit. The most brilliant student without any of these qualifications is of no use. We want leaders: we have very good men at the top, but we want men amongst the rank and file to take the initiative and show the men what to do. Don't forget your men's lives are just as valuable as your own. Take an interest in their affairs and troubles—show your men that you are capable of looking after men and then you will get their loyalty. You have been promoted as some think that you are above the average. I hope you will be worthy of the Canada who has put us all here, true to the Canadian Corps and to your men.

Odlum noted, "You can not live too close to your men. Know them, know their families, know their troubles. You will have won only when they come [to you] if things are wrong before they go to their padres. You will have lost if they do not."[16]

Defence Minister J.L. Ralston offered similar advice in the fall of 1942:

> Set yourself to learn immediately the names of the men, where they come from and a little something at least of their background, what they did before they came into the Army; what their fathers did; something about their families and something about their ambitions. [Learning their names] will make you more human. It will help you get the best out of them. [A platoon commander is more than just] a commander of men ... He is a guide, counselor and friend as well ... A man who has to keep aloof from his men to maintain his prestive [sic] isn't the kind of stuff to make a good Canadian officer. They [the soldiers] don't want to be babied, but they have a right to expect your constant and vigilant interest in their welfare.[17]

All of this must have seemed rather abstract for young officers with no soldiers to train.

In April 1943 the Commandant of OTC Gordon Head noted of Jones: "This candidate is a hard worker, possessing initiative and good leadership qualities. Displayed fair instructional ability and a very fair general military knowledge. Will make a good offr, either in the fd [field] or in an Administrative capacity."[18] Provisional Second Lieutenant Jones was then off to the Canadian (Advanced) Infantry Training Centre in Farnham, Quebec, where instructional duties may have provided some chance to handle troops. In May 1943, Jones's commandant at Farnham observed: "Knowledge well applied. Serious, hard worker, with more practical experience should make a good officer." Jones became a full lieutenant in July 1943. Armed with his daily ration allowance of 50 cents, he took two weeks' leave and was married. In November 1943, Jones took a refresher course in Brockville, where he also spent six days in the Brockville Military Hospital with influenza.

Lieutenant Jones arrived in the United Kingdom in February 1944 to join the thousands of officer reinforcements waiting to join their units. For the next six months he spent much of his time attached to the 4th Canadian Infantry Reinforcement Unit, where he took more courses in gas, the use of wireless, and driving. He also continued as an instructor. By any standard then set by the Canadian Army, Lieutenant Jones was a well-trained reinforcement army officer.

Lieutenant Jones arrived in France on 6 September 1944. He was just weeks from joining the Black Watch, which, together with the Régiment de Maisonneuve and the Calgary Highlanders, formed the infantry component of the 5th Brigade of the 2nd Canadian Infantry Division. Since arriving in Normandy in the first week of July 1944, the brigade had faced terrible fighting in the battles south of Caen. Between 19 and 24 July, the Black Watch lost two of its four rifle company commanders, one dead; and eight platoon commanders, three killed and five wounded.[19] Then came Phase II of Operation Spring. On the morning of 25 July 1944 the Black Watch lost 121 killed, 119 wounded, and 82 taken prisoner on Verrières Ridge south of Caen. With another 14 officer casualties the battalion had lost 63 percent of its officer establishment in less than two weeks of fighting. These losses included two commanding officers: Lieutenant-Colonel S.S.T. Cantlie and his immediate replacement, Major E.P. Griffin, both died in the battle for Verrières Ridge.[20]

The reality of battle was far worse than the estimates. The British Army had anticipated that infantry formations would lose just 24 percent of their officers and 19 percent of their other ranks in thirty days of operations. In June 1944 British infantry battalions lost 61 percent of their officers and 55 percent of their other ranks. The respective loss rates dropped slightly between July and September 1944, to 55 percent for officers and 47 percent for other ranks, but such casualties reinforced how the British Army had underestimated the disproportionate roles played (and the casualties suffered) by both the infantry and the armoured corps.[21]

First Canadian Army faced an even heavier proportionate burden. Between 6 June and 1 October 1944, Canada's two infantry divisions committed to Normandy suffered the highest casualties of any divisions in 21 Army Group.[22] Colonel Stacey long ago cited these figures to reinforce the notion that First Canadian Army (particularly its battlefield officers) did not measure up to the demands of the Normandy battlefield. But Terry Copp argues that such losses point instead to the higher number of days that the Canadians saw intense combat. Each of seven British divisions each experienced an average of nearly eighteen days of intense combat between D-Day and 30 September 1944. Through that time the two Canadian infantry divisions each endured over thirty days of intense combat.[23]

Such figures strengthen Copp's observation that the Allied armies placed an "enormous burden" on their junior officers, who "were expected, indeed required, to lead from the front."[24] Lieutenant-General Guy Simonds conceded that the problem of battle exhaustion within his 2nd Canadian Corps during August 1944 was partly due to "a high proportion of reinforcement officers, short of regimental experience and with very little opportunity to get to know their men before they are actively engaged with the enemy."[25] Simonds offered no solutions to the problem. Lieutenant Joe Nixon graduated from McGill's COTC contingent and, like Lieutenant Jones, was chosen to be a Black Watch officer cadet. Nixon found the battalion widely dispersed in August 1944, giving him little chance to review the events of July 1944, except at an occasional Orders Group. The new commanding officer, Major Frank Mitchell, who was busy rebuilding the battalion, advised Nixon to learn from an experienced NCO. In Sergeant Barney Benson, Nixon found a mentor, and they worked "closely together" until Benson, all of twenty-four years of age, was killed on 9 September 1944 outside of Dunkirk.[26]

The strategic realities that arose through the fall of 1944 gave the soldiers of First Canadian Army little respite. On 17 September 1944, American and British formations launched Operation Market Garden to drive a salient into the eastern Netherlands and force a crossing over the Rhine at Arnhem. This left First Canadian Army, "Cinderella on the Left," with a difficult set of tasks. First, it had to wrest the French Channel ports from stubborn German garrisons. Then as Market Garden faltered and the operation continued to draw on vital resources into October, the Canadians faced the imposing job of opening the Scheldt Estuary, which joined the vital port of Antwerp to the North Sea.

Neither personnel files nor war diaries offer a clear picture of Lieutenant Jones after he joined the Black Watch on 28 September 1944. We do not know to what company and platoon he was assigned. A year earlier Jones may have read some tips to new Canadian officers that stressed appearances, obedience, and initiative. A note in the *Canadian Army Training Memorandum* warned against buying cheap clothing and boots and advised that officers know how to wear their new uniforms properly. It further stressed that "THE FIRST DUTY OF A SOLDIER IS TO OBEY ORDERS." Without orders or instructions, one was to do what one's commanding officer would do. Following the lead of another officer was further counselled. This advice was repeated for emphasis: "Don't talk too much. Keep your eyes and ears open and your mouth shut."[27]

The advice made only partial sense in October 1944. The new commanding officer of the Black Watch, Lieutenant-Colonel Bruce Ritchie, replaced Frank Mitchell in late September after a failed attack over the Albert Canal north of Antwerp. Ritchie was likely too preoccupied to offer much advice to Lieutenant Jones. Lieutenant Nixon had done well learning from experienced sergeants, but seasoned officers like Captain John Orr of the carrier platoon, or B Company commander Major Robert Slater were also good men to watch closely. Perhaps a platoon of tired veterans and nervous newcomers told their new lieutenant to forget all previous counsel and look as little like an officer as possible.

Everyone realized that the relationship between officers and men had a notable impact on morale, but British reports pointed to army officers with little experience in or willingness to improve what was then known as "man management." Cross-posting officers weakened a unit's esprit des corps, while soldiers resented their officers' privileges and felt that officers did not show enough interest in their welfare.[28] Canadian troops may have held similar complaints, though anecdotes hint that Canadian regimental officers may have done a better job than their British opposites at bridging the divide that rank imposed.[29]

On the other hand, British medical studies from the time conceded that the reinforcement officer faced a difficult psychological challenge. His was a "dual" problem: his "emotional organization" was divided

> between self-preservation on the one hand and responsibility on the other. [The officer faced] quasi-abstract considerations as organising a party of men for action, keeping up their courage and sense of urgency, and other imponderable cognitive and emotional aspects of leadership. These latter demands are what put a particular strain on the officer; for he is obliged to maintain high-level awareness on a multitude of issues. [The private soldier could] react on a more primitive level, showing at such a level a primitive awareness of danger and opportunity for offensiveness. To the soldier his supports are his pals, whose example of endurance alongside him is a spur and a comfort. The officer must often rise above this.[30]

Clearly, there was much to learn.

Just days after Lieutenant Jones joined the Black Watch, on the morning of 1 October 1944, Lieutenant-Colonel Ritchie led an assault towards the village of Brecht. The unit war diarist boasted of the results:

> The ground over which the attack went in had been carefully recced [sic] the previous evening, and everyone was fully aware at all times of the plan, the objectives, and what the flanks were doing. The success of the attack had been assured in advance by the unit having had plenty of time to plan and execute a careful attack. The enemy put up determined resistance in the town, but the artillery and mortars had a terrific effect on him even before we went in.[31]

The war diarist had reason to brag, for even if the unit's performance has not impressed all historians, careful preparation, coordination, and plenty of fire power worked well for the Canadians. The next day, 2 October 1944, the acting army commander Guy Simonds ordered First Canadian Army to clear the Scheldt Estuary. The 3rd Division was to attack "Scheldt Fortress South" along the estuary's southern banks west of Antwerp; the 2nd Division was to continue north of Antwerp to seal off the "eastern end of the Zuid [South] Beveland Isthmus."[32]

In the next days, Ritchie ordered a series of patrols to remain in contact with the enemy. Canadian officers who were later questioned about such things felt they were good at patrolling, but only if they explained their purpose to their men. Night operations of the kind Ritchie ordered were especially difficult, for almost three-quarters of officers interviewed observed that they had never trained for night patrols.[33]

Against these demands the battlefield began to prey on the unit's morale. At a brigade meeting on 2 October, Ritchie took the unusual step of raising issues about "training, morale, tactics and the reinforcement situation." He pointed out "how many men there were who had not been trained for the jobs they were called upon to do in an Infantry Battalion." Perhaps this was just griping. Everyone knew that a crisis over conscription was then brewing in Ottawa. Two days later the Black Watch war diarist noted that the added threat of German artillery, mortar, and sniper fire was "nerve-racking" and was "beginning to tell on some of the men. Each day sees the strength of each company being gradually whittled down." Ritchie took quick action. The next day, the paymaster arrived and a movie was screened "to a packed house." Both brought "a most welcome relief … To know that there is no possibility of a visitor in field-gray edging in to share one's slit trench during the hours of darkness is more conducive to easy slumber than any sedative yet concocted."[34] A sense of humour helped.

By 7 October 1944, Canadian intelligence reports were predicting that German forces would not defend the islands along the northern shore of the Scheldt that the 2nd Division was then fighting to reach. That same day, General Gustav-Adolf Von Zangen declared to his Fifteenth German Army that "the defence of the approaches to Antwerp represents a task which is decisive for the further conduct of the war."[35] The Black Watch's battle for the Dutch village of Hoogerheide on 8 October recorded the first contact with "Battle Group Chill," whose orders were to stop the Allies from reaching South Beveland Island to the west. It was a difficult day. Despite support from armour, artillery, and heavy mortars, a company of the Black Watch had to fight for its start line against "an enemy [that] was well dug in, in well sited positions, and supported by artillery, mortar, heavy m.g. [machine guns], and scores of snipers." A German counterattack that came down Hoogerheide's main street early in the evening was fought off with the help of the carrier platoon: "heavy fighting ensued and it was over two hours before the enemy decided that he had had enough. We lost no ground, and accounted for many Germans in the engagement." The Canadians knew how to deal with German counterattacks, but they still held a begrudging respect for their opponents. "The troops we are now meeting are very definitely the cream of the crop. The[y] belong to the paratroop bns. [battalions], with a sprinkling of glider troops and Luftwaffe personel [sic]. They range in age from 20 to 26 years, are fine physical specimens, keen to fight and with excellent morale."[36]

Heavy German artillery, mortar, and sniper fire anticipated another counterattack into Hoogerheide, which the Canadians broke up late on the afternoon of 9 October. "For a while things were again very sticky, but once again this attack was repulsed without the loss of any ground. There has been very close co-operation today between the artillery and our forward companies, and our guns have been firing continually upon targets directed by the companies." At a brigade O Group later that evening, the acting II Corps Commander Major-General Charles Foulkes, urged an attack, but then changed his mind when Brigadier W.J. Megill, commander of the 5th Brigade, explained "the amount of opposition concentrated on this front."[37]

Lieutenant-Colonel Ritchie then returned to his battalion headquarters, a schoolhouse in Hoogerheide, to brief his company commanders. The war diarist noted that "on his way back to tell his Carrier Platoon after the meeting, Capt. [John Ethelbert] Orr, one of the most courageous officers this unit has ever known, was killed by a sniper's bullet, no more than thirty yards from B.H.Q. [Battalion Headquarters]."[38] The next day, the war diary observed that B Company commander Major Robert Gordon Slater had gone missing. A series of searches failed to find him. Rumours ran through the unit that he had been killed by a mortar blast.[39]

War diaries routinely mention specific officers, but losing senior and well-respected ones so suddenly seems to have rattled the war diarist. He listed eighty-one Black Watch casualties in the battle for Hoogerheide, which nearly equalled the strength of one of its four rifle companies. At noon on 10 October the battalion pulled out of the village for a brief respite. "The men had their first full night's sleep in four nights and felt, and looked much better for it. The constant wakefulness had sapped quite a bit of their strength, in addition to the strenuous fighting they had been doing."[40] Earlier in the year the army had commented on the effects of fatigue, especially on officers. They were "encouraged to learn to snatch short periods of sleep during the day whenever possible in order that they may visit posts during the night without gross fatigue."[41] It was good advice, but difficult to follow.

On the morning of Friday, 13 October 1944, the Black Watch led off during the opening phases of Operation Angus. The objective was a dyke embankment to the northwest of the village of Woensdrecht that swung west towards the South Beveland peninsula. It could only be reached across several hundred metres of open, sodden fields. The Black Watch took the lead under the gunfire of three artillery regiments, smoke, mortars, flamethrowers, anti-tank guns, and attacks from fighter-bombers. Despite repeated efforts, the four rifle companies could not hold their objective. The fighting cost the battalion 145 casualties: 56 were killed or died of wounds; a further 27 became prisoners of war. "Black Friday" was the second worst day the battalion suffered during its ten months in Northwest Europe.[42]

Lieutenant Jones's war ended at Woensdrecht. A medical report dated 13 October 1944 noted that his unit "got into heavy action and had to withdraw ... losing a no. [number] of men. He himself momentarily stunned by a mortar blast and when he returned to H.Q. he was badly shaken up." His commanding officer noted that "this man has lost confidence in his ability to lead his men, and as a result can not carry on with his duties. This officer is quite shaken." Jones reportedly sought out his commanding officer and "told him how he felt about the situation."[43]

Had Lieutenant Jones been a subaltern during the First World War, his diagnosis might have been very different. Many still consider Lord Moran's 1945 volume, *The Anatomy of Courage*, a classic for the way its author compared courage to a bank account upon which individuals could draw only so much. But the work draws heavily from Moran's experiences as a battalion medical officer during the First World War. In Moran's view, one's social class, breeding, and masculine demeanour anticipated one's ability to withstand the stress of battle. The author described with a weary arrogance two officers who had broken down. They "went about wearing labels for all to read ... They had about them the marks known to our calling of the incomplete man, the stamp of degeneracy. The whole miserable issue could have been foretold, the man was certain to crack when the strain came." One reinforcement officer's "large irregular features" signalled his imminent collapse. A company commander removed another "plainly worthless" officer during the latter's second day in the trenches: "He showed none of the extreme signs of fear, he was just a worthless chap, without shame, the worst product of the towns."[44]

A medical report dated 17 October 1944 said nothing of Lieutenant Jones's upbringing or the shape of his head. Instead, divisional psychiatrists observed that Jones was "aggrieved & disgruntled, critical of his immediate superiors & of general policy, labours under a felt injustice ... The officer's aggressive criticism is partly a rationalisation for his own sense of fear & inferiority."[45] These comments were consistent with contemporary studies which posited that officers broke down because of a feeling that they could not exercise their responsibility.[46]

As Terry Copp and Bill McAndrew concluded in their study of battle exhaustion, "There was no psychological breathalyzer or litmus test that accurately predicted which individuals might withstand the stress of battle and for how long."[47] The same was true at the unit level. At the end of the Normandy campaign the units of the 2nd Division showed no clear correlations among casualties, exhaustion figures, and a battalion's performance.[48]

Lieutenant Jones's record is thus difficult to characterize. Inexperience, fatigue, and the bewilderment of first command likely played a role here. Jones was also unlucky to join his regiment during a week of sustained operations, which climaxed in a battle that caused terrible casualties for little gain. By the measures of the time, however, he had been disobedient, possibly insubordinate. A psychiatrist observed that "[Jones] is unlikely to give satisfactory service under the stress of battle conditions." He recommended that Jones be evacuated to England where a medical board decided to send him home to Canada. In the meantime, he was treated for "psychoneurosis anxiety state" at 23 Canadian General Hospital, Leavesden, Watford, UK. This likely meant a stint of rest, therapy, and exercise to help him regain his confidence. When he sailed for Canada on 30 December 1944, he was not alone: a partial list of fifty officers on board shows that Jones and twenty-three others shared some form of the diagnosis, "psychoneurosis anxiety state."[49]

To his credit, Lieutenant Jones did not leave the army once he returned to Canada in January 1945. The following month he was gaining high marks for his instruction at an Infantry Corps Training Centre. Not until 23 August 1946 was he struck off strength of the Canadian Army Active Force in Montreal, Quebec, returning to reserve status under the King's Regulations for Canada.

The search for leadership continues to evolve, even though current attempts to measure a Canadian officer's "cultural" or "emotional" intelligence resemble the moral qualities that aging generals and politicians spoke of over seventy years ago.[50] Such concepts are difficult to measure. Wartime army planners tried to assess Lieutenant Jones's "moral equipment" through his church and sporting background, as well as his "very good personality, good approach and very serious manners." Examiners saw Jones as the "right type," someone who was intelligent, "keen" and "enthusiastic," able to make up for his lack of military experience by his own initiative. The wartime army found it easier to gauge Lieutenant Jones's "technical" aptitude by his high school and university education, as well as by his time in the cadet corps and the COTC. In many ways, Lieutenant Jones stood up well against a vision of the English-Canadian middle-class male.

Unfortunately, the battlefields that Lieutenant Jones faced in October 1944 were far more dangerous and difficult places than anyone had anticipated. Casualty rates that were three times heavier than expected placed an enormous weight on young men to demonstrate leadership. Army officials hoped that reinforcement officers could ease into the routine to better acquaint themselves with their men and conditions. But Jones was unlucky, for this was not possible in the first half of October 1944. In the event, a young infantry lieutenant could watch, learn, keep his mouth shut, and hope to do what he was expected to do. But the nearly constant fighting against a determined enemy took its toll. An earlier generation might well have judged Lieutenant Jones's behaviour at Woensdrecht more harshly, but the psychiatrists who treated him understood that a soldier's reactions in battle were difficult to predict. That he was not alone offered, perhaps, some solace to a young man whose background and training gave him little chance to prepare for the harsh realities he faced on the battlefields of Northwest Europe.

Notes

1. C.P. Stacey, *Six Years of War: The Army in Canada, Britain, and the Pacific* (Ottawa: E. Cloutier, Queen's Printer, 1957), 141-44.
2. Ibid., 127-32, 138-41.
3. Emanuel Miller, "Psychiatric Casualties Among Officers and Men from Normandy," *The Lancet* 245, no.6343 (n.d.), 364.
4. For reasons of privacy, I do not refer to Lieutenant Jones's real name. Quotes from his service record, which is in the author's possession, are cited as "Military Service Record, Lieutenant Jones."
5. Neil Sutherland, *Children in English-Canadian Society: Framing the Twentieth-Century Consensus* (Toronto: University of Toronto Press, 1978; Waterloo: Wilfrid Laurier University Press, 2000), 239-41.
6. Mark Moss, *Manliness and Militarism: Educating Young Boys in Ontario for War* (Don Mills: Oxford University Press, 2001), 9.
7. Samuel Hynes, *The Soldiers' Tale: Bearing Witness to Modern War* (New York: Penguin, 1997), 108-10; undated, unpublished manuscript of James Fletcher Swayze, in the possession of the author.
8. Stephen John Harris, *Canadian Brass: The Growth of the Canadian Military Profession 1860-1919* (Durham: Duke University Press, 1985), 208; John A. English, *The Canadian Army and the Normandy Campaign: A Study of Failure in High Command* (New York: Praeger, 1991), 46.
9. "Military Service Record, Lieutenant Jones."
10. Ibid.
11. See G. Hayes, "Science and the Magic Eye: Innovations in the Selection of Canadian Army officers, 1939-1945," *Armed Forces and Society* 22, no.2 (Winter 1995-96), 275-95.
12. On localized officer training, see Kim Beattie, *Dileas: History of the 48th Highlanders of Canada 1929-1956* (Toronto: 48th Highlanders of Canada, 1957).
13. Stacey, *Six Years of War*, 138.
14. Officer Training Centre (OTC), Brockville, "Block Standard Syllabus," April 1941, Library and Archives Canada [LAC], Record Group [RG] 24, vol.16,934.
15. See, for example, OTC, Brockville, May/June 1942, LAC, RG 24, vols. 16,935-36.
16. "Address by General Victor Odlum," 11 April 1941, Officer Cadet Training Unit, OCTU, Canadian OCTU overseas. Bordon Camp, Hants, LAC, RG 24, vol. 16,852.
17. "Minister Ralston's address to the OTC Graduating Class, Brockville, 7 November 1942," LAC, RG 24, 16,936, folder 7, vol. 21, 8-9.
18. "Military Service Record, Lieutenant Jones."
19. Terry Copp, *The Brigade: The Fifth Canadian Infantry Brigade in World War II* (Stoney Creek: Fortress Publications, 1992), 59.
20. Terry Copp and Bill McAndrew, *Battle Exhaustion: Soldiers and Psychiatrists in the Canadian Army, 1939-1945* (Montreal and Kingston: McGill-Queen's University Press, 1990), 126.

21 H.G. Gee, *Battle Wastage Rates, British Army, 1940–45*, Military Operational Research Series 2 (Waterloo: Laurier Centre for Military Strategic and Disarmament Studies, 2010), 8, 14–15. The officer loss rates are 2.54 times higher than estimated. The loss rates for other ranks are 2.89 times higher than the estimates.
22 C.P. Stacey, *The Victory Campaign: The Operations in North-West Europe, 1944–1945* (Ottawa: Queen's Printer, 1960), 271.
23 Terry Copp, "To the Last Canadian? Casualties in 21 Army Group," *Canadian Military History* 18, no.1 (Winter 2009), 8. Averages are calculated from Table 1.
24 Copp, *The Brigade*, 59.
25 Simonds Directive, 29 August 1944, cited in Copp and McAndrew, *Battle Exhaustion*, 134.
26 Copp, *The Brigade*, 91. Sergeant Bernard F. Arnold Benson of Montreal was killed on 9 September 1944. He is buried in Calais cemetery.
27 *Canadian Army Training Memorandum* (CATM), 24 March 1943, 10.
28 See Jeremy Crang, "The British Soldier on the Home Front: Army Morale Reports, 1940–45," in Paul Addison and Angus Calder, eds., *Time to Kill: The Soldier's Experience of War in the West* (London: Pimlico, 1997), 65–68.
29 Lieutenant J.F. Wallace recalled speaking with two British soldiers in Sicily. "When we told them that we were Lieutenants they pretty nearly passed out over our entirely casual way in which we engaged them in conversation." Lieutenant J.F. Wallace, MC, "A Diary of the Sicilian Campaign (1943)," n.d., 28, LAC, Manuscript Group (MG) 30, E 211.
30 Miller, "Psychiatric Casualties," 364.
31 "War Diary, Royal Highland Regiment of Canada (Black Watch)," n.d., 1 October 1944, http://victorian.fortunecity.com/finsbury/764/oct_44.htm.
32 Cited in Copp, *The Brigade*, 133.
33 Robert Engen, *Canadians Under Fire: Infantry Effectiveness in the Second World War* (Montreal and Kingston: McGill–Queen's University Press, 2009), 115, 120.
34 "War Diary, Royal Highland Regiment of Canada (Black Watch)," 2, 4, 5 October 1944.
35 Cited in Copp, *The Brigade*, 138.
36 "War Diary, Royal Highland Regiment of Canada (Black Watch)," 8, 9 October 1944.
37 Ibid., 9 October 1944.
38 Ibid.
39 Ibid. Major Slater was thirty-two years old and from Toronto. His date of death is recorded as 19 October 1944. He is buried in Bergen op Zoom Canadian War Cemetery.
40 "War Diary, Royal Highland Regiment of Canada (Black Watch)," 9, 10 October 1944.
41 Cited in Copp and McAndrew, *Battle Exhaustion*, 109–10.
42 Copp, *The Brigade*, 149.
43 "Military Service Record, Lieutenant Jones."
44 Lord Moran, *The Anatomy of Courage* (London: Constable and Co. 1945), 20, 21.
45 "Military Service Record, Lieutenant Jones."
46 Miller, "Psychiatric Casualties," 364.
47 Copp and McAndrew, *Battle Exhaustion*, 151.

48 Ibid., 139.
49 "Military Service Record, Lieutenant Jones."
50 See, for example, Kimberly-Anne Ford, Sarah E. Winton, and Karen D. Davis, *Measuring "Cultural Intelligence" and "Emotional intelligence": An Annotative Bibliography* (Canadian Forces Leadership Institute, 2009).

19

A Biography of Major Ronald Edmond Balfour

Michelle Fowler

In 1985 the town of Cleve, Germany, recognized a former enemy soldier with a local award. Major Ronald Balfour was awarded the Johanna Sebus medal in recognition of his efforts to protect artifacts during the Second World War. Forty years earlier, in February and March 1945, the battles of the Rhineland had ravaged Cleve and other towns of the Lower Rhine, such as Goch, Emmerich, Xanten, and Kalkar. Forty-one-year-old Ronald Edmond Balfour found himself at the front lines, attached to the First Canadian Army as a civil affairs specialist. Despite heavy fighting, Balfour worked to ensure that this part of the Lower Rhine kept much of its recorded history, artifacts, and some architecture preserved. Balfour, a man of unorthodox methods, extraordinary brilliance and fierce dedication, typified the ideal officer candidate for civil affairs.

Ronald Edmond Balfour was born in 1904 into a family that served its country when duty called. His father, Lieutenant-Colonel K.R. Balfour, and his brother, Major Kenneth Balfour, served with the Royal Dragoons. He was educated at Eton and King's College Cambridge, where he was awarded double first class honours in history and theology. In 1928 his Master's dissertation explored "Church and State in France under the Third Republic: The Reactions of Clericalism and Anti-Clericalism."[1] That year he became a Fellow of King's and a lecturer.

Balfour combined deep religious faith with a wide intellectual curiosity. While at Cambridge he noted in his diary a list of readings, including an essay written on W.H. Mallock's "The New Republic" and the G.K.

Chesterton lecture "The Superstitions of the Skeptic."² In 1928 he attended a service at a "Temple of Humanity" in Liverpool, a church based on the nineteenth-century secular religion, simply for the experience.³ He was a voracious reader; his personal library compiled during his tenure at King's grew to more than 10,000 volumes. At the outbreak of war his greatest fear was that it would be destroyed.⁴

Ronald Balfour joined the French desk at the Ministry of Information in 1939. This proved wearisome, so he enlisted in the British Army the following year and was soon commissioned and sent to Yorkshire to interview recruits.⁵ Balfour was in

Ronald Balfour as a student at Eton College, near Windsor, in England.

his mid-thirties when the war broke out, but he was eager to serve across the Channel, and a university friend provided that opportunity. Geoffrey Webb, who headed the Monuments, Fine Arts, and Archives (MFAA) at Supreme Headquarters Allied Expeditionary Force (SHAEF), offered Balfour a chance to serve as one of the "Monuments Men."

Supreme Commander Dwight D. Eisenhower best articulated the mission of the Monuments Men when he declared: "Historical monuments and cultural centers will come across our path that symbolize to the world all we are fighting to preserve. It is our responsibility to respect and protect these symbols whenever possible."⁶ Ronald Balfour served on a staff of thirty officers of different nationalities with backgrounds in history, architecture, art history, archaeology, and sculpture. Their responsibility was to protect monuments, works of art, repositories, buildings, and archives of historical significance from unnecessary damage in enemy territory. They were also to make temporary repairs to damaged monuments, safeguard monuments from misuse by Allied troops, record all theft of works of art by the enemy, and collect evidence to help in their recovery.⁷

The most recent scholarship does not paint a particularly flattering picture of the Monuments Men. Historian Nicola Lambourne argues that a significant gap divides the words of governments and the work done to protect artifacts.[8] Lambourne correctly notes that the MFAA was understaffed, underfunded, and underprioritized.[9] But Lambourne's argument that the division emphasized protection as a propaganda tool does not properly situate its role in the context of the greater war effort. The war needed to be won, and then humanitarian assistance had to be undertaken, before the MFAA received enough resources to do its work.[10]

Ronald Balfour and the other MFAA officers understood their responsibilities and took their duties extremely seriously. Balfour well appreciated that the Allies should not abstain from bombing certain places, and he put his trust in the decisions of his commanders. But Balfour also knew the value of art, monuments, and archival resources to the cultural integrity and morale of all European nations. In an undated draft lecture presumably delivered before June 1944, he spoke to an audience of soldiers about the value of the historic buildings in which they might soon be billeted.[11] He cautioned them not to carve their names into buildings nor, referencing incidents in North Africa, to drive a tank into a Roman ruin.[12] Balfour's sense of preservation encompassed things of great historical significance to both enemy and ally. He eloquently explained: "No age lives entirely alone; every civilization is formed not merely by its own achievements but by what it has inherited from the past. If these things are destroyed, we have lost a part of our past, and we shall be the poorer for it." He assessed the importance of preserving all of the continent's past. "Even if they [monuments] do belong to Germany, they don't belong to Germany alone— they belong to all of us."[13]

Major Ronald Balfour, King's Royal Rifle Corps.

Balfour arrived in France in August 1944, where crowded roads, no transport, and destroyed bridges delayed his detachment to First Canadian Army.[14] The Anglo-American armies worked closely in civil affairs. Assignments given to civil affairs officers depended on the particular needs of a unit or formation, as determined by SHAEF, not nationality. It was not unusual to find British officers in Canadian units and vice versa. Balfour finally found "his Canadians" on 9 September and issued his first report from Rouen to the Senior Civil Affairs Officer (SCAO), First Canadian Army. His meticulous attention to detail and his all-out effort to obtain information from as many sources as possible provide the first hints of his dedication. He carefully surveyed the three types of damage suffered within the city: that resulting from German air bombardment in 1940, from Allied bombardment in 1944, and from the retreating enemy. Balfour met with local historians and archivists to ascertain the history of the damage and the potential locations of repositories. He inspected many buildings, providing much more than an assessment of damage. He considered temporary solutions, tried to liaise with departmental and municipal authorities to prioritize repairs, and outlined any special actions that civil affairs staff needed to take.

Balfour then followed instructions to report to detachments at Ypres and Bruges in Belgium, which had been liberated by the Allies in early September.[15] Ever cognizant of the manpower shortages facing the MFAA, he made the most of his trek into Belgium, reporting also on conditions in Dieppe, Amiens, Abbeville, and Montreuil-sur-Mer. Of utmost concern for Balfour and his Monuments Men was the condition of cathedrals and other medieval buildings in France. Surprisingly, though the centre of Amiens had been razed during the German bombings of 1940, the cathedral was untouched. Unfortunately, Abbeville had suffered great losses from air raids with incendiary bombs in May 1940.[16] Having interviewed inhabitants of Abbeville, Balfour reported with some surprise that German soldiers passing through in more recent months understood that the responsibility for Abbeville's damage fell squarely on the British.[17]

Balfour tried to be fair in his assessments. When asked by Geoffrey Webb to investigate claims that the Germans had damaged First World War memorials in Belgium, Balfour wrote back that most of the cemeteries were in good shape, cared for by locals or by British nationals in hiding. In his formal report to First Canadian Army, Balfour noted how local legend attributed to overzealous Germans the destruction of the French Memorial at Steenstraate in Belgium, which commemorated the first gas attack in the Great War. According to locals, the Germans felt that the Allies had been responsible for the first gas attack and that destroying the French monument vindicated that belief.[18] Balfour provided some reasonable doubt as to the accuracy of local folklore when he noted that the Canadian monument at St-Julien, which commemorated the same event, had not been touched.

On 3 October 1944, Balfour wrote the first of many reports to First Canadian Army complaining that a lack of transport prevented him from doing his job. This was a common concern for all men serving in civil affairs roles. He noted that he had hitchhiked from Rouen to Belgium, wasting precious time. "Problems require personal inspection and discussion; a monuments officer must be mobile and independent."[19] Despite these encumbrances, Balfour continued to interview local architects, asking them to summarize the level of destruction of their hometowns and countries. He painstakingly recorded their observations, as well as his own surveys of damage to all monuments (art, archives, churches, museums, libraries), and in his official reports, he assessed the ease with which they might be restored.

First Canadian Army supplied Balfour with a vehicle in October, but breakdowns continued to impede his efforts to cover ground. A German historian observed that "with some 15000 square miles to patrol, in one of the richest cultural areas of the land, was one lonely officer with no transportation."[20] Historian Leslie Poste estimates that there were "two and a half Monuments Fine Arts and Archives officers, [who] averaged 125 sites and 60 towns per man per month."[21] The vast distances were too much to cover. In late autumn of 1944, Balfour suggested that there was enough "work to justify the appointment of a second Monuments, Fine, Arts and Archives officer attached to Headquarters Line of Communications (HQ L of C) who can devote himself to Belgium."[22]

Many civil affairs officers believed that Belgium posed a unique problem. Balfour concurred, observing that "materially Belgium appears to have suffered very little from the war. It is doubtful whether the people fully realize that the rapidity of the Allied advance spared them the horrors of being fought over, but they are inclined to exaggerate the amount of destruction caused by Allied bombing earlier in the year ... The statement that towns are a third or half damaged is wildly exaggerated, but people are still apt to refer to a town which has lost a few dozen houses as having suffered horribly."²³ Balfour and others strongly suggested to SHAEF that the scale of war damage and restrictions in England be conveyed to give some perspective to the people of Belgium.

For Balfour, Hoogstraeten, a village north of Antwerp, represented one small and bittersweet victory. On hearing that Belgian authorities were anxious to protect the Church of Ste-Catherine at Hoogstraeten, Balfour immediately notified the SCAO. By all accounts, the Allies heeded his advice, and commanders strongly suggested that this Belgian monument not be targeted with direct fire, even though the Germans were using it as an observation post.²⁴ On 23 October 1944, the Germans destroyed the tower and the Hoogstraeten city hall.²⁵ The heartbreak of the architectural loss only meant more work for Balfour. He reported the incident to First Canadian Army Headquarters as well as to the office of Political and Psychological Warfare.²⁶ This diligent officer also made efforts to minimize potential public relations damage to the Allied war effort. Follow-up visits by Balfour to Hoogstraeten in early November 1944 ensured that salvage operations were carried out with the approval of local Belgian authorities.

A traffic accident put Balfour in hospital with a broken ankle in late November 1944. It would be nearly two months before he reported back to First Canadian Army Headquarters. Captain Marvin Ross, a member of the US Marine Corps Reserve and a Monuments Man attached to SHAEF, stated in a memo that Balfour's reports were deeply missed. "It will be good to be receiving your reports again. The OR's are so funny about them. They like yours best and always grin with delight when they get yours to type."²⁷ Balfour was an intellectual powerhouse with a wit to match, and admiration for him ran deep. A frustrated Balfour sought out information about other Monuments Men and their experiences. He made countless attempts to stay apprised of his colleagues' work in Florence and other parts of Italy. He waited patiently, despite consistent promises that the information would be forwarded, but reports rarely arrived. Balfour wrote emphatically in a letter to Marvin Ross, "I don't think anyone at SHAEF quite realizes how cut off we are in the field, and how much we long for information about what is going on elsewhere."²⁸

In January 1945, back with "his Canadians," Balfour attached himself to the 1st British Corps and pursued information on Michelangelo's sculpture,

Madonna and Child, which German radio reported had been taken by German troops from the Church of Notre Dame in Bruges "to safeguard … for Europe."[29] The case sent Balfour on a journey through the province of Zeeland in the Netherlands. His report, dated 24 February 1945, discussed his visit to Walcheren Island and his inspection of monuments at Goes, Middleburg, Flushing, and Veere. At Flushing he made inquiries about the sculpture; it was believed that the Germans had hidden it on a Red Cross ship and transported it through the port at Flushing. His interviews led nowhere, but the sculpture was returned to Bruges after the war.

Denied the simple tools to carry out much of his good work, a frustrated Balfour carried on with his tasks during January and February 1945. Transportation remained difficult to obtain. Those with whom he had worked so closely at Army Headquarters had moved, and their successors "were much more sticky with the rules."[30] He wrote to a British colleague, Squadron Leader J.E. Dixon-Spain: "I've been back a week now but grounded without transport again, doing best to cover the area by getting attachments to each Corps in turn, but difficult to get to smaller and isolated places." He continued his efforts to gain "independent transport before any big advance."[31] Making the most of a difficult situation, he spent a great deal of time reviewing his notes and conducting interviews. He requested that previously unlisted museums and buildings be added to the protected list. And he began to consider the problems that he and other Monuments Men would face in Germany.

Despite the frustration, Balfour's service did not go unnoticed in Britain. His academic achievements were widely known and respected, but as John Clapham, Vice Provost of King's College, suggested, Balfour's "conduct and work in the war brought out all that was best in him."[32] Rumours circulated that Balfour was a possible future Provost at King's.[33]

When First Canadian Army's area of operations grew to include the towns of the Lower Rhine in Germany, Balfour's mood changed considerably. Though exasperated by the extent of looting on German soil by Allied troops, he persevered, doing his best to post warning notices or to safeguard the valuables himself.[34] He thrived on being less than a mile from the front. On 3 March 1945 he wrote to Webb describing his first week in Germany as grand—he finally felt achievement in his work: "[There is] no civil authority to worry about and … quick decisions are one's own responsibility."[35] He joked about the unorthodox way in which he attempted to preserve the archives at Goch. It would make any archivist's "hair stand on end." When a fourteenth-century gate in Goch blocked the advance of heavy tanks, he convinced commanders to demolish a less significant adjacent building instead. The tanks got through, and today Goch retains its ancient gate with its unique stone door. Regarding his makeshift repository at Cleve, Balfour joked: "[It] would not meet with approval in Washington, an upper room of a building occupied by troops and refugees, without any proper protection, and shells intermittently falling in the neighborhood, but it is the only building in town which possesses a roof, doors and windows, and a resident friar, in whose custody I can leave them when I go away."[36] Goch, Cleve, Kranenburg, and Xanten still have their complete medieval records thanks to Balfour's dedication. Goch's town museum is filled with statues, carvings, and other vestments that Balfour salvaged from the ruins of the Rhineland towns.[37]

Just one week after he wrote to Webb, shrapnel from a shell burst killed Major Ronald Balfour. The fourteenth-century Stifts-Kirche in Cleve came under heavy fire on 10 March just as he ran from it with two altarpieces in hand. He died instantly and became one of only a handful of civil affairs officers to be killed in action.

The loss of Ronald Balfour reverberated in almost every community he touched. The multitude of condolence letters directed to his family from colleagues at Cambridge and in the army are an incredible memorial to the man. Sir Ernest Barker, a professor at King's and a colleague, wrote affectionately: "He was not only a scholar of the first order, especially in all matters of the history and thought of France: he was also a lover of beautiful things, and ... a great gentleman."[38] Letters of admiration from his army colleagues and other Monuments Men reaffirmed Balfour's dedication to and passion for his work. A fellow Monuments Man wrote: "It was so like Ronald to be carrying out his duty to the fullest possible extent. He had a real contempt for danger, and no personal considerations would weigh with him beside the responsibility for doing his job."[39] From Webb, his old friend and the head of MFAA: "He had a quality of clear headedness and practical common sense and a knowledge of the army combined with the obvious distinction of his mind that gave him a special position among Monuments officers. Both British and Americans felt that they could talk things over with him."[40]

Not just his colleagues felt the need to honour him. As West Germany began to take shape and rebuild, the once "hostile" towns of the Lower Rhine began to compile a picture of the man to whom they owed their preserved collective history. Newspapers in the small Rhineland cities began to tell the story that German burgomasters and architects had figured out: one British officer serving with First Canadian Army had helped save the recorded history of their towns. This revelation became a matter of public record when, in 1955, the town of Goch dedicated an archives room in their famous fourteenth-century Steintor building to Ronald Balfour. A photograph provided by the Balfour family had an epitaph underneath that read: "To his memory."[41] On 7 February 1955, the *Rheinische Post* ran the story with the headline, "An Opponent—But No Enemy."[42] The article told of how in June 1945 the city of Goch archivist heard that during the battle the previous March, a British officer had hidden archival records in a large circular area of the monastery. On investigation, Goch officials discovered a room filled with archival materials, and three truckloads of records were returned to the city archives.[43]

Balfour's story does not appear to have been widely known outside the Rhineland or the very small circle of veteran Monuments Men. However, the archive did receive several British visitors during the 1950s. In the fall of 1955, after frequent correspondence between the Balfour family and the City of Goch, Ronald's brother Kenneth and his mother visited the newly dedicated archive room as well as Ronald Balfour's grave at the Reichswald Forest War Cemetery. That trip initiated a decades-long relationship between the city of Goch and the Balfour family. Letters held by the city of Goch also reveal that F.S.V. Donnison, the author of the British official history of civil affairs, inquired about visiting the archives. The visit must have made an impression, for amidst the typical official history debriefing on civil affairs activities in Northwest Europe, half a paragraph is dedicated specifically to Ronald Balfour and his work.[44]

The Johanna Sebus medal is named for a young heroine from a small village near Cleve who in the early nineteenth century saved the lives of local villagers when a dam broke, unleashing the Rhine and flooding local towns and villages. Its posthumous awarding to Major Ronald Balfour in 1985 brought a new round of attention to his story. Again the newspapers of the Lower Rhine towns told of his heroic actions. There were eyewitness interviews, and more honours: a local street was named after him, and a plaque was affixed to the fourteenth-century stone gate in Goch that Balfour had saved from destruction. Members of the Balfour family returned to Goch.

Ronald Balfour's dedication and unorthodoxy typified the ideal civil affairs candidate; his frustrations were shared by civil affairs officers across all the specialist fields. Many of the officers who made up the civil affairs branch, like Balfour, spoke several languages; many were older; many were intellectuals, successful academics and businessmen in civilian life. Their careers after the war in higher education, business, and politics reflected the unique capabilities they brought to their civil affairs duties. After the war, Balfour might have become Provost at King's College, Cambridge University. Balfour's dedication in war provides insight into the work of civil affairs officers. Considered a hero in many German towns, Balfour has received little attention in his native Britain or from "his Canadians." His service to preserve the treasures of France, Belgium, and the Netherlands and his death saving the treasures of Germany is a poignant addition to the story of the Allied campaign of liberation in Northwest Europe.

The grave of Major Ronald Balfour, Reichswald Forest War Cemetery, Germany.

Notes

1 King's College Archive Centre, Cambridge [KCACC], Papers of Ronald Edmond Balfour [REB], REB/5/7.
2 KCACC, REB/1/2/8.
3 KCACC, REB/1/2/8.
4 John Clapham, "Ronald Edmond Balfour 1904–1945," *Cambridge Review*, 26 May 1945. Found in REB/6/3.
5 Ibid.

6   Library and Archives Canada [LAC] RG 24, vol.10588, Department of National Defense Memo, "Protected Monuments," dated 26 May 1944.
7   Paul Ayshford Methuen, *Normandy Diary: Being a Record of Survivals and Losses of Historical Monuments in North-Western France, together with those in the Island of Walcheren and in that Part of Belgium Traversed by 21st Army Group in 1944–1945* (London: Robert Hale, 1952), xvi.
8   Nicola Lambourne, *War Damage in Western Europe: The Destruction of Historic Monuments during the Second World War* (Edinburgh: Edinburgh University Press, 2001), 6.
9   Ibid., 123.
10 Leslie I. Poste, *The Development of US Protection of Libraries and Archives in Europe During WWII* (Fort Gordon, GA: US Army Civil Affairs School, 1958), 159.
11 KCACC, REB 3/1/1, "Draft Lecture," undated but believed to be pre-June 1944, 9.
12 Ibid., 19.
13 Ibid., 11.
14 Methuen, *Normandy Diary*, 7.
15 KCACC, REB/3/1/2.
16 KCACC, REB/3/1/2, fortnightly report from Ronald Balfour to SCAO, First Canadian Army, 17 September 1944.
17 Ibid.
18 KCACC, REB/3/1/2, fortnightly report ending 16 September 1944.
19 KCACC, REB/3/1/2, second report from Balfour to SCAO, First Canadian Army, dated 3 October 1944.
20 Opritsa D. Popa, *Bibliophiles and Bibliothieves: The Search for the Hildebrandslied and the Willehalm Codex* (Berlin: 2003), 51.
21 Poste, *The Development*, 159.
22 KCACC, REB 3/1/2.
23 KCACC, REB 3/1/2, fifth report, Period Ending 25 November 1944 from Ronald Balfour to SCAO, First Canadian Army, 26 November 1944.
24 Guido De Werd, *Around the Swan Tower: Address at the Presentation of the Johan Sebus Medal*, http://www.klevischer-verein.de/schwanenturm/1985/balfour_03.htm, accessed 28 April 2010. Also in KCACC, REB 3/1/2, second report from Balfour to SCAO, First Canadian Army, dated 3 October 1944.
25 KCACC, REB 3/1/2, report from Balfour to SCAO, First Canadian Army, Appendix A, dated 2 November 1944.
26 Ibid.
27 KCACC, REB/3/1/4, memo from Captain Marvin Ross at SHAEF to Balfour, dated 6 February 1945.
28 Ibid., memo from Balfour to Captain Marvin Ross, dated 2 February 1945.
29 KCACC, REB 3/1/2 Fourth report from Balfour to SCAO, First Canadian Army, dated 2 November 1944.
30 KCACC, REB 3/1/4, letter dated 17 February 1945 to Geoffrey Webb.

31 KCACC, REB 3/1/4, letter dated 28 January 1945 to Squadron Leader J.E. Dixon-Spain.
32 KCACC, REB/6/2, letter dated 20 March 1945 from John Clapham to Mrs. Balfour.
33 KCACC, REB/3/1/4, letter dated 27 December 1944 from C.S Phillips to Balfour.
34 KCACC, REB/3/1/4, letter dated 3 March 1945 from Balfour to Webb.
35 KCACC, REB/3/1/4, letter dated 3 March 1945, Balfour to Webb.
36 KCACC, REB/3/1/4, letter from Balfour to Webb dated 3 March 1945.
37 KCACC, REB/6/3.
38 KCACC, REB/6/2, letter to Mrs. Balfour from Sir Ernest Barker, 24 March 1945.
39 KCACC, REB/6/2, letter to Mrs. Balfour from Jack W. Goodison, 19 March 1945.
40 KCACC, REB/6/2 letter to Mrs. Balfour from Webb, n.d.
41 Goch City Archives, letter to Stadtdirektor Goch from Kenneth Balfour, 28 August 1954.
42 Goch City Archives, "Ein Gegner—aber kein Feind," *Rheinische Post,* 7 February 1955.
43 Ibid.
44 F.S.V. Donnison, *History of the Second World War: Civil Affairs and Military Government North-West Europe 1944–1946* (London: HMSO, 1961), 212.

20

The Personality of Memory
The Process of Informal Commemoration in Normandy

Matt Symes

"We can't ignore events that cost the lives of young Canadians who were not required to come and who were volunteers that did not return to Canada. I believe it's our responsibility, no, it's even more than a responsibility, it's a duty. We had the chance to be free, to live free, and this is the least we can do to remember them."[1] This reflection by the mayor by Le Mesnil-Patry, Roger Alexandre, is at the heart of the informal commemoration that adorns the seaside settlements and farming hamlets that make up the French coast of Normandy. Between Cherbourg and Le Havre, sites of memory honouring Americans, British, Polish, French, Canadians, and others are everywhere. The commemorative symbols, from streets named after liberating regiments to school playgrounds that feature monuments, form part of daily Norman life. In the absence of an official government effort, memory in the Canadian sector of Normandy has been driven less by the historical record than by key personalities and the relationships they have developed and maintained over time.

Other chapters in this volume have noted that Colonel C.P. Stacey's official history of the Canadian Army in the Second World War faulted the Canadians' performance in Normandy. "The D Day achievement was magnificent," he maintained, though "one may be permitted to inquire whether it is not conceivable that we could have accomplished even more on the 6th of June. Was it really impossible to reach the inland objectives?"[2] Historians like Terry Copp and Marc Milner later questioned Stacey's wider verdict, giving weight to the regimental historians who emphasized the combined efforts of individual courage and enterprise that carried the Canadian regiments towards their D-Day objectives. By the end of the first day, the Queen's Own Rifles had fought all the way to Anisy, about 10 kilometres inland. The North Shore (New Brunswick) Regiment had pushed to Tailleville, where they encountered the German regimental headquarters and the forward defences of the Douvre Radar Station. The overly ambitious plan had been for the North Shores to push to Anguerny on the first day. They had fallen short of this; however, the soldiers from northern New Brunswick had encountered what the rest of the Allied armies faced on D+2 and D+3 and had much to be proud of and much to be remembered for. They had broken through Hitler's Atlantic Wall, had secured the eastern flank of the Canadian advance, and, most significantly, in Tailleville had battled their way through the "strongest secondary position on Juno Beach."[3] The historic battle to end Hitler's control of Europe came at a severe cost. By the time the Allies gained a foothold in Caen on 10 July 1944, neither the North Shores nor the Queen's Own looked much like the regiments that had stormed the beaches in early June. In the process, village names such as Bernières-sur-Mer, Tailleville, Le Mesnil-Patry, and Carpiquet found a permanent place in the lore of the regiments of New Brunswick, Ontario, and Quebec. Yet there remains a discrepancy between both the number of monuments and, more important, the commemorative attention each regiment receives.

The existing literature on war and memory examines national and multinational understandings of constructed memory. From Paul Fussell's now classic *The Great War and Modern Memory* to more recent studies by scholars such as Jay Winter, Michael Kamaan, James Young, and Jonathan Vance, the focus remains fixed on national memory.[4] Vance cuts to the heart of this understanding with one succinct sentence where he argues that memory of the Great War in Canada was produced through "a mythic version of the events ... from a complex mixture of fact, wishful thinking, half truth, and outright invention."[5] The same can be said of memory in general. Kirk Savage shaped his overview of the field around what he views as the three principle questions that studies of memory contend with: "Who guides the process of remembering and to what end? Why do specific commemorative projects take particular forms? How do commemorative practices actually shape social relations and cultural beliefs (rather than simply reflecting them)?"[6] Only on this methodological or theoretical level does the available literature help us understand how memory has been constructed in Normandy, where there are no formal sites of commemoration.

The process of commemoration that followed the Second World War differed greatly from what followed the First World War. The Government of Canada did not embark on a plan of overseas commemoration as it had after the Great War when it erected monuments in honour of the Canadian Expeditionary Force. As Jonathan Vance argues in his chapter in this collection, ridding the world of Nazi persecution was not a task that required justification afterwards. Instead, dates and names were added to the First World War monuments that already dotted the Canadian landscape. The language used to commemorate the fallen was cloaked in the same rhetoric as that of the previous generation, and 11 November came to represent a day to reflect on both world wars. Memorials in honour of the Second World War were progressive in nature, with a look to the positive future, and took root in parks, arenas, and hospitals.[7]

Commemorating the Canadians in Normandy took a different path. Only once the veterans of the Second World War reached their retirement years did the commemorative landscape of Normandy start to develop in earnest. The veterans, part of a generation that had lived through a period of unequalled prosperity, returned to the landing sites and began to cultivate relationships with the citizens of Normandy. Monuments honouring the regiments in Normandy had been raised as early as 1947, but it was for the 40th, 50th, and 60th anniversaries of D-Day that monument construction and commemoration truly began. It is within this complex reality of the postwar era that the memory of Canadian regiments involved in the battle for Normandy emerged in a fickle, informal, and unofficial manner that relied almost solely on a few key personalities.

Between the beaches and Caen there are thirty-seven sites of memory that commemorate one or more of the three regiments of the 8th Canadian Infantry Brigade. There are five monuments—two in Carpiquet, two in Caen, and one at a roundabout in Bretteville-l'Orgueilleuse—that mention all three regiments. Of the remaining thirty-two sites, thirteen commemorate Le Régiment de la Chaudière, twelve the Queen's Own, and seven the North Shores. The numbers alone are misleading.[8]

In 1999, the Canadian Minister of Heritage, Sheila Copps, unveiled the first sanctioned Canadian monument outside of Canada to commemorate an action of the Second World War.[9] It was not until 2003 that the newly constructed Juno Beach Centre in Courseulles-sur-mer became the site of Canada's "official" D-Day commemorations. At the official opening, Prime Minister Jean Chrétien said "The world needed a memorial so that the memory and the story of Canada's military and civilian contributions and efforts during the Second World War would never be forgotten. Until now, there has been no significant Canadian memorial to mark their achievements, anywhere."[10] The previous lack of a Canadian national commemorative presence like the Juno Beach Centre had resulted in a vacuum in the commemoration process; as a result, sites of varying degrees of historical importance led by individuals (both French and Canadian) "competed" to tell their stories of liberation and tragedy. One of the most enduring commemorations is found farther east, where members of the Queen's Own Rifles of Canada stormed the beaches at Bernières-sur-Mer. There five monuments honour the regiment, including a private home where a rich personal collaboration has taken place between a French family and Canadian veterans.

The Queen's Own Rifles House in 1944.

The building's appearance in newsreel footage made it well known to Canadians for many years. But not until 1984, during the 40th anniversary of the D-Day landings, did the Hoffer family learn, through their bilingual son who had conversed with the Queen's Own veterans, of the symbolic importance of a summer home they had owned since 1936. Since that first meeting between the Hoffers and members of the Queen's Own, the house has become an unofficial museum for the Queen's Own Rifles of Canada. On its walls the Hoffer family carefully displays photographs and mementoes that veterans have gratefully donated. The Hoffers also keep a detailed book listing the casualties suffered by the Queen's Own Rifles; another copy is kept in the local church.

The Canadian unit and the French family grew even closer in 1997 when members of the Queen's Own asked the Hoffer family if they would be willing to place a plaque in front of the house to inform people of its significance. The family agreed.[11] Canadian and French citizens worked on the text, which suggests that the house "may well have been the first house on French soil

The Queen's Own Rifle House in 2007.

liberated by seaborne allied forces."[12] The plaque's unveiling had a noticeable impact on how the town now commemorates the events of 6 June 1944. Before 1984 the only ceremony in Bernières centred on a German concrete gun position, where unit plaques are displayed. Since the plaque, the ritual, supported heavily by the Queen's Own Rifles, has migrated along the beach boardwalk to the Hoffers' summer home. Increased visibility coupled with the openness of the Hoffers has made the house a destination for tourists. The house is now featured in Canada's pre-eminent guidebook to Normandy.[13]

The ongoing relationship between the Hoffer family and the Queen's Own demonstrates that the Riflemen are able and willing to make a considerable financial commitment. For generations their ranks have been able to secure private donations to build memorials across Europe, maintain a museum in Toronto, publish a quarterly journal, and support other commemorative projects for both world wars.[14] Other Queen's Own memorial projects planned for the immediate future include the building of three First World War monuments.[15]

The commemorative footprint of the Queen's Own contrasts sharply with that of the North Shore (New Brunswick) Regiment. Unlike the men of Toronto's Queen's Own, the soldiers of the North Shore Regiment made their living in the forests and fields and on the waters of northern New Brunswick.[16] The regiment's history dates to the 1870s, but unlike the Queen's Own Rifles, its name did not survive much past the Second World War.[17] The only semblance of a regimental museum is in the basement of an avid militaria collector in Miramichi, New Brunswick. The regimental association organizes reunions and local ceremonies. The Honorary Colonel has financed trips to Normandy for North Shore veterans, but the organization has done little else to develop commemorations overseas of the kind found at Bernières-sur-Mer.[18]

The Hoffer residence, often referred to as the Queen's Own House, provides a striking contrast to the first house liberated by the North Shore (New Brunswick) Regiment between Bernières-sur-Mer and St-Aubin-sur-Mer. It too still stands near the coast, but there is no way to know that the house is anything more than a summer residence. There are no plaques, nor is there any mention whatsoever that this house has special meaning, and for those reasons it does not feature in any battlefield guidebook. Yet this house is visible in what is now the iconic film footage of the D-Day landings. As Marc Milner relates, historians and veterans have long misidentified both

The first house liberated by the North Shore (New Brunswick) Regiment on D-Day.

the regiment in the video as well as the exact location of the North Shore landings.[19] The confused history of the landings partly explains why the structure remains a simple beach house and why there has never been an attempt by the North Shores to engage in relationships of the sort fostered by the Queen's Own.

Three of the seven monuments dedicated to the North Shores in Normandy are at St-Aubin-sur-Mer. The contribution made by that regiment, though, has been obscured by the role of a British unit, the 48th Royal Marine Commando. The Commandos in their plywood landing craft, no match for the German mortars and machine guns, arrived after the Canadians as the tide was rising, with the result that less than half their original contingent made it ashore.[20] Despite the horrific losses, they provided the link between the Canadian and British beaches and have much to be commended for. In 1948, one of the earliest monuments commemorating the landings was erected to honour both the 48th Commando and the North Shores. But for reasons of geographic proximity, the veterans of the 48th Commando have been the most prominent participants at perhaps the most moving beachside ceremony every 6 June. And while the Commandos give proper mention of the role of the Canadians, the public memory of the invasion in St-Aubin has focused on the Commandos. Another monument in the village credits the 48th with the liberation of St-Aubin-sur-Mer and wholly neglects the contribution of the North Shores.[21] The commemorative disparity at St-Aubin has led Marc Milner to conclude that "the Commandos stormed the beach in 1944 and have held on ever since."[22]

Citizens of St-Aubin have tried to keep the memory of the Canadians alive through street names, such as Rue du North Shore Regiment (ironically the most convenient access is via Voie du 48eme Commando).[23] But without a personal relationship of the kind that exists between the Queen's Own and the Hoffer family, it is difficult to establish more meaningful commemorations.

The 2006 edition of the annual ceremony in honour of the 48 Royal Commando in St-Aubin-sur-Mer.

When the village of St-Aubin sought the names of the North Shores who died on D-Day, they could find no answers. An inquiry to their sister town in Bathurst, New Brunswick—the heart of the old North Shore Regiment—did not help. Reluctantly, the town used the names of the North Shores who were buried in the Canadian War Cemetery in Beny-sur-Mer with recorded deaths on 6 June 1944. This option, their only recourse, neglected those who had been wounded on D-Day and who later died from their injuries. The fact that a few soldiers were missed still bothers the long-time mayor of St-Aubin.[24]

The ficklenness of memory is further demonstrated in the village of Tailleville. In 1944 the small village was the headquarters of a German battalion and "was a warren of prepared defences and underground structures held by a company of infantry."[25] While the Queen's Own marched around the strongpoint on their way to Anisy, the North Shores became embroiled in hard fighting that would characterize the next month in Normandy. The defences, many of them recognizable to this day, compelled the North

Shores to assault the enemy no less than six times at a terrible cost.[26] Near the Tailleville château leading into the village, five members of the North Shores, including the grandfather of the regiment, forty-two-year-old Major Archie McNaughton, were killed by the hidden defences that protected the German regimental headquarters.

Yet present-day visitors will find no mention of these fatalities, nor will they find an understanding of the military obstacle that Tailleville presented in 1944. Instead, they may ponder a machine-gun turret that sits beside a flower bed in the centre of the village that displays the Canadian flag when in bloom. A sign overhead reads simply: "Place Alphonse Noël: un soldat blessé ici en 1944."[27] Noël was one of many who were injured by the German machine-gun fire on that corner. During the 40th anniversary of the landings in 1984, he revisited the spot where he had been wounded and met Monsieur Cassigneul, the owner of the château, who had been a child during the war. The meeting resulted in a friendship that has lasted to this day through their children. When the family heard that Alphonse Noël would be returning for the 60th anniversary in 2004, the Cassigneuls asked if they could do something in his honour. Noël agreed.

The result seems odd, for this small monument in Tailleville says nothing of the five men of the North Shores who were killed nearby. Instead it demonstrates the enduring strength of personal connections. When pressed,

M. Cassigneul stands in front of Place Alphonse Noël in Tailleville, 2007.

Monsieur Cassigneul shared that the memorial symbolizes the end of German occupation in his village as well as a chance to honour a friend.[28] Other informal commemorations are found nearby. A roundabout in Tailleville is improperly labelled "Place du Royal North Shore." The aging sign is overshadowed by a larger monument to the residents of Tailleville who gave their lives to France in both World Wars. Perhaps more ironic, Place du North Shore is located on Rue de la Chaudières.

Of the thirteen Norman sites that mention the North Shores, the lone monument that commemorates just the New Brunswick regiment as a unit is found in Carpiquet—and the old guard certainly earned the commemorative monument that bears their regimental insignia. The initial attack across more than 2500 yards of flat, open terrain started shortly after 0500 on 4 July 1944. Allied gunners, drawing their tactics from the First World War, tried to "lift" their barrage at regular intervals to "walk" the North Shores to Carpiquet village. But advanced technology allowed the Germans to put up a counterbarrage that forced the North Shores into a small pocket. In one grueling hour, the North Shores marched uphill through a maelstrom of fire and shrapnel across an open, smoking field "where every step forward meant possible death."[29] Once they reached the village, the North Shores and the Chaudières endured some of the fiercest shelling in Normandy with the full understanding that a German counterattack would follow. The next morning, the notorious 12 SS Hitler Youth Division led the first of five counterattacks, all but one directed on the North Shores. "With rifle companies down to about half strength,

The North Shore Monument in Carpiquet, the graveyard of the regiment, 2009.

overlooked and blasted from three sides by everything the elite Nazi forces could throw at them," the North Shores held firm.[30]

The cost was grim: the North Shores suffered 289 casualties, including 77 dead, during those two days in July.[31] That the North Shores were able to hold Carpiquet forced C.P. Stacey to conclude that Operation Windsor was a "partial success" though it "had been dearly bought."[32] Terry Copp broadened our understanding of the defensive victory, noting that the defence of Carpiquet decimated the only available operational German reserve in the sector, which allowed for the eventual capture of Caen.[33] Further research by Marc Milner has revealed that while the operation was costly on manpower, contrary to what is usually viewed as an example of the lopsided losses the allies endured, the casualty levels on the Germans side were about the same.[34]

It is unlikely that the people of Carpiquet knew much about this broader debate when they built a granite monument to the North Shore Regiment in 1987. Myles Hickey, the inspirational wartime padre of the NSR, spoke at the unveiling. Sadly, or prophetically, he died that night in his sleep. For the next seventeen years the monument played host to Carpiquet's annual commemorations. During the 60th anniversary celebrations in 2004, the people of Carpiquet unveiled a new monument that honoured all the regiments who had fought for the liberation of their town. There is no question that the new monument better reflects the total Canadian effort to capture Carpiquet, but its existence has overshadowed the monument that honours the North Shores. The 1987 monument honouring the North Shores now sits in the middle of the village as one of five, and its significance will undoubtedly continue to fade with the passage of time. With only limited resources and sporadic connections between New Brunswick and France, the legacy of the North Shores is often shared with and overshadowed by other regiments or monuments.

An obvious comparison to make is between the North Shores who fell at Carpiquet and the Queen's Own Rifles who were massacred at Le Mesnil-Patry. On 11 June 1944, the Queen's Own was hastily paired with the tanks of London Ontario's 1st Hussars to lead an assault on Le Mesnil-Patry in support of the British 50th Division. The two regiments had never worked together and had no time for proper planning. The attack was an abysmal failure. The operation, "conceived in sin and born of iniquity," cost the Queen's Own over sixty dead and took the same toll on the men of the 1st Hussars.[35]

Before the war, the small Norman hamlet could boast a population of less than 125.³⁶ In 1944, Roger Alexandre was a fourteen-year-old boy growing up in Le Mesnil-Patry. Sixty years on, he has long served as the mayor. He is also the president of the "Friends of the Juno Beach Centre" and has always worked to preserve the memory of the Canadians, first in Bernières-sur-Mer and then in his own small hamlet. Since 2007 he has organized the many ceremonies held each year in honour of the Queen's Own Rifles of Canada.

The relationship began in 1988, when members of the Queen's Own asked Alexandre if it was possible to erect a monument in memory of those who were killed on 11 June 1944. Alexandre and the people of Le Mesnil-Patry welcomed the memorial, and on the 45th anniversary, many members of the regiment joined a number of local residents for the official unveiling. As the years passed, the ceremonies continued and the relations between the regiment and Alexandre developed further. Alexandre has been to Canada more than once and has been received by both the Riflemen in Toronto and the 1st Hussars in London. When the Queen's Own returned for the 50th anniversary, Alexandre planted his crop to form a gold Maple Leaf against the green field. He then arranged for members of the regiment to see his work from the air. For the 60th anniversary the small hamlet of Le Mesnil-Patry

Tjarko Pot (left) and Roger Alexandre (right) stand in front of the monument in Le Mesnil-Patry, 2007. The 2004 addition sits atop the 1989 monument which forms the base.

decided to increase the stature of the monument, and from the community's coffers added all the names of those who died on 11 June 1944.

The addition was warmly received by the regimental membership, and they were easily able to provide the names of those who paid the ultimate sacrifice. Since the unveiling of the original monument, Alexandre has held as many as ten ceremonies per year for a host of guests ranging from teachers' tours to battlefield tours as well as tours put on by the Queen's Own. And always, there are ceremonies on 8 May, V-E Day, and 11 June, the anniversary of the massacre of the Canadians in the town. The flowers are always prepared well in advance by Alexandre's wife, and the children from the village are in charge of placing these flowers. The initial contact came from the Queen's Own, but the relationship between the regiment and the mayor and the people of the town has allowed for a flourishing commemorative effort in Le Mesnil-Patry.[37]

In the end, the efforts of the Queen's Own Rifles of Canada to preserve the memory of their own regiment are remarkable. Members of the regimental association have worked hard to overcome a language barrier to gain recognition. Lieutenant-Colonel Steve Brand and Padre Craig Cameron continue to dedicate a great deal of time to the remembrance in Europe,

A 1994 postcard showcasing the Roger Alexandre's farm from the air. Alexandre laughed at his mistake when he accidentally ran the tractor over a portion of the maple leaf.

strengthening relationships with passionate residents in places that are important to the Queen's Own. The brass of the Queen's Own have embraced the commemorative work of others, who include Tjarko Pot, a Dutch national and the regiment's European representative, who is young and enthusiastic about preserving the memory of the regiment. The regiment was a key contributor to the Juno Beach Centre, which gained widespread support through the purchase of name plates commemorating Canadian soldiers. The QOR purchased these plates for every member who served in Normandy. It was the only regiment to do so. Most important, the Queen's Own Rifles of Canada were among the first and most active in all the anniversaries of the Normandy campaign—Bill Ross, a veteran of the QOR who landed on D-Day, asked rhetorically at the 2007 Juno Beach Centre ceremony how he could expect anyone to remember his fallen comrades if he was not willing to make the effort himself.[38] Through the very effective promotion of their own history, the Queen's Own Rifles are easily the most visible and active Canadian regiment in Normandy.

For the North Shores, there is no champion of remembrance, no personality to drive the process of commemoration, and no supporting organizational structure to safeguard their memory. In St-Aubin, the 48th Commando have largely taken on the role of liberators. In Tailleville, the roundabout that bears the regiment's name is obscured by other monuments and Place d'Alphonse Noël does not reflect the historical significance of the town or the total sacrifice of Archie McNaughton's Company. In Carpiquet there exists a simple plaque on a forgotten monument that fails to do justice to both the cost of the battle and the significance of the defensive victory. Visitors to Normandy could easily be forgiven for not noticing the North Shores at all. They are the least commemorated regiment of the 8th Canadian Infantry Brigade, and even where they are memorialized, they are often overshadowed. Perhaps this should come as little surprise. The regimental historian, Will Bird, argued that the North Shores suffered a similar fate during the war, always lacking "equal representation at brigade or division level, with the result that lesser units were given publicity and received awards."[39]

Despite a common language and ancestry, Le Régiment de la Chaudière and their place in Norman lore is an anomaly. For political and financial reasons the regiment has put little sustained effort into preserving their memory in Normandy.[40] However, almost every community the Chauds passed through remembers the French-speaking "Tommies" with street signs, individual plaques, and monuments.[41] Yet there is no evidence of annual ceremonies, nor is there a long-standing relationship between the regiment and the local population. In fact, the main ceremony attended by those members of the Chaudières who make the trek back to Normandy is at Bernières-sur-Mer in front of the Queen's Own House. Ultimately, their sites of memory seem to have grown out of a local desire to acknowledge the sacrifices of the Chaudières, an interest that re-emerged with several new monuments unveiled during the 50th anniversary celebrations in 1994. Nevertheless, there is little to suggest that the regiment has been directly linked to the process or that the monuments represent anything more than sites for socially significant anniversaries.

This examination, though, is not about regional or even historical imbalance. The ease of commemoration also owes much to Canada's international reputation and the good relations the two countries have enjoyed since the Second World War. For the citizens of Normandy, a memorial to an Ontario regiment or a single New Brunswicker is a memorial to the Canadian effort. This case study has identified the fickle nature of informal memory and how that memory is nurtured. The comparison between the memory of the Queen's Own Rifles of Canada and that of the North Shore (New Brunswick) Regiment provides an important understanding of how memory is constructed and preserved through the continuous commitment of passionate individuals and the relationships they maintain over time.

Historical interpretation relies on highlighting certain events over others; the construction of memory and memorials depends on a similar selection process. Historians ask questions and examine evidence for answers. The final product is judged on, and academic integrity hinges on, the interpretation of that evidence. Those who construct memorials and who guide the process of remembrance are not bound by the same adherence to historical accuracy. To borrow from Vance, the constructed memory of the 8th Canadian Infantry Brigade on the beaches and inland is a complex mixture of fact, half-truths, exaggeration, and key personalities. On the coast of Normandy, the evidence suggests that the process of preserving memory hinges on a complex and uneven web of personal and always changing connections between Canadian and French citizens that has endured for almost seventy years.

Notes

This chapter draws its research from my Master's Major Research Paper, which was completed in August 2007 under the supervision of John Laband at Wilfrid Laurier University. Further refinements were made after presenting a version of this research in May 2007 at the 18th Canadian Military History Colloquium in Waterloo, Ontario. The arguments contained in this chapter benefited a great deal from collegial discussions with Marc Milner, Roger Sarty, Krista Elliott, Mark Humphries, and especially Vanessa McMackin, who has recently published her own work on war and memory in *Canadian Military History*. Special thanks is owed to Geoffrey Hayes whose thorough edit helped turn this from a graduate paper into a chapter. During my MA I had the good fortune of becoming acquainted with Terry Copp and the Laurier Centre for Military Strategic and Disarmament Studies (LCMSDS). I could not have asked for a more supportive, personally challenging, and inspirational mentor.

1. Roger Alexandre, interview by author, 10 February 2007, Le Mesnil Patry, France. Recorded.
2. C.P. Stacey, *The Victory Campaign: The Operations in North-West Europe, 1944–1945* (Ottawa: Queen's Printer, 1960), 118.
3. Marc Milner, *D-Day to Carpiquet: The North Shore Regiment and the Liberation of Europe* (Fredericton: Goose Lane Editions, 2007), 69.
4. Paul Fussell, *The Great War and Modern Memory* (New York: Oxford University Press, 2000). For a counterargument to Fussell, see Jay Winters, *Sites of Memory, Sites of Mourning: The Great War in European Cultural History* (Cambridge: Cambridge University Press, 1995); Michael Kammen, *Mystic Chords of Memory: The Transformation of Tradition in American Culture* (New York: Random House, 1991). For a look at the way the Holocaust has been shaped in different countries, see James Young, *The Texture of Memory: Holocaust, Memorials, and Meaning* (New Haven: Yale University Press, 1993). For an interesting look at the increase in memory studies at university, see Jay Winter, "The Memory Boom in Contemporary Historical Studies," *Raritan* 21, no.1 (2001).
5. Jonathan Vance, *Death So Noble: Memory, Meaning, and the First World War* (Vancouver: UBC Press, 1997), 3.
6. Kirk Savage, "History, Memory, and Monuments: An Overview of the Scholarly Literature on Commemoration" (2006), http://www.nps.gov/history/history/resedu/savage.htm, accessed 30 October 2006.
7. See Jonathan Vance's chapter in this collection.
8. The research for this piece comes from the benefit of having been a part of the 2006 Canadian Battlefields Foundation (CBF) tour led by Marc Milner, from a subsequent personal trip to revisit the sites and interview the key players, and then from serving as an instructor on the 2009 Cleghorn Battlefield tour (a joint tour between Wilfrid Laurier University and the Université de Montréal) funded by John Cleghorn. Those familiar with the CBF know of Terry Copp's influential role in its beginnings. The Cleghorn Tour is a direct result of the generous donation made by John Cleghorn after

he toured the battlefields with Terry. Those tours expose students to two intense weeks of this "informed memory." The commemorative landscape of the North Shore (New Brunswick) Regiment and the Queen's Own Rifles of Canada is a testament to this need.

9   The burst of public interest in the international celebrations of the 50th anniversary of Normandy in 1994 (and the VE campaign in 1995) caught the Canadian government by surprise. The result was an extension of the Historic Sites and Monuments Board's mandate to include overseas sites. In 1999, Roger Sarty, then chief historian for the Canadian War Museum, was charged with leading a pilgrimage to Normandy on behalf of Veteran's Affairs which included the Minister of Heritage, Sheila Copps. On the tour, Copps unveiled the first official government memorial in Normandy at Bernières-sur-mer on behalf of the Historic Sites and Monuments Board of Canada. For the official press release see http://www.pc.gc.ca/APPS/CP-NR/release_e.asp?id=23&andor1=nr.
10 Jean Chretien, 6 June 2003, Courseulles-sur-mer. Video. http://www.ctv.ca/CTVNews/TopStories/20030607/juno_beach_memorial_030606/, accessed 30 November 2010.
11 M. Hoffer, interview by author, 12 February 2007, Le Mesnil Patry, France. Recorded.
12 Inscription on the plaque outside the Queen's Own Rifles House, Bernières-sur-mer, France.
13 Terry Copp and Mike Bechthold, *The Canadian Battlefields in Normandy: A Visitor's Guide*, 3rd ed. (Waterloo: LCMSDS Press, 2008), 24–26.
14 Lieutenant-Colonel Steve Brand, interview by author, 14 April 2007, Toronto, Ontario. Recorded.
15 Ibid.
16 Milner, *D-Day to Carpiquet*.
17 In September 1954, the North Shore (New Brunswick) Regiment and 28 Field Artillery Battery were amalgamated. The unit became the 2nd Battalion, The Royal New Brunswick Regiment (North Shore) in 1956.
18 Some have surmised that the French–English rivalries within the regiment during the war may have lessened the organization's ability to organize significant overseas commemoration.
19 Marc Milner, *In Search of the Lost Brigade: The North Shore Regiment from D-Day to Carpiquet*, paper presented at the 18th Canadian Military History Colloquium, Waterloo, Ontario, 2007.
20 Terry Copp, *Fields of Fire: The Canadians in Normandy* (Toronto: University of Toronto Press, 2004), 48.
21 A prime example is the information pole that gives information about the town's Second World War history. It mentions only the 48th Commando as having landed on the beach.
22 Milner, *In Search of the Lost Brigade*.
23 Copp, *Fields of Fire*, 48.
24 Jean-Alain Tranquart, interview by author, 9 February 2007, St-Aubin-sur-mer, France. Recorded.

25 Milner, *D-Day to Carpiquet*, 65.
26 Ibid., 67.
27 Place Alphonse Noël: A soldier wounded here in 1944.
28 M. Cassigneul, interview by author, 14 February 2007, Tailleville, France. Recorded.
29 Major Anderson as quoted in Milner, *D-Day to Carpiquet*, 101.
30 Milner, *D-Day to Carpiquet*, 109.
31 Ibid., Chapter 5.
32 Stacey, *The Victory Campaign*, 155.
33 Milner, *D-Day to Carpiquet*, 109. Terry Copp mistakenly gives this credit to the Chaudières for this accomplishment in *Fields of Fire*, 100.
34 Milner, *D-Day to Carpiquet*, 113–14.
35 William Thomas Barnard, *The Queen's Own Rifles of Canada, 1860–1960: One Hundred Years of Canada* (Toronto: Ontario Pub., 1960), 201.
36 Alexandre, interview, 2 October 2007.
37 Ibid.
38 Mike Vernon, *School Trip to Juno Beach: A Diary*, produced for CBC Online, http://www.cbc.ca/news/background/dday/juno-trip-diary.html, accessed 2 August 2007.
39 Will Bird, *North Shore (New Brunswick) Regiment* (Fredericton: Brunswick Press, 1963), 23.
40 Sébastien Vincent, in *Laissé dans l'Ombre: Les Québécois engage volontairres de 39–45* (Montréal: VLB Editeur, 2004), contends, quite convincingly, that the political opposition to conscription has overshadowed the actions of Quebec volunteers and their accomplishments during the Second World War and by extension has done an injustice to their memory. In fact, Béatrice Richard contends that Les Fusiliers Mont-Royal, because of the political capital of the failed Dieppe raid, are the only known regiment in Quebec in Béatrice Richard, *La Mémoire de Dieppe: Radioscopie d'un mythe* (Montéal: VLB Éditeur, 2002).
41 Copp and Bechthold, *The Canadian Battlefields in Normandy*, 26.

21

An Open Door to a Better Future
The Memory of Canada's Second World War

Jonathan F. Vance

In the town of Aylmer, in Southern Ontario, a bronze statue of a weeping woman adorns the war memorial; one hand is at her downcast face, while the other holds a wreath. On either side of her, etched into the stone, are the names of fifty-five men from Aylmer and Malahide Township who were killed during the First World War—including Clark and Leslie Haight of Aylmer South, brothers who died seven months apart but are commemorated together on the Vimy Memorial. Under the platform on which the weeping woman stands is another list, this one of the twenty-six local men who died during the Second World War, among them the Wilson brothers of Aylmer West—John, who lost his life on air operations in 1941, and Bruce, killed in action in Normandy with the British Columbia Regiment.

The haunting memorial, its stark white stone contrasting the tragedy implicit in the figure, is meaningful on two levels. First, that the town lost far more young men in the First World War than in the Second reflects the national story. On a deeper level, the memorial reveals the degree to which the dead of the First World War have dominated Canada's collective memory of war in the twentieth century. Those who gave their lives between 1939 and 1945 have always been overshadowed by the soldiers who died in the earlier war, just as the twenty-six names on the base of the monument are dominated by the fifty-five names above them.

Even in the 1940s, it was evident that the two world wars were inextricably intertwined. The seeds of the Second World War lie in the First, leading some historians to argue that they really constitute a single conflict, interrupted by a twenty-five-year ceasefire.¹ Even without carrying the argument so far, one cannot deny the continuities between the two, even in something as amorphous as memory. In the two decades after VE-Day and VJ-Day, Canada's collective memory of the Second World War emerged in a form that was strikingly similar to the memory of the First. It was less extensive— reminders of death in war were not omnipresent in the 1950s, as they had been in the 1920s and 1930s—but the themes and symbols that were used to understand the tragedy of Flanders were mobilized again to remember Hong Kong, Dieppe, and Normandy.

War and soldiering have always been a part of Canada's history, but the First World War was entirely unprecedented. Although a few thousand Canadians had signed up to fight the Boers in South Africa in 1899, never before had the nation assembled a major overseas expeditionary force. The first 30,000-man contingent left Canada for Europe in October 1914, and by the end of the war as many as 700,000 Canadians had enlisted for service or been conscripted, from a population of just over seven million.² They proved themselves in battle, with the Canadian Corps, a robust formation of four over-strength divisions, becoming known as the shock troops of the British Army.

A generation later, it was all done again. Canada's response in September 1939 was just as rapid as it had been twenty-five years earlier, and by war's end over 1.1 million men and women had served in uniform, out of a population of roughly 11 million.³ In 1945, the nation that had started the war with a pathetically small military boasted the fourth-largest air force and the third-largest navy in the world.

But the price was heavy: as many as 70,000 dead in the First World War, over 42,000 in the Second.⁴ And the difference is more than it seems. Canada in 1914 was young and a little naïve; to lose so many of its youth in its first major war constituted a profound psychic shock. But in 1939, the nation was hardened by a decade of Depression; there was little of the wide-eyed enthusiasm of 1914, and none of the naïveté. There is no question that 42,000 dead was a heavy price, but they came from a much larger population and military, and from a country that was all too familiar with death in war.

In these circumstances, it is hardly surprising that the Great War continued to exercise such a powerful hold over collective memory and that the memory of the Second World War often resembled that of its predecessor. In 1942,

Frank Scott, a Quebec legal scholar whose brother was killed in action in 1916 and whose father had been the senior chaplain of the Canadian Expeditionary Force (CEF), complained bitterly that very little had changed since 1918. Commenting on *Voices of Victory*, an anthology of Second World War poetry, he lamented "the utter lack on the part of these Canadian writers of the sense of impending change ... and of any new outlook on the contemporary world. Judging by this volume, nothing has altered in the realm of poetry or politics."[5]

Scott was a brilliant observer and he must have noticed that, in the broader realm of collective memory, very little had changed as well. After the First World War, Canadians had, both consciously and unconsciously, crafted a memory that stressed utility and goodness. The war had been fought to preserve Christianity, freedom, and right from a German dark age. The meaning of death in war became more important than the means, so the horrors of the Western Front were glossed over to emphasize a number of themes that cast the war in positive terms: the comparison of the soldier with Christ, the gift of comradeship in the trenches, the traditional martial values that twentieth-century soldiers shared with medieval knights, Canada's soldiers as the personification of the nation, battle as a refiner's fire that produced a better man, the war as a nation-building experience that overcame divisions of class, religion, ethnicity, and region. This interpretation suffused every aspect of Canadian society, from literature, art, and music to advertising and consumer goods, to war memorials and commemorative observances, to veterans' organizations and schools. The memory was not fashioned by elites and foisted on Canada as a means of social control; it emerged in thousands of Canadian communities as a way to provide consolation and

The war memorial in Aylmer, Ontario. [J. Peter Vance, photo]

explanation for a loss that seemed unfathomable.[6] In creating that memory, Canadians in the 1910s and 1920s had looked back to the Victorian age for frames of reference to comprehend the Great War. So it is hardly surprising that Canadians of the 1940s looked back to the 1910s for inspiration. They found that their parents' war themes and modes of remembrance could easily be updated by doing little more than changing the place names. Sometimes not even that was necessary.

Indeed, many of the conduits of memory had already been constructed. Canada's veterans' organizations, which had played such a critical role in shaping how Canadians remembered the First World War, had been through twenty years of growing pains by 1939 and were firmly set in their ways; although Second World War veterans were quick to assume leadership positions in the Canadian Legion (the first came in 1944 when Allan Piper of the Stormont, Dundas, and Glengarry Highlanders, who had lost both hands in a training accident, was elected Third Vice-President), the rank and file did not immediately follow. And when they did, they were sometimes made to feel very much like novices. "My father and his cronies ran the organization from a room over his store," recalled Bob Smellie of the Royal Winnipeg Rifles. "They let us in, but they made all the decisions."[7] In 1954, fully two-thirds of the Legion's members were First World War veterans; it would be well into the 1960s before they no longer dominated the membership rolls and the Legion ceased to be, for all intents and purposes, the Great War Veterans' Association.[8] A glimpse at any issue of *The Legionary* from the two decades after the end of the Second World War bears this out, and confirms Scott's fears that very little had changed. Readers of the December 1950 issue, for example, were introduced to the new Dominion Chairman, Erle Burgess of St. Thomas, Ontario, who had enlisted with the 4th Divisional Cyclists in March 1916. A report from the meeting of the National Council in Ottawa noted that a committee had been struck to prepare plans for battlefield pilgrimages in 1952, to recapture the success of the 1936 Vimy Pilgrimage. Douglas How's short story "The Fall of Private O'Quirk" bore more than a passing resemblance to Will Bird's tales of Private Timothy Fergus Clancy, the inveterate schemer who was the hero of Bird's 1930 novel; the accompanying cartoon featured the lovable Everyman Herbie, the Second World War descendant of Old Bill. There was also the regular column "Five Nines and Whiz Bangs" by the Orderly Sergeant (W.W. Murray), which had been a favourite almost since *The Legionary* began publishing. In December 1950, the Orderly Sergeant reflected on the death of Colonel H.M. Urquhart, biographer of Arthur Currie and historian of the 16th Battalion, and offered an anecdote about Milton Gregg, who had won a Victoria Cross near Cambrai in 1918. In that issue of *The Legionary*, as in many others, there was relatively little that pertained to the interests and experiences of Second World War veterans.

Furthermore, there is little indication that the veterans' movement, or indeed veterans themselves, were any less susceptible to the same strong sense of nostalgia that characterized ex-soldiers' activities in the 1920s and 1930s. Scholars of collective memory argue that nostalgia as a mode of remembering points to a perceived deficiency in the present—one looks back fondly at the past because it is believed to be the repository of positive values and ideals that no longer exist.[9] For ex-soldiers, nostalgia was also a celebration of the gift of comradeship, the close relations between fighting men that allowed them to endure common trials. These notions certainly describe the world view of the veterans' movement in the interwar era. But in contrast to that world view, where an idealization of the past was accompanied by a bitter lament about the present, post-1945 veteran nostalgia has no such negativity. There are few complaints about a shallow and grasping postwar world, about high ideals that had been betrayed. Instead, there is simply a fond recollection of good times spent with true friends that made the horrors bearable. *The Legionary* after 1945 featured Doug Macbeth's regular column "Remember When? Service Trails, 1939–45," a direct descendant of Will Bird's *Thirteen Years After* (1932) and *The Communication Trench* (1933), the clearest expressions of the nostalgic impulse among Great War veterans.

Yet despite the nostalgic tone of much of *The Legionary*'s content in the two decades after the end of the Second World War, it is always difficult to determine whether such a publication reflects the opinion of the average veteran. By the same token, many Second World War regimental histories were written by veterans or historians of the First World War—Kim Beattie (48th Highlanders), Will R. Bird (North Nova Scotia Highlanders), R.C. Fetherstonhaugh (Royal Montreal Regiment), G.R. Stevens (Royal Canadian Regiment). Can we deduce from the tone or content of those histories how Second World War veterans remembered their experiences? Without resorting to oral history (which has its own pitfalls), how can we glean the memories of the average veteran? One example of a better gauge is a copy of a regimental chronicle, *The Six Years of 6 Canadian Field Regiment*, that has been carefully annotated in clear, strong handwriting by Gunner F.R. MacDonald.[10] The book itself is unexceptional. Published in the Netherlands immediately after the war, it is a straightforward account from the mobilization of the unit in Manitoba to its time in the Netherlands in 1945. The book celebrates the regiment's achievements, mourns its dead, and recalls its high points and low points. But in MacDonald's annotations, we see what a probably typical ex-gunner wanted to remember about the war. During the regiment's training in England, the annotations are not surprising—a typical note reads: "Harkhurst—cleaned boys in poker. Left on leave with 40£. Took another 18£ on my return shooting craps." In early July 1944, the regiment moved to France, and here MacDonald's notes become more interesting. On 13 July the unit had its first casualty, yet on the relevant page, MacDonald wrote, "Found old piano in the rubble of town. Had a merry time for awhile after changing position." On 23 July the regiment fired six hundred rounds per gun in support of the Cameron Highlanders of Canada. It must have been a brutally exhausting day, so MacDonald's comment is not surprising: "Celebrated the last of the 600 with a good shot of salvaged Calvados, what a hair raiser." Of a difficult deployment to Montreuil-sur-Mer in September 1945, he wrote nothing of adversity or discomfort, but that "Dragon [probably one of MacDonald's fellow gunners—he is never identified more fully] won all the dough, loot & otherwise. Back of a Quad with H.E. [High Explosive] box for a table is not of the best for the good old game." And his annotation gives a new perspective on the liberation of Holten, in the Netherlands, in April 1945: "Dragon got stuck in Holten while looting before it had been taken. Had to lay down a heavy barrage to get him clear. Result—loss of 60 days pay & wk's guard at R.H.Q. [Regimental Headquarters] What a character."

    A number of conclusions might be drawn from MacDonald's notes. In the first place, there is the natural human preference for good memories over bad—there should be no wonder that he wanted to balance the shock of the battery's first battle death with a recollection of an impromptu singalong. It is probably also true that MacDonald was keen to liven up the rather bland text of the chronicle with his own memories. But the memories he chose to record are instructive in that they cover, almost without exception, pleasant interludes spent with comrades. No matter how much Bob Smellie and other veterans like him may have chafed at their continued subordination to veterans of their fathers' war, they implicitly embraced a central element of their fathers' nostalgic mode of remembering.

As it was for the living, so it was for the dead. Both administratively and aesthetically, the First World War had already determined how the fallen of the Second would be buried; many of them would be interred in Great War cemeteries with the dead of their fathers' generation. Even the new cemeteries that were built after 1945 conformed to the principles and design elements that had been enunciated in 1917 and put into place in the early 1920s—headstone epitaphs chosen by Rudyard Kipling ("Known unto God" and "Their glory shall not be blotted out"), Reginald Blomfield's Cross of Sacrifice, and Edwin Lutyens' Stone of Remembrance (bearing another inscription suggested by Kipling, "Their name liveth for evermore"). In every sense, the Second World War cemeteries bore the creative stamp of nineteenth-century British imperial culture.

In Canada there were countless communities like Aylmer, Ontario, where the dead of 1939–1945 were memorialized simply with an addition to the earlier memorial. This was certainly a reasonable course for practical purposes—what community needs two cenotaphs when the first one can be amended? But even so, there was scarcely a rush to make those amendments. Not until 1982, for example, were the dates 1939–1945 added to the National War Memorial in Ottawa. The governments of the British Commonwealth even debated moving Remembrance Day from 11 November to a date that had a closer connection to the Second World War (and, not incidentally, better weather), such as 6 June, the date of the D-Day landings, or 15 September, Battle of Britain Day. But all of the possibilities were found wanting. The anniversary of VE-Day or VJ-Day was rejected because to select one would lead to endless questions about why the other was unsuitable. The anniversary of the beginning of the war was out of the question since not all Commonwealth countries entered the war on the same date—Australia and New Zealand joined Britain in declaring war on 3 September, but South Africa joined the war three days later and Canada inconveniently waited until the 10th. In any case, it seemed a little perverse to mark the *beginning* of six years of bloodshed. The 6th of June meant very little in Australia, New Zealand, or South Africa, whose troops did not join the campaign in Northwest Europe. In the end, the governments elected to make no change.

The dead of the Second World War would continue to be commemorated on the anniversary of the end of the First World War.

Honouring the dead by naming things after them, an immensely popular practice in Canada in the 1920s and 1930s, continued, but even there the Great War continued to exert a powerful influence. David Hornell Junior School in Mimico, Ontario, was named after a local man who won a posthumous Victoria Cross for an attack on a German U-boat in 1944, while Andrew Mynarski VC Junior High School in Winnipeg commemorated an airman who died while trying to save the life of a crewmate trapped in their burning bomber. The Hornell and Mynarski schools were a rarity; even after 1945, the heroes of the First World War were honoured with new memorial schools twice as frequently as those of the Second. There was a similar trend in the practice of using the war as a source for street and place names, something that had taken off in the 1920s and 1930s. In 1948, the district of Cascade Heights in Vancouver, British Columbia, was given war-inspired street names, including Falaise Avenue, Malta Place, and Matapan Crescent. But the planners of the subdivision could not resist doing homage to the earlier war—so Dieppe Drive intersects with Vimy Crescent and Anzio Drive crosses Mons Drive.

In a country with literally tens of thousands of unnamed physical features (Manitoba alone has over 100,000 lakes, only a fraction of which are named), such commemoration was not confined to urban areas. In 1947, the Geographical Names Board of Canada, a federal government committee that approves all nomenclature in Canada, authorized the provincial directors of surveying to name lakes, islands, bays, and rivers after the war dead. In Saskatchewan, where nearly 3,700 physical features in the northern part of the province became war memorials, the program was applied only to the dead of 1939–1945; in neighbouring Manitoba, over 4,200 men and women have been so recognized—not only Second World War casualties, but the dead of the First World War and the Korean War as well.[11]

It was not only in commemoration where the dead of the Second World War were denied their own distinct identity. In literature, too, the dead of the First World War became an interpretive lens through which the dead of the Second could be understood. Poets made much of the device of the soldier of 1939 following in the footsteps of his soldier-father of 1914, particularly when those footsteps led to the grave. "The sons shall sleep beneath the soil that holds their father's dust," wrote amateur poet Robert D. Little of Willowdale, Ontario.[12] Wynne Bunning of Blenheim, Ontario, imagined herself as a mother whose son had been posted missing in action, and reflected on the continuity: "He was never afraid, our soldier lad / He was too much like his soldier dad."[13] But in few places is that continuity clearer than in John Nixon's "Veteran of 1914-18: Bombed and Drowned at Dunkirk":

> Chance at Ypres and the Somme
> Saw me through and safely home;
> Shell and shrapnel passed me by;
> Young, I thought I could not die;
> Why did God, who made them miss,
> Hold me in His hand for this?[14]

Indeed, in culture and the arts generally, one sees very clearly the continuities that had bothered Frank Scott. A language of memory had become entrenched through the 1920s and 1930s, a language of Victorian adjectives, historical references, traditional metaphors, and religious symbolism. Paul Fussell argued that such Big Words, those euphemisms that cloaked the horrific and the mundane elements of the war in bright colours and positive overtones, had been made irrelevant by the experience of the First World War.[15] Canadians, however, still found Big Words and traditional concepts useful in making sense of the Second World War. Indeed, one can only marvel at the persistence of classical, medieval, Victorian, and Christian imagery after 1945.

For example, it might be tempting to discount as an aberration Eric Aldwinckle and A.E. Cloutier's recruiting poster showing a very modern Canadian soldier riding a motorcycle superimposed on a ghostly image of an enormous medieval knight on his rearing steed[16]—except that medieval imagery was not at all uncommon during and after the Second World War. In his 1946 history of the Royal Canadian Regiment, Strome Galloway saw nothing out of place in resorting to the language of medieval warfare in referring to blots on the regimental escutcheon being cleansed by the blood and sweat of Canadian soldiers.[17] And the authors of the chronicle of the 13th Field Regiment, in searching for an epigram for the unit history, settled upon a prayer that was uttered by Sir Francis Drake before he sailed into Cadiz Harbour to sink the Spanish Armada in 1587.[18]

When the occasion demanded a poetic response, the influences and work of earlier generations were preferred to those of the recent war. When he returned from three years' captivity in Germany, infantry officer Tom Melville (captured at Dieppe) published a collection of verses written while he was a prisoner of war. In it, he offered acknowledgments to the poets who had most influenced his work—Rudyard Kipling, Joyce Kilmer, Robert Service, and W.A. Drummond, all of them born in the nineteenth century and all of them resolutely traditional in style—and included selections that would "be easily recognized by 'old sweats' of the 16th and 43rd Battalions, C.E.F."[19] The short official histories published in the series *The Canadian Army at War* tended to be spare and matter-of-fact, but had verse sprinkled throughout. None of it was recent. There was Kipling, Hillaire Belloc (whose journalism had been ridiculed by soldiers during the Great War for having so little resemblance to their own experience), Shakespeare's *Henry V*, Robert Browning's "Childe Roland to the Dark Tower Came" (1855), and a sketch by Bernard Partridge, one of the most popular graphic illustrators of the First World War, thrown in for good measure.[20] There is something to be learned from the fact that, when the Canadian Legion chose a verse to adopt as its Act of Remembrance, it followed the lead of veterans' organizations throughout the British Commonwealth by turning not to the Second World War but to the First, to Laurence Binyon's "For the Fallen," originally published in *The Times* in September 1914: "They shall grow not old, as we that are left grow old: / Age shall not weary them, nor the years condemn. / At the going down of

Eric Aldwinckle and A.E. Cloutier, "Canada's New Army Needs Men Like You" (LAC C-087430)

the sun and in the morning, / We will remember them." The Closing Ritual to be used at the conclusion of formal Legion gatherings reaches even further into imperial history. It is a line from Rudyard Kipling's poem "Recessional," which first appeared in *The Times* in 1897: "Lord God of Hosts, be with us yet, / Lest we forget – lest we forget." Clearly, the tone of the Victorian and Edwardian world was more appropriate than anything that came later. And John McCrae's poem "In Flanders Fields" remained by popular consent the most important Canadian war poem ever written. If anything was going to come close to unseating it after 1945, it would not be something from the body of modernist verse, such as A.M. Klein's "The Hitleriad," Earle Birney's "The Road to Nijmegen," or Frank Scott's "For R.A.S. 1925–1943," but John Gillespie Magee's "High Flight," a poem as replete with Big Words as anything published during the First World War.

The language of the past can be found in many different contexts throughout the memory of the Second World War. In glimpsing those moments of memory, even in a random and entirely unscientific way, one can only be struck by the degree to which the Second World War was passed over in favour of language and symbols from the First. The notion of war as a game that toughened and improved the players remained current, with Captain the Reverend David Marshall, a military chaplain in the CEF, effortlessly falling into a metaphor from his war. In a speech at the dedication of Guelph, Ontario's war memorial arena in 1948, he expressed the hope that "those who use this building play the game in the future as these men have done in the days of old."[21] The poet Dorothy Dumbrille, embracing another trope of the First World War, could easily envision the dead of Dieppe walking in ranks with the fallen of Flanders and Vimy Ridge, with the entire procession being led by Christ: "And He who walks at the head of the host / Has wounded feet and hands."[22] At Vancouver's 1944 Remembrance Day ceremony, one would have expected thoughts to be turned to the casualties sustained in the fighting in Italy and Northwest Europe. But the keynote speaker, R. Rowe Holland, gave an entire address that made no explicit reference at all to the Second World War, but many references to the First, including Rupert Brooke's seminal poem "1914: The Dead," the "knight-errants" who fought on the Western Front, and "the chilling mud of Flanders." The German capture of the island of Lemnos in April 1941 was of critical strategic importance because it brought the Nazis perilously close to the Dardanelles and the possibility of cutting off access to the Black Sea. But for poet Dorothy Dumbrille, the short battle was remarkable chiefly for the fact that Rupert Brooke was buried on Lemnos.[23]

Even a cursory glance at the subject, such as this essay provides, suggests that the dominance of the First World War in Canada's collective memory was largely a consequence of size. The memory of that war was omnipresent in the 1920s and 1930s; even if society had wanted to flee from the past, it was impossible, for there were reminders at every turn. After the Second World War, the situation was very different. In short, there was much less of everything. Nowhere is this clearer than with regard to print. Concerning the interwar era, the notion of a decade-long pause before people were willing to write about the war is the stuff of myth. In fact, there had been an enormous demand for war-related books between 1914 and 1918, and there was little decline in that demand after the Armistice. Memoirs, poetry collections, novels, biographies, popular histories, regimental chronicles—all poured forth from Canada's authors from 1919 through to the late 1930s.

There was no such boom after 1945. It is a moot point whether no one wanted to write such books, or no one wanted to read them—either way, one can only be struck by the dearth of war-related publishing in the two decades after the end of the Second World War. War poetry anthologies of any kind (not just the variety that so annoyed Frank Scott) were few and far between, a noteworthy fact even when one takes into account that the generation of 1939 was less poetic than the generation of 1914. As Tim Cook notes, few potential memoirists were inclined to share their memories in the two decades after 1945.[24] There was William Pugsley's *Saints, Devils, and Ordinary Seamen* (1945), Peter Simonds's *Maple Leaf Up, Maple Leaf Down* (1946), Farley Mowat's *The Regiment* (1955), and Donald Pearce's *Journal of a War* (1965), but not until the late 1970s (Murray Peden's excellent *A Thousand Shall Fall* appeared in 1979) did memoirs start to emerge in significant numbers. Even then, though the memoirs tended towards realism, rather than the romanticism of many Great War memoirs, it was usually not the realism of Charles Yale Harrison and Erich Maria Remarque. On the contrary, their tone was much closer to the tone adopted by Will Bird. For memoirists like Dave McIntosh (*Terror in the Starboard Seat*, 1980), Doug Harvey (*Boys, Bombs, and Brussels Sprouts*, 1981), and George Blackburn (*The Guns of Normandy*,

1997), war was hell, but there was always idealism, comradeship, humour, and heroism in sufficient measure to temper the agony.

Novelists, too, showed little interest in tackling the Second World War. Beyond Ralph Allen's *Home Made Banners* (1946), Earle Birney's *Turvey* (1949), Jean Vaillancourt's *Les Canadiens errants* (1954), Lionel Shapiro's *The Sixth of June* (1955), Colin McDougall's *Execution* (1958), and a handful of other novels, distinguished and undistinguished, there was little of note, and certainly nothing to match the war book boom of the late 1920s and early 1930s. It is worth mentioning that the two most important Canadian novels published during the Second World War, Hugh MacLennan's *Barometer Rising* (1941) and *Two Solitudes* (1945), both deal with the First World War. Even regimental associations, such as they existed, tended to be idle. In the two decades after 1945, only two or three dozen army unit histories were published, including some that covered more than just the recent war. In contrast, in the two decades after 1918, more than twice as many unit histories were published.

What was behind this striking contrast? Why did the Generation of 1914 show so much interest in its past, and the Generation of 1939 so little? The answer lies in the peace rather than the war. After 1918, it was difficult to point to a tangible gain that had emerged from the First World War. There was rising unemployment, labour strife, worrisome inflation, political turmoil, and many other conditions that the war was supposed to solve. With a depressing present and a future that seemed to hold little hope, the past alone offered promise. It could be controlled, and transformed into something that offered meaning and comfort. So a complex myth emerged that provided a balm to grieving

The Legionary, October 1964: Twenty years after the Second World War and still featuring the First.

Canadians at the same time as it explained the importance of the intangibles for which their loved ones had fought and died. In this myth, the elevated rhetoric of the past provided the consolation that so many people sought, and became a refuge from a disappointing peace.

After 1945, the fruits of victory were everywhere and no such refuge was needed. There could be no thought that the 44,000 dead of the Second World War had given their lives in vain. Nazi Germany and Imperial Japan had been utterly crushed, and Canada could enjoy its time in the sun—full employment, a rising GNP, a burgeoning consumer economy, the security of the social welfare state, and political stability. Mackenzie King was virtually the only Western leader to remain in office after the war—his Liberal Party was not defeated at the polls until 1957, the sure sign of a satisfied electorate. The present was all that Canadians could have hoped for, and the future promised only more of the same. In such a society, what need was there to fall back upon the past? For those few people who seem interested in revisiting the war, the language of memory inherited from the First World War would suffice; for everyone else, there was only the future.

This explains why, in the contexts in which a different memory of the recent war emerged after 1945, it was explicitly forward-looking. Despite (or perhaps because of) the nostalgia that still characterized the pages of *The Legionary*, new veterans who joined the Canadian Legion began to push it away from the past and towards the future. The organization had done important social service work during the Second World War (through the Canadian Legion War Services and Canadian Legion Educational Services), and some new members believed that it had to continue on that road. At the Dominion Convention in Montreal in 1952, one committee report mused on the organization's future. It noted that unit-based veterans' groups had little appeal for new veterans and that if the Legion continued in that direction, it would soon wither into irrelevancy. Instead, they should embrace community service, particularly working with youth and sport.[25] The message was simple: the Legion had to stop looking to the past and must instead direct its gaze towards the future.

More significant, those communities that erected new war memorials after the Second World War took a decidedly different course than communities had in the 1920s. New war memorials tended to be modest and locally made—there was little appetite to spend thousands of dollars on an imported bronze soldier or marble angel. And where large, ambitious commemorations were built, they were almost always utilitarian memorials—libraries, arenas, community centres, parks—rather than cenotaphs or statues. Not only did most communities see no need for a traditional aesthetic memorial, but such a thing was incompatible with the spirit of the times. "The cenotaph is a gate closing on the past," observed literary critic W.A. Deacon in an editorial supporting plans for a war memorial library; "the library is an open door to a better future."[26]

Social memory is all about the creation of a usable past, but in the two decades after 1945, Canadians did not have much need for the past. The present seemed all too good, and the future too promising, for people to want to take refuge in the war that had just ended. Nor did they show any great need to make sense of it. For now, it was enough to enjoy a booming economy, the most generous veterans' benefits in the world, the burgeoning suburbs, the new cars, refrigerators, and patio furniture that churned off production lines, the strip malls filled with affordable consumer goods. In time, the postwar dream might prove itself a myth, but until then it seemed a fair reward for the nation's sacrifice. For the time being, Canadians were happy to close a gate on the past and direct their gaze through the open door to a better future.

Notes

1 See, for example, J.M. Roberts, *A History of Europe* (New York: Allen Lane, 1996), esp. Book 5.
2 The only reliable statistics that exist pertain to the Canadian Expeditionary Force (CEF), in which 619,636 men and women served. G.W.L. Nicholson, *Canadian Expeditionary Force, 1914-1919: Official History of the Canadian Army in the First World War* (Ottawa: Queen's Printer, 1962), appendix C. I estimate that as many as 70,000 Canadians enlisted in other formations, such as the Royal Flying Corps, the Royal Canadian Navy, the British Army, and units of Canada's Non-Permanent Active Militia.
3 The most reliable figures can be found in J.L. Granatstein and Peter Neary, eds., *The Good Fight: Canadians and World War II* (Toronto: Copp Clark, 1995), appendix B. Again, this number does not include Canadians serving outside of the Canadian forces, perhaps as many as 50,000.

4 Nicholson, *Canadian Expeditionary Force*, states that the CEF sustained 59,544 fatal casualties during the First World War, and I estimate that another 10,000 Canadians died while serving outside of the CEF. Granatstein and Neary, *The Good Fight*, give a figure of 42,043 fatal casualties sustained by the Canadian forces in the Second World War.
5 F.R. Scott, "A Note on Canadian War Poetry" (review of *Voices of Victory*, 1941) in *Preview* 9 (November 1942), 4.
6 For a full discussion, see Jonathan F. Vance, *Death So Noble: Memory, Meaning, and the First World War* (Vancouver: UBC Press, 1997).
7 Quoted in James Hale, *Branching Out: The Story of The Canadian Legion* (Ottawa: Royal Canadian Legion, 1995), 94.
8 Hale, *Branching Out*, 274.
9 See, for example, Malcolm Chase and Christopher Shaw, eds., *The Imagined Past: History and Nostalgia* (Manchester: Manchester University Press, 1989).
10 R.B. Dale Harris, *The Six Years of 6 Canadian Field Regiment, Royal Canadian Artillery—September, 1939–September, 1945* (Bilthoven, Holland, 1945). The annotated copy is in the D.B. Weldon Library at the University of Western Ontario.
11 Doug Chisholm, *Their Names Live On: Remembering Saskatchewan's Fallen in World War II* (Regina: Canadian Plains Research Center, 2001); *A Place of Honour: Manitoba's War Dead Commemorated in Its Geography* (Winnipeg: Manitoba Conservation, 2002).
12 Robert D. Little, "Sleeping Far from Home," in *Rhymes and Reason* (Willowdale: author, 1946), 43.
13 Wynne Bunning, "Missing," in *Dear Mom* (Blenheim: author, 1945), 42.
14 John Nixon, "Veteran of 1914–18: Bombed and Drowned at Dunkirk," in *Canadian Poetry Magazine* 6, no.1 (December 1941), 29.
15 Paul Fussell, *The Great War and Modern Memory* (Oxford: Oxford University Press, 1975), 21ff.
16 Marc H. Choko, *Affiches de guerre canadiennes, 1914–1918, 1939–1945* (Ottawa: Meridien, 1994), 139.
17 Strome Galloway, *55 Axis, with the Royal Canadian Regiment* (Montreal: Provincial Publishing, 1946), 216.
18 *The History of 13 Canadian Field Regiment, Royal Canadian Artillery, 1940–1945* (privately published, 1945).
19 Lt. Tom Melville, *Barbed Wire Ballads* (Regina: School Aids and Text Book Publishing, 1946), 3.
20 *The Canadians in Britain, 1939–1944* (Ottawa: King's Printer, 1945); C.P. Stacey, *Canada's Battle in Normandy: The Canadian Army's Share in the Operations, 6 June–1 September 1944* (Ottawa: King's Printer, 1946).
21 *Guelph Mercury*, 11 November 1948.
22 Dorothy Dumbrille, "The Deathless Host: Remembrance Day, November 11th 1942," in *Stairway to the Stars* (Toronto: Thomas Allen, 1946), 61.
23 Dumbrille, "Forever England," in *Stairway to the Stars*, 10.

24 Tim Cook, *Clio's Warriors: Canadian Historians and the Writing of the World Wars* (Vancouver: UBC Press, 2006), 190–91.
25 Hale, *Branching Out*, 114–15.
26 "The Fly Leaf," in the *Globe and Mail*, 5 June 1943, 11.

Contributors

Mike Bechthold is the managing editor of *Canadian Military History* and the communications director of the Laurier Centre for Military Strategic and Disarmament Studies. He teaches military history at Wilfrid Laurier University. He has published three guides on the Canadian battlefields in Normandy and Northwest Europe with Terry Copp and is the co-editor of *Vimy Ridge: A Canadian Reassessment* (2007).

Mark Bourrie is a 17-year member of the Parliamentary Press Gallery and has won numerous awards for journalism. He holds a PhD in History from the University of Ottawa. His thesis *The Fog of War*, Bourrie's tenth book, was published in the summer of 2011 by Douglas & McIntyre.

Angelo Caravaggio is an officer in the Canadian Forces and is currently the Director, Centre for National Strategic Studies at the Canadian Forces College in Toronto. His article, "The British Attack at Taranto: Tactical Success, Operational Failure," won the United States Naval War College, Edward S. Miller award for best historical essay for 2006.

Cynthia Comacchio is a professor of history at Wilfrid Laurier University. Her interests in early twentieth-century Canadian sociocultural history, especially family, childhood and youth, have led her to a particular focus on the critical generational impact of the world wars. Her most recent book is *The Dominion of Youth: Adolescence and the Making of Modern Canada* (Wilfrid Laurier University Press, 2006).

Douglas E. Delaney is the author of *The Soldiers' General: Bert Hoffmeister at War* (2005), which won the 2007 C.P. Stacey Prize in Canadian Military

History. His latest work, *Corps Commanders* (2011), examines Canadian and British generals who commanded corps for Canada during the Second World War. A retired infantry officer with over 27 years of service, Delaney is currently Chair of the War Studies program at the Royal Military College of Canada.

Michelle Fowler works as a freelance writer and researcher in Phoenix, Arizona, and is currently undertaking doctoral studies at Arizona State University in US historiography. Michelle's current research focus is the role of civil affairs officers in 21 Army Group during the liberation of Northwest Europe, 1944–45. Michelle has published articles in *War and Society* and *Canadian Military History*. In 2009, Michelle completed *A Duffle Bag, Close Friends and Lots of Memories: A Photo Diary* of Marion Swinton, W.R.C.N.S.

Andrew Godefroy, is a strategic analyst and historian with the Department of National Defence as well as the Editor-in-Chief of the *Canadian Army Journal*. He holds a PhD is War Studies from the Royal Military College of Canada and was the 2009–10 Canadian Visiting Research Fellow in the Changing Character of War Programme at the University of Oxford. The author of several works on military strategy, thought, and innovation, his latest book, *Defence & Discovery: Canada's Military Space Program, 1945–74* (2011) examined Canada's Cold War–era defence research and development of rocketry, missiles, and space technology.

Geoffrey Hayes took part in Terry Copp's first graduate seminar in Canadian military history at Wilfrid Laurier University. Shaun Brown and Rob Campbell were the better students. Hayes went on to complete his PhD at the University of Western Ontario under A.M.J. Hyatt. His book, *The Lincs: A History of the Lincoln and Welland Regiment* (1986, 2007), grew from his Master's thesis under Terry's direction. Hayes is currently an associate professor at the University of Waterloo, where he teaches Canadian political and military history.

Mark Osborne Humphries is an Assistant Professor in the Department of History at Memorial University of Newfoundland, where he teaches military history. Mark has published five books and over a dozen articles and book chapters, one of which won the 2010 Canadian Historical Review Prize. Mark was one of Terry's last BA thesis students, working on a history of the 38th Battalion, and he also co-supervised Mark's MA thesis with Roger Sarty on shell shock in the CEF. Mark and Terry have since written a book together, *Combat Stress in the 20th Century: the Commonwealth Experience* (2010) and continue to collaborate on a number of projects.

Andrew Iarocci earned his doctorate under the supervision of Professor Terry Copp. He recently completed a research fellowship at the Canadian War Museum, where he also served as Collections Manager, Transportation and Artillery. Iarocci is the author of *Shoestring Soldiers: The 1st Canadian Division at War, 1914–1915* (2008), and co-editor of *Vimy Ridge: A Canadian Reassessment.* He is currently writing *Chariots of Mars*, a study of mechanization and transportation in the Canadian Expeditionary Force during the First World War. He teaches history at the University of Western Ontario and with the Royal Military College of Canada.

Marc Milner is Director of the Brigadier Milton F Gregg, VC Centre for the Study of War and Society at the University of New Brunswick. He is best known for his work on naval history, including *North Atlantic Run* (1985), *The U-Boat Hunters* (1995), *Canada's Navy: The First Century* (1999 and 2009) and *Battle of the Atlantic* (2003), which won the C.P. Stacey Prize, and he writes a regular column on Canadian naval history for *Legion Magazine*. His chapter here derives from his ongoing research on the Normandy campaign of 1944.

Jason Ridler, PhD, is the author of *Maestro of Science: Omond McKillop Solandt and Government Science in War and Hostile Peace, 1939–1956*, forthcoming from University of Toronto Press. His academic work has appeared in such journals as *Diplomacy and Statecraft*, *Canadian Military History*, and *The International Journal of Canadian Studies*, among others. A published writer of over forty short stories, Ridler is currently a Visiting Scholar at the University of California, Berkeley, and is working on a biography of counter-insurgency pioneer Charles Bohannan. His writing blog is www.jridler.com.

Roger Sarty was head of historical research and exhibits at the Canadian War Museum in 1998–2003, and led exhibition and program development for the museum's new building. Since 2004 he has taught at Wilfrid Laurier University. He is editor-in-chief of *Canadian Military History* and editor of the *Northern Mariner/Le marin du nord*. He has won Canadian and American awards for *'Tin Pots' and Pirate Ships* (1991, co-authored with Michael Hadley), *Guardian of the Gulf* (2000, co-authored with Brian Tennyson), and was a senior author of two volumes of the official history of the *Royal Canadian Navy, No Higher Purpose* (2004) and *A Blue Water Navy* (2007).

R. Scott Sheffield, PhD, teaches in the History Department of the University of the Fraser Valley in Abbottsford, BC. He has published *The Red Man's on the Warpath: The Image of the 'Indian' and the Second World War* (2004), in addition to a number of other books, government reports, chapters, and journal articles on the subject of Indigenous peoples and the Second World War in Canada and New Zealand.

Matt Symes is a PhD candidate at Wilfrid Laurier University. He is the Online Editor for canadianmilitaryhistory.ca. and the Publications Manager for the Laurier Centre for Military Strategic and Disarmament Studies. With Eric McGeer, Symes has published three Battlefield Guides on the Italian Campaign in the Second World War. His most recent work, with Terry Copp and Nick Lachance, is *Canadian Battlefields 1915–1918: A Visitor's Guide* (LCMSDS/WLU Press 2011).

Yves Tremblay, PhD, is an historian with the Directorate of History and Heritage, Department of National Defence in Ottawa and part-time lecturer at the University of Ottawa. He is the author of two studies published by Athéna éditions on operational and tactical training in the Canadian Army during the Second World War. He is completing an official history of Canadian participation in ONUC (Congo, 1960–64) and has started a project on suicides in the Canadian Army from 1939 to 1947.

Jonathan F. Vance holds the J.B. Smallman Chair in the Department of History at The University of Western Ontario, where he teaches military history, Canadian history, and social memory. A native of Waterdown,

Ontario, he holds degrees from McMaster University, Queen's University, and York University. He is the author of many books and articles, most recently *Maple Leaf Empire: Canada, Britain and Two World Wars* (2011).

Randall Wakelam, PhD, retired from the Canadian Forces College in 2009 and is currently an assistant professor of History at the Royal Military College of Canada. He is one of a handful of air force historians in Canada and in addition to studies of Canadian air power has written extensively on issues of command, leadership, military culture, and military education. He has published two monographs: *The Science of Bombing: Operational Research in RAF Bomber Command* (2009) and *Cold War Fighters: Canadian Aircraft Procurement, 1945–54* (2011).

Lee Windsor, PhD, teaches history at the University of New Brunswick and is Deputy Director of the Brigadier Milton F. Gregg, VC Centre for the Study of War and Society. He was lead author of *Kandahar Tour: Turning Point in Canada's Afghan Mission* (2008). His most recent book is *Steel Cavalry: The 8th New Brunswick Hussars at War in Italy* (2011). Since the first Canadian Battlefields Foundation Study Tour in 1995, he has served alongside Terry Copp to expand the program across Canada.

James A. Wood, PhD, teaches history and is a SSHRC Post-Doctoral Fellow in the Department of History at the University of Victoria, where he is also Assistant Director of the Veterans' Oral History Program. His recent books include and *We Move Only Forward: Canada, the United States, and the First Special Service Force* (2006) and *Militia Myths: Ideas of the Canadian Citizen Soldier, 1896–1921* (2010).

Terry Copp: A Select Bibliography

Books

Copp, Terry, and Mike Bechthold. *The Canadian Battlefields in Northern France: Dieppe and the Channel Ports*. Waterloo: Laurier Centre for Military Strategic and Disarmament Studies, 2011.

———, Matt Symes, and Nick Lachance. *Canadian Battlefields, 1915–1918: A Visitor's Guide*. Waterloo: Laurier Centre for Military Strategic and Disarmament Studies, 2011.

———, and Mike Bechthold. *The Canadian Battlefields in Belgium, the Netherlands and Germany: A Visitor's Guide*. Waterloo: Laurier Centre for Military Strategic and Disarmament Studies, 2011.

———, and Eric McGeer with Matt Symes. *The Canadian Battlefields in Italy: Sicily and Southern Italy*. Waterloo: Laurier Centre for Military Strategic and Disarmament Studies, 2009.

———, and Mike Bechthold. *The Canadians Battlefields in Normandy: A Visitor's Guide*, 3rd edition. Waterloo: Laurier Centre for Military Strategic and Disarmament Studies, 2008.

———. *Cinderella Army: The Canadians in Northwest Europe 1944–1945*. Toronto: University of Toronto Press, 2007.

———. *The Brigade: The Fifth Canadian Infantry Brigade, 1939–1945*. Stoney Creek: Fortress Publications, 1992; Mechanicsburg, PA: Stackpole Books, 2007.

———, and Dennis and Shelagh Whitaker. *Victory at Falaise: The Soldiers' Story*. Toronto: HarperCollins, 2000. Republished as *Normandy: The Real Story*. Presidio Press, 2004.

———. *A Nation at War 1939–1945: Essays from Legion Magazine*. Waterloo: Laurier Centre for Military Strategic and Disarmament Studies, 2004.

———. *Fields of Fire: The Canadians in Normandy*. Toronto: University of Toronto Press, 2003.

———. *No Price Too High: Canadians in the Second World War*. Toronto: McGraw-Hill Ryerson, 1995.

———. *The Canadian Battlefields in Normandy*. Waterloo: Laurier Centre for Military Strategic and Disarmament Studies, 1994; translated as *Guide Canadien des*

Champs de Bataille de Normandie Waterloo: Laurier Centre for Military Strategic and Disarmament Studies, 1994.

———, and Bill McAndrew. *Battle Exhaustion: Soldiers and Psychiatrists in the Canadian Army 1939–1945*. Montreal and Kingston: McGill-Queen's University Press, 1990.

———, and Robert Vogel. *Maple Leaf Route: Victory*. Alma: Maple Leaf Route, 1988.

———, and Robert Vogel. *Maple Leaf Route: Scheldt*. Alma: Maple Leaf Route, 1985.

———, and Robert Vogel. *Maple Leaf Route: Antwerp*. Alma: Maple Leaf Route, 1984.

———, and Robert Vogel. *Maple Leaf Route: Falaise*. Alma: Maple Leaf Route, 1983.

———, and Robert Vogel. *Maple Leaf Route: Caen*. Alma: Maple Leaf Route, 1983.

———, and Desmond Morton. *Working People*. Ottawa: Deneau and Greenberg, 1980.

———. *The IUE in Canada*. Elora: Cumnock Press, 1980; translated as *Le Site au Canada*. Elora: Cumnock Press, 1980.

———. *The Anatomy of Poverty: The Condition of the Working Class in Montreal*. Toronto: McClelland and Stewart, 1974; translated as *Class ouvrière et pauvreté*. Montreal: Boréal Express, 1978.

———, and T.D. Tait. *The Canadian Response to War, 1914–1917*. Toronto: Copp Clark, 1969.

———, and Marcel Hamelin. *Confederation: 1987*. Toronto: Copp Clark, 1966.

Edited Works

———. *1st Canadian Radar Battery 1944–45*. Waterloo: Laurier Centre for Military Strategic and Disarmament Studies, 2010.

———, and Mark Humphries. *Combat Stress: The Commonwealth Experience*. Kingston: Canadian Defence Academy, 2009.

———. *Guy Simonds and the Art of Command*. Kingston: Canadian Defence Academy, 2007.

———, with Gordon Brown. *Look to Your Front: Regina Rifles: A Regiment at War, 1944–1945*. Waterloo: Laurier Centre for Military Strategic and Disarmament Studies, 2001.

———. *Montgomery's Scientists: Operational Research in Northwest Europe*. Waterloo: Laurier Centre for Military Strategic and Disarmament Studies, 2000.

———. *Industrial Unionism in Kitchener, 1937–47*. Elora, 1976.

Articles, Essays, and Chapters in Books

———. "Workers and Soldiers: Adventures in History." *Canadian Historical Review* 93 no.3 (2012).

———. "The Decision to Reinforce Hong Kong: September 2011." *Canadian Military History* 20, no.2 (Spring 2011), 3–11.

———. "Combat Stress: The Commonwealth Experience." *Canadian Military History* 18, no.3 (Summer 2009), 3–7.

———. "To the Last Canadian?: Casualties in 21st Army Group." *Canadian Military History* 18, no.1 (Winter 2009), 3–6.

———. "21st Army Group in Normandy: Towards a New Balance Sheet." In John Buckley, ed., *Normandy: Sixty Years On*. London: Cass, 2006.

———. "Operation Spring: An Historian's View." *Canadian Military History* 12, nos.1–2 (Winter 2003), 63–70.

———. "The Defence of Hong Kong: December 1941." *Canadian Military History* 10 no.4 (Autumn 2001), 5–20.

———. "Le Regiment de Maisonneuve: A Profile Based on Personnel Records." *Canadian Military History* 8, no.4 (Autumn 1999), 17–25.

———. "General Simonds Speaks: Canadian Battle Doctrine in Normandy." *Canadian Military History* 8, no.2 (Spring 1999), 69–80.

———. "Official History in the 1990s." *Canadian Military History* 7, no.3 (Summer 1998), 58–60.

———. "From Neurasthenia to Post-Traumatic Stress Disorder: Canadian Veterans and the Problem of Persistent Emotions Disorders." In Peter Neary and J.L. Granatstein, eds., *The Veterans Charter*. Montreal and Kingston: McGill-Queen's, 1998.

———. "If This War Isn't Over ... First Canadian Army: Feb.–March 1945." In Paul Addison and Angus Calder, eds., *A Time to Kill*. London: Pimlico, 1997.

———. "Ontario 1939: The Decision for War." In Norman Hilmer, ed., *A Country of Limitations*. Ottawa, 1996.

———. "Counter-Mortar Operational Research in 21 Army Group." *Canadian Military History* 3, no.2 (Autumn 1994), 45–52.

———. "Operation Research and 21 Army Group." *Canadian Military History* 3, no.1 (Spring 1994), 71–84.

———. "Fifth Brigade at Verrières Ridge." *Canadian Military History* 1, nos.1–2 (Autumn 1992), 45–63.

———. "Return to Dieppe: September 1944." *Canadian Military History* 1, nos.1–2 (Autumn 1992), 71–78.

———. "Scientists and the Art of War: Operational Research in 21 Army Group." *RUSI Journal* 136, no.4 (Winter 1991), 65–69.

———. "The Child Welfare Movement in Montreal 1897—1914." In D.C.M. Platt, ed., *Social Welfare, 1850-1950: Australia, Argentina and Canada Compared*. London: Macmillan, 1989.

———. "Battle Exhaustion and the Canadian Soldier in Normandy." *British Army Review* 85 (April 1987), 46–54.

———. "The Health of the People: Montreal in the 1930's." In *Norman Bethune: His Life, His Legacy*. Ottawa: Canadian Public Health Association, 1982.

———, and Robert Vogel. "No Lack of Rational Speed: First Canadian Army September 1944." *Journal of Canadian Studies*, Fall–Winter 1981.

———. "Public Health." In E.B. Shortt, ed., *Medicine in Canadian Society*. Montreal and Kingston: McGill-Queen's, 1980.

———. "Montreal's Municipal Government and the Crisis of the 1930's." In Alan F.J. Artibise and Gilbert A. Stelter, eds., *The Useable Urban Past: Planning and Politics in the Modern Canadian City*. Toronto: Macmillan, 1979.

———. "The Pattern of Industrial Unionism in Four Ontario Towns 1937–1951." *Bulletin*, Canadian Committee on Labour History, no.6 (Autumn 1978).

———. "The Montreal Working Class in Prosperity and Depression." *Canadian Issues*, vol. I, no. 1. (1976).

———. "The Condition of the Working Class in Montreal 1897–1920." Canadian Historical Association *Historical Papers*, 1972. Reprinted in Michiel Horne and Ronald Sabourin, eds., *Studies in Canadian Social History*. Toronto: McClelland and Stewart, 1974.

———. "The Whig Interpretation of Canadian History. *Canadian Dimension*, 1969. Reprinted in G. Milburn, ed., *Teaching History in Canada*. Toronto: McGraw-Hill, 1972.

Since 1994 Terry has written a regular series of articles on Canadian military history covering both the First and Second World Wars for *Legion Magazine*. To date, this series comprises over 100 articles.